Feature Papers in Mathematical and Computational Applications 2025

Feature Papers in Mathematical and Computational Applications 2025

Guest Editors

Gianluigi Rozza
Oliver Schütze
Nicholas Fantuzzi

MDPI

Basel • Beijing • Wuhan • Barcelona • Belgrade • Novi Sad • Cluj • Manchester

Guest Editors
Gianluigi Rozza
SISSA MathLab
International School for Advanced Studies
Trieste
Italy

Oliver Schütze
Departamento de Computacion
Cinvestav
Mexico City
Mexico

Nicholas Fantuzzi
Department of Civil, Chemical, Environmental, and Materials Engineering
University of Bologna
Bologna
Italy

Editorial Office
MDPI AG
Grosspeteranlage 5
4052 Basel, Switzerland

This is a reprint of the Special Issue, published open access by the journal *Mathematical and Computational Applications* (ISSN 2297-8747), freely accessible at: https://www.mdpi.com/journal/mca/special_issues/W4RX4KB07G.

For citation purposes, cite each article independently as indicated on the article page online and as indicated below:

Lastname, A.A.; Lastname, B.B. Article Title. *Journal Name* **Year**, *Volume Number*, Page Range.

ISBN 978-3-7258-7438-5 (Hbk)
ISBN 978-3-7258-7439-2 (PDF)
https://doi.org/10.3390/books978-3-7258-7439-2

Contents

Preface

This volume is a reprint of the Special Issue that comprises the fifth collection of papers submitted by both the Editorial Board Members (EBMs) of the journal *Mathematical and Computational Applications (MCA)* and the outstanding scholars working in the core research fields of *MCA*. This reprint consists of 17 chapters coming from the 16 research articles of the Special Issue and the corresponding editorial. The order of the presented chapters is organized chronologically by the publication of the respective research papers. We hope that this volume can serve as a contemporary reference to the core fields of *MCA*.

We warmly thank all authors who submitted a work to this Special Issue. Finally, we thank MDPI and *MCA* for allowing us to edit the Special Issue and this volume.

Gianluigi Rozza, Oliver Schütze, and Nicholas Fantuzzi
Guest Editors

Mathematical and Computational Applications

MDPI

Editorial

Feature Paper Collection of Mathematical and Computational Applications—2025

Gianluigi Rozza [1], Oliver Schütze [2,*] and Nicholas Fantuzzi [3]

1 SISSA MathLab, International School for Advanced Studies, Office A-435, Via Bonomea 265, 34136 Trieste, Italy; gianluigi.rozza@sissa.it

2 Computer Science Department, Cinvestav, Mexico City 07360, Mexico

3 Department of Civil, Chemical, Environmental, and Materials Engineering, University of Bologna, Viale del Risorgimento 2, 40136 Bologna, Italy; nicholas.fantuzzi@unibo.it

* Correspondence: schuetze@cs.cinvestav.mx

This Special Issue comprises the fifth collection of papers submitted by both the Editorial Board Members (EBMs) of the journal *Mathematical and Computational Applications* (*MCA*) and the outstanding scholars working in the core research fields of *MCA*. Therefore, this collection typifies the most insightful and influential original articles that discuss key topics in these fields. More precisely, this issue contains 16 research articles published in *MCA* between February and December 2025. All papers are briefly outlined below, organized chronologically by publication.

Gandomirouzbahani et al. [1] developed a patient-specific head model to address the impact of the brain's constitutive model and loading location on head impact. More precisely, two hyperelastic constitutive models and one hyper-viscoelastic constitutive model were developed for brain tissue. The results regarding the impact on the head and critical regions can help in the development of protective features, such as helmets and airbags.

Lau et al. [2] developed and analyzed machine learning (ML) models that can identify patients at risk of requiring red blood cell transfusion. The retrospective cohort study was conducted at a tertiary northern Portuguese hospital between 2018 and 2023. The considered ML models demonstrate the potential to improve the accuracy of transfusion prediction at hospital admission, despite the absence of key variables such as surgeon identity and anaemia diagnosis.

Sarfraz et al. [3] investigated how regime shifts during the COVID-19 pandemic influenced variable annuity pricing in the Indian stock market. Advanced methodologies, including regime-switching hidden Markov models, artificial neural networks, and Monte Carlo simulations, were applied to analyze pre- and post-COVID-19 market behavior. The regime-switching hidden Markov models can effectively capture latent market regimes and their transitions, which traditional models often overlook, while neural networks can provide flexible functional approximations that enhance pricing accuracy in highly non-linear environments. The findings highlight the effectiveness of regime-switching models in capturing market dynamics, particularly during periods of economic uncertainty and turbulence.

Rocha et al. [4] studied risk factors that lead to psychological problems, using data from primary health care centers in the region of Aveiro. A significant increase in number of appointments was observed in 2021 and 2022, revealing an increase in mental health problems, resulting in more medical consultations for psychological reasons. Risk factors included being female and having chronic conditions such as cancer. The findings provide insights into the burden of mental health issues in the region, highlighting the need for effective mental health interventions and resources to address health inequalities and support at-risk groups.

López-Lobato et al. [5] proposed a generalization of the induction process of a Convolutional Decision Tree (CDT) with the Differential Evolution (DE) algorithm for image segmentation. More precisely, this new approach considered color images, while previous methods were restricted to grayscale images due to the higher computational cost. The efficacy of the novel techniques were evaluated using two datasets, resulting in favorable outcomes in terms of the segmentation performance of the induced CDTs, and the processing time and memory required for the induction process.

Herrera-Sánchez et al. [6] proposed an automated multiple-feature construction approach for image segmentation, working with magnetic resonance images, computed tomography, and RGB digital images. Genetic programming is used to automatically create and construct pipelines to extract meaningful features for segmentation tasks. Additionally, a co-evolution strategy is proposed within the evolution process to increase diversity without affecting segmentation performance. Numerical results on some benchmark problems show that the novel method is highly competitive with state of the art algorithms.

López-Lobato et al. [7] proposed a procedure to identify the colors of heterogeneous color bean landraces based on the information from their digital images. This classification is of particular interest since the color of these plants is associated with the nutritional components present in their seeds. The novel approach facilitates the acquisition of representative information for the colors of a bean landrace. Furthermore, the method can be trained with these punctual representations to identify colors, yielding satisfactory results on landraces with homogeneous and heterogeneous seeds.

Morales-Reyes et al. [8], propose a methodology for classifying bean landrace samples using three two-dimensional histograms with data in the CIE L*a*b* color space while additionally integrating chroma (C*) and hue (h°) to develop a new proposal from histograms, employing deep learning for the classification task. It is shown that the new color characterization approach presents a viable solution for classifying common bean landraces of both homogeneous and heterogeneous colors.

Temizel et al. [9] addressed the problem of accurate permeability predictions for the understanding of fluid flows in porous media. To this end, they introduced a new paradigm, employing vision transformers (ViTs)—a recent advancement in computer vision—for this crucial task. The prediction results suggest that, with adequate training data, ViTs can match or surpass the predictive accuracy of CNNs, especially in rocks exhibiting significant heterogeneity. The study underscores the potential of ViTs as an innovative tool in permeability prediction, paving the way for further research and integration into mainstream reservoir characterization workflows.

Barradas-Palmeros et al. [10] tested various efficient evaluation methods (EEMs) in the Deep Genetic Algorithm (DeepGA), including early stopping, population memory, and training-free proxies. This is carried out with the aim of reducing the computational resources for Neural Architecture Search (NAS). A comparison of the architectures and hyperparameters obtained with the different algorithm configurations is presented. The training-free search processes resulted in deeper architectures with more fully connected layers and skip connections than the ones obtained with accuracy-guided search configurations.

Bertolo et al. [11] developed a second-order Kurganov–Tadmor scheme in curvilinear coordinates to analyze the external supersonic flow over bodies of various shapes. This scheme is capable of handling interfaces across different regions of the domain. A fourth-order Runge–Kutta temporal integrator is used and several test cases are conducted to validate the performance of the new scheme. The results indicate that the new method

https://doi.org/10.3390/mca31010026

produces highly accurate outcomes.

Ratner et al. [12] presented a systematic literature review of data envelopment analysis (DEA) models used to evaluate circular economy (CE) practices. The analysis shows that DEA models provide valuable insights when assessing circular strategies. Over 40% of the surveyed literature focuses on China, with nearly 20% on the European Union. Other regions are sparsely represented within the sample, highlighting a potential gap in the current research landscape.

Martines-Arano et al. [13] examined the contrast in the nonlinear dynamics of Thrinax radiata Lodd. ex Schult. & Schult. f. (known as chit palm in the Yucatán Peninsula). Simulations reveal heat transfer of approximately 1 °C in central regions, closely correlating with observed changes in chaotic attractor morphology. These findings pave the way for future applications and highlight the potential of chaos theory for the early detection of structural and bioelectrical changes induced by external energy inputs, thereby contributing to sample protection.

Bolle et al. [14] utilized κ-mathematics for the analysis of complex systems. Specifically, the mathematical framework in the context of a first-order decay κ-differential equation was investigated, facilitating an in-depth examination of the κ-mathematical structure. This framework serves as a foundational platform, representing the simplest non-trivial setting for such inquiries, which are demonstrated for the first time in the literature. In conclusion, possible paths of future research are discussed.

Kamran et al. [15] presented a comparative analysis of tumor growth models based on logistic, exponential, and Gompertz formulations. Their response to therapeutic intervention was examined to identify which model shows better behavior with minimal decline of immune cells. Numerical simulations indicate that the logistic model provides more favorable treatment outcomes compared to the exponential and Gompertz models. The results also show a faster decline of immune cell populations in the exponential and Gompertz models than in the logistic model under varying drug flux.

Finally, Tavakoli et al. [16] presented an integrative framework based on Evolutionary Stackelberg Game Theory to model the strategic interaction between a physician, acting as a rational leader, and a heterogeneous population of treatment-sensitive and treatment-resistant breast cancer cells. It is shown that this framework offers a biologically interpretable tool for guiding evolution-aware, patient-tailored cancer therapies toward improved long-term outcomes.

Conflicts of Interest: The authors declare no conflicts of interest.

References

1. Gandomirouzbahani, A.; Taghizadeh, H.; Oskui, I.Z.; Fernandes, F.A.O. Impact Loading on a Patient-Specific Head Model: The Significance of Brain Constitutive Models and Loading Location. *Math. Comput. Appl.* **2025**, *30*, 21. [CrossRef]
2. Lau, B.; Ramos, D.; Afreixo, V.; Silva, L.M.; Tavares, A.H.; Felgueiras, M.M.; Castro Paupério, D.; Firmino-Machado, J. Predicting Red Blood Cell Transfusion in Elective Cardiac Surgery: A Machine Learning Approach. *Math. Comput. Appl.* **2025**, *30*, 22. [CrossRef]
3. Sarfraz, M.; D'Amico, G.; Selvamuthu, D. Market Regime Identification and Variable Annuity Pricing: Analysis of COVID-19-Induced Regime Shifts in the Indian Stock Market. *Math. Comput. Appl.* **2025**, *30*, 23. [CrossRef]
4. Rocha, F.; Silva, C.J.; Pinheiro, S.J.; Afreixo, V.; Leitão, R.P.; Felgueiras, M. Characterization of the Appointment's Reasons for "P—Psychological" on the ICPC-2 Scale in Primary Health Care Services. *Math. Comput. Appl.* **2025**, *30*, 28. [CrossRef]
5. López-Lobato, A.-L.; Acosta-Mesa, H.-G.; Mezura-Montes, E. Induction of Convolutional Decision Trees for Semantic Segmentation of Color Images Using Differential Evolution and Time and Memory Reduction Techniques. *Math. Comput. Appl.* **2025**, *30*, 53. [CrossRef]
6. Herrera-Sánchez, D.; Fuentes-Tomás, J.-A.; Acosta-Mesa, H.-G.; Mezura-Montes, E.; Morales-Reyes, J.-L. Multiple-Feature Construction for Image Segmentation Based on Genetic Programming. *Math. Comput. Appl.* **2025**, *30*, 57. [CrossRef]

https://doi.org/10.3390/mca31010026

7. López-Lobato, A.-L.; Avendaño-Garrido, M.-L.; Acosta-Mesa, H.-G.; Morales-Reyes, J.-L.; Aquino-Bolaños, E.-N. Color Identification on Heterogeneous Bean Landrace Seeds Using Gaussian Mixture Models in CIE L*a*b* Color Space. *Math. Comput. Appl.* **2025**, *30*, 64. [CrossRef]
8. Morales-Reyes, J.-L.; Aquino-Bolaños, E.-N.; Acosta-Mesa, H.-G.; Pérez-Castro, N.; Chavez-Servia, J.-L. Classification of Common Bean Landraces of Three Species Using a Neuroevolutionary Approach with Probabilistic Color Characterization. *Math. Comput. Appl.* **2025**, *30*, 66. [CrossRef]
9. Temizel, C.; Odi, U.; Li, K.; Liu, L.; Tutun, S.; Santos, J. Permeability Prediction Using Vision Transformers. *Math. Comput. Appl.* **2025**, *30*, 71. [CrossRef]
10. Barradas-Palmeros, J.-A.; López-Herrera, C.-A.; Mezura-Montes, E.; Acosta-Mesa, H.-G.; López-Lobato, A.-L. Testing Neural Architecture Search Efficient Evaluation Methods in DeepGA. *Math. Comput. Appl.* **2025**, *30*, 74. [CrossRef]
11. Bertolo, S.; Elaskar, S.; Gutiérrez Marcantoni, L. Application of the Kurganov–Tadmor Scheme in Curvilinear Coordinates for Supersonic Flow. *Math. Comput. Appl.* **2025**, *30*, 92. [CrossRef]
12. Ratner, S.V.; Lychev, A.V.; Muravleva, E.D.; Muravlev, D.M. Measuring Circular Economy with Data Envelopment Analysis: A Systematic Literature Review. *Math. Comput. Appl.* **2025**, *30*, 102. [CrossRef]
13. Martines-Arano, H.; Vera-Ku, M.; Álvarez-Espino, R.; Vivanco-Benavides, L.E.; Martínez-González, C.L.; Torres-Torres, C. Thrinax radiata Seed Germplasm Dynamics Analysis Assisted by Chaos Theory. *Math. Comput. Appl.* **2025**, *30*, 113. [CrossRef]
14. Bolle, R.; Jarra, I.; Secrest, J.A. An Exposition on the Kaniadakis κ-Deformed Decay Differential Equation. *Math. Comput. Appl.* **2025**, *30*, 115. [CrossRef]
15. Kamran, M.; Abdullah, J.Y.; Ahmad Satmi, A.S.; Genisa, M.; Majeed, A.; Nadeem, T. Mathematical Modeling and Analysis of Tumor Growth Models Integrating Treatment Therapy. *Math. Comput. Appl.* **2025**, *30*, 119. [CrossRef]
16. Tavakoli, F.; Mohammadpur, D.; Sartakhti, J.S.; Manshaei, M.H. Reinforcement Learning-Driven Evolutionary Stackelberg Game Model for Adaptive Breast Cancer Therapy. *Math. Comput. Appl.* **2025**, *30*, 134. [CrossRef]

https://doi.org/10.3390/mca3101002€

Mathematical and Computational Applications

MDPI

Article

Impact Loading on a Patient-Specific Head Model: The Significance of Brain Constitutive Models and Loading Location

Amirhossein Gandomirouzbahani [1,2], Hadi Taghizadeh [3,*], Iman Z. Oskui [4,*] and Fábio A. O. Fernandes [1,2,*]

1 TEMA—Centre for Mechanical Technology and Automation, Department of Mechanical Engineering, University of Aveiro, Campus de Santiago, 3810-193 Aveiro, Portugal; amirhossein.gandomi@ua.pt
2 LASI—Intelligent Systems Associate Laboratory, 4800-058 Guimarães, Portugal
3 Tissue Mechanics Laboratory, Faculty of Biomedical Engineering, Sahand University of Technology, Tabriz 51335/1996, Iran
4 Biomechanical Engineering Group, Faculty of Biomedical Engineering, Sahand University of Technology, Tabriz 51335/1996, Iran
* Correspondence: taghizadeh@sut.ac.ir (H.T.); zoljanahi@sut.ac.ir (I.Z.O.); fabiofernandes@ua.pt (F.A.O.F.); Tel.: +9841-33-458-415 (H.T.); +9841-33-458-412 (I.Z.O.)

Abstract

Head impacts are common incidents that may cause traumatic brain injury (TBI), which imposes significant economic and social burdens. This study developed a patient-specific head model to address the significance of the brain's constitutive model and loading location on head impact. Two hyperelastic (Model I and Model II) constitutive models and one hyper-viscoelastic (Model III) constitutive model for the brain tissue were developed. In Models II and III, white and gray matter heterogeneities were included. Respective volumetric and deviatoric responses were compared for a frontal head impact. Then, the load was applied to the head's frontal, lateral, and posterior regions to report location-wise outcomes. The findings indicated that Model I, which was based on almost quasi-static experiments, underestimated the deviatoric responses. Although the pressure contours were similar for Models II and III, the latter included viscous effects and provided more accurate deviatoric responses. Lateral loading indicated a significantly higher risk of TBI. Interestingly, the deviatoric responses and strain energy density of the brain did not decay with relaxation of the impact load. Hence, the incidence of TBI should be explored after load relaxation.

Keywords: traumatic brain injury; hyper-viscoelastic constitutive modeling; deviatoric and volumetric response; stress analysis; finite element analysis

1. Introduction

According to a report by the Centers for Disease Control and Prevention, 1.7 million cases of traumatic brain injuries (TBIs) occur annually in the United States, and TBI was associated with 30.5% of all injury-related deaths [1]. The most common causes of TBI are falling, collisions with obstacles or objects, and vehicle accidents [2]. Respective treatment and rehabilitation costs are among the factors that seriously increase TBI's economic burden [1].

Human head models are computational tools and representations of the head that provide the possibility of detailed mechanical investigations using simulations. Essential anatomical components for developing finite element head models include the skull, brain tissue, and cerebrospinal fluid region [3,4].

Computational models of head impact conditions, including those addressing the heterogeneities of brain components and the incidence of TBI have been studied and explored [5,6]. The finite element method has great potential in addressing different scenarios of head impact loading. Accurate model outcomes depend on accurate geometries, reliable mechanical properties (MPs), and realistic loading and boundary conditions.

Brain tissue mechanics researchers have demonstrated the brain tissue's nonlinear and different tension/compression responses [7,8], apparent homogenous behavior in certain regions, such as the cerebral cortex [9], and incompressibility [10]. Brain tissue is composed of white and gray matter; the stiffer behavior of the former [11] is complemented by the significantly more compliant response of the latter [12]. Therefore, the risk of TBI in different brain regions varies [13]. Newer studies, in which more evolved models were used to integrate nonlinear and time-dependent features to show the significant regional and temporal variability in brain tissue mechanics across various loading modes, have supported these findings [14]. While testing on tissue samples has been utilized for extraction of nonlinear and time-dependent behaviors of the brain [11,12], further advancements have also demonstrated the utility of magnetic resonance elastography as a non-invasive way to quantify such properties [15,16].

While some studies have examined more basic non-human models [17,18], with the progress of computing systems, complex models of human head dynamics, with sophisticated geometrical features and nonlinear MPs, have been proposed. Adding facial features improves the accuracy of the models [19]. In addition, adopting more complex geometries can partially improve the accuracy of simulation outcomes [20,21]. Some studies have also focused on more specific conditions, such as the mechanical behavior of cranial implants under impact loading in a finite element head model [22]. Furthermore, the integration of finite element models with advanced methods, like machine learning, has also been studied for practical aspects like functional outcomes in TBI [23].

Allocating suitable MPs for the heterogeneous and soft brain tissue is the pivotal point of head impact studies [19]. Earlier studies assumed linear elastic behavior for the head model components, including the brain [24]. Zhou et al. [25] stated the importance of mechanical differences between the white and gray matter in the impact response of the head model, and such differences have been further looked into in more recent studies [26]. Some other studies scaled the stiffness of the gray matter by a constant factor to obtain the MPs of the white matter [27]. For TBI simulations, such assumptions are inadequate, and separate allocation of material parameters for the white and gray matter is necessary.

Considering the time-dependent and viscoelastic characteristics observed from the brain tissue [12,28], viscoelastic constitutive models have been favored for mechanical description of the brain tissue [20,21,29–32], but, as mentioned above, hyper-viscoelastic models more accurately reflect the MPs of brain tissue. While nonlinear and time-dependent properties were considered for the white and gray matter in further improved head models, in some studies, a single constitutive model was considered for the whole brain [5,31–34]. In some other studies, high rates of impact loadings were neglected in proposed constitutive models [22,33,35], since these models are based on quasi-static experiments of the brain tissue [10,36].

To apply impact loading to the models, the head encounters impact from objects directed at specific regions [5,20,25] or collides with obstacles at defined velocities and positions [20,37]. In the modeling environment, impact conditions are established by applying force amplitude directly to a region of the head model over a specific period as a distributed load [21,29]. Furthermore, collision data are reconstructed in the laboratory to inform subsequent simulations, incorporating factors like acceleration [33,38]. In the recreation of blast exposures, pressure shocks are employed in shock tube simulations [34].

The location and direction of the impact loading on the head play principal roles in determining the extent of brain tissue damage. Some comprehensive studies in the literature have addressed these parameters [37–40]. However, simplified geometries [39,41] or undemanding elastic and viscoelastic properties for the brain [24,38,40,42] are drawbacks of these studies. Also, some head models have been created for a specific group, such as infants [37], as this limits the adoption of the reported outcomes for general TBI cases.

The current study proposes a new finite element head model to address some of the mentioned limitations in the literature on head impact biomechanics and TBI investigation. The aim was to evaluate the influence of mechanical properties of brain tissue and loading locations on the brain's mechanical responses during head impacts, focusing on critical factors of TBI risk investigation. In this study, coefficients for constitutive models of brain tissue were determined to ensure suitable performance in investigating impact loading conditions.

The geometry of the head was imported into the numerical modeling environment with reasonable accuracy. In the investigation process, three constitutive models were examined to select a refined model for the brain for impact simulations. The white and gray matter heterogeneities were incorporated in the proposed model with different MPs, including rate-dependent parameters. After the developed head model was verified, it was subjected to frontal, lateral, and posterior impact loadings, and the risks of TBI were investigated.

2. Materials and Methods

2.1. Head Model Geometry

Magnetic resonance (MR) scans, including 870 images with 250 μm thick slices, were obtained from the online database provided by Lüsebrink et al. [43] and were used to generate the geometry of the head model. Using 3D Slicer 5.0.1 software, the skull bone was identified by the provided segmentation tools and created as a single component. Then, the brain tissue was also identified from the image stacks, shown in Figure 1a, along the skull bone. The white and gray matter were also detected separately by appropriate thresholding (Figure 1a). The space between the skull and brain tissue were regarded as the cerebrospinal fluid (CSF) (Figure 1a). In addition, the facial bones were included in the model as a rigid part (Figure 1b), and the scalp was assumed as a nonstructural mass over the superior and posterior surfaces of the skull. Considering the vital functions of the midbrain and the prevalence of respective injuries in TBI investigations [3,4,44], it was regarded as an anatomical landmark (Figure 1a) to evaluate probable injury onset.

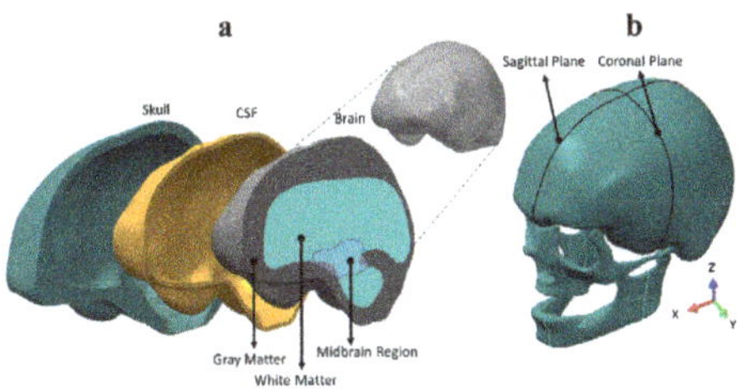

Figure 1. (**a**) An illustration of the major parts of the developed head model and the approximate anatomical location of the midbrain. (**b**) The geometry of the whole model, including the facial bones and mandible. The origin of the coordinate system is positioned at the midpoint of the line between the auditory meatus in the midsagittal plane. The Y-axis coincides with this line, with its positive direction from right to left. The Z-axis is in the midsagittal plane and is positive along the superior direction. Hence, the X-axis is positive anteriorly. It is represented outside the origin and next to the head model to visualize the directions better. The sagittal and coronal planes coincide with the X–Z and Y–Z planes, respectively.

Scalp and facial bone masses influence the physical properties of the head model, such as the total mass, center of gravity (COG), and moments of inertia. These mass values were determined based on previous studies, and are consistent with those reported in the literature [25]. The total mass, the center of gravity (COG), and the moments of inertia of the presented head model were calculated, and are shown next to the experimental evidence from Yoganandan et al. [45] in Table 1.

Table 1. Physical features of the head model and experimental measurements presented by Yoganandan et al. [45], based on the coordinate system of Figure 1.

	Mass (kg)	COG Coordinates (cm) X	Y	Z	I_{XX} (kg.cm^2)	I_{YY} (kg.cm^2)	I_{ZZ} (kg.cm^2)
Head Model	3.92	1.4	−0.2	3.4	159	230	129
Experimental Measurement [45]	3.88 ± 0.47	1.3 ± 0.28	−0.1 ± 0.13	2.5 ± 1.08	174.9 ± 45.2	219.3 ± 50.8	159 ± 25.7

A right-hand coordinate system was used for physical measurements of the head model, similar to the study by Yoganandan et al. [45] (Figure 1). Through this validation step, the close association of the present model data with the experimental evaluations indicates the potential of the proposed model for TBI investigations.

2.2. Model MPs

Due to the importance of brain tissue mechanics in studying dynamic responses of the brain in the present head model, the CSF and skull were assumed to behave as linear elastic materials (Table 2). Although these assumptions may have affected the results, they favored a reduction in the computational complexity to help increase focus on the brain tissue. The choice of elastic properties for the CSF is common in similar previous studies [20,27,35], and it has been characterized as a very soft and incompressible material here (Table 2). Practically, the elastic behavior of the CSF was determined based on the assumption of incompressibility, with a bulk modulus of 2.16 GPa and a Poisson's ratio of 0.4999 [18]. Also, the density of the brain tissue was considered to be 1040 kg/m^3 [20,33].

Table 2. The physical and mechanical properties of the skull and CSF in the head model.

Model Components	Elastic Modulus (MPa)	Poisson's Ratio	Density (kg/m^3)	References
Skull	10,000	0.21	1800	[46,47]
CSF	1.314	0.4999	1040	[20]

Due to its very soft nature and its high water content, brain tissue has shown hyperelastic, time-dependent, and incompressible behaviors [11–13,48]. In order to investigate the effects of the brain tissue MPs on the head model behavior, three different constitutive models were allocated from previous studies on the brain tissue.

In "Model I", the mechanical behavior of the brain tissue was assumed to be nonlinear elastic with material coefficients, based on Mihai et al. [48]. In this model, the same MPs were assigned for the white and gray matter. Also, the allocated material parameters of Model I were not extracted at impact loading rates.

Therefore, for Model II the nonlinear elastic properties of the white and gray matter were taken into account based on the experimental data of Jin et al. [11]. The mentioned data were collected at a strain rate of 30/s, which resembles head impact loading rates [44]. Model III incorporates the hyperelastic behavior in Model II, and also includes time-dependent characteristics of the white and gray matter. In the latter case, the material parameters of the hyper-viscoelastic constitutive model were obtained by interpolating the data from the stress relaxation experiments of Finan et al. [12]. Indeed, a hyper-viscoelastic constitutive model was considered for Model III, with the instantaneous response of Model II. It is worth mentioning that all of the chosen data sets (for Models II and III) were gathered from experimental studies of human brain samples [11,12]. However, one limitation of the present study was the use of data collected from different individuals' brain tissue. Data were either from post-mortem experiments [11] or from brain samples obtained during epilepsy surgery [12]. For ethical reasons, such limitations exist in testing human brain tissue and affect the data. However, in the study by Finan et al. [12], an attempt was made to use healthy, non-epileptic samples that were collected as surgical waste from surgery procedures.

A general expression for the equation of motion can be represented through momentum balance, as follows:

$$\rho \frac{\partial^2 v}{\partial t^2} = \text{div}\ \sigma + \rho b \tag{1}$$

where ρ is the mass density, v is the displacement vector, σ is the stress tensor, so the divergence of this tensor would account for the internal force per unit volume, and b represents body forces per unit volume.

It is noteworthy that Equations (2)–(7) are presented below for further explanations regarding the process of determining coefficients of the constitutive models based on experimental data sets. The Ogden strain energy density function (SEDF) has been popular in brain tissue constitutive modeling [10,14,48] and head impact simulations [5,33]. The Ogden SEDF is expressed as a function of principal stretches (λ_1, λ_2, and λ_3), as follows:

$$U = \sum_{i=1}^{N} \frac{2\mu_i}{\alpha_i{}^2}\left(\lambda_1{}^{\alpha_i} + \lambda_2{}^{\alpha_i} + \lambda_3{}^{\alpha_i} - 3\right) \tag{2}$$

where N denotes the order of the Ogden SEDF, and μ_i and α_i are the material parameters. In the present study, N was chosen to be 4. Using the Ogden SEDF, in theory, the three principal values of the Cauchy stresses can be computed as follows:

$$\sigma_j = -p + \lambda_j \frac{\partial U}{\partial \lambda_j} = -p + \sum_{i=1}^{N} \frac{2\mu_i}{\alpha_i}\left(\lambda_j{}^{\alpha_i}\right)\ ;\ j = 1.2.3 \tag{3}$$

where p is an unknown scalar in this theoretical representation that must be determined from the equilibrium equations and the boundary conditions.

Under uniaxial tensile test conditions, with the stretch ratio given as λ_1, and considering the assumption of incompressibility of the brain tissue [10] ($\lambda_1\lambda_2\lambda_3 = 1$) and equal stretch ratios in the transverse directions ($\lambda_2 = \lambda_3 = \lambda_1{}^{-\frac{1}{2}}$), the Ogden SEDF is simplified as follows:

$$U = \sum_{i=1}^{N} \frac{2\mu_i}{\alpha_i{}^2}\left(\lambda_1{}^{\alpha_i} + 2\lambda_1{}^{-\frac{\alpha_i}{2}} - 3\right) \tag{4}$$

The associated principal Cauchy stress along the uniaxial testing direction (σ_1) is obtained according to the boundary conditions of the uniaxial tensile test ($\sigma_2 = \sigma_3 = 0$), as follows:

$$\sigma_1 = \sum_{i=1}^{N} \frac{2\mu_i}{\alpha_i}\left(\lambda_1{}^{\alpha_i} - \lambda_1{}^{-\frac{\alpha_i}{2}}\right) \tag{5}$$

Furthermore, the principal nominal stress along the uniaxial testing direction (P_1) is calculated as follows:

$$P_1 = \sum_{i=1}^{N} \frac{2\mu_i}{\alpha_i}\left(\lambda^{\alpha_i - 1} - \lambda^{-\frac{\alpha_i}{2} - 1}\right) \tag{6}$$

Also, the shear time-dependent behavior of the brain tissue was represented by the Prony series of the generalized Maxwell model for the relative shear modulus:

$$g(t) = \frac{G(t)}{G_0} = \left(1 - \sum_{i=1}^{M} g_i \left(1 - e^{\frac{-t}{\tau_i}}\right)\right) \tag{7}$$

where $G(t)$ is the shear relaxation modulus, G_0 is the initial shear modulus, M indicates the number of branches with viscous terms, g_i is the relaxation coefficient, τ_i represents the relaxation times, which, for the generalized Maxwell, are the parameters for each branch, and t denotes time. In this study, M was set to 3, which was appropriate to capture the observed brain tissue's relaxation behavior in the obtained experimental data (Figure 2b,c).

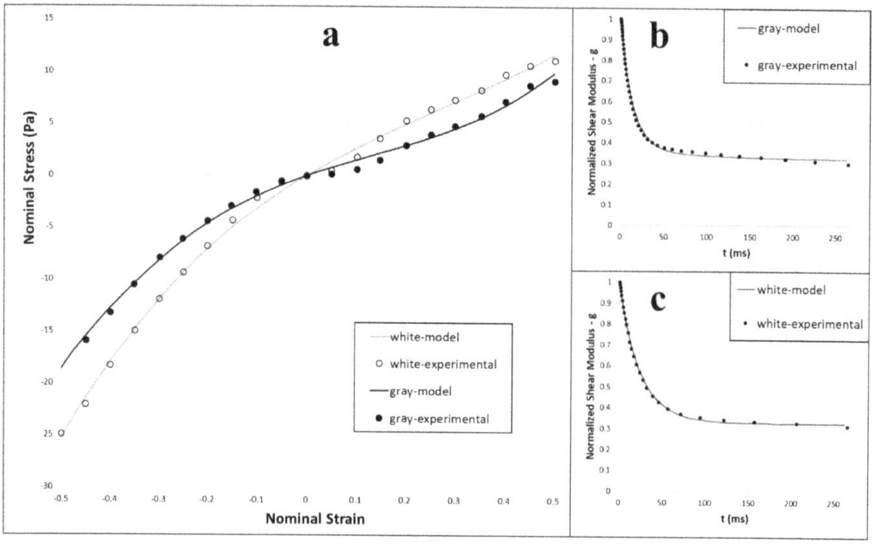

Figure 2. (**a**) Uniaxial extension–compression data for the gray and white matter (from [11]) and their respective fits with the Ogden hyperelastic SEDF. (**b**,**c**) Normalized relaxation data (from [12]) and the interpolated viscoelastic response for the gray and white matter, respectively.

The parameter μ represents the shear behavior in the Ogden SEDF. Therefore, in the resulting hyper-viscoelastic constitutive model based on it (Model III), μ is considered the time-dependent shear modulus, upon which the relaxation behavior is defined through the Prony series, as follows:

$$\mu(t) = \mu_0 \left(1 - \sum_{i=1}^{M} g_i \left(1 - e^{\frac{-t}{\tau_i}}\right)\right) \tag{8}$$

where $\mu(t)$ is the above-mentioned material parameter at each moment, and μ_0 is its initial or instantaneous value.

In order to allocate the material constants of the brain tissue from experimental data, curve fitting was carried out using a nonlinear optimization algorithm in MATLAB 2022 software. An objective function (x) was proposed as the difference between the model and empirical data, and the material parameters were allocated to minimize the objective function (interested readers can find more detail on the soft tissue constitutive modeling optimization procedure in [49]). In general, the optimization algorithm for determining the material parameters of the constitutive model required minimizing the objective error function, according to the following equation:

$$x = \sum_{i=1}^{n} (C_m - C_e)^2 \tag{9}$$

where n represents the number of experimental data, C_e represents the experimental data, and C_m represents the parameters corresponding to the material models. In the case of the Ogden SEDF, the C parameter represents the nominal stress, and in the viscoelastic equation, it represents the relative shear modulus.

The experimental stress data for the white and gray matter [11] were fitted with the Ogden hyperelastic constitutive model (Figure 2a), and respective material parameters were determined (Table 3). Also, the fitted normalized relaxation of the generalized Maxwell model (Equation (7)) to the experimental data of Finan et al. [12] is represented in Figure 2 (panes b and c), respectively, for the gray and white matter. The allocated material parameters for the proposed three brain tissue models are reported in Table 3.

Table 3. MPs of the brain tissue in three constitutive models.

Model Type	Brain Component	Ogden Material Parameters								Viscoelastic Parameters in Prony Series					
		μ_1 (Pa)	α_1 (-)	μ_2 (Pa)	α_2 (-)	μ_3 (Pa)	α_3 (-)	μ_4 (Pa)	α_4 (-)	g_1 (-)	τ_1 (ms)	g_2 (-)	τ_2 (ms)	g_3 (-)	τ_3 (ms)
Model I (hyperelastic)	Gray matter White matter	−5877	2	5043	−2	2322	4	−1002	−4	-	-	-	-	-	-
Model II (hyperelastic)	Gray matter	45,670	1	−55,270	3	22,150	5	−6976	−2	-	-	-	-	-	-
	White matter	22,860	1	−15,790	3	7356	5	−4928	−2	-	-	-	-	-	-
Model III (hyper-viscoelastic)	Gray matter	45,670	1	−55,270	3	22,150	5	−6976	−2	0.1091	10	0.5237	15	0.0474	100
	White matter	22,860	1	−15,790	3	7356	5	−4928	−2	0.0578	15	0.6116	25	0.0082	250

2.3. *Interface and Boundary Conditions*

For all model components, continuity conditions were imposed at their interfaces, which is a common approach in similar studies [29,35,47]. This means that a common surface was defined between each pair of components in contact, causing no relative movement between them. As a result, it is implied that the mechanical parameters at these boundaries are consistent and shared among the contacting components. Although similar studies have employed the continuity conditions mentioned above, this option differs from realistic conditions with the possibility of relative movements. Therefore, such simplification represents a limitation of the present study, and future investigations can benefit from incorporating more complex definitions in this regard.

Furthermore, the facial bones and mandible area were tied to the skull. The effects of the neck joints on head dynamics were almost insignificant for the impact loading conditions [24]; hence, a free boundary condition without any constraint was acquired for this area in the present study.

2.4. *Loading Conditions*

The applied loading profile is shown in Figure 3a. The proposed loading regime was based on experiments by Nahum et al. [50]. In that experimental study, a seated human cadaver was hit on the head, specifically with impacts directed at the frontal bone along the midsagittal plane. Then, the intracranial pressure was measured at different spots over time, including a site behind the frontal bone near the impact area. The pressure in this spot was called the coup pressure. The coup pressure data from the experiments by Nahum et al. [50] are utilized to validate the present head model performance in the next section.

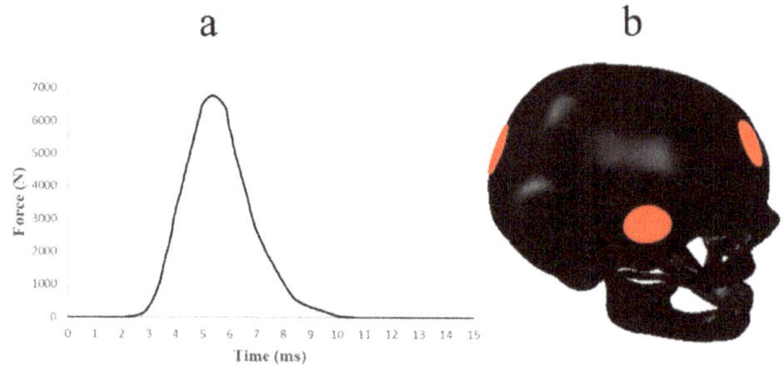

Figure 3. (**a**) The impact loading profile based on the Nahum et al. [50]. (**b**) The locations of different areas on the head subjected to impact loading.

The location of the impact is a determining factor in the biomechanics of the head. Hence, three mentioned loading profiles were applied on three sides of the head, namely the frontal, lateral (near the temporal area), and posterior (near the occipital bone) sides of the head (Figure 3b).

Mechanical analysis of the head model was carried out using ABAQUS 2017 software and the explicit dynamic method. The explicit solver is suitable for the simulation of dynamic cases, like high-speed head impacts, because it can better handle high strain rates, nonlinearities, rapidly changing stress and strain states, and large deformations or material damages; this is because it does not require an implicit tangent stiffness matrix and it does not involve checking iterations or convergence criteria [31].

However, a limitation of an explicit method is its inability to strictly enforce incompressibility, unlike implicit approaches that may solve for pressure as a separate field variable. Explicit methods approximate near-incompressible properties through constitutive responses of the material, which may influence predictions of the pressure response. Despite this limitation, explicit approaches have been commonly used for studying head impact dynamics [5,20,29,31,34,35,37], providing computational efficiencies and the possibility of investigating the mechanics of head components like brain tissue.

Mesh-convergence was attained with 106,372 quadratic tetrahedral elements. In this process, to investigate whether the results were independent of the mesh used, the impact on the head model was performed in cases of different numbers of elements. By gradually increasing the number of elements, the maximum internal energy values of the head model were analyzed. Then, the desired number of elements was selected when the differences decreased and reached an almost stable state where variations were less than 0.5%.

To verify the performance of the head model, after the frontal loading, coup pressure was gathered from beneath the impact site in the CSF region and compared with the results of Nahum et al. [50]. The values obtained for the constitutive Model I were utilized in the verification step. In the next step, responses from Models I, II, and III were investigated under the same frontal loading. Then, the effects of loading location (the frontal, posterior, and lateral sides of the head) were studied on Model III, incorporating the viscous effects.

As mentioned in the study by Chen and Ostoja-Starzewski [29] regarding the decoupling of dilatation (pressure) and distortion (shear) or deviatoric parts in the equation of motion of a homogeneous material, the mechanical response of the brain can be separated into dilatational (related to volume changes) and deviatoric (related to shape changing without volume alteration) behaviors. Pressure, as an important dilatational variable [42], and von Mises stresses, as the representative deviatoric behavior [29], were studied for the proposed head model. Pressure is defined as the mean value of the three principal stresses, while the von Mises stress, as a measure of deviatoric response, is based on the differences between the principal stresses. These two mechanical measures are represented as follows:

$$Pressure = \frac{\sigma_1 + \sigma_2 + \sigma_3}{3} \tag{10}$$

$$\sigma_{von\ Mises} = \sqrt{\frac{1}{2}\left((\sigma_1 - \sigma_2)^2 + (\sigma_2 - \sigma_3)^2 + (\sigma_1 - \sigma_3)^2\right)} \tag{11}$$

where $\sigma_{von\ Mises}$ is the von Mises stress, and σ_1, σ_2, and σ_3 denote the principal stresses.

For a more comprehensive investigation of deviatoric responses at different loading locations, the stress values were compared along specific pathlines for the three loading cases. These pathlines started near the impact site, spanning the head COG (near the corpus callosum), and reached the opposite side of the brain (Figure 4). Each pathline included a set of 30 elements with approximately 4 mm steps selected, and stress values were extracted. In each case, the first element in the impact site was numbered 1, and the last element on the opposite side was numbered 30.

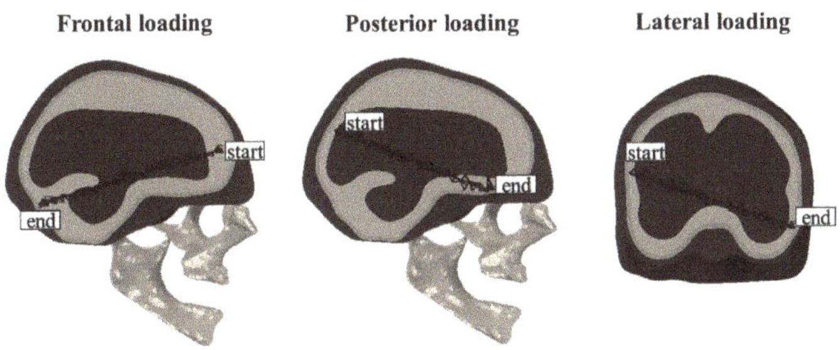

Figure 4. Data extraction pathlines, including the start and end points for each of the frontal and posterior loadings (sagittal view) and the lateral loading (coronal view).

3. Results and Discussion

3.1. Model Verification

The coup pressure profile of the head model (Model I) was compared against the experimental results of Nahum et al. [50], as shown in Figure 5. Using this experimental data for the performance validation of different head models is also common in other studies [5,20,24]. The agreement between the model and the experimental data was assessed using metrics such as the difference in peak pressure magnitude, being a low value of about 23 kPa. Also, a difference of less than 0.5 milliseconds was observed regarding the timing of the peak pressure value.

Although the maximum pressure value of the model is about 13% higher than the respective experimental pressure, the general agreement between the simulation and experiment outcomes indicates the validity of the proposed head model for further head impact studies.

Using the mentioned impact data to investigate the performance of head models by comparing it with experimental conditions is common in similar studies [3,5,20,21,29,47,51]. However, the limitations caused in this regard include the fact that the Nahum et al. [50] study was not recent and was conducted on cadavers.

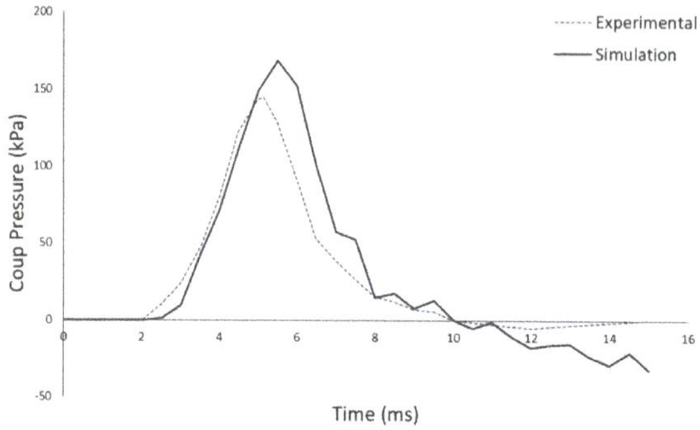

Figure 5. The coup pressure trend for the proposed head model (using Model I) and the cadaver experiments by Nahum et al. [50]. For both cases, the same frontal regions of the skull were loaded with the impact loading profile shown in Figure 3a.

3.2. *Significance of Brain MPs*

In Figure 6, the distributions of brain pressure for the three proposed models are presented on the sagittal plane at time steps of 3, 5, 7, 9, and 11 ms. For the three models with different brain MPs, no apparent differences in respective pressure distribution were noticeable (Figure 6). Such similar pressure contours for the three models are most likely due to the incompressibility constraint of the brain tissue. The high bulk modulus provided a nearly incompressible state for the brain tissue. Such behavior was associated with considerably high dilatational wave speeds [29]. Hence, even for short time intervals in the order of milliseconds, as seen in impact loading, the dilatational pressure waves would have many reflections in the bounded environment of the skull. As a result, at any instant of loading time, a dynamic equilibrium state is depicted, mostly independent of the brain MPs (Figure 6). Noticeable negative pressure at the opposite side of the impact in the 4–7 ms period might also have injured the respective regions [52].

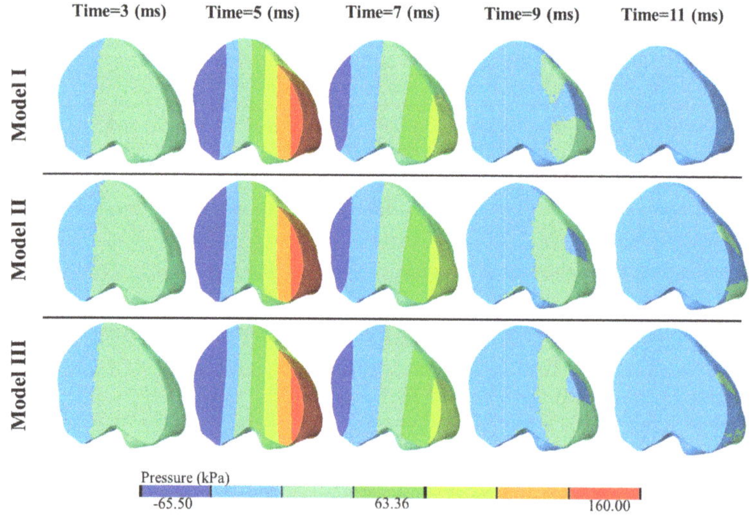

Figure 6. Brain pressure regimes for the three models of the brain at different time steps during the impact loading. For the range of proposed constitutive models, the maximum pressure values are observed at 5 ms, which coincides with the time of peak impact load.

Based on the von Mises stress contours of the brain at different time steps in Figure 7, shear waves moved from the surface of the gray matter toward the inner white matter region. Despite the respective dilatational behaviors, the brain's deviatoric responses mainly depended on the proposed constitutive models.

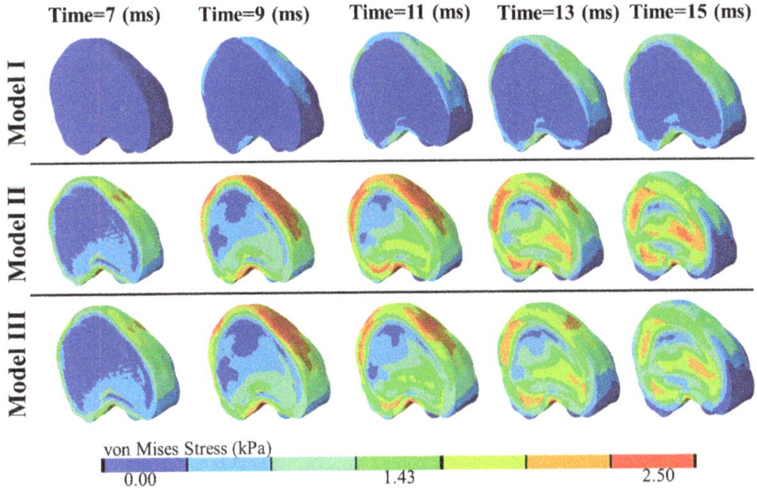

Figure 7. Von Mises stress contours of the brain models during the 15 ms interval. The impact loading diminishes after 10 ms, but the shear waves still exist after 15 ms. Markedly lower stress values for Model I are evident. The viscoelastic behavior of the gray and white matter in Model III proposes lower von Mises stresses than the respective hyperelastic model (Model II).

The observed differences between the deviatoric and dilatational behaviors arise from the lower speed of the shear waves compared to the dilatational waves [29]. Such lower wave speed made it possible to observe the differences between the performances of the constitutive models (especially Model I) in short periods of impact loadings. Notably, propagated shear waves did not diminish even after unloading at 10 ms, and von Mises stresses keep fluctuating in the brain (t = 13 ms and t = 15 ms in Figure 7).

In the case of Model I, the von Mises stress values were significantly lower compared to the respective time steps of the other two models (Figure 7). Noticeably, lower stress values for the inner brain regions in Model I were observed because the respective constitutive model is not based on impact experiments, and hence underestimates the brain tissue stresses in impact loading.

Although the overall patterns of deviatoric behavior were similar for the respective time steps of Models II and III, lower von Mises stresses were observed in the case of Model III, especially for the last 4 milliseconds (Figure 7). The viscous damping characteristics of Model III led to the observed lower stress values compared to Model II. The brain tissue and its main components were proven to demonstrate nonlinear elastic and time-dependent responses [12,13], and viscous effects were part of their nature.

It could be concluded that Model III (hyper-viscoelastic) is the most suitable here for studying head impacts and investigating TBI incidence. However, this is based on the specific experimental data that indicates material parameters. It is acknowledged that this finding may have limitations in its application for broad accident scenarios. Therefore, further investigation is encouraged under varying conditions as well.

The maximum shear stress of the midbrain area (as a valid used injury criterion) in Models II and III was 2.44 kPa and 2.13 kPa, respectively, while in Model I, such stress

(0.64 kPa) was less than the other two cases. According to the criteria of TBI occurrence [3], in Models II and III, the brain tissue was more near to the borderline of damage incidence.

It was shown that brain pressures did not provide enough detail on the time steps of the impact (in the order of milliseconds), and they rapidly reached an equilibrium state, while the shear waves existed in the head even after the impact. Therefore, deformations and deviatoric behaviors were crucial for these studies.

Although care was taken to select appropriate experimental data and indicate models for the brain tissue so that the present model could have good performance in general investigations of head impacts, there are still differences between individuals regarding the properties of their brain tissue, which may cause differences between studies using a single head model. Such differences are among the limitations of using a patient-specific head model, which affect their practicality aspect, besides their applicability.

3.3. *Effect of Loading Location*

Figure 8 depicts the von Mises stress contours of shear wave propagation during the impact loading in different locations. Stress values for the lateral loading were significantly higher than the other two loading cases. To perform a neat comparison of the cases, maximum values of brain pressures, von Mises stresses, and nominal strains in the midbrain area for all impact cases were collected, as shown in Table 4. The differences between the lateral loading and the other two cases are remarkable. The maximum pressure in the lateral loading case is more than twice that of the other cases, and the maximum von Mises stresses and nominal strains are more than three times their respective parameters in the frontal and posterior impact cases.

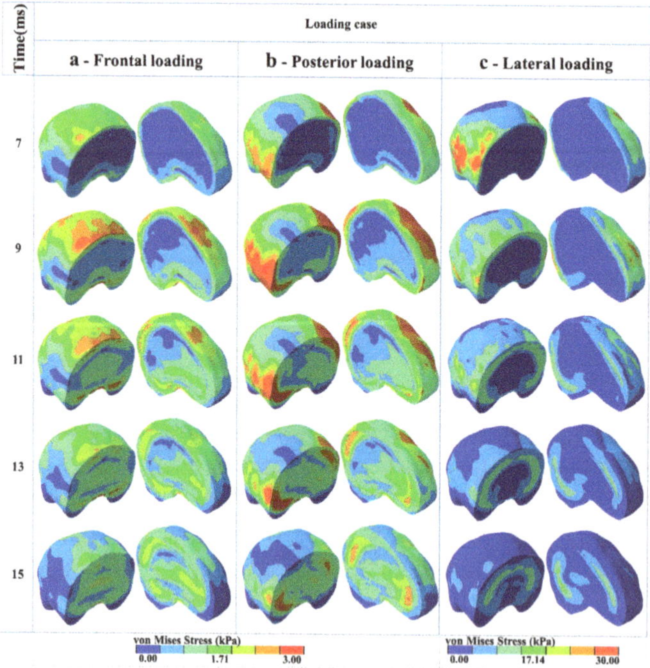

Figure 8. Von Mises stresses distribution for impact loading on frontal, posterior, and lateral locations on the head. The contours of the lateral loading have a different scale because of one-order-higher stress values.

Table 4. The maximum values of brain pressure, von Mises stress, and nominal strain in the midbrain area for impact loading on three different head locations.

Load Case	Frontal	Posterior	Lateral
Maximum brain pressure (kPa)	159.4	178.8	467.9
Maximum von Mises stress of midbrain (kPa)	1.9	2.2	7.7
Maximum nominal strain of midbrain	0.078	0.089	0.284

Based on the previous literature, a brain pressure of 173 kPa poses a minimal risk of damage, while pressures exceeding 200 kPa are associated with high risks of contusions, edema, and hematoma [4]. According to the values given in Table 4, the maximum pressure for the posterior impact case is within the injury threshold, and the lateral loading case demonstrates severe TBI incidence. Strains beyond 0.26 in the midbrain are reported to increase the incidence of mild traumatic brain injury or concussion by 25% [4]. However, the maximum strain values in the frontal and posterior loadings do not pose such risks of brain injury, though the strain for the lateral loading case is beyond the given threshold.

To observe the trend of stress changes more closely, the pathlines defined earlier were focused on (Figure 4). Accordingly, von Mises stress curves are reported for the second half of the loading interval, which is associated with peak values of the stress wave in the brain (Figure 8). These curves can represent the considerable effects of shear waves on the internal areas of the brain. For the frontal loading, stresses over the entire pathline increase in the first two time steps of 7 and 9 ms. Following the effect of deviatoric waves, the maximum stress values do not reduce noticeably at subsequent time steps (Time = 11 to 15 ms, Figure 9a). In the gray matter near the two endpoints, no considerable stress changes are evident after 11 ms (Figure 9a).

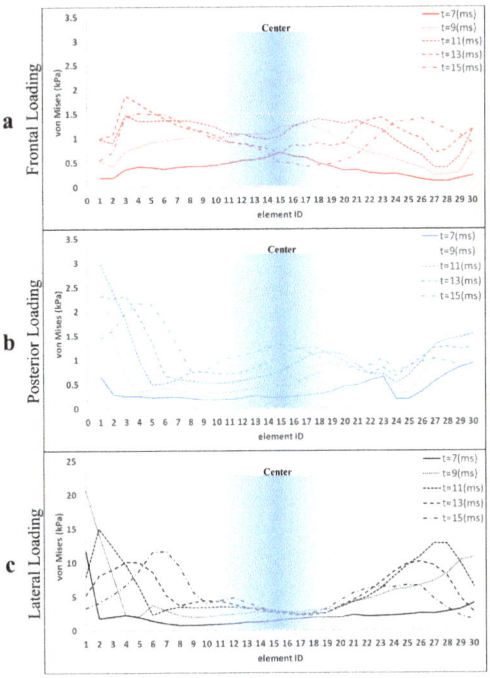

Figure 9. Changes in von Mises stress along the introduced pathlines for the head's frontal, posterior, and lateral loading. A different set of axis limits was adopted for the lateral loading, because of much higher von Mises stresses in this case.

For the posterior loading (Figure 9b), near the impact site, the stresses are significantly higher than in the center. In addition, shear waves are observable near the two endpoints of the pathline, especially for the 11–15 ms range. Consistently with the general trend (posterior loading in Figure 8b), a shift in local shear wave peaks toward the center and slightly reduced stress values are also noticeable.

The incidence of stress peaks near the corpus callosum indicates shear wave propagation into the white matter areas. In the frontal loading, the initially observed inner wave peak moves away from the center over time (Figure 9a, t = 11 to 15 ms). However, for the loading on the posterior side of the head, the peak is observed close to the end of the curve (far from the loading site), and it moves toward the center and reaches the corpus callosum area at the final time step (Figure 9b, t = 15 ms). In both the frontal and posterior loadings, the inner peak stresses relocate towards the back of the head. The peak magnitude increases slightly for the posterior loading case. However, the central areas demonstrate lower stresses compared to the endpoints, showing low shear wave propagations into these areas.

For the loading on the lateral side, stresses near both endpoints rapidly rise and show faster decay. For most of the inspected interval, shear waves remain out of the central areas of the brain. Only in the last 4 ms, after the relaxation of impact loading, do the waves advance toward the corpus callosum area (~pathline center), although the stress values in this area are minimal compared to the endpoints (Figure 9c). The shear waves propagate more rapidly in the lateral and posterior loadings. This is compatible with general observations of stress contours (Figure 8b,c) and highlights the importance of shear waves in the cortex areas and the gray matter, while propagations into the white matter areas are lower in these two loadings. On the other hand, compared to the other two loading scenarios, stress values near the corpus callosum are higher than the endpoints for the frontal loading (Figure 9a). Therefore, the corpus callosum and other internal components of the brain are more susceptible to damage accumulation and consequent adversities.

The observed distinctions for the studied impact locations arise from the asymmetric and complex geometry of the head and its compartments. Because of the higher stiffness of the skull compared to other components of the head, respective stress wave transmissions are much faster than those of the brain tissue. With the given complications of the head model, observed differences in stress patterns are due to these heterogeneities. However, these observations underline the importance of designing more sophisticated head protection devices, as the brain's resulting stress state depends on the location of impact loading.

The loading conditions used in the present study give a general idea of head impacts, but they are based on simpler scenarios, and might not fully represent the complexity of real-world incidents. Vast variability in factors like the loading angle, force, and duration of the impact, or variations in individual body structures, could lead to more complex conditions.

4. Conclusions

This study focused on allocating appropriate constitutive models of the brain tissue for impact loading conditions. A patient-specific finite element head model was developed for this purpose. The von Mises stresses, as a deviatoric response, denoted marked differences between the brain constitutive models. Model I was unsuitable for reflecting the brain response under impact loading, since it was not based on impact experiments, and its respective stiffness was lower than the other models. The hyper-viscoelastic Model III provided a reasonably accurate framework for studying brain deviatoric responses and investigating TBI occurrence. In addition, among the impact loadings on the head's frontal, lateral, and posterior regions, lateral loading indicated a significantly higher risk of TBI incidence, with much higher stress values. The impact consequences are not confined to the impact time, and stress fluctuations after the relaxation of the impact load might also lead to TBI. The reported head impact results and critical regions can help in the development of protective features such as helmets and airbags.

Author Contributions: Conceptualization, H.T. and I.Z.O.; methodology, A.G., H.T. and I.Z.O.; software, A.G.; validation, A.G., H.T. and I.Z.O.; formal analysis, A.G., H.T. and I.Z.O.; investigation, A.G. ; resources, H.T. and I.Z.O.; data curation, A.G.; writing—original draft preparation, A.G.; writing—review and editing, A.G., H.T., I.Z.O. and F.A.O.F.; visualization, A.G.; supervision, H.T. and I.Z.O.; project administration, H.T., I.Z.O. and F.A.O.F.; funding acquisition, F.A.O.F. All authors have read and agreed to the published version of the manuscript.

Funding: This article was supported by the projects UIDB/00481/2020 and UIDP/00481/2020—Fundação para a Ciência e a Tecnologia, DOI: 10.54499/UIDB/00481/2020 and DOI: 10.54499/UIDP/00481/2020.

Data Availability Statement: The original contributions presented in this study are included in the Article. Further inquiries can be directed to the corresponding authors.

Conflicts of Interest: The authors declare no conflicts of interest.

References

1. Nguyen, R.; Fiest, K.M.; McChesney, J.; Kwon, C.S.; Jette, N.; Frolkis, A.D.; Atta, C.; Mah, S.; Dhaliwal, H.; Reid, A.; et al. The international incidence of traumatic brain injury: A systematic review and meta-analysis. *Can. J. Neurol. Sci.* **2016**, *43*, 774–785. [CrossRef]
2. Taylor, C.A.; Bell, J.M.; Breiding, M.J.; Xu, L. Traumatic brain injury–Related emergency department visits, hospitalizations, and deaths—United States, 2007 and 2013. *MMWR Surveill. Summ.* **2017**, *66*, 1–16. [CrossRef]
3. Tse, K.M.; Lim, S.P.; Tan, V.B.C.; Lee, H.P. A Review of Head Injury and Finite Element Head Models. *Am. J. Eng. Technol. Soc.* **2015**, *1*, 28–52.
4. Fernandes, F.A.O.; Alves de Sousa, R.J.; Ptak, M. *Head Injury Simulation in Road Traffic Accidents*; Springer International Publishing: Berlin/Heidelberg, Germany, 2018.
5. Fernandes, F.A.; Tchepel, D.; de Sousa, R.J.A.; Ptak, M. Development and validation of a new finite element human head model: Yet another head model (YEAHM). *Eng. Comput.* **2018**, *35*, 477–496. [CrossRef]
6. Cinelli, I.; Destrade, M.; McHugh, P.; Trotta, A.; Gilchrist, M.; Duffy, M. Head-to-nerve analysis of electromechanical impairments of diffuse axonal injury. *Biomech. Model. Mechanobiol.* **2019**, *18*, 361–374. [CrossRef] [PubMed]
7. Miller, K.; Chinzei, K. Constitutive modelling of brain tissue: Experiment and theory. *J. Biomech.* **1997**, *30*, 1115–1121. [CrossRef] [PubMed]
8. Miller, K.; Chinzei, K. Mechanical properties of brain tissue in tension. *J. Biomech.* **2002**, *35*, 483–490. [CrossRef]
9. Coats, B.; Margulies, S.S. Material properties of porcine parietal cortex. *J. Biomech.* **2006**, *39*, 2521–2525. [CrossRef] [PubMed]
10. Franceschini, G.; Bigoni, D.; Regitnig, P.; Holzapfel, G. Brain tissue deforms similarly to filled elastomers and follows consolidation theory. *J. Mech. Phys. Solids* **2006**, *54*, 2592–2620. [CrossRef]
11. Jin, X.; Zhu, F.; Mao, H.; Shen, M.; Yang, K.H. A comprehensive experimental study on material properties of human brain tissue. *J. Biomech.* **2013**, *46*, 2795–2801. [CrossRef]
12. Finan, J.D.; Sundaresh, S.N.; Elkin, B.S.; McKhann, G.M.; Morrison, B. Regional mechanical properties of human brain tissue for computational models of traumatic brain injury. *Acta Biomater.* **2017**, *55*, 333–339. [CrossRef]
13. Budday, S.; Sommer, G.; Birkl, C.; Langkammer, C.; Haybaeck, J.; Kohnert, J.; Bauer, M.; Paulsen, F.; Steinmann, P.; Kuhl, E.; et al. Mechanical characterization of human brain tissue. *Acta Biomater.* **2017**, *48*, 319–340. [CrossRef] [PubMed]
14. Budday, S.; Sommer, G.; Haybaeck, J.; Steinmann, P.; Holzapfel, G.; Kuhl, E. Rheological characterization of human brain tissue. *Acta Biomater.* **2017**, *60*, 315–329. [CrossRef] [PubMed]
15. Murphy, M.C.; Huston, J.; Ehman, R.L. MR elastography of the brain and its application in neurological diseases. *NeuroImage* **2019**, *187*, 176–183. [CrossRef] [PubMed]
16. Arani, A.; Manduca, A.; Ehman, R.L.; Huston, J. Harnessing brain waves: A review of brain magnetic resonance elastography for clinicians and scientists entering the field. *Br. J. Radiol.* **2021**, *94*, 20200265. [CrossRef]
17. Ueno, K.; Melvin, J.W.; Li, L.; Lighthall, J.W. Development of Tissue Level Brain Injury Criteria by Finite Element Analysis. *J. Neurotrauma* **2009**, *12*, 695–706. [CrossRef]
18. Miller, K.; Chinzei, K.; Orssengo, G.; Bednarz, P. Mechanical properties of brain tissue in-vivo: Experiment and computer simulation. *J. Biomech.* **2000**, *33*, 1369–1376. [CrossRef]

19. Claessans, M.; Sauren, F.; Wismans, J. Modeling of the human head under impact conditions: A parametric study. In *Stapp Car Crash*; SAE International: Warrendale, PA, USA, 1997; pp. 315–328.
20. Tse, K.M.; Bin Tan, L.; Lee, S.J.; Lim, S.P.; Lee, H.P. Development and validation of two subject-specific finite element models of human head against three cadaveric experiments. *Int. J. Numer. Methods Biomed. Eng.* **2014**, *30*, 397–415. [CrossRef]
21. Yang, B.; Tse, K.-M.; Chen, N.; Tan, L.-B.; Zheng, Q.-Q.; Yang, H.-M.; Hu, M.; Pan, G.; Lee, H.-P. Development of a finite element head model for the study of impact head injury. *BioMed Res. Int.* **2014**, *2014*, 1–14. [CrossRef] [PubMed]
22. Garcia-Gonzalez, D.; Jayamohan, J.; Sotiropoulos, S.; Yoon, S.-H.; Cook, J.; Siviour, C.; Arias, A.; Jérusalem, A. On the mechanical behaviour of PEEK and HA cranial implants under impact loading. *J. Mech. Behav. Biomed. Mater.* **2017**, *69*, 342–354. [CrossRef]
23. Schroder, A.; Lawrence, T.; Voets, N.; Garcia-Gonzalez, D.; Jones, M.; Peña, J.M.; Jerusalem, A. A Machine Learning Enhanced Mechanistic Simulation Framework for Functional Deficit Prediction in TBI. *Front. Bioeng. Biotechnol.* **2021**, *9*, 587082. [CrossRef]
24. Ruan, J.S.; Khalil, T.; King, A.I. Dynamic response of the human head to impact by three-dimensional finite element analysis. *J. Biomech. Eng.* **1994**, *116*, 44–50. [CrossRef]
25. Zhou, C.; Khalil, T.B.; King, A.I. *A New Model Comparing Impact Responses of the Homogeneous and Inhomogeneous Human Brain*; SAE Transactions: Warrendale, PA, USA, 1995; pp. 121–137.
26. Garcia-Gonzalez, D.; Race, N.S.; Voets, N.L.; Jenkins, D.R.; Sotiropoulos, S.N.; Acosta, G.; Cruz-Haces, M.; Tang, J.; Shi, R.; Jérusalem, A. Cognition based bTBI mechanistic criteria; a tool for preventive and therapeutic innovations. *Sci. Rep.* **2018**, *8*, 1–14. [CrossRef]
27. Zhang, L.; Yang, K.H.; Dwarampudi, R.; Omori, K.; Li, T.; Chang, K.; Hardy, W.N.; Khalil, T.B.; King, A.I. Recent Advances in Brain Injury Research: A New Human Head Model Development and Validation. *SAE Tech. Pap.* **2001**. [CrossRef]
28. Tzschätzsch, H.; Kreft, B.; Schrank, F.; Bergs, J.; Braun, J.; Sack, I. In vivo time-harmonic ultrasound elastography of the human brain detects acute cerebral stiffness changes induced by intracranial pressure variations. *Sci. Rep.* **2018**, *8*, 17888. [CrossRef] [PubMed]
29. Chen, Y.; Ostoja-Starzewski, M. MRI-based finite element modeling of head trauma: Spherically focusing shear waves. *Acta Mech.* **2010**, *213*, 155–167. [CrossRef]
30. Gomez-Cruz, C.; la Torre, M.F.; Lachowski, D.; Prados-De-Haro, M.; Hernández, A.E.d.R.; Perea, G.; Muñoz-Barrutia, A.; Garcia-Gonzalez, D. Mechanical and Functional Responses in Astrocytes under Alternating Deformation Modes Using Magneto-Active Substrates. *Adv. Mater.* **2024**, *36*, 2312497. [CrossRef] [PubMed]
31. Deng, X.; Du, Z.; Feng, H.; Wang, S.; Luo, H.; Liu, Y. Investigation on the Modeling and Reconstruction of Head Injury Accident Using ABAQUS/Explicit. *Bioengineering* **2022**, *9*, 723. [CrossRef]
32. Abdi, H.; Sánchez-Molina, D.; García-Vilana, S.; Rahimi-Movaghar, V. Revealing the role of material properties in impact-related injuries: Investigating the influence of brain and skull density variations on head injury severity. *Heliyon* **2024**, *10*, e29427. [CrossRef] [PubMed]
33. Kleiven, S. Predictors for traumatic brain injuries evaluated through accident reconstructions. *Stapp Car Crash J.* **2007**, *51*, 81–114. [CrossRef]
34. Subramaniam, D.R.; Unnikrishnan, G.; Sundaramurthy, A.; Rubio, J.E.; Kote, V.B.; Reifman, J. Cerebral Vasculature Influences Blast-Induced Biomechanical Responses of Human Brain Tissue. *Front. Bioeng. Biotechnol.* **2021**, *9*, 744808. [CrossRef] [PubMed]
35. Li, X.; Zhou, Z.; Kleiven, S. An anatomically detailed and personalizable head injury model: Significance of brain and white matter tract morphological variability on strain. *Biomech. Model. Mechanobiol.* **2021**, *20*, 403–431. [CrossRef] [PubMed]
36. Franceschini, G. *The Mechanics of Human Brain Tissue*; The University of Trento: Trento, Italy, 2006.
37. Li, X.; Sandler, H.; Kleiven, S. The importance of nonlinear tissue modelling in finite element simulations of infant head impacts. *Biomech. Model. Mechanobiol.* **2017**, *16*, 823–840. [CrossRef] [PubMed]
38. Elkin, B.S.; Gabler, L.F.; Panzer, M.B.; Siegmund, G.P. Brain tissue strains vary with head impact location: A possible explanation for increased concussion risk in struck versus striking football players. *Clin. Biomech.* **2019**, *64*, 49–57. [CrossRef] [PubMed]
39. Giudice, J.S.; Park, G.; Kong, K.; Bailey, A.; Kent, R.; Panzer, M.B. Development of Open-Source Dummy and Impactor Models for the Assessment of American Football Helmet Finite Element Models. *Ann. Biomed. Eng.* **2018**, *47*, 464–474. [CrossRef] [PubMed]
40. Takhounts, E.G.; Ridella, S.A.; Hasija, V.; Tannous, R.E.; Campbell, J.Q.; Malone, D.; Danelson, K.; Stitzel, J.; Rowson, S.; Duma, S. Investigation of traumatic brain injuries using the next generation of simulated injury monitor (SIMon) finite element head model. *Stapp Car Crash J.* **2008**, *52*, 1–31. [CrossRef] [PubMed]
41. Takhounts, E.G.; Eppinger, R.H.; Campbell, J.Q.; Tannous, R.E.; Power, E.D.; Shook, L.S. *On the Development of the SIMon Finite Element Head Model*; SAE Tech Pap 2003-Octob; SAE: Warrendale, PA, USA, 2003. [CrossRef]
42. Ruan, J.S.; Khalil, T.B.; King, A.I. Finite element modeling of direct head impact. In Proceedings of the Stapp Car Crash Conference Warrendale, PA, USA, 1 November 1993.
43. Lüsebrink, F.; Sciarra, A.; Mattern, H.; Yakupov, R.; Speck, O. T1-weighted in vivo human whole brain MRI dataset with an ultrahigh isotropic resolution of 250 μm. *Sci. Data* **2017**, *4*, 170062. [CrossRef] [PubMed]

44. Viano, D.C.; Casson, I.R.; Pellman, E.J.; Zhang, L.; King, A.I.; Yang, K.H. Concussion in professional football: Brain responses by finite element analysis: Part 9. *Neurosurgery* **2005**, *57*, 891–916. [CrossRef] [PubMed]
45. Yoganandan, N.; Pintar, F.A.; Zhang, J.; Baisden, J.L. Physical properties of the human head: Mass, center of gravity and moment of inertia. *J. Biomech.* **2009**, *42*, 1177–1192. [CrossRef] [PubMed]
46. Mao, H.; Gao, H.; Cao, L.; Genthikatti, V.V.; Yang, K.H. Development of high-quality hexahedral human brain meshes using feature-based multi-block approach. *Comput. Methods Biomech. Biomed. Eng.* **2013**, *16*, 271–279. [CrossRef]
47. Belingardi, G.; Chiandussi, G.; Gaviglio, I. Development and validation of a new finite element model of human head. In Proceedings of the 19th International Technical Conference of the Enhanced Safety of Vehicle (ESV), Washington, DC, USA, 6–9 June 2005.
48. Mihai, L.A.; Chin, L.; Janmey, P.A.; Goriely, A. A comparison of hyperelastic constitutive models applicable to brain and fat tissues. *J. R. Soc. Interface* **2015**, *12*, 20150486. [CrossRef] [PubMed]
49. Taghizadeh, H.; Tafazzoli-Shadpour, M.; Shadmehr, M.B.; Fatouraee, N. Evaluation of biaxial mechanical properties of aortic media based on the lamellar microstructure. *Materials* **2015**, *8*, 302–316. [CrossRef]
50. Nahum, A.M.; Smith, R.; Ward, C.C. Intracranial pressure dynamics during head impact. In Proceedings of the Stapp Car Crash Conference Proceedings, New Orleans, LO, USA, 19–21 October 1977.
51. Abdi, H.; Sanchez-Molina, D.; Garcia-Vilana, S.; Rahimi-Movaghar, V. Quantifying the effect of cerebral atrophy on head injury risk in elderly individuals: Insights from computational biomechanics and experimental analysis of bridging veins. *Injury* **2023**, *54*, 111125. [CrossRef] [PubMed]
52. Martin, G. Traumatic brain injury: The first 15 milliseconds. *Brain Inj.* **2016**, *30*, 1517–1524. [CrossRef] [PubMed]

Mathematical and Computational Applications

MDPI

Article

Predicting Red Blood Cell Transfusion in Elective Cardiac Surgery: A Machine Learning Approach

Beatriz Lau [1,*], Daniel Ramos [1], Vera Afreixo [1], Luís M. Silva [1], Ana Helena Tavares [1], Miguel Martins Felgueiras [1,2], Diana Castro Paupério [3,4] and João Firmino-Machado [3,4,5]

1 Centre for Research and Development in Mathematics and Applications, University of Aveiro, 3810-193 Aveiro, Portugal; danielsramos@ua.pt (D.R.); vera@ua.pt (V.A.); lmas@ua.pt (L.M.S.); ahtavares@ua.pt (A.H.T.); mfelg@ipleiria.pt (M.M.F.)

2 Polytechnic of Leiria and Centre for Statistics and Applications, University of Leiria, 2411-901 Leiria, Portugal

3 Local Health Unit of Vila Nova de Gaia Espinho, 4434-502 Vila Nova de Gaia, Portugal; diana.gomes@gmail.com (D.C.P.); firmino@ua.pt (J.F.-M.)

4 Egas Moniz Health Alliance Academic Clinical Centre, 3810-193 Aveiro, Portugal

5 Department of Medical Sciences, University of Aveiro, 3810-193 Aveiro, Portugal

* Correspondence: beatrizlau@ua.pt

Abstract

The benefits of Patient Blood Management can vary depending on a patient's risk profile for requiring a blood transfusion. The objective of this study is to develop and analyse machine learning models that can identify patients at risk of requiring red blood cell transfusion. This retrospective cohort study was conducted at a tertiary northern Portuguese hospital between 2018 and 2023. Two machine learning algorithms, extreme gradient boosting and neural networks, were employed due to their efficiency in handling complex feature interactions. Shapley additive explanations values were analysed to assess the contribution of each feature to the predictions generated by the models. The neural network achieved an accuracy of 0.735 and an area under the receiver operating characteristic curve of 0.798 (95% CI 0.747 to 0.849). The extreme gradient boosting model achieved an accuracy of 0.700 and an area under the receiver operating characteristic curve of 0.762 (95% CI 0.707 to 0.817). An analysis of Shapley additive explanations values revealed that the most important variable was preoperative haemoglobin levels, which can be optimised through the Patient Blood Management approach. These machine learning models demonstrate the potential to improve the accuracy of transfusion prediction at hospital admission, despite the absence of key variables such as surgeon identity and anaemia diagnosis.

Keywords: machine learning; cardiac surgery; blood transfusion

1. Introduction

Cardiac surgery is well established as being associated with a considerable risk of perioperative blood loss and the need for allogeneic blood transfusions. This is due to the invasive nature of the procedures themselves, the necessity for high-dose anticoagulation, and exposure to cardiopulmonary bypass [1]. Despite its common practice, an increasing body of evidence suggests that the transfusion of one or more allogeneic blood components may be associated with an increased risk of prolonged hospital length-of-stay, morbidity, and mortality [2]. Moreover, the financial burden of transfusions is increasing, while the discrepancy between the supply and demand for this scarce resource is widening [3].

In response to this paradigm, there has been a shift in focus from the intervention itself to the patient's needs, which has led to the emergence of Patient Blood Management

(PBM) [4]. PBM is an approach that has been recognised by the World Health Organisation as representing the 'best clinical practice' [5]. It aims to preserve the patient's own blood [6] by adopting pre-operative, intra-operative, and post-operative measures, in accordance with the three pillars established by Goodnough and Shander: optimising erythropoiesis, minimising blood loss, and managing tolerance to anaemia [7]. In this way, PBM contributes to improving patient outcomes and to the reduction in healthcare costs [5]. While this approach confers benefits on all individuals undergoing cardiac surgery, the magnitude of these benefits may vary as the impact of a PBM intervention in a patient with an already low risk of blood transfusion will be less than in a patient with a high risk of blood transfusion [8]. As such, the identification of patients who are at an increased risk of requiring a blood transfusion throughout the perioperative and postoperative periods is crucial to prioritise PBM interventions.

Machine learning (ML) models, defined as algorithms capable of improving through experience and data [9,10], have shown promise in predictive tasks across different disciplines [11]. Among these, extreme gradient boosting (XGBoost) and neural networks have gained increasing attention in recent years due to their high computational efficiency and predictive accuracy [12,13]. In cardiac surgery, decision-making is a complex and important process, as it involves balancing multiple risk factors and individual patient characteristics. ML models can enhance outcomes by predicting high-risk patients, enabling healthcare providers to be more proactive and vigilant [14].

Several studies have explored the application of ML in predicting red blood cell (RBC) transfusion needs. For example, Mitterecker et al. [10] demonstrated that ML models, including gradient boosting and neural networks, achieved excellent predictive performance in predicting the need for at least one RBC transfusion across various types of surgeries, with an area under the receiver operating characteristics curve (AUROC) exceeding 0.9. Additionally, Tschoellitsch et al. [15] specifically focused on cardiac surgery and predicted massive perioperative transfusions ($\geq$10 red blood cells), with random forest and gradient boosting models achieving AUROCs of 0.810. However, despite the existence of many studies predicting red blood cell transfusion [16–24], none of these specifically focus on elective cardiac surgery, consider the context of the Portuguese National Healthcare Service, or incorporate a database that distinguishes between the presence and absence of PBM practices.

Therefore, the present study aims to develop and analyse machine learning models capable of identifying patients who underwent elective cardiac surgery and were at risk of requiring one or more red blood cell transfusions, thereby supporting healthcare professionals in assessing patients' risk levels of transfusion with and without PBM practices in a northern Portuguese healthcare setting.

2. Materials and Methods

2.1. Study Design

A prospective observational cohort study was conducted among patients who underwent elective cardiac surgery at a tertiary hospital—Vila Nova de Gaia-Espinho. Data collected from medical records were used to train and test machine learning models. This manuscript was prepared in accordance with the Strengthening the Reporting of Observational Studies in Epidemiology (STROBE) guidelines [25].

2.2. Settings and Participants

The study was conducted on individuals aged 18 years or older who underwent elective cardiac surgery between 2018 and 2022 at Vila Nova de Gaia-Espinho Hospital. Prior to 2019, the Patient Blood Management (PBM) approach was not applied to any patient scheduled for elective cardiac surgery, with only anaemia screening being performed immediately before surgery.

Individuals with cognitive impairment, pregnant women, and those without data regarding allogeneic red blood cell transfusion were excluded. Reoperations were also excluded.

The data were obtained through extraction from the electronic medical records and through manual collection by an anesthesiologist.

Ethics Approval

The study was conducted in accordance with the Declaration of Helsinki, and approved by the ULSGE Ethical Health Committee, assigned with the number 196/2023. Patient consent was waived since this is an observational study (Law No. 21/2014 of April 16, amended by Law No. 73/2015 of July 27, Article 6, No. 2), and the data were fully anonymized.

2.3. Data Pre-Processing

2.3.1. Data Overview

An overview of the most important demographic and preoperative data included is presented in Table 1. The data preprocessing and cleaning were performed as follows:

1. From an initial sample of 1038 subjects, patients who had no information about the number of RBC transfused were removed, resulting in a sample of 1036 individuals;
2. Variables that contain information collected after admission were removed, as the objective was to develop a predictive model at admission time at the hospital. Moreover, variables with no information in the pre- and post-PBM datasets were also excluded. This procedure led to the final set of 14 features: age, sex, New York Heart Association classification (NYHA), Canadian Cardiovascular Society grading of angina pectoris (CCS), American Society of Anesthesiologists physical status classification (ASA), type of surgery, diagnosis of diabetes mellitus type II, hypertension and chronic kidney disease, glomerular filtration rate, creatinine, PBM approach implementation, preoperative haemoglobin level (g/L), and number of RBC transfusion;
3. NYHA, CCS, and ASA variables, were grouped into high level (III and IV), low level (I and II) and "not applicable", due to the low number of observations in levels I and IV. This led to more robust conclusions, impossible to achieve without a minimum number of observations in each category;
4. The number of RBC transfusions was recorded as a binary variable to specify the occurrence of transfusion (RBC > 0 coded as "with-transfusion") or not (RBC = 0 coded as "without-transfusion"). This transformation enabled the application of a classification model to predict the risk of an individual requiring RBC transfusion, which is the primary objective of this study;
5. All numerical variables (age, preoperative haemoglobin, glomerular filtration rate, and creatinine) were standardised using the Z-score approach, with the goal of adjusting the scales so that variables with high variance do not dominate the entire process;
6. All categorical variables were one-hot encoded, a technique that converts categorical data into binary vectors. Each vector uniquely represents a category, where a value of 1 signifies its presence, and 0 is its absence.

The models were firstly trained using the original data; however, due to the number of missing values and the imbalance between groups (with the group of patients who did not require transfusion being considerably larger), the models' performance was not acceptable, having AUROC close to 0.5. Hence, to obtain the best models, multiple imputation and data balancing techniques were applied.

Table 1. Sociodemographic and clinical data.

Characteristic	With Transfusion, N = 334 [1]	Without Transfusion, N = 702 [1]	p-Value [2]
Age—median [IQR]	73 [10]	69 [13]	**<0.001**
Sex—n (%)			**<0.001**
Female	204 (61%)	209 (30%)	
Male	130 (39%)	493 (70%)	
NYHA [3]—n (%)			0.183
High level (III and IV)	101 (30%)	187 (27%)	
Low level (I and II)	233 (70%)	515 (73%)	
CCS [4]—n (%)			0.200
High	68 (20%)	169 (24%)	
Low	266 (80%)	533 (76%)	
ASA [5]—n (%)			0.410
High	327 (98%)	681 (97%)	
Low	7 (2.1%)	21 (3.0%)	
High blood pressure—n (%)			0.270
No	57 (17%)	140 (20%)	
Yes	277 (83%)	562 (80%)	
Diabetes type II—n (%)			0.935
No	229 (69%)	479 (68%)	
Yes	105 (31%)	223 (32%)	
Chronic kidney disease—n (%)			**<0.001**
No	211 (63%)	556 (79%)	
Yes	123 (37%)	146 (21%)	
Dyslipidemia—n (%)			0.206
No	86 (26%)	152 (22%)	
Yes	248 (74%)	550 (78%)	
Creatinine—median [IQR]	0.90 [0.45]	0.89 [0.30]	0.104
Glomerular filtration rate—median [IQR]	65 [34]	79 [36]	**<0.001**
Pre-op haemoglobin—median [IQR]	13.00 [1.98]	14.30 [1.70]	**<0.001**
Patient blood management—n (%)			**<0.001**
Pre PBM	93 (28%)	109 (16%)	
Post PBM	241 (72%)	593 (84%)	
Surgery with extracorporeal circulation—n (%)			**<0.001**
Yes	308 (92%)	481 (69%)	
No	26 (7.8%)	221 (31%)	

[1] Median [IQR]; n (%); [2] Wilcoxon rank sum test; Pearson's Chi-squared test; [3] NYHA—New York Heart Association classification; [4] CCS—Canadian Cardiovascular Society grading of angina pectoris; [5] ASA—American Society of Anesthesiologists physical status classification.

2.3.2. Multiple Imputation

Data imputation is an important step for improving data quality and model performance [26]. For this purpose, multivariate imputation by chained equation (MICE) has emerged as one of the main methods in the statistical literature, as it is very flexible and can handle variables of different types and complexity [27]. In this study, MICE was applied separately for the pre- and post-PBM datasets to account for potential differences in the relationships among variables. In the pre-PBM dataset, 2 out of 14 variables had more than 5% missing values, while in the post-PBM dataset, only 1 out of 14 variables had more than 5% missing values (see Figure A1 in the Appendix A). We use predictive mean matching for continuous variables, logistic regression for binary variables, and polytomous logistic regression for unordered categorical variables. Data were imputed using the **mice** package.

2.3.3. Data Balancing

The number of patients who required RBC transfusion and those who did not was imbalanced, with only 334 out of 1036 (32%) in the "with-transfusion" class. Imbalanced data can interfere with the development of effective classifiers because the lower representativeness of the minority class may lead to inadequate learning, resulting in poor predictive performance for that class [28]. In addition, it can make it difficult for evaluation metrics to accurately assess the model's performance [28].

The initial experiments with the original data showed a reduced discriminative capability of the machine learning models. To improve their predictive ability, we applied an oversampling technique called Synthetic Minority Oversampling Technique (SMOTE) to balance the classes. This technique generates synthetic samples for the minority class, increasing its size until it reaches a more balanced proportion with the majority class [29].

2.4. *Models*

We use the variables presented in Table 1 as inputs to develop our machine learning models. Training and test sets were created with an 80:20 ratio. A five-fold cross-validation scheme was used in the training phase to fine-tune the models, with the best hyperparameters being empirically selected in an iterative manner (see Table A1 in the Appendix A). The best model was selected according to the accuracy values obtained.

2.4.1. Extreme Gradient Boosting (XGBoost)

XGBoost belongs to the class of ensemble models and is an implementation of the more traditional gradient boosting machines focused on computational efficiency [30]. It is essentially an additive model of the form as shown below:

$$Y_B = \sum_{b=1}^{B} \alpha_b y_b$$

where each base model y_b is a decision tree. B is the number of trees in the model (usually in the order of hundreds or thousands) while the scalars α_b weigh the corresponding base model y_b in the sum according to its performance. The optimisation technique relies on a sequential application of the gradient descent method where at step m, α_m and the y_m parameters (splits and nodes of the tree) are optimised in order to correct the errors of the current model by minimising the following:

$$\sum_{n=1}^{N} E(t_n, Y_{m-1} + \alpha_m y_m)$$

over a training set of size N. $E(x, y)$ is an appropriate measure of the discrepancy between x and y and Y_{m-1} is fixed. XGBoost employs regularisation strategies (controlled by several hyperparameters) to mitigate overfitting, which is an excessive fitting of the model to the training data, leading to poor generalisation of unseen data [30,31]. The hyperparameters tuned were *max_depth*, *eta*, *gamma*, *subsample*, *min_child_weight* and *nrounds*. In the current study, the XGBoost model was developed using the **xgboost** package, while the hyperparameter tuning was using the **caret** package (for the final model, see Table A1 in the Appendix A).

2.4.2. Neural Network (NNs)

Neural networks are among the best-performing models for a large set of problems. Mathematically, a neural network is a composition of linear and non-linear functions that can be represented as a set of interconnected layers of simple processing units, called neurons. As Figure 1 illustrates, NNs have an input layer (whose non-processing units simply represent the input variables), one to many intermediate (hidden) layers and an output layer of neurons, constituting the architecture of the NN.

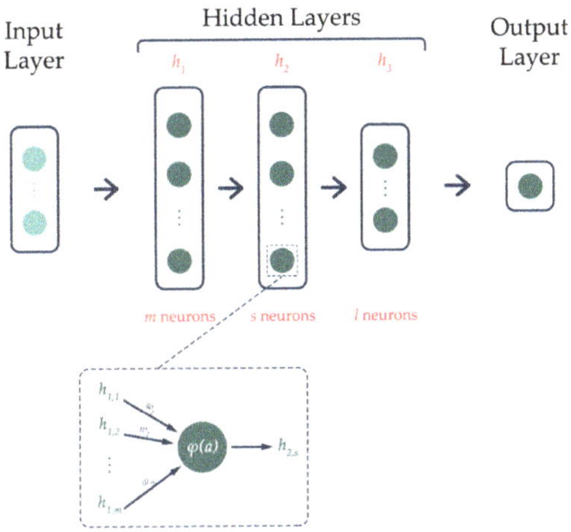

Figure 1. Schematic representation of a neural network with three hidden layers.

Each neuron computes a linear combination of its inputs (from the previous layer) followed by a non-linear function φ, the so-called activation function, enabling the algorithm to learn complex patterns and perform computationally intensive tasks [32]. For example, the output of the sth neuron in the hidden layer h_2 is

$$h_{2,s} = \varphi(a) = \varphi(w_1 h_{1,1} + w_2 h_{1,2} + \cdots + w_m h_{1,m} + w_0)$$

which is then fed to the neurons of the following layer.

The optimisation of the model's weights (parameters) w_j is usually performed by gradient descent techniques, iteratively reducing the average error between the predicted and true outcome values as measured by a specific loss function. Regularisation techniques are also employed in NN training to prevent overfitting.

In this study, the NN has a single neuron at the output to cope with the 2-class nature of the problem, acting as a logistic regression layer. The NN model was developed using the **TensorFlow** and **Keras** packages. Hyperparameter tuning included adjusting the learning rate with the Adam optimizer, applying Lasso regularisation to prevent overfitting, and testing different activation functions (SoftPlus, ReLU, and ArcTan) (for the final model, see Table A1 in the Appendix A).

2.4.3. Interpretability

After training and testing the selected models, variable importance and interpretation were analysed using the Shapley additive explanations (SHAP) values. Derived from game theory, SHAP values provide an importance score for each feature, reflecting its contribution to the model's prediction. Positive SHAP values indicate that a feature increases the value of the dependent variable, if it is numeric, or increases the probability of a particular event occurring if it is categorical. Conversely, negative SHAP values suggest that the feature has the opposite effect. The magnitude of the SHAP values represents the strength of each feature's effect on the outcome [33].

2.5. Statistical Analysis

To assess the normality of continuous variables, the Shapiro–Wilk test and QQ plot analysis were conducted. As the data did not meet the assumptions of normality, the Wilcoxon rank-sum test was used to compare median differences between groups (with- and without-transfusion). For categorical variables, the Pearson chi-squared test was applied.

Multiple imputation, data balancing, model training and testing were then carried out, with a seed of 1234 to guarantee reproducibility. The models were evaluated using different performance metrics such as accuracy, recall, specificity, area under the receiver operating characteristics curve (AUROC), F1 score and average precision (AP; the area under the precision–recall curve). To study the differences between the two AUROCs, the DeLong test was performed.

All analyses were performed using R version 4.4.1 with a significance value of 0.05.

3. Results

For the purpose of this work, we studied a cohort of patients eligible for elective cardiac surgery between 2018 and 2022 (n = 1036). Within this sample, 334 (32.2%) patients required the transfusion of at least one unit of red blood cells, while 702 patients did not. An overview of the demographic and clinical data is given in Table 1.

The median patient age was 73 for the with-transfusion group and 69 for the without-transfusion group (interquartile range of 10 and 13 years, respectively), and 39.9% of patients were women. As expected, preoperative haemoglobin was lower in the transfused group (13.00 [1.98] versus 14.30 [1.70], p-value < 0.001), as patients with lower haemoglobin levels tend to require more red blood cells transfusions.

Our predictive models only partially predicted who needed transfusion of at least one unit of RBCs. Using XGBoost and NNs the AUROC was 0.762 and 0.798, respectively. Although they were different, the DeLong test showed no significant difference between those performances (p-value = 0.343). The F1 scores were 0.770 and 0.807 and the accuracies were 0.700 and 0.736, respectively (for details see Table 2 and Figure 2). Although the NN model had the best performance, its specificity is only fair (0.582), indicating that the model has more difficulty in correctly predicting the need for at least one transfusion. On the other hand, it performs well in identifying patients who did not require a transfusion (0.807).

Table 2. Evaluation of predictive models for transfusion of at least one RBC unit.

	Accuracy (Recall, Specificity)	AUROC (95% IC)	F1-Score
Neural Network	0.736 (0.807, 0.582)	0.798 (0.747–0.849)	0.807
XGBoost	0.700 (0.736, 0.622)	0.762 (0.707–0.817)	0.770

Although these two models perform similarly, the XGBoost model appears to predict with a higher probability the individuals who will require one or more RBC transfusions. This is clear in Figure 3, where a greater density of blue points is observed near the value 1 in the XGBoost model. In contrast, the neural network model exhibits a more dispersed distribution of blue points with no discernible region of higher density. However, the neural network model demonstrates a higher degree of certainty in predictions when the probability is greater than 80%, as evidenced by a reduced number of false positives at this threshold.

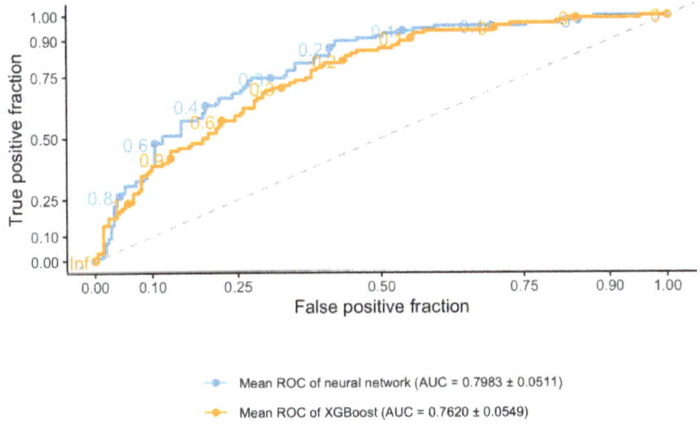

(**a**)

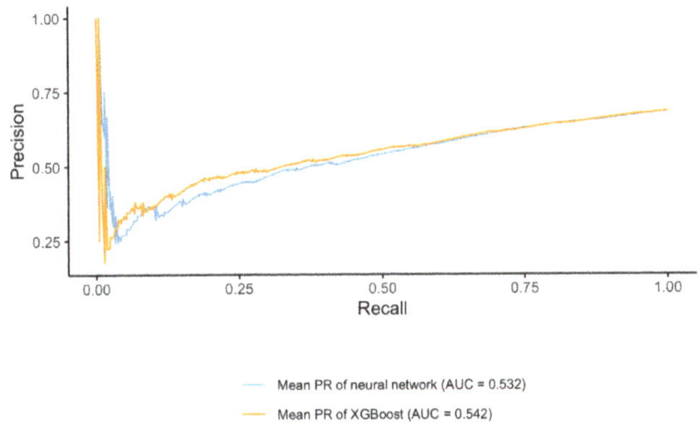

(**b**)

Figure 2. Performance comparison of the models (**a**): ROC curves; (**b**): precision–recall curves.

The most important variables in predicting the need for transfusion of at least one unit of RBCs were preoperative haemoglobin and glomerular filtration rate (see Figure 4). Preoperative haemoglobin was negatively associated with transfusion requirement, with higher values decreasing the likelihood of transfusion requirement. This is illustrated in the graphic by the red bar extending towards the negative side. A decrease in glomerular filtration rate was associated with an increase in the likelihood of transfusion, as reflected by the negative SHAP value and a positive contribution indicated by the green bar pointing towards the positive side of the graphic.

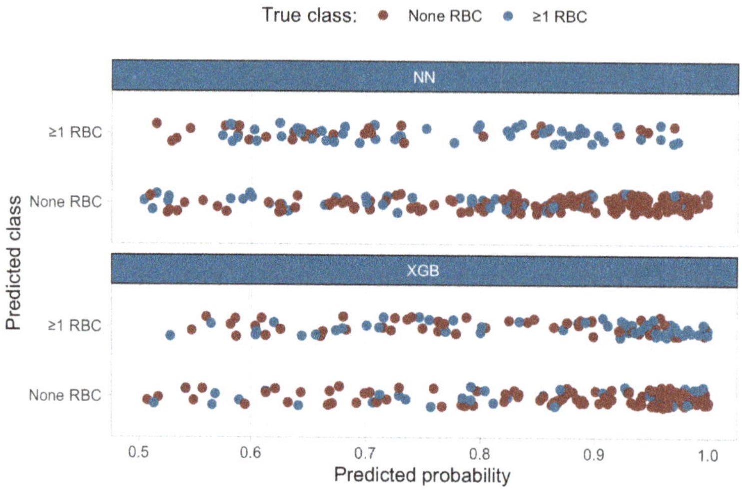

Figure 3. Prediction probabilities of the XGBoost and Neural Network models in the test set.

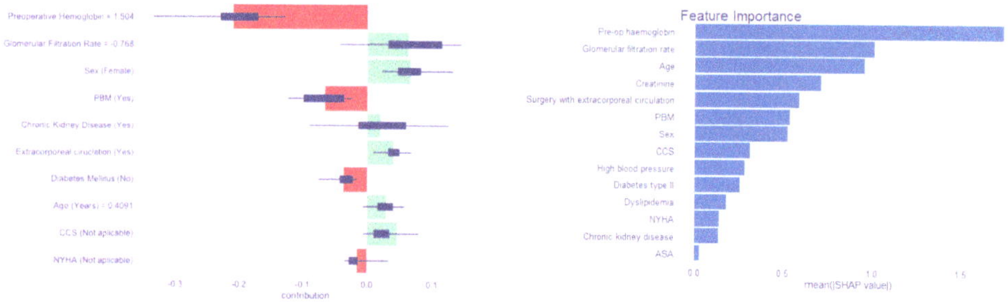

(a) (b)

Figure 4. Feature importance (using SHAP values) for transfusion of at least one RBC unit. (**a**): Neural Network model; (**b**): XGBoost model.

4. Discussion

Our models showed a moderate ability to effectively predict which patients would need a transfusion and which would not, with the most important variable being the haemoglobin level measured immediately before surgery.

Both of our models achieved an AUROC above 0.75, with the lower bound of the 95% confidence interval above 0.5, indicating a statistically significant ability to predict transfusion risk. In addition, our models showed similar performance to the Transfusion Risk Understanding Scoring Tool (TRUST) [34], a well-known risk score widely used in clinical practice, with the added benefit of incorporating information on the use of PBM interventions.

Nevertheless, the ability to predict at least one red blood cell transfusion could be improved. In our dataset, condition severity-related data were not explicitly available, which may have limited our models' performance. The only variable indirectly indicating it was the type of surgery. Extracorporeal circulation—known to stimulate a systemic inflammatory response following cardiac surgery, triggering complement activation, pro-inflammatory cytokine secretion, and leukocyte activation [35,36], resulting in cellular damage, bleeding disorders, anaemia, acute kidney injury, respiratory failure, haemodynamic instability, and neurological complications [37]—was performed in 92% of patients requiring transfusion. This variable was among the top 10 most important in our models based on SHAP values, reflecting its positive association with transfusion requirements. However, it ranked below the top three features, suggesting its influence, while notable, may not be the primary determinant in our setting.

During data preprocessing, key variables such as platelet count, ferritin levels, transferrin saturation, and the International Normalised Ratio (INR)—a known predictor of transfusion requirements [38]—had to be excluded due to missing information on the pre-PBM dataset. Given the established associations of these variables with transfusion needs, their inclusion might have enhanced the models' predictive accuracy. Furthermore, collecting additional data, such as the surgical team responsible could also improve performance, as these are well-recognised factors influencing transfusion outcomes [38,39].

In both models, the most important feature identified was the haemoglobin level measured immediately before surgery, where a higher haemoglobin level was associated with a reduced need for transfusions. A principal distinction of the PBM approach in comparison to standard of care, is the preoperative anaemia assessment which identifies patients with or at risk for anaemia, enabling proactive intervention to correct haemoglobin levels before surgery. By increasing preoperative haemoglobin levels, the requirement for transfusion decreases, subsequently reducing the incidence of transfusion-associated risks, improving patient outcomes in the postoperative period [2,40]. This is a particularly relevant conclusion, as it highlights the efficacy of implementing the PBM approach within the Portuguese National Health Service.

Providing healthcare professionals with a tool able to predict the risk (probability) of requiring an allogeneic RBC transfusion, in the post-operative period, at the time of hospital admission, allows them to support the decision of prioritising high-risk individuals to receive PBM intervention. This targeted approach not only ensures personalised and patient-centred care but also helps to reduce the workload of healthcare professionals and improve overall hospital resource management through more efficient use of blood and PBM resources [41].

Strengths and Limitations

To the best of our knowledge, this is the first study to focus on predicting the need for at least one RBC transfusion in patients undergoing elective cardiac surgery using machine learning algorithms. In addition, the inclusion of individuals who underwent cardiac surgery before, during, and after the implementation of the PBM process allowed us to capture real-world clinical practice, increasing the generalisability of the results to other hospitals in the country currently adopting this approach. It is also the first study of its kind to use data from the Portuguese National Health Service. Nevertheless, certain limitations in our methodology must be acknowledged.

The limited automation in data collection resulted in a considerable number of variables with a high proportion of missing data, which prevented quality imputation, and consequently, restricted the model's predictive capacity.

Additionally, the smaller sample size, compared to other similar studies, may have further limited the model's performance.

The absence of variables that are well-established as being associated with the need for blood transfusion limited the predictive power of both models tested.

Finally, the lack of computational power prevented a more comprehensive and appropriate tuning of the hyperparameters, which had to be conducted through an iterative, empirical trial-and-error process. We believe that the employment of a more extensive grid of values for hyperparameter tuning would have resulted in an enhanced predictive capacity for both models, as well.

5. Conclusions

The application of contemporary machine learning algorithms has the potential to enhance the accuracy of transfusion prediction at the time of hospital admission. Both the XGBoost and neural network models demonstrated an AUC exceeding 0.75, despite the absence of critical core variables such as the surgical team and the diagnosis of anaemia. Despite the limited predictive capacity of the model, the interpretation of variable importance through SHAP values revealed that the implementation of the PBM approach has a significant impact on reducing transfusion needs. This, in turn, contributes to improved postoperative outcomes and more effective management of blood resources, which ultimately reduces the financial costs associated with blood transfusions. Future studies should focus on incorporating additional variables that are strongly associated with transfusion needs and using greater computational power, thereby allowing the development of a more effective tool to assist clinicians in making informed decisions regarding PBM implementation.

Author Contributions: Conceptualization, B.L. and D.R.; data collection, D.C.P. and J.F.-M.; methodology, B.L. and D.R.; formal analysis, B.L. and D.R.; writing—original draft preparation, B.L. and D.R.; writing—review and editing, V.A., L.M.S., A.H.T., M.M.F., J.F.-M., and D.C.P.; supervision, V.A., L.M.S., A.H.T., and M.M.F. All authors have read and agreed to the published version of the manuscript.

Funding: This research was partially supported by Portuguese funds through CIDMA, The Center for Research and Development in Mathematics and Applications of the University of Aveiro, and the Portuguese Foundation for Science and Technology (FCT—Fundação para a Ciência e a Tecnologia), within projects UIDB/04106/2020 (https://doi.org/10.54499/UIDB/04106/2020) and UIDP/04106/2020 (https://doi.org/10.54499/UIDP/04106/2020). B. Duarte and D. Ramos were supported by a Research Grant of the Thematic Line Biomathematics of CIDMA.

Data Availability Statement: The data used in this study were obtained from medical records collected by the author, Dr. Diana Castro Paupério, an anesthesiologist at Vila Nova de Gaia-Espinho Hospital, and are subject to ethical and privacy restrictions. To request access to the data, please contact the corresponding author.

Conflicts of Interest: The authors declare no conflicts of interest.

Appendix A

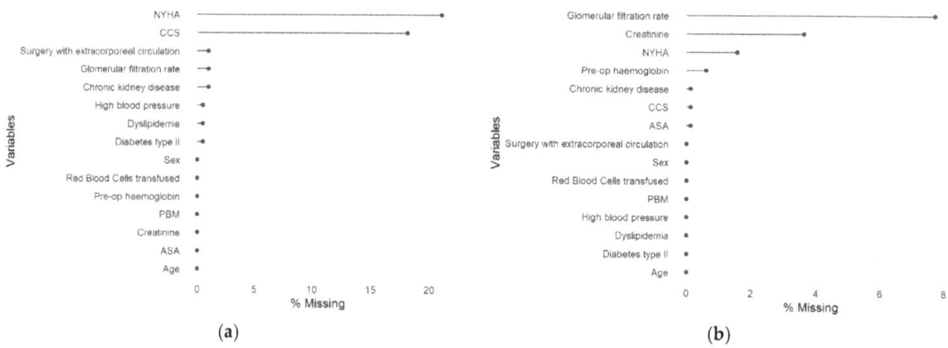

Figure A1. Missing data. (**a**): Pre-PBM dataset. (**b**): Post-PBM dataset.

Table A1. Final model.

Models	Hyperparameters	Values
Neural Network	Layers	3
	Neurons of the first layer	16
	Activation function of the first layer	ReLu
	Neurons of the second layer	16
	Activation function of the second layer	ArcTan
	Neurons of the third layer	10
	Activation function of the third layer	ReLu
	Lasso regularisation	5×10^{-5}
	Learning rate	0.004
	Epoch	500
XGBoost	max_depth	10
	eta	0.1
	gamma	0.1
	subsample	0.8
	min_child_weight	0.1
	nrounds	1000

References

1. Boer, C.; Meesters, M.I.; Milojevic, M.; Benedetto, U.; Bolliger, D.; von Heymann, C.; Jeppsson, A.; Koster, A.; Osnabrugge, R.L.; Ranucci, M.; et al. 2017 EACTS/EACTA Guidelines on Patient Blood Management for Adult Cardiac Surgery. *J. Cardiothorac. Vasc. Anesth.* **2018**, *32*, 88–120. [CrossRef] [PubMed]
2. Paone, G.; Likosky, D.S.; Brewer, R.; Theurer, P.F.; Bell, G.F.; Cogan, C.M.; Prager, R.L. Transfusion of 1 and 2 Units of Red Blood Cells Is Associated With Increased Morbidity and Mortality. *Ann. Thorac. Surg.* **2014**, *97*, 87–94. [CrossRef] [PubMed]
3. Kilic, A.; Whitman, G.J.R. Blood Transfusions in Cardiac Surgery: Indications, Risks, and Conservation Strategies. *Ann. Thorac. Surg.* **2014**, *97*, 726–734. [CrossRef]
4. Desai, N.; Schofield, N.; Richards, T. Perioperative Patient Blood Management to Improve Outcomes. *Anesth. Analg.* **2018**, *127*, 1211–1220. [CrossRef] [PubMed]
5. World Health Organization. *The Urgent Need to Implement Patient Blood Management: Policy Brief*; World Health Organization: Geneva, Switzerland, 2021.
6. Shander, A.; Hardy, J.-F.; Ozawa, S.; Farmer, S.L.; Hofmann, A.; Frank, S.M.; Kor, D.J.; Faraoni, D.; Freedman, J. A Global Definition of Patient Blood Management. *Anesth. Analg.* **2022**, *135*, 476–488. [CrossRef]
7. Goodnough, L.T.; Shander, A.; Riou, B. Patient Blood Management. *Anesthesiology* **2012**, *116*, 1367–1376. [CrossRef]
8. Klein, A.A.; Collier, T.; Yeates, J.; Miles, L.F.; Fletcher, S.N.; Evans, C.; Richards, T. The ACTA PORT-Score for Predicting Perioperative Risk of Blood Transfusion for Adult Cardiac Surgery. *Br. J. Anaesth.* **2017**, *119*, 394–401. [CrossRef]
9. Helm, J.M.; Swiergosz, A.M.; Haeberle, H.S.; Karnuta, J.M.; Schaffer, J.L.; Krebs, V.E.; Spitzer, A.I.; Ramkumar, P.N. Machine Learning and Artificial Intelligence: Definitions, Applications, and Future Directions. *Curr. Rev. Musculoskelet. Med.* **2020**, *13*, 69–76. [CrossRef]
10. Mitterecker, A.; Hofmann, A.; Trentino, K.M.; Lloyd, A.; Leahy, M.F.; Schwarzbauer, K.; Tschoellitsch, T.; Böck, C.; Hochreiter, S.; Meier, J. Machine Learning–Based Prediction of Transfusion. *Transfusion* **2020**, *60*, 1977–1986. [CrossRef] [PubMed]
11. Meier, J.M.; Tschoellitsch, T. Artificial Intelligence and Machine Learning in Patient Blood Management: A Scoping Review. *Anesth. Analg.* **2022**, *135*, 524–531. [CrossRef] [PubMed]
12. Mavrogiorgou, A.; Kiourtis, A.; Kleftakis, S.; Mavrogiorgos, K.; Zafeiropoulos, N.; Kyriazis, D. A Catalogue of Machine Learning Algorithms for Healthcare Risk Predictions. *Sensors* **2022**, *22*, 8615. [CrossRef] [PubMed]
13. Mateo, J.; Rius-Peris, J.M.; Maraña-Pérez, A.I.; Valiente-Armero, A.; Torres, A.M. Extreme Gradient Boosting Machine Learning Method for Predicting Medical Treatment in Patients with Acute Bronchiolitis. *Biocybern. Biomed. Eng.* **2021**, *41*, 792–801. [CrossRef]
14. Goodnough, L.T.; Maggio, P.; Hadhazy, E.; Shieh, L.; Hernandez-Boussard, T.; Khari, P.; Shah, N. Restrictive Blood Transfusion Practices Are Associated with Improved Patient Outcomes. *Transfusion* **2014**, *54*, 2753–2759. [CrossRef] [PubMed]
15. Tschoellitsch, T.; Böck, C.; Mahečić, T.T.; Hofmann, A.; Meier, J. Machine Learning-Based Prediction of Massive Perioperative Allogeneic Blood Transfusion in Cardiac Surgery. *Eur. J. Anaesthesiol.* **2022**, *39*, 766–773. [CrossRef]

16. Levi, R.; Carli, F.; Arévalo, A.R.; Altinel, Y.; Stein, D.J.; Naldini, M.M.; Grassi, F.; Zanoni, A.; Finkelstein, S.; Vieira, S.M.; et al. Artificial Intelligence-Based Prediction of Transfusion in the Intensive Care Unit in Patients with Gastrointestinal Bleeding. *BMJ Health Care Inform.* **2021**, *28*, e100245. [CrossRef] [PubMed]
17. Pieri, M.; Nardelli, P.; De Luca, M.; Landoni, G.; Frassoni, S.; Melissano, G.; Zangrillo, A.; Chiesa, R.; Monaco, F. Predicting the Need for Intra-Operative Large Volume Blood Transfusions During Thoraco-Abdominal Aortic Aneurysm Repair. *Eur. J. Vasc. Endovasc. Surg.* **2017**, *53*, 347–353. [CrossRef] [PubMed]
18. Attali, E.; Many, A.; Kern, G.; Reicher, L.; Kahana, A.; Shemer, A.; Kagan, G.; Gamzu, R.; Yogev, Y.; Zakar, L. Predicting the Need for Blood Transfusion Requirement in Postpartum Hemorrhage. *J. Matern.-Fetal Neonatal Med.* **2024**, *35*, 7911–7916. [CrossRef] [PubMed]
19. Kadar, A.; Chechik, O.; Steinberg, E.; Reider, E.; Sternheim, A. Predicting the Need for Blood Transfusion in Patients with Hip Fractures. *Int. Orthop.* **2013**, *37*, 693–700. [CrossRef]
20. Li, Q.; Lv, H.; Chen, Y.; Shen, J.; Shi, J.; Zhou, C.; Yan, F. Development and Validation of a Machine Learning Prediction Model for Perioperative Red Blood Cell Transfusions in Cardiac Surgery. *Int. J. Med. Inform.* **2024**, *184*, 105343. [CrossRef] [PubMed]
21. Wang, Z.; Zhe, S.; Zimmerman, J.; Morrisey, C.; Tonna, J.E.; Sharma, V.; Metcalf, R.A. Development and Validation of a Machine Learning Method to Predict Intraoperative Red Blood Cell Transfusions in Cardiothoracic Surgery. *Sci. Rep.* **2022**, *12*, 1355. [CrossRef] [PubMed]
22. Liu, S.; Zhou, R.; Xia, X.-Q.; Ren, H.; Wang, L.-Y.; Sang, R.-R.; Jiang, M.; Yang, C.-C.; Liu, H.; Wei, L.; et al. Machine Learning Models to Predict Red Blood Cell Transfusion in Patients Undergoing Mitral Valve Surgery. *Ann. Transl. Med.* **2021**, *9*, 530. [CrossRef]
23. Chen, D.X.; Wang, Y.S.; Yan, M.; Du, L.; Li, Q. A Model Based on Electronic Health Records to Predict Transfusion Events in On-Pump Cardiac Surgery. *iScience* **2023**, *26*, 107798. [CrossRef] [PubMed]
24. Ranucci, M.; Castelvecchio, S.; Frigiola, A.; Scolletta, S.; Giomarelli, P.; Biagioli, B. Predicting Transfusions in Cardiac Surgery: The Easier, the Better: The Transfusion Risk and Clinical Knowledge Score. *Vox Sang.* **2009**, *96*, 324–332. [CrossRef] [PubMed]
25. Cuschieri, S. The STROBE Guidelines. *Saudi J. Anaesth.* **2019**, *13*, 31. [CrossRef] [PubMed]
26. Hasan, M.K.; Alam, M.A.; Roy, S.; Dutta, A.; Jawad, M.T.; Das, S. Missing Value Imputation Affects the Performance of Machine Learning: A Review and Analysis of the Literature (2010–2021). *Inform. Med. Unlocked* **2021**, *27*, 100799. [CrossRef]
27. Azur, M.J.; Stuart, E.A.; Frangakis, C.; Leaf, P.J. Multiple Imputation by Chained Equations: What Is It and How Does It Work? *Int. J. Methods Psychiatr. Res.* **2011**, *20*, 40–49. [CrossRef] [PubMed]
28. Japkowicz, N.; Stephen, S. The Class Imbalance Problem: A Systematic Study. *Intell. Data Anal.* **2002**, *6*, 429–449. [CrossRef]
29. Chawla, N.V.; Bowyer, K.W.; Hall, L.O.; Kegelmeyer, W.P. SMOTE: Synthetic Minority Over-Sampling Technique. *J. Artif. Intell. Res.* **2002**, *16*, 321–357. [CrossRef]
30. Chen, T.; Guestrin, C. XGBoost. In *Proceedings of the 22nd ACM SIGKDD International Conference on Knowledge Discovery and Data Mining*; ACM: New York, NY, USA, 2016; pp. 785–794.
31. Tarwidi, D.; Pudjaprasetya, S.R.; Adytia, D.; Apri, M. An Optimized XGBoost-Based Machine Learning Method for Predicting Wave Run-up on a Sloping Beach. *MethodsX* **2023**, *10*, 102119. [CrossRef] [PubMed]
32. Akanbi, L.A.; Oyedele, A.O.; Oyedele, L.O.; Salami, R.O. Deep Learning Model for Demolition Waste Prediction in a Circular Economy. *J. Clean. Prod.* **2020**, *274*, 122843. [CrossRef]
33. Rodríguez-Pérez, R.; Bajorath, J. Interpretation of Machine Learning Models Using Shapley Values: Application to Compound Potency and Multi-Target Activity Predictions. *J. Comput. Aided Mol. Des.* **2020**, *34*, 1013–1026. [CrossRef] [PubMed]
34. Alghamdi, A.A.; Davis, A.; Brister, S.; Corey, P.; Logan, A. Development and Validation of Transfusion Risk Understanding Scoring Tool (TRUST) to Stratify Cardiac Surgery Patients According to Their Blood Transfusion Needs. *Transfusion* **2006**, *46*, 1120–1129. [CrossRef] [PubMed]
35. Fromes, Y. Reduction of the Inflammatory Response Following Coronary Bypass Grafting with Total Minimal Extracorporeal Circulation. *Eur. J. Cardio-Thorac. Surg.* **2002**, *22*, 527–533. [CrossRef] [PubMed]
36. Kraft, F.; Schmidt, C.; Van Aken, H.; Zarbock, A. Inflammatory Response and Extracorporeal Circulation. *Best. Pract. Res. Clin. Anaesthesiol.* **2015**, *29*, 113–123. [CrossRef] [PubMed]
37. Bical, O.M.; Fromes, Y.; Gaillard, D.; Fischer, M.; Ponzio, O.; Deleuze, P.; Gerhardt, M.-F.; Trivin, F. Comparison of the Inflammatory Response between Miniaturized and Standard CPB Circuits in Aortic Valve Surgery. *Eur. J. Cardio-Thorac. Surg.* **2006**, *29*, 699–702. [CrossRef] [PubMed]
38. Karkouti, K.; O'Farrell, R.; Yau, T.M.; Beattie, W.S. Prediction of Massive Blood Transfusion in Cardiac Surgery. *Can. J. Anesth./J. Can. D'anesthésie* **2006**, *53*, 781–794. [CrossRef] [PubMed]
39. Ferraris, V.A.; Ferraris, S.P.; Saha, S.P.; Hessel, E.A.; Haan, C.K.; Royston, B.D.; Bridges, C.R.; Higgins, R.S.D.; Despotis, G.; Brown, J.R.; et al. Perioperative Blood Transfusion and Blood Conservation in Cardiac Surgery: The Society of Thoracic Surgeons and The Society of Cardiovascular Anesthesiologists Clinical Practice Guideline. *Ann. Thorac. Surg.* **2007**, *83*, S27–S86. [CrossRef]

40. Karkouti, K.; Wijeysundera, D.N.; Yau, T.M.; Beattie, W.S.; Abdelnaem, E.; McCluskey, S.A.; Ghannam, M.; Yeo, E.; Djaiani, G.; Karski, J. The Independent Association of Massive Blood Loss with Mortality in Cardiac Surgery. *Transfusion* **2004**, *44*, 1453–1462. [CrossRef] [PubMed]
41. Munting, K.E.; Klein, A.A. Optimisation of Pre-Operative Anaemia in Patients before Elective Major Surgery—Why, Who, When and How? *Anaesthesia* **2019**, *74*, 49–57. [CrossRef]

Mathematical and Computational Applications

MDPI

Article

Market Regime Identification and Variable Annuity Pricing: Analysis of COVID-19-Induced Regime Shifts in the Indian Stock Market

Mohammad Sarfraz [1,†], Guglielmo D'Amico [2,*,†]

1 Department of Mathematics, Indian Institute of Technology Delhi, Hauz Khas, New Delhi 110016, India; maz198787@maths.iitd.ac.in (M.S.); dharmar@maths.iitd.ac.in (D.S.)
2 Department of Economics, University G. d'Annunzio of Chieti-Pescara, Viale Pindaro, 65127 Pescara, Italy
* Correspondence: g.damico@unich.it
† These authors contributed equally to this work.

Abstract

Understanding how crises like the COVID-19 pandemic affect variable annuity pricing is crucial, especially in emerging markets like India. The motivation is that financial stability and risk management in these markets depend heavily on accurate pricing models. While prior research has primarily focused on Western markets, there is a significant gap in analyzing the impact of extreme volatility and regime-dependent dynamics on variable annuities in emerging economies. This study investigates how regime shifts during the COVID-19 pandemic influence variable annuity pricing in the Indian stock market, specifically using the Nifty 50 Index data from 7 September 2017 until 7 September 2023. Advanced methodologies, including regime-switching hidden Markov models, artificial neural networks, and Monte Carlo simulations, were applied to analyze pre- and post-COVID-19 market behavior. The regime-switching hidden Markov models effectively capture latent market regimes and their transitions, which traditional models often overlook, while neural networks provide flexible functional approximations that enhance pricing accuracy in highly non-linear environments. The Expectation–Maximization (EM) algorithm was employed to achieve robust calibration and enhance pricing accuracy. The analysis showed significant pricing variations across market regimes, with heightened volatility observed during the pandemic. The findings highlight the effectiveness of regime-switching models in capturing market dynamics, particularly during periods of economic uncertainty and turbulence. This research contributes to the understanding of variable annuity pricing under regime-dependent dynamics in emerging markets and offers practical implications for improved risk management and policy formulation.

Keywords: variable annuity pricing; hidden Markov model; regime switching; Monte Carlo; calibration; EM algorithm; Nifty 50 Index data; neural networks; emerging markets

JEL Classification: C13; C32; C45; G22; N25

1. Introduction

Over the last ten years, the life insurance sector has been modifying its product designs to meet client demands more effectively. Traditional life insurance products, such as pure endowments, death-deferred capital, and unit-linked insurance, have transformed into more adaptable options known as variable annuities (VAs). These VA products are tax-deferred and provide customers the choice to deploy their funds to investing methods before or after retirement, ensuring a lifelong income or death capital while protecting against market downturns.

In recent years, VAs have witnessed substantial sales volumes, surpassing 20 billion per quarter. This surge in popularity is driven mainly by the inclusion of rider features, which offer enhanced benefits and customization options to policyholders. However, the incorporation of rider features in VAs introduces a spectrum of risks for issuers, spanning financial risks, mortality or longevity risks, and surrender risks. Additionally, navigating the complexities of a low- or negative-interest-rate environment, market interconnections, and risk interactions poses challenges in accurately valuing life insurance contracts with embedded guarantees (see [1]). GMxB is a common abbreviation for these guarantees, where x represents the kind of benefit. A few of the most common examples are the GMDB, GMAB, GMWB, and GMIB, which guarantee a minimum death benefit, minimum accumulation benefit, minimum withdrawal benefit, and minimum income benefit, respectively. As a result of intense competition, insurers have increased the scope of these guarantees.

Researchers have extensively studied life insurance contracts with embedded guarantees for many years.

Most VA issuers suffered significant losses during the credit crisis that lasted from October 2007 until March 2009. The sources of these losses were found to be rising guarantee values, decreased earnings from mutual fund fees, negative hedging results, and exceeding hedging expenses. To reduce the risk of financial losses for VA issuers, it is critical to incorporate economic regime variations into the valuation framework while also taking into account the benefits of VAs during periods of economic boom and recession.

Furthermore, understanding market behavior during different economic conditions is crucial for accurate valuation and risk management. For example Figure 1 represents the trajectory of the Nifty 50 Index price before and after the COVID-19 pandemic. The price movements display relatively stable behavior before COVID-19, with moderate levels of volatility. However, after COVID-19, the price processes exhibit a significantly higher level of volatility. Table 1 presents the descriptive statistics for Nifty 50 Index prices before COVID-19 and after the COVID-19 pandemic. Before COVID-19, the Nifty 50 Index exhibited relatively stable behavior, with a mean price of 7200 and a low degree of volatility (standard deviation of 2468.981). A higher mean price (15718) and standard deviation (2992.078) after COVID-19 show that there was a significant increase in volatility. The negative skewness before and after COVID-19 suggests a left-tailed distribution, indicating more frequent lower index values, whereas the full dataset's slight positive skewness reflects a small rightward asymmetry. The negative kurtosis values across all cases indicate a platykurtic distribution, suggesting fewer extreme price fluctuations compared to a normal distribution. The properties of time series (spikes) render the widely used class of jump-diffusion models ineffective, as they cannot depict successive spikes with the regularity seen in market data.

The complexity and flexibility of these products can be solved by using a regime-switching model. Hardy [2] and Sui et al. [3] discussed how to value and hedge long-term investment guarantees within the context of regime-switching models. Elliott et al. [4] introduced a novel approach to option pricing by proposing a switching jump-diffusion process. Building upon this work, Boyarchenko and Levendorskii [5] extended Carr's randomization procedure to evaluate American options in the context of regime-switching models. Lin et al. [6] examined the valuation of equity-indexed annuities (EIAs) and VAs by employing a regime-switching model that modeled the dynamics of the reference investment fund value as a geometric Brownian motion, modulated by a continuous-time, finite-state Markov chain. Ng and Li [7] were pioneers in exploring the valuation of VA guarantees using a multivariate regime-switching model. Fan et al. [8] studied the valuation of VAs with Guaranteed Minimum Death Benefits (GMDBs) using a Markov-modulated geometric Brownian motion for the investment fund. Mohammad et al. [9] applied a regime-switching local volatility model for pricing VAs with embedded GMABs. Bargos and Claro Romão [10] investigated the integration of machine learning techniques with risk and return performance measures, providing a data-driven framework for identifying investment opportunities in equity funds.

Table 1. Descriptive statistics for Nifty 50 Index prices.

	Mean	Std. Dev.	Kurtosis	Skewness
Before COVID-19	7200	2468.981	−0.86	−0.35
After COVID-19	15,718	2992.078	−0.29	−0.88
Full Data	13,043.61	3503.70	−1.28	0.43

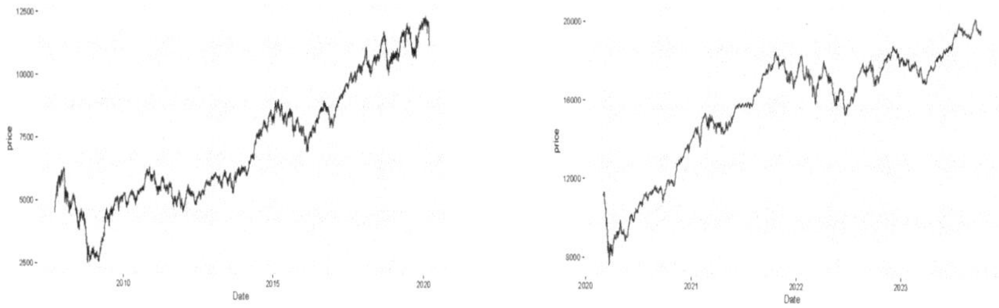

(**a**) (**b**)

Figure 1. Nifty 50 Index price (INR) from September 2007 to September 2023. (**a**) Before COVID-19 pandemic. (**b**) After COVID-19 pandemic.

However, the majority of the current work on the valuation of financial assets using regime-switching models assumes that the model parameters vary with respect to the modulating observable Markov chain. There has been relatively less attention given to regime-switching hidden Markov models (HMMs). The main idea behind hidden Markov models (HMMs) is to characterize the observed stochastic behavior of a given time series using two or more different states or regimes with different underlying stochastic processes. HMMs have gained popularity in this domain due to their relative simplicity and ability to capture the distinguishing features of index pricing.

The econometric literature has devoted considerable attention to modeling economic cycles using hidden Markov chains. Our article directly aligns with this research line, drawing insights from previous studies. Guidolin and Timmermann [11] provide empirical evidence of enduring 'bull' and 'bear' periods in the returns of UK stocks and bonds. In Shahzad et al. [12], the daily return spillover of 18 cryptocurrencies is examined under low- and high-volatility regimes, with consideration given to three price parameters and the impact of the COVID-19 pandemic. It is shown that the regime-dependent spillover results provide better ways to manage portfolio diversification strategies. S.Y. Tchoumi et al. [13] formulated a mathematical model incorporating infective immigrants and vaccination to study the impact of imported infections on COVID-19 dynamics. De Blasis et al. [14] examined the impact of stablecoin design on market behavior during turbulent periods and found significant contagion effects from the TerraUSD collapse. Using an event study approach, Wu et al. [15] investigated how the COVID-19 outbreak affected stock price movements of China's tourism industry. The findings indicated that the crisis had a negative impact on stocks in the tourism sector. Mazur et al. [16] investigates the US stock market performance during the crash of March 2020 triggered by COVID-19. MC Belili et al. [17] analyzed the dynamics of a discrete-time SIRS epidemic model, focusing on the stability of the endemic state and bifurcations. Using COVID-19 data from the USA, they applied optimal control strategies, demonstrating their effectiveness in mitigating the pandemic's spread.

As Silva [18], who examined exchange rate and stock price behavior in developing nations using the Markov Switching Vector Autoregressive model, shows, the adoption of regime-switching models has been shown to be an efficient method in catching structural changes in financial markets. In order to assess the performance of sustainability-oriented indexes in India, Jasuja et al. [19] also used a Markov regime-switching technique, therefore underlining the need to include regime changes into financial modeling. Xie et al. [20] have pointed out that the COVID-19 epidemic emphasizes the need for including such models, as market discipline and risk management in developing nations were clearly disrupted. Reiterating the need for regime-dependent techniques in actuarial and financial modeling, Zhong et al. [21] showed, in the context of VA pricing, the efficacy of regime-switching jump-diffusion models in capturing mortality and surrender risks. This work uses regime-switching models and machine learning approaches to improve the accuracy of VA pricing in developing countries considering the higher volatility and structural changes brought about by crises such as COVID-19.

Building upon the framework established by prior researchers who have utilized regime-switching models, this study seeks to address critical questions regarding the impact of the COVID-19 pandemic on the pricing of VAs in emerging markets, focusing on the Indian stock market. Specifically, this research investigates how market volatility induced by the pandemic influenced VA pricing and assesses the suitability of regime-switching HMMs in capturing these dynamics. Key research questions include the following: How did the pandemic affect VA pricing in an emerging market?; Can regime-switching models effectively capture price variations under extreme market conditions? Previous studies have largely focused on VA pricing in developed markets or under stable economic conditions, leaving a gap in understanding how emerging markets respond to significant financial disruptions. By addressing this gap, this study aims to provide insights into VA pricing in volatile contexts, using the Nifty 50 Index to model market shifts and analyze pricing behavior pre- and post-COVID-19. This analysis contributes to a deeper understanding of how crisis-induced regime shifts affect VA pricing, offering valuable implications for financial risk management in similar contexts.

The NIFTY 50 Index was selected as the benchmark for this study due to its broad market representation, liquidity, and relevance in the Indian financial market. As India's premier stock market index, NIFTY 50 comprises the 50 most liquid and large-cap stocks across various sectors, making it a strong indicator of overall market performance. Unlike broader indices such as NIFTY 500 or sector-specific indices, NIFTY 50 strikes a balance between comprehensive market coverage and efficient trading activity, ensuring that the findings remain both representative and practical. Additionally, it is widely used by institutional and retail investors as a benchmark for portfolio performance, derivatives trading, and economic analysis. Given its significance in capturing market sentiment and macroeconomic shifts, NIFTY 50 provides a robust framework for analyzing the impact of economic events, such as the COVID-19 pandemic, on the Indian stock market.

This research utilizes a mean-reverting model to examine the impact of COVID-19 on the evaluation of VA contracts. The primary objective of this research is to analyze how the VA contract price changed during the COVID-19 pandemic, specifically using Indian stock market data. We employ a well-known model to answer this question across different market conditions, which, to the best of our knowledge, has not been previously explored. By applying these methodologies, we aim to fill this gap and provide a comprehensive answer to how variable annuity pricing is affected during the pandemic. Our main purpose is not to develop a new methodology but to use existing ones to address this specific issue under varying market regimes.

The second contribution of our work is the application of the modeling technique proposed by Janczura and Weron [22] to a specific financial domain. We utilize Expectation–Maximization (EM) algorithm techniques to extract significant information and determine the regime-switching parameters from real-world data. By employing this regime-switching model, we are able to obtain a significant level of precision in our valuation methodology.

At present, India has one of the most rapidly developing emerging stock markets in the world, and although many scholars have shown strong interest in its market (see Selvamuthu et al. [23]), the impact of COVID-19 on variable annuity pricing in the Indian context has received scant attention. Therefore, analyzing Indian stock market data provides a unique opportunity to fill the gap in the extant literature on government policy responses to India's stock markets and identify whether such responses had a mitigating effect on the relationship between COVID-19 and variable annuity pricing. In the context of the Indian stock market, these methodologies have not been implemented in VA market evaluation. The MRS model is applied to the pricing of variable annuities in India in our research, which has not been previously investigated. The potential of this model to capture regime shifts and their impact on VA pricing under the unique dynamics of the Indian market is demonstrated through its implementation. This innovative application expands the application of well-established methods, providing insights that can improve the accuracy of VA pricing models in emerging markets like India.

There is a noticeable difference in prices before and after the COVID-19 pandemic. Our findings demonstrate that the pandemic has significantly affected the fair prices of VA contracts across different guarantee frameworks and market regimes. Prior to the pandemic, fair prices were higher, but they dropped considerably afterward, indicating changes in investor sentiment and risk perception due to heightened market volatility and unpredictability. Furthermore, during the COVID-19 period, prices remained stable across regimes, suggesting that the pandemic had a uniform impact on the market, diminishing regime-specific variations.

The paper is structured as follows. Section 2 explains the model's description. Next, Section 3 describes the model calibration methodology for Markov regime-switching models. Then, in Section 4, an application of the proposed approach to Nifty 50 Index data is discussed. In Section 5, the valuation of VAs with GMAB and GMDB riders is discussed. Section 6 discusses the numerical results and sensitivity analysis. Finally, in Section 7, we conclude and provide suggestions for future work.

2. Model Description

A Markov regime-switching model (MRS) represents the observed stochastic behavior of a time series by two separate states or regimes, each characterized by different underlying stochastic processes. The transition process between states is intended to be a hidden Markov chain. These models have attracted significant attention in recent years, not only in the field of econometrics but also in several other scientific domains, such as option pricing (Elliott et al. [24,25]), life insurance policies (Siu [26]), and electricity spot pricing (Janczura and Weron [22]).

Let $(\Omega, \mathcal{F}, (\mathcal{F}_t)_{t\geq 0}, \mathbb{P})$ be a filtered probability space satisfying the standard filtration conditions of completeness and right-continuity, with $\mathcal{F}_0 = \{\emptyset, \Omega\}$. An MRS model is based on an unobservable continuous-time homogeneous Markov chain $\mathbf{X}(t) = \{\mathbf{X}(t), t \in T\}$, defined for $t \in T$ with a time horizon $T \in [0, \infty)$. This chain enables transitions between distinct states or regimes, governed by a transition probability matrix $\mathbf{P}$. The entries of $\mathbf{P}$, denoted as $p_{ij} = \mathbb{P}(\mathbf{X}(t+1) = j \mid \mathbf{X}(t) = i)$, specify the likelihood of moving from regime i at time t to regime j at time $t+1$. For a two-state model, where $i, j \in \{1, 2\}$, the transition matrix is structured as

$$\mathbf{P} = \begin{pmatrix} p_{11} & p_{12} \\ p_{21} & p_{22} \end{pmatrix} = \begin{pmatrix} 1 - p_{12} & p_{12} \\ p_{21} & 1 - p_{21} \end{pmatrix}. \tag{1}$$

The Markov property ensures that the current state $\mathbf{X}(t)$ relies solely on the immediately preceding state $\mathbf{X}(t-1)$, simplifying the complexity of state dependencies over time.

This study focuses on two widely used MRS models in economics, both based on a discretized version of mean-reverting heteroskedastic processes, originally proposed by Janczura and Weron [22] to model electricity spot price processes, for modeling investment risk or the underlying processes $S(t)$. These processes are described by the following stochastic differential equation:

$$dS(t) = (\alpha - \beta S(t))dt + \sigma |S(t)|^{\gamma} dW(t), \tag{2}$$

where γ is a constant. In this model, volatility is influenced by the current stock price level, denoted as $S(t)$. When γ is positive, higher stock prices are associated with larger price fluctuations, meaning that volatility increases as the stock price rises. Conversely, when γ is negative, lower stock prices correspond to greater price fluctuations, implying that volatility is higher when the stock price declines. This relationship highlights how the magnitude of price changes varies depending on the price level and the sign of γ. In the context of financial data, γ can be interpreted as a parameter representing the 'degree of inverse leverage'. The inverse leverage effect captures the observation that positive shocks to asset prices tend to increase volatility more than negative shocks, which contrasts with the traditional leverage effect observed in financial markets.

The absolute value is required to manage cases where the process may take negative values, e.g., the return series of underlying stock. The first model configuration involves parameter switching, where the model parameters switch depending on the regime. The second configuration separates the regimes into distinct processes, each governed independently.

In the first case, i.e., the parameter-switching setup, the process $S(t)$ evolves as

$$S(t) = \alpha_{\mathbf{X}(t)} + \left(1 - \beta_{\mathbf{X}(t)}\right) S(t-1) + \sigma_{\mathbf{X}(t)} |S(t-1)|^{\gamma_{\mathbf{X}(t)}} \epsilon(t), \tag{3}$$

with $\epsilon(t)$ representing random shocks drawn from a standard normal distribution. The same random innovations apply across all regimes in this formulation.

For the second case, the process $S(t)$ is explicitly defined for each regime as

$$S(t) = \begin{cases} S(t,1) & \text{if } \mathbf{X}(t) = 1, \\ S(t,2) & \text{if } \mathbf{X}(t) = 2, \end{cases} \tag{4}$$

where at least one of the regimes is characterized as

$$S(t,i) = \alpha_i + (1 - \beta_i) S(t-1,i) + \sigma_i |S(t-1,i)|^{\gamma_i} \epsilon(t,i), \quad i = 1 \vee i = 2. \tag{5}$$

While this study specifically examines a two-regime model, the framework can be easily extended to include additional regimes, allowing for a more comprehensive representation of complex processes. This flexibility makes MRS models a robust tool for capturing dynamic behavior across various regimes. The adoption of a two-regime model is well supported by empirical evidence, as highlighted in [27,28], where regime-switching techniques effectively capture shifts in market behavior.

Although MRS models have shown success in reflecting changes in financial regimes, they are not without limitations. Especially with a small sample size, problems like state misclassification and overfitting may develop. Under such conditions, inadequate data might cause the model to overfit to noise, instead of accurately identifying real structural changes, and assign observations to inappropriate regimes. But in our analysis, we gain from an enormous dataset that greatly allays these issues. Having enough data helps to reduce overfitting and misclassification risks, therefore guaranteeing a stronger and more consistent estimate of regime shifts.

3. Calibration Methodology of MRS Models

Calibrating MRS models is challenging since the regimes are hidden and hence not easily identifiable. Hamilton [29] offered an application of the Expectation–Maximization method initially proposed by Dempster et al. [30]. This application involves a two-step iterative approach starting from the initial set of parameters, denoted as Θ. To initiate the EM algorithm, an appropriate initial set of parameters must be selected. A reasonable approach is to use estimates obtained through alternative estimation methods, such as the method of moments, to define the initial values for the parameter vector. This section gives a general description of the estimate technique and offers explicit estimators for the model parameters provided by Equation (2). We apply the calibration process as used by Janczura and Weron [22], which serves as a basis for estimating the parameters in this model.

3.1. Parameter-Switching Variant

To start the estimation procedure, first an initial parameter vector is needed. We assume the following initial parameter vector:

$$\Theta^{(0)} = \left(\alpha_i^{(0)}, \beta_i^{(0)}, \sigma_i^{(0)}, \gamma_i^{(0)}, \mathbf{P}^{(0)}, \rho_i^{(0)}\right), \tag{6}$$

for $i = 1, 2$, where $\rho_i^{(0)} = \mathbb{P}(\mathbf{X}(1) = i)$ and the remaining parameters are defined by Equations (1), (2) and (5).

At the beginning of the iterative procedure, i.e., the E-step, estimates about the hidden-state process are calculated. Since $\mathbf{X}(t)$ is unobservable, only the expected values of the state process, conditioned on the observed data, $\mathbb{E}\left(\mathbb{I}_{\mathbf{X}(t)=j} \mid s(1), s(2), \ldots, s(T); \Theta\right)$, can be determined. Where $s(1), s(2), \ldots, s(T)$ are the realizations of the processes $S(t)$ for $t = 1, 2, \ldots T$. These expectations provide smoothed inferences, which are the conditional probabilities $\mathbb{P}(\mathbf{X}(t) = j \mid s(1), s(2), \ldots, s(T); \Theta)$, indicating the probability of the system being in regime j at time t. In the following step, i.e., the M-step, new estimates for the parameter vector Θ are computed using the maximum likelihood approach, based on the smoothed inferences derived in the E-step. These two steps are repeated iteratively until the likelihood function converges to its local maximum. A detailed explanation of this algorithm is provided below.

3.1.1. The E-Step

Assume the vector of parameters at the nth iteration $\Theta^{(n)}$, calculated in the M-step during the previous iteration, is known. Now, the first part of the E-step is called filtering.

1. Filtering: Compute regime probabilities using the Bayes formula. Let $\mathbf{s}(t) = (s(1), s(2), \ldots, s(t))$. Therefore, we have
$$\mathbb{P}\Big(\mathbf{X}(t) = i \mid \mathbf{s}(t); \Theta^{(n)}\Big) = \frac{\mathbb{P}\big(\mathbf{X}(t)=i|\mathbf{s}(t-1);\Theta^{(n)}\big) f\big(s(t)|\mathbf{X}(t)=i;\mathbf{s}(t-1);\Theta^{(n)}\big)}{\sum_{i=1}^{2} \mathbb{P}\big(\mathbf{X}(t)=i|\mathbf{s}(t-1);\Theta^{(n)}\big) f\big(s(t)|\mathbf{X}(t)=i;\mathbf{s}(t-1);\Theta^{(n)}\big)},$$
where $f\Big(s(t) \mid \mathbf{X}(t) = i; \mathbf{s}(t-1); \Theta^{(n)}\Big)$ is the density of the $S(t)$ process conditional on the ith regime. Observe that
$$f\Big(s(t) \mid \mathbf{X}(t) = i; \mathbf{s}(t-1); \Theta^{(n)}\Big) \sim \mathcal{N}(\alpha_i + (1-\beta_i)S(t-1),\ \sigma_i^2 |S(t-1)|^{2\gamma_i}).$$
$$\mathbb{P}\Big(\mathbf{X}(t+1) = i \mid \mathbf{s}(t); \Theta^{(n)}\Big) = \sum_{j=1}^{2} p_{ji}^{(n)} \mathbb{P}\Big(\mathbf{X}(t) = j \mid \mathbf{s}(t); \Theta^{(n)}\Big),$$
until $\mathbb{P}\Big(\mathbf{X}(t) = i \mid \mathbf{s}(T); \Theta^{(n)}\Big)$ is calculated. The starting point for the iteration is chosen as $\mathbb{P}\Big(E_1 = i \mid \mathbf{s}_0; \Theta^{(n)}\Big) = \rho_i^{(n)}$.
2. Smoothing: Starting from $t = T-1$ and moving backward to $t = 1$, perform iterations on the following steps:
$$\mathbb{P}\Big(\mathbf{X}(t) = i \mid \mathbf{s}(T); \Theta^{(n)}\Big) = \sum_{j=1}^{2} \frac{\mathbb{P}\big(\mathbf{X}(t)=i|\mathbf{s}(t);\Theta^{(n)}\big)\mathbb{P}\big(\mathbf{X}(t+1)=j|\mathbf{s}(T);\Theta^{(n)}\big) p_{ij}^{(n)}}{\mathbb{P}\big(\mathbf{X}(t+1)=j|\mathbf{s}(t);\Theta^{(n)}\big)}.$$
The procedure mentioned above requires the derivation of the conditional probability distribution function (pdf),
$$f\Big(s(t) \mid \mathbf{X}(t) = i; \mathbf{s}(t-1); \Theta^{(n)}\Big),$$
which is used in the filtering. The model definition Equation (3) states that $S(t)$, given $S(t-1)$, follows a conditional Gaussian distribution with a mean of $\alpha_i + (1-\beta_i)S(t-1)$ and a standard deviation of $\sigma_i |S(t-1)|^{\gamma_i}$. This distribution is described by the following probability distribution function:
$$f\Big(s(t) \mid \mathbf{X}(t) = i; \mathbf{s}(t-1); \Theta^{(n)}\Big) = \frac{1}{\sqrt{2\pi}\sigma_i^{(n)} |s(t-1)|_i^{\gamma_i^{(n)}}} \cdot \exp\left\{ -\frac{\Big(s(t) - \Big(1-\beta_i^{(n)}\Big)s(t-1) - \alpha_i^{(n)}\Big)^2}{2\Big(\sigma_i^{(n)}\Big)^2 |s(t-1)|^{2\gamma_i(n)}} \right\}.$$

3.1.2. The M-Step

In the second step of the EM algorithm, updated maximum likelihood estimates, $\Theta^{(n+1)}$, are computed for all model parameters with greater precision. Unlike standard maximum likelihood estimation, which maximizes the log-likelihood function for a given probability density function (pdf) f, this approach incorporates weights based on smoothed inferences. These weights account for the fact that each observation is associated with a specific regime, determined probabilistically. The model defined in Equation (3) allows explicit parameter estimates to be derived by solving the system of equations obtained by setting the partial derivatives of the log-likelihood function to zero. This results in the following system of equations:

$$\hat{\alpha}_i = \frac{\sum_{t=2}^{T}\left[\mathbb{P}\left(\mathbf{X}(t) = i \mid \mathbf{s}(T);\Theta^{(n)}\right)|s(t-1)|^{-2\gamma_i}\left(s(t) - (1-\hat{\beta}_i)s(t-1)\right)\right]}{\sum_{t=2}^{T}\left[\mathbb{P}(\mathbf{X}(t) = i \mid \mathbf{s}(T);\Theta^{(n)})|s(t-1)|^{-2\gamma_i}\right]},$$

$$\hat{\beta}_i = \frac{\sum_{t=2}^{T}\left\{\mathbb{P}\left(\mathbf{X}(t) = i \mid \mathbf{s}(T);\Theta^{(n)}\right)s(t-1)|s(t-1)|^{-2\gamma_i}B_1\right\}}{\sum_{t=2}^{T}\left[\mathbb{P}(\mathbf{X}(t) = i \mid \mathbf{s}(T);\Theta^{(n)})s(t-1)|s(t-1)|^{-2\gamma_i}B_2\right]},$$

$$B_1 = s(t) - s(t-1) - \frac{\sum_{t=2}^{T}\mathbb{P}\left(\mathbf{X}(t) = i \mid \mathbf{s}(T);\Theta^{(n)}\right)|s(t-1)|^{-2\gamma_i}(s(t) - s(t-1))}{\sum_{t=2}^{T}\mathbb{P}(\mathbf{X}(t) = i \mid \mathbf{s}(T);\Theta^{(n)})|s(t-1)|^{-2\gamma_i}},$$

$$B_2 = \frac{\sum_{t=2}^{T}\mathbb{P}\left(\mathbf{X}(t) = i \mid \mathbf{s}(T);\Theta^{(n)}\right)s(t-1)|s(t-1)|^{-2\gamma_i}}{\sum_{t=2}^{T}\mathbb{P}(\mathbf{X}(t) = i \mid \mathbf{s}(T);\Theta^{(n)})|s(t-1)|^{-2\gamma_i}} - s(t-1),$$

$$\hat{\sigma}_i^2 = \frac{\sum_{t=2}^{T}\left\{\mathbb{P}\left(\mathbf{X}(t) = i \mid \mathbf{s}(T);\Theta^{(n)}\right)|s(t-1)|^{-2\gamma_i}\left(s(t) - \hat{\alpha}_i - (1-\hat{\beta}_i)s(t-1)\right)^2\right\}}{\sum_{t=2}^{T}\mathbb{P}(\mathbf{X}(t) = i \mid \mathbf{s}(T);\Theta^{(n)})}.$$

The parameter γ_i is determined through the numerical maximization of the log-likelihood function.

Following the approach outlined by [29], the updated estimate for $\rho_i^{(n+1)}$ is given by $\rho_i^{(n+1)} = \mathbb{P}\left(\mathbf{X}(1) = i \mid \mathbf{s}(T);\Theta^{(n)}\right)$. Additionally, the transition probabilities are calculated using the formula proposed by [31].

$$\begin{aligned} p_{ij}^{(n+1)} &= \frac{\sum_{t=2}^{T}\mathbb{P}\left(\mathbf{X}(t) = j, \mathbf{X}(t-1) = i \mid \mathbf{s}(T);\Theta^{(n)}\right)}{\sum_{t=2}^{T}\mathbb{P}(\mathbf{X}(t-1) = i \mid \mathbf{s}(T);\Theta^{(n)})} \\ &= \frac{\sum_{t=2}^{T}\mathbb{P}\left(\mathbf{X}(t) = j \mid \mathbf{s}(T);\Theta^{(n)}\right)\frac{p_{ij}^{(n)}\mathbb{P}(\mathbf{X}(t-1)=i|\mathbf{s}(t-1);\Theta^{(n)})}{\mathbb{P}(\mathbf{X}(t)=j|\mathbf{s}(t-1);\Theta^{(n)})}}{\sum_{t=2}^{T}\mathbb{P}(\mathbf{X}(t-1) = i \mid \mathbf{s}(T);\Theta^{(n)})}, \end{aligned}$$

where $p_{ij}^{(n)}$ is the transition probability from the previous iteration.

All values obtained in the M-step are then used as a new parameter vector $\Theta^{(n+1)} = \left(\hat{\alpha}_i, \hat{\beta}_i, \hat{\sigma}_i, \hat{\gamma}_i, \mathbf{P}^{(n+1)}, \rho_i^{(n+1)}\right), i = 1,2$, in the next iteration of the E-step. Although the latent states rely on the whole history of the process, which makes the standard EM algorithm computationally demanding, we use a computationally effective method to solve this problem. Specifically, we approximately estimate the latent state expectations depending on the available information at every time step instead of considering all feasible paths of the state process. Inspired by Gray [32], this approach substitutes the unobserved past-state values with their expected values, hence lowering the E-step's computational complexity. This improves practicality for big datasets by significantly reducing the memory needs from an exponential dependency on sample size to a more reasonable form. It has been demonstrated that this type of approximation can enhance computational efficiency while simultaneously maintaining estimation accuracy.

Remark 1. *The standard EM algorithm was utilized in this study without the application of any acceleration techniques. To ensure convergence and avoid premature termination, a stringent stopping criterion was adopted, terminating the iterative process only when the relative change in log-likelihood fell below* 10^{-12}*, ensuring high precision. To address challenges associated with multi-factor optimization, the initial parameter values were determined using alternative estimation methods, such as the method of moments, to improve stability and convergence. Additionally, multiple initializations were tested to mitigate local optima issues, and numerical stability was maintained by constraining transition probabilities and applying regularization where necessary. The robustness of the estimated parameters was further verified through multiple calibration trials and consistency checks.*

4. Application to Nifty 50 Index Data

In this study, we demonstrate how the methods outlined in Section 3 are able to effectively calibrate the MRS models to the Nifty 50 Index data. We use the daily returns of the Nifty 50 Index data from September 2017 to September 2023. To enable accurate comparisons of market behavior before and after COVID-19, daily price data for the Nifty 50 Index were divided into two sets: pre-pandemic (September 2017 to February 2020) and post-pandemic (February 2020 to September 2023). Each dataset was standardized to ensure comparability, equalizing factors such as mean and variance to allow for meaningful analysis of regime shifts induced by the pandemic. Calibration of the regime-switching HMM was achieved using the Expectation–Maximization algorithm, which iteratively optimizes model parameters for hidden regimes within the data. However, calibration presented challenges due to the increased volatility in post-COVID-19 data, which affected the convergence and stability of parameter estimates. To address these issues, we carefully selected initial values and performed multiple runs to ensure robustness. This expanded methodological approach provides greater transparency on data handling and calibration, ensuring that the model reliably captures shifts in VA pricing across different market regimes.

In order to achieve consistency and make meaningful comparisons in statistical analysis, it is crucial to standardize both datasets. This uniformity allows for a fair assessment of market behavior and allows researchers to accurately distinguish the distinct impacts of the COVID-19 epidemic on the performance of the Nifty 50 Index. By equalizing the datasets, we ensure that statistical methods can be consistently applied to both time periods, which improves the reliability and validity of the research. It is crucial to ensure parity between the datasets in order to derive significant conclusions about the influence of the pandemic on financial markets.

While the World Health Organization (WHO) officially declared COVID-19 a pandemic in March 2020, financial markets and economic activity in India started reacting to the outbreak much earlier. By February 2020, global supply chain disruptions had already begun affecting the Indian economy, particularly due to India's trade dependence on China, which imposed lockdown measures in January 2020. The Indian stock market also showed early signs of distress, with the benchmark indices (SENSEX and NIFTY 50) experiencing increased volatility and declines in February 2020, reflecting global uncertainties. Additionally, the first confirmed COVID-19 case in India was reported on 30 January 2020, leading to heightened concerns and precautionary measures by businesses and investors. Hence, February 2020 is chosen as the cut-off date, as it marks the initial financial market reactions and economic disruptions in India, making it a more relevant point for distinguishing the pre- and post-pandemic periods.

In what follows, the returns series of the underlying stock prices has been considered for the analysis. Returns series tend to be easier to model with the models discussed in this article rather than the prices themselves.

Let us consider the stochastic process $S(t)$ a return series of the underlying prices, which is determined by a Markov regime-switching model consisting of two independent states:

$$S(t) = \begin{cases} S_{t,1} & \text{if } \mathbf{X}(t) = 1 \\ S_{t,2} & \text{if } \mathbf{X}(t) = 2 \end{cases}$$

The mean-reverting, heteroskedastic process with Equation (7) represents the base regime, i.e., regime 1, which defines the normal pricing behavior:

$$S(t,1) = \alpha_1 + (1-\beta_1)S(t-1,1) + \sigma_1 |S(t-1,1)|^{\gamma_1} \epsilon(t), \tag{7}$$

where $\epsilon(t)$ is the standard normally distributed random variable. Regime 2, or the spike regime, which is represented by independent and identically distributed random variables from the shifted log-normal distribution, is characterized by sudden price surges (spikes) due to unexpected changes in the market:

$$log(S(t,2) - S(q2)) \sim \mathcal{N}(\alpha_2, \sigma_2^2), \quad S(t,2) \geq S(q2) \tag{8}$$

In the above Equation (8), $S(q2)$ represents the third quantile of the dataset. In general, the choice for $q2$ is arbitrary, but in this section, we assume $q2$ is 0.75, i.e., the third quartile. The reason for this is the statistical nature of the model, where the base regime's dynamics drive small deviations, and only large deviations are driven by the spike regime's dynamics.

Our approach categorizes prices as spikes based on certain criteria related to the probabilities of market regimes. More precisely, we define a spike as an event where the likelihood of being in regime 2, represented by $\mathbb{P}(\mathbf{X}(t) = 2 \mid s(1), s(2), \ldots, s(T))$, is greater than 0.5. When analyzing the historical data till time t, if the probability of the market being in regime 2 is more than 50%, we categorize the observed price at time t as a spike.

This classification technique enables us to identify cases in which the market exhibits evident support for regime 2, indicating a substantial departure from its usual pattern. Regime 2 may indicate periods characterized by high volatility, intense market sentiment, or sudden shifts in economic conditions.

Tables 2 and 3 show the calibrated model parameters. For instance, $\beta_1 = 0.3784$ suggests a relatively fast mean-reversion rate in the base regime's pre-COVID-19 data as compared to $\beta_1 = -0.2548$ in the base regime's post-COVID-19 data. A negative value of γ is responsible for the positive leverage effect, meaning that as the value of the asset declines, volatility increases. Finally, by evaluating the probability p_{ii} of remaining in the same regime, relatively high values are observed for each of the base regimes, ranging from 0.8469 for pre-COVID-19 data to 0.9083 for the post-COVID-19 data in Nifty 50 returns series. As a result, there are numerous successive observations from the same regime on average. Based on the findings presented in Table 4, it is evident that the Akaike information criterion (AIC) and Bayesian information criterion (BIC) values for the two-regime model are lower in comparison to those without the regime model. This implies that the two-regime model provides a better fit.

Table 2. Calibration results for MRS models with (two) independent regimes fitted to the Nifty 50 Index returns before COVID-19.

Parameters							Probabilities	
$\hat{\alpha}_1$	$\hat{\beta}_1$	$\hat{\sigma}_1^2$	$\hat{\gamma}_1$	$\hat{\alpha}_2$	$\hat{\gamma}_2$	$\hat{\sigma}_2^2$	$\hat{p}_{11}$	$\hat{p}_{22}$
−0.2227	0.3784	0.0158	−0.1468	−5.3880	0.0005	1.6526	0.8469	0.1440

Table 3. Calibration results for MRS models with (two) independent regimes fitted to the Nifty 50 Index returns after COVID-19.

Parameters							Probabilities	
$\hat{\alpha}_1$	$\hat{\beta}_1$	$\hat{\sigma}_1^2$	$\hat{\gamma}_1$	$\hat{\alpha}_2$	$\hat{\gamma}_2$	$\hat{\sigma}_2^2$	$\hat{p}_{11}$	$\hat{p}_{22}$
0.1037	−0.2548	0.0336	−0.1690	−6.0557	0.0014	2.2115	0.9083	0.2492

Table 4. Comparing best-fit model: AIC and BIC values without regime and with two regimes.

	Without Regime	With Two Regimes
AIC	25.99	19.74
BIC	42.00	35.74

Regime Classification Measure

Traditional specification tests for regime-switching (RS) models have predominantly focused on examining the properties of residuals or utilizing score-based approaches. However, these methods do not directly assess the precision of regime classification. To address this gap, Ang and Bekaert [33] introduce a summary statistic that quantifies the effectiveness of regime classification in RS models.

In an RS framework, the underlying state of the system at any given time is assumed to follow a latent regime structure, where the regime is observable to economic agents but remains unobserved by the econometrician. The inference about the prevailing regime is typically based on smoothed (ex-post) regime probabilities, denoted as p_t. When an RS model is well specified, it should assign high confidence to specific regimes, implying that p_t should be close to either 0 or 1. If, instead, the probabilities hover around 0.5, the model struggles to distinguish between regimes, suggesting weak regime identification and potential misspecification.

To formally evaluate the accuracy of regime classification, we use the Regime Classification Measure (RCM), which quantifies the extent to which the estimated probabilities provide clear separation between regimes. For a two-state model, the RCM is defined as

$$\text{RCM} = 400 \times \left(\frac{1}{T} \sum_{t=1}^{T} p_t(1 - p_t) \right), \tag{9}$$

where the constant ensures that the measure is normalized to the range $[0, 100]$. A lower RCM value indicates a higher degree of confidence in regime classification. Since the true regime follows a Bernoulli distribution, the RCM statistic serves as an empirical estimate of its variance.

For models incorporating multiple regimes (K), the generalized form of the RCM is expressed as

$$\text{RCM}(K) = 100K^2 \left(\frac{1}{T} \sum_{t=1}^{T} \left(\prod_{i=1}^{K} p_{i,t}^2 \right) \right), \tag{10}$$

where $p_{i,t} = \mathbb{P}(\mathbf{X}(t) = i \mid \mathcal{F}_T)$ represents the smoothed probability of being in regime i at time t. The measure extends naturally to higher-order regime-switching models and provides a direct assessment of how well the model differentiates between regimes.

The regime classification measure analysis reveals a shift in regime dynamics when comparing pre- and post-COVID-19 periods. Prior to the COVID-19 pandemic, the RCM was estimated at 49.301, indicating a moderate level of information revealed about the regimes under consideration and a degree of uncertainty in their classification. In contrast, the RCM post-COVID-19 was calculated to be 33.314, a notable decrease. This lower RCM value suggests a more distinct regime classification following the pandemic, implying that the factors influencing the regimes have become more pronounced or that the regimes themselves have become more clearly differentiated. This could be attributed to the significant disruptions and shifts in various sectors caused by the pandemic, leading to more defined patterns and behaviors within the data

5. Variable Annuity Pricing

This section explores the pricing of variable annuity contracts, focusing on a detailed description of the contracts' features including their guarantees and terms, and methodologies for valuation.

5.1. Contract Description

The Guaranteed Minimum Death Benefit (GMDB) and Guaranteed Minimum Accumulation Benefit (GMAB) represent two key features of the VA contract analyzed in this research work. Under this contract, policyholders make a single premium payment of $h_0 > 0$ in exchange for benefits tied to the performance of the investment portfolio. The insurance policy incurs fees to cover management expenses, including mortality fees, management fees, and other fees related to contract riders. An annual proportion of $m > 0$ is charged to the account value of the VA contract by the insurer. Consequently, the insured's fund value $F(t)$ at time $t \in [0, T]$ is determined by the following equation:

$$\frac{F(t)}{F(0)} = e^{-mt} \frac{S(t)}{S(0)}, \tag{11}$$

where the initial values are $F(0) = S(0) = h_0$.

Furthermore, let $\omega \geq 0$ represent the guaranteed roll-up rate utilized to reset the premium throughout the duration of the VA contract. This contract provides a lump sum payout upon its expiration date and a minimum guaranteed benefit in the event of death. It is assumed that withdrawals and surrenders are prohibited during the contract's lifetime. Accordingly, the benefits are defined as follows.

GMDB: In the event of death before the maturity time T, the insurer pays out the higher of the fund value and a guaranteed amount. At the time of death t_d, $t < t_d \leq T$, the death benefit is calculated as $D_b(t_d) = \max(F(t_d), G(t_d))$, where $G(0) \in (0, h_0]$ and the common guaranteed amount $G(t_d)$ in the market is either of the following:

1. The roll-up of the premium at the guaranteed roll-up rate ω:

$$G(t_d) = G(t)e^{\omega(t_d - t)} \tag{12}$$

2. The highest account value recorded every year before death, known as the ratchet guarantee:

$$G(t_d) = \max_{k \in \{1, \cdots, \lfloor t_d \rfloor\}} (G(t), F(t + k)). \tag{13}$$

GMAB: If the policyholder is still alive on the expiration date T, they receive the maximum of the policy fund value and the guaranteed amount. Therefore, the living benefit is given by

$$L_b(T) = \max\{F(T), G(T)\},$$

where the guaranteed amount $G(T)$ is defined similarly as in the case of death (see Equations (12) and (13)).

5.2. Valuation of VAs

Assume $\mathcal{P}(S(0), G, T)$ as the present value of the embedded guarantee in the VA contract written on S, with an initial value $S(0)$, with guaranteed amount G, and time to maturity T. In this article, we rely on the no-arbitrage principle and thus consider a risk-adjusted measure $\tilde{\mathbb{P}}$. As we concentrate on market risk, it is assumed that mortality risk may be diversified away. Hence, $\mathbb{P}$ and $\tilde{\mathbb{P}}$ coincide on occurrences relating to mortality.

It is also assumed that the financial and mortality risks are independent under $\tilde{\mathbb{P}}$. Hence, the present values of the death benefit and the living benefit at time $t = 0$ are as follows:

$$\mathcal{P}(S(0), G, T) = \mathbb{E}_{\tilde{\mathbb{P}}}\Big(e^{-rt}\mathbb{I}_{\{\tau_d<T\}}D_b(\tau_d) + e^{-rT}\mathbb{I}_{\{\tau_d>T\}}L_b(T)\Big). \tag{14}$$

In the preceding expression, the indicator function $\mathbb{I}_{\{t_d>T\}}$ ensures that the insured is still alive at time T and $\mathbb{E}_{\tilde{\mathbb{P}}}$ denotes an expectation under the risk-neutral Esscher measure $\tilde{\mathbb{P}}$ (refer [34]). It is assumed that the policyholder dies at the end of the year. Therefore, the death payment is paid out at the end of the year of death. Hence, the present value of the death benefit is then given by

$$\begin{aligned}\mathcal{P}_D(t) &= \mathbb{E}_{\tilde{\mathbb{P}}}\Big(e^{-rt}\mathbb{I}_{\{\tau_d<T\}}D_b(\tau_d) \mid \mathcal{F}_t\Big)\\ &= \sum_{k=0}^{T-t-1} {}_kp_{x+t}q_{x+t+k}\mathbb{E}_{\tilde{\mathbb{P}}}\Big(e^{-r(t+k+1)}D_b(t+k+1) \mid \mathcal{F}_t\Big),\end{aligned}$$

where $t+1, t+2, \ldots, T$ represent the potential payment dates for death benefits up to the maturity date T, while the present value of the living benefit is determined by

$$\begin{aligned}\mathcal{P}_L(T) &= \mathbb{E}_{\tilde{\mathbb{P}}}\Big(e^{-rT}\mathbb{I}_{\{\tau_d>T\}}L_b(T) \mid \mathcal{F}_t\Big)\\ &= {}_Tp_{x+t}\mathbb{E}_{\tilde{\mathbb{P}}}\Big(e^{-rT}L_b(T) \mid \mathcal{F}_t\Big).\end{aligned}$$

The living benefit $L_b(T) = \max\{F(T), G(T)\}$ is valued based on the two kinds of guarantees considered. Equation (12) describes the guaranteed amount $G(T)$, which takes into account the roll-up guarantee. The maximum value of a random variable and a fixed constant can determine the living benefit. Thus, the present value of living benefits may be calculated as

$$\begin{aligned}\mathcal{P}_L(T) &= {}_Tp_{x+t}\mathbb{E}_{\tilde{\mathbb{P}}}\Big(e^{-rT}\max\{F(T), G(t)e^{\omega(T-t)}\} \mid \mathcal{F}_t\Big)\\ &= {}_Tp_{x+t}\mathbb{E}_{\tilde{\mathbb{P}}}\left(e^{-r(T-t)}\left(F(t)e^{-m(T-t)}\frac{S(T)}{S(t)}\right)\right.\\ &\qquad \left. + \left(G(t)e^{\omega(T-t)} - F(t)e^{-m(T-t)}\frac{S(T)}{S(t)}\right)_+ \mid \mathcal{F}_t\right)\\ &= {}_Tp_{x+t}\mathbb{E}_{\tilde{\mathbb{P}}}\left(e^{-rT}\left(S(T)e^{-mT} + \left(G(0)e^{\omega T} - S(T)e^{-mT}\right)_+\right) \mid \mathcal{F}_t\right)\\ &= {}_Tp_{x+t}e^{-mT}\left(\mathbb{E}_{\tilde{\mathbb{P}}}\Big(e^{-rT}S(T) \mid \mathcal{F}_t\Big) + \mathbb{E}_{\tilde{\mathbb{P}}}\Big(e^{-rT}\Big(G(0)e^{(m+\omega)T} - S(T)\Big)_+ \mid \mathcal{F}_t\Big)\right)\\ &= {}_Tp_{x+t}e^{-mT}\Big(S(0)e^{-rT} + p_T(t)\Big),\end{aligned} \tag{15}$$

where the last step is due to the discounted process $(e^{-rt}S(t))$ being a martingale, $p_T(t)$ represents the price of a European put option having maturity T and strike price $G(0)e^{(m+\omega)T}$, and for any real number $(x, x)_+ = max(x, 0)$.

In the case of a ratchet guarantee, the living benefit is calculated using the maximum value of account F observed each year till maturity T. The martingale property does not apply since the account value at any point in time is determined by the state of the chain.

Hence, a closed-form expression cannot be deduced in this scenario. Thus, the present value of the living benefits in this case will be

$$\mathcal{P}_L(T) = {}_T p_{x+t} \mathbb{E}_{\tilde{\mathbb{P}}}\left(e^{-rT} \max\{F(T), \max_{k \in \{1,\cdots,T-t-1\}} (G(t), F(t+k))\} \mid \mathcal{F}_t \right). \quad (16)$$

The Monte Carlo (MC) technique is used to evaluate Equation (16).

5.3. Pricing with Neural Networks: An Efficient Approach

The neural network methodology has proven its validity in making predictions in several research fields; see, e.g., Atomsa and Zhou [35]. Finance is not an exception, and the use of neural network pricing methodology provides an efficient way to assess liabilities without requiring repeated MC simulations. This approach involves training a neural network model to make predictions on liability using only a certain set of input factors. In contrast to the extensive data inputs needed for MC simulations, the neural network specifically targets the parameters that are pertinent to the calculation of liabilities.

The process commences by choosing suitable input factors that have a substantial impact on the liability. The inputs are utilized to train the neural network model, which acquires the ability to comprehend the intricate connections between the inputs and the related liabilities. The training data usually comprise historical data that include pairings of inputs and outputs, where the inputs represent the chosen parameters and the outputs reflect the related liabilities.

During the training process, the neural network continuously modifies its internal parameters in order to minimize the discrepancy between the predicted and real liabilities. This optimization process persists until the model attains adequate performance on the training dataset, as assessed by suitable metrics such as loss functions.

After undergoing training, the neural network model is capable of accurately forecasting liabilities using novel sets of input variables. This enables quick and precise evaluations of liabilities without the computing effort associated with MC simulations. Furthermore, the pricing approach of the neural network can be adjusted and optimized to accommodate variations in input variables or include other elements as required, offering flexibility and scalability in the calculation of liabilities. Inputs for neural network pricing:

- Time until contract maturity (T).
- Interest rate (r).
- Nifty 50 Index returns.
- Fund value ($F(T)$).
- Nifty 50 volatility (σ).
- Guaranteed amount ($G(T)$).
- The calibrated model's parameter values.
- Regime probabilities.

The neural network used in this study is designed to predict the present value of the VA contract, with one hidden layer consisting of 10 neurons. This architecture, denoted as 10-10-1, was chosen based on a heuristic approach that matches the hidden layer neurons to the neurons in the input layer. Moller [36] employed this approach with successful outcomes and without encountering issues of overfitting. While experimenting with alternative architectures, we observed that expanding the number of hidden-layer nodes resulted in only slight improvements in performance, but with the drawback of longer training durations.

Training Neural Networks: Optimization Algorithms and Data Partitioning

An essential component of training neural networks consists of modifying the weights that separate nodes in order to improve the network's comprehension of the correlation between inputs and outcomes. Commonly, the gradient descent algorithm computes, with respect to each weight, the derivative of an error function (typically the sum of squares for regression or cross-entropy for classification). Scaled by the learning rate, the weights are subsequently revised by repositioning them in the opposite direction to their gradients. Nevertheless, determining an optimal learning rate is a difficult task; if the rate is too high, the network might fail to converge and fail to detect minima, whereas if it is too low, training could be considerably prolonged.

Resilient backpropagation (RPROP)-scaled conjugate gradient descent (SCGD), and the Broyden–Fletcher–Goldfarb–Shanno (BFGS) algorithm are alternative gradient descent optimization algorithms. RPROP updates weights based solely on gradient signs, adjusting step sizes dynamically. SCGD employs second-order approximations to determine optimal learning rates, while BFGS offers a more comprehensive second-order approach, with line searches for step size determination (see [36]).

For this analysis, we utilized the BFGS algorithm, implemented in the *nnet* package in R.

The dataset was partitioned into training and testing sets, with 80% allocated for training and 20% for testing, randomly selecting data points for each set. This split is a common practice in neural network applications for data partitioning. Table 5 summarizes the neural network training time, resource utilization, and hardware specifications, highlighting key metrics such as total training time, GPU usage, and memory consumption.

Table 5. Neural network training time and resource utilization.

Metric	Value	Remarks
Total Training Time	3.0 h	Convergence achieved via early stopping
Average Time per Epoch	3.6 min	Estimated over ∼50 epochs
Number of Epochs	∼50	Training iterations until convergence
GPU Utilization	85%	Peak utilization during training
Maximum GPU Memory Usage	8 GB	Monitored during training
Hardware Specifications	MacBook Air M2 with 8 GB RAM, running macOS Sonoma 14.6.1.	System details

6. Numerical Results and Sensitivity Analysis

This section provides a description of the data used in the numerical calculation and the corresponding numerical results for the proposed model.

Data Description

This paper considers Nifty 50 Index daily returns data from the Indian market for numerical analysis. The index was selected on the basis of available data. We considered information from 7 September 2017 until 7 September 2023. The data for the Nifty 50 Index is taken from Bloomberg Terminal.

The Gompertz–Makeham distribution is used to model the mortality rate (see Makeham [37]). With this setting, a closed-form expression of the survival probability can be derived. The mortality rate $\nu(x)$ is given by the following equation for an individual age x at time zero:

$$\nu(x) = A_\nu + B_\nu C_\nu^x, \text{ with } B > 0, A \geq -B, C > 1 \text{ and } x \geq 0.$$

The mortality rate due to accidents is denoted as A_ν, while the term related to aging is represented by $B_\nu C_\nu^x$. The survival probability of an individual aged x at time zero is determined by the death time, denoted as t_d, given as follows:

$$_tp_x = \mathbb{P}(t_d > t) = e^{-\int_0^t \nu(x+u)du}, \forall t \geq 0,$$

where ν is the mortality intensity. We use the following mortality parameters obtained by Melnikov and Romaniuk [38]:

$$A = 9.5666 \times 10^{-4}, \quad B = 5.162 \times 10^{-5}, \quad C = 1.09369.$$

The Gompertz–Makeham mortality model is selected due to its extensive use in actuarial studies and VA pricing. Although we do not apply it to a specific dataset, its parameters serve as a benchmark for numerical analysis, ensuring that the results are consistent with the existing literature. This model is an appropriate choice for our pricing framework because it effectively depicts mortality dynamics that are pertinent to VA contracts. The financial parameters are derived through the process of calibrating the model using the Nifty 50 Index data. This is performed to demonstrate how two different economic conditions, namely, a spike regime characterized by high volatility and low returns and a base regime characterized by low volatility and high returns, impact pricing performance.

Specifically, the equity components (funds) of the VA guarantees being evaluated are based on the Nifty 50 Index data (India) from September 2017 to September 2023. Unless otherwise stated, the values for the model parameters are given in Tables 2 and 3. The management fee is $m = 0.2$ percent (see Sun et al. [39]). The insured age is $x = 50$ years (see Mamon et al. [40]) at the beginning of the contract. An INR 100 premium is invested in the referenced portfolio, which has an initial fund value of $F(0) = 100$. The interest rate is $r = 3$ percent. The initial guarantee $G(0)$ is assumed to be 100 percent of the initial fund value (see Mamon et al. [40]).

Tables 6 and 7 display the fair pricing of VAs with embedded Guaranteed Minimum Accumulation Benefits (GMABs) during two different market regimes before the COVID-19 outbreak. It assumes a roll-up rate ($\omega = 0$) and the guaranteed benefit $G = F(0)$. The prices are classified into three distinct regimes: the base regime, the spike regime, and without any particular regime.

Table 6. Fair price of GMAB with two regimes before COVID-19, considering roll-up rate $\omega = 0$ and G = F(0).

Base Regime		Spike Regime		Without Regime	
T (Years)	Price (INR)	*T* (Years)	Price (INR)	*T* (Years)	Price (INR)
5	139.2658	5	163.5337	5	152.068
10	113.6701	10	129.0237	10	118.554
15	90.6150	15	107.9259	15	106.343

Table 7. Fair price of GMAB with two regimes before COVID-19, considering ratchet guarantee.

Base Regime		Spike Regime		Without Regime	
T (Years)	Price (INR)	*T* (Years)	Price (INR)	*T* (Years)	Price (INR)
5	147.3695	5	164.9542	5	153.250
10	133.2425	10	141.4670	10	140.4530
15	128.4624	15	140.0761	15	139.5820

In the base regime, which represents a relatively stable market environment with lower volatility, the fair prices of GMAB are generally the lowest across all time horizons (5, 10, and 15 years) compared to the spike regime. For instance, with a roll-up rate $\omega = 0$ and initial guarantee $G = F(0)$, the fair price at a 5-year maturity is INR 139.27, which then decreases to INR 113.67 and INR 90.62 at 10 and 15 years, respectively, as shown in Table 6. This pattern aligns with the expectations in a stable market, where investors may perceive lower risk and therefore demand a smaller premium for guaranteed accumulation benefits. In stable market conditions, investors place relatively less importance on the need for guarantees since the likelihood of adverse market movements is lower, which results in lower fair prices for GMAB.

In contrast, the spike regime, which is characterized by increased market volatility and sudden price surges, produces significantly higher GMAB prices. For instance, under the same roll-up and guarantee conditions, the 5-year fair price in the spike regime is INR 163.53, considerably higher than the INR 139.27 seen in the base regime (Table 6). This pattern remains consistent across longer time horizons. The increased prices reflect the increased risk premium associated with volatile markets, where investors are willing to pay more for GMABs to secure their returns against sudden market downturns. The literature on regime-switching models (see [3,6]) suggests that in times of elevated volatility, the valuation of guarantees increases as investors seek protection from potential losses, thereby driving up the fair price of these products.

In the without regime scenario, which serves as a baseline for GMAB pricing without accounting for specific market dynamics, the prices fall between those observed in the base and spike regimes. For example, the 5-year fair price is INR 152.07 (Table 6). This intermediate pricing level suggests that without clear regime patterns, the model reflects a balanced valuation that partially accounts for the average risk level but lacks the specificity of regime-dependent adjustments. In Table 7, which considers the ratchet guarantee, the fair prices similarly show an increase under the spike regime compared to the base regime, with the without regime scenario yielding intermediate prices. This scenario aligns with findings in the literature indicating that fair prices calculated without accounting for regime-specific volatility are typically higher than those in stable conditions but lower than in high-volatility scenarios (see [7]).

The pricing behavior across these regimes underscores the importance of incorporating regime-switching mechanisms in VA pricing models, as different market conditions significantly influence investor demand for guarantees and consequently the fair price of GMABs. This insight supports the theoretical and empirical conclusions from prior studies, which emphasize that regime-dependent pricing better captures the risk–return trade-off perceived by investors under varying market conditions (see [8,24]).

Moreover, in order to compare the price for the roll-up guarantee with the ratchet guarantee, using the MC technique, the prices of the GMAB contract for different maturities, specifically $T = 5, 10, 15$ years, are calculated. The results, shown in Table 6, demonstrate that the prices for the roll-up guarantee are less compared to the yearly ratchet guarantee (Table 7). The extra cost associated with ratchet options is the reason for this variation in prices.

Upon conducting a comparative analysis of the fair prices of GMABs prior to and subsequent to the COVID-19 pandemic, it becomes apparent that the occurrence had a substantial influence on the pricing dynamics within various guarantee frameworks and market regimes. As shown in Tables 6 and 7, fair prices appear to have been higher prior to COVID-19, irrespective of the guarantee framework. Conversely, fair prices witnessed a significant drop after the commencement of the pandemic, as illustrated in Tables 8 and 9. This implies that investor sentiment and risk perceptions underwent a transformation, possibly impacted by the increased market volatility and unpredictability instigated by the pandemic. The substantial price fluctuations after the epidemic may be primarily ascribed to increased market volatility, influenced by economic uncertainty, policy changes, and investor state of mind. The disruptions caused by the pandemic resulted in significant swings in asset values, characterized by phases of severe volatility followed by stabilization as markets adapted to new circumstances. Heightened risk perception among investors led to elevated implied volatility, impacting asset values and pricing models.

Table 8. Fair price of GMAB with two regimes after COVID-19, considering roll-up rate $\omega = 0$ and $G = F(0)$.

Base Regime		Spike Regime		Without Regime	
T (Years)	Price (INR)	T (Years)	Price (INR)	T (Years)	Price (INR)
5	137.5320	5	145.4734	5	141.2034
10	110.1768	10	114.4784	10	111.4890
15	89.4207	15	106.9060	15	103.0897

Table 9. Fair price of GMAB with two regimes after COVID-19, considering ratchet guarantee.

Base Regime		Spike Regime		Without Regime	
T (Years)	Price (INR)	T (Years)	Price (INR)	T (Years)	Price (INR)
5	146.003	5	150.4295	5	148.3564
10	131.5893	10	137.7056	10	134.3098
15	113.0430	15	116.4080	15	112.5052

These modifications underscore the criticality for insurers and financial institutions to consistently assess and adjust pricing strategies in order to efficiently mitigate risk and satisfy investor requirements in ever-changing financial landscapes, especially in times of crisis. More study is necessary to thoroughly examine the fundamental elements that are causing these price patterns and to formulate adaptable risk management approaches customized to the financial environment following the pandemic. It is worth mentioning that these computed prices appear to be rational and typically align with the prices derived from earlier research on comparable VA guarantees. However, because of the diverse range of product structures, methodologies, and assumptions used, making direct comparisons is challenging.

The main objective of this study was to perform a comprehensive analysis of the fair prices of variable annuity contracts with embedded GMABs under different market regimes to see the impact of the COVID-19 pandemic, and also to examine the effectiveness of using a neural network technique for valuation and to compare with the prices calculated by MC simulations. Convincing evidence has been found that the neural network performs better and faster than the usual MC simulation methods. The neural network predictions are examined using the R^2 measure, which is a measure regularly used by researchers (refer to N. Hattab [41]) to determine the performance of neural networks. Table 10 displays the R^2 values obtained by comparing the neural network's outcomes with those produced by the MC simulations. For both the pre- and post-COVID-19 data, across the base and spike regimes, one can see that the neural network performs well using the R^2 metric. However, the spike regime performs significantly worse than the base regime in both datasets, owing to the existence of a few outliers. The primary benefit of using the neural network approach instead of the MC method is in the possible time efficiency during computations. On the specific computer used in this analysis, the computation of the pricing of VAs with embedded GMABs over 5-, 10-, and 15-year durations using MC simulations takes around six hours. Conversely, the neural network technique performs the same computation in little more than one minute. To train a neural network, each training input is fed in sequentially, the gradients of the network weights throughout the whole dataset are evaluated, and the weights are modified accordingly. As a consequence, when networks and datasets are bigger, the time required for training is often greater. However, once the neural network has been trained, evaluating the outcomes of the entire set of data occurs very fast and is proportional to its magnitude rather than to the quantity of data used for training. This is in contrast to approaches like kriging, which need distance computations and hence become more challenging as the quantity of the training data rises. Although the neural network approach may have somewhat lower accuracy compared to methods like kriging, its substantial time savings make it attractive.

Table 10. Values of R^2 for GMAB with two regimes before and after COVID-19.

	Before COVID-19		After COVID-19	
	Base Regime	**Spike Regime**	**Base Regime**	**Spike Regime**
GMAB	0.996	0.988	0.993	0.985

Figures 2 and 3 illustrate that when the initial guarantee amount $G(0)$ decreases, the fair price also decreases. The inverse relationship between the fair price and the initial guaranteed amount suggests that lower guaranteed amounts are associated with lower fair prices. Nevertheless, it is crucial to acknowledge that when there are positive returns in the market, the relationship may be reduced, leading to prices that may not perfectly follow this inverse trend. However, contracts with higher guaranteed amounts generally have higher fair prices, which are impacted by positive market yields. Especially for contracts of short duration, the decrease in the initial guaranteed payment significantly reduces the fair price because of the increased uncertainty over the contract's duration.

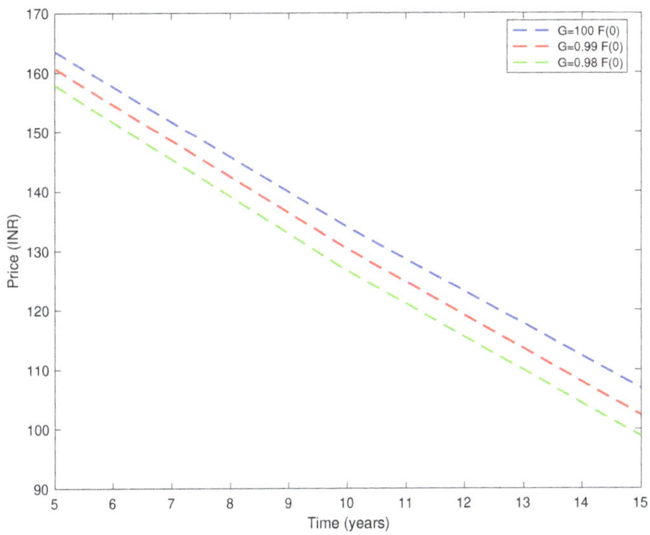

Figure 2. Sensitivity of GMAB price with respect to time to maturity for different guaranteed values in spike regime.

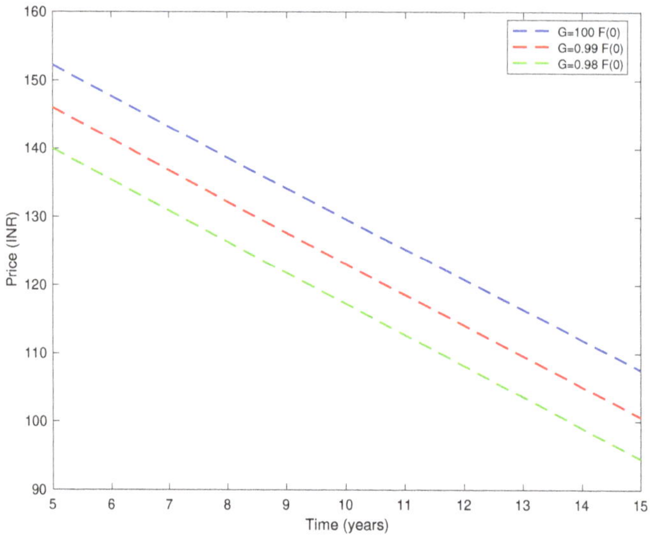

Figure 3. Sensitivity of GMAB price with respect to time to maturity for different guaranteed values in the base regime.

7. Conclusions and Future Work

This study investigates the impact of the COVID-19 pandemic on the pricing of variable annuities (VAs) within the Indian stock market, using a regime-switching HMM framework combined with artificial neural networks and Monte Carlo simulations. By focusing on the Nifty 50 Index data split into pre- and post-COVID-19 periods, this study sheds light on how extreme market conditions can influence VA pricing. The results highlight that the pandemic had a significant effect on the pricing of VA products, with increased volatility leading to notable price shifts across market regimes. Fair prices of VAs dropped significantly after COVID-19, reflecting changes in investor sentiment and risk perceptions due to the heightened unpredictability during this period.

The findings underscore the utility of regime-switching models in capturing market regime dynamics, especially under conditions of economic turbulence. In stable market conditions, regime-switching models show significant variation in pricing dynamics, while during catastrophic events like the COVID-19 pandemic, the models show less variation across regimes. This observation suggests that crisis conditions might dampen regime-specific influences, with overall volatility overshadowing differences in pricing behavior. This insight is crucial for insurers and financial institutions, as it emphasizes the need for adaptable pricing models that can effectively manage risks in times of crisis and better align with changing market dynamics.

This study also demonstrates the efficiency of neural network pricing approaches in the VA context, offering a faster alternative to Monte Carlo simulations. The comparison shows that neural networks can provide accurate VA pricing with significant computational advantages, particularly when applied across portfolios. These findings reinforce the importance of integrating advanced computational techniques into VA pricing models, as they can enhance accuracy and efficiency under varying market conditions. Furthermore, the best-fitted model was compared using well-known methods based on the AIC and BIC, suggesting that the model with two regimes was best fitted. These findings may assist regulators and insurers in enhancing risk management methods, modifying capital reserves, and formulating more robust pricing frameworks to mitigate future market disruptions.

Despite these contributions, the study has limitations. It focuses exclusively on the Indian stock market, which may limit the generalization of the findings to other emerging markets. Additionally, the reliance on historical data restricts the ability to capture longer-term pandemic-related market behaviors. Future research could extend this analysis to other emerging markets and explore alternative modeling techniques, such as semi-Markov processes or ensemble machine learning approaches, to better capture regime-dependent dynamics with more complexity. Moreover, expanding the scope to analyze VA pricing under various macroeconomic shocks could provide deeper insights into managing financial risks in highly volatile markets.

Author Contributions: They equally contributed to this research paper. All authors have read and agreed to the published version of the manuscript.

Funding: This research received no external funding.

Data Availability Statement: The data that support the findings of this study are available from Bloomberg but restrictions apply to the availability of these data, which were used under license for the current study, and so are not publicly available.

Conflicts of Interest: The authors declare that they have no known competing financial interests or personal relationships that could have appeared to influence the work reported in this paper.

Abbreviations

VAs	Variable annuities
GMxB	Guaranteed Minimum Benefit
GMDB	Guaranteed Minimum Death Benefit
GMAB	Guaranteed Minimum Accumulation Benefit
GMWB	Guaranteed Minimum Withdrawal Benefit
GMIB	Guaranteed Minimum Income Benefit
EIAs	Equity-indexed annuities
HMMs	Hidden Markov models
MRS	Markov regime-switching model
NN	Neural network
RPROP	Resilient backpropagation
SCGD	Scaled conjugate gradient descent
BFGS	Broyden-Fletcher-Goldfarb-Shanno algorithm
AIC	Akaike information criterion
BIC	Bayesian information criterion
MC	Monte Carlo

References

1. Fontana, C.; Rotondi, F. Valuation of general GMWB annuities in a low interest rate environment. *Insur. Math. Econ.* **2023**, *112*, 142–167. [CrossRef]
2. Hardy, M.R. A regime-switching model of long-term stock returns. *N. Am. Actuar. J.* **2001**, *5*, 41–53. [CrossRef]
3. Siu, T.K.; Lau, J.W.; Yang, H. Pricing participating products under a generalized jump-diffusion model. *J. Appl. Math. Stoch. Anal.* **2008**, *2008*, 474623. [CrossRef]
4. Elliott, R.J.; Kuen Siu, T.; Chan, L. Pricing volatility swaps under Heston's stochastic volatility model with regime switching. *Appl. Math. Financ.* **2007**, *14*, 41–62. [CrossRef]
5. Boyarchenko, S.; Levendorskii, S. American options in regime-switching models. *SIAM J. Control Optim.* **2009**, *48*, 1353–1376. [CrossRef]
6. Lin, X.S.; Tan, K.S.; Yang, H. Pricing annuity guarantees under a regime-switching model. *N. Am. Actuar. J.* **2009**, *13*, 316–332. [CrossRef]
7. Ng, A.C.Y.; Li, J.S.H. Valuing variable annuity guarantees with the multivariate Esscher transform. *Insur. Math. Econ.* **2011**, *49*, 393–400. [CrossRef]

8. Fan, K.; Shen, Y.; Siu, T.K.; Wang, R. Pricing annuity guarantees under a double regime-switching model. *Insur. Math. Econ.* **2015**, *62*, 62–78. [CrossRef]
9. Mohammad, S.; Arunachalam, V.; Selvamuthu, D. Pricing Variable Annuity Contract with GMAB Guarantee Under a Regime Switching Local Volatility Model. *Comput. Econ.* **2024**, 1–22.. [CrossRef]
10. Bargos, F.F.; Claro Romão, E. Enhanced Forecasting of Equity Fund Returns Using Machine Learning. *Math. Comput. Appl.* **2025**, *30*, 9. [CrossRef]
11. Guidolin, M.; Timmermann, A. Economic implications of bull and bear regimes in UK stock and bond returns. *Econ. J.* **2005**, *115*, 111–143. [CrossRef]
12. Shahzad, S.J.H.; Bouri, E.; Kang, S.H.; Saeed, T. Regime specific spillover across cryptocurrencies and the role of COVID-19. *Financ. Innov.* **2021**, *7*, 5. [CrossRef] [PubMed]
13. Tchoumi, S.Y.; Rwezaura, H.; Diagne, M.L.; González-Parra, G.; Tchuenche, J. Impact of infective immigrants on COVID-19 dynamics. *Math. Comput. Appl.* **2022**, *27*, 11. [CrossRef]
14. De Blasis, R.; Galati, L.; Webb, A.; Webb, R.I. Intelligent design: Stablecoins (in) stability and collateral during market turbulence. *Financ. Innov.* **2023**, *9*, 85. [CrossRef]
15. Wu, W.; Lee, C.C.; Xing, W.; Ho, S.J. The impact of the COVID-19 outbreak on Chinese-listed tourism stocks. *Financ. Innov.* **2021**, *7*, 22. [CrossRef]
16. Mazur, M.; Dang, M.; Vega, M. COVID-19 and the march 2020 stock market crash. Evidence from S&P500. *Financ. Res. Lett.* **2021**, *38*, 101690.
17. Belili, M.C.; Sahari, M.L.; Kebiri, O.; Zeghdoudi, H. Analyzing bifurcations and optimal control strategies in SIRS epidemic models: insights from theory and COVID-19 data. *Math. Comput. Appl.* **2024**, *29*, 69. [CrossRef]
18. da Silva, C.A.G. The Regime Changing Behavior of Exchange Rates and Stock Market Prices of Selected Emerging Countries: An application of the Markov Switching Vector Autoregressive model (MS-VAR). *Am. J. Econ. Bus. Innov.* **2023**, *2*, 2832–4862. [CrossRef]
19. Jasuja, D.; Prosad, J.M.; Nautiyal, N. A Comparative Performance Analysis of Sustainability Themed Indices in India: Markov Regime Switching Approach. *FIIB Bus. Rev.* **2021**.. [CrossRef]
20. Xie, X.; Mirza, N.; Umar, M.; Ji, X. COVID-19 and market discipline: Evidence from the banking sector in emerging markets. *Int. Rev. Econ. Financ.* **2024**, *89*, 612–621. [CrossRef]
21. Zhong, W.; Zhang, Z.; Cui, Z. Efficient valuation of variable annuities under regime-switching jump diffusion models with surrender risk and mortality risk. *Commun. Nonlinear Sci. Numer. Simul.* **2024**, *138*, 108246. [CrossRef]
22. Janczura, J.; Weron, R. Efficient estimation of Markov regime-switching models: An application to electricity spot prices. *ASTA Adv. Stat. Anal.* **2012**, *96*, 385–407. [CrossRef]
23. Selvamuthu, D.; Kumar, V.; Mishra, A. Indian stock market prediction using artificial neural networks on tick data. *Financ. Innov.* **2019**, *5*, 16. [CrossRef]
24. Elliott, R.J.; Chan, L.; Siu, T.K. Option pricing and Esscher transform under regime switching. *Ann. Financ.* **2005**, *1*, 423–432. [CrossRef]
25. Elliott, R.J.; Aggoun, L.; Moore, J.B. *Hidden Markov Models: Estimation and Control*; Springer Science & Business Media: Berlin/Heidelberg, Germany, 2008; Volume 29.
26. Siu, T.K. Fair valuation of participating policies with surrender options and regime switching. *Insur. Math. Econ.* **2005**, *37*, 533–552. [CrossRef]
27. Chkili, W.; Nguyen, D.K. Exchange rate movements and stock market returns in a regime-switching environment: Evidence for BRICS countries. *Res. Int. Bus. Financ.* **2014**, *31*, 46–56. [CrossRef]
28. Naik, N.; Mohan, B.R. Stock Price Volatility Estimation Using Regime Switching Technique-Empirical Study on the Indian Stock Market. *Mathematics* **2021**, *9*, 1595. [CrossRef]
29. Hamilton, J.D. Analysis of time series subject to changes in regime. *J. Econom.* **1990**, *45*, 39–70. [CrossRef]
30. Dempster, A.P.; Laird, N.M.; Rubin, D.B. Maximum likelihood from incomplete data via the EM algorithm. *J. R. Stat. Soc. Ser. B (Methodol.)* **1977**, *39*, 1–22. [CrossRef]
31. Kim, C.J. Dynamic linear models with Markov-switching. *J. Econom.* **1994**, *60*, 1–22. [CrossRef]
32. Gray, S.F. Modeling the conditional distribution of interest rates as a regime-switching process. *J. Financ. Econ.* **1996**, *42*, 27–62. [CrossRef]
33. Ang, A.; Bekaert, G. Regime switches in interest rates. *J. Bus. Econ. Stat.* **2002**, *20*, 163–182. [CrossRef]
34. Yang, H. Esscher Transform. In *Encyclopedia of Actuarial Science*; John Wiley & Sons: Hoboken, NJ, USA, 2006.
35. Atomsa, G.A.; Zhou, Y. Application of neural network to model rainfall pattern of Ethiopia. *Stat. Theory Relat. Fields* **2023**, *7*, 69–84. [CrossRef]
36. Møller, M.F. A scaled conjugate gradient algorithm for fast supervised learning. *Neural Netw.* **1993**, *6*, 525–533. [CrossRef]
37. Makeham, W.M. On the law of mortality and the construction of annuity tables. *J. Inst. Actuar.* **1860**, *8*, 301–310. [CrossRef]

38. Melnikov, A.; Romaniuk, Y. Evaluating the performance of Gompertz, Makeham and Lee–Carter mortality models for risk management with unit-linked contracts. *Insur. Math. Econ.* **2006**, *39*, 310–329. [CrossRef]
39. Sun, J.; Shevchenko, P.V.; Fung, M.C. The impact of management fees on the pricing of variable annuity guarantees. *Risks* **2018**, *6*, 103. [CrossRef]
40. Mamon, R.; Xiong, H.; Zhao, Y. The valuation of a guaranteed minimum maturity benefit under a regime-switching framework. *N. Am. Actuar. J.* **2021**, *25*, 334–359. [CrossRef]
41. Hattab, N.; Hambli, R.; Motelica-Heino, M.; Mench, M. Neural network and Monte Carlo simulation approach to investigate variability of copper concentration in phytoremediated contaminated soils. *J. Environ. Manag.* **2013**, *129*, 134–142. [CrossRef]

Mathematical and Computational Applications

MDPI

Article

Characterization of the Appointment's Reasons for "P—Psychological" on the ICPC-2 Scale in Primary Health Care Services

Filipa Rocha [1], Cristiana J. Silva [2,3], Sofia J. Pinheiro [1,2], Vera Afreixo [1,2], Rui Pedro Leitão [4] and Miguel Felgueiras [2,5,*]

[1] Department of Mathematics, University of Aveiro, 3810-193 Aveiro, Portugal; filipasarreira@ua.pt (F.R.); spinheiro@ua.pt (S.J.P.); vera@ua.pt (V.A.)
[2] Center for Research and Development in Mathematics and Applications (CIDMA), Department of Mathematics, University of Aveiro, 3810-193 Aveiro, Portugal; cjoaosilva@ua.pt
[3] Department of Mathematics, ISTA, Iscte-Instituto Universitário de Lisboa, Avenida das Forças Armadas, 1649-026 Lisbon, Portugal
[4] Public Health Unit, ACES Baixo Vouga, 3800-120 Aveiro, Portugal; rpleitao@ulsra.min-saude.pt
[5] ESTG, Polytechnic Institute of Leiria and CEAUL, Faculty of Sciences, University of Lisbon, 1749-016 Lisboa, Portugal
* Correspondence: mfelg@ipleiria.pt

Abstract

(1) Background: Mental health significantly impacts personal relationships and societal integration. Portugal faces a high prevalence of psychiatric illnesses and psychological distress, which the COVID-19 pandemic might have exacerbated. Therefore, this study aims to study risk factors that lead to psychological problems, using data available in the primary health care centers of the region of Aveiro. (2) Methods: This observational and retrospective study analyzes data from 2009 to 2022 on psychological consultations in the Aveiro municipalities. Variables considered are municipality, International Classification of Primary Care problem, sex, and comorbidities (cancer, obesity, and diabetes). Summary statistics and graphs were employed for data understanding, with R software used for analysis. Regression models, odds ratios, and association tests were calculated. Also, cluster analysis was performed on municipalities. (3) Results: A new, significant increase in the appointment growth rate was observed in 2021 and 2022. Anxiety and depressive disorders contribute to the identified growth. Women reported more problems than men. Cancer was the most present comorbidity. (4) Conclusions: The study reveals increased mental health problems, with primary health care users in Aveiro experiencing worsened psychosocial health, resulting in more medical consultations for psychological reasons. Risk factors included being female and having chronic conditions such as cancer. The findings provide insights into the burden of mental health issues in the region, highlighting the need for effective mental health interventions and resources to address health inequalities and support at-risk groups.

Keywords: health care systems; health promotion; mental health services; regional differences

1. Introduction

Mental health has been a topic of constant concern. In recent years, mental health's important role in achieving global development goals has been recognized. This recognition is illustrated, for example, by the inclusion of mental health in the World Health Organization's (WHO) Sustainable Development Goals: "By 2030, reduce premature mortality from non-communicable diseases by one-third through prevention and treatment, and promote mental health and well-being" [1,2].

However, in recent years, mental health and substance use disorders have increased by around 13%. The two most common mental health problems are depressive disorders and anxiety disorder [2]. According to information from the National Coordination for Mental Health, epidemiological studies have revealed that psychiatric disorders and mental health problems have become the leading cause of disability and morbidity in our societies. Of the ten leading causes of disability, five are psychiatric [3]. People with severe mental health problems tend to die prematurely due to preventable physical conditions. Globally, it is estimated that about 20% of children and adolescents have a mental health problem, and suicide is highlighted as the second leading cause of death among people aged 15–29 years [2]. Despite this information, the average global government spending on mental health is less than 2%. Many of these problems can even be treated efficiently at a relatively low cost; however, adequate treatment coverage remains extremely low, and, in addition, there is still a significant difference between people who need care and those who have access to it [2].

According to the Portuguese Society of Psychiatry and Mental Health, Portugal has Europe's second-highest prevalence rate of psychiatric illnesses (22.9%). Other studies show that 57% of the Portuguese population has psychological distress [2,3]. According to the "Health at a Glance 2019" report of the Organization for Economic Cooperation and Development (OECD), Portugal is the second OECD country with the highest consumption of N04A antidepressants (1505 doses per thousand habitants) [4].

Since the COVID-19 pandemic emerged, an increased annual prevalence of mental health problems in the adult population has been reported, with the most frequent being depression, anxiety, mood disorders, post-traumatic stress, and obsessive-compulsive disorders [5]. Although the pandemic arose from the viral disease COVID-19, it turned out to be a crisis that affected the population at various levels: physical, mental, social, and economic. Therefore, it had a widespread impact, inducing, among other things, considerable levels of fear, restlessness, and concern. Some have referred to the growing burden on mental health as the "second" or "silent" pandemic [6].

Even though the negative consequences for mental health affect everyone, young people have been among populations with a higher risk of developing poor mental health, together with health professionals and females. The risk of poor mental health is also generally higher in individuals with pre-existing mental health problems [6].

The 2021 World Happiness Report indicates that the pandemic has been associated with a substantial increase in symptoms of mental illness, further noting that this period has contributed to the rise in inequalities in mental health, both within the population and among social groups [7]. In addition, four main types of mechanisms were identified with the various stressors associated with the pandemic. The four mechanisms that may affect mental health can be presumed as: (1) health-related anxieties directly resulting from COVID-19, such as the probability of being infected, the possibility of being hospitalized or dying, the probability of infecting others, and the possibility of loved ones becoming infected or dying; (2) the mental health consequences of concerns resulting from how the pandemic may affect a person's financial situation, both in the short and long term; (3) complications resulting from domestic family arrangements during quarantine periods; and (4) the direct mental health effects of the loss or restriction of activities caused by the pandemic and the various quarantine policies [7].

The International Classification of Primary Care (ICPC) opened new horizons when it was published in 1987 by WONCA (World Organization of Colleges, Academies, and Academic Associations of General Practitioners/Family Physicians), now better known as the World Organization of Family Physicians. For the first time, health professionals had the means to classify, using only one classification, three essential elements of an appointment: reasons that led to the appointment, diagnoses or problems, and procedures. The link between these elements allows categorization from the beginning of the appointment to its conclusion [8].

The ICPC is a document with a simple structure based on two parts. One part comprises seventeen chapters, each with an alpha code. The other part contains seven identical components numbered with two-digit codes. This structure allows for specific categorization of the three elements of an appointment, facilitating manual classification systems. The rational and comprehensive structure of the ICPC makes it a classification model for present and future international classifications [8]. Since its publication, the ICPC has progressively received worldwide recognition as an appropriate classification for general and family medicine and primary care. It has been used intensively in some parts of the world, notably in Europe and Australia [8].

The reasons that lead patients to seek primary health care are found within the scope of general and family medicine. These reasons can present several natures, including symptoms, administrative procedures, diseases, established medical diagnoses, or even psychosocial problems. The latter can influence the course of a consultation, especially regarding correct medical diagnoses or managing the patient's disease [9,10]. General and family medicine appointments are based on a "patient-centered" approach, which attends not only to the clinical response to the signs and symptoms presented but also to the expectations and fears of the user [10,11].

The Baixo Vouga Health Centre Group (Aveiro region), for general and family medicine, comprises eleven municipalities: Águeda, Albergaria-a-Velha, Anadia, Aveiro, Estarreja, Ílhavo, Murtosa, Oliveira do Bairro, Ovar, Sever do Vouga, and Vagos. There is a total of 74 parishes where, approximately estimated, three hundred and thirty thousand people live [12,13]. Its mission is to provide primary health care to the population in its geographical area with efficiency and quality, seeking to maintain the principles of equity and accessibility in a multidisciplinary manner and coordination with other national health services to enhance health gains. The mission also includes epidemiological surveillance, participation in teaching and training health professionals, and developing projects and programs in health and health services [13].

The present study was based on the ICPC classification of general and family medicine appointments between 2009 and 2022, with the goal of characterizing the population and identifying risk factors concerning mental health. Moreover, this study aimed to obtain more information on where municipalities stand regarding the impact of the pandemic on the mental health of their populations and, hence, adequate future mental health strategies and action plans in the area. In the analyzed dataset, each patient may have simultaneous diagnostic ICPC problems. Therefore, different rows can have information about the same patient.

According to the prioritization made in the Local Health Plan of the Region of Aveiro, the Public Health Unit chose to study three comorbidities (cancer, diabetes, and obesity) to better allocate resources to the population groups that will most benefit from its interventions.

2. Materials and Methods

The present epidemiological study is observational, analytical, and has a retrospective nature. The data under analysis refers to the collected data during medical consultations in which the codifications of the chapter "P—Psychological" of the International Classification of Primary Care (ICPC-2) were used. Data was collected between 2009 and 2022 in the municipalities that belong to the ACeS Baixo Vouga. Variables "Year", "Municipality", "ICPC-2 Code", "ICPC-2 Title", "Sex", "N_Total", and "Comorbidities" were considered.

Data regarding comorbidities were extracted separately by filtering the database to obtain the above mentioned variables, crossed with "P—Psychological" code and also with each comorbidity (T89 and T90 for diabetes, T82 for obesity, and B74, B75, D74, D75, D76, D77, D78, F74, H75, K72, L71, L97, N74, N75, N76, R84, R85, R86, R92, S77, S79, T71, T72, T73, U75, U76, U77, U78, U79, W72, W73, X75, X76, X77, X79, X80, X81, Y77, Y78, and Y79 for cancer). To obtain the final data for analysis, the different datasets were crossed through the variables "Year", "Municipality", "ICPC-2 Code", "ICPC-2 Title", and "Sex" to match the number of people who also had comorbidities. Variables for "Total_Diabetes", "Total_Cancer", and "Total_Obesity" were created.

The present study uses aggregated data considering the "ICPC-2 Title" and the "ICPC-2 Code" variables. All datasets were filtered according to ICPC-2 codification (variable ICPC-2 Code) regarding the diseases in question; only codes beginning with seven or higher were kept, as they refer to the diagnoses and diseases component.

Several statistical analyses were performed, including growth rate for the total number of problems, the individual analysis of each problem, and the number of problems with comorbidities.

$$\text{growth rate} = \frac{(\text{present count} - \text{previous count})}{\text{previous count}}$$

The number of problems per year was analyzed by municipality, gender, and comorbidity. To visualize the data, scatterplots with fitted lines, dendograms, and geospatial graphs (maps) were constructed. Geospatial graphs illustrate the district of Aveiro and its municipalities, colored through a coded gradient in parallel with the number of problems registered; standardization was performed according to the number of residents [14].

Pearson correlation, and, after that, a linear regression model, was used to study the relationship between the annual number of problems and the registration year. Association measures, e.g., odds ratio (OR), between binary variables were calculated, namely for measuring the association between sex and psychological problems and between comorbidities and psychological problems. For the association between each psychological problem and its occurrence in the municipalities, and the strength of that association, Cramér's V coefficient was calculated [15]. When required, assumptions were validated for all performed tests and analyses. Finally, a cluster analysis was performed with the goal of checking differences between municipalities.

All analyses were performed using the R software (version 4.0.2) through the RStudio interface. In addition, the analyses were conducted with a 5% significance level as a reference.

3. Results

3.1. Frequency Tables

Table A1 (Appendix A) reveals the number of psychological problems ICPC2 registered each year between 2009 and 2022. In 14 years, more than 1 million problems involving the chapter P—Psychological (all codes considered) of ICPC-2 were registered in the health centers of the ACeS Baixo Vouga, with an annual increase in reported problems since 2009.

It should be noted that these results are not cumulative but refer to the number of problems registered every 12 months. The column "Growth in Percentage (%)" shows a general trend of decreasing growth rate, as revealed by the values of the percentages that decrease from year to year. However, in 2021 and 2022, this decrease did not occur, and a new increase in this percentage was observed (highlighted). The column "Number of patients of the ACeS" [16] presents data publicly accessible since 2016. Unfortunately, information before 2016 was unavailable. Here, an increase in the number of enrolled users from 2017 is verified.

When seeking to understand the nature of reported problems, the numbers of each ICPC-2 psychological problem recorded in each year and the respective growth rates were registered in Tables A2 and A3 (Appendix A). These results helped to find which ICPC-2 psychological problems contributed most to the increase in percentage growth recorded in the last two years. Thus, anxiety disorder/anxiety state, phobia and compulsive disorder, hyperkinetic disorder, depressive disorder, post-traumatic stress, and nervous anorexia/bulimia showed considerable increases. Depressive and anxious/anxiety disorders were the most common diagnoses. The growth of hyperkinetic disorders has become more prominent over the years.

The percentage of all three comorbidities (cancer, diabetes, and obesity) present in the data was also recorded. For the last year (2022), 10.7% of the individuals with psychological problems had diabetes, 21.2% of the individuals had obesity, and 25.1% of the individuals had cancer. Therefore, cancer emerged as the more common comorbidity in 2022.

3.2. Results by Sex

Women report more than double men's psychological problems in primary health care consultations in the Aveiro region. The growth rate by sex is similar, with men's growth rate always slightly bigger than women's growth rate, but almost equal in recent years (Figure 1). Both results are not contradictory since the total number of psychological problems is much bigger for women; even with a higher growth rate, the total number of reported problems for men is growing far apart from the total number of reported problems for women.

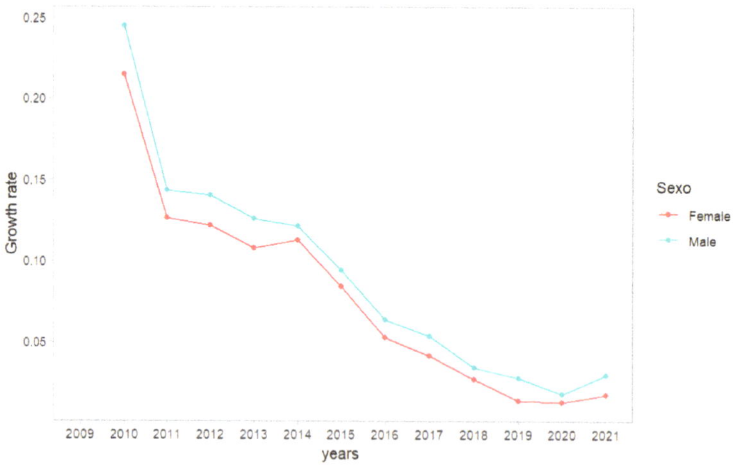

Figure 1. Growth rate of total number of problems registered per year in the ACeS BV according to gender.

The association with each ICPC-2 psychological problem was also verified, and the results are shown in Table 1, which presents ORs for different psychological problems according to sex. The female gender was used as the reference group. Therefore, an OR above 1 indicates that men have a higher possibility of developing a particular psychological problem. On the other hand, an OR below indicates the reverse situation. When the confidence interval for OR includes 1, the differences are not statistically significant [17]. In our analysis, all the reported problems had significant ORs. Nervous anorexia and bulimia (0.26), depressive disorders (0.49), and somatization (0.95) are the only ones that are more associated with the female gender since the OR is lower than 1. This does not contradict Figure 1 because depressive and anxiety disorders are clearly the most common problems (see Tables A2 and A3). On the contrary, hyperkinetic disorders (9.07), schizophrenia (5.26), and post-traumatic stress (4.47) are problems that are more associated with males, but they are much more uncommon problems than depressive and anxiety disorders.

Table 1. Calculated Odds Ratio (OR) for each psychological disorder and sex from August 2009 to August 2022.

Type of Psychological Problem	OR	95% CI
Personality Changes	2.58 *	(2.47–2.68)
Nervous Anorexia, Bulimia	0.26 *	(0.23–0.29)
Mental Retardation	3.01 *	(2.92–3.11)
Dementia	1.18 *	(1.15–1.21)
Anxiety Disorder/Anxiety State	1.09 *	(1.08–1.10)
Schizophrenia	5.26 *	(5.07–5.45)
Phobia, Compulsive Disorder	1.93 *	(1.84–2.02)
Neurasthenia, Surmenage	1.06 *	(1.03–1.10)
Other Psychological Disorders	2.55 *	(2.49–2.60)
Other Organic Psychosis	2.79 *	(2.66–2.92)
Other Psychosis	1.02 *	(2.73–2.87)
Hyperkinetic Disorder	9.07 *	(8.74–9.40)
Depressive Disorders	0.49 *	(0.48–0.49)
Affective Psychosis	1.51 *	(1.46–1.57)
Somatization	0.95 *	(0.93–0.97)
Post-Traumatic Stress	4.47 *	(4.19–4.77)
Suicide/Attempted Suicide	1.19 *	(1.13–1.25)

Notes: * means significant (1 is out of the obtained CI). The reference group used was the female gender.

3.3. *Results by Comorbidities*

In this subsection, we present the results concerning the OR calculated to test the association between comorbidities (diabetes, cancer, and obesity) and reported psychological disorders. Note that authors present unadjusted odds ratios, as confounders were not measured, implying caution in interpretations. More accurate results would be obtained for odds ratios adjusted by age and gender. The reference category represents the absence of the comorbidity. Thence, an OR above 1 yields a direct relation between the comorbidity and the psychological disorder, as an OR below 1 stands for the inverse situation. For example, for the more common problem (depressive disorders), all the OR are significant and above 1, indicating that patients with comorbidities are more likely to have depressive disorders than patients without comorbidities. Table 2 contains the results for the aforementioned comorbidities and psychological problems. The results with greater strength of association with diabetes are dementia (3.29), nervous anorexia and bulimia (0.10), and hyperkinetic disorder (0.07). The association between diabetes and dementia is well-known from the literature since blood sugar control can lead to hypoglycemia and damage the hippocampus [18]. The results with greater strength of association with cancer are nervous anorexia and bulimia (0.15), mental retardation (0.28), and hyperkinetic disorder (0.05). Finally, the results obtained regarding obesity present more non-significant ORs and values closer to 1.

Table 2. Calculated Odds Ratio (OR) for each psychological disorder and comorbidity from August 2009 to August 2022.

Type of Psychological Problem	OR (Diabetes)	95% CI	OR (Cancer)	95% CI	OR (Obesity)	95% CI
Personality Changes	1.07	(0.99–1.14)	0.67 *	(0.64–0.71)	0.95	(0.89–1.01)
Nervous Anorexia, Bulimia	0.10 *	(0.08–0.12)	0.15 *	(0.14–0.17)	0.20 *	(0.18–0.23)
Mental Retardation	0.61 *	(0.57–0.65)	0.28 *	(0.26–0.29)	0.98	(0.94–1.03)
Dementia	3.29 *	(3.20–3.38)	1.26 *	(1.22–1.29)	0.79 *	(0.76–0.82)
Anxiety Disorder/ Anxiety State	0.84 *	(0.83–0.86)	1.12 *	(1.11–1.13)	0.98 *	(0.97–0.99)
Schizophrenia	1.06 *	(1.01–1.13)	0.34 *	(0.31–0.36)	1.09 *	(1.04–1.15)
Phobia, Compulsive Disorder	0.60 *	(0.54–0.66)	0.77 *	(0.72–0.82)	1.00	(0.93–1.07)
Neurasthenia, Surmenage	0.48 *	(0.45–0.52)	0.79 *	(0.76–0.83)	0.63 *	(0.60–0.66)
Other Psychological Disorders	0.64 *	(0.61–0.67)	0.43 *	(0.41–0.45)	0.57 *	(0.55–0.59)
Other Organic Psychosis	1.40 *	(1.31–1.51)	0.66 *	(0.62–0.71)	0.96	(0.89–1.03)
Other Psychosis	1.25 *	(1.15–1.35)	0.54 *	(0.50–0.59)	1.10 *	(1.03–1.19)
Hyperkinetic Disorder	0.07 *	(0.06–0.08)	0.05 *	(0.04–0.06)	0.35 *	(0.33–0.38)
Depressive Disorders	1.11 *	(1.09–1.13)	1.17 *	(1.15–1.18)	1.17 *	(1.16–1.19)
Affective Psychosis	1.36 *	(1.29–1.43)	0.95 *	(0.91–0.99)	1.54 *	(1.47–1.60)
Somatization	0.87 *	(0.84–0.91)	1.26 *	(1.23–1.29)	0.88 *	(0.86–0.91)
Post-Traumatic Stress	1.56 *	(1.43–1.71)	0.99	(0.91–1.07)	1.16 *	(1.06–1.26)
Suicide/ Attempted Suicide	1.16 *	(1.08–1.26)	0.79 *	(0.74–0.85)	1.10 *	(1.02–1.17)

Note: * means significant (1 is out of the obtained CI).

3.4. Results by Municipalities

To visually compare the number of problems registered, maps of the district of Aveiro were built where the municipalities belonging to the ACeS Baixo Vouga were colored through a coded gradient in parallel with the number of problems registered each year. The darker the color, the more problems were registered; however, the municipalities colored in lighter colors registered fewer problems. A rate was also obtained (standardized according to the resident population) to make it possible to directly compare the number of problems recorded between municipalities without the number of residents being a source of bias. These results are illustrated in Figure 2. The municipality with more psychological problems registered in 2022 was Ovar. On the other hand, Albergaria-a-Velha was the municipality with the fewest registered psychological problems per 100,000 inhabitants.

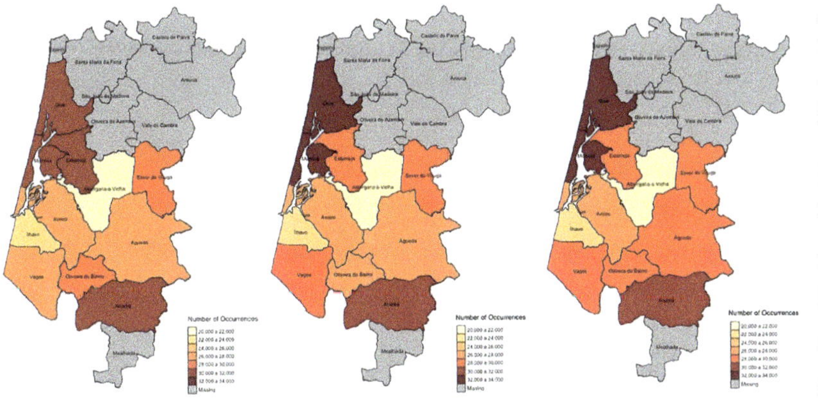

Figure 2. Maps for 2020, 2021, and 2022, from left to right, respectively, with the municipalities belonging to the ACeS Baixo Vouga colored by a gradient representing the number of problems registered (from lighter to darker); results per 100,000 residents.

When testing independence between municipalities and mental illness, all Chi-square tests proved to be significant ($p < 0.05$), but Cramer's V pointed to weak associations. Thus, no ICPC-2 psychological illness is strongly associated with its specific occurrence in the municipalities, despite the statistical relevance of this weak association.

A cluster analysis was also conducted to determine if the occurrence profiles of psychological problems reported in each municipality were similar over the years. Ward's method for clustering [19] was used since it is a general agglomerative hierarchical clustering procedure already implemented in R software. The results illustrated in Figure 3 reveal two clusters, with the first one consisting of Murtosa, Ovar, Estarreja, and Anadia, and the second one consisting of Sever do Vouga, Oliveira do Bairro, Ílhavo, Aveiro, Albergaria-a-Velha, Vagos, and Águeda. The results show that some municipalities have a similar behavior when considering the number of psychological problems over the years. The cluster analysis results are supported by grouping the municipalities with the most psychological problems recorded consistently over the years (Group 1).

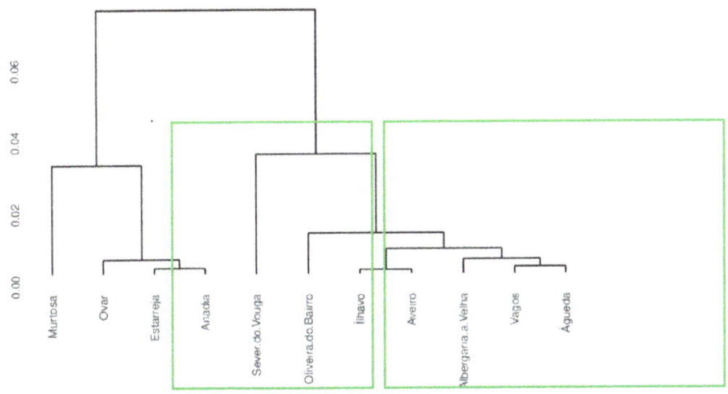

Figure 3. Dendrogram for cluster analysis of occurrence profiles of psychological problems reported in each municipality.

3.5. Results by Year

A significant correlation of −0.92 ($p < 0.01$) between the variables' growth rate and year was verified. Figure 4 illustrates the growth in percentage by year. The obtained linear regression line, plotted in blue, considers the percentage growth values between 2010 and 2021 because the objective was to understand if the increase in the number of problems recorded in consultations in 2022 would be significantly higher to the point of reversing this downward trend that was being observed. It must be highlighted that the percentage growth in the number of problems, compared to the previous year, has decreased until 2020, despite an increase in the total number of reported problems (see Table A1). From this year onwards, the percentage growth was higher than in the previous year.

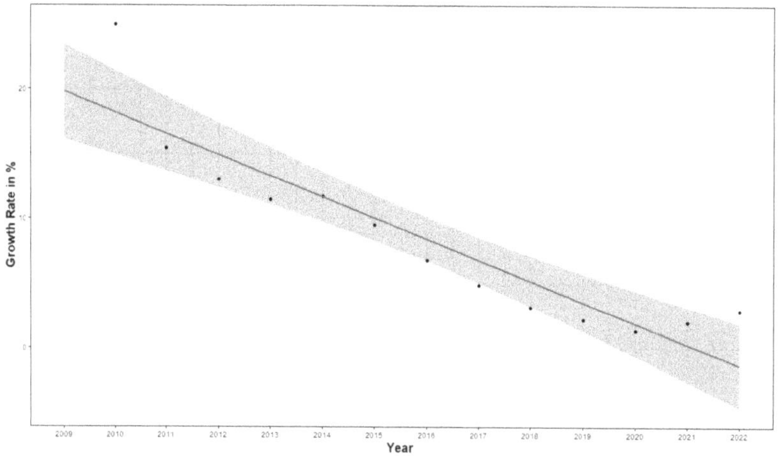

Figure 4. Scatter plot for percentage growth of the number of problems per year with fit line and 95% CI.

By analyzing the obtained graph, the number of problems registered in 2022 is higher than predicted since the point is outside and above the calculated confidence interval (shown in gray); therefore, this growth is significant. The model estimated an increase in percentage for the year 2022 of −1.37% (−4.64%, 1.91%), while the actual value recorded was 2.86%. Therefore, there will likely be an increase in mental health problems due to the pandemic from 2020 onwards.

4. Discussion

Some limitations are present in this study, as only aggregated data was studied. The inherent limitations of aggregated data can impact the depth and accuracy of the conclusions that were drawn. This can be particularly problematic when studying mental health dynamics, where individual experiences and circumstances vary widely. Additionally, important variables such as age, socioeconomic status, and educational background were not available as they are not routinely collected in the National Health Service. While health care access is free and primary care units are distributed according to population needs, factors such as referral patterns and sociocultural influences could not be controlled. Therefore, this study offers a broad overview and facilitates high-level comparisons, but it is essential to analyze the obtained results with caution, recognizing the study's potential to oversimplify complex realities and overlook critical nuances. Despite that, we believe that the results are useful as they can highlight several characteristics of mental health in the Aveiro region (major problems, gender differences, comorbidities influence, geographical patterns, and general tendency over the years).

Our work shows that primary health care users in the Aveiro region (Baixo Vouga Health Centre Group) have worsened their psychosocial health by increasing the number of medical consultations with a "P—Psychological" reason. Over the years, more psychological problems have been recorded in primary health care appointments. These results are general and do not consider if more than one psychological problem was mentioned per consultation or how many times a single patient visited the primary health care centers each year. However, as already stated, family doctors tend to send their patients to specialized appointments, leading to a small number of appointments with the same combination of patient and psychological problem in primary health care. It should also be noted that, in 2008, there was a reorganization of the national health service (SNS), which led to the digitalization of data, leading to greater awareness on the part of health professionals for improving clinical records [20,21].

Among the psychological problems recorded under the 'P—Psychological' chapter of the ICPC-2 classification in Aveiro, depressive disorders and anxiety disorders were the most frequently reported. These results are consistent with both the country's and the world's results regarding the prevalence of psychological problems [22]. Being female and having chronic conditions such as cancer seem to be risk factors associated with a higher likelihood of having more common psychological problems, especially for depressive disorders that represent about half of the reported problems.

The results reveal (Section 3.2) that women report more than twice as many psychological problems as men. The reported ORs are usually higher for men, but they concern more uncommon problems. Depressive disorders represent most of the reported problems each year, and, for that problem, women have an OR more than two times higher than men. We should point out that, in Portugal, there is some stigma and discrimination in mental health [23] affecting males, which may explain the lack of data concerning that gender. However, although this may be a plausible explanation, women represent a slightly higher proportion of primary health care center users. The higher prevalence of mental health disorders, psychological distress, and psychiatric drug use among women compared to men has been largely attributed to sex and gender differences [24,25]. Our results did not consider this difference due to the lack of available information.

To study psychological problems associated with comorbidities, diabetes, cancer, and obesity were chosen. The results revealed that 25% of individuals with at least one psychological problem have cancer. This percentage may be related to the fact that a cancer patient rarely closes the process regarding this disease, as it is chronic and usually always associated with active problems, and we may be facing a bias in the results. Cancer is a known significant stressor that can lead to increased psychological distress, such as anxiety and depressive disorders [26,27]. On the other hand, ageing may also be a plausible explanation since older people are more likely to develop psychological problems and cancer. For all the comorbidities, an association with depressive disorders has been shown since confidence intervals for OR are always above 1.

Regarding the low OR values of the association of each ICPC-2 psychological problem with cancer, these results may be due to greater difficulty in the clinical follow-up of patients with schizophrenia and mental retardation. Another noteworthy result is the hyperkinetic disorder, which is very much associated with children, hence the low OR value observed. Depressive and anxiety disorders are diseases that will hardly be considered surpassed, i.e., an "end" date is not attributed to the problem. Being relatively frequent pathologies, they will eventually lead to an accumulation of "active problems" without necessarily corresponding to the true prevalence of the problem.

A result highlighted with the diabetes comorbidity was the OR obtained for dementia (OR = 3.29). This is a high result indicating a strong association. However, it is most likely due to the age of the patients and the increased prevalence of type 2 diabetes in older people, as they are also more likely to develop psychological problems.

Concerning obesity, several results with a reduced effect may indicate a negligible association. Regarding this comorbidity, it should be noted that some drugs used in this group of diseases are associated with weight gain. For these reasons, it could be an interesting analysis, and it may be an alternative to study the overweight category instead of obesity.

Our study revealed that some municipalities behave similarly, considering the number of psychological problems reported over the years. The cluster analysis results are supported by grouping the municipalities with more reported psychological problems, which a greater presence of the elderly population, local social dynamics, or better primary care services can explain. No high association values were found using Cramer's V coefficient for measuring the association between mental problems and municipalities, although independence was rejected ($p < 0.05$).

From Section 3.5, we can conclude that the percentage growth in the number of problems, compared to the previous year, has decreased until 2020. From this year onwards, the percentage growth was higher than in the previous year. Many reasons may explain this result, namely, the pandemic crisis. Also, the use of electronic medical records was not a standard from 2009 to 2022. Electronic records were increasingly adopted in the following decade, with many contributing factors: the expansion of family health units, the retirement of older physicians and their replacement with a younger generation, improvements in the electronic health record, and increased familiarity with ICPC-2. It was also expected that the registrations in 2022 were higher since there was an effort on the part of primary health care at the national level to again improve the access of users to the National Health Service with extraordinary work to catch up on the backlog of consultations that were suspended and postponed during the pandemic period. The number of patients enrolled in the ACeS Baixo Vouga has been increasing since 2017; however, there was only an increase in the growth rate in 2021.

The number of problems recorded in 2022 is higher than expected when applying the regression model to the percentage growth values between 2010 and 2021, as it is outside the confidence interval, and it can be concluded that this growth is significant. This behavior has been commonly identified as a striking feature of the COVID-19 pandemic, as a correlation between confinement, COVID-19, and mental problems is already well known [28–31].

5. Conclusions and Future Work

Major mental health strategies and action plans highlight the importance of mental health. However, interventions in the area are punctual and are not sustained over time [32]. Over 14 years of study, a notable surge in consultations has been observed in the Aveiro region, with particular evidence in the years 2021 and 2022, where unexpected increases in growth percentages were recorded. Depressive and anxiety disorders emerge as primary concerns. Gender disparities reveal that women seek psychological support more than twice as often as men, with certain disorders showing significant associations with gender. Geospatial analysis reveals variations in psychological burdens across municipalities, with Ovar notably reporting the highest number of cases. Additionally, cluster analysis elucidates distinct behavioral patterns among municipalities, paving the way for tailored strategies. Overall, these findings provide a nuanced understanding of psychological health dynamics in the Aveiro region, crucial for informed resource allocation in primary health care services. The results reinforce the importance of implementing community intervention programs and projects in mental health.

Future research should aim to incorporate individual-level data in order to account for confounding factors such as socioeconomic status, educational background, health care access, and age distribution. Additionally, longitudinal studies assessing post-pandemic trends and exploring specific mechanisms linking chronic diseases and mental health outcomes are suggested.

Author Contributions: Conceptualization, F.R., C.J.S., S.J.P., V.A., M.F. and R.P.L.; methodology, F.R., C.J.S., S.J.P., V.A., M.F. and R.P.L.; validation, F.R., C.J.S., S.J.P., V.A., M.F. and R.P.L.; formal analysis, F.R., C.J.S., S.J.P., V.A., M.F. and R.P.L.; investigation, F.R., C.J.S., S.J.P., V.A., M.F. and R.P.L.; data curation, R.P.L.; writing—original draft preparation, F.R., C.J.S., S.J.P., V.A., M.F. and R.P.L.; writing—review and editing, F.R., V.A. and M.F. All authors have read and agreed to the published version of the manuscript.

Funding: This work is supported by CIDMA under the FCT (Portuguese Foundation for Science and Technology) Multi-Annual Financing Program for R&D Units. Filipa Rocha was supported by a Research Grant of the Thematic Line Biomathematics of CIDMA. This work is partially financed by national funds through FCT—Fundação para a Ciência e a Tecnologia under the projects UID/00006/2025 and UIDB/00006/2020. https://doi.org/10.54499/UIDB/00006/2020. C.J.S. was also supported by the project "Mathematical Modelling of Multi-scale Control Systems: applications to human diseases (CoSysM3)", 2022.03091.PTDC (https://doi.org/10.54499/2022.03091.PTDC), financially supported by national funds (OE), through FCT/MCTES.

Data Availability Statement: The original contributions presented in this study are included in the article. Despite being a secondary anonymized dataset extracted from the local database of the Public Health Unit of ACES BV, the dataset that supports the findings of this study is not publicly available because it may contain information that could compromise the normal operations of the data owner institution, but is available upon reasonable request to the coordination of Public Health Unit of ACES Baixo Vouga (usp.bv@arscentro.min-saude.pt).

Conflicts of Interest: The authors declare no conflicts of interest.

Appendix A

Table A1. Representative table of the number of problems registered each year, the percentage growth rate related to the previous year, and the number of patients registered in the ACeS Baixo Vouga.

Year (September to August)	Number of Problems	Growth Percentage (%)	Number of Patients of the ACeS
2009	39,800		
2010	49,755	25.0%	—
2011	57,436	15.4%	—
2012	64,932	13.1%	—
2013	72,379	11.5%	—
2014	80,869	11.7%	—
2015	88,543	9.5%	—
2016	94,537	6.8%	384,303
2017	99,096	4.8%	380,145
2018	102,191	3.1%	384,967
2019	104,433	2.2%	391,411
2020	105,870	1.4%	393,881
2021	107,967	1.9%	396,232
2022	111,063	2.8%	402,526
Total	1,178,871	—	—

Table A2. Number of problems registered each year by disease, and the respective percentage growth rate regarding the previous year (part I).

Year	Personality Changes		Nervous Anorexia & Bulimia		Mental Retardation		Dementia		Anxiety Disorder/ Anxiety State		Schizophrenia		Phobia, Compulsive Disorder		Neurasthenia, Surmenage		Other Psycho-logical Disorders	
	N	%	N	%	N	%	N	%	N	%	N	%	N	%	N	%	N	%
2009	328		125		644		937		11,891		630		240		652		1605	
2010	436	32.9	157	25.6	770	19.6	1209	29.0	14,742	24.0	742	17.8	322	34.2	887	36.0	1989	23.9
2011	491	12.6	182	15.9	873	13.4	1492	23.4	16,894	14.6	817	10.1	381	18.3	1021	15.1	2271	14.2
2012	593	20.8	201	10.4	997	14.2	1634	9.5	18,906	11.9	899	10.0	424	11.3	1181	15.7	2510	10.5
2013	649	9.4	223	10.9	1073	7.6	1861	13.9	20,774	9.9	941	4.7	479	13.0	1318	11.6	2685	7.0
2014	737	13.6	246	10.3	1162	8.3	2082	11.9	23,060	11.0	1021	8.5	513	7.1	1438	9.1	2923	8.9
2015	791	7.3	268	8.9	1268	9.1	2354	13.1	25,134	9.0	1066	4.4	565	10.1	1517	5.5	3034	3.8
2016	842	6.4	276	3.0	1378	8.7	2607	10.7	26,866	6.9	1115	4.6	610	8.0	1599	5.4	3032	−0.1
2017	871	3.4	294	6.5	1464	6.2	2786	6.9	28,550	6.3	1179	5.7	647	6.1	1687	5.5	3052	0.7
2018	914	4.9	300	2.0	1546	5.6	2898	4.0	29,921	4.8	1207	2.4	678	4.8	1805	7.0	3073	0.7
2019	945	3.4	299	−0.3	1614	4.4	3043	5.0	30,968	3.5	1240	2.7	700	3.2	1829	1.3	3035	−1.2
2020	978	3.5	299	0.0	1628	0.9	2994	−1.6	31,851	2.9	1239	−0.1	712	1.7	1810	−1.0	2987	−1.6
2021	1014	3.7	316	5.7	1647	1.2	3093	3.3	33,087	3.9	1255	1.3	738	3.7	1715	−5.2	2929	−1.9
2022	1039	2.5	330	4.4	1689	2.6	3183	2.9	34,583	4.5	1256	0.1	774	4.9	1687	−1.6	2923	−0.2

Table A3. Number of problems registered each year by disease and the respective percentage growth rate regarding the previous year (part II).

Year	Other Organic Psychosis		Other Psychosis		Hyperkinetic Disorder		Depressive Disorders		Affective Psychosis		Somatization		Post-Traumatic Stress		Suicide/ Attempted Suicide	
	N	%	N	%	N	%	N	%	N	%	N	%	N	%	N	%
2009	328		270		304		19,205		435		1846		153		207	
2010	393	19.8	316	17.0	461	51.6	24,072	25.3	545	25.3	2251	21.9	190	24.2	273	31.9
2011	431	9.7	344	8.9	599	29.9	27,987	16.3	627	15.0	2503	11.2	199	4.7	324	18.7
2012	460	6.7	366	6.4	778	29.9	31,970	14.2	741	18.2	2665	6.5	225	13.1	382	17.9
2013	491	6.7	405	10.7	961	23.5	36,005	12.6	850	14.7	2946	10.5	281	24.9	437	14.4
2014	533	8.6	446	10.1	1163	21.0	40,526	12.6	974	14.6	3244	10.1	305	8.5	496	13.5
2015	577	8.3	478	7.2	1389	19.4	44,635	10.1	1086	11.5	3497	7.8	325	6.6	559	12.7
2016	590	2.3	496	3.8	1535	10.5	47,796	7.1	1178	8.5	3676	5.1	345	6.2	596	6.6
2017	622	5.4	513	3.4	1666	8.5	49,707	4.0	1253	6.4	3799	3.3	369	7.0	637	6.9
2018	626	0.6	534	4.1	1782	7.0	50,587	1.8	1315	4.9	3963	4.3	388	5.1	654	2.7
2019	630	0.6	550	3.0	1889	6.0	51,250	1.3	1368	4.0	3999	0.9	404	4.1	670	2.4
2020	623	−1.1	555	0.9	1959	3.7	51,747	1.0	1385	1.2	4007	0.2	411	1.7	685	2.2
2021	626	0.5	544	−2.0	2046	4.4	52,642	1.7	1404	1.4	3826	−4.5	409	−0.5	676	−1.3
2022	609	−2.7	560	2.9	2191	7.1	54,042	2.7	1443	2.8	3624	−5.3	432	5.6	698	3.3

References

1. United Nations. The Sustainable Development Goals Report 2022. Available online: https://unstats.un.org/sdgs/report/2022/ (accessed on 30 December 2024).
2. World Health Organization. Mental Health. Available online: https://www.who.int/health-topics/mental-health#tab=tab_1 (accessed on 30 December 2024).
3. Relatório de Atividades UCC "Nós". Available online: https://bicsp.min-saude.pt/pt/biufs/3/833/30019/3152671/O%20QUE%20FAZEMOS/Relato%CC%81rio%20de%20Atividades%20USF%20QM%202022.pdf (accessed on 30 December 2024).
4. OECD Pharmaceutical Market: Pharmaceutical Consumption. 2022. Available online: https://stats.oecd.org/ (accessed on 30 December 2024).
5. Baltazar, C. Mental Healthcare in Portugal: Support, Options, and More. Available online: https://www.expatica.com/pt/healthcare/healthcare-services/mental-health-portugal-104327/ (accessed on 30 December 2024).

6. Scholz, N. Mental Health and the Pandemic. 2021. Available online: https://www.europarl.europa.eu/thinktank/en/document/EPRS_BRI(2021)696164 (accessed on 30 December 2024).
7. Helliwell, J.; Layard, R.; Sachs, J.; Neve, J.E.; Aknin, L.; Wang, S. World Happiness Report. 2021. Available online: https://happiness-report.s3.amazonaws.com/2021/WHR+21.pdf (accessed on 30 December 2024).
8. World Organization of Family Doctors. *International Classification of Primary Care: ICPC-2*; Oxford University Press: Oxford, UK, 2003.
9. Rodrigues, J. Porque consultam os utentes o seu médico de família. *Rev. Port. Med. Geral Fam.* **2000**, *16*, 442–452.
10. Gulbrandsen, P.; Fugelli, P.; Sandvik, L.; Hjortdahl, P. Influence of social problems on management in general practice: Multipractice questionnaire survey. *BMJ* **1998**, *317*, 28. [CrossRef] [PubMed]
11. Rebelo, L.P. O médico de família do futuro: Três modelos de actuação, cinco atributos e cinco aptidões essenciais-parte II. *Rev. Port. Med. Geral Fam.* **2001**, *17*, 159–162.
12. População Residente: Total. Available online: https://www.pordata.pt/municipios/populacao+residente+total-359 (accessed on 30 December 2024).
13. Relatório Atividades ACES Baixo Vouga. 2022. Available online: https://bicsp.min-saude.pt/pt/biufs/2/20019/Pages/default.aspx (accessed on 30 December 2024).
14. População Residente. Available online: https://www.ine.pt/xportal/xmain?xpid=INE&xpgid=ine_indicadores&contecto=pi&indOcorrCod=0011628&selTab=tab0 (accessed on 30 December 2024).
15. Liebetrau, A.M. *Measures of Association*; Sage Publications Newbury Park: Thousand Oaks, CA, USA, 1983.
16. Utentes Inscritos em Cuidados de Saúde Primários. Available online: https://transparencia.sns.gov.pt/explore/dataset/utentes-inscritos-em-cuidados-de-saude-primarios/table/?flg=pt&disjunctive.ars&disjunctive.aces&sort=periodo (accessed on 30 December 2024).
17. Morris, J.A.; Gardner, M.J. Calculating confidence intervals for relative risks (odds ratios) and standardised ratios and rates. *Br. Med. J. Clin. Res. Ed.* **1988**, *296*, 1313–1316. [CrossRef] [PubMed]
18. Cao, F.; Yang, F.; Li, J.; Guo, W.; Zhang, C.; Gao, F.; Sun, X.; Zhou, Y.; Zhang, W. The relationship between diabetes and the dementia risk: A meta-analysis. *Diabetol. Metab. Syndr.* **2024**, *16*, 101. [CrossRef] [PubMed]
19. Ward, J.H. Hierarchical Grouping to Optimize an Objective Function. *JASA* **1963**, *58*, 236–244. [CrossRef]
20. Diário da República Portugal. Decreto-Lei n.o 28/2008, de 22 de Fevereiro. 2008. Available online: https://diariodarepublica.pt/dr/detalhe/decreto-lei/28-2008-247675 (accessed on 30 December 2024).
21. Diário da República Portugal. Decreto-Lei n.o 19/2010, de 22 de Março. 2010. Available online: https://diariodarepublica.pt/dr/detalhe/decreto-lei/19-2010-611341 (accessed on 30 December 2024).
22. Institute of Health Metrics and Evaluation. Global Health Data Exchange. Available online: https://ghdx.healthdata.org/ (accessed on 30 December 2024).
23. Di Fazio, N.; Morena, D.; Delogu, G.; Volonnino, G.; Manetti, F.; Padovano, M.; Fineschi, V. Mental Health Consequences of COVID-19 Pandemic Period in the European Population: An Institutional Challenge. *Int. J. Environ. Res. Public Health* **2022**, *19*, 9347. [CrossRef] [PubMed]
24. Maestre-Miquel, C.; López-de-Andrés, A.; Ji, Z.; de Miguel-Diez, J.; Brocate, A.; Sanz-Rojo, S.; Zamorano-León, J.J. Gender differences in the prevalence of mental health, psychological distress and psychotropic medication consumption in Spain: A nationwide population-based study. *Int. J. Environ. Res. Public Health* **2021**, *18*, 6350. [CrossRef] [PubMed]
25. Otten, D.; Tibubos, A.N.; Schomerus, G.; Brähler, E.; Binder, H.; Kruse, J.; Beutel, M.E. Similarities and differences of mental health in women and men: A systematic review of findings in three large German cohorts. *Front. Public Health* **2021**, *9*, 553071. [CrossRef] [PubMed]
26. Forbes, H.; Carreira, H.; Funston, G.; Andresen, K.; Bhatia, U.; Strongman, H.; Bhaskaran, K. Early, medium and long-term mental health in cancer survivors compared with cancer-free comparators: Matched cohort study using linked UK electronic health records. *EClinicalMedicine* **2024**, *76*, 102826. [CrossRef] [PubMed]
27. Pitman, A.; Suleman, S.; Hyde, N.; Hodgkiss, A. Depression and anxiety in patients with cancer. *BMJ* **2018**, *361*, k1415. [CrossRef] [PubMed]
28. Larson, P.; Bergmans, R. Impact of the COVID-19 pandemic on temporal patterns of mental health and substance abuse related mortality in Michigan: An interrupted time series analysis. *Lancet Reg. Health–Am.* **2022**, *10*, 100218. [CrossRef] [PubMed]
29. Lopes, S.; Soares, P.; Sousa, J.; Rocha, J.; Boto, P.; Santana, R. Effect of the COVID-19 pandemic on the frequency of emergency department visits in Portugal: An interrupted time series analysis until July 2021. *J. Am. Coll. Emerg. Phys.* **2023**, *4*, e12864. [CrossRef] [PubMed]
30. Silva-Valencia, J. Effect of the COVID-19 pandemic on mental health visits in primary care: An interrupted time series analysis from nine INTRePID countries. *EClinicalMedicine* **2024**, *70*, 102533. [CrossRef] [PubMed]

31. Zhou, Q.; Hu, J.; Hu, W. Interrupted time series analysis using the ARIMA model of the impact of COVID-19 on the incidence rate of notifiable communicable diseases in China. *BMC Infect. Dis.* **2023**, *23*, 375. [CrossRef] [PubMed]
32. Center for Disease Control and Prevention. About Mental Health. Available online: https://www.cdc.gov/mental-health/about/index.html (accessed on 30 December 2024).

Mathematical and Computational Applications

MDPI

Article

Induction of Convolutional Decision Trees for Semantic Segmentation of Color Images Using Differential Evolution and Time and Memory Reduction Techniques

Adriana-Laura López-Lobato *, Héctor-Gabriel Acosta-Mesa and Efrén Mezura-Montes

Artificial Intelligence Research Institute, University of Veracruz, Campus Sur, Calle Paseo Lote II, Sección Segunda No. 112, Nuevo Xalapa 91097, Mexico; heacosta@uv.mx (H.-G.A.-M.); emezura@uv.mx (E.M.-M.)

* Correspondence: adrilau17@gmail.com

Abstract

Convolutional Decision Trees (CDTs) are machine learning models utilized as interpretable methods for image segmentation. Their graphical structure enables a relatively simple interpretation of how the tree successively divides the image pixels into two classes, distinguishing between objects of interest and the image background. Several techniques have been proposed to induce CDTs. However, they have primarily been focused on analyzing grayscale images due to the computational cost of the Differential Evolution (DE) algorithm, which is employed in these techniques. This paper proposes a generalization of the induction process of a CDT with the DE algorithm using color images, implementing two techniques to reduce the computational time and memory employed in the induction process: the median selection technique and a memory of previously evaluated solutions. The first technique is applied to select a representative sample of pixels from an image for the model's training process, and the second technique is implemented to reduce the number of evaluations in the fitness function considered in the DE process. The efficacy of these techniques was evaluated using the Weizmann Horse and DRIVE datasets, resulting in favorable outcomes in terms of the segmentation performance of the induced CDTs, and the processing time and memory required for the induction process.

Keywords: semantic segmentation; image segmentation; convolutional decision tree; differential evolution; SHADE

1. Introduction

Semantic segmentation is a process that involves the labeling of image pixels to distinguish between objects of interest and the background of the image; see Figure 1. This task is challenging since the analyzed images have variations that can add noise to the segmentation process.

Image segmentation has numerous applications in computer vision, including analyzing medical images for diagnostic purposes [1,2]. Many methodologies have been devised to address this issue [3]; however, contemporary research has demonstrated a marked predilection for deploying Convolutional Neural Networks (CNNs) [4]. This is primarily because CNNs have been shown to yield optimal performance across a diverse array of applications. Nevertheless, CNNs are often characterized as "black boxes" due to the complexity of their internal processes, making it challenging to comprehend their decision-making processes [5]. This limitation is particularly problematic in domains where explainability is paramount, such as medicine.

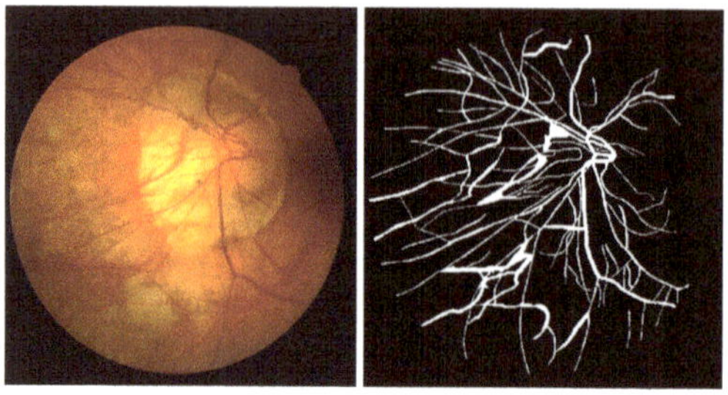

Figure 1. Semantic segmentation technique applied to retinal vessel detection *. * https://drive.grand-challenge.org/DRIVE/ (accessed on 7 May 2025).

Convolutional Decision Trees (CDTs) [6] present a viable alternative to CNNs for image segmentation. This method involves the construction of a multivariate decision tree, where a convolution kernel defines each condition on the tree nodes. These kernels are learned in a supervised manner by solving an optimization problem that aims to maximize the classification accuracy of the pixels in the segmentation of grayscale images.

Several techniques have been proposed to induce CDTs, considering different approaches to maximize the accuracy in classifying the image pixels for the segmentation task. The original approach uses an analytical process to maximize the information gain function on each node of the tree [6]. Consequently, it is a local greedy search that partitions the data (pixels) on each node of the CDT, but it can result in overfitting during the learning process. To conduct a global search approach, in [7], the capabilities of the differential evolution (DE) algorithm are analyzed to identify competitive convolution kernels to induce CDTs that maximize the F1-score in the classification task. The DE algorithm is a metaheuristic search strategy to solve optimization problems by exploring the problem domain with several parameters and stochastic elements that must be adapted to the specific problem [8]. In [7], each individual in the DE algorithm represents all the kernels of a CDT, so a set of CDTs are obtained to select the one with the best F1-score.

Both techniques consider CDTs with kernels of the same size in the tree's nodes. In [9], a local search is performed using the DE algorithm to identify the optimal convolution kernel size and the convolution kernel that maximizes the F1-score on each node of the CDT. So, this technique obtains a unique CDT with convolutional kernels of different sizes.

Since the DE algorithm requires several parameters that must be adapted to the specific dataset (images in the training set) employed to induce a CDT, in [10], the SHADE algorithm is used instead of the traditional DE algorithm. SHADE saves the values of the successful parameters that guide the optimization process in a historical memory H, so the best values are considered for the DE process. This approach facilitates the attainment of comparable or superior results without establishing two parameters for the evolutionary process.

It is important to note that all the aforementioned methods necessitate substantial computational time and memory during the induction process. This is due to the requirement to classify each image pixel in the training set to evaluate the fitness function. This classification process is essential regardless of the method employed, be it an analytical approach or a search with differential evolution. Additionally, the nature of the search, whether local or global, influences the evaluation process. For local searches, evaluations are conducted for each kernel node, while, for global searches, evaluations are performed on all the proposed CDTs.

For this reason, in [11], two techniques for selecting a representative sample of pixels from an image for the model's training process are proposed: raw selection and median selection. The results in the cited work demonstrate that these techniques reduce the computational time required for CDT induction while maintaining or enhancing the precision of the resulting segmentation.

Despite the advancements mentioned above, previous studies have indicated that numerous segmentation databases comprise color images, necessitating their conversion to grayscale to execute CDT induction processes. This conversion procedure often results in the loss of critical information. Consequently, this work proposes a comprehensive enhancement to the induction process of a CDT, considering the use of color images within the learning process and applying the median selection technique to reduce the computational cost that this generalization may entail.

So, the primary objective of this project is to implement a color image segmentation algorithm based on CDTs using the SHADE algorithm, operating under the hypothesis that it is possible to characterize the kernels corresponding to the CDT with the SHADE process by considering chromosomes as vectors that represent the three channels of the convolution kernels of the CDT nodes. The novel aspect of this project lies in its potential to broaden the scope of knowledge about semantic segmentation and CDT-based learning, by leveraging color images and three-channel tree structures, in contrast to the prevailing practice of grayscale image utilization.

The performance of the proposed model was evaluated using the "Weizmann Horse dataset" and "Digital Retinal Images for Vessel Extraction" (DRIVE) dataset, resulting in favorable outcomes regarding the segmentation performance of the induced CDTs, and a significant reduction in the processing time and memory required for the induction process when compared with previous works [6,7,9–11]. The findings of this study underscore the significance of incorporating color characterization into the segmentation process for CDTs. Moreover, the proposal facilitates the comprehension of the methodology employed for image pixel classification given the intuitive nature of the graphical representation of decision trees compared to the approach used by CNNs.

The remainder of the paper is structured into four sections. Section 2 describes the DE algorithm and highlights the most relevant characteristics of the Convolutional Decision Trees. This section also presents the details of the median selection technique employed for the reduction in computational time and memory and the proposal for the induction of CDTs with color images. Section 3 is dedicated to the experiments and results obtained. Finally, Sections 4 and 5 offer a detailed discussion, conclusion, and consider future work.

2. Materials and Methods

In this section, the main subjects of the project are presented: the differential evolution algorithm and SHADE. Also, a description of the Convolutional Decision Trees (CDTs) and the methodology proposed for CDT induction using SHADE on color images is presented.

2.1. Differential Evolution Algorithm and SHADE

Differential Evolution (DE) algorithm is a stochastic research strategy for optimization problems [12]. In the DE process, a competitive solution for a given fitness function is found by perturbing a population of feasible solutions through an iterative process composed of three operators: crossover, mutation, and selection. There are several DE strategies [8,13], but the DE/rand/1/bin strategy is described in detail next.

For a given fitness function f, a population $\mathcal{P} = \{x_i\}_{i=1}^{NP}$ of NP feasible solutions (individuals) is randomly generated. Then, a mutant vector v_i is obtained for each target vector x_i in the population with the mutation operator described in Equation (1), where x_{r_0}, x_{r_1}, and x_{r_2} are individuals randomly selected from the population, and F is the scale factor defined by the user.

$$v_i = x_{r_0} + F(x_{r_1} - x_{r_2}). \quad (1)$$

The mutant vector v_i and its corresponding target vector x_i are used as parents to generate a trial vector u_i, called offspring, by selecting between the parents' coordinates, with the process described in Equation (2). If a random number rnd_j is less than a Crossing Rate CR, defined by the user, or the coordinate position j corresponds to one previously determined by chance (j_{rnd}), the component takes the value from v_i. Otherwise, it takes the value from x_i.

$$u_{ij} = \begin{cases} v_{ij}, & \text{if } (rnd_j \leq CR) \text{ o } (j = j_{rnd}); j = 1, \ldots, |x_i|. \\ x_{ij}, & \text{otherwise.} \end{cases} \tag{2}$$

Once the trial vector v_i is generated, a binary tournament between it and the corresponding target vector x_i is performed to determine what vector survives to the next generation, selecting the one with the best fitness. If the trial vector has the best fitness, it replaces the corresponding target vector in the next generation. Otherwise, the target vector remains in the population, and the trial vector is discarded.

This process is performed NG times (generations), so the population is becoming better or remains the same concerning fitness but never worse; see Figure 2.

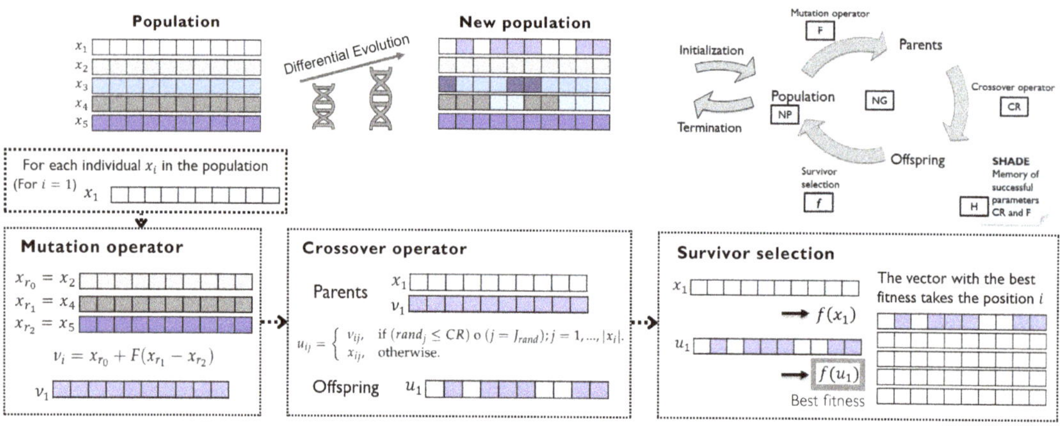

Figure 2. DE algorithm with SHADE.

In the DE algorithm, the parameters CR, F, NP, and NG are problem-dependent and significantly influence the performance of the process [14]. Consequently, it is imperative to calibrate these parameters when implementing the algorithm in real-world scenarios to achieve optimal outcomes. For these reasons, numerous self-adaptive mechanisms to adjust these parameters have been the focus of academic study, including JADE [15], SHADE [16], and L-SHADE [17].

The present study focuses on the Success-History-Based Adaptive Differential Evolution (SHADE) algorithm. SHADE is a technique that regulates the DE algorithm parameters, CR and F, through an adaptive parameter control mechanism. This technique uses a historical memory of size H with successful parameters to modify and adapt the values during the search process; see Figure 2. Further details about SHADE can be found in [16].

2.2. Convolutional Decision Trees

The Convolutional Decision Tree (CDT) is a supervised machine learning model employed for image segmentation [6]. It has the graphical structure of an oblique (multivariate) decision tree, which is easy to interpret [9,10].

The input of a CDT is a digital image composed of pixels with specific positions and hues. Until this work, the images used to induce a CDT were restricted to grayscale images, which are two-dimensional arrays where each pixel has a unique integer value between 0 and 255 (the range of values that an 8-bit number can represent); see Figure 3.

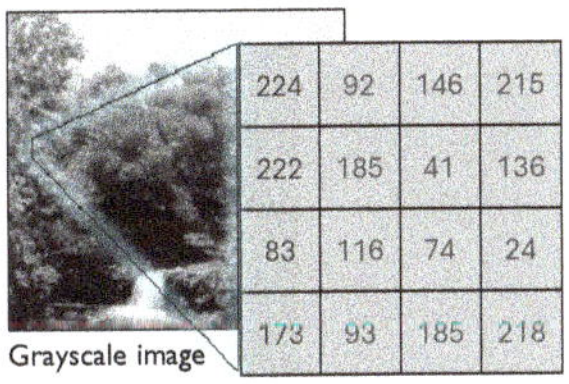

Figure 3. Grayscale image.

Convolution kernels represent the primary components of CDTs. They are square arrays of discrete numbers, known as weights, that function as feature extractors through the convolution operation they execute. The convolution process entails transferring a kernel over an image, thereby integrating the information from both sets. This integration is achieved by applying a dot product between the kernel values and the corresponding values of the image region the kernel covers. The resultant pixel value is derived from this product in conjunction with the bias associated with the filter, thus generating an output feature map; see Figure 4. This process is repeated until the convolution kernel has passed through all pixels of the input image, at which point the full convolution is complete. The result is a filtered version of the image.

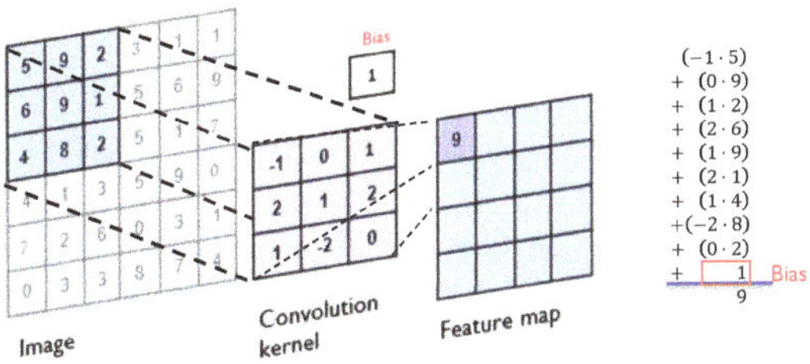

Figure 4. Convolution process on a 6×6 image with a 3×3 kernel.

CDT employs the values obtained in the feature map to classify the pixels in the image according to a predefined criterion, called predicated ϕ. It is a function that has two output values, 0 or 1, depending on whether the value in the feature map is less than or equal to zero or greater than zero, respectively. This is represented in Equation (3), where β denotes the convolution kernel and x is the information of a pixel and its neighboring pixels, which together form an array of the same size of the kernel.

$$\phi(x) = \begin{cases} 0, & \text{if } x^T \cdot \beta \leq 0, \\ 1, & \text{if } x^T \cdot \beta > 0. \end{cases} \quad (3)$$

In this manner, each node of the CDT is represented by a convolutional kernel that partitions the data into two subsets of pixels. The ϕ value of a pixel serves as a directive, guiding toward the subsequent branch of the tree. Pixels with ϕ values equal to zero go to the left branch, and pixels with ϕ values equal to 1 go to the right branch. Consequently, the kernels within a CDT execute successive classifications of each pixel until a leaf node is reached, as illustrated in Figure 5. The ϕ value obtained in a leaf node of a CDT is the label or class assigned to the pixel.

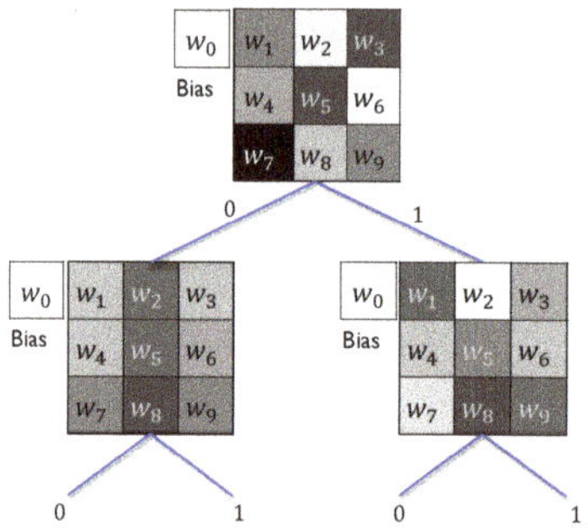

Figure 5. Convolutional Decision Tree with kernels of size 3 and depth 2.

The values of the weights of these kernels are learned in a supervised manner. The initial method proposed for the CDT induction is a local greedy search [6]. To enhance performance, the methods proposed in [7,9] use the DE algorithm to induce a CDT. However, these methods have parameters that must be defined by the user and directly affect the model's performance. So, the use of the SHADE algorithm is proposed in [10] to auto-calibrate the parameters in the DE process.

Another challenge that all these proposals have to deal with is the computational cost of performing the learning process in terms of time and memory, so, in [11], two techniques were proposed (row and median selection). With these techniques, a representative subset of pixels in the images of the training set are selected, speeding up the learning process while maintaining and even improving the performance of the CDT.

In this study, an adaptation of the SHADE-CDT technique will be employed for the induction of a CDT that enables the segmentation of color images, using the median selection technique to reduce the computational cost of the process. The following sections will provide a concise description of these subjects.

2.2.1. SHADE-CDT Technique for CDT Induction

The SHADE-CDT technique performs a global search to induce a CDT [10]. It uses the variant of the differential evolution called SHADE algorithm. This variant tunes the values for the parameters of the crossover and mutation operators in the differential evolution process, described in Section 2.1, by adding a memory of successful parameters.

In the SHADE-CDT technique, each individual in the population conforms to a CDT, so they are vectors of size $(s^2+1)(2^d-1)$ with possible weights for the kernels in the internal nodes of the CDT, obtained randomly between -255 and 255. In Figure 6, an example of a node kernel encoding for a CDT of depth $d=3$ with kernels of size $s=3$ is shown. In this case, each kernel node has $s^2+1=10$ values, and there are $2^d-1=7$ nodes, so, each individual for the SHADE-CDT technique is a vector with $(s^2+1)(2^d-1)=70$ values randomly obtained between -255 and 255.

The DE algorithm employs the F1-score metric to evaluate the accuracy of a model's label assignment. This is achieved by comparing the predicted labels with the actual labels of the instances. To calculate the F1-score value, it is necessary to obtain the labels assigned to each pixel on the images in the training dataset with each individual of the population (representing a CDT) and compare them with the actual labels of the pixels. To achieve this, the images in the training dataset are preprocessed to obtain pixel representations as coded vectors. The corresponding encoded vector for a pixel is formed by the values of the pixels in the neighborhood of size $s \times s$ surrounding it. The length of this vector depends on the kernel size s provided by the user, with a value of 1 added as a bias value; see Figure 7.

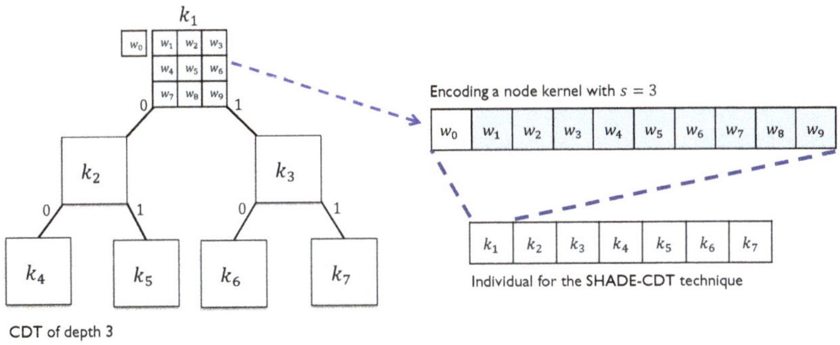

Figure 6. Encodings of a kernel and an individual for the SHADE-CDT technique to induce a CDT of depth 3 with kernels of size 3.

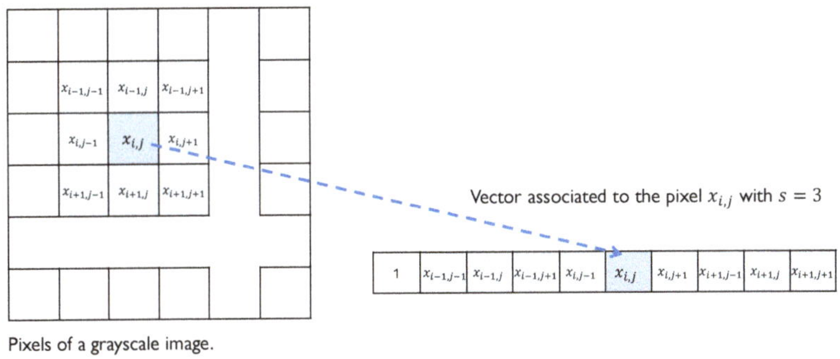

Figure 7. Coding of a pixel-associated instance.

After encoding the pixel information and the kernel structure as vectors of equivalent size, a dot product is performed between them. The resulting value is then processed by an activation function. For the particular case of the SHADE-CDT method, the sigmoid function, defined in Equation (4), is employed.

$$S(x) = \frac{1}{1 + e^{-x}}, \text{ with } x \in \mathbb{R}. \tag{4}$$

This function returns a value between 0 and 1. This value undergoes a classification step in which value 1 is assigned to values greater or equal to 0.5 and 0 to values less than 0.5. The tree node where the instance needs to go is then decided based on this classification step, considering the label 0 for the branch on the left side of the node and 1 for the branch on the right side. This procedure is repeated until a leaf node is reached, at which point a label is assigned to the instance, as illustrated in Figure 8.

Subsequent to the acquisition of all the labels for all the pixels in the images in the training dataset, the F1-score metric, also known as Dice coefficient, is employed to evaluate the fitness of the corresponding CDT. The F1-score is calculated with Equation (5), where TP is the total of true positive cases, FP is the total of false positives, and FN is the total of false negatives.

$$F1\text{-}score = \frac{2 \times TP}{2 \times TP + FN + FP}. \tag{5}$$

An F1-score value approaching zero is indicative of poor segmentation, whereas a value approaching one is indicative of good segmentation.

This process is performed on each individual in the population under consideration for the SHADE process to identify the individual (CDT) with the highest F1-score after multiple generations.

As is made evident by the process, it envolves a substantial amount of computational time and memory. For this reason, two techniques to address this issue were proposed in [11]: the raw selection and the median selection techniques. Given the results obtained with these methods, the median selection technique is employed in this work as considering color images directly affects the amount of information taken into account in the learning process.

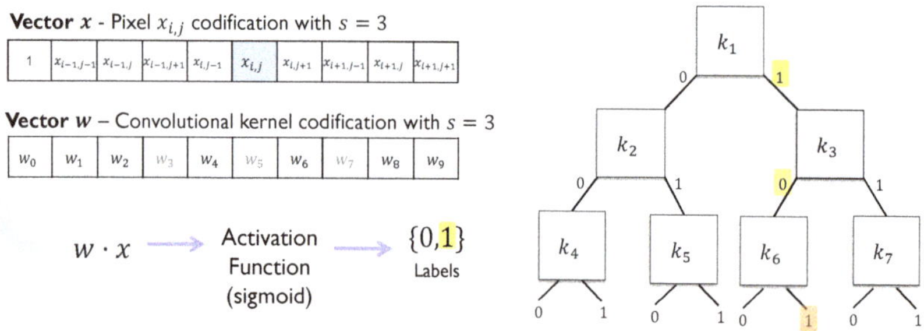

Figure 8. SHADE-CDT process employing the codification of the pixel-associated instance (x) and the codification of the convolutional kernels (w) in the nodes of a CDT. The dot product between x and w is evaluated in the sigmoid function to obtain a value between 0 and 1. In this example, this evaluation is greater than 0.5, so the label assigned for the root node, denoted as k_1, is 1, highlighted in the CDT, directing the pixel information to the node k_3. The same process is repeated with the codification of node k_3 to obtain the label 0, directing the pixel information to the leaf node k_6. With its vectorial codification, the process obtains the final label 1 for the pixel under consideration.

Also, it is important to mention that, for this method, five parameters are user-defined:

- For the SHADE-CDT algorithm: the population size (NP), the number of generations (NG), and the memory size (H).
- For the CDT structure: the size (s) of the kernels and the depth (d) of the tree.

Further details on the SHADE-CDT method can be found in [10].

2.2.2. Median Selection Technique for CDT Induction

The median selection technique involves the selection of samples of representative pixels from each of the two classes to be segmented in the images of the training set [11]. With the median selection technique, a partition of the dataset is performed to obtain the median vector with the representative information of each subset in the partition.

In this technique, a proportion value $\mathcal{P}$ is needed. This value indicates the quantity or proportion of the total image information sampled for the induction process. So, if the user establishes $\mathcal{P} = 0.2$, this means that the process will find the representative information equivalent to only 20% of the total information. For example, in Figure 9, a grayscale image and its ground truth are presented. Remember that the ground truth contains the labels for each pixel from the original image, considering two classes: 0 (black) and 1 (white). This image has dimensions 15×26, yielding a total of 390 pixels, 82 of which are classified as class 1 (white) and 308 as class 0 (black). Assuming that $\mathcal{P} = 0.2$ for the median technique, the image information will go through the corresponding process that results in the extraction of the representative information, as if the image were composed at most of 78 pixels, equivalent to 20% of the total pixels ($390 \times 0.2 = 78$).

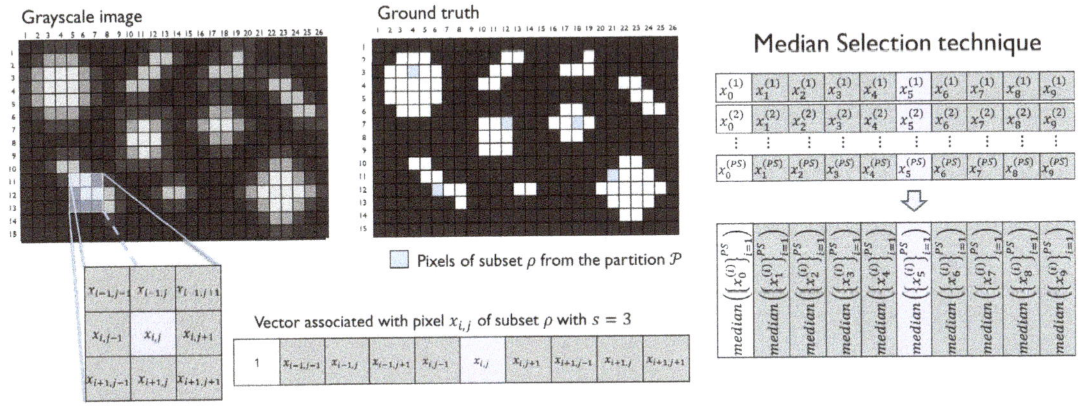

Figure 9. Grayscale image and its ground truth on the left, and a representation of the obtention of a representative vector for the analyzed subset ρ with the median selection technique.

A distinctive feature of this process is preserving the proportion between the classes. In the example of Figure 9, approximately 21% of the pixels in the original image are designated as class 0, while 79% are labeled as class 1. To maintain this ratio, the technique generates pixels equivalent to 20% of each class, i.e., 16 pixels for class 1 and 61 pixels for class 0 ($82 \times 0.2 = 16.4$ and $302 \times 0.2 = 61.6$), consequently maintaining the proportion 21%/79% between classes and a total of 77 representative pixels for this image.

The generation of pixels is achieved through the implementation of a partitioning technique, which divides each class into a predefined number of subsets of the same size if possible. The number of subsets is equivalent to the number of pixels desired for each class. So, for the example, class 1 has 82 pixels, but, with the technique at 20%, only 16 pixels of this class are required. So, the pixels of this class are partitioned into 16 disjoint subsets: 15 subsets of size 5 and 1 subset of size 7 (7 ($15 \times 5 + 7 = 82$). The pixels on each subset are randomly selected from the pixels of class 1, but, remembering that a partition is a division of a set into a family of subsets where each element in the original set is present only in one of the subsets and all the subsets together contain all the members of the original set, once a pixel is selected for a subset, it cannot be in any other subset. This process is repeated for the class 0 pixels, resulting in the acquisition of information for only 61 pixels out of 308 pixels that were originally present. Consequently, the partition of this class is constituted by 61 disjoint subsets, 60 subsets of size 5, and 1 subset of size 8 ($60 \times 5 + 8 = 308$). As in the other class, the pixels within each subset are randomly selected from the pixels of class 0.

Following the implementation of this partition, denoted by $\mathcal{P}$, a total of 77 subsets are obtained, 16 of class 1 and 61 of class 0. For each subset, denoted by ρ, the vectors associated with each pixel in the grayscale image are obtained, considering the kernel size s of the CDT that is sought to be obtained, as illustrated in Figure 9. Subsequent to the acquisition of these vectors, the representative vector of this subset is formed by the median value calculated by coordinates and depicted in the right image of Figure 9. These "mean vectors" have the class of the subset from which they were derived.

Subsequent to the completion of the process of obtaining representative vectors of each image in the training set, the new training set for the induction process of a CDT will consist of all these vectors. The pseudocode of the median selection technique is presented in Algorithm A1 of Appendix B.

As demonstrated in the experiments performed in [11], this technique has been shown to reduce the computational time required to induce a CDT on grayscale images. This reduction is due to a decrease in the number of training instances. In addition, it has been shown to improve the quality of the segmentation results by minimizing the risk of overfitting in the learning process. For these reasons, the median selection technique is used in this work to induce CDTs using color images (with three color channels). This generalization to color images was not even considered because the process triples the number of elements in the training dataset. However, the median selection technique allows datasets with color images to perform the CDT induction process without losing critical information when converted to grayscale images.

The following sections describe images in color spaces and the proposed process to induce CDTs in three color channels.

2.3. Color Images and Color Spaces

For this work, the images used as an input are color images. Usually, to represent color in digital images, the RGB color space is used. The RGB color space is an additive model, wherein colors are created through the combination of three primary colors (red (R), green (G), and blue (B)). So, the RGB model can be conceptualized as a cube whose coordinate axes correspond to R, G, and B; see Figure 10a. All RGB values are constrained to the interval [0, 255]. Consequently, each possible color corresponds to a unique point in the RGB cube with coordinates $(Red, Green, Blue)$ in the space $[0, 255] \times [0, 255] \times [0, 255]$. For instance, the black and white colors are located at (0, 0, 0) and (255, 255, 255), respectively, in the RGB color space. This indicates that the white color is representative of an absence of the three primary colors, while the white color is itself a combination of the three colors.

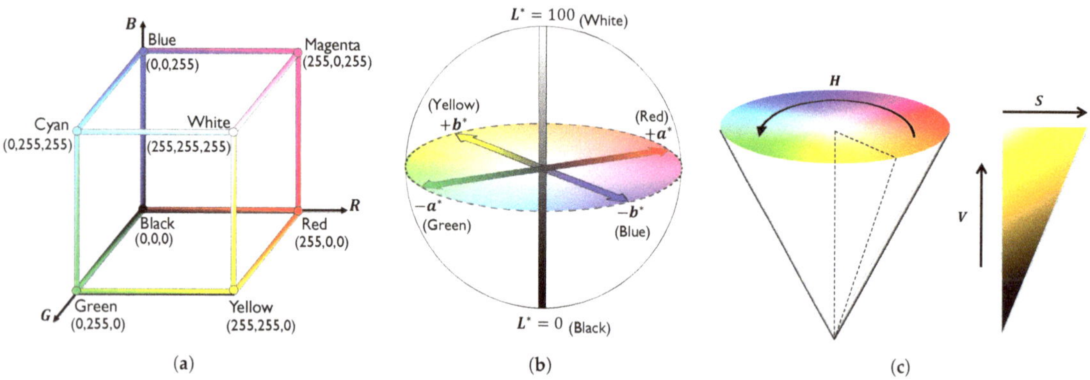

Figure 10. Color spaces analyzed in this work: (**a**) RGB. (**b**) CIE L*a*b*. (**c**) HSV.

The RGB color space can be converted to other color spaces, such as L*a*b* and HSV, to obtain different color representations; see Figure 10. These alternative representations can help to extract color features and patterns [18]. For this reason, the following sections will briefly describe the CIE L*a*b* and HSV color spaces.

2.3.1. CIE L*a*b* Color Space

The CIE L*a*b* color space is a mathematical transformation of the colorimetric system in which the numerical differences between colors consistently correspond to the visual perception of the human eye [19,20]. The CIE L*a*b* space is three-dimensional. The vertical axis represents the lightness L*, with values ranging from 0 (black) to 100 (white). The primary color axes extend from red to green (a* axis) and from yellow to blue (b* axis), as illustrated in Figure 10b. In the a* axis, a positive number indicates a redder color, and a negative number indicates greener color. In the b* axis, a positive number indicates yellower color, and a negative number indicates bluer color.

Consequently, each possible color corresponds to a unique point (L^*, a^*, b^*) in the space $[0, 100] \times [-128, 127] \times [-128, 127]$. For example, the colors white and black are located in the coordinates (0, 0, 0) and (100, 0, 0), respectively, and the primary colors red, green, and blue are located (approximately) in the coordinates (53.24, 80.09, 67.2), (87.73, −86.18, 83.18), and (32.3, 79.19, −107.86), respectively.

2.3.2. HSV Color Space

In the HSV color space, color information is represented through three components: hue (H), saturation (S), and value (V). This model is commonly depicted as an inverse pyramid, where the vertical axis represents the value (V), the horizontal distance, with the V axis used as a reference point, corresponds to the saturation (S), and the angle, with the V axis acting as the rotation point, defines the hue (H) [21]. Refer to Figure 10c for a visual representation. In this color space, the parameters on H are color indicators with angular dimensions. The black color in the HSV space is located at the apex of the pyramid, while white occupies the center of the base. Within the base, the three fundamental colors (red, green, and blue) and their respective combinations are distributed.

So, each possible color corresponds to a unique point in the HSV space with coordinates $(Hue, Saturation, Value)$ in the space $[0, 360] \times [0, 100] \times [0, 100]$. For example, the colors white and black have the coordinate values (0, 0, 100) and (0, 0, 0), respectively. The fundamental colors are located at the base of the pyramid at positions (0, 100, 100) for red, (120, 100, 100) for green, and (240, 100, 100) for blue.

2.3.3. Representation of Color Images

Images in the previously described color spaces are structured in three dimensions since the color values of each pixel are described as a vector with three coordinates, as in Equation (6).

$$color = (x_{Channel_1}, y_{Channel_2}, z_{Channel_3}) \tag{6}$$

Thus, a composition by channels can be used to describe the structure of a color image C considering a representation of three matrices of the same size as C, denoted by C_1, C_2, and C_3; see Equation (7).

$$C = \{C_!, C_2, C_3\}. \tag{7}$$

These matrices have as element in the position (x, y) the corresponding color channel value of the pixel at the same position in the original image, as shown in Figure 11 and in Equation (8).

$$C(x, y) = (C_1(x, y), C_2(x, y), C_3(x, y)). \tag{8}$$

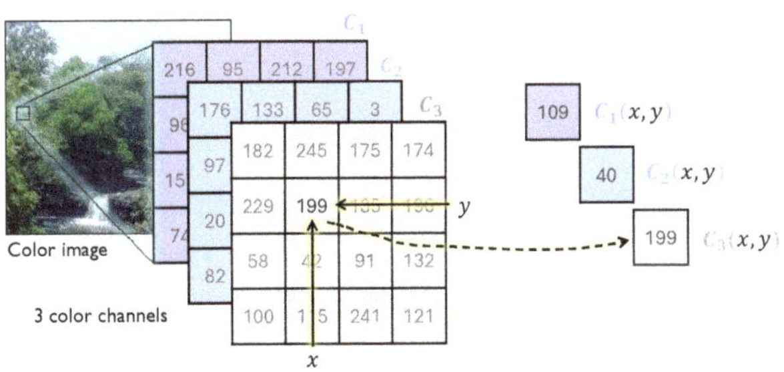

Figure 11. Composition of a color image by channels.

Thus, any color image can be represented by three two-dimensional matrices that display the values of the corresponding coordinate channels at the corresponding pixel locations.

The subsequent section presents a detailed description of the convolutional process on images with three channels. This provides a structured framework for the proposal outlined in this work.

2.4. Convolution Process on Images with Three Channels of Color

In the convolution process, it is essential that the dimensions of the convolutional kernel be matched to the image's dimensions, ensuring proper coverage.

For images with three color channels, such as in RGB, CIE L*a*b, and HSV, the convolutional kernels must be represented as arrays of three dimensions (height, width, and depth). In Figure 12, a $3 \times 3 \times 3$ kernel performs the convolution process on an image with three color channels.

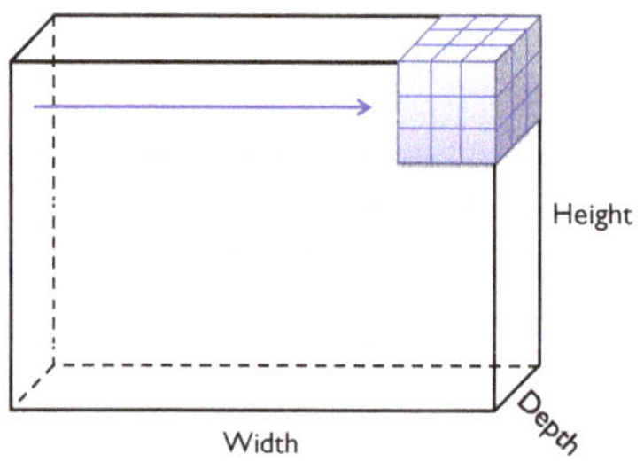

Figure 12. $3 \times 3 \times 3$ convolutional kernel process on an image with three channels of color.

In this scenario, the convolution process is performed for each depth layer, where each dimension of the image representing a color channel is subjected to the convolution process using the corresponding kernel dimension. Subsequently, three convolution processes are performed, whose results, in conjunction with the value of the bias assigned to the kernel, are aggregated to obtain the value of the output pixel. Notably, although the convolution process is executed on a three-dimensional image, the result will have only one dimension. An illustration of this process can be found in Figure 13.

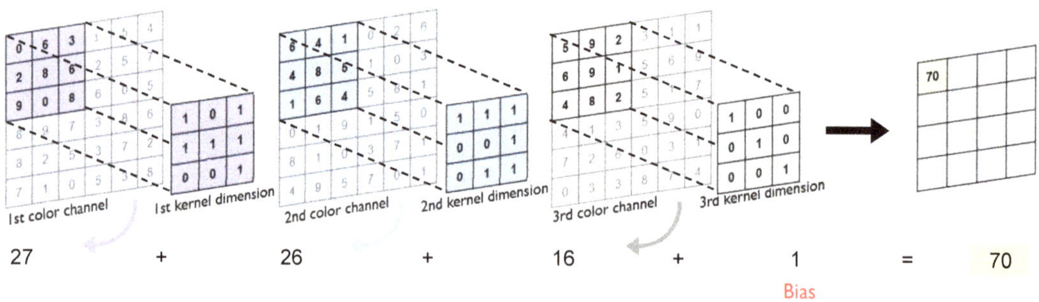

Figure 13. Convolution process on an image with three color channels with a kernel of size $3 \times 3 \times 3$.

2.5. Proposed Model: CDT Induction Using SHADE with Color Images ($SHADE\text{-}CDT_{color}$)

In this work, the $SHADE\text{-}CDT_{color}$ search strategy is proposed. This model employs the SHADE algorithm to find the kernels that serve as conditions in the nodes of a CDT, with the particularity that these kernels are directed to the convolution process in color spaces; that is, they have three channels.

In this model, the CDT structure is defined by two parameters: the size of the kernels, denoted by s, and the depth of the tree, denoted as d. The objective is to perform a global search to maximize the classification accuracy of the CDT, measured with the F1-score metric.

In the $SHADE\text{-}CDT_{color}$ model, the pixels in the images and the kernels for the CDT are encoded separately for each channel. To encode a pixel (instance) of the image, the hues of the pixels in the neighborhood of size s surrounding it are used in each channel. Similarly, the weights of a node kernel of the CDT in each channel are encoded as a vector of size s^2. These coding processes are illustrated in Figure 14.

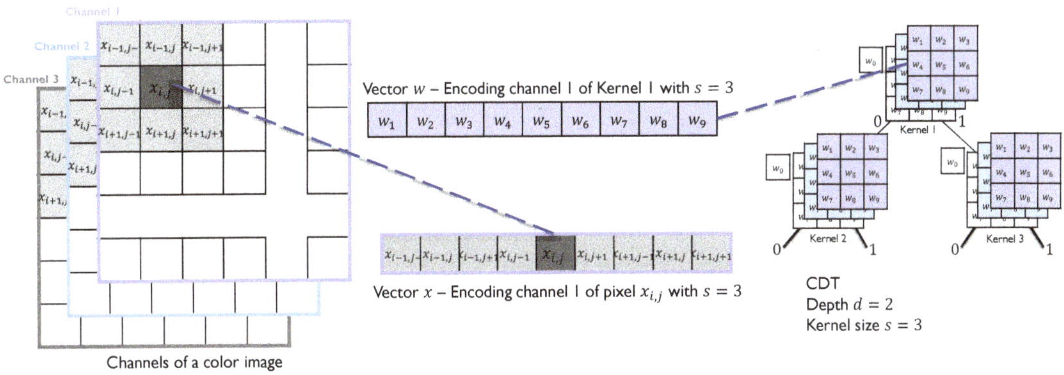

Figure 14. Encodings of a kernel and an instance by color channel.

In the SHADE process, each individual in the population is represented by a vector of real values that correspond to the weights of the kernels of the CDT to be found; see Figure 15. The length of this vector is dependent on the kernel size s and the depth d of the CDT under consideration. For instance, when a kernel with three channels is considered at each of the three nodes, $3s^2$ values are required, along with a single value for the bias of the convolution process (see Figure 13 for a description of the convolution process on a three-color-channel image). This sum of values must then be multiplied by the number of kernels in the CDT, which is calculated as $2^d - 1$. So, for the SHADE process, each individual in the population is a vector of real values of size $(3s^2 + 1)(2^d - 1)$. These values are randomly generated between -255 and 255.

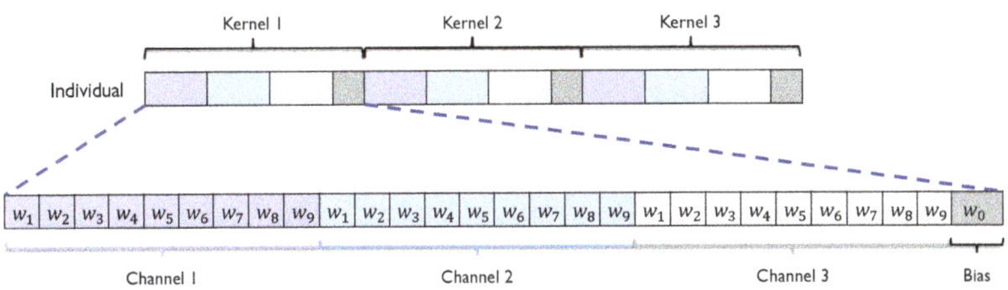

Figure 15. Individual considered in the SHADE process for the induction of a CDT with kernel size $s = 3$ and depth $d = 2$ (vector of length $(3s^2 + 1) \cdot (2^d - 1) = 84$).

A perceptron structure is employed to ascertain the appropriate branch of the tree to pursue during the classification of an instance. To accomplish this, the final pixel (instance) encoding is a vector with the encodings of the channels appended as a vector, incorporating a value of 1 for the bias; see Figure 16.

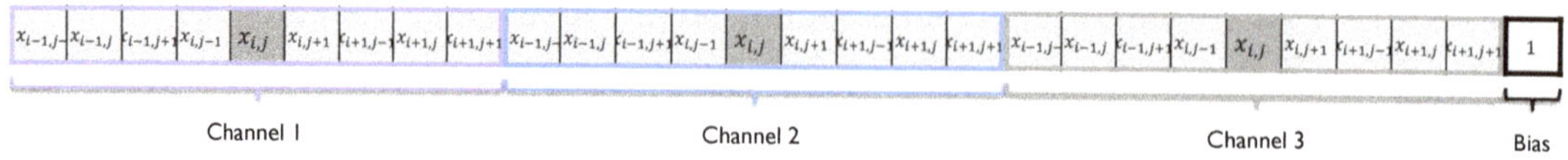

Figure 16. Information of the pixel $x_{i,j}$ structured for the SHADE process considering a kernel of size $s = 3$.

In the perceptron structure, the dot product of the vector with the values of the encoded instance (as in Figure 16) with the vector corresponding to the encoding of the kernel (as in Figure 15) is passed through the sigmoid activation function, defined by Equation (4). This function returns a value between 0 and 1, and, as in the SHADE-CDT method, if this value is smaller than or equal to 0.5, the label 0 is assigned; if the value is higher than 0.5, the label 1 is assigned. The tree node to which the instance should be directed is then determined based on this label, with label 0 assigned to the node on the left side and label 1 assigned to the node on the right side. This procedure is repeated until a leaf node is reached, at which point a label is assigned to the instance (pixel).

After the acquisition of all the labels for the pixels in the images of the training dataset, the F1-score metric is utilized to evaluate the fitness of the corresponding CDT.

The pseudocode describing the process for determining the fitness value of an individual using the $SHADE\text{-}CDT_{color}$ method can be found in Algorithm A2 of Appendix B.

As previously indicated, the one-dimensional process ($SHADE\text{-}CDT$) necessitates considerable computational time and memory when considering only grayscale images. However, when color images are incorporated, the learning process involves tripling the amount of information due to the convolution performed in each color channel. Consequently, the median selection technique is a powerful tool employed in the $SHADE\text{-}CDT_{color}$ method proposed in this study. This technique facilitates reducing information during the learning process by selecting a sample of representative pixels, as Section 2.2.2 outlines, but, in the three-channel version, the associated vector for each pixel is obtained as depicted in Figure 16.

Also, to reduce the computational time required for the learning process of the $SHADE\text{-}CDT_{color}$ method, another modification considered was the utilization of a memory of previously evaluated individuals for the SHADE algorithm. In this memory, the individuals of the initial population and their fitness values are stored, and, for the subsequent generation, solely the recently generated individuals resulting from the mutation, crossover, and selection operators are evaluated and substituted for the defeated individuals. This process is repeated for subsequent generations until the DE algorithm is complete, as illustrated in Figure 17. This modification has been demonstrated to reduce the number of individual evaluations and the time required to complete the induction process, even when considering the three color channels.

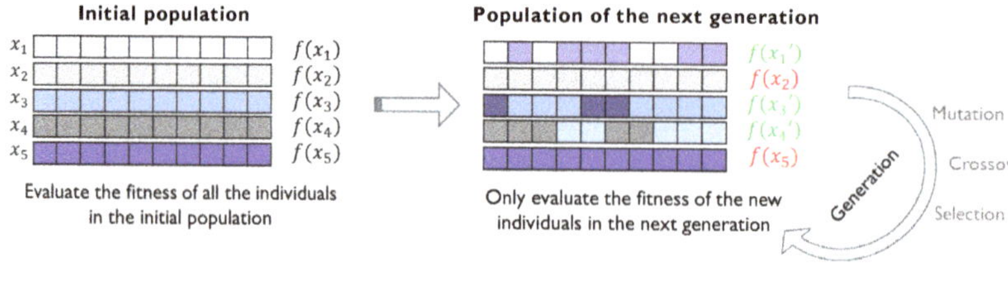

Figure 17. The memory implemented for the $SHADE\text{-}CDT_{color}$ method calculates the fitness for all individuals in the initial population, and, for subsequent populations, only the fitness for the new individuals in the immediate next generation is calculated, reducing the computational time of the induction process.

The pseudocode of the proposed model for CDT induction using SHADE with color images ($SHADE\text{-}CDT_{color}$ method) is presented in Algorithm A3 of Appendix B.

It is important to acknowledge the critical role of the median selection technique in reducing information during the learning process and the proposed memory to reduce individual evaluations. These approaches enable the execution of the experiments described in the following section implemented in the Matlab R2023b software on a computer with the same characteristics as the one used in [10,11]; see Table 1. This facilitates a comparative analysis of the outcomes, showing that the proposed methodology reduces the memory and time of the induction process of a CDT compared to previous works while improving the F1-scores in the segmentation task by incorporating color images instead of grayscale images.

Table 1. Computer specifications.

Operating System	Windows 11 Pro 23H2
RAM	64 GB
Processor	AMD Ryzen 5 5600G
Processor speed	3.90 GHz

3. Experiments and Results

This section describes the experiments performed to analyze the performance of the CDT induction process for the segmentation of color images proposed in this work. The images from the "Weizmann Horse dataset" [22] are used to compare the proposal results considering the different color spaces described in Section 2.3. Once the best color space for induction is identified, the "Digital Retinal Images for Vessel Extraction" (DRIVE) dataset (https://drive.grand-challenge.org/DRIVE/ (accessed on 7 May 2025)) is employed to conduct a comparative analysis of the induction time and precision between the $SHADE\text{-}CDT$ method, employing grayscale images, and the $SHADE\text{-}CDT_{color}$ technique, using color images. The selection of these datasets allows the comparison of the results with those described in [6,10,11].

3.1. Comparison of Color Spaces with the Weizmann Horse Dataset

The Weizmann Horse dataset was used in experiments to compare the three color spaces under consideration (RGB, CIE L*a*b*, and HSV). This dataset comprises 327 manually segmented images of horses, which were resized to 40% of their original size for the experimental procedures. The images were divided into training and test sets, with 33 and 295 images, respectively. Subsequently, controlled experiments were conducted to compare the segmentations obtained in each color space. These experiments consider as a primary approach the following parameters: 100 generations, population size with 100 individuals, and a memory of size 100 for the SHADE algorithm, and depths ranging from 1 to 5 and kernel sizes of 3, 5, 7, 9, and 11 were considered for the CDT structure.

The results obtained for the segmentation of the images in the test dataset employing the $SHADE\text{-}CDT_{color}$ method with the median technique, with $\mathcal{P} = 0.3$, are presented in Table 2. This $\mathcal{P}$ value was selected after performing controlled experiments considering proportions of 10%, 20%, 30%, 40%, and 50%, obtaining the best results with 30%, so this value was maintained for the subsequent experiments. The training and test datasets were the same in these experiments to ensure consistency in the comparison between the color spaces and the different configurations of tree depth and kernel size in the structure of the CDTs.

Table 2. Results for the Weizmann Horse dataset segmentation with the $SHADE\text{-}CDT_{color}$ method employing the median technique with $\mathcal{P} = 0.3$, and, for the SHADE algorithm, 100 individuals, 100 generations, and a memory size of 100. The best F1-score by kernel size, considering the color space, is shown in bold numbers, and the best result by kernel size is highlighted.

CDT Structure		RGB			CIE L*a*b*			HSV		
s	*d*	F1-Score	Accuracy	Time (min)	F1-Score	Accuracy	Time (min)	F1-Score	Accuracy	Time (min)
3	1	0.5415	0.7632	6.39	0.5466	0.7653	6.18	0.3996	0.7383	6.64
3	2	0.5346	0.7509	10.6	0.548	0.7645	10.44	0.5239	0.7675	10.82
3	3	**0.5718**	0.773	14.23	0.5654	0.7664	14.27	0.5143	0.7692	14.36
3	4	0.5534	0.7492	18.08	**0.5689**	0.7692	18.25	0.5353	0.7623	18.7
3	5	0.5664	0.7669	22.39	0.5664	0.7648	24.62	**0.5455**	0.7689	22.16
5	1	0.5562	0.7702	7.26	0.5567	0.7647	7.16	0.4087	0.7331	6.65
5	2	0.5544	0.7694	11.22	0.581	0.76	11.37	0.4966	0.7457	11.72
5	3	0.5769	0.7484	15.41	0.5686	0.7528	15.68	0.5152	0.7484	15.81
5	4	**0.5793**	0.7502	19.58	**0.593**	0.7778	20.13	**0.5359**	0.7486	19.33
5	5	0.5666	0.7557	23.6	0.592	0.7703	24.91	0.512	0.7528	23.04
7	1	0.563	0.7689	8.51	0.5641	0.7635	8.83	0.4127	0.7235	8.61
7	2	0.5669	0.7694	13.25	**0.5942**	0.7667	13.22	0.5115	0.7425	13.82
7	3	0.5825	0.7532	18.16	0.5923	0.7672	17.30	0.5226	0.7513	18.46
7	4	**0.5918**	0.7567	22.76	0.5865	0.756	23.15	**0.5312**	0.7363	21.79
7	5	0.5671	0.74	28.09	0.5642	0.7385	26.13	0.5275	0.7337	26.44
9	1	0.5548	0.7586	11.8	0.5707	0.7631	11.62	0.4387	0.7183	11.23
9	2	**0.5946**	0.7502	18.38	**0.6042**	0.769	17.8	0.5063	0.7258	16.75
9	3	0.5936	0.7545	24.48	0.5897	0.7567	21.91	0.5214	0.7202	22.22
9	4	0.5898	0.7503	31.26	0.5699	0.7441	26.69	**0.53**	0.7376	29.41
9	5	0.5848	0.758	32.14	0.5915	0.7648	31.98	0.5234	0.7012	32.31
11	1	0.5559	0.7519	12.62	0.5806	0.763	12.43	0.4407	0.7134	15.09
11	2	0.5503	0.7458	19.69	**0.6052**	0.7585	18.26	0.5088	0.7129	20.65
11	3	**0.5891**	0.7393	23.71	0.5903	0.7591	23.68	0.5225	0.7166	25.76
11	4	0.5623	0.7411	29.76	0.5954	0.7507	28.39	0.5255	0.7179	30.07
11	5	0.5749	0.7437	35.69	0.5624	0.7354	35.64	**0.5315**	0.7118	35.49

To perform more in-depth experiments, the CDT structure with the highest F1-score value by kernel size was used. For this reason, a graphical representation of the information in Table 2 is presented in Figure 18, where the subfigures are line plots in two dimensions considering the depth of the CDT and their corresponding F1-scores, fixing the kernel size in each subfigure.

As demonstrated in Figure 18, the comparison lines facilitate the identification of the depth value, *d*, and the color space corresponding to the higher F1-score for each kernel size *s*. In Figure 18a, the maximum F1-score attained by a CDT with a kernel size of 3 is achieved when the depth is 3 in the RGB color space. Figure 18b illustrates that a higher F1-score is obtained by a CDT with a kernel size of 5 when the depth is 4 in the CIE L*a*b* color space. Furthermore, Figure 18c–e demonstrate that the best F1-score outcomes achieved with the CDTs employing fixed kernel sizes 7, 9, and 11, correspondingly, are attained when the trees have a depth of 2 in the CIE L*a*b* color space.

Five experiments were conducted to induce a CDT with each of the structures previously enumerated and for each space color, so, in total, 75 experiments were performed (25 for each color space). For these experiments, the same training and test sets were used to ensure a consistent comparison with the median selection technique.

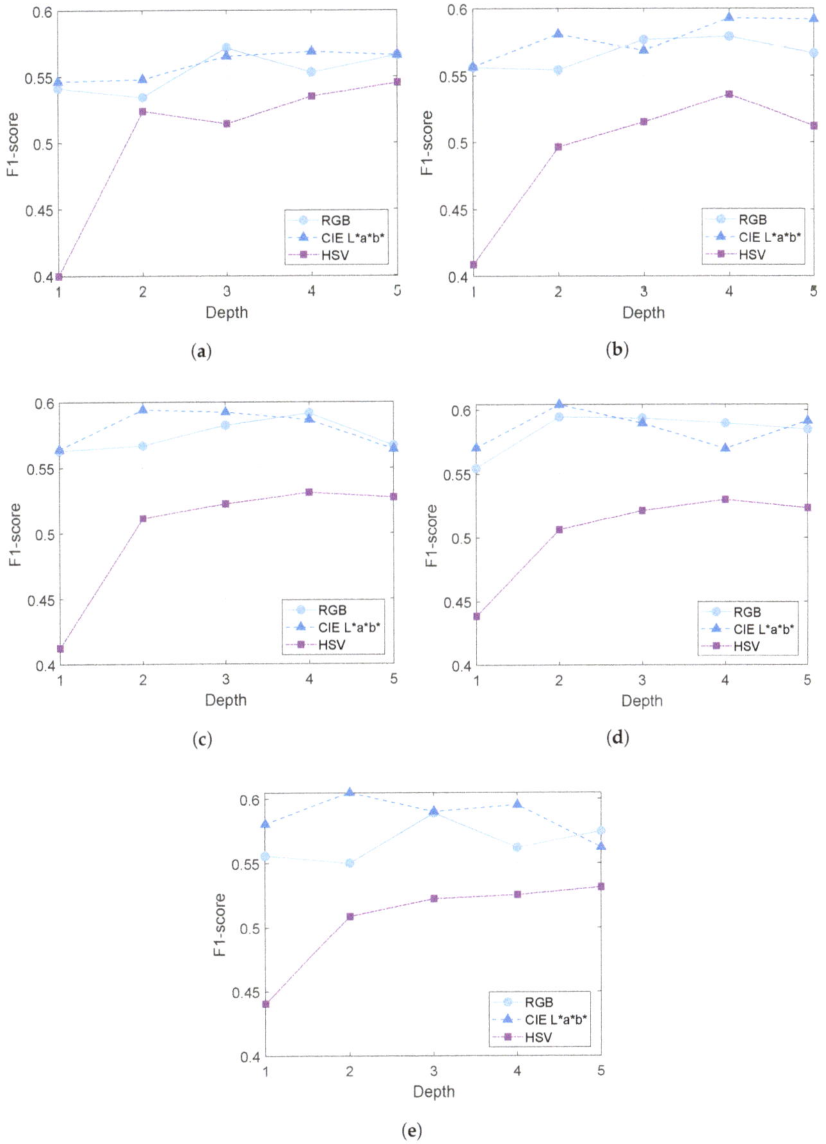

Figure 18. Line plots in two dimensions considering the depth d of the CDTs and their corresponding F1-scores, fixing the kernel size s. (**a**) CDTs with $s = 3$. (**b**) CDTs with $s = 5$. (**c**) CDTs with $s = 7$. (**d**) CDTs with $s = 9$. (**e**) CDTs with $s = 11$.

In Table 3, the minimum, maximum, and mean $\pm$ standard deviation of the image segmentation precision, measured by the F1-score, of the images in the test set are presented.

The Shapiro–Wilk statistical test was employed for each CDT configuration within each color space to verify the normal distribution of the F1-score results obtained from the five executions. The corresponding p-values are also presented in Table 3.

Table 3. Results of 5 experiments with the Weizmann Horse dataset in the three color spaces employing the median technique with $\mathcal{P} = 0.3$, and for the SHADE algorithm 100 individuals, 100 generations, and a memory size of 100. The table presents the minimum, maximum, mean ± standard deviation, and median of the F1-scores obtained in each color space and with the specified CDT structure. Additionally, the mean time and two *p*-values for the statistical tests, namely the Shapiro–Wilk test and the one-way ANOVA test, are included, with a significance level of $\alpha = 0.05$ applied to all tests. The values in bold represent the results with the best segmentation, with two highlighted values when the differences between the corresponding color spaces are not statistically significant.

CDT structure	Metrics	RGB	CIE L*a*b*	HSV
	Min / Max	0.5445 / 0.5777	0.5654 / 0.5843	0.5143 / 0.5416
$s = 3$	Mean ± St.D.	**0.5612 ± 0.0143**	**0.5714 ± 0.0075**	0.5276 ± 0.0103
$d = 3$	Median	0.5627	0.5697	0.5288
	Time (min)	15.81	15.4	14.48
Shapiro–Wilk	*p*-value	0.6189	0.0660	0.9871
One-way ANOVA	*p*-value		1.08×10^{-4} *	
	Min / Max	0.5462 / 0.5793	0.5723 / 0.5930	0.5028 / 0.5386
$s = 5$	Mean ± St.D.	**0.5678 ± 0.0133**	**0.5823 ± 0.0075**	0.5246 ± 0.0150
$d = 4$	Median	0.5706	0.5817	0.5297
	Time (min)	21.31	21.15	19.54
Shapiro–Wilk	*p*-value	0.3067	0.9548	0.4637
One-way ANOVA	*p*-value		2.33×10^{-5} *	
	Min / Max	0.5562 / 0.5845	0.591 / 0.6057	0.5023 / 0.5119
$s = 7$	Mean ± St.D.	0.5660 ± 0.011	**0.598 ± 0.006**	0.5077 ± 0.0041
$d = 2$	Median	0.5615	0.5966	0.5078
	Time (min)	14.5	14.33	13.7
Shapiro–Wilk	*p*-value	0.1777	0.7977	0.5394
One-way ANOVA	*p*-value		1.12×10^{-9} *	
	Min / Max	0.5559 / 0.5946	0.5699 / 0.6064	0.5063 / 0.5149
$s = 9$	Mean ± St.D.	**0.5819 ± 0.0152**	**0.5951 ± 0.0147**	0.5110 ± 0.0038
$d = 2$	Median	0.5880	0.5984	0.5101
	Time	17.68	17.21	17.42
Shapiro–Wilk	*p*-value	0.0952	0.0687	0.3659
One-way ANOVA	*p*-value		3.18×10^{-7} *	
	Min / Max	0.5503 / 0.5884	0.5978 / 0.6122	0.4906 / 0.5192
$s = 11$	Mean ± St.D.	0.5696 ± 0.0174	**0.6041 ± 0.0054**	0.5096 ± 0.0115
$d = 2$	Median	0.5719	0.6041	0.5116
	Time	19.94	19.6	20.34
Shapiro–Wilk	*p*-value	0.3384	0.857	0.2049
One-way ANOVA	*p*-value		1.81×10^{-7} *	

* The differences between some of the mean F1-scores of color spaces are significant at the 95% confidence level.

In Figure 19, the boxplots of each color space are presented for each analyzed configuration.

The following observations can be made with reference to Figure 19:

- In Figure 19a–c, the values obtained with the CIE L*a*b* color space demonstrate less variability when compared to the other two color spaces. This is because the corresponding boxes are comparatively short. Conversely, the boxes corresponding to the RGB and HSV color spaces are comparatively tall.
- As illustrated in Figure 19c,d, the values obtained with the CIE L*a*b* color space demonstrate less variability when compared to the other two color spaces. However, in these instances, the boxes corresponding to the RGB and CIE L*a*b* color spaces do not exhibit significant variability.
- As illustrated in Figure 19a,b, two values are positioned on the upper whiskers of the boxplots, corresponding to the CIE L*a*b* and RGB color spaces, respectively. This

observation suggests the presence of outliers in their corresponding values. However, it should be noted that these values are above the median F1-score.

- Conversely, in Figure 19b,d,e, the outliers are values that fall below the median F1-scores since they appear in the lower whiskers of the RGB, RGB and CIE L*a*b*, and HSV color spaces, respectively. However, in these cases, the comparative superiority of the RGB and CIE L*a*b* color spaces over the HSV color space is evident.
- The boxplots demonstrate that the CIE L*a*b* color space consistently yields the highest mean F1-score values and exhibits minimal variability. However, a one-way ANOVA test was conducted to ascertain the disparities among the means of the various color spaces.

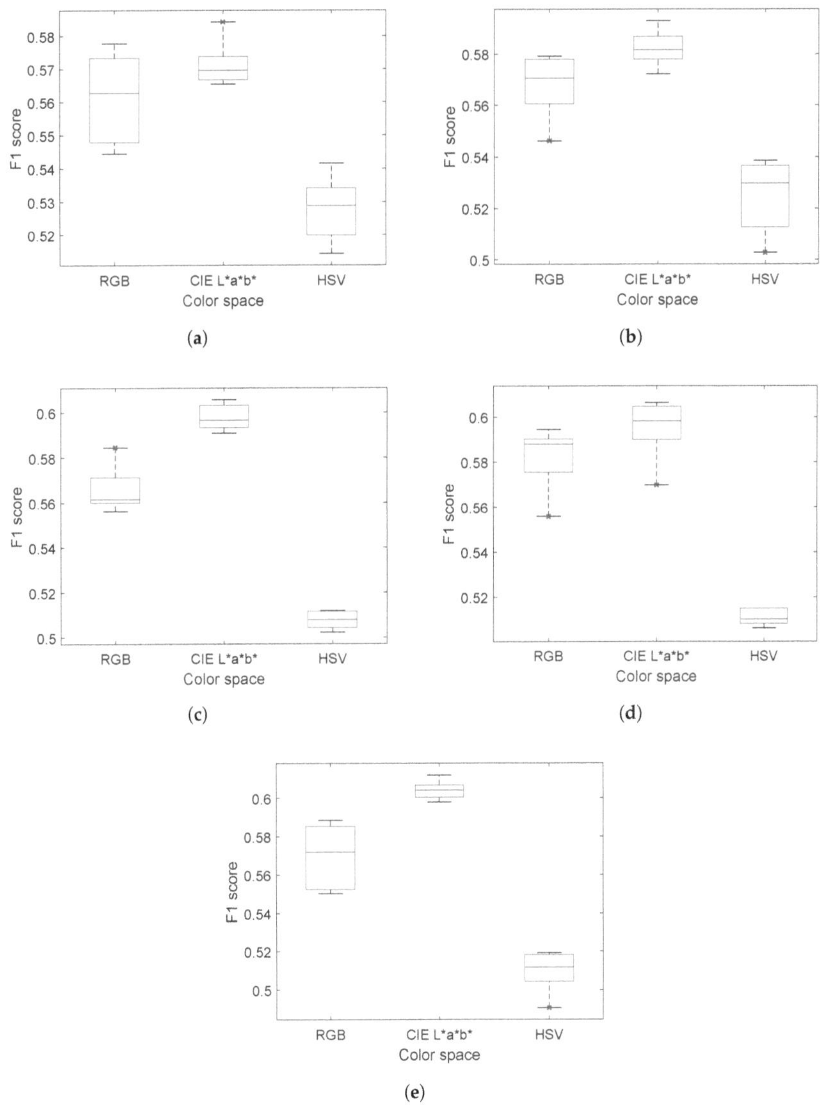

Figure 19. Boxplots of the F1-scores obtained in five experiments in each color space and in each of the following CDT structures: (**a**) CDTs with $s = 3$ and $d = 3$. (**b**) CDTs with $s = 5$ and $d = 4$. (**c**) CDTs with $s = 7$ and $d = 2$. (**d**) CDTs with $s = 9$ and $d = 2$. (**e**) CDTs with $s = 11$ and $d = 2$.

Subsequently, the one-way ANOVA test was performed to ascertain whether the differences between the means of the color spaces are statistically significant for each CDT structure. The p-values for these tests are also presented in Table 3. As these p-values were lower than the pre-determined significance level of $\alpha = 0.05$, it can be concluded that the differences observed between the means of some of the methods are indeed statistically significant.

Tukey's Honestly Significant Difference Procedure was employed as a post hoc multiple comparison test to ascertain which color spaces' means are distinct on each CDT structure since the ANOVA test rejected the null hypothesis that all the method means are equal. The test results are illustrated in Figure 20. Additionally, a spider graph is provided in Figure 21 to facilitate a visual representation of the performance on each color space. This graph considers the three analyzed color spaces (RGB, CIE L*a*b*, and HSV) and the different CDT structures outlined in Table 3. The value of 1 indicates that the color space has obtained the best segmentation result in the corresponding CDT structure. Conversely, the value of 0 indicates that the mean F1-score obtained by the color space is not the best in the corresponding CDT structure.

The following observations can be made with reference to Figures 20 and 21:

- For the CDT structures with kernel sizes 3, 5, and 9 in Figure 20a, 20b, and 20d, respectively, the differences between the RGB and CIE L*a*b* color spaces are not significant. In Figure 21, the RGB and CIE L*a*b* color spaces have a value of 1 in the corresponding CDT structures, indicating that the best segmentation results are achieved in these color spaces.
- For the CDT structures with kernel sizes of 7 and 11, significant differences are presented between the three color spaces in Figure 20a and 20b, respectively. The spider graph in Figure 21 shows that those CDT structures' best segmentation results are obtained in the CIE L*a*b* color space.
- In Figure 20, the means for the RGB and CIE L*a*b* color spaces are always significantly different from those of the HSV color space. This assertion can be made since the lines corresponding to the HSV color space are positioned more to the left on the horizontal axis and do not overlap with the lines corresponding to the other color spaces.
- These figures demonstrate the comparative superiority of the CIE L*a*b* color space over the other color spaces. As illustrated in Figure 20, in all the subfigures, the lines corresponding to the CIE L*a*b* color space are positioned more to the right on the horizontal axis. This finding indicates that optimal segmentation outcomes are attained within this color space. This is represented in Figure 21 since the CIE L*a*b* color space has a value of 1 in all the CDT structures.

These results demonstrate that a CDT induced with the information of the images in the CIE L*a*b* color space produces superior segmentation results in comparison to a CDT induced with information in other color spaces.

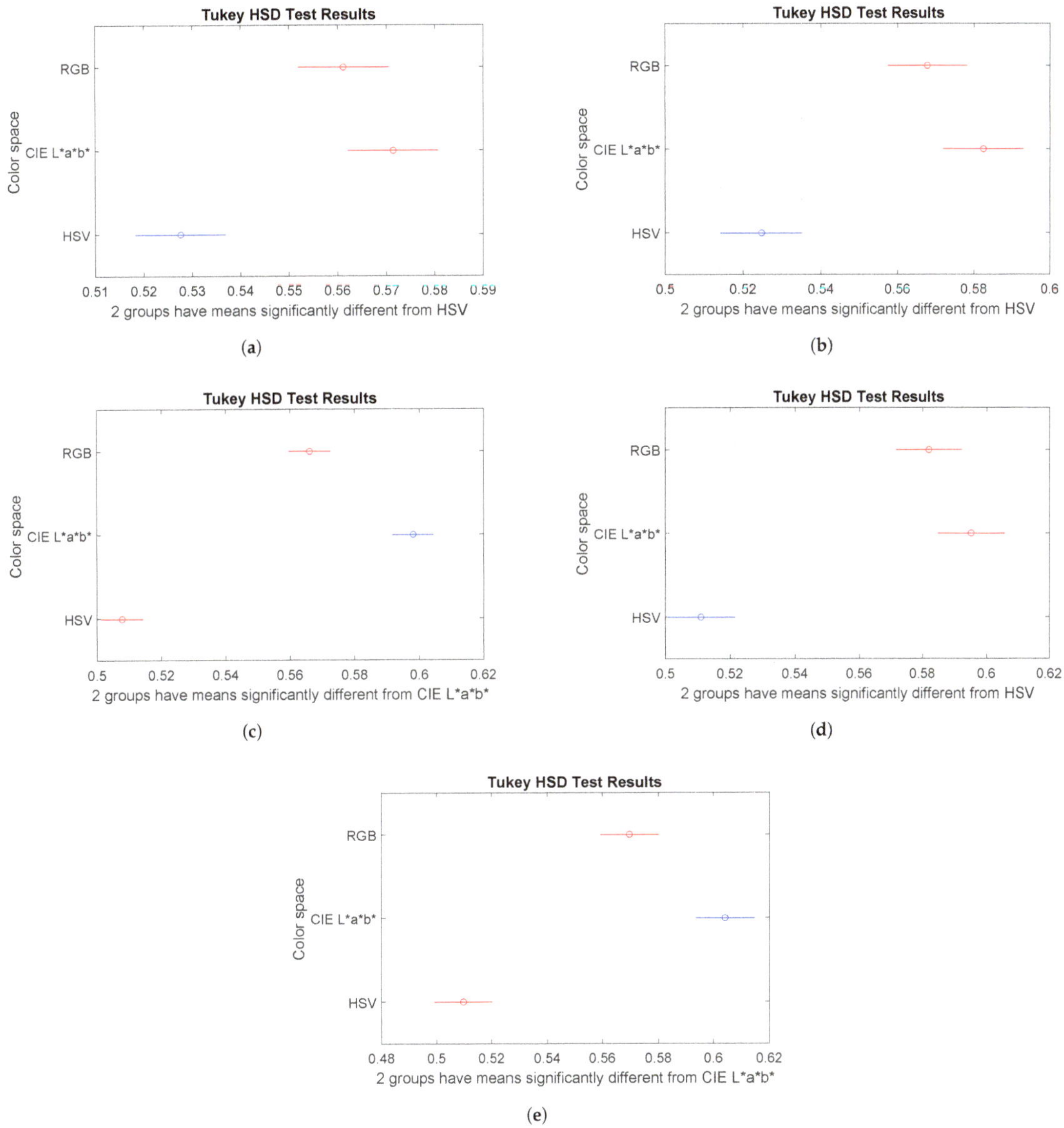

Figure 20. Multiple comparison test between the color spaces analyzed in each of the following CDT structures: (**a**) CDTs with $s = 3$ and $d = 3$. (**b**) CDTs with $s = 5$ and $d = 4$. (**c**) CDTs with $s = 7$ and $d = 2$. (**d**) CDTs with $s = 9$ and $d = 2$. (**e**) CDTs with $s = 11$ and $d = 2$.

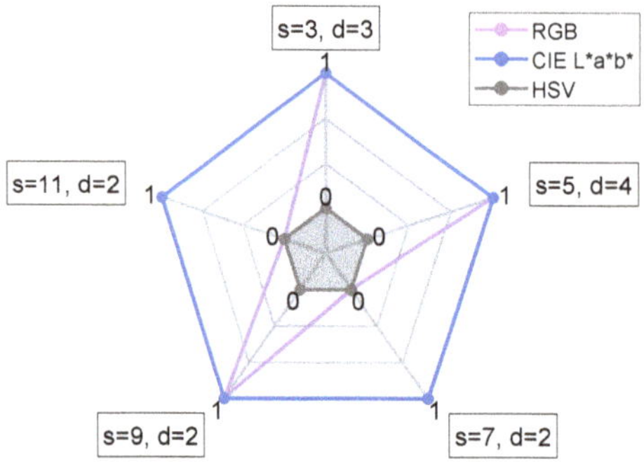

Figure 21. Spider graph of the results obtained with the three analyzed color spaces (RGB, CIE L*a*b*, and HSV) and the different CDT structures (kernel size s and depth d). Value 1 indicates that the color space has obtained the best segmentation result in the corresponding CDT structure. Value of 0 indicates the contrary case.

$SHADE\text{-}CDT$ vs. $SHADE\text{-}CDT_{color}$

A comparison of the results obtained with the $SHADE\text{-}CDT_{color}$ technique and those obtained with the $SHADE\text{-}CDT$ method is conducted in this study.

The best results reported in [10] per kernel size for the $SHADE\text{-}CDT$ technique are presented in Table 4. These results were documented following the implementation of a singular execution of the $SHADE\text{-}CDT$ technique. Given the absence of computational reduction approaches for the induction process, the volume of information for the training process was substantial. Consequently, multiple experiments with different kernel sizes and depths were not feasible, even when grayscale images were considered.

In the same Table 4, the best results with the $SHADE\text{-}CDT_{color}$ method are reported. These values were obtained from Table 3 considering the CIE L*a*b* color space with the corresponding CDT structure.

In both methods, the median selection technique was employed with a proportion of 0.3, and, for the SHADE algorithm, 100 individuals and a memory size of 100 were used. For the number of generations, 200 were considered for the $SHADE\text{-}CDT$ approach, while 100 were considered for the $SHADE\text{-}CDT$ method.

In Figure 22, a visual representation of the information in Table 4 is presented. The comparison between the F1-score and induction time results with each method ($SHADE\text{-}CDT$ and $SHADE\text{-}CDT_{color}$) is presented as a plot line, indicating the kernel size considered on each point.

As indicated in Table 4 and Figure 22, the precision values obtained with the $SHADE\text{-}CDT$ technique are lower than those obtained with the $SHADE\text{-}CDT_{color}$ method. In Table 4, the F1-scores in column 3 are less than 0.53, while the scores in column 5 are greater than 0.56, with some exceeding 0.6. This assertion is corroborated by Figure 22, which illustrates that the points representing the $SHADE\text{-}CDT$ method results are positioned more to the left along the horizontal axis, corresponding to the F1-score, in comparison to the points for the $SHADE\text{-}CDT_{color}$ method.

Table 4. The best results per kernel size using the *SHADE-CDT* approach in [10] for image segmentation on the Weizmann Horse dataset, and the corresponding CDT structure results employing the $SHADE\text{-}CDT_{color}$ technique in the CIE L*a*b* color space. In both methods, the median selection technique was employed with a proportion of 0.3, and, for the SHADE algorithm, 100 individuals and a memory size of 100 were used. For the number of generations, 200 were considered for the *SHADE-CDT* approach, while 100 were considered for the *SHADE-CDT* method.

CDT Structure		*SHADE-CDT*		$SHADE\text{-}CDT_{color}$	
s	*d*	F1-Score	Time (min)	F1-Score	Time (min)
3	4	0.4789	48.87	0.5689	18.25
5	4	0.4981	56.95	0.5930	20.13
7	4	0.5151	66.6	0.5865	23.15
9	2	0.5220	86.4	0.6042	17.8
11	2	Not available	Not available	0.6052	18.26

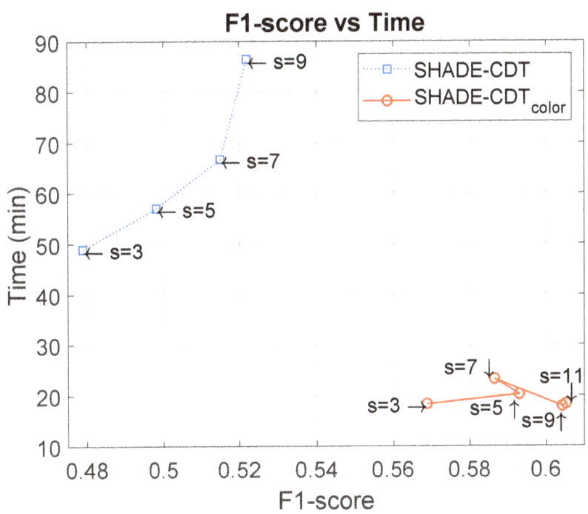

Figure 22. Plot line to compare the F1-scores and the induction time results with each method (*SHADE-CDT* and $SHADE\text{-}CDT_{color}$), indicating the kernel size *s* considered on each point.

Concerning the induction time, none of the experiments employing the $SHADE\text{-}CDT_{color}$ technique exceeded 24 min in execution, whereas the *SHADE-CDT* method reported execution times over 48 min for identical structures. This hypothesis is corroborated by Figure 22 since the points representing the *SHADE-CDT* method are located higher along the vertical axis, corresponding to the induction time, in comparison to the points for the $SHADE\text{-}CDT_{color}$ method.

It is important to note that the median selection technique and the modification in the SHADE process for the $SHADE\text{-}CDT_{color}$ technique have significantly reduced the learning process time and memory in experiments that utilize information from three color channels for induction. As demonstrated in Figure 22, the behavior of the induction time for the *SHADE-CDT* method appears to be exponential. In contrast, for the $SHADE\text{-}CDT_{color}$ method, the induction time is not as variable and is entirely dependent on the number of new individuals generated in the SHADE algorithm.

It is also noteworthy that the SHADE algorithm process involved 200 generations with the *SHADE-CDT* technique and only 100 generations with the $SHADE\text{-}CDT_{color}$ method. This discrepancy precludes a precise time induction comparison between the methods. In the following section, an accurate comparison of times will be performed in the experiments conducted with the DRIVE dataset, considering only the CIE L*a*b* color space.

It should be noted that experiments with kernels of size 11 are not documented in [10]. This is likely due to the computer specifications described in Table 2 being inadequate for executing the induction of CDT, or due to the experimental time required for these structures, even when grayscale images were considered. In contrast, the $SHADE\text{-}CDT_{color}$ method, in conjunction with the median selection technique, has yielded favorable outcomes for CDTs with kernels of size 11 and color images, requiring a small amount of time for the induction process.

3.2. Comparison of Induction Time and Precision with the DRIVE Dataset Considering the CIE L*a*b* Color Space

In this section, the "Retinal Vessel Segmentation" dataset was employed to analyze several CDT structures' induction times and performance with the $SHADE\text{-}CDT_{color}$ technique. This dataset comprises 20 retinal images with their corresponding segmentation masks or ground truths. The selection of these images was guided by the findings reported in [11], which detailed the segmentation outcomes obtained by applying the $SHADE\text{-}CDT$ method with the median selection technique to induce CDTs with this dataset.

Replicating the characteristics mentioned in [11] was considered in these experiments. Consequently, the resolution of the images, which previously was 565×584, was changed to 256×256. Furthermore, the same images utilized for the training and test sets in [11] were considered, with proportions of 70% and 30%, respectively. The parameter settings for the experiments are presented in Table 5. In this work, these values were applied to the $SHADE\text{-}CDT_{color}$ technique, considering 10 independent executions, enabling a comparison of the computational time for the induction by employing the median selection technique.

Table 5. Parameter settings for the $SHADE\text{-}CDT$ and $SHADE\text{-}CDT_{color}$ methods with the median selection technique.

Population Size NP	Number of Generations NG	Memory Size H	Kernel Size k	Tree Depth d	Proportion $\mathcal{P}$
100	200	100	5	2	0.3 (30%)

In Table 6, the outcomes of the image segmentation process utilizing both methodologies are presented. The results with the full training data ($SHADE\text{-}CDT_{full}$) and with the $SHADE\text{-}CDT$ method were obtained from [11].

Table 6. F1-score results and mean time obtained using the $SHADE\text{-}CDT$ technique with the full training set ($SHADE\text{-}CDT_{full}$), and with the $SHADE\text{-}CDT$ and $SHADE\text{-}CDT_{color}$ methods employing the median selection technique. The parameter values specified in Table 6 were employed for the three methods.

Method	Mean F1-Score ± St.D.	Mean Time
$SHADE\text{-}CDT_{full}$	0.6283 ± 0.0089	85.8 min
$SHADE\text{-}CDT$	0.6415 ± 0.0069	27.21 min
$SHADE\text{-}CDT_{color}$	0.5511 ± 0.0260	38.67 min

As demonstrated in Table 6, the findings reveal that, for a given CDT configuration (kernel size and depth), the time required to induce a CDT using the median selection technique, with images in a single color channel (grayscale images for the $SHADE\text{-}CDT$ technique) or three color channels (color images for the the $SHADE\text{-}CDT_{color}$ technique), is consistently less than the induction process that incorporates all the information of the grayscale images present in the training set ($SHADE\text{-}CDT_{full}$).

It is important to mention that, although the $SHADE\text{-}CDT_{color}$ technique increases the length of individuals and kernel weights by a factor of three for the SHADE algorithm, the induction time is not tripled compared to the $SHADE\text{-}CDT$ method. This is attributable to the incorporation of a memory of previously evaluated individuals, which reduces the number of evaluations in the fitness function.

Furthermore, experimentation with the $SHADE\text{-}CDT_{color}$ technique incorporating all the information of the color images present in the training set was not feasible with the computer available. Consequently, a direct comparison of the technique in three color channels with the full training data and the median selection technique, as in [11], was not possible.

As previously indicated, these experiments were conducted to analyze the computational time required for these processes, not the precision, given that the CDT induction using the $SHADE\text{-}CDT_{color}$ technique did not correspond to the ideal parameter values. Initially, the structure employed in [11] was used to compare the times for both techniques. So, to evaluate the precision of the CDT induced with the $SHADE\text{-}CDT_{color}$ technique, several experiments were performed considering different parameters for the SHADE algorithm, the CDT structure, and the proportion $\mathcal{P}$ for the median selection technique. The best results were obtained with CDTs induced with the parameters presented in Table 7.

Table 7. Best parameter settings found for the $SHADE\text{-}CDT_{color}$ method using the median selection technique to induce a CDT with the DRIVE dataset.

Population Size NP	Number of Generations NG	Memory Size H	Kernel Size k	Tree Depth d	Proportion $\mathcal{P}$
200	350	100	5	2	0.3 (30%)

A total of ten independent experiments were conducted to induce CDTs using the $SHADE\text{-}CDT_{color}$ technique, with the parameter values given in Table 7. The minimum, maximum, and mean ± standard deviation of the F1-scores obtained are presented in Table 8. The results obtained in [11] with the $SHADE\text{-}CDT$ technique using the parameter values in Table 5 are also reported in the same table to facilitate the comparison. The p-values obtained when performing the Shapiro–Wilk statistical test are included in both cases.

Table 8. Best results obtained with the $SHADE\text{-}CDT$ and $SHADE\text{-}CDT_{color}$ methods for the image segmentation of the images in the DRIVE dataset, with the parameter values presented in Tables 6 and 7, respectively.

Method	Min	Max	Mean ± St.D.	Time	p-Value (Shapiro–Wilk)
$SHADE\text{-}CDT$	0.6318	0.6502	0.6415 ± 0.0069	27.21 min	0.1650
$SHADE\text{-}CDT_{color}$	0.6468	0.6808	0.6608 ± 0.0141	131.54 min	0.0095

The Shapiro–Wilk statistical test was performed to verify the normal distribution on the F1-score results obtained in the ten executions of each of the two methods ($SHADE\text{-}CDT_{color}$ and $SHADE\text{-}CDT$). The p-values indicate that the distribution of F1-scores obtained with the $SHADE\text{-}CDT_{color}$ technique is non-parametric, so, in order to identify if the samples of both methods exhibit significant differences, the Mann–Whitney U test was conducted, obtaining a value of 0.0017. Since this p-value is lower than the significance level $\alpha = 0.05$, it is concluded that the difference between the two methods is significant.

So, it is accurate to assert that the $SHADE\text{-}CDT_{color}$ method, employing the median selection technique, yields superior outcomes compared to the $SHADE\text{-}CDT$ method, utilizing the same technique, when the induction parameters are calibrated. This assertion is substantiated by the median values of 0.6520 and 0.6392 for the $SHADE\text{-}CDT_{color}$ and $SHADE\text{-}CDT$ methods, respectively, and the means in Table 8.

Regarding temporal requirements, the $SHADE\text{-}CDT_{color}$ method necessitated a greater investment of time than the $SHADE\text{-}CDT$ approach. This is because the $SHADE$ algorithm process incorporates a population of 200 individuals and 350 generations in the first method as opposed to the 100 individuals and 200 generations employed in the second method. This suggests that there is a compromise between the temporal demands of the processes and their performance. Nevertheless, the induction times reported in this work are shorter than those documented in [6] and [7]. In those papers, the process required at least 12 hours of execution. This represents a significant and noteworthy enhancement regarding the CDT induction process.

4. Discussion

As reported in previous studies, the induction of CDTs for the segmentation task employs grayscale images and analytic or evolutive processes to perform local or global searches to obtain the kernels of the nodes of the CDTs, respectively [6,7,9–11]. The present study explores the integration of color images in the induction process of a CDT.

In this direction, three color spaces were employed in the initial stages of the investigation to establish the most effective channels for characterizing the colors of the images in the induction process. A comparison of the RGB, CIE L*a*b*, and HSV color spaces, three of the most relevant color spaces, was undertaken, and it was found that the CIE L*a*b* color space rendered the best three channels in all the experiments of induction of the CDTs considered (see Tables 2 and 3). Consequently, this color space was utilized to compare the outcomes obtained through the conventional induction of CDTs with grayscale images in a single channel and the proposed approach with color images and CDTs with three channels.

This study considered two types of analysis: one to analyze the execution time and the other to analyze the segmentation task's precision.

Regarding temporal considerations, the proposed methodology employs the median selection technique and a memory of previously evaluated individuals for the SHADE algorithm in the learning process. This modification reduces the number of individual evaluations and the time required to complete the induction process (see Table 6). The induction times reported in this study (with a maximum of 131.54 min for the induction process) are shorter than those previously reported in other studies (which involved 12 h of experimentation with lower F1-scores).

Regarding precision, the proposal enhances the F1-scores obtained for the Weizmann Horse and DRIVE datasets when considering the CIE L*a*b* color space and the appropriate parameter settings for the SHADE algorithm in the induction process (see Tables 4 and 8). These enhancements signify a substantial and noteworthy advancement in the CDT induction processes.

Regarding the so-called explainability of the CDTs, the structures proposed in this work have the same performance as the classical single-channel CDT structures. In the segmentation process, the information of each pixel of the image to be segmented passes through the classification process determined by the convolution on each node of the CDT, and its final label is obtained when the pixel reaches a leaf node. Thus, classifying a pixel with label 0 or 1 can be directly observed. It is also possible to characterize the pixels that reach the same leaf node of the CDT or to analyze why the F1-score values are high or low in different images. Appendix A shows some examples of analyses performed using the inherent explanatory power of the CDTs.

5. Conclusions and Future Work

This work proposes implementing and analyzing a color image segmentation algorithm based on CDTs using differential evolution. In this proposal, the SHADE algorithm was utilized in the learning process, where multiple individuals (CDTs) were randomly proposed and evolved to ascertain the weights of the CDT kernels, which were structured with three channels. The final CDT is the individual with the best F1-score in the training dataset.

The proposal further considers an analysis of three spaces of color to identify the one with the optimal structure for the CDT induction in three color channels, demonstrating the most favorable results in the CIE L*a*b* color space.

The results demonstrated the significance of considering the three color channels in the induction of CDTs, resulting in enhanced segmentation outcomes. The implementation of the median selection technique, in conjunction with the memory of previously evaluated individuals, exhibited a significant contribution, as evidenced by a substantial reduction in the computational time required for the induction process.

This study demonstrated that color characterization is a critical factor in enhancing the efficacy of the segmentation task performed with the induced CDTs since the precision increased by at least 8% between the experiments with grayscale and color images.

Future work will examine other color spaces, including L*C*h*, which have exhibited substantial outcomes in prior studies investigating color. Moreover, restricting the analysis to two channels and two-dimensional structures could be a viable approach to reduce computational time. Consequently, a thorough investigation into the two most representative channels for color space is warranted. Another approach that merits consideration is translating the color information to an optimal color space, where the pixels of the different classes (0 and 1) are separated by techniques such as Linear Discriminant Analysis. In addition, the performance of the CDT in comparison with other segmentation techniques that employ CNNs is proposed.

Author Contributions: Conceptualization, A.-L.L.-L., H.-G.A.-M., and E.M.-M.; Data curation, A.-L.L.-L.; Formal analysis, A.-L.L.-L.; Investigation, A.-L.L.-L.; Methodology, A.-L.L.-L., H.-G.A.-M., and E.M.-M.; Resources, A.-L.L.-L., H.-G.A.-M., and E.M.-M.; Software, A.-L.L.-L.; Supervision, H.-G.A.-M. and E.M.-M.; Validation, H.-G.A.-M. and E.M.-M.; Visualization, A.-L.L.-L.; Writing—original draft, A.-L.L.-L.; Writing—review and editing, A.-L.L.-L., H.-G.A.-M., and E.M.-M. All authors have read and agreed to the published version of the manuscript.

Funding: This research received no external funding.

Institutional Review Board Statement: Not applicable.

Informed Consent Statement: Not applicable.

Data Availability Statement: Data derived from public domain resources: the *Weizmann Horse dataset* from Kaggle at https://www.kaggle.com/datasets/ztaihong/weizmann-horse-database/data, and the *Digital Retinal Images for Vessel Extraction* (DRIVE) at https://drive.grand-challenge.org/DRIVE/ (accessed on 7 May 2025).

Acknowledgments: The first author acknowledges the Secretaría de Ciencia, Humanidades, Tecnología e Innovación (SECIHTI) of Mexico for the support provided through scholarship 712182, which was awarded for postdoctoral studies at the Artificial Intelligence Research Institute at the University of Veracruz.

Conflicts of Interest: The authors declare no conflicts of interest.

Abbreviations

The following abbreviations are used in this manuscript:

CNN	Convolutional Neural Network
CDT	Convolutional Decision Tree
DE	Differential Evolution
SHADE	Success-History-Based Adaptive Differential Evolution

Appendix A. Explainability in CDTs of Three Channels

The segmentation process performed with a CDT can be analyzed by following the partitions performed on each CDT node. This approach facilitates the analysis of the corresponding subsets, thereby enabling the determination of the characteristics the CDT identifies on each branch. In this section, a detailed description regarding explainability with the CDT with the best F1-score for the Weizmann Horse and DRIVE datasets is provided.

Appendix A.1. Weizmann Horse Dataset

The following description of results was conducted by considering the CDT induced with the best F1-score in Section 3.1, with a kernel size of 11 and a depth of 2 (refer to Table 2).

As illustrated in Figure A1, the considered CDT is displayed, with red, green, and blue borderlines denoting the three channels in the structure and a small square indicating the bias value. The left-hand branch is applied to pixels labeled 0 in the root node, while the right-hand branch is applied to pixels labeled 1.

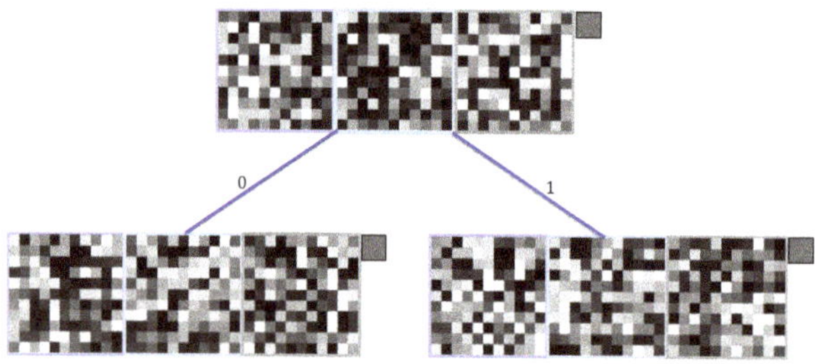

Figure A1. CDT induced to segment the images in the Weizmann Horse dataset.

In Figure A2, the best segmentation achieved on an image from the Weizmann Horse dataset is shown. It attains an F1-score of 0.9141. The partitions obtained on each node are displayed, with white representing the pixels labeled as the corresponding class. For instance, kernel 1 partitions the pixels into 0 and 1, where the background is labeled as 0 and depicted with the white pixels on the left branch, and the horse is labeled as class 1 and depicted with the white pixels on the right branch. The original image, its ground truth, and the segmentation obtained are shown on the right side.

As demonstrated in Figure A2, the first kernel performs a very good segmentation as the horse shape is clearly distinguishable on the pixels labeled as class 1. However, the subsequent investigation into the partitions of the following kernels suggests that certain regions of the horse's head, chest, and tail were erroneously classified as part of the background as their color is brighter than the typical brown hue of the horse. Kernel 2 detects these pixels and labels them as class 1. Conversely, kernel 3 does not appear to perform another partition as no pixels are labeled as class 0.

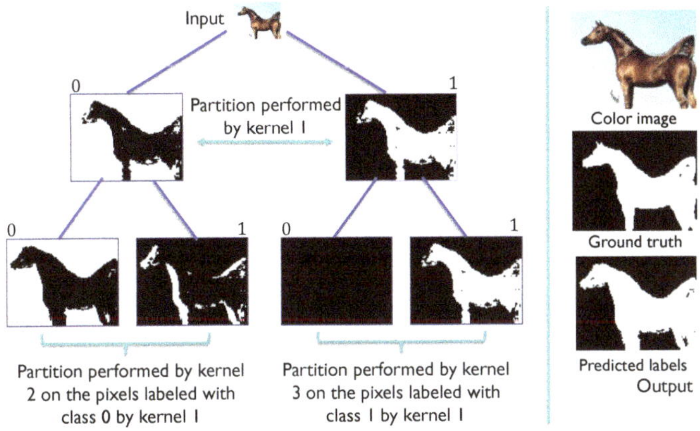

Figure A2. Best segmentation performed on an image from the Weizmann Horse dataset. The image on the left side of the figure displays the partitions that were performed on each node of the CDT. The image on the right presents the original image, its ground truth, and the segmentation obtained with the CDT.

In this instance, the objective of the partitions was to detect the brown pixels in the original image.

Figure A3 shows the worst segmentation of an image of the Weizmann Horse dataset (F1-score = 0.1076). In this case, the performance of kernel 1 is substandard as the pixels corresponding to the horse are labeled as class 0, along with the pixels corresponding to the ground, and remain in that class after passing through kernel 2. Conversely, the pixels representing the sky are classified as class 1.

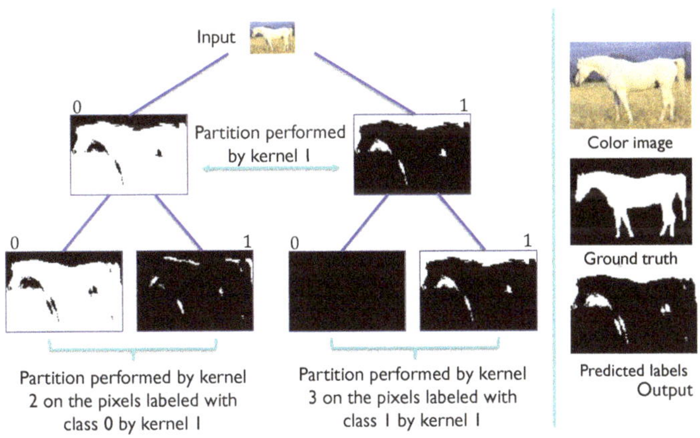

Figure A3. Worst segmentation performed on an image from the Weizmann Horse dataset. The image on the left side of the figure displays the partitions that were performed on each node of the CDT. The image on the right presents the original image, its ground truth, and the segmentation obtained with the CDT.

Figure A4 provides more in-depth insight into the process performed by the CDT. In this representation, the white regions of the horse are designated as class 0, while the darkest regions are labeled as class 1. Consequently, the CDT demonstrates effective segmentation in images depicting black and brown horses but exhibits suboptimal performance in images featuring light-colored horses. This hypothesis can be validated by analyzing the training dataset, which exhibits a paucity of light-colored horses.

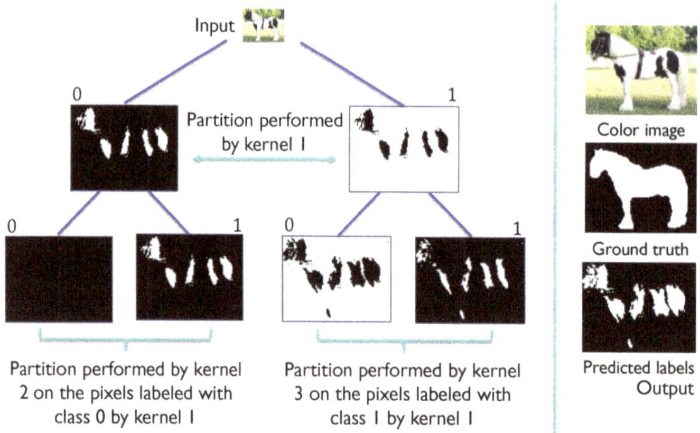

Figure A4. Analysis of segmentation on an image of the Weizmann Horse dataset. The image on the left side of the figure displays the partitions that were performed on each node of the CDT. The image on the right presents the original image, its ground truth, and the segmentation obtained with the CDT.

Appendix A.2. DRIVE Dataset

The following description of results was conducted by considering the CDT induced with the best F1-score in Section 3.2, with a kernel size of 5 and a depth of 2 (refer to Table 8).

In Figure A5, the CDT under consideration is displayed, with red, green, and blue borderlines denoting the three channels in the structure and a small square indicating the bias value.

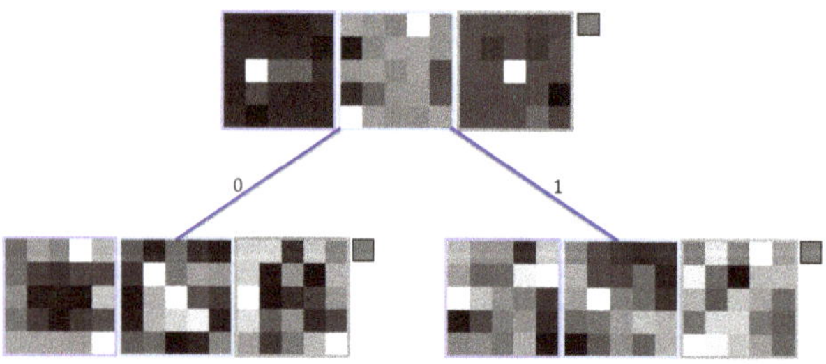

Figure A5. CDT induced to segment the images in the DRIVE dataset.

Figures A6 and A7 present the best and worst segmentation results on the images of the DRIVE dataset, respectively, with F1-scores of 0.7339 and 0.6085.

In these cases, it is evident that kernel 1 performs a partition that discriminates the interior and exterior of the retina, with subsequent kernels conducting the detailed classification of the veins. In particular, kernel 3 is responsible for the most detailed classification step. A subsequent analysis of the results reveals that the CDT consistently achieves lower F1-scores because the pixels designated as class 1 exceed the original number, as the CDT identifies all the veins in the retina, in contrast to the number identified in the ground truth.

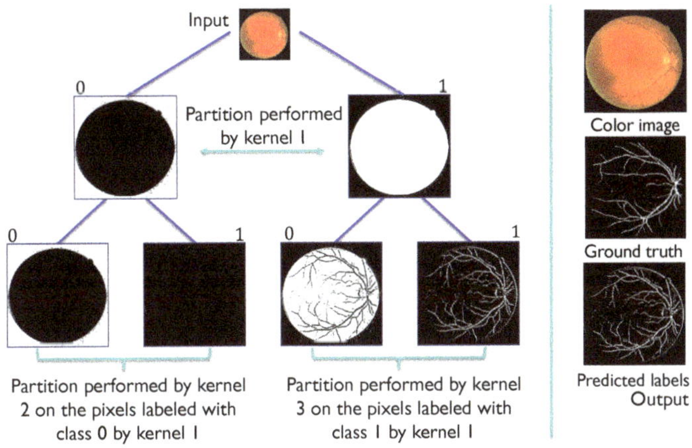

Figure A6. Best segmentation performed on an image of the DRIVE dataset. The image on the left side of the figure displays the partitions that were performed on each node of the CDT. The image on the right presents the original image, its ground truth, and the segmentation obtained with the CDT.

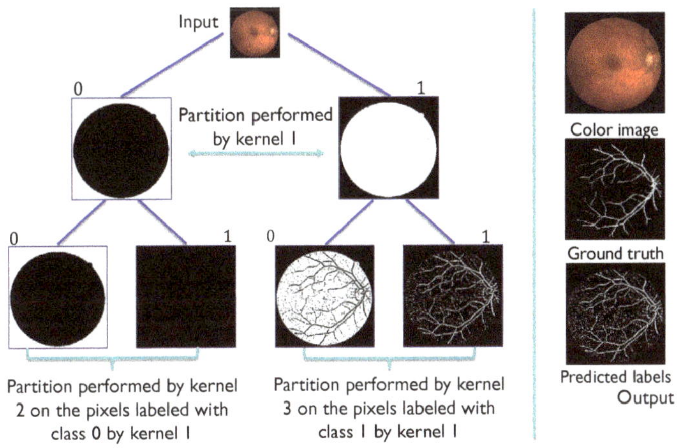

Figure A7. Worst segmentation performed on an image of the DRIVE dataset. The image on the left side of the figure displays the partitions that were performed on each node of the CDT. The image on the right presents the original image, its ground truth, and the segmentation obtained with the CDT.

Appendix A.3. Description and future analysis

In the context of performing segmentation of color images with CDTs, the structures exhibited in Appendices A.1 and A.2 appear to execute a binary classification of the two primary colors in the image on the root node. In the other leaf nodes, a characterization of subcolors present in the corresponding partitions is evident. This analysis provides a foundation for understanding the factors that contribute to suboptimal performance of CDTs on various images, as illustrated in Figures A3 and A7.

In addition, the analysis of sub-structures can be considered in future studies, as illustrated by the partition observed in Figure A8, where a liver is segmented with a CDT and the pixels from different leaf nodes are identified with different colors. This analysis will facilitate the observation and subsequent description of the various colorations present on the liver, with the intensity of color serving as a distinguishing feature. This approach will generate a model for identifying regions of interest that has the potential to contribute to several fields of science.

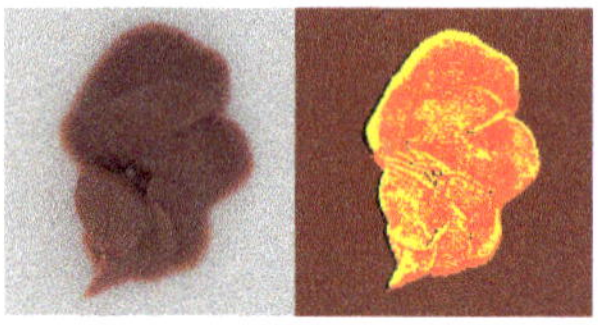

Figure A8. Segmentation of a liver image [23] performed with a CDT and considering the partition performed by branch, not for binary class.

Appendix B. Pseudocodes

The pseudocodes that describe the $SHADE\text{-}CDT_{color}$ method for CDT induction proposed in this paper are presented in this section to facilitate the reproducibility of the process.

Algorithm A1 delineates the median selection technique described in Section 2.2.2. Algorithm A2 details the process employed to classify the pixels of an image with a CDT encoded as a vector (*individual*) to obtain the corresponding CDT's fitness. This process is employed in the SHADE algorithm. Finally, the pseudocode of the $SHADE\text{-}CDT_{color}$ method is presented in Algorithm A3.

Algorithm A1: Median selection technique

Input: Dataset of color images CI and their corresponding ground truth images GT. The CDT structure parameters: kernel size s and depth d. The median selection technique parameter: proportion ρ.
Output: Matrix M with the vector representation associated with the pixels of CI and vector $labels$ with the real labels of the pixels.

// Initialization
Initialize matrix $M \leftarrow [\,]$;
Initialize vector $labels \leftarrow ()$;
Calculate $aux \leftarrow$ smaller integer that is nearest to $s/2$;
// Process
for *(image, ground truth image) in* (CI, GT) **do**
  Initialize matrixes M_{image}, M_1, $M_0 \leftarrow [\,]$;
  Initialize vector $labels_{image} \leftarrow ()$;
  Get $[rows, cols] \leftarrow$ image dimension;
  Set $row \leftarrow 1$;
  for $label \leftarrow 0$ **to** 1 **do**
    Find $indexes_{label} \leftarrow$ Set with the indexes (i, j) of the pixels of the *ground truth image* of class $label$, with $aux + 1 \leq i \leq rows - aux$ and $aux + 1 \leq j \leq cols - aux$;
    Calculate $NS_{label} \leftarrow$ Number of subsets for the partition of $indexes_{label}$ considering the smaller integer that is nearest to $|indexes_{label}| \cdot \rho$;
    Get $Partition_{label} \leftarrow$ Partition of the set $indexes_{label}$ with NS_{label} subsets of the same size if possible;
    for *subset in* $Partition_{label}$ **do**
      Get $vectors_{subset} \leftarrow$ Matrix of vectors associated with the pixels corresponding to the indexes in $subset$ as rows;
      Calculate $Median_{subset} \leftarrow$ median vector of $vectors_{subset}$ matrix;
      Set $M_{label}[row, :] \leftarrow Median_{subset}$;
      Set $row \leftarrow row + 1$;
    end
  end
  Get $M_{image} \leftarrow$ matrices M_1 and M_0 merged by rows;
  Get $labels_{image} \leftarrow$ vector with NS_1 values 1 and NS_0 values 0;
end
Get $M \leftarrow$ all matrices M_{image} merged by rows;
Get $labels \leftarrow$ all vectors $labels_{image}$ merged as vector;
Return: M, $labels$

Algorithm A2: F1-score of an individual (fitness)

Input: Matrix M with the pixel encodings as rows vectors and their corresponding $labels$. Vector $individual$ with the convolutional kernels of the CDT, and the kernel size s and depth d of the CDT.
Output: F1-score $fitness$ of the CDT decoded as $individual$.

```
// Initialization
```
Initialize list $kernels \leftarrow \{ \}$;
Initialize vector $labels_{predicted} \leftarrow ()$;
```
// Process
```
for $index \leftarrow 1$ **to** $(2^d - 1)$ **do**
  Set $kernels\{index\} \leftarrow$ first $(3s^2 + 1)$ elements of $individual$ vector;
  $individual \leftarrow$ remove the first $s^2 + 1$ elements of $individual$ vector;
end
Get $rows \leftarrow$ number of rows in M ;
for $i \leftarrow 1$ **to** $rows$ **do**
  Set $pixel \leftarrow i$-th row of matrix M;
  Set $current\ depth \leftarrow 1$;
  Set $index \leftarrow 1$;
  while $current\ depth \leq d$ **do**
    Set $Kernel \leftarrow kernels\{index\}$;
    Calculate $convolution \leftarrow$ dot product of the $pixel$ encoding and the $Kernel$;
    Calculate $\phi \leftarrow$ sigmoid of $convolution$ value;
    if $\phi \leq 0.5$ **then**
      Set $index \leftarrow 2 * index$
    else
      Set $index \leftarrow 2 * index + 1$
    end
    Set $current\ depth \leftarrow current\ depth + 1$;
  end
  if $index$ *is even* **then**
    $labels_{predicted}(pixel) \leftarrow 0$;
  else
    $labels_{predicted}(pixel) \leftarrow 1$;
  end
end
Set $fitness \leftarrow F1score(labels, labels_{predicted})$;
Return: $fitness$

Algorithm A3: $SHADE\text{-}CDT_{color}$ method (CDT induction with color images)

Input: Dataset of color images CI and their corresponding ground truth images GT. CDT structure parameters: kernel size s and depth d. SHADE parameters: population size NP, number of generations NG, memory size H, and fitness function f. Median selection technique parameter: proportion ρ.
Output: $individual_{best}$ with the kernel values of the CDT with the best F1-score value $fitness_{best}$.

```
// Initialization
```
Generate $population \leftarrow NP$ vectors of size $(3s^2 + 1) * (2^d - 1)$ with random values chosen from -255 to 255;
```
// Process
```
Get $[M, labels] \leftarrow$ training dataset M and its corresponding $labels$ vector generated with the median selection technique applied to CI and GT, with parameters s, d, ρ;
Get $[individual_{best}, fitness_{best}] \leftarrow$ by applying the SHADE algorithm to the $population$, with the parameters NG, H, and F1-score as fitness function f, considering the memory of previously evaluated individuals described in Section 2.5 (see Figure 17);
Return: $individual_{best}, fitness_{best}$

References

1. Patil, D.D.; Deore, S.G. Medical image segmentation: A review. *Int. J. Comput. Sci. Mob. Comput.* **2013**, *2*, 22–27.
2. Zhu, C.; Ni, J.; Li, Y.; Gu, G. General tendencies in segmentation of medical ultrasound images. In Proceedings of the 2009 Fourth International Conference on Internet Computing for Science and Engineering, Harbin, China, 21–22 December 2009; IEEE: Piscataway, NJ, USA, 2009; pp. 113–117.
3. Lateef, F.; Ruichek, Y. Survey on semantic segmentation using deep learning techniques. *Neurocomputing* **2019**, *338*, 321–348. [CrossRef]
4. Minaee, S.; Boykov, Y.; Porikli, F.; Plaza, A.; Kehtarnavaz, N.; Terzopoulos, D. Image segmentation using deep learning: A survey. *IEEE Trans. Pattern Anal. Mach. Intell.* **2021**, *44*, 3523–3542. [CrossRef] [PubMed]
5. Molnar, C. *Interpretable Machine Learning: A Guide for Making Black Box Models Explainable*, 2nd ed. Available online: https://christophm.github.io/interpretable-ml-book (accessed on 15 April 2025).
6. Laptev, D.; Buhmann, J.M. Convolutional decision trees for feature learning and segmentation. In Proceedings of the German Conference on Pattern Recognition, Munster, Germany, 2–5 September 2014; Springer: Cham, Switzerland, 2014; pp. 95–106.
7. Barradas Palmeros, J.A.; Mezura Montes, E.; Acosta Mesa, H.G.; Márquez Grajales, A.; Rivera López, R. Induction of Convolutional Decision Trees with Differential Evolution for Image Segmentation. In Proceedings of the Congreso Mexicano de Inteligencia Artificial, Guadalajara, Mexico, 30 May–3 June 2023; Volume 8.
8. Eiben, A.E.; Smith, J.E. *Introduction to Evolutionary Computing*; Springer: Berlin/Heidelberg, Germany, 2015.
9. López-Lobato, A.L.; Acosta-Mesa, H.G.; Mezura-Montes, E. Blood Cell Image Segmentation Using Convolutional Decision Trees and Differential Evolution. In *Advances in Computational Intelligence. MICAI 2023 International Workshops, Proceedings of the WILE 2023, HIS 2023, and CIAPP 2023, Yucatan, Mexico, 13–18 November 2023*; Springer Nature: Cham, Switzerland, 2024; pp. 315–325.
10. López-Lobato, A.L.; Acosta-Mesa, H.G.; Mezura-Montes, E. Induction of Convolutional Decision Trees with Success-History-Based Adaptive Differential Evolution for Semantic Segmentation. *Math. Comput. Appl.* **2024**, *29*, 48. [CrossRef]
11. López-Lobato, A.L.; Acosta-Mesa, H.G.; Mezura-Montes, E. Computational Time Reduction in the Induction of Convolutional Decision Trees. In *Advances in Computational Intelligence. MICAI 2024 International Workshops, Proceedings of the HIS 2024, WILE 2024, and CIAPP 2024, Tonantzintla, Mexico, 21–25 October 2024*; Martínez-Villaseñor, L.; Ochoa-Ruiz, G.; Montes Rivera, M.; Barrón-Estrada, M.L.; Acosta-Mesa, H.G., Eds.; Springer: Cham, Switzerland, 2025; pp. 99–111.
12. Storn, R.; Price, K. Differential evolution-a simple and efficient heuristic for global optimization over continuous spaces. *J. Glob. Optim.* **1997**, *11*, 341–359. [CrossRef]
13. Price, K.; Storn, R.M.; Lampinen, J.A. *Differential Evolution: A Practical Approach to Global Optimization*; Springer Science & Business Media: Berlin/Heidelberg, Germany, 2006.
14. Ahmad, M.F.; Isa, N.A.M.; Lim, W.H.; Ang, K.M. Differential evolution: A recent review based on state-of-the-art works. *Alex. Eng. J.* **2022**, *61*, 3831–3872. [CrossRef]
15. Zhang, J.; Sanderson, A.C. JADE: Adaptive differential evolution with optional external archive. *IEEE Trans. Evol. Comput.* **2009**, *13*, 945–958. [CrossRef]
16. Tanabe, R.; Fukunaga, A. Success-history based parameter adaptation for differential evolution. In Proceedings of the 2013 IEEE Congress on Evolutionary Computation, Cancun, Mexico, 20–23 June 2013; IEEE: Piscataway, NJ, USA, 2013; pp. 71–78.
17. Tanabe, R.; Fukunaga, A.S. Improving the search performance of SHADE using linear population size reduction. In Proceedings of the 2014 IEEE Congress on Evolutionary Computation (CEC), Beijing, China, 6–11 July 2014; IEEE: Piscataway, NJ, USA, 2014; pp. 1658–1665.
18. Phuangsaijai, N.; Jakmunee, J.; Kittiwachana, S. Investigation into the predictive performance of colorimetric sensor strips using RGB, CMYK, HSV, and CIELAB coupled with various data preprocessing methods: A case study on an analysis of water quality parameters. *J. Anal. Sci. Technol.* **2021**, *12*, 1–16. [CrossRef]
19. Korifi, R.; Le Dréau, Y.; Antinelli, J.F.; Valls, R.; Dupuy, N. CIEL* a* b* color space predictive models for colorimetry devices–Analysisof perfume quality. *Talanta* **2013**, *104*, 58–66. [CrossRef] [PubMed]
20. Vodyanitskii, Y.N.; Kirillova, N. Application of the CIE-L* a* b* system to characterize soil color. *Eurasian Soil Sci.* **2016**, *49*, 1259–1268. [CrossRef]
21. Cuevas, E.; Zaldívar, D.; Pérez-Cisneros, M. *Procesamiento Digital de Imágenes Usando Matlab & Simulink*; Alfaomega: Ciudad de Mexico, Mexico, 2010; Volume 479,

22. Borenstein, E.; Sharon, E.; Ullman, S. Combining top-down and bottom-up segmentation. In Proceedings of the 2004 Conference on Computer Vision and Pattern Recognition Workshop, Washington, DC, USA, 27 June–2 July 2004; IEEE: Piscataway, NJ, USA, 2004; p. 46.
23. Herrera-Sánchez, D.; Acosta-Mesa, H.G.; Mezura-Montes, E.; Herrera-Meza, S.; Rivadeneyra-Domínguez, E.; Zamora-Bello, I.; Almanza-Domínguez, M.F. Imaging Estimation for Liver Damage Using Automated Approach Based on Genetic Programming. *Math. Comput. Appl.* **2025**, *30*, 25. [CrossRef]

Mathematical and Computational Applications

MDPI

Article

Multiple-Feature Construction for Image Segmentation Based on Genetic Programming

David Herrera-Sánchez [1], José-Antonio Fuentes-Tomás [1], Héctor-Gabriel Acosta-Mesa [1,*], Efrén Mezura-Montes [1] and José-Luis Morales-Reyes [2]

1 Artificial Intelligence Research Institute, University of Veracruz, Xalapa 91097, Mexico; hersan19@hotmail.es (D.H.-S.); josefuentes.at@gmail.com (J.-A.F.-T.); emezura@uv.mx (E.M.-M.)
2 Centre for Food Research and Development, University of Veracruz, Xalapa 91190, Mexico; jluismorey@hotmail.com
* Correspondence: heacosta@uv.mx

Abstract

Within the medical field, computer vision has an important role in different tasks, such as health anomaly detection, diagnosis, treatment, and monitoring medical conditions. Image segmentation is one of the most used techniques for medical support to identify regions of interest in different organs. However, performing accurate segmentation is difficult due to image variations. In this way, this work proposes an automated multiple-feature construction approach for image segmentation, working with magnetic resonance images, computed tomography, and RGB digital images. Genetic programming is used to automatically create and construct pipelines to extract meaningful features for segmentation tasks. Additionally, a co-evolution strategy is proposed within the evolution process to increase diversity without affecting segmentation performance. The segmentation is addressed as a pixel classification task; in this way, a wrapper approach is used, and the classification model's segmentation performance determines the fitness. To validate the effectiveness of the proposed method, four datasets were used to measure the capability of the proposal to deal with different types of medical images. The results demonstrate that the proposal achieves values of the DICE similarity coefficient of more than 0.6 in MRI and C.T. images. Additionally, the proposal is compared with *SOTA* GP-based methods and the convolutional neural networks used within the medical field. The method proposed outperforms these methods, achieving improvements greater than 20% in DICE, specificity, and sensitivity. Additionally, the qualitative results demonstrate that the proposal accurately identifies the region of interest.

Keywords: image segmentation; genetic programming; multiple-feature construction

1. Introduction

Computer vision has been an important and relevant tool within the medical field. The capabilities of computer vision systems that involve images play an important role in clinical care and treatment. Also, these systems can support medical staff and decision-making, particularly for personnel with limited experience. Furthermore, medical images can effectively help doctors evaluate the size of different disease tumors and analyze the images obtained before and after treatment. Numerous approaches for different tasks have been developed over the last several years, such as image classification [1–6], image segmentation [7–12], and image estimation [13]. These tasks involve medical imaging, and typically, the images used are obtained via Magnetic Resonance Imaging (MRI), X-ray, and Computerized Tomography (C.T.) [14]. Working with medical imaging, grayscale images are commonly used because most medical image acquisition systems naturally produce grayscale output based on intensity values corresponding to tissue density or signal response [15]. The grayscale comprises an image where each pixel can take a value between 0 and 255. The lowest value (0) represents black, and the highest (255) represents white.

The segmentation process separates an image into representative regions according to certain criteria shared in a specific area. It differentiates digital image pixels belonging to an object from those corresponding to the background [7]. Image segmentation has several grades of complexity according to the different coarse and fine granularities of segmentation [3]. The lowest complexity is the semantic segmentation, where each pixel has a label that determines whether it belongs to the object [16], also known as binary segmentation. For example, the task is to identify an object from the rest of the image. The medium complexity is the instance segmentation, which allocates a pixel label for objects and separates them from each other; in other words, it separates the per-object mask and localizes varying numbers of instances presented in the image [17], for example, when identifying cars in traffic, each vehicle has its own label. The highest complexity is panoptic segmentation, which generalizes and combines instance segmentation and semantic segmentation. The task is to identify individual objects and their backgrounds, for example, to identify trees in a landscape and also the sky or the ground [18].

To perform these tasks adequately, the object/interest region needs to be separated from the background, which is not an easy task. Firstly, one of the most common issues is the low quality or noise within the images caused by the acquisition of the source device. In this way, noise can influence determining which region belongs to the background and the Region Of Interest (ROI). Secondly, determining which techniques or functions of image processing are the most adequate to perform the segmentation requires expertise.

Several approaches have been proposed within the *state of the art*. The well-known convolutional neural networks are the most popular deep learning models, such as U-net [9] and U-net++ [19]. These architectures are relevant within the medical field, which is the interest of this research. Despite the good performance of these models, designing and implementing them requires knowledge about artificial neural networks. Additionally, they are known as "black boxes", and the big models lack information about how they perform tasks, making it difficult for humans to analyze and interpret the procedure. However, several efforts have been reported in the area of evolutionary computation (EC), specifically within the field of Genetic Programming (GP) for image classification and segmentation, where the approaches work as "white boxes" [20].

In this way, this work proposes an automated approach for multiple-feature construction for medical image segmentation. Based on Darwin's metaphor, evolutionary computation is employed to perform a guided search for selecting image processing functions such as filters, morphological operators, and pixel operations, which modify the raw data until meaningful features are extracted. Selecting by hand the set of functions for feature extraction in the images requires effort and is time-consuming. In contrast, the automated approach for multiple-feature construction significantly reduces processing time, improves efficiency and precision, and allows for adaptation using different images. For this reason, the automated approach for multiple-feature construction saves time in the trial and error phases.

The proposed approach, Genetic Programming Multiple-Image Feature Construction (GP-MIFC), extracts five different features from the raw images, and then the segmentation is performed as a pixel classification task. In this way, a classification model is employed in the pipeline. The contributions of this research can be summarized as follows:

- Multiple features are constructed independently from the raw grayscale images.
- A co-evolution strategy is adapted to evolve five different populations, and each one constructs a feature used for the segmentation step.
- The binarization for segmentation is performed as a pixel classification task using an Iterative Dichotomiser 3 (ID3) classifier [21].
- Images are segmented from different acquisition systems such as Computed Tomography (C.T.), Magnetic Resonance Imaging (M.R.I.), and digital images.

2. Background and Related Work

2.1. Basics of Genetic Programming

GP is a paradigm of EC known for evolving computer programs. It has gained relevance in recent years due to its capability to deal with problems in different research areas mainly due to its flexibility to adapt problems to tree representations, including complex functions or computer programs. Additionally, it enhances the transparency of the solutions, making them more *interpretable* for humans. Each solution is easy to replicate via analysis. Furthermore, unlike other optimization techniques based on the gradient, GP can be optimized in non-differentiable or discontinuous functions. GP can be considered as an automated learning method—the evolutionary process supports the automatic search.

The paradigm of GP is based on Darwin's evolutionary theory, where a population of programs (individuals) lives within a specific environment. Within this environment, the individuals contend among themselves, and those that perform better according to the environmental conditions are selected for reproduction. This selection process ensures that the individuals with the highest fitness and who are most capable of solving problems have a high probability of producing offspring.

The offspring inherit features from their parents with some variations. Through generations, the offspring will be able to adapt to the environment, ensuring that future generations evolve to solve problems. To determine which individuals are the most promising for solving problems, an evaluation process is performed to assess their aptitude. The individuals are then selected to create new individuals. The fitness function assesses each individual and assigns a corresponding performance score according to how well the individual solves the problem.

The evolutionary process involves two selection mechanisms. First, the individuals are evaluated and selected as potential individuals to generate offspring through crossover and mutation operators. These are responsible for exploring the search space by introducing variations and maintaining diversity within the population. The other selection step is performed during the replacement strategy to determine which individuals will remain in the population and survive for the next generation. This way, the crossover and mutation operators introduce new solutions along the evolution process. The evolutionary process can be observed within Figure 1.

John Koza proposed GP [22], where the individual is represented as a tree. Other approaches of GP have arisen, such as Cartesian Genetic Programming (CGP) [23], Grammar-Guided Genetic Programming (GG-GP) [24], and Linear Genetic Programming (LGP) [25]. For our work, we use tree-based GP. As part of the representation, trees contain internal and leaf nodes, and the length and size of the trees can be different.

Considering the representation, the nodes in the tree can be functions, variables, and constants. The internal nodes can be used to implement and represent a computational program, arithmetic functions, or another function the programmer implements as needed. On the other hand, the leaf nodes always contain variables and constants. The scope of our method is to make a feature extraction and construction from the images. In this way, the set of functions to construct the individuals correspond to image processing filters, pixel operations, and morphological operators. According to the aforementioned, the leaf nodes correspond to the raw image data for our implementation, acting as the individuals' inputs. The final result is the set of functions used to extract the most representative information to perform the segmentation.

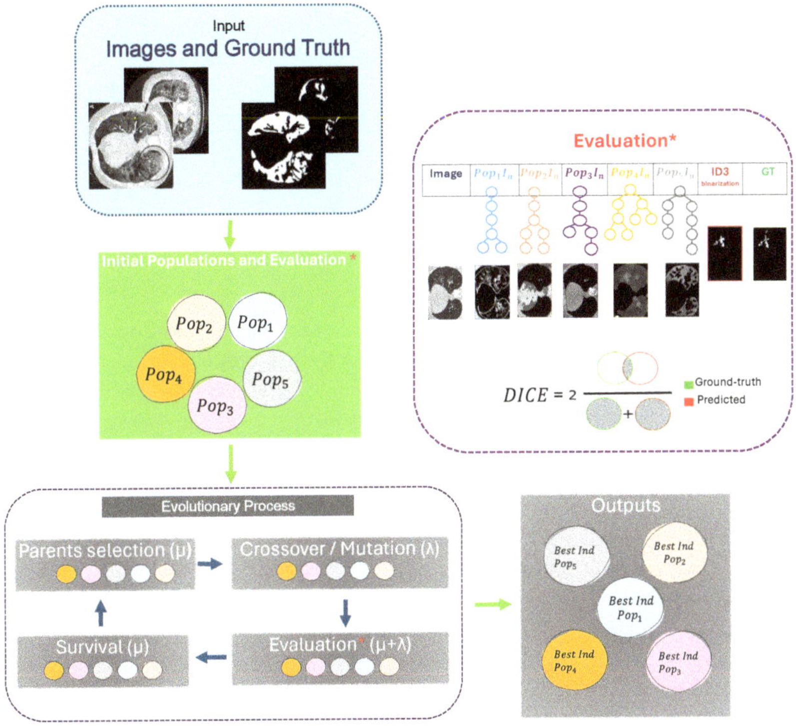

Figure 1. General workflow of GP-MIFC.

2.2. GP for Feature Construction and Image Segmentation

GP has also been applied in image segmentation tasks. StronglyGP, CoevoGP, and TwostageGP methods are proposed in [26], employing preprocessing and postprocessing techniques, such as histogram equalization and morphological operations. In [27,28], a semi-automatic method transforms a segmentation problem into a classification problem by taking sub-images of the test image. They use Gabor features, extraction, feature construction, and a voting scheme to generate the segmented image. Ref. [29] uses GP to construct a model to measure the blurriness of pixels using a linear binary pattern along with high-frequency multiscale fusion and sort transform (HiSFT) with different window sizes. Then, an adaptive threshold based on a support vector machine generates the segmented image. Using smoothing and edge detection operators, a speckle noise-reduction model based on GP is proposed in [30]. Moreover, the authors propose a fitness function to prevent the uncontrolled height of trees. The Kartezio method [31] leverages the interpretability of CGP [23] to evolve image pipelines employing 42 operators and trained with limited data.

M2GP [32] is a wrapper-based multidimensional feature transformation method for multiclass classification. It employs a root node as a collector of tree-based GP solutions, each representing the attributes transformed to a scalar. Therefore, each individual is described as a set of d-evolved transformations. To overcome the fixed d hyperparameter, the M3GP method [33] adapts the number of dimensions of the evolved feature transformations. The M4GP [34] method employs a stack-based representation. It encodes each GP solution with a postfix notation, allowing multiple outputs without specialized instructions. Recent works have aimed to develop parallelizable models capable of running on GPUs [35] and multi-objective approaches [36] that consider the structural complexity of the trees in addition to the classification performance.

Despite the demonstrated applicability of GP in image segmentation [26–28], most existing methods rely on preprocessing techniques for feature extraction as well as threshold-based and if–then rules for pixel classification. In addition, it has been observed that employing multi-tree-structured [32–36] solutions can lead to a collection of evolved feature transformations, improving future learned representations. However, its applications have been limited to tabular data classification and regression tasks. Our proposal focuses on the image segmentation task, employing a set of domain spatial functions and a simple co-evolution approach.

3. The Proposed Approach

Considering the importance of segmentation tasks within the medical field, our method leverages the tree-based representation of genetic programming, where more than one tree can be generated and evolved to construct and extract more efficient features to perform segmentation tasks. Additionally, our method addresses the segmentation task as a form of pixel classification. In this way, a classifier is used instead of classical techniques such as Otsu or threshold binarization methods. To perform the segmentation, it is necessary to work with the original image and the image already segmented by an expert, also known as Ground Truth (G.T.).

In this manner, we can asses the performance of each individual at the binarization/segmentation step. The proposal uses a wrapper method where the learning algorithm's performance is used as the evaluation criterion.

Typically, the evolution process involves only one population to evolve. The result from the evolution returns only one individual with the highest fitness according to the metric used during evaluation.

Our method evolves simultaneously and in isolation into five populations. Each population returns one pipeline containing the necessary functions for the feature extraction/construction of the raw grayscale images. These five features are fed into the classifier to perform the pixel classification. Each featured image is converted to a column vector to match the pixel label for the ROI in the G.T. Figure 1 shows the framework of the segmentation based on the features constructed by GP.

First, the data used contain the original images in grayscale. Then, the evolution process includes five populations. The five initial populations are generated using the *Full* method [22]. This method randomly produces individuals with the same depth in all branches. Then, the five populations are evaluated as if they were one population. For each population, one individual is taken and performs the feature construction/extraction in the images. Then, after processing the images with the functions for each individual, they are converted into a feature vector, where each pixel has its own label.

At this stage, six features are considered for the classifier model. The first is the original grayscale image, and the rest correspond to each feature constructed for each individual selected from the five populations.

The fitness of those individuals is shared among them, i.e, individual 1 in population one shares the same fitness as individual 1 in the other populations.

At this point, the way they are paired for the evaluation and fitness sharing is based on the index of the initial population. The order across populations during the evolution is static, meaning that the individuals keep the same index and remain consistent across generations.

The variation operators, such as crossover and mutation, are performed internally in each population. The $\mu + \lambda$ strategy is adopted into our approach. μ represents the number of individuals to select for the next generation during the evolutionary process, while λ is the number of offspring to generate each generation. This ensures that at the time of evaluation, the offspring for the five populations will be the same number of new individuals.

The final result of the evolutionary process is the best individual for each population. The five individuals contain the set of functions of image processing that help the classifier to perform the segmentation. The GP-MIFC pseudocode is shown in Algorithm 1.

Algorithm 1 GP-MIFC algorithm

Input: Grayscale images
Output: Five individuals, one from each population, with image processing functions for segmentation

$G \leftarrow 0$;
$P_{i_G} \leftarrow$ Initialize five populations $\mathcal{P}_1, \mathcal{P}_2, \ldots, \mathcal{P}_5$ using the *Full* method by Koza [22], each with $\mu = 100$ individuals;
for *each population* $\mathcal{P}_{i_G}$ **do**
  Select one individual I_i from $\mathcal{P}_{i_G}$;
  Apply I_i to the images to extract features (image processing functions);
  Construct a per-pixel feature vector with six features:;
    - Original grayscale image;
    - One feature extracted by each individual I_i from populations $i = 1$ to 5;
  Evaluate the classifier's performance (segmentation model);
  Assign the same fitness score to individuals $I_1, I_2, \ldots, I_5$;
end
while $G <$ *Max Generations* **do**
  for *each population* $\mathcal{P}_{i_G}$ **do**
    $O_j \leftarrow$ Generate $\lambda = 50$ offspring using crossover and mutation within $\mathcal{P}_{i_G}$;
    for *j in* O_j **do**
      Select a set of individuals $Inew_1, \ldots, Inew_5$);
      Apply them to the images to extract features;
      Build the feature vector and evaluate the classifier;
      Assign the fitness score to O_j (shared across all positions);
    end
    Combine parents and offspring: $\mathcal{P}_{i_G} \cup \lambda_i$;
    Select the best $\mu = 100$ individuals to form the next generation $\mathcal{P}_{i_G}$;
  end
  $G \leftarrow G + 1$;
end
Select the best individual from each population as the final result;

3.1. Representation

As mentioned earlier, the representation used throughout our proposal is trees and five populations within the evolutionary process. The tree-based representation of individuals contains functions, and the leaf nodes involve the variables, which correspond to grayscale images. We use this representation because of its ability to efficiently perform the co-evolution. Also, it is easy to interpret and replicate the pipeline of image processing functions.

Figure 2 shows the individual tree representation.

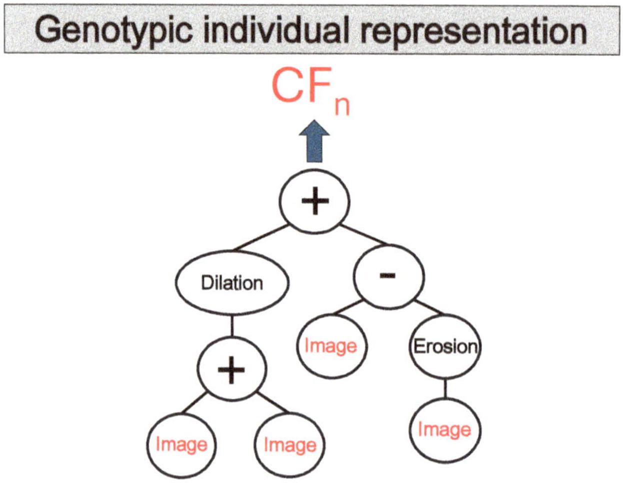

Figure 2. Individual representation.

3.2. Function and Terminal Set

The set of functions used in GP-MIFC is listed in Table 1. The function set is divided into pixel, filter, and morphological operation, as suggested in [8].

Table 1. Function set and terminal definitions used in the Genetic Programming framework.

Function	Definition
Addition	Pixel-wise summation: $I(x,y) + I(x,y)$. Useful for combining two images.
Subtraction	Pixel-wise difference: $I(x,y) - I(x,y)$. Highlights contrast.
Erosion	Morphological operation that removes pixels on object boundaries.
Dilation	Morphological operation that adds pixels to object boundaries.
Opening	Erosion followed by dilation, removes small objects/noise.
Closing	Dilation followed by erosion, fills small holes.
Mask (from [8])	Thresholding function: sets pixel to 0 if $I(x,y) <$ threshold.
Gaussian Filter	Smoothes the image using a Gaussian kernel to reduce noise.
Canny Edge Detector	Detects edges based on gradient magnitude.
Gabor Filter	Detects texture patterns using sinusoidal functions modulated by Gaussian.
Invert Values	Transforms intensity: $\|255 - I(x,y)\|$ to highlight complementary features.
	Terminal Set
Grayscale Image (Im)	Input 2D grayscale image used as the terminal node in the tree.

The pixel operation only considers the pixel value, and the neighborhood is discarded. Each new value depends on the original pixel value in the same position. The new values are calculated following $f[I(x,y)] \rightarrow I'(x,y)$. The arithmetic operation functions, such as addition, subtraction, mask [8], and invert values, are used as pixel operations. The addition and subtraction work as a feature construct function. They can mix different features from different filters used in the same image.

The filter functions include the Gaussian and Canny using the default parameters [37]. Gabor filters can take one of five possible frequency values: 0.2, 0.4, 0.6, and 0.8. Likewise, for orientation degrees, one of the following is taken: $15^\circ, 30^\circ, 45^\circ, 75^\circ$, and 90°.

Morphological operators included are *opening*, *closing*, *erosion*, and *dilation*. The structure element employed for operation is a disk using a kernel size of 7×7 pixels. It is known that morphological operators work well with grayscale and binary images.

The unique terminal used is called *Im*. It contains the input for the individual, which is the grayscale image.

3.3. Fitness Function

The proposal focuses on the segmentation task; the most important metric is the DICE coefficient. This metric evaluates the model's performance on pixel classification in the test set of images and is assigned to individuals. Another reason to use this metric is that it performs well for binary classification and can deal with unbalanced data. Additionally, it is the most common metric used for segmentation. The DICE coefficient is expressed by

$$DICE = \frac{2TP}{2TP + FP + FN} \tag{1}$$

where TP is the total of true positives, FN is the total of false negatives, and FP is the total of false positives. The value 0 indicates that the segmentation is poor, and the maximum value of 1 indicates that the segmentation is excellent.

In medical image segmentation, the interpretation of the value of DICE varies according to the images and the difficulty in distinguishing the ROI by humans in different anatomic structures [38]. Typically, working with RMI images and CT, a 0.6 value of the metric DICE can be categorized as satisfactory, especially due to the visual features that can be complex and require major effort to segment. Additionally, in sample visualization, comparing the annotation by the expert with the prediction by the segmentation allows for avoiding a statistical bias [38]. Values higher than 0.7 of DICE can be categorized as good and excellent segmentation, respectively.

Supporting the above, suppose that the ROI of the image covers 100 pixels (G.T.) and the result of the segmentation gives the following values for TP = 50 (pixels correctly segmented), FP = 50 (pixels wrongly segmented), and FN = 50 (pixels not segmented that belong to the ROI). Applying the metric, the value of DICE is 0.5.

Another segmentation case takes the following values: TP = 50, FP = 0, and FN = 50; additionally, the value of the metric DICE is ≈ 0.67. In both cases, the TP was 50, which means that 50% of the ROI was correctly segmented. However, it does mean that 50% correctly segmented is equal to 0.5 of the DICE metric.

4. Experimental Design

4.1. Parameter Settings and Experiment Configuration

The number of populations used within the co-evolution process was fixed to 5. The objective was to create five features from the raw images instead of only one from the typical evolution process. Five populations are enough to give the necessary information to the classifier model and cover the search space, whereas only one population does not cover it. Additionally, including more than five populations represents consuming more computational resources. The time to construct a feature was multiplied by the number of populations evolved.

The five populations used the same terminals and function, and the primitives gave the search space. At this point, we could not ensure that the final solutions for each population were completely orthogonal. The same parameters were also applied for the five populations, all listed in Table 2. In this way, the objective was to explore the search space in different regions, not other search spaces. This is why each population evolved independently, and only the fitness was shared among the individuals according to the initial index. Even though the five populations used the same functions, different regions could be explored by the randomness of the initialization populations and the variation operators applied separately on each population. This allowed each population to explore different regions of the search space.

The parameter settings for each population were set as follows. Considering the number of evolved individuals in preliminary research [8] and based on the performance obtained given the experimentation research, our method also used the same parameters of 100 generations and 100 individuals for each population. The $\mu + \lambda$ values were set to 100 and 50, respectively.

Additionally, the crossover and mutation rates were set to 0.75 and 0.25. The crossover operator was *one-point*, and mutation was the *uniform* [22]. The maximum and minimum depths of the initial trees were set to 15 and 5, respectively. The tournament was the selection method with a size of 5 individuals.

Table 2. Configuration details for the Genetic Programming (GP) setup.

Parameter	Value	Description
Number of generations	100	Total evolutionary iterations.
Population size	100	Number of solutions.
Initialization strategy	Full method	Same depth in each branch
Min/Max tree depth	5–15	Defines the range of depth for the expression trees used in evolution.
Selection strategy	Tournament (size = 5)	Selects the fittest individual among five randomly chosen candidates.
Crossover probability	0.75	Probability of recombining subtrees from two parents during evolution.
Mutation probability	0.25	Probability of randomly modifying a subtree to introduce variation.
Reproduction strategy	$(\mu, \lambda) = (100, 50)$	Evolutionary strategy where 50 children are created from a parent population of 100.

The model classifier that performed the segmentation throughout the pixel classification was the ID3 decision tree. The maximum depth was set to 5 to avoid overfitting. As part of the wrapper approach, the datasets were split into training and test sets, 70% and 30%, respectively.

The proposal was implemented in Python 3, using DEAP [39], OpenCV [40], Scikit-image [37], and Scikit-learn [41] libraries. The experimentation was performed on a server with 64 Intel Xeon Silver 4216 2.1 GHz CPU's, 264 GB of memory, and Linux OS. The GP-MIFC was run 10 times for each dataset due to the limited time available on the server, and each execution took more than 5 h. The executions were carried out in a serial configuration.

4.2. Benchmark Datasets

In this paper, we evaluate the performance of the proposed method using four medical datasets. The datasets were selected according to the objective of dealing with different modalities of medical images, such as C.T., MRI, and digital images from cameras. The first dataset is the COVID-19 dataset [42], which contains the computed tomography of lungs affected by COVID-19 with the corresponding mask. This dataset contains 100 images with the corresponding G.T.

The second and third datasets are DRIVE [43] and ISIC [44], which contain 20 and more than 1200 color images, respectively. Finally, the fourth dataset, Intracranial Hemorrhage (MRI-IH) [45], contains MRI. This dataset includes more than 2000 slices of images of brain MRI; however, only 318 MRI images contain the G.T. For experimentation only, 100 images were used for each dataset, except for DRIVE (it only contains 20 images). In the case of those datasets that contain more than 100 images, the selection was performed randomly with different seeds to ensure a fair comparison with other methods. The reason for using only 100 images was to save computational resources. This configuration and seeds are also used for benchmark methods.

4.3. Benchmark Methods

The proposal was compared with four methods. Two of them are based on Genetic Programming. The first one is *StronglyGP*, and the second is *TwoStageGP*, both taken from [26]. *StronglyGP* highlights using the updated version of GP where the set of functions are typed according to a certain type of data. *TwostageGP* evolves two subpopulations, where the first one uses grayscale images, which are then binarized, in such a way that the second one employs binary image operators.

On the other hand, the well-known CNN's U-net [9] and U-net++ [19] were used to compare our method. Each model considered a maximum number of 500 epochs using an early stopping strategy with 10 tolerance epochs to save computational cost, and the learning rate was 1×10^{-4}.

5. Results and Discussion

This section is divided into two subsections. Section 5.1 refers to the results of the proposed method evaluated in different datasets and briefly discusses the performance achieved. In Section 5.2, we compare our method with *SOTA* methods in the datasets mentioned above.

5.1. Performance for Each Dataset

Table 3 and Figure 3 show the performance statistics of GP-MIFC corresponding to different datasets. The listed values correspond to the performance in the test set. The dataset where GP-MIFC performs better is in the COVID-19 and DRIVE datasets, achieving median values of more than 0.74 of DICE. The dataset where GP-MIFC performs badly is with MRI-IH, achieving mean and median values lower than 0.35 regarding the DICE metric. The best value of segmentation is for the COVID-19 dataset, with a DICE value of 0.81. On the other hand, the worst proposal performance is in the MRI-IH, with a DICE value of 0.31.

Table 3. Performance of GP-MIFC in four datasets.

	DICE Performance in Datasets			
Statistic	**COVID-19**	**ISIC**	**DRIVE**	**MRI-IH**
Best	0.81	0.78	0.74	0.56
Worst	0.71	0.71	0.24	0.31
Mean	0.75	0.75	0.58	0.44
Median	0.74	0.76	0.65	0.43
Std. Dev.	0.02	0.03	0.18	0.09

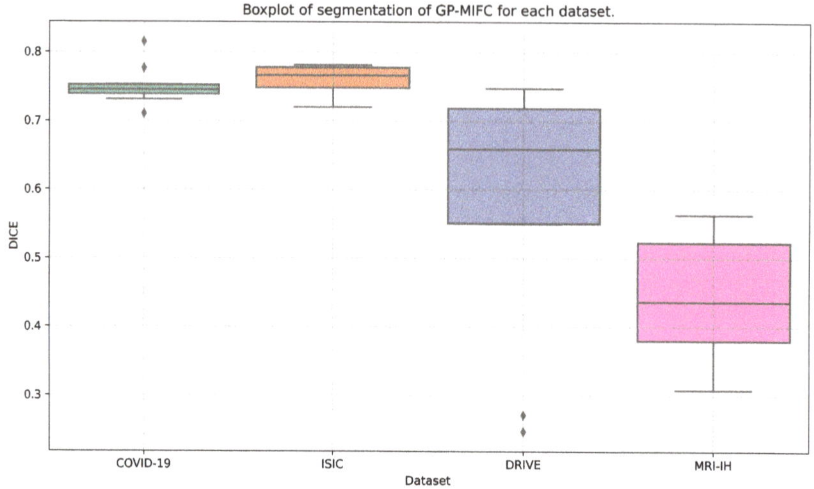

Figure 3. Boxplot of segmentation performance from GP-MIFC for each dataset.

Figure 4 shows four examples of the results obtained from the five best individuals after the evolution process. The original image is also considered a feature for the pixel classification made by the ID3. FC_1, FC_2, FC_3, FC_4, and FC_5 are the image features constructed/extracted according to the individual, which contains the pipeline for the image processing.

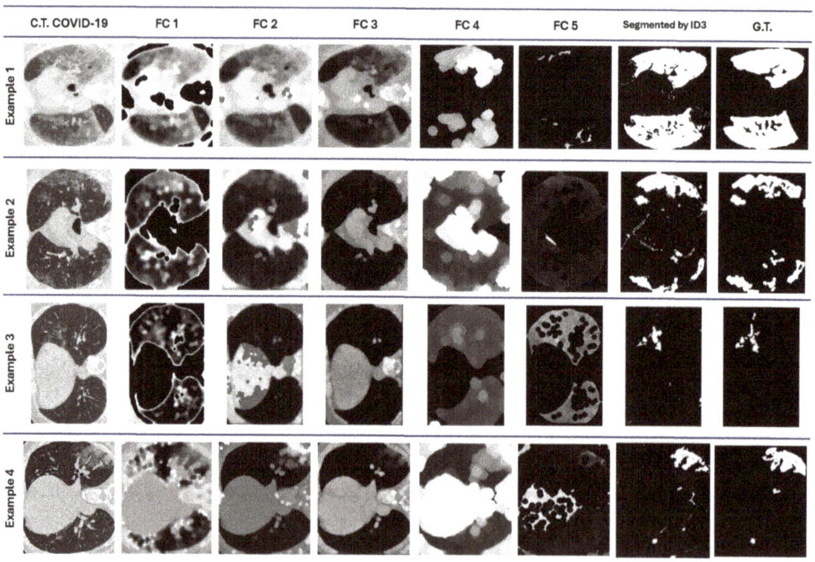

Figure 4. COVID-19 dataset results. The first column contains the original images. $FC_{1...5}$ are the images processed by each best individual for each evolved population. The ID3 column contains the images segmented by the model at the pixel level. The G.T. column contains objective images.

We can observe that comparing qualitative results in Figure 4 with the quantitative performance with DICE in Table 3 demonstrates that the ROI is marked successfully in some cases, such as in examples 1 and 3. However, in examples 2 and 4, some regions are also marked as ROI even though they are not.

For the performance of the ISIC dataset, the best DICE value achieved is 0.78, and the worst is around 0.72. However, according to the DICE metric, the mean and median are greater than 0.76. The standard deviation demonstrates that the GP-MIFC performs more stably with COVID-19, MRI-IH, and ISIC datasets. Two datasets correspond to C.T. and MRI sources, where, naturally, the images are in grayscale. However, in the ISIC dataset, the algorithm is also stable. The algorithm works without outliers with images originally in grayscale, such as the MRI-IH dataset. It is well known that moving from RGB colors to grayscale results in information loss. As mentioned in [1], the color gives more information as part of the features related to the image content. Surprisingly, the RGB DRIVE dataset achieves values that are higher than 0.65, but it also shows a higher standard deviation than in the grayscale datasets.

For the DRIVE dataset, the mean and median are 0.58 and 0.65, respectively, and the best and worst values obtained are 0.747 and 0.24, respectively. This dataset's mean and median results are higher than the MRI-IH dataset.

Finally, in the MRI-IH, the algorithm performance achieves a mean and median value of 0.44 and 0.43, respectively. This dataset was the most challenging part of the proposal. The best value achieved is the lowest compared to the other datasets, with only a 0.56 DICE value. Also, it has the second-lowest value for the worst performance in the different datasets. The visual results with this dataset are shown in Figure 5. In example 1, the segmentation results show some regions marked as ROI, according to the G.T. Examples 3 and 4 show a good visual performance. However, some regions are discarded and include areas that do not correspond to the ROI.

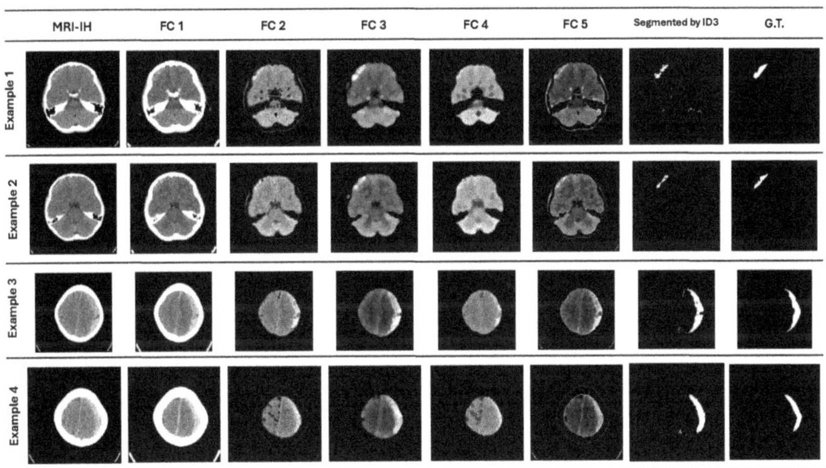

Figure 5. MRI-IH dataset results. The first column contains the original images. $FC_{1...5}$ are the images processed by each best individual for each evolved population. The ID3 column contains the images segmented by the model at the pixel level. The G.T. column contains objective images.

The variability among the segmentations by the model and the G.T. given by an expert can be high, mainly due to human bias. This can be attributed to the fact that human segmentations may be influenced by the expert's experience with a specific imaging modality and their individual visual perception. The variability is present in both cases, in humans and computer programs. The results demonstrate that the variability of our method is present in different percentages according to the dataset.

The significant variability is present in the DRIVE dataset, where some outliers exist and correspond to the worst and lowest values. As we can observe in Figure 3, the MRI-IH dataset reflects the difficulty for our method to perform the segmentation, where the ROIs are small regions that are hard to segment.

Regarding ISIC and COVID-19 datasets, the distribution is lower. However, the COVID-19 dataset has some outliers.

Figure 3 demonstrates the variability, which is highly related to the image complexity of each dataset.

5.2. Comparison with Benchmark Methods

Given the results obtained regarding segmentation quality, a comparison was made between the proposed algorithm and other *state-of-the-art* methods designed for image segmentation. Two of these methods follow the genetic programming approach, both taken from [26]: StronglyGP and TwostageGP. These were considered in the comparison due to their recent development and the fact that they were tested on various image datasets, obtaining competitive results. It is worth noting that both algorithms were configured using the parameters reported in [26].

On the other hand, the comparison also includes two well-known methods used for medical image segmentation: the convolutional neural networks U-Net [9] and U-Net++ [19]. Table 4 reports the median values for each method compared. Each method was executed 10 times. The values marked with ↑ for only the DICE metric indicate the best result, according to the Mann–Whitney U statistical test with a 95% confidence level. The results for the metrics specificity (SPC), sensitivity (SEN), and Hausdorff Distance are also reported in detail. The highest median values for each method and metric are highlighted in bold.

Table 4. Comparison with benchmark methods for each dataset. The values reported correspond to the medians of ten executions.

Dataset	Method	DICE	SPC/SEN	HD
COVID-19	GP-MIFC	**0.74** ↑	0.95/**0.80**	**7.90**
	StronglyGP	0.40	**0.96**/0.33	2045.26
	TwostageGP	0.45	0.89/0.48	16,233.66
	Unet	0.43	0.91/0.63	2300.48
	Unet++	0.54	0.95/0.71	2091.99
ISIC	GP-MIFC	**0.76** ↑	0.90/**0.85**	**126.39**
	StronglyGP	0.23	0.63/0.19	1680.96
	TwostageGP	0.45	0.81/0.40	1851.13
	Unet	0.19	0.78/0.27	948.09
	Unet++	0.32	**0.90**/0.34	2157.25
DRIVE	GP-MIFC	**0.65** ↑	0.95/**0.87**	**9.01**
	StronglyGP	0.54	0.93/0.53	2087.34
	TwostageGP	0.44	**0.96**/0.31	2697.37
	Unet	0.10	0.91/0.51	1152.01
	Unet++	0.15	0.91/0.66	980.59
MRI-IH	GP-MIFC	**0.43** ↑	0.99/**0.81**	**3.93**
	StronglyGP	0.13	0.99/0.07	2650.29
	TwostageGP	0.16	0.98/0.11	2542.92
	Unet	0.10	0.99/0.05	2337.89
	Unet++	0.10	0.99/0.05	2396.68

Figure 6 contains a radar chart for each dataset, where the benchmark methods are compared with our method GP-MIFC in terms of DICE, specificity, and sensitivity metrics.

For the first dataset containing COVID-19 images, GP-MIFC showed favorable results regarding segmentation performance. As seen in Table 4, the values achieved are outstanding compared to the other methods. Regarding StronglyGP, its performance was not favorable due to its use of Otsu's method for binarization, which led to less competitive segmentation in a portion of the images. In contrast, TwostageGP achieved better performance than StronglyGP.

The performance of the CNNs is also noteworthy, with UNet++ reaching a value of 0.54038. UNet++ outperformed UNet, TwostageGP, and StronglyGP, but not GP-MIFC. Visually, the results do not clearly show the affected lung area, as some final images appear completely dark.

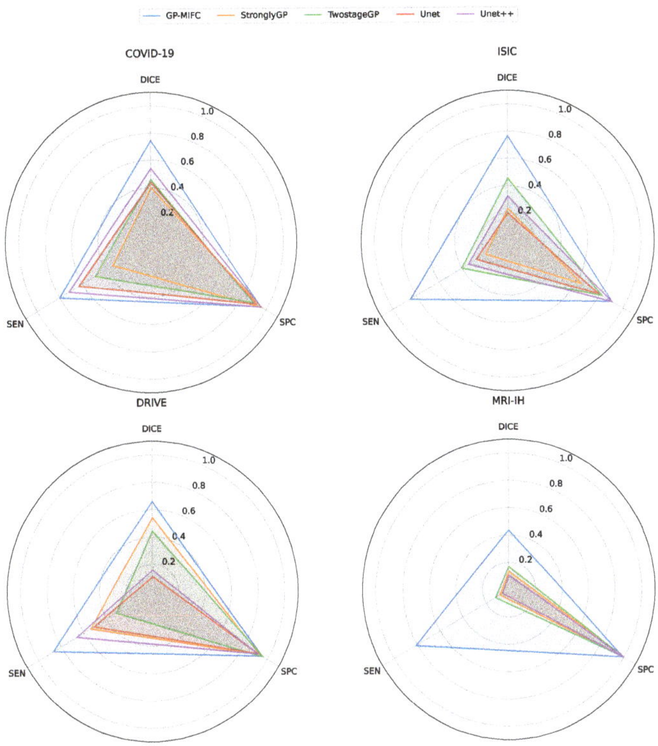

Figure 6. Radar chart for median performance comparison with benchmark methods. Each axis represents a metric. The greater the area covered by the line, the better the performance.

The proposed algorithm significantly outperformed the other algorithms in the ISIC dataset. The second-best performance was obtained by TwostageGP, which benefits from applying certain operations and filters in the first stage and then processing the already-binarized image in the second stage. The performance of UNet and UNet++ was unfavorable; although some of the resulting images visually resemble the target image, the DICE metric indicates otherwise.

The third dataset used for comparison is DRIVE. For GP-MIFC, both visual- and segmentation-level performances were favorable. The method achieved a DICE score above 0.60, surpassing the other methods. Interestingly, the genetic programming-based methods performed more competitively than the CNNs. For this dataset, StronglyGP outperformed TwostageGP. The CNNs showed poor segmentation performance and visual interpretation of the resulting images.

Lastly, none of the comparison methods reached a DICE value of 0.2 for the MRI-IH dataset. Even GP-MIFC did not perform as well on the other datasets. Moreover, due to the nature of the images, accurately identifying the hemorrhage area is challenging, as it represents a very small portion of the entire image. Despite this challenge, GP-MIFC still achieved a meaningful level of performance compared to the other methods, with some resulting images clearly showing the area of interest. This was not the case for the other methods, which failed to approach the target image.

Based on the results and comparisons between all methods, it is evident that the proposed GP-MIFC algorithm performs competitively compared to *state-of-the-art* methods. Additionally, the visual perception of the resulting images allows for the easy identification of the area of interest, making this tool capable of constructing the necessary features to perform accurate segmentation. Figure 7 shows the comparison results with benchmark methods in the four datasets.

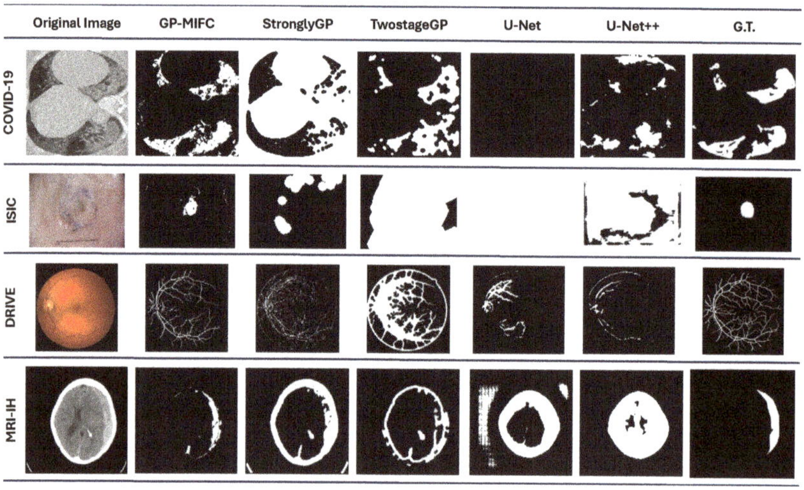

Figure 7. Comparison results with the benchmark methods in four datasets.

6. Conclusions

Based on the results obtained in this work, it is clear that the capability of evolutionary algorithms can achieve competitive results. Although they do not guarantee finding the optimal solution, they offer one or more solutions that can effectively address the problem. In this work, genetic programming provided the opportunity to create solutions using programs and image processing functions to perform the feature construction process, enabling adequate segmentation of the ROI and demonstrating competitiveness compared to various current algorithms that tackle the segmentation problem.

In this work, the design of the GP-MIFC algorithm, which performs automatic feature construction to achieve competitive segmentation and identify the ROI in the images, was presented. The proposed method achieved competitive values, with segmentation performance exceeding 0.7 regarding the DICE metric. Moreover, the ROI was identified clearly and concisely.

With the obtained results, comparisons were made with other *SOTA* methods that perform the image segmentation task. Two of them were based on genetic programming, and the remaining two were based on convolutional neural networks.

Part of our future work is to use the updated version of GP, Strongly Genetic Programming, to include the classifiers within the individual. Additionally, strategies such as surrogate models or inheritance can speed up the image processing during individual evaluation since the evolutionary process takes a long time. It is important to consider reducing the computational cost without affecting the segmentation performance. Future research would be appropriate to explore changing the search space for each population, modifying the primitive set for each, and using different parameters for the variation operators to ensure orthogonality across the final co-evolution solutions.

Author Contributions: Conceptualization, D.H.-S., J.-A.F.-T., H.-G.A.-M., E.M.-M. and J.-L.M.-R.; methodology, D.H.-S., J.-A.F.-T., H.-G.A.-M., E.M.-M. and J.-L.M.-R.; software, D.H.-S.; validation, D.H.-S., J.-A.F.-T., H.-G.A.-M., E.M.-M. and J.-L.M.-R.; formal analysis, D.H.-S., J.-A.F.-T., H.-G.A.-M. and E.M.-M.; investigation, D.H.-S.; resources, D.H.-S., J.-A.F.-T., H.-G.A.-M. and E.M.-M.; data curation, D.H.-S.; writing—original draft preparation, D.H.-S.; writing—review and editing, D.H.-S., J.-A.F.-T., H.-G.A.-M., E.M.-M. and J.-L.M.-R.; visualization, D.H.-S.; supervision, D.H.-S., J.-A.F.-T., H.-G.A.-M. and E.M.-M. All authors have read and agreed to the published version of the manuscript.

Funding: This research received no external funding.

Data Availability Statement: The data are available in references [42–45].

Acknowledgments: The first and second authors acknowledge support from Secretaría de Ciencia, Humanidades, Tecnología e Innovación (SECIHTI) of Mexico, through scholarships to pursue graduate studies at the University of Veracruz.

Conflicts of Interest: The authors declare no conflicts of interest.

Abbreviations

The following abbreviations are used in this manuscript:

MRI	Medical Resonance Imaging
CT	Computerized Tomography
EC	Evolutionary Computation
GP	Genetic Programming
GP-MIFC	Genetic Programming Multiple-Image Feature Construction
CGP	Cartesian Genetic Programming
GC-GP	Grammar-Guided Genetic Programming
LGP	Linear Genetic Programming
MRI-IH	Medical Resonance Imaging–Intracranial Hemorrhage
G.T.	Ground Truth
ROI	Region Of Interest
CNN	Convolutional Neural Network

References

1. Herrera-Sánchez, D.; Acosta-Mesa, H.G.; Mezura-Montes, E.; Márquez-Grajales, A. Shifting Color Space for Image Classification using Genetic Programming. In Proceedings of the GECCO 2024 Companion—Proceedings of the 2024 Genetic and Evolutionary Computation Conference Companion, Melbourne, VIC, Australia, 14–18 July 2024; pp. 283–286. [CrossRef]
2. Ling, Y.; Wang, Y.; Dai, W.; Yu, J.; Liang, P.; Kong, D. MTANet: Multi-Task Attention Network for Automatic Medical Image Segmentation and Classification. *IEEE Trans. Med. Imaging* **2024**, *43*, 674–685. [CrossRef] [PubMed]
3. Liu, X.; Song, L.; Liu, S.; Zhang, Y.; Feliu, C.; Burgos, D. A Review of Deep-Learning-Based Medical Image Segmentation Methods. *Sustainability* **2021**, *13*, 1224. [CrossRef]
4. Lensen, A.; Al-Sahaf, H.; Zhang, M.; Xue, B. Genetic Programming for Region Detection, Feature Extraction, Feature Construction and Classification in Image Data. In *Genetic Programming. EuroGP 2016. Lecture Notes in Computer Science*; Springer: Cham, Switzerland, 2016; Volume 9594, pp. 51–67. [CrossRef]
5. Bi, Y.; Xue, B.; Zhang, M. Dual-Tree Genetic Programming for Few-Shot Image Classification. *IEEE Trans. Evol. Comput.* **2022**, *26*, 555–569. [CrossRef]
6. Sun, Y.; Zhang, Z. Automatic Feature Construction-Based Genetic Programming for Degraded Image Classification. *Appl. Sci.* **2024**, *14*, 1613. [CrossRef]
7. Fuentes-Tomás, J.A.; Mezura-Montes, E.; Acosta-Mesa, H.G.; Márquez-Grajales, A. Tree-Based Codification in Neural Architecture Search for Medical Image Segmentation. *IEEE Trans. Evol. Comput.* **2024**, *28*, 597–607. [CrossRef]

8. Herrera-Sánchez, D.; Fuentes-Tomás, J.A.; Acosta-Mesa, H.G.; Mezura-Montes, E. Experimental Study for Automatic Feature Construction to Segment Images of Lungs Affected by COVID-19 Using Genetic Programming. *Lect. Notes Comput. Sci.* **2025**, *15465 LNAI*, 155–166. [CrossRef]
9. Ronneberger, O.; Fischer, P.; Brox, T. U-Net: Convolutional Networks for Biomedical Image Segmentation. In *Medical Image Computing and Computer-Assisted Intervention—MICCAI 2015. MICCAI 2015. Lecture Notes in Computer Science*; Springer: Cham, Switzerland, 2015; Volume 9351, pp. 234–241. [CrossRef]
10. Cai, Y.; Yuan, J. A Review of U-Net Network Medical Image Segmentation Applications. In Proceedings of the 2022 5th International Conference on Artificial Intelligence and Pattern Recognition (AIPR '22), Xiamen, China, 23–25 September 2022; pp. 457–461. [CrossRef]
11. Naser, M.A.; Deen, M.J. Brain tumor segmentation and grading of lower-grade glioma using deep learning in MRI images. *Comput. Biol. Med.* **2020**, *121*, 103758. [CrossRef]
12. Liang, Y.; Zhang, M.; Browne, W.N. Image Segmentation: A Survey of Methods Based on Evolutionary Computation. In *Simulated Evolution and Learning. SEAL 2014. Lecture Notes in Computer Science*; Springer: Cham, Switzerland, 2014; Volume 8886, pp. 847–859. [CrossRef]
13. Herrera-Sánchez, D.; Acosta-Mesa, H.G.; Mezura-Montes, E.; Herrera-Meza, S.; Rivadeneyra-Domínguez, E.; Zamora-Bello, I.; Almanza-Domínguez, M.F. Imaging Estimation for Liver Damage Using Automated Approach Based on Genetic Programming. *Math. Comput. Appl.* **2025**, *30*, 25. [CrossRef]
14. Miller, C.G.; Krasnow, J.; Schwartz, L.H. Medical imaging in clinical trials. In *Medical Imaging in Clinical Trials*; Springer: London, UK, 2013; pp. 1–420. ISBN 9781848827103. [CrossRef]
15. Mahesh, M. The Essential Physics of Medical Imaging. *Med. Phys.* **2013**, *40*, 077301. [CrossRef]
16. Guo, Y.; Nie, G.; Gao, W.; Liao, M. 2D Semantic Segmentation: Recent Developments and Future Directions. *Future Internet* **2023**, *15*, 205. [CrossRef]
17. Liu, S.; Qi, L.; Qin, H.; Shi, J.; Jia, J. Path Aggregation Network for Instance Segmentation. In Proceedings of the IEEE Computer Society Conference on Computer Vision and Pattern Recognition, Salt Lake City, UT, USA, 18–23 June 2018; pp. 8759–8768. [CrossRef]
18. Kirillov, A.; He, K.; Girshick, R.; Rother, C.; Dollar, P. Panoptic segmentation. In Proceedings of the IEEE Computer Society Conference on Computer Vision and Pattern Recognition, Long Beach, CA, USA, 15–20 June 2019; pp. 9396–9405. [CrossRef]
19. Zhou, Z.; Rahman Siddiquee, M.M.; Tajbakhsh, N.; Liang, J. Unet++: A nested u-net architecture for medical image segmentation. In *Lecture Notes in Computer Science (Including Subseries Lecture Notes in Artificial Intelligence and Lecture Notes in Bioinformatics)*; Springer International Publishing: Berlin/Heidelberg, Germany, 2018; Volume 11045 LNCS, pp. 3–11. [CrossRef]
20. Mei, Y.; Chen, Q.; Lensen, A.; Xue, B.; Zhang, M. Explainable Artificial Intelligence by Genetic Programming: A Survey. *IEEE Trans. Evol. Comput.* **2023**, *27*, 621–641. [CrossRef]
21. Quinlan, J.R. Induction of decision trees. *Mach. Learn.* **1986**, *1*, 81–106. [CrossRef]
22. Koza, J.R. Genetic Programming On the Programming of Computers by Means of Natural Selection. *Stat. Comput.* **1994**, *4*, 87–112. [CrossRef]
23. Miller, J.F. Cartesian Genetic Programming. In *Cartesian Genetic Programming*; Springer: Berlin/Heidelberg, Germany, 2011; pp. 17–34. [CrossRef]
24. Mckay, R.I.; Hoai, N.X.; Whigham, P.A.; Shan, Y.; O'Neill, M. Grammar-based Genetic Programming: A survey. *Genet. Program. Evolvable Mach.* **2010**, *11*, 365–396. [CrossRef]
25. Brameier, M.F.; Banzhaf, W. Linear Genetic Programming. In *Linear Genetic Programming*; Springer: Berlin/Heidelberg, Germany, 2007. [CrossRef]
26. Liang, J.; Wen, J.; Wang, Z.; Wang, J. Evolving semantic object segmentation methods automatically by genetic programming from images and image processing operators. *Soft Comput.* **2020**, *24*, 12887–12900. [CrossRef]
27. Liang, Y.; Zhang, M.; Browne, W.N. Image feature selection using genetic programming for figure-ground segmentation. *Eng. Appl. Artif. Intell.* **2017**, *62*, 96–108. [CrossRef]
28. Liang, Y.; Zhang, M.; Browne, W.N. Figure-ground image segmentation using feature-based multi-objective genetic programming techniques. *Neural Comput. Appl.* **2019**, *31*, 3075–3094. [CrossRef]
29. Mahmood, M.T. Defocus Blur Segmentation Using Genetic Programming and Adaptive Threshold. *Comput. Mater. Contin.* **2021**, *70*, 4867–4882. [CrossRef]
30. Yuan, D.; Zhang, D.; Yang, Y.; Yang, S. Automatic construction of filter tree by genetic programming for ultrasound guidance image segmentation. *Biomed. Signal Process. Control* **2022**, *76*, 103641. [CrossRef]
31. Correia, J.; Rodriguez-Fernandez, N.; Vieira, L.; Romero, J.; Machado, P. Towards Automatic Image Enhancement with Genetic Programming and Machine Learning. *Appl. Sci.* **2022**, *12*, 2212. [CrossRef]

32. Ingalalli, V.; Silva, S.; Castelli, M.; Vanneschi, L. A Multi-dimensional Genetic Programming Approach for Multi-class Classification Problems. In *Genetic Programming. EuroGP 2014. Lecture Notes in Computer Science*; Springer: Berlin/Heidelberg, Germany, 2014; Volume 8599, pp. 48–60. [CrossRef]
33. Muñoz, L.; Silva, S.; Trujillo, L. M3GP—Multiclass Classification with GP. In *Genetic Programming. EuroGP 2015. Lecture Notes in Computer Science*; Springer: Cham, Switzerland, 2015; Volume 9025, pp. 78–91. [CrossRef]
34. La Cava, W.; Silva, S.; Vanneschi, L.; Spector, L.; Moore, J. Genetic Programming Representations for Multi-dimensional Feature Learning in Biomedical Classification. In *Applications of Evolutionary Computation. EvoApplications 2017. Lecture Notes in Computer Science)*; Springer: Cham, Switzerland, 2017; Volume 10199 LNCS, pp. 158–173. [CrossRef]
35. Cárdenas Florido, L.; Trujillo, L.; Hernandez, D.E.; Muñoz Contreras, J.M. M5GP: Parallel Multidimensional Genetic Programming with Multidimensional Populations for Symbolic Regression. *Math. Comput. Appl.* **2024**, *29*, 25. [CrossRef]
36. Batista, J.E.; Rodrigues, N.M.; Vanneschi, L.; Silva, S. M6GP: Multiobjective Feature Engineering. In Proceedings of the 2024 IEEE Congress on Evolutionary Computation, CEC 2024—Proceedings, Yokohama, Japan, 30 June–5 July 2024. [CrossRef]
37. Van Der Walt, S.; Schönberger, J.L.; Nunez-Iglesias, J.; Boulogne, F.; Warner, J.D.; Yager, N.; Gouillart, E.; Yu, T. Scikit-image: Image processing in python. *PeerJ* **2014**, *2014*, e453. [CrossRef] [PubMed]
38. Müller, D.; Soto-Rey, I.; Kramer, F. Towards a guideline for evaluation metrics in medical image segmentation. *BMC Res. Notes* **2022**, *15*, 210. [CrossRef]
39. Kim, J.; Yoo, S. Software review: DEAP (Distributed Evolutionary Algorithm in Python) library. *Genet. Program. Evolvable Mach.* **2019**, *20*, 139–142. [CrossRef]
40. Bradski, G. The OpenCV Library. *Dr. Dobb's J. Softw. Tools* **2000**, *25*, 120–123.
41. Pedregosa, F.; Varoquaux, G.; Gramfort, A.; Michel, V.; Thirion, B.; Grisel, O.; Blondel, M.; Prettenhofer, P.; Weiss, R.; Dubourg, V.; et al. Scikit-learn: Machine learning in Python. *J. Mach. Learn. Res.* **2011**, *12*, 2825–2830.
42. MedSeg; Jenssen, H.B.; Sakinis, T. MedSeg Covid Dataset 1. Available online: https://doi.org/10.6084/m9.figshare.13521488.v2 (accessed on 16 April 2025).
43. Staal, J.; Abràmoff, M.D.; Niemeijer, M.; Viergever, M.A.; Van Ginneken, B. Ridge-based vessel segmentation in color images of the retina. *IEEE Trans. Med. Imaging* **2004**, *23*, 501–509. [CrossRef]
44. Gutman, D.; Codella, N.C.F.; Celebi, E.; Helba, B.; Marchetti, M.; Mishra, N.; Halpern, A. Skin Lesion Analysis toward Melanoma Detection: A Challenge at the International Symposium on Biomedical Imaging (ISBI) 2016, hosted by the International Skin Imaging Collaboration (ISIC). *arXiv* **2016**, arXiv:1605.01397.
45. Hssayeni, M.D.; Croock, M.S.; Salman, A.D.; Al-Khafaji, H.F.; Yahya, Z.A.; Ghoraani, B. Intracranial Hemorrhage Segmentation Using a Deep Convolutional Model. *Data* **2020**, *5*, 14. [CrossRef]

Mathematical and Computational Applications

MDPI

Article

Color Identification on Heterogeneous Bean Landrace Seeds Using Gaussian Mixture Models in CIE L*a*b* Color Space

Adriana-Laura López-Lobato [1,*], Martha-Lorena Avendaño-Garrido [2], Héctor-Gabriel Acosta-Mesa [1], José-Luis Morales-Reyes [3] and Elia-Nora Aquino-Bolaños [3]

1 Artificial Intelligence Research Institute, University of Veracruz, Xalapa 91097, Mexico; heacosta@uv.mx
2 Faculty of Mathematics, University of Veracruz, Xalapa 91097, Mexico; maravendano@uv.mx
3 Center for Food Research and Development, University of Veracruz, Xalapa 91190, Mexico; jluismorey@hotmail.com (J.-L.M.-R.); eliaquino@uv.mx (E.-N.A.-B.)
* Correspondence: adrilau17@gmail.com

Abstract

The classification of bean landraces based on their coloration is of particular interest, as the color of these plants is associated with the nutritional components present in their seeds. In this paper, the authors propose a procedure to identify the colors of heterogeneous color bean landraces based on the information from their digital images. The proposed methodology employs a three-dimensional histogram representation of the estimated color, expressed in the CIE L*a*b* color space, with an unsupervised learning method called the Gaussian Mixture Model. This approach facilitates the acquisition of representative information for the colors of a bean landrace, represented as points in the CIE L*a*b* color space. Furthermore, the *K-nn* method can be trained with these punctual representations to identify colors, yielding satisfactory results on landraces with homogeneous and heterogeneous seeds.

Keywords: bean landrace analysis; Gaussian Mixture Model; Gini index; CIE L*a*b* color space; optimization

1. Introduction

The common bean (*Phaseolus vulgaris* L.) is an important legume in Mexico and Central America, due to its high consumption and significant nutritional value, including proteins, fiber, and other components with antioxidant properties [1]. These properties are well-documented for their ability to prevent cardiovascular diseases and chronic degenerative conditions such as diabetes, obesity, and cholesterol [2,3].

The identification of bean varieties intended for commercial consumption is typically based on the morphology and pigmentation of the seeds, with only those varieties exhibiting similarities between grains being considered [4]. However, there are bean varieties that are cultivated domestically for private consumption, and which exhibit divergent characteristics due to their adaptation to different agricultural practices and the conditions of the rural communities, as altitude, climate and soil [5–8]. These bean varieties are known as common bean landraces and their seeds can be either homogeneous (exhibiting similar coloration) or heterogeneous (different or variegated colors or patterns) [3], see Figure 1. This diversity makes it very difficult to classify.

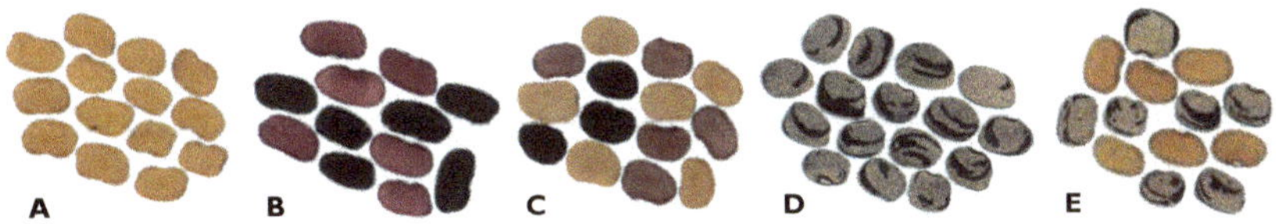

Figure 1. Common bean landraces with homogeneous and heterogeneous seeds. Bean landraces with (**A**) yellow color seeds (homogeneous), (**B**) black and red color seeds (heterogeneous), (**C**) black, yellow and pink color seeds (heterogeneous), (**D**) variegated seeds (heterogeneous), and (**E**) yellow and variegated seeds (heterogeneous).

Also, it has been established that there is a direct correlation between the chemical composition of common bean landraces and their colorimetric properties [9]. Dark bean landraces (black, red, or a mixture of dark grains) present higher levels of anthocyanin content and antioxidant activity in comparison to white or yellow bean landraces [2]. Furthermore, proanthocyanidins, flavonol glycosides, and anthocyanins have been identified as the compounds responsible for the coloration of bean seeds [10]. Consequently, it is imperative to classify bean landraces according to their coloration and utilize this classification as a reference point for the potential health benefits to the consumer.

The spectrometry laboratory technique has been employed to characterize the color of bean landraces. However, it should be noted that this device only illuminates an area of 8 mm diameter when observing an object, thus only a small portion of the seed surface can be sampled to determine color. Consequently, an average of these measurements may not represent the entire seed [2,11]. This only considers seeds of homogeneous color; therefore, the worst-case scenario would occur if the bean landrace contains seeds of heterogeneous color [11].

Several works have proposed the acquisition of color directly from a digital camera image [12–17]. These studies have focused on the analysis of color in fruits, such as grapes and strawberries, and in bean seeds, primarily because a digital image is capable of providing a complete color distribution of the individual analyzed. In the bean landrace case, the color distribution of the seed or a set of seeds can be obtained.

The utilization of digital images in the analysis of the colorimetric properties for classification and characterization involves the employment of numerous computer vision systems. An example of this is the use of color averages in a specific region of interest to represent an individual and determine their classification as a particular variety [16]. However, it has been observed that such averages are unable to adequately represent the color distributions observed in bean landraces [2]. Consequently, studies that utilize these metrics in conjunction with seed color patches [18,19] or morphological characteristics, such as seed shape and size [20], are regarded as more comprehensive. The methodologies employed to analyze the shape and texture of each bean sample encompass the use of Fourier elliptic descriptors [21], the Principal Component Analysis of grey histograms of a bean color region [22], and the dominant color technique on each bean [23].

It has been observed that the primary challenge encountered in the analysis and classification of bean landraces pertains to the heterogeneity in coloration among the seeds of a particular landrace [24]. Consequently, it is more appropriate to consider color distributions within the landraces. The utilization of probability distributions to characterize the color of bean landraces has been documented in [12,25], where two-dimensional and three-dimensional histograms were employed to describe the coloration of a set of seeds.

The work most closely related to this project is presented in [26], where an unsupervised learning model was employed to concentrate the information of these three-dimensional histograms into points in the CIE L*a*b* color space. This information compression allows for efficient classification of bean landraces with homogeneous color seeds based on their color and variety.

An adaptation of the technique proposed in [26] is employed in this work to address the challenge of classifying common bean landraces with heterogeneous colored seeds. This project uses the three-dimensional histogram in the CIE L*a*b* color space representing the landrace color information to fit a Gaussian Mixture Model (GMM). The GMM is a parametric model whose density function is a linear combination of K multivariate normal (Gaussian) distributions. In this context, the number of Gaussians must correspond to the number of colors in the bean landrace analyzed. For this purpose, the Gini Index (GI) algorithm [27,28] is employed, since it is distinguished by its ability to identify the number of Gaussian components present in the dataset. Consequently, in the event of the bean landrace exhibiting seeds of heterogeneous color, the GI algorithm identifies as many Gaussian components as colors, and the representative color information of the bean landrace is characterized by the means of the Gaussian components found.

To our knowledge, the classification of common bean landraces with heterogeneous seeds characterized by points of representative colors in the CIE L*a*b* color space has not yet been explored; therefore, this work aims to demonstrate that the color information on landraces with homogeneous and heterogeneous color seeds can be characterized as points in the CIE L*a*b* color space using their corresponding GMMs fitted with the GI algorithm. Then, the *K-nn* method can be trained to classify/identify the colors present in the landraces of heterogeneous seeds.

The novel approach proposed in this work for color characterization, which employs the information of the Gaussian components of a GMM as points in the CIE L*a*b* color space, offers a significant reduction in computational cost when compared with previous techniques that manage the information of two-dimensional and and three-dimensional histograms.

The remaining sections of the paper are organized as follows. Section 2 details the image acquisition, segmentation, and extraction of color information. In addition, a description of the Gaussian Mixture Model and the GI algorithm is provided, along with the proposed methodology. Section 3 presents the obtained results, and Section 4 describes the discussion based on these results. The conclusions are presented in Section 5, and Section 6 is added to complement and clarify the drawbacks and limitations of the proposed methodology. Finally, future work is presented in Section 7.

2. Materials and Methods

This section provides a concise overview of the process employed to acquire bean landrace images, the segmentation of the seeds, and the representation utilized to obtain the color information. It also presents a detailed exposition of the Gaussian Mixture Model and the Gini Index (GI) algorithm, along with the proposed methodology for color identification in heterogeneous bean landrace seeds.

2.1. Bean Landraces: Image Acquisition, Segmentation, and Extraction of Color Information

The common bean landraces utilized in this study were procured from rural communities in Oaxaca, Mexico. A total of 60 g of seeds, exhibiting diverse coloration patterns, were employed to represent each of the 168 bean landraces analyzed.

The classification of seeds according to their color is divided into seven distinct categories: black, brown, pink, purple, red, white, and yellow. Illustrative examples of the bean landraces associated with these color categories are presented in Figure 2.

Figure 2. Color categories considered for seeds.

To obtain a digital image of the bean landraces that closely resembled the color of their seeds, the artificial illumination environment and color image reproduction workflow delineated in [12,25] were employed. Once the digital images on the CIE L*a*b* color space are obtained, a segmentation step is considered to extract the color information of the bean landraces seeds as three-dimensional histograms (3D histograms) of color. The subsequent subsections will describe this process, with the relevant visual representation provided in Figure 3.

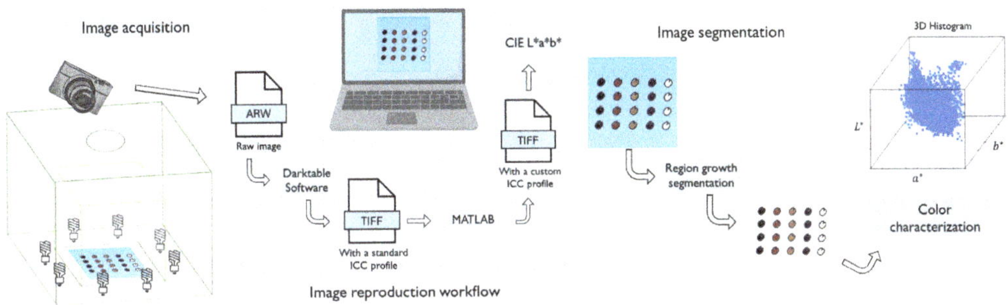

Figure 3. Process performed to obtain the color information of the bean landraces seeds as 3D histograms in the CIE L*a*b* color space.

2.1.1. Artificial Illumination Environment

The illumination configuration comprises a controlled lighting system that ensures uniform illumination, mitigates glare, and reduces specular brightness for shiny bean landraces. The setup, depicted in Figure 4, consists of an aluminum box measuring 68 cm × 68 cm for the base and 60 cm in height (Figure 4A). A diffusion box inside this aluminum box decreases the specular reflexes and shadows among seeds (Figure 4B). The dimensions of the diffusion box are 38 cm × 38 cm for the base and 45 cm in height. Eight fluorescent bulbs are distributed between the boxes to illuminate the environment with a color temperature of 6500 K. A hole at the top of the box allows for the camera lens placement (Figure 4C).

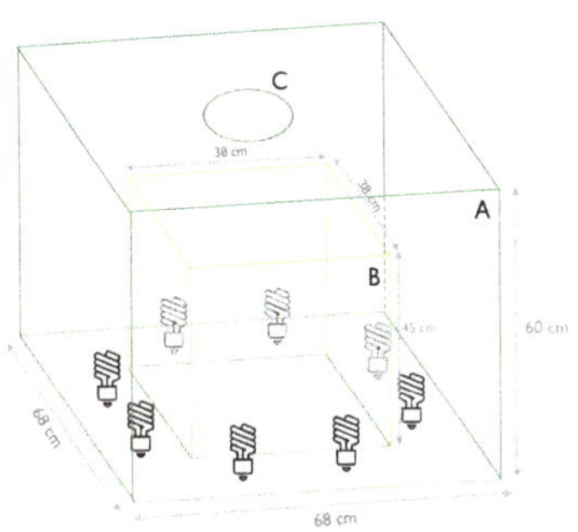

Figure 4. Prototype for the image acquisition process.

2.1.2. Image Acquisition: The Color Image Reproduction Workflow

The image acquisition process entailed meticulously placing the seeds on a sliding base within the aluminum box to ensure the collection of unobstructed and well-lit images. The blue color was strategically employed to differentiate the seeds from their background to achieve optimal visual contrast, see Figure 5.

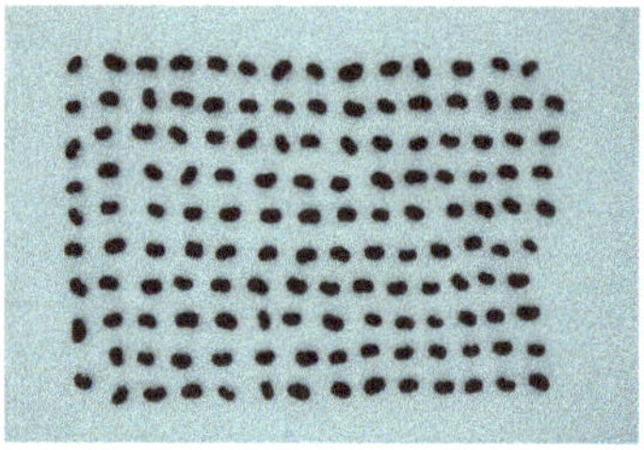

Figure 5. Visual contrast between the bean landrace and the background of the image in blue color.

A camera configured for RAW image acquisition was employed. The ARW file format retains the complete data captured by the camera sensor. Darktable Software (Version 4.4.2) was then used to export each image from the ARW format to the TIFF format without compression. During this process, each TIFF image is assigned a standard ICC profile. ICC profiles are imperative in image conversion to the color space of a disparate device, given that each device possesses its own distinct color space. Finally, Matlab software (Version 2023b) replaced the standard ICC profile with a custom ICC profile. The custom ICC profile used corresponds to the one reported in [12]. This profile was converted from the RGB color space to the CIE L*a*b* color space. For a more detailed description of this process, please refer to [12,25].

The CIE L*a*b* color space is utilized in this study, as it is intended to investigate the chromaticity channels of luminosity. Furthermore, it is acknowledged as the color space most frequently used in numerous laboratory devices for measuring color. Several studies have demonstrated that this particular space is well-suited for characterizing the color of bean landraces, thereby ensuring enhanced precision in the results obtained [25]. Furthermore, it is the color space that most closely aligns with human vision perception.

The CIE L*a*b* color space is three-dimensional. The vertical axis represents the luminance L*, with values ranging from 0 (black) to 100 (white). The primary color axes range from red to green (the a* axis) and from yellow to blue (the b* axis). This is illustrated in Figure 6.

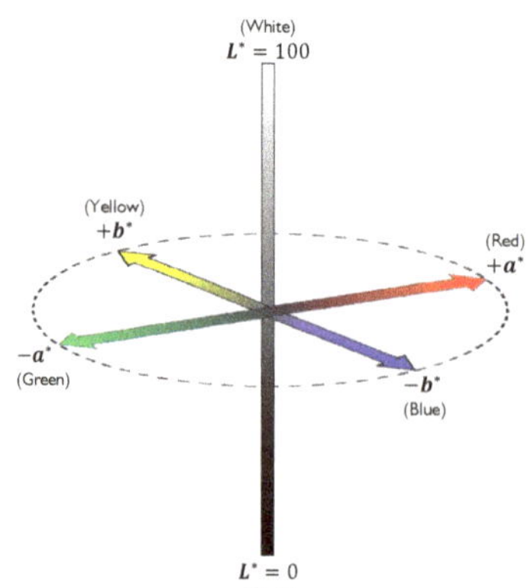

Figure 6. CIE L*a*b* color space.

Within this color space, each possible color is represented by a unique point in the coordinate system (L*, a*, b*). For example, the colors white and black are located at coordinates (0, 0, 0) and (100, 0, 0), respectively.

2.1.3. Image Segmentation

The subsequent step was to identify the regions of interest. To this end, the region growth segmentation algorithm was employed, which utilizes the Euclidean distance as a criterion of similarity between pixels. For this algorithm it is imperative to designate a seed pixel as the initial point, from which the region will expand if the neighboring pixels exhibit a degree of similarity. Given the homogeneity of the background, the seed pixel was selected in that area.

The segmentation process yields a binary image (see Figure 7), thus facilitating the identification of regions of interest, in this case, the bean landraces seeds, which are represented by the color black regions in the binary image. This enables the accurate acquisition of color information of the bean landrace seeds.

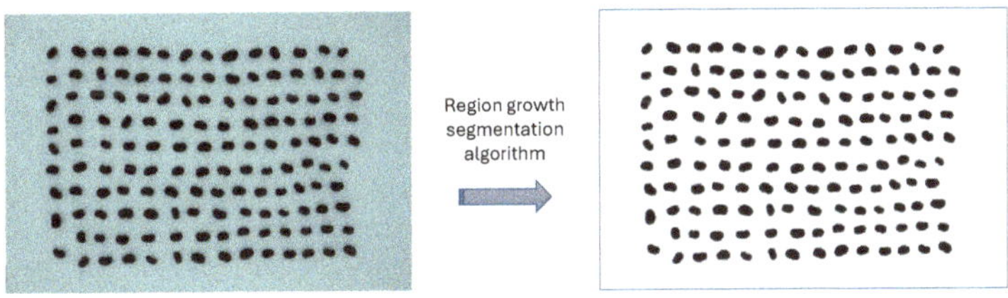

Figure 7. Original and binary image obtained with the region growth segmentation algorithm. The black regions obtained correspond to the region of interest, i.e., the bean landrace seeds.

2.1.4. Extraction of Color Information: 3D Histograms

In the context of a digital image, a three-dimensional histogram (3D histogram) can be derived by using the three channels on the CIE L*a*b* color space. The color histogram bins are calculated by discretizing the CIE L*a*b* chromaticity channels into 256 values (2^8). This discretization was necessary because the range of channels a* and b* lies within $[-128, 127]$. The values for the L* channel were normalized and scaled to 256 values. Consequently, each 3D histogram is represented as a three-dimensional matrix of size $256 \times 256 \times 256$, as illustrated in Figure 8.

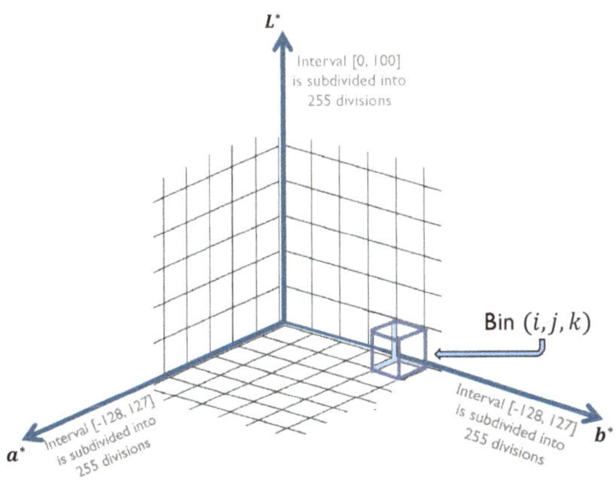

Figure 8. 3D histogram divisions considering the CIE L*a*b* color space.

The frequency of each color bin, denoted by f_{ijk}, is specified in Equation (1), where p_{ijk} denotes the number of pixels with color channel values belonging to a bin (i, j, k), and N is the total number of pixels in the image.

$$f_{ijk} = \frac{p_{ijk}}{N} \tag{1}$$

The values f_{ijk} define a joint probability mass function $f(X, Y, Z)$, since the conditions presented in Equations (2) and (3) are fulfilled when $f(X = i, Y = j, Z = k) = f_{ijk}$.

$$f_{ijk} \geq 0, \ \forall (i, j, k) \in X \times Y \times Z. \tag{2}$$

$$\sum_{i \in X} \sum_{j \in Y} \sum_{k \in Z} f_{ijk} = 1. \tag{3}$$

To characterize the color of a set of seeds, the corresponding joint probability mass function is defined solely with the pixels of the image that correspond to the seeds. So, the segmentation step is necessary to capture the colorimetric representation of each bean landrace as the joint probability distribution of their pixel color values. An example of a bean landrace 3D histogram is presented in Figure 9, where the blue squares represent bins of the color space with frequencies greater than 0. These are the colors present in the seeds of this bean landrace.

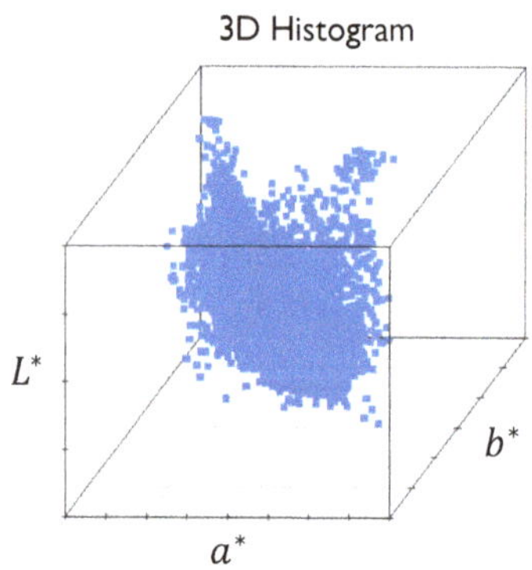

Figure 9. 3D histogram of a bean landrace in the CIE L*a*b* color space.

A subsequent examination of the scatterplots of the 3D histograms revealed a concentration of points in several regions of the CIE L*a*b* color space. This representation facilitates the implementation of a statistical approach known as the Gaussian Mixture Model (GMM). This model enables the description of the color behavior in the bean landrace through a mixture of Gaussian distributions, using the "means" of these distributions as representative information, or indicators, of the colors present in the bean landrace.

The subsequent section provides detailed descriptions of the GMM and the Gini Index (GI) algorithm, which are necessary for the methodology proposed in this work.

2.2. Gaussian Mixture Model and Gini Index Algorithm

The Gaussian Mixture Model (GMM) is a parametric, multimodal model widely utilized for unsupervised learning problems, specifically density estimation [29]. The objective of density estimation is to employ a parametric distribution to model the behavior of a given dataset, as illustrated in Figure 10. The Figure 10a presents the plots of a dataset in dimension 2, where concentrations of dots are observed in specific regions. In contrast, the Figure 10b offers a graphical representation of a continuous density function derived from a GMM learned with this dataset. This function is characterized by peaks or hills corresponding to the points' concentrations in the analyzed set, providing a concise depiction of the data's behavior.

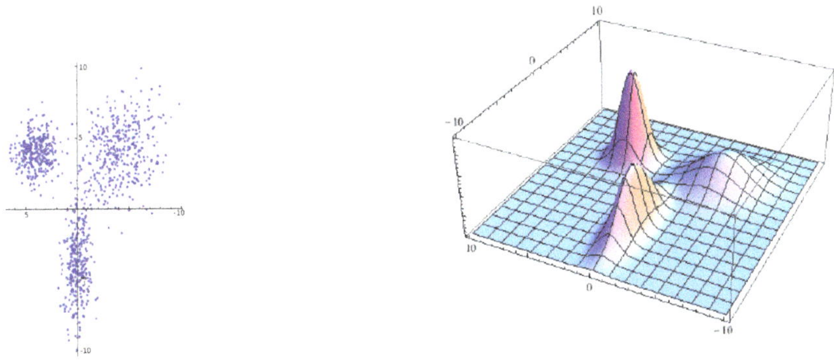

(**a**) (**b**)

Figure 10. Example of (**a**) a dataset dispersion in $\mathbb{R}^2$, and (**b**) its corresponding fitted Gaussian mixture distribution.

The parametric density function employed for a Gaussian Mixture Model is a linear combination of K multivariate normal distributions, as illustrated in Equation (4). In this equation, the mean μ_k and the covariance matrix Σ_k of the k-th Gaussian component f_{θ_k} are denoted by $\theta_k = (\mu_k, \Sigma_k)$, for $k = 1, \ldots, K$. The parameters denoted by the letter ϕ_k represent the weights or mixing proportions required to satisfy the restrictions presented in Equation (5).

$$\sum_{k=1}^{K} \phi_k f_{\theta_k}(\cdot), \text{ with } f_{\theta_k} = \frac{1}{2\pi\sqrt{\Sigma_k}} e^{-\frac{1}{2}(x-\mu_k)^T \Sigma_k^{-1}(x-\mu_k)}. \tag{4}$$

$$0 \leq \phi_k \leq 1, \text{ for } k = 1, \ldots, K, \text{ and } \sum_{k=1}^{K} \phi_k = 1. \tag{5}$$

The GMM facilitates the modeling of dataset behavior by estimating the parameter $\theta = \{\phi_k, \theta_k\}_{k=1}^{K}$.

One method of determining the values of these parameters is to employ Fisher's maximum likelihood method, using the log-likelihood function $\mathcal{L}$, as shown in Equation (6), where $\{x_m\}_{m=1}^{M}$ denotes the dataset. This approach facilitates the implementation of the EM algorithm, which in turn enables the identification of the target values [29]. However, it should be noted that this algorithm is subject to certain limitations and performance concerns [30].

$$\mathcal{L} = \sum_{m=1}^{M} \log\left(\sum_{k=1}^{K} \phi_k f(x_m \mid \mu_k, \Sigma_k) \right). \tag{6}$$

Consequently, in 2006, there was a significant increase in the use of distances between probability distributions involving optimal transportation problems, such as the Kantorovich metric and the Gini index problem, for solving density estimation problems [31]. The approach adopted in this study for estimating the values of the GMM parameters for a given dataset is the GI algorithm, which utilizes the Gini index problem as the basis for the calculation [27,28].

The Gini index (GI) is the optimal value obtained by resolving a variant of the optimal transportation problem. In the GI problem [32,33], two probability distributions, denoted by ν_1 and ν_2, are considered within a random variable Y. A distance d in Y is employed as a cost function. The GI problem is structured in Equation (7), where the set of joint probability distributions in $Y \times Y$ with marginals ν_1 and ν_2 in the first and second factors, respectively, is denoted by $\Pi(\nu_1, \nu_2)$.

$$GI(\nu_1, \nu_2) = \min_{\pi \in \Pi(\nu_1,\nu_2)} \left\{ \int_{Y \times Y} d(y_1, y_2) d\pi \right\}. \tag{7}$$

From a graphical perspective, the objective is to identify a joint distribution function, denoted by π, in $Y \times Y$ such that the projections of π onto the axes coincide with the distributions ν_1 and ν_2, see Figure 11.

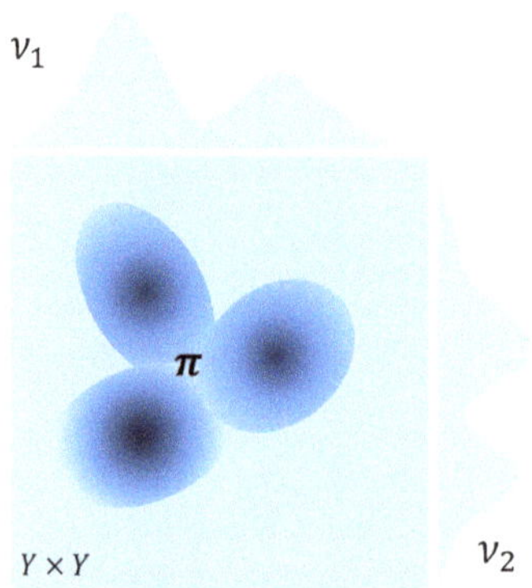

Figure 11. Graphical representation of a joint distribution function π whose projections onto the axes are the distributions ν_1 and ν_2 .

The Gini index $GI(\nu_1, \nu_2)$ is a distance between the probability distributions ν_1 and ν_2 [34]. So, the objective of the GI algorithm is to calculate the parameters of the GMM by minimizing the distance, measured by the Gini index, between an empirical distribution of the analyzed data and the density function of the GMM [27,28,31].

In the model proposed in [27,28], the dataset P is utilized to delineate the three principal components of the GI problem. These components are the random variable Y, the distribution ν_1, and the shape of the parametric distribution ν_2. The distribution ν_2 is hypothesized to be a GMM of independent multivariate normal distributions, that is, Gaussians whose covariance matrices are diagonal.

Once the GI problem has been established with these three characteristics, the Lagrange multiplier method is used to identify Equations (8) and (9), defining the GI algorithm, for a dataset $P = \{p_i\}_{i=1}^{M}$, with $p_i = \left(p_1^{(m)}, p_2^{(m)}, \ldots, p_N^{(m)}\right) \in \mathbb{R}^N$, where the mean μ_k is a real vector in $\mathbb{R}^N$, and the covariance matrix Σ_k is a positive definite diagonal matrix of dimension $N \times N$, see Equation (10).

$$\mu_{tr} = \frac{\sum_{m=1}^{M} p_r^{(m)} \exp\left(-\frac{\left(p_r^{(m)} - \mu_{tr}\right)^2}{2\sigma_{tr}^2}\right)}{\sum_{m=1}^{M} \exp\left(-\frac{\left(p_r^{(m)} - \mu_{tr}\right)^2}{2\sigma_{tr}^2}\right)}, \text{ for } 1 \leq t \leq K \text{ and } 1 \leq r \leq N, \tag{8}$$

$$\sigma_{tr} = \frac{\sum_{m=1}^{M} \left(p_r^{(m)} - \mu_{tr}\right)^2 \exp\left(-\frac{\left(p_r^{(m)} - \mu_{tr}\right)^2}{2\sigma_{tr}^2}\right)}{\sum_{m=1}^{M} \exp\left(-\frac{\left(p_r^{(m)} - \mu_{tr}\right)^2}{2\sigma_{tr}^2}\right)}, \text{ for } 1 \leq t \leq K \text{ and } 1 \leq r \leq N. \tag{9}$$

$$\mu_k = \begin{pmatrix} \mu_{k1} \\ \mu_{k2} \\ \vdots \\ \mu_{kN} \end{pmatrix} \text{ and } \Sigma_k = \begin{pmatrix} \sigma_{k1}^2 & 0 & \dots & 0 \\ 0 & \sigma_{k2}^2 & \dots & 0 \\ \vdots & \vdots & \ddots & \dots \\ 0 & 0 & \dots & \sigma_{kN}^2. \end{pmatrix} \quad (10)$$

For the mixture proportions ϕ_k, the Law of Total Probability and Bayes' Theorem are employed to calculate the conditional probabilities $P(f_{\theta_k} \mid p_m)$, for $k = 1, 2, \dots, K$. These values indicate the probability that the point p_m originates from the Gaussian f_{θ_k}. The membership of each point is identified by considering the maximum conditional probability of that point and each Gaussian component. Therefore, the values of the mixture proportions, ϕ_k, are obtained by quantifying the elements in each class and normalizing them.

By assigning initial values to the parameters being sought and following several iterations, these expressions will converge to the values of the means, covariance matrices and mixture proportions that most accurately reflect the behavior of the data [35]. The pseudocode of the GI algorithm is presented in Algorithm A1 of the Appendix A. Further details about the GI algorithm can be found in [27,28].

The experiments conducted in [27,28] demonstrated the efficacy of the GI algorithm when utilizing both real and synthetic data under various conditions. These conditions encompass variations in quantity, the intersection of classes, dimensionality, and non-normal conditions. This finding supports the assertion that the GI algorithm is a robust methodology for fitting a GMM.

Also, it is essential to consider the critical advantage of the GI algorithm over the EM algorithm. Both of these approaches allow for estimating the parameters of a GMM. However, the GI algorithm is distinguished by its ability to identify the number of Gaussian components present in a dataset, a difference from the classical EM algorithm that always found the K components established by the user.

The present paper puts forward the proposal of the GI algorithm for the identification of as many Gaussian components as there are colors in a bean landrace. The information delivered by the vector means obtained in the adjustment of the GMM represents the information of the colors in a bean landrace as points in the CIE L*a*b* color space. This color characterization enables a substantial reduction in computational cost when compared with previous techniques of color identification that manage all the information presented in two-dimensional and three-dimensional histograms. The subsequent section will describe the methodology employed to perform this process.

2.3. Proposed Methodology

In this section, the methodology proposed in this work is described. The GI algorithm is used to concentrate the bean landrace 3D histogram information in several 3D points in the CIE L*a*b* color space. These points are representative of the colors observed in each bean landrace.

Subsequent to the acquisition of these points, the K nearest neighbors' method, denoted as *K-nn* [29], will be employed to classify them. This method has been demonstrated to be both simple and effective for small datasets [36,37], as is the case in the present situation. Moreover, the theoretical framework employed in the implementation of this method, which considers the proximity between instances, aligns with the hypothesis that points representing the colors of the bean landraces exhibiting analogous colors are closer together.

The following steps constitute the methodological framework of the color analysis:

1. Data cleansing on the bean landrace 3D histogram.
The dataset P is obtained by considering positions whose normalized frequencies exceed a predefined threshold. This threshold is determined by dividing the maximum value of the normalized frequencies of the histogram in 3D by a parameter t given by the user. In Figure 12, a graphical representation of the variation in the number of positions that are taken into consideration before the thresholding process (Figure 12A) and after the thresholding process (Figure 12B) is presented. After thresholding, the representative positions constitute a dataset P for the specific landrace.

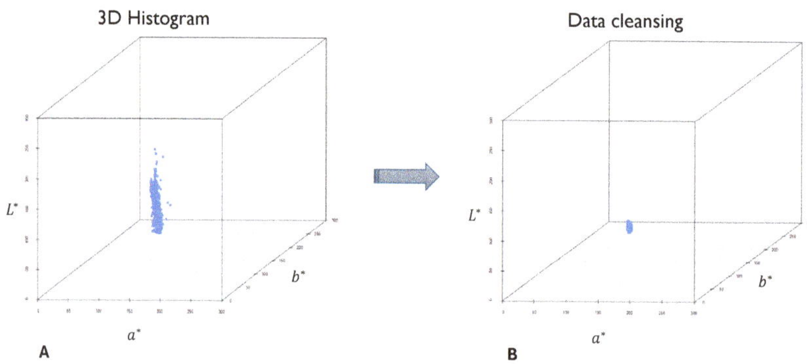

Figure 12. Process of data cleansing using thresholding on a 3D histogram of a bean landrace. (**A**) presents the positions considered in the original 3D histogram and (**B**) the positions that remain after the thresholding process.

2. Transfer of data to space $[0,100] \times [0,100] \times [0,100]$.
The information of each of the three axes (L*, a*, and b*) of the dataset P is transferred to the interval $[0,100]$ to apply the GI algorithm, defined over a squared domain $Y \times Y \times Y$. Consequently, the information is obtained in the space $[0,100] \times [0,100] \times [0,100]$.
3. Gaussian fitting with the GI algorithm.
The GI algorithm is employed to fit K Gaussians in the dataset P, where K is the number of colors sought in the analyzed landrace. This approach enables the estimation of the means, the diagonal covariance matrices, and the mixture proportions for each color. Notably, the GI algorithm's effectively identifies the diversity of colors exhibited by bean landraces. This is due to its ability to overcome challenges denoted as "open set classification problems", wherein the number of classes (colors) is not known in advance. In this step of the process, consideration is given exclusively to those Gaussian components for which the mixture proportions are greater than zero.
4. Return the mean values to the CIE L*a*b* color space.
The mean values equivalence in the CIE L*a*b* color space is computed with the operation described in Equation (11), where $k = 1,2,\ldots,K'$ correspond to the K' Gaussian components whose mixture proportions are greather than zero, and the columns of the dataset in the CIE L*a*b* color space are denoted by C_j, $j = 1,2,3$. The minimum and maximum values of the analyzed axis C_j are denoted by MC_j and mC_j, respectively.

$$\mu_{kC_j} = \frac{\mu_{kj}}{100} \cdot (MC_j - mC_j) + mC_j. \tag{11}$$

The pseudocode of the proposed methodology is presented in Algorithm A2 of the Appendix A.

The procedure outlined in this section is employed to obtain representative information of the analyzed bean landrace, expressed as the corresponding means in the CIE L*a*b* color space. The landrace means, in the CIE L*a*b* color space obtained through this methodology, serves as indicators of the colors of the corresponding landrace. By replicating this process for each landrace, it is possible to compare the information of all the landraces under consideration using some learning method, such as the K nearest neighbors method (K-nn), and identify the seed colors of bean landraces.

2.4. General Experiment Design

This section describes the experiments conducted to validate the performance of the proposed methodology. The project involves the identification of the colors of bean landraces' seeds, considering seven colors: black, brown, pink, purple, red, white, and yellow (see Figure 2).

As a preliminary approximation, the bean landraces considered for these experiments have seeds of different colors but not exceeding three colorations on the same landrace (see Figure 13). Furthermore, landraces exhibiting variegated coloration were excluded from the study. The final sample comprises two hundred and six bean landraces with these characteristics. The number of landraces exhibiting the specific number of colorations is enumerated in Table 1.

Table 1. Number of bean landraces that have one, two, or three colors on their seeds.

Number of Colors	Number of Landraces
One	130
Two	42
Three	34
Total	206

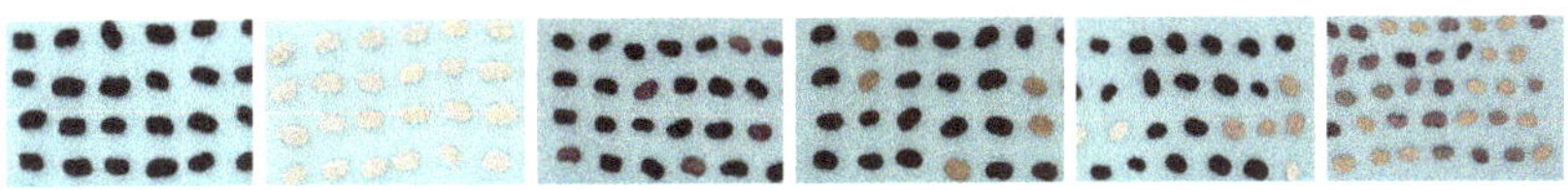

Figure 13. Bean landraces with seeds of heterogeneous colors, considering one, two or three colors in each landrace.

To execute the experimental process, the following steps are performed 20 times for each value of K for the K-nn method, considering values from 1 to 10. Consequently, the total number of executions is 200. The experimental process is illustrated in Figure 14.

(A) Acquisition of the training dataset (See Figure 14A)
Given that the bean landraces under analysis possess different seed colors, the training dataset is structured with the color information of individual seeds previously labeled with one of the seven colors to be analyzed. The 3D histogram of each digital image seed is obtained, and the methodology proposed in Section 2.3 is employed, with one Gaussian component in the GI algorithm and a thresholding value t of 100, to get a single point (the median of the Gaussian component) in the CIE L*a*b* color space with the representative color information of the seed. An example of the process performed with the information of one seed of a bean landrace is shown in Figure 15. The information of several seeds labeled with the considered colors enables the characterization of the color space with groups of points, wherein the points with identical labels must be closer to each other (see Figure 16).
In the present study, a set of 762 images of single seeds of various colors is utilized in the experimental setup. Given the substantial information these bean landrace seeds

can provide, a random selection of 10% of the seeds by color constitutes the training dataset for each experiment performed. The number of seeds and the number of seeds included in the training dataset by color are presented in Table 2.

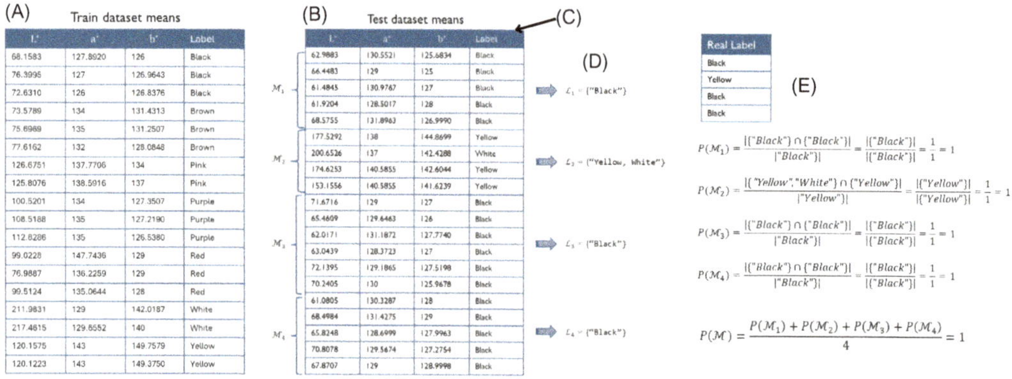

Figure 14. Example of the steps performed for the general design of the experiments. The training dataset (**A**) is structured by the single-point means of 3D histograms of individual seeds that have been labeled with one of seven colors considered. The test dataset (**B**) comprises the means with a mixture proportion greater than zero delivered by the GI algorithm for the bean landraces analyzed. The labels predicted by the *K-nn* method for the test dataset (**C**) are obtained, and the label assignment for each bean landrace (**D**) is considered as the set of colors identified by the *K-nn* method in their respective means. To evaluate the performance of the proposed method, the precision of each bean landrace, $P(\mathcal{M}_i)$, and the general precision, $P(\mathcal{M})$, (**E**), are considered.

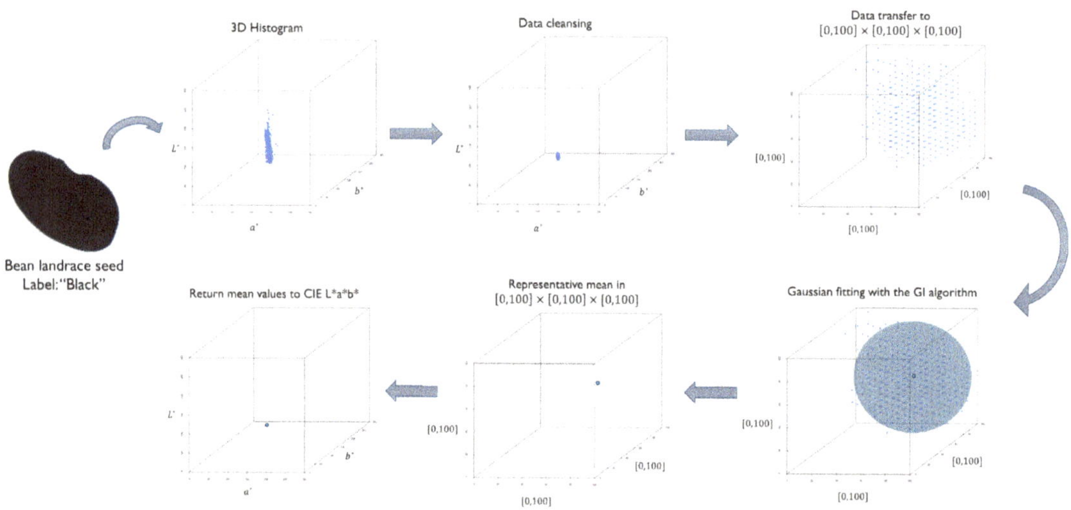

Figure 15. Process performed in one bean landrace seed of homogeneous color to obtain its representative mean in the CIE L*a*b* color space.

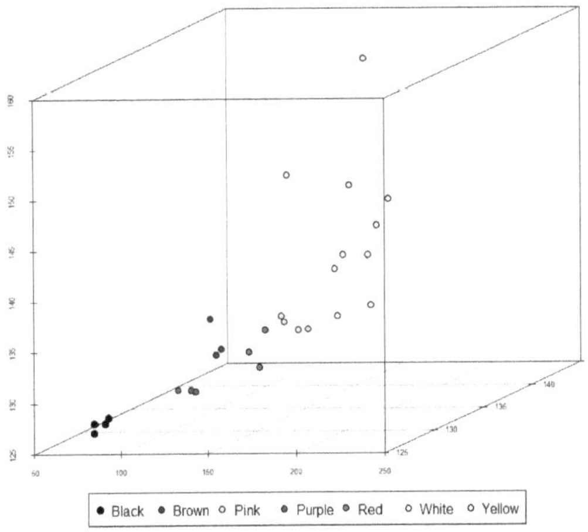

Figure 16. Example of the representative means for a training dataset in the CIE L*a*b* color space.

Table 2. Number of bean landrace seeds used in the experimental setup and training dataset, categorized by color.

Color	Number of Seeds	Number of Seeds for Training (10%)
Black	108	11 *
Brown	135	14 *
Pink	48	5 *
Purple	110	11
Red	166	17 *
White	66	7 *
Yellow	129	13 *
Total	762	78

* Numbers are rounded to the nearest integer.

(B) Acquisition of the test dataset (See Figure 14B)
Two experiments are considered to acquire the test dataset. Firstly, 3D histograms of landraces with one- and two-color bean seeds are employed. Secondly, 3D histograms of landraces with one-, two-, and three-color seeds are employed. This distinction enables the analysis of whether the complexity of the classification process is increasing in correspondence with the number of colors and bean landraces considered. The study focuses on 172 bean landraces in the initial case, while the subsequent case encompasses 206 bean landraces (refer to Table 1 for details).
For both cases, the methodology described in Section 2.3 is employed on each bean landrace. A threshold value t of 500 is used to cleanse the data, thereby ensuring that the most visible colors are well identified, and 7 Gaussians are considered in the GI algorithm since seven colors are being sought. Consequently, seven means are obtained for each distinct bean landrace, along with a standard deviation matrix of size seven and seven mixture proportions. As previously stated in Section 2.2, the GI algorithm can identify Gaussian components with mixture proportion of zero. Consequently, the focus is directed towards those medians from the Gaussian components that have a proportion greater than zero, since this is indicative of concentration of information in those components (See Figure 17). This process results in the acquisition of a set of means with mixture proportion greater than zero for a bean landrace i, denoted by $\mathcal{M}_i$, within the CIE L*a*b* color space.

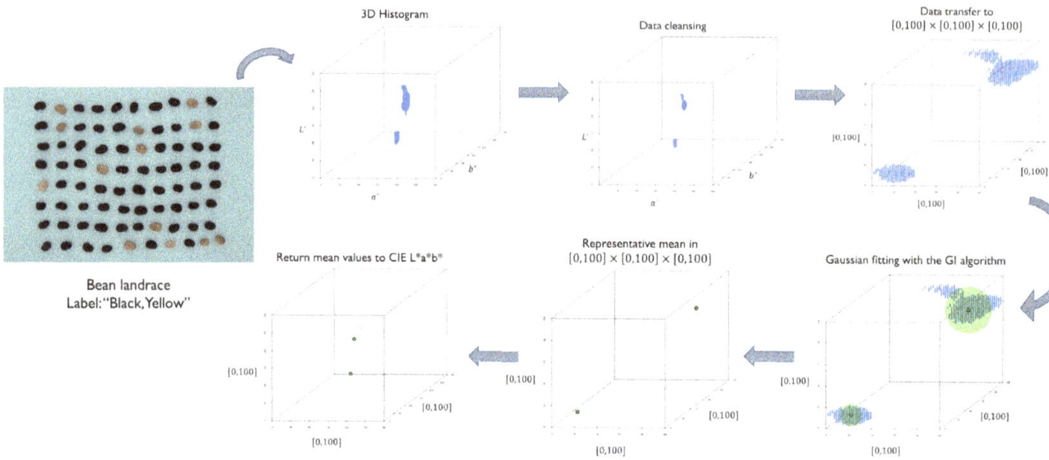

Figure 17. Process performed in one bean landrace of heterogeneous color to obtain its representative means in the CIE L*a*b* color space.

The test dataset, denoted by $\mathcal{M}$, is conform by all the medians with mixture proportion greater than zero in all the bean landraces considered.

It is imperative to elucidate that the bean landraces utilized for the test set were previously categorized by experts based on the colors visually discerned in their seeds. This classification will facilitate a comparison between the colors predicted by the proposed process and the actual colors observed, thereby enabling the estimation of the precision achieved by implementing the proposed methodology.

(C) Application of the *K-nn* method (See Figure 14C)

Following the acquisition of the training and test datasets, the *K-nn* method is employed to classify all the means in $\mathcal{M}$. The *K-nn* method calculates the distance between each test mean and all training means, selects the K nearest neighbors based on these distances and assigns the majority class to the test mean analyzed. With this method the labels predicted for the means in $\mathcal{M}$, denoted by $\mathcal{L}$, is obtained.

(D) Bean landrace label assignment (See Figure 14D)

After executing the aforementioned class assignment, the label predicted for each bean landrace i is the set of colors identified by the *K-nn* method in their representative means, denoted by $\mathcal{L}_i$. It is imperative to note that a set is defined as a collection of distinct elements. Consequently, if different means in the bean landrace i have the same label color, this color will only appear once in the set $\mathcal{L}_i$.

(E) Calculate precision (See Figure 14E)

The performance of the proposed process is evaluated through the utilization of the functions presented in Equations (12) and (13), where $\mathcal{L}_i$ is the set of labels predicted for the means in $\mathcal{M}_i$, $\mathcal{A}_i$ is the set of actual colors observed by the expert on the bean landrace i, I is the number of bean landraces analyzed, and $|\cdot|$ denotes the cardinality of a set (the number of elements in it).

$$P(\mathcal{M}_i) = \frac{|\mathcal{L}_i \cap \mathcal{A}_i|}{|\mathcal{A}_i|} \tag{12}$$

$$P(\mathcal{M}) = \frac{\sum_{i=1}^{I} P(\mathcal{M}_i)}{I} \tag{13}$$

Equation (12) calculates the precision for each bean landrace $\mathcal{M}_i$, taking into account the number of colors found by the proposed method that match the colors seen by the expert. If the colors found by the process match the actual colors, the value of this function is one. Suppose the process found more colors than the actual colors. In that case, this is also considered with a value of one, as it indicates that the algorithm found colors that are imperceptible by simple visual observation. Conversely, the value zero is found when the colors found by the proposed method do not match the actual colors, and the values are between zero and one when the proposed method finds some of the actual colors but not all the colors seen by the expert.
The Equation (13) quantifies the general precision obtained for the test dataset of the experiment under consideration. This is achieved by calculating the mean of all the precisions obtained in the bean landraces.

The implementation of the proposed methodology and the experiments are performed in the R project software (Version R 4.3.2) on a computer with the characteristics presented in Table 3.

Table 3. Computer specifications.

Operating System	Windows 11 Pro 23H2
RAM	64 GB
Processor	AMD Ryzen 5 5600G
Processor speed	3.90 GHz

The general precisions $P(\mathcal{M})$ obtained for each of the 20 executions with each K value between 1 and 10 are documented, and their corresponding statistical descriptions are presented in the following section. The relevant statistical tests and an analysis of the results obtained are also included.

3. Results and Analysis

3.1. Experiments with Bean Landraces with One- or Two-Color Seeds and Fitting 7 Gaussians

In Table 4, the results obtained with the methodology proposed in this work are presented, considering 7 Gaussian components in the GI algorithm and bean landraces with one- and two-color seeds. The minimum, maximum, mean and standar deviation of the precisions of twenty experiments for each K value for the K-*nn* method are reported along with the mean time needed to obtain the training and test datasets for the experimental process (steps (A) and (B)). Even though the times employed for the K-*nn* method have been obtained, the results show that the mean time is 0.00059 s when using the *knn()* function of the R project software. Therefore, these times are not specified due to their low values.

The Shapiro-Wilk statistical test was performed to verify the normal distribution on the precisions obtained in the twenty executions of each K value. The p-values are also included in Table 4 and indicate that the distributions are non-parametric, so, in order to identify if the samples exhibit significant differences, the Kruskal-Wallis rank sum test was conducted, obtaining a p-value of 0.03162. Since this p-value is smaller than the significance level $\alpha = 0.05$, it is concluded that the differences between the precision results obtained with the different K values for the K-*nn* method are significant, so, a post-hoc test for non-parametric comparison must be performed. However, the post-hoc analysis using Dunn's test with bonferroni adjustment for multiple comparisons showed no significant differences between any of the K values at a significance level $\alpha = 0.05$.

Table 4. Results of the experiments considering bean landraces with seeds of one and two colors, searching for 7 Gaussian components with the GI algorithm.

K	Min	Max	Mean ± St.D.	Train/Test Mean Time (min)	p-Value (Shapiro-Wilk)
1	0.7209	0.9477	0.8974 ± 0.0651	4.05/8.67	2.51×10^{-5} *
2	0.7384	0.9419	0.9041 ± 0.0437	4.34/8.40	1.50×10^{-5} *
3	0.7529	0.9477	0.8953 ± 0.0645	4.17/8.45	3.16×10^{-5} *
4	0.7616	0.9506	0.9161 ± 0.0414	4.04/8.45	1.88×10^{-5} *
5	0.7878	0.9477	0.9164 ± 0.0400	4.18/8.47	2.37×10^{-6} *
6	0.8488	0.9477	0.9256 ± 0.0236	4.06/8.42	3.46×10^{-5} *
7	0.8256	0.9564	0.9230 ± 0.0279	4.07/8.46	5.92×10^{-4} *
8	0.7471	0.9622	0.9231 ± 0.0435	4.09/8.48	5.09×10^{-7} *
9	0.7500	0.9622	0.9259 ± 0.0437	4.12/8.50	6.95×10^{-7} *
10	0.8692	0.9506	0.9279 ± 0.0192	4.16/8.52	8.05×10^{-3} *

* Cases where there is a 95% confidence that the precisions does not fit a normal distribution.

As illustrated in Figure 18, the boxplots are employed to visually represent the outcomes and the corresponding median for each K value. A comprehensive analysis of Figure 18 determined that the value of K would be set at 9 to analyze the specific results obtained. This determination was made on the basis that the median value obtained with $K = 9$ was the highest.

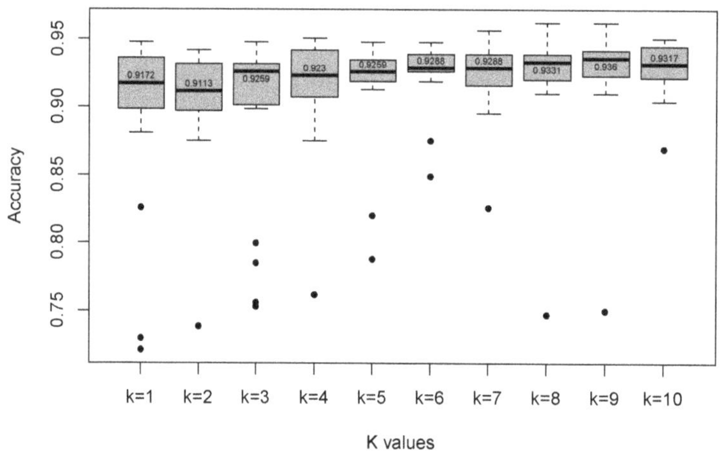

Figure 18. Boxplots of the results obtained considering bean landraces with one- and two-color seeds and the different K values for the K-nn method with the proposed methodology, fitting 7 Gaussians with the GI algorithm. The median for each K value is displayed in the corresponding boxplot.

A closer look at the results is warranted, given that the fitness function employed for the process exhibits a specific characterization. Consequently, five types of classifications are considered and enlisted with examples next:

1. The colors in the real and predicted labels are the same.

   Example: Real label = "Black Yellow", Predicted label = "Black Yellow"

2. The colors in the real label are contained in the predicted label.

   Example: Real label = "Black", Predicted label = "Black Purple"

3. The colors in the predicted label are contained in the real label.

   Example: Real label = "Black Purple Red", Predicted label = "Purple Red"

4. Some colors in the real and predicted labels are the same.
 Example: Real label = "Black Brown Yellow", Predicted label = "Brown White"
5. The colors in the real and predicted labels are different.
 Example: Real label = "Black Purple", Predicted label = "Brown Red"

By considering these types of classifications on the optimal result with value $K = 9$, corresponding to the precision 0.9622, the performance described in Table 5 is demonstrated.

Table 5. Analysis of labels obtained with the proposed methodology considering bean landraces with one- and two-color seeds.

Description	Number of Bean Landraces
Same colors	99
Predicted colors contain real colors	60
Real colors contain predicted colors	3
Some colors are the same	10
Different colors	0
Total	172

Table 5 shows the number of bean landraces that fit the types of classifications previously described. 99 of the bean landraces were labelled with the same colors as observed by the expert, while the remaining 73 have colors in common between the predicted and real colors. It is important to note that there is no bean landrace where the predicted colors completely differed from the real colors in this experiment. However, the 60 bean landraces where the predicted colors contain the real colors must be analyzed, since if the proposed methodology assigned to a bean landrace the 7 colors searched for, the precision for this bean landrace would be 1, without the real colors presented on the bean landrace being relevant.

In the following section, examples of the types of classifications are presented to analyze if the additional colors predicted with the methodology or if the colors not detected by the same are justified.

3.1.1. Analysis of Results Obtained by Type

This section analyzed a random selection of bean landraces to determine whether the colors predicted by the methodology are adequate compared to the real colors. In each case, the corresponding bean landrace image is displayed to analyze the colors on the seeds.

The case where the predicted and real colors are identical is not considered by the analysis, and, in this particular instance, no discrepancies were observed between the predicted and real colors of the bean landraces. Consequently, the analysis for the classification of types 1 and 5 is omitted.

The colors in the real labels are contained in the predicted labels (Type 2)

In this type of classification, the methodology proposed identifies the colors observed by the expert and additional colors. In such instances, the fitness function invariably yields a value of 1. This decision is justified by the premise that the methodology identifies colors the expert could not perceive. However, in such cases, it is important to analyze how the methodology assigns the additional colors.

To this end, Table 6 presents the number of bean landraces where the real colors are contained in the predicted colors, considering the number of colors in each case. The findings presented in this table demonstrate that, in certain instances, a maximum of two additional colors can be identified by implementing the proposed methodology in specific bean landraces.

Table 6. Analysis of bean landraces where the real colors are contained in the predicted colors.

Real Colors	Predicted Colors	Number of Bean Landraces
1	2	33
1	3	7
2	3	16
2	4	4

Figure 19 shows three examples of bean landraces, each with a single-color real label. The proposed methodology identifies two colors (Figure 19A,B) or three colors (Figure 19C) in these cases. By analyzing the seeds on Figure 19A, there is a noticeable differentiation between the yellow tones, some darker than the others. These seeds were probably sufficient to contribute significantly to a new Gaussian whose means are closer to the brown color means in the training dataset. In the Figure 19B, the purple colors added by the proposed method are also visible in some seeds. This could be due to the lighting environment. The same happens in Figure 19C, where several tonalities can be perceived with the blue background and the accommodation of the bean seeds, so the methodology's addition of the brown and purple colors can be justified.

Figure 19. Examples of bean landraces with single-color seeds (according to the expert), where the proposed methodology identifies the color, and one (**A**,**B**) or two colors more (**C**).

Figure 20 shows two examples of bean landraces, each with two colors in their real labels. However, the proposed methodology identifies three colors. The additional colors, yellow and pink, added with the proposed methodology on Figure 20A and Figure 20B, respectively, are perceptible but in a smaller quantity than the other colors. This is probably why the expert does not consider these colors on the bean landraces.

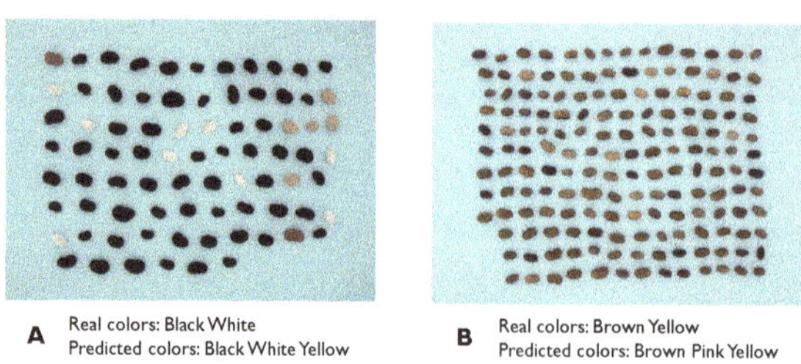

Figure 20. Examples of bean landraces characterized by the presence of two colors on their seeds (according to the expert), where the proposed methodology identifies these colors and one more color.

In Figure 21, two examples of bean landraces with two colors in their real labels are presented. However, the proposed methodology identifies four colors. As in the previous case, the two added colors, pink and red for Figure 21A, and pink and purple for Figure 21B, are present in the corresponding bean landraces, but in a lower quantity of seeds, so the expert does not consider the presence of those colors.

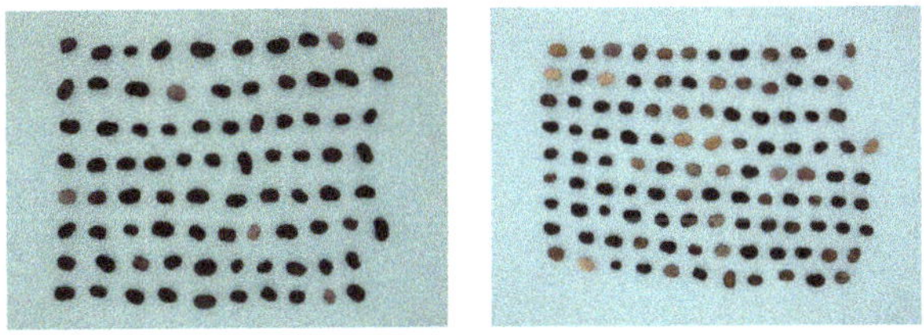

A Real colors: Black Brown
Predicted colors: Black Brown Pink Red

B Real colors: Black Brown
Predicted colors: Black Brown Pink Purple

Figure 21. Examples of bean landraces characterized by the presence of two colors on their seeds (according to the expert), where the proposed methodology identifies these colors and two more colors.

The colors in the predicted labels are contained in the real labels (Type 3)

In this type of classification, the methodology proposed identifies fewer colors than those observed by the expert. Consequently, the fitness function invariably yields a value lower than 1. The three bean landrace images that fulfil this characterization are presented in Figure 22.

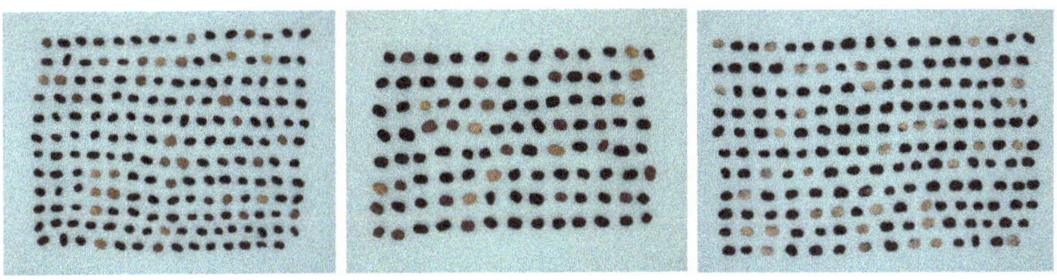

A Real colors: Black Brown
Predicted colors: Brown

B Real colors: Black Brown
Predicted colors: Brown

C Real colors: Black Yellow
Predicted colors: Black

Figure 22. Examples of bean landraces characterized by the presence of two colors on their seeds (according to the expert), where the proposed methodology only identifies one of these colors.

As illustrated in Figure 22, the proposed methodology identifies the brown color in Figure 22A,B, despite the black color being the more prevalent color in the seeds. In such instances, the GI algorithm identifies means that are more proximate to the information of the brown means in the training dataset. This phenomenon could be attributed to the fact that the black and brown colors are in proximity and on the same level in the training dataset locations, as illustrated in Figure 16. So, the means obtained for these bean landraces with the GI algorithm are at the same level and between the concentration of black and brown points means of the training dataset but closer to the brown ones.

Conversely, in Figure 22C it is evident that the proportions of seeds between colors are significantly imbalanced. So, the information of the pixels corresponding to the yellow seeds probably was eliminated during the thresholding process performed by the methodology proposed.

Some colors in the real and predicted labels are the same (Type 4)

In this type of classification, the methodology proposed does not identify all the colors observed by the expert and adds others. In such cases, the fitness function has a value lower than 1.

In Figure 23, three examples of bean landraces are presented, each bearing two colors in their real labels. In these cases, the proposed methodology identifies one of the colors and adds one or two more for the predicted label.

Figure 23. Examples of bean landraces characterized by the presence of two colors on their seeds (according to the expert), where the proposed methodology only identifies one of these colors and assigns two colors (**A**,**B**) or one color (**C**) more.

As illustrated in Figure 23, the methodology identifies the presence of yellow in certain seeds of the bean landrace on Figure 23A. However, the black color is excluded despite its observable presence in some seeds. A more in-depth analysis of the image reveals the presence of more than two colors in the seeds, although the estimation performed with the proposed model identifies red and brown as the means instead of black, likely because these colors are spatially close to black in the CIE L*a*b* color space. This substitution of brown for red is also evident in Figure 23C. In Figure 23B, the yellow color identified by the proposed methodology is consistent with the presence of seeds of this color in the bean landrace, and the brown color is also present. However, the black color is substituted by the red one for the same reasons as the other images: the black and brown colors are found in proximity in the CIE L*a*b* color space.

3.1.2. General Conclusions for the First Set of Experiments Considering Bean Landraces with One- or Two-Color Seeds and the Adjustment of 7 Gaussians

After analyzing the types of classifications, the following implications can be made:

- The classification of type 2, which corresponds to cases where the real labels are contained in the predicted labels, occurs when the expert does not perceive the additional colors due to their observations being performed without a unified background. Alternatively, the expert may consider that the additional colors found by the methodology are in lower quantities than the other colors and, therefore, are not included in the real label.
- The classification of type 3, corresponding to cases where the colors in the predicted labels are contained in the real labels, occurs when there is a confusion between the black and brown colors due to the proximity of the means of the training dataset in the CIE L*a*b* color space, or when some color is directly eliminated during the thresholding process.
- The classification of type 4, corresponding to cases where some colors in the real and predicted labels are the same, occurs when the additional colors found by the methodology substitute the other colors considered in the real label, considering their spatial proximity in the CIE L*a*b* color space.

It can be posited that the proposed methodology is subject to critical errors in the classification of type 4, given that in such instances, certain visible colors are substituted by others that are proximate in the CIE L*a*b* color space. However, this is well penalized in the precision function, which gives values lower than 1 in these cases, considering the colors that are visually present but not found by the process.

The subsequent section will present a detailed exposition of the second set of experiments. These experiments will involve the analysis of bean landraces with one-, two-, and three-color seeds. The objective of this analysis is to ascertain whether the incorporation of bean landraces with more than two color seeds results in a significant enhancement of the complexity of the process.

3.2. Experiments with Bean Landraces with One-, Two-, or Three-Color Seeds and Fitting 7 Gaussians

In Table 7, the results obtained with the methodology proposed considering 7 Gaussian components in the GI algorithm and bean landraces with one-, two- and three- color seeds are shown. The minimum, maximum, mean and standar deviation of the precisions of twenty experiments for each K value for the *K-nn* method are reported along with the mean time needed to obtain the training and test datasets for the experimental process (steps (A) and (B)).

Table 7. Results of the experiments considering bean landraces with seeds of one, two and three colors, searching for 7 Gaussian components with the GI algorithm.

K	Min	Max	Mean ± St.D.	Train/Test Mean Time (min)	p-Value (Shapiro-Wilk)
1	0.6610	0.8989	0.8408 ± 0.0656	4.17/10.37	9.56×10^{-5} *
2	0.6731	0.8859	0.8459 ± 0.0564	4.19/10.36	1.73×10^{-5} *
3	0.6683	0.8859	0.8503 ± 0.0568	4.32/10.38	3.37×10^{-6} *
4	0.6820	0.8908	0.8590 ± 0.0524	4.29/10.42	1.12×10^{-6} *
5	0.7112	0.9094	0.8704 ± 0.0403	4.19/10.47	1.64×10^{-6} *
6	0.7751	0.8997	0.8725 ± 0.0268	4.20/10.50	1.04×10^{-4} *
7	0.7961	0.9037	0.8765 ± 0.0235	4.34/10.50	9.22×10^{-4} *
8	0.8139	0.9013	0.8741 ± 0.0207	4.20/10.51	8.09×10^{-3} *
9	0.8390	0.9013	0.8765 ± 0.0166	4.27/10.60	3.30×10^{-1} *
10	0.8341	0.8989	0.8739 ± 0.0173	4.29/10.64	2.94×10^{-1} *

* Cases where there is a 95% confidence that the precisions does not fit a normal distribution.

In this instance, the p-values of the Shapiro-Wilk statistical test shown in Table 7 indicate that the distributions of the precisions obtained in the twenty executions of each K value for the *K-nn* method are non-normal. Therefore, in order to identify if the samples exhibit significant differences, the Kruskal-Wallis test was conducted, obtaining a value of 0.3802. As this p-value exceeds the significance level of 0.05, it can be concluded that the differences between the values of K for the *K-nn* method are not statistically significant.

In Figure 24, the boxplots for these results are presented with the corresponding median for each K value. As in the previous set of experiments, the value of K is selected considering the highest median obtained. So the value of K is set at 7 to analyze the specific results in this case.

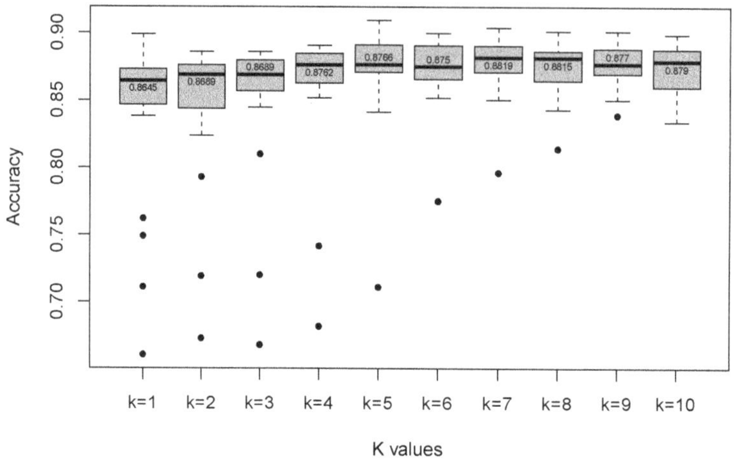

Figure 24. Boxplots of the results obtained considering bean landraces with one-, two-, and three-color seeds and the different K values for the K-nn method with the proposed methodology, and fitting 7 Gaussians with the GI algorithm. The median for each K value is displayed in the corresponding boxplot.

In this case, the five types of classifications are also considered on the best result with $K = 7$, corresponding to the precision 0.9037. Table 8 shows the number of bean landraces that fit the types of classifications, and it is observed that 118 of the bean landraces were labeled with the same colors as observed by the expert, while the remaining 88 have colors in common between the predicted and real labels. In this experiment, there is no bean landrace where the predicted colors completely differed from the real colors. However, the following section will analyze the types of classifications obtained with the methodology compared to the real colors observed by the expert.

Table 8. Analysis of labels obtained with the proposed methodology considering bean landraces with one-, two-, and three-color seeds.

Description	Number of Bean Landraces
Same colors	118
Predicted colors contain real colors	47
Real colors contain predicted colors	9
Some colors are the same	32
Different colors	0
Total	206

3.2.1. Analysis of Results Obtained by Type

This section analyzes a random selection of bean landraces to determine whether the colors predicted by the methodology are adequate compared to the real colors., adding the corresponding bean landrace image to visually analyze the colors on the seeds.

In this case, the analysis for the classification of types 1 and 5 is also omitted since there is no need to analyze the cases where the predicted colors and the real colors are the same, and no discrepancies were observed between the predicted and real colors of the bean landraces, respectively.

The colors in the real labels are contained in the predicted labels (Type 2)

Table 9 shows the number of bean landraces where the real colors are included in the predicted colors, considering the number of colors in each case. In this set of experiments, the same behavior is observed as in the previous set of experiments. The proposed methodology finds at most two additional colors in some cases, so 5 colors are found in some bean landraces.

Table 9. Analysis of bean landraces where the real colors are contained in the predicted colors.

Real Colors	Predicted Colors	Number of Bean Landraces
1	2	18
1	3	5
1	4	3
2	3	11
2	4	5
3	4	4
3	5	1

In Figure 25, three examples of bean landraces are presented, wherein the actual labels exhibit a single color, whereas the proposed methodology discerns two distinct colors. In these images, discerning at least two different intensity levels of color on each bean landrace is facilitated by the blue background incorporated during the image acquisition. In Figure 25A, the black coloration appears to have been added to accentuate the deep brown hue of certain seeds. In contrast, brown coloration was introduced in Figure 25B,C to create a contrasting effect with the light red seeds.

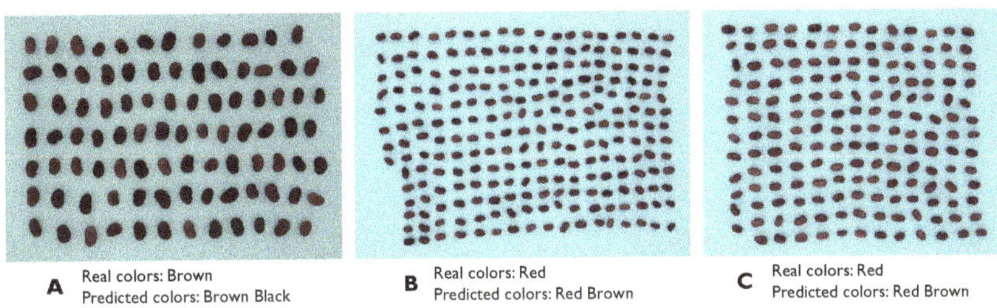

Figure 25. Examples of bean landraces where the real color observed by the expert is included in the corresponding set of predicted colors with the proposed methodology, with two colors.

Figures 26 and 27 contain examples of bean landraces where the expert discerns single-color seeds. However, the proposed methodology identifies three- and four-color seeds, respectively.

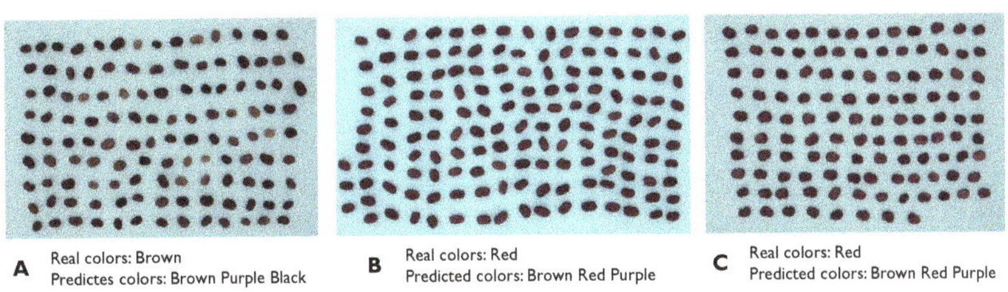

Figure 26. Examples of bean landraces where the real color observed by the expert is included in the corresponding set of predicted colors with the proposed methodology, with three colors.

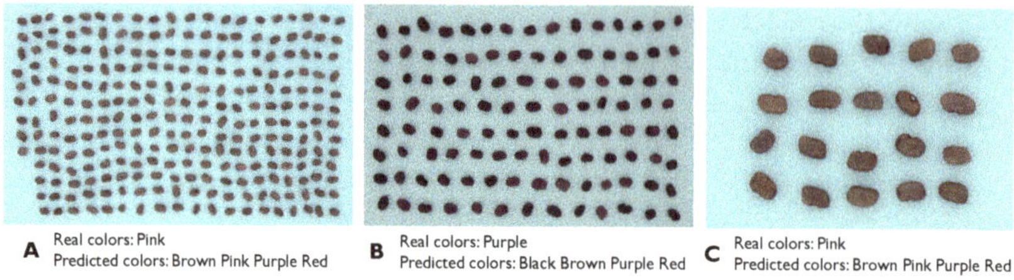

Figure 27. Examples of bean landraces where the real color observed by the expert is included in the corresponding set of predicted colors with the proposed methodology, with four colors.

Image **A** in Figure 26 exhibits at least three distinct color intensity levels. For this reason the proposed methodology assigns three colors. Conversely, in images **B** and **C**, the variation in the red intensity can be structured at most in two intensities of red, yet the predicted colors exhibit brown and purple hues. This phenomenon can be attributed to the proximity of these colors to the red color in the CIE L*a*b* color space.

In Figure 27, the three bean landraces with a single-color real label that the methodology predicted to have a four-color label are displayed. These could be the three most critical errors performed by the proposed methodology since the predicted colors on images **A**, **B**, and **C** add three colors that cannot be perceived visually. The proximity of the colors in the CIE L*a*b* color space may be a contributing factor to this phenomenon, given the number of seeds, and the dispersion of their real colors.

On Figure 28, three examples of images are presented, with the predicted labels exhibiting three colors, while the real labels display two colors. A visual analysis of these bean landraces reveals that the colors indicated with the methodology are distinguishable on the corresponding images. In this case, the proposed methodology successfully identifies colors that the expert cannot perceive without the uniform background.

Figure 28. Examples of bean landraces where the two real colors observed by the expert are included in the corresponding set of predicted colors with the proposed methodology, with three colors.

This phenomenon is also observed in the bean landrace images depicted in Figures 29 and 30. The methodology employed identifies all the colors observed in the seeds of the images **A**, **B**, and **C** of both Figures. It is possible that the expert may not have considered these colors due to the limited number of seeds or perhaps due to the difficulty in discerning the colors in the absence of a blue background and under the conditions of the illumination environment.

The only case where the methodology found five colors in a bean landrace previously labeled with three colors is shown in Figure 31. It is evident from this figure that the five colors predicted by the methodology are present in the seeds, but some in smaller quantities than the others.

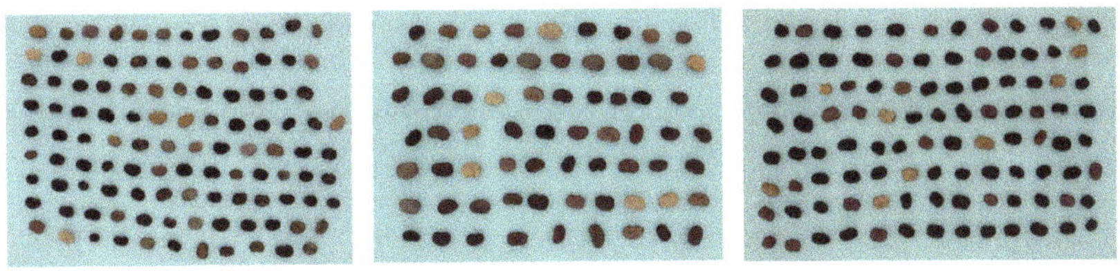

Figure 29. Examples of bean landraces where the two real colors observed by the expert are included in the corresponding set of predicted colors with the proposed methodology, with four colors.

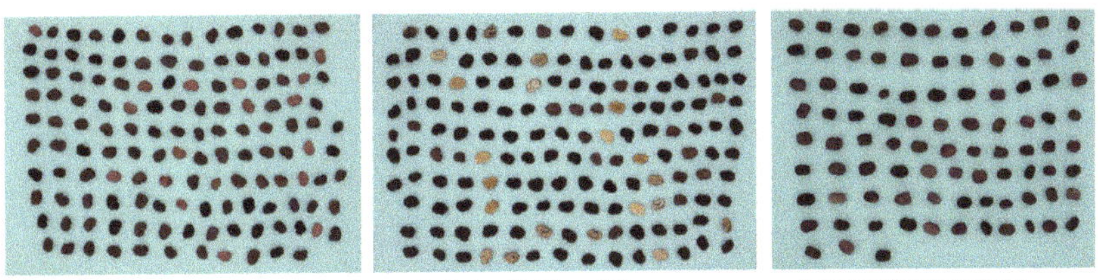

Figure 30. Examples of bean landraces where the three real colors observed by the expert are included in the corresponding set of predicted colors with the proposed methodology, with four colors.

Figure 31. Bean landrace where the three real colors observed by the expert are included in the corresponding set of predicted colors with the proposed methodology, with five colors.

The colors in the predicted labels are contained in the real labels (Type 3)

In this classification, the methodology identifies fewer colors than those observed by the expert. The number of images with this characterization is documented in Table 10. Nine images of bean landraces are included in this classification, all exhibiting three colors as observed by the expert. However, the methodology detects only one or two colors on the seeds.

Table 10. Analysis of bean landraces where the predicted colors are contained in the real colors.

Real Colors	Predicted Colors	Number of Bean Landraces
3	1	2
3	2	7

As illustrated in Figure 32, the two images of bean landraces display three colors in their labels, yet the methodology identifies only one color. In this case, the three colors of the seeds are perceptible visually; however, in image **A**, the reduced seed quantity in this sample relative to the other bean landraces examined can potentially influence the outcomes of the methodology. This is particularly salient in the thresholding process, where the color of the seeds not detected by the procedure may be filtered out. A similar scenario might occur in image **B**, where yellow seeds may have been removed, resulting in a dataset predominantly comprising black and brown seeds that are more closely aligned in terms of spatial distribution with the brown color means of the training dataset.

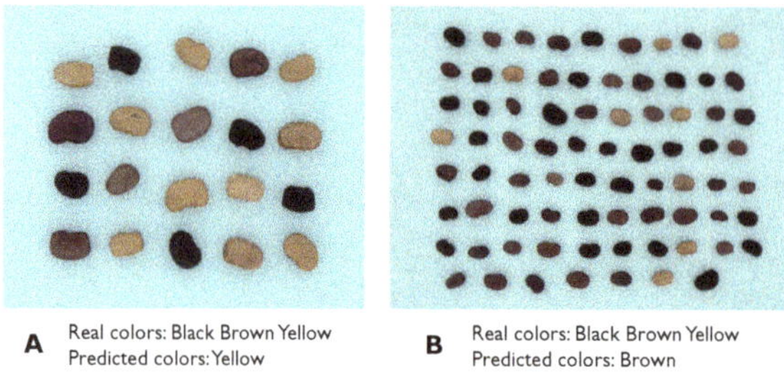

Figure 32. Examples of bean landraces where the predicted color with the proposed methodology is included in the corresponding set of real colors observed by the expert, with three colors.

In Figure 33, three examples of bean landrace images are presented, in which the methodology identified two colors instead of the three indicated in the actual label. Notably, distinguishing more than two colors on the seeds in images **A** and **C** is significantly challenging. However, the expert adds red and purple colors, respectively. On the other hand, the image labeled as **B** presents a case in which the brown and purple seeds are grouped as a single brown category.

Figure 33. Examples of bean landraces where the two predicted colors with the proposed methodology are included in the corresponding set of real colors observed by the expert, with three colors.

Some colors in the real and predicted labels are the same (Type 4)

In this type of classification, the expert and the methodology coincide in some colors of the analyzed bean landraces, but not in all, so a proper subset of colors is not presented as in the previous types of classification.

In Figure 34, three examples of bean landraces are presented, each exhibiting this characterization. In image **A**, the color indicated in both labels is black. A visual inspection of the landrace seeds reveals the presence of at least three distinct colors, with yellow being particularly notable. However, the proposed methodology erroneously identifies brown, pink, and red colors, even when the number of yellow seeds is significant. This discrepancy indicates a critical error in the methodology. In image **B**, both labels exhibit brown and yellow colors, while the pink color in the real colors is substituted by a combination of purple and red colors. This phenomenon can be attributed to the proximity of these three colors in the CIE L*a*b* color space. Furthermore, this proximity can provide a potential explanation for the labels in image **C**, where the red color observed by the expert is replaced by the purple color delivered by the methodology.

Figure 34. Examples of bean landraces where the set of predicted colors with the proposed methodology and the set of real colors observed by the expert have one or two colors in common.

3.2.2. General Conclusions for the Second Set of Experiments Considering Bean Landraces with One-, Two-, or Three-Color Seeds and the Adjustment of 7 Gaussians

After analyzing the types of classifications of this set of experiments, it is observed that there are more critical errors by considering those populations with three colors on their seeds. The following implications can be made in this case:

- The classification of type 2, in which the colors perceived by the expert are contained within the colors generated by the methodology, necessitates more cases for analysis compared to the previous set of experiments. However, a distinguishing feature of this classification is that the methodology identifies no more than two additional colors beyond the actual colors. Consequently, the methodology identifies a maximum of five colors. As in the previous set of experiments, the presence of additional colors can be attributed to the expert's inability to perceive the colors in the absence of a plain background and an illumination environment, or to the expert's perception that the additional colors found by the methodology are present in smaller quantities compared to the other colors. However, there are instances where the addition of colors by the methodology is not evident, as observed in images A and B of Figure 27. This phenomenon can be attributed to the proximity of the predicted colors in the CIE L*a*b* color space.
- The classification of type 3, in which the colors in the predicted labels are contained in the actual labels, occurs in nine images previously analyzed by the expert with seeds of three different colors. In these cases, the methodology identified only one or two colors due to the proximity of the means in the CIE L*a*b* color space or when some color is directly eliminated during the thresholding process due to the number of seeds analyzed on the bean landrace.
- The classification of type 4 corresponds to cases where some colors in the real and predicted labels are the same. In such instances, the supplementary colors identified by the methodology supplant the other colors specified in the real label, with their spatial proximity in the CIE L*a*b* color space being considered.

The proposed methodology exhibits a higher incidence of critical errors in this set of experiments compared to the previous one. The incorporation of bean landraces with three distinct colors serves to augment the complexity of the process due to the characteristics of these new images, some of which have a lower quantity of seeds, and since the thresholding process considers the same number t for all the images in the test dataset to clean the information, some colors disappear in this step (step (B) on Section 2.4).

It is also noteworthy that these cases are adequately penalized by the fitness function proposed. As in both sets of experiments, the analysis of the classification of types 3 and 4 employs the distribution of the training dataset in the CIE L*a*b* color space as justifications; the subsequent section will present a brief analysis of these datasets.

3.3. Analysis of the Means in the Training Dataset

As previously stated in step (A) of Section 2.4, the training dataset for the *K-nn* method considers the information of the means obtained from 3D histograms of individual seeds previously labeled with one color. Consequently, the information of multiple seeds of a single color is utilized to characterize the CIE L*a*b* color space with a group of points. Ideally, points with identical labels would be positioned closer to each other, as illustrated in Figure 16. However, the results obtained suggest that this phenomenon was not observed in the training datasets. So, this is an unconsidered factor that influences the outcomes.

The plots of four training datasets are presented in Figure 35.

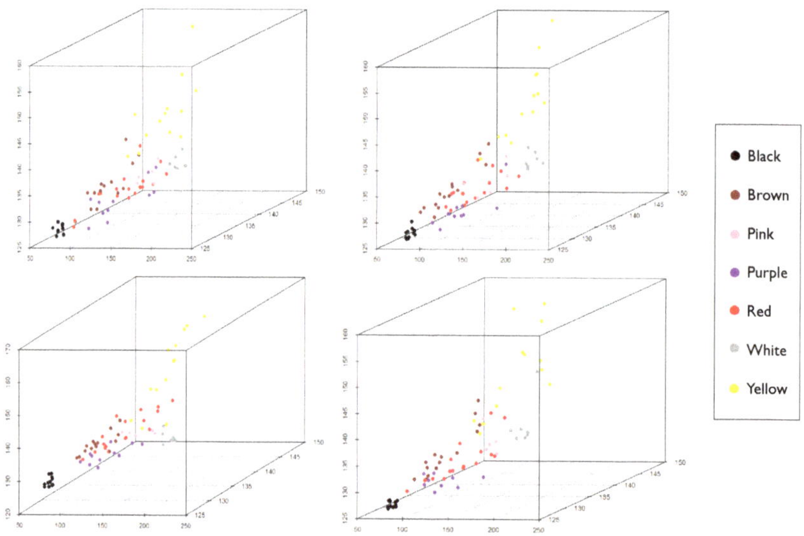

Figure 35. Examples of training datasets considered in the experiments of the proposed methodology.

As demonstrated in Figure 35, the points corresponding to the means of black, white, and occasionally yellow colors appear to be distributed evenly. That is to say, the points with these colors are close, or there is an absence of other color points overlapping their spatial structure. Conversely, for the colors brown, pink, purple, and red, there is an overlap of concentrations of points. This observation is further substantiated by the analysis of results, which reveals instances of color combination or substitution among these hues employing the *K-nn* method for the classification of the means in the test dataset.

4. Discussion

As established in preceding studies, identifying color in bean landraces is paramount, given the demonstrated correlation between the chemical composition and health benefits of the seeds and their colorimetric properties. However, the diversity of colors present in bean landrace seeds poses a challenge to classification.

Previous studies have employed various analytical techniques, including laboratory and digital images, to analyze the color properties of bean landraces. Contemporary investigations have highlighted the employment of probability distributions to characterize the colors of bean landraces on histograms in two and three dimensions in a color space, such as the CIE L*a*b* color space. The present study employs this approach, but instead of utilizing the complete information of these histograms in the learning process, a compression of information is considered with the GMM and the GI algorithm. This model facilitates capturing information regarding the colors in the bean landraces with the means vectors obtained for the GMM.

Characterizing the colors of heterogeneous bean landraces by points in the CIE L*a*b* color space is the novel approach employed in this study. In addition to the favorable outcomes achieved with the proposed methodology, the process facilitates a substantial computational cost reduction in terms of temporal requirements and memory when contrasted with antecedent techniques that employ numerous two-dimensional histograms for each bean landrace, along with a considerable amount of time in the learning process.

The proposed methodology involves the compression of information from each bean landrace into a maximum of seven points in the CIE L*a*b* color space (since seven colors are considered as base) in comparison with several 2D histograms of size 255×255 employed in other works.

Concerning the computational time required to conduct experiments of the proposed methodology, the compression of information from a set of 3D histograms from singular seeds with one color requires less than five minutes. The compression of information from a set of 3D histograms corresponding to the bean landraces analyzed employs 8 or 11 min, depending on the number of colors considered in the seeds. After the compression stage, the *K-nn* method is employed to classify the information of the bean landraces using the information of the single seeds as a training dataset. This process takes no more than 0.0006 s. Consequently, the total duration of the experiment is no more than 16 min. This represents a substantial reduction compared to alternative approaches that employ convolutional neural networks and more sophisticated techniques, which require greater information, more computational time, and a process where structures must be found first.

In contrast, the proposed process involves only two considerations to obtain each dataset (training and test): the number of Gaussians for the GMM that the GI algorithm must search for and the thresholding value t. The former is employed to restrict the search to the maximum number of colors considered for the bean landraces. At the same time, the latter is used to enhance the clarity of the color agglomerations in the CIE L*a*b* color space and eliminate noise information from the 3D histograms for the GI algorithm. However, more room of improvement was found in this regard, since the critical errors performed by the proposed methodology are part of the characterization of these parameters.

Regarding precision, the proposed methodology and experimentation setup obtained favorable results considering the proposed fitness function.

These enhancements signify a substantial and noteworthy advancement in the color identification of heterogeneous bean landraces.

5. Conclusions

The proposed methodology has yielded favorable outcomes in identifying colors in bean landraces with seeds of heterogeneous color. Employing the means obtained with the GMM and the GI algorithm for each seed (training dataset) and each bean landrace (test dataset) is a good approach to identifying the colors with the help of the *K-nn* method.

The analysis of the results of this study, considering the five types of classification, along with examples of the "errors" committed by the proposed methodology, enables the description of the main challenges presented in this identification process.

Firstly, the involvement of an expert in the pre-labeling process is paramount since several cases of type 2 occur when the expert does not perceive certain colors in the seeds due to suboptimal lighting and environmental conditions during observation. Additionally, the expert may overlook certain colors due to their minimal presence in a particular bean landrace.

Secondly, it is crucial to analyze the distribution of the means in the training dataset, as cases of types 3 and 4 occur when the means of different colors overlap in the CIE L*a*b* color space, as described in Section 3.

Thirdly, the quantity of seeds shown in the images is relevant to the process. In most images depicting bean landraces, 60 g of seeds are considered, as this is the specified value reported in several studies utilizing the pH differential method to measure the anthocyanin concentration of the landrace. Notably, the anthocyanin concentration is closely associated with the coloration of the seeds. However, it was observed that several errors in the proposed methodology resulted in the display of a lower quantity of seeds for some bean landraces. This phenomenon can be attributed to the threshold value t employed during the cleansing process, eliminating the information of the seeds with the color less pronounced.

Still, with these limitations, the proposed methodology achieves a high level of precision, with values exceeding 90%.

6. Drawbacks and Limitations of the Proposed Methodology

The methodology proposed in this work is subject to certain limitations:

- The first and critical drawback results from the specific characteristics of the 3D histograms used as inputs for the methodology. As demonstrated in Section 2.1, these are derived from images obtained with the process described therein, where the photos are captured in optimal lighting conditions, with reduced specular brightness and a uniform background. In particular, as demonstrated in [12], experiments conducted on low-quality bean landrace images have yielded unsatisfactory results due to the presence of noise that can manifest as new or different colors. Consequently, the methodology employed in this study may be susceptible to errors in the GMM fitting process when employing low-quality images, which could lead to the discovery of more colors than the real ones and potentially result in diminished outcomes. However, the model's objective is to achieve concordance with the outcomes of laboratory-based chemical analyses that measure anthocyanin levels without incurring the financial expense of reagents. Consequently, the structured imaging process, which is already in place in a regulated environment, offers the optimal conditions for the algorithm to achieve the most optimal results.
- Another characteristic to consider is the limited number of bean landrace samples available for specific colors and varieties. For example, in this project, the bean landraces of variegate colors were not considered for this reason. However, it is essential to recognize that these legumes play a crucial role in the diets of local farmers and communities with limited resources.

7. Future Work

There is room for improvement by considering the following proposals:

- A significant step in the process is to consider 3D histograms from images of low quality, such as those resulting from poorly illuminated conditions, to assess the robustness of the proposed methodology.

- It is imperative to incorporate bean landraces with variegated seeds in this study. The compilation, image acquisition, segmentation, and extraction of information regarding these specific bean landraces must be performed to facilitate a comprehensive analysis of the proposed methodology's behavior.
- Identify the appropriate parameters for the methodology by performing more experiments:
  - The thresholding values t employed in the cleansing process should be analyzed, even considering different values between bean landraces, depending on the quantity of seeds in the images.
  - Further experimentation could be conducted by reducing the number of Gaussians considered for the GMM. In this case, 7 Gaussian was considered since that is the number of searched colors. However, given the understanding that, in some cases, the GI algorithm is capable of identifying a maximum of five colors, this number should be employed in subsequent studies to fit the GMM.
- Furthermore, the utilization of 3D histograms in alternative color spaces, such as RGB, LCh, and HSV, is imperative for subsequent analysis. Alternatively, it can be considered the translation of color information to an optimal color space, where pixels of different colors are separated through techniques such as Linear Discriminant Analysis.

Author Contributions: Conceptualization, A.-L.L.-L. and M.-L.A.-G.; Data curation, A.-L.L.-L. and J.-L.M.-R.; Formal analysis, A.-L.L.-L.; Investigation, A.-L.L.-L.; Methodology, A.-L.L.-L. and M.-L.A.-G.; Resources, H.-G.A.-M., J.-L.M.-R. and E.-N.A.-B.; Software, A.-L.L.-L.; Supervision, M.-L.A.-G., H.-G.A.-M., J.-L.M.-R. and E.-N.A.-B.; Validation, M.-L.A.-G.; Visualization, A.-L.L.-L.; Writing—original draft, A.-L.L.-L.; Writing—review & editing, M.-L.A.-G., H.-G.A.-M., J.-L.M.-R. and E.-N.A.-B. All authors have read and agreed to the published version of the manuscript.

Funding: This research received no external funding.

Data Availability Statement: The datasets employed in this article are not readily available since they are part of an ongoing study. Requests for access to the datasets should be directed to eliaquino@uv.mx and heacosta@uv.mx.

Acknowledgments: The first author acknowledges the Secretaría de Ciencia, Humanidades, Tecnología e Innovación (SECIHTI) of Mexico for the financial support provided through scholarship 712182, which was awarded for postdoctoral studies at the Artificial Intelligence Research Institute at the University of Veracruz. The authors also express their gratitude to José Luis Chávez Servia for providing the samples of bean landraces employed in this study.

Conflicts of Interest: The authors declare no conflicts of interest.

Abbreviations

The following abbreviations are used in this manuscript:

GMM	Gaussian Mixture Model
GI algorithm	Gini Index algorithm

Appendix A. Pseudocodes

In this section, the pseudocodes for the GI algorithm and the proposed methodology are presented to facilitate the reproduction of the process.

The Gini Index algorithm, described in Section 2.2, is outlined in Algorithm A1. The methodology proposed in Section 2.3 for identifying the colors present in a bean landrace using the GMM and the GI algorithm is presented in Algorithm A2.

Algorithm A1: Gini index algorithm (GI algorithm)

Input: Dataset P, number of Gaussian components K, initial values for the parameters $\theta = \{\phi_k, \theta_k\}_{k=1}^{K}$.

Output: Parameters $\hat{\theta}$.

Notation: $P = \{p_m = (p_1^{(m)}, p_2^{(m)}, \ldots, p_N^{(m)})\}_{m=1}^{M}$:= Dataset with M observations in dimension N. ϕ_k := Proportion of the k-th Gaussian component. $\mu_k = (\mu_{k1}, \mu_{k2}, \ldots, \mu_{kN})$:= Mean vector of the k-th Gaussian component. $diag(\Sigma_k) = (\sigma_{k1}^2, \sigma_{k2}^2, \ldots, \sigma_{kN}^2)$:= Diagonal of the k-th Gaussian component's covariance matrix. $\theta_k = (\mu_k, \Sigma_k)$:= Parameters of the k-th Gaussian component.

`// Process`

repeat

  `// Update the mean and covariance matrix parameters of the Gaussian components.`

  for $t \leftarrow 1$ **to** K **do**

    for $r \leftarrow 1$ **to** N **do**

$$\mu_{tr} = \frac{\sum_{m=1}^{M} p_r^{(m)} \exp\left(-\frac{\left(p_r^{(m)} - \mu_{tr}\right)^2}{2\sigma_{tr}^2}\right)}{\sum_{m=1}^{M} \exp\left(-\frac{\left(p_r^{(m)} - \mu_{tr}\right)^2}{2\sigma_{tr}^2}\right)};$$

$$\sigma_{tr} = \frac{\sum_{m=1}^{M} \left(p_r^{(m)} - \mu_{tr}\right)^2 \exp\left(-\frac{\left(p_r^{(m)} - \mu_{tr}\right)^2}{2\sigma_{tr}^2}\right)}{\sum_{m=1}^{M} \exp\left(-\frac{\left(p_r^{(m)} - \mu_{tr}\right)^2}{2\sigma_{tr}^2}\right)};$$

    end

  end

  `// Get the conditional probabilities` $P(f_{\hat{\theta}_k} | p_m)$.

  for $k \leftarrow 1$ **to** K **do**

    for $m \leftarrow 1$ **to** M **do**

$$P(f_{\hat{\theta}_k} | p_m) = \frac{\phi_k f_{\theta_k}(p_m)}{\sum_{j=1}^{K} \phi_j f_{\theta_j}(p_m)}$$

    end

  end

  `// Find the class of each data point` p_m

  for $m \leftarrow 1$ **to** M **do**

    $Cl_{p_m} = \arg\max_k \{P(f_{\theta_k} | p_m) | k = 1, 2, \ldots, K\}$

  end

  `// Update the Gaussian proportions` ϕ_k

  for $k \leftarrow 1$ **to** K **do**

    $\hat{\phi}_k = \frac{\sum_{m=1}^{M} I(Cl_{p_m} = k)}{M}$

  end

  Establish $\hat{\theta} = \{\hat{\phi}_k, \hat{\theta}_k\}_{k=1}^{K}$ with $\hat{\theta}_k = \{\hat{\mu}_k, \hat{\Sigma}_k\}$.

until *convergence is reached according to the minimum distance criterion between the vectors' values* $\hat{\theta} = (\hat{\phi}_1, \hat{\mu}_1, diag(\hat{\Sigma}_1), \ldots, \hat{\phi}_K, \hat{\mu}_K, diag(\hat{\Sigma}_k))$ *of successive iterations.*;

Return: $\hat{\theta}$

Algorithm A2: Methodology

Input: Set $\{(i,j,k), f_{ijk}\}$ with the 3D histogram information of the bean landrace (or seed) in the CIE L*a*b* color space, number of Gaussian components K, threshold value t, initial values for the parameters $\theta = \{\phi_k, \theta_k\}_{k=1}^{K}$.

Output: Means of the Gaussian components, with mixture proportion greater than zero, in the CIE L*a*b* color space $\hat{\mu}_{L^*a^*b^*}$.

Notation: $P[r,c]$:= element in the row r and column c of the dataset P.

// Process
// 1) Data cleansing - Obtention of the dataset P
Get $threshold \leftarrow \frac{\max\{f_{ijk}\}}{t}$;
Get $P_{threshold} \leftarrow \{(i,j,k) | f_{ijk} > threshold\}$ (See Equation (1)) ;
Get $P \leftarrow$ array with three columns, where each column corresponds to the coordinates of the elements in $P_{threshold}$;
// 2) Transfer to space $[0,100] \times [0,100] \times [0,100]$
for $j \leftarrow 1$ **to** 3 **do**
    Set $C_j \leftarrow j$-th column of dataset P ;
    $MC_j \leftarrow \max\{C_j\}$;
    $mC_j \leftarrow \min\{C_j\}$;
    for $m \leftarrow 1$ **to** $|P|$ **do**
        $P[m,C_j] \leftarrow 100 * \frac{P[m,C_j]-mC_j}{MC_j - mC_j}$;
    end
end
// 3) Gaussian fitting with the GI algorithm
$\hat{\theta} = GI\text{-}algorithm(P, K, \theta = (\phi_k, \theta_k)_{k=1}^{K})$;
// 4) Return the mean values to the $CIE\ L^*a^*b^*$ color space
Set $K' \leftarrow$ number of Gaussian components with ϕ_k values greater than 0 ;
for $j \leftarrow 1$ **to** 3 **do**
    for $k \leftarrow 1$ **to** K' **do**
        $\hat{\mu}_{kC_j} = \frac{\hat{\mu}_{kj}}{100} \cdot (MC_j - mC_j) + mC_j$
    end
end
for $k \leftarrow 1$ **to** K' **do**
    $\hat{\mu}_k = (\hat{\mu}_{kC_1}, \hat{\mu}_{kC_2}, \hat{\mu}_{kC_3})$;
end
Set $\hat{\mu}_{L^*a^*b^*} \leftarrow \{\hat{\mu}_k\}_{k=1}^{K'}$;
Return: $\hat{\mu}_{L^*a^*b^*}$

References

1. Aquino-Bolaños, E.N.; Garzón-García, A.K.; Alba-Jiménez, J.E.; Chávez-Servia, J.L.; Vera-Guzmán, A.M.; Carrillo-Rodríguez, J.C.; Santos-Basurto, M.A. Physicochemical Characterization and Functional Potential of *Phaseolus vulgaris* L. and *Phaseolus coccineus* L. Landrace Green Beans. *Agronomy* **2021**, *11*, 803. [CrossRef]
2. Aquino-Bolaños, E.N.; García-Díaz, Y.D.; Chavez-Servia, J.L.; Carrillo-Rodríguez, J.C.; Vera-Guzmán, A.M.; Heredia-García, E. Anthocyanins, polyphenols, flavonoids and antioxidant activity in common bean (*Phaseolus vulgaris* L.) landraces. *Emir. J. Food Agric.* **2016**, *28*, 581–588. [CrossRef]
3. Chávez-Servia, J.L.; Heredia-García, E.; Mayek-Pérez, N.; Aquino-Bolaños, E.N.; Hernández-Delgado, S.; Carrillo-Rodríguez, J.C.; Gill-Langarica, H.R.; Vera-Guzmán, A.M. Diversity of common bean (*Phaseolus vulgaris* L.) landraces and the nutritional value of their grains. In *Grain Legumes*; InTech: Rijeka, Croatia, 2016; pp. 1–33.
4. Singh, S.P. Broadening the genetic base of common bean cultivars: A review. *Crop Sci.* **2001**, *41*, 1659–1675. [CrossRef]

5. Bitocchi, E.; Nanni, L.; Bellucci, E.; Rossi, M.; Giardini, A.; Zeuli, P.S.; Logozzo, G.; Stougaard, J.; McClean, P.; Attene, G.; et al. Mesoamerican origin of the common bean (*Phaseolus vulgaris* L.) is revealed by sequence data. *Proc. Natl. Acad. Sci. USA* **2012**, *109*, E788–E796. [CrossRef]
6. Espinoza-García, N.; Martínez-Martínez, R.; Chávez-Servia, J.L.; Vera-Guzmán, A.M.; Carrillo-Rodríguez, J.C.; Heredia-García, E.; Velasco-Velasco, V.A. Contenido de minerales en semilla de poblaciones nativas de frijol común (*Phaseolus vulgaris* L.). *Rev. Fitotec. Mex.* **2016**, *39*, 215–223. [CrossRef]
7. Capistrán-Carabarin, A.; Aquino-Bolaños, E.N.; García-Díaz, Y.D.; Chávez-Servia, J.L.; Vera-Guzmán, A.M.; Carrillo-Rodríguez, J.C. Complementarity in Phenolic Compounds and the Antioxidant Activities of *Phaseolus coccineus* L. and *P. vulgaris* L. Landraces. *Foods* **2019**, *8*, 295. [CrossRef]
8. Hernández-Delgado, S.; Muruaga-Martínez, J.S.; Vargas-Vázquez, M.L.P.; Martínez-Mondragón, J.; Chávez-Servia, J.L.; Gill-Langarica, H.R.; Mayek-Pérez, N. Advances in genetic diversity analysis of Phaseolus in Mexico. *Mol. Approaches Genet. Divers.* **2015**, *1*, 47–73.
9. Chávez-Servia, J.L.; Carrillo-Rodríguez, J.C.; Guzmán, A.M.V.; Aquino-Bolaños, E.N.; Hernández-Delgado, S.; Mayek-Pérez, N.; Lobato-Ortiz, R. Traditional family production and nutritional-nutraceutical value of common beans (*Phaseolus vulgaris* L.) in Southeast Mexico. In *Phaseolus vulgaris: Cultivars, Production and Uses*; Nova Science Publishers, Inc.: Hauppauge, NY, USA, 2018.
10. Campos-Vega, R.; Bassinello, P.Z.; Santiago, R.d.A.C.; Oomah, B.D. Dry beans: Processing and nutritional effects. In *Therapeutic, Probiotic, and Unconventional Foods*; Elsevier: Amsterdam, The Netherlands, 2018; pp. 367–386.
11. Chávez-Mendoza, C.; Hernández-Figueroa, K.I.; Sánchez, E. Antioxidant capacity and phytonutrient content in the seed coat and cotyledon of common beans (*Phaseolus vulgaris* L.) from various regions in Mexico. *Antioxidants* **2018**, *8*, 5. [CrossRef]
12. Morales Reyes, J.L.; Acosta Mesa, H.G.; Aquino Bolaños, E.N.; Herrera Meza, S.; Cruz Ramírez, N.; Chávez Servia, J.L. Classification of Bean (*Phaseolus vulgaris* L.) Landraces with Heterogeneous Seed Color using a Probabilistic Representation. In Proceedings of the 2021 IEEE International Autumn Meeting on Power, Electronics and Computing (ROPEC), Ixtapa, Mexico, 10–12 November 2021; IEEE: Piscataway, NJ, USA, 2021; Volume 5, pp. 1–7.
13. Fernandes, A.M.; Franco, C.; Mendes-Ferreira, A.; Mendes-Faia, A.; da Costa, P.L.; Melo-Pinto, P. Brix, pH and anthocyanin content determination in whole Port wine grape berries by hyperspectral imaging and neural networks. *Comput. Electron. Agric.* **2015**, *115*, 88–96. [CrossRef]
14. Grimm, E.; Kuhnke, F.; Gajdt, A.; Ostermann, J.; Knoche, M. Accurate quantification of anthocyanin in red flesh apples using digital photography and image analysis. *Horticulturae* **2022**, *8*, 145. [CrossRef]
15. Yoshioka, Y.; Nakayama, M.; Noguchi, Y.; Horie, H. Use of image analysis to estimate anthocyanin and UV-excited fluorescent phenolic compound levels in strawberry fruit. *Breed. Sci.* **2013**, *63*, 211–217. [CrossRef] [PubMed]
16. Del Valle, J.C.; Gallardo-López, A.; Buide, M.L.; Whittall, J.B.; Narbona, E. Digital photography provides a fast, reliable, and noninvasive method to estimate anthocyanin pigment concentration in reproductive and vegetative plant tissues. *Ecol. Evol.* **2018**, *8*, 3064–3076. [CrossRef] [PubMed]
17. Djoulde, K.; Ousman, B.; Hamadjam, A.; Bitjoka, L.; Tchiegang, C. Classification of pepper seeds by machine learning using color filter array images. *J. Imaging* **2024**, *10*, 41. [CrossRef] [PubMed]
18. Kılıç, K.; Boyacı, I.H.; Köksel, H.; Küsmenoğlu, İ. A classification system for beans using computer vision system and artificial neural networks. *J. Food Eng.* **2007**, *78*, 897–904. [CrossRef]
19. Nasirahmadi, A.; Behroozi-Khazaei, N. Identification of bean varieties according to color features using artificial neural network. *Span. J. Agric. Res.* **2013**, *11*, 670–677. [CrossRef]
20. Venora, G.; Grillo, O.; Ravalli, C.; Cremonini, R. Identification of Italian landraces of bean (*Phaseolus vulgaris* L.) using an image analysis system. *Sci. Hortic.* **2009**, *121*, 410–418. [CrossRef]
21. Koklu, M.; Ozkan, I.A. Multiclass classification of dry beans using computer vision and machine learning techniques. *Comput. Electron. Agric.* **2020**, *174*, 105507. [CrossRef]
22. Tormena, C.D.; Campos, R.C.S.; Marcheafave, G.G.; Bruns, R.E.; Scarminio, I.S.; Pauli, E.D. Authentication of carioca common bean cultivars (*Phaseolus vulgaris* L.) using digital image processing and chemometric tools. *Food Chem.* **2021**, *364*, 130349. [CrossRef]
23. De Araújo, S.A.; Pessota, J.H.; Kim, H.Y. Beans quality inspection using correlation-based granulometry. *Eng. Appl. Artif. Intell.* **2015**, *40*, 84–94. [CrossRef]
24. Morales-Reyes, J.L.; Aquino-Bolaños, E.N.; Acosta-Mesa, H.G. Color Quantification in Common Bean Landraces Using a Supervised Learning Technique. In *Proceedings of the Mexican International Conference on Artificial Intelligence*; Springer: Berlin/Heidelberg, Germany, 2024; pp. 167–178.
25. Morales-Reyes, J.L.; Aquino-Bolaños, E.N.; Acosta-Mesa, H.G.; Márquez-Grajales, A. Estimation of Anthocyanins in Heterogeneous and Homogeneous Bean Landraces Using Probabilistic Colorimetric Representation with a Neuroevolutionary Approach. *Math. Comput. Appl.* **2024**, *29*, 68. [CrossRef]

26. López-Lobato, A.L.; Avendaño-Garrido, M.L.; Acosta-Mesa, H.G.; Morales-Reyes, J.L.; Aquino-Bolaños, E.N. Bean Landraces Color Identification Through Image Analysis and Gaussian Mixture Model. In *Proceedings of the Mexican International Conference on Artificial Intelligence*; Springer: Berlin/Heidelberg, Germany, 2024; pp. 112–124.
27. López-Lobato, A.L.; Avendaño-Garrido, M.L. Using the Gini index for a Gaussian Mixture Model. In Proceedings of the Advances in Computational Intelligence: 19th Mexican International Conference on Artificial Intelligence, MICAI 2020, Mexico City, Mexico, 12–17 October 2020; Proceedings, Part II 19; Springer: Berlin/Heidelberg, Germany, 2020; pp. 403–418.
28. López-Lobato, A.L.; Avendaño-Garrido, M.L. Fitting a Gaussian mixture model through the Gini index. *Int. J. Appl. Math. Comput. Sci.* **2021**, *31*, 487–500. [CrossRef]
29. Bishop, C.M. *Pattern Recognition and Machine Learning*; Springer: Berlin/Heidelberg, Germany, 2006.
30. Vaida, F. Parameter convergence for EM and MM algorithms. *Stat. Sin.* **2005**, *15*, 831–840.
31. Bassetti, F.; Bodini, A.; Regazzini, E. On minimum Kantorovich distance estimators. *Stat. Probab. Lett.* **2006**, *76*, 1298–1302. [CrossRef]
32. Gini, C. Variabilità e mutabilità. In *Reprinted in Memorie di Metodologica Statistica*; Pizetti, E., Salvemini, T., Eds.; Libreria Eredi Virgilio Veschi: Rome, Italy, 1912.
33. Gini, C. Sulla misura della concentrazione e della variabilità dei caratteri. *Atti R. Ist. Veneto Sci. Lett. Arti* **1914**, *73*, 1203–1248.
34. Villani, C. *Optimal Transport: Old and New*; Springer Science & Business Media: Berlin/Heidelberg, Germany, 2008; Volume 338.
35. López Lobato, A.L.; Avendaño Garrido, M.L. Convergence of parameter estimation of a Gaussian mixture model minimizing the Gini index of dissimilarity. *Commun. Stat.-Theory Methods* **2024**, *53*, 6030–6037. [CrossRef]
36. Guo, G.; Wang, H.; Bell, D.; Bi, Y.; Greer, K. KNN model-based approach in classification. In Proceedings of the On The Move to Meaningful Internet Systems 2003: CoopIS, DOA, and ODBASE: OTM Confederated International Conferences, CoopIS, DOA, and ODBASE 2003, Catania, Italy, 3–7 November 2003; Proceedings; Springer: Berlin/Heidelberg, Germany, 2003; pp. 986–996.
37. Hand, D.J. Principles of data mining. *Drug Saf.* **2007**, *30*, 621–622. [CrossRef]

Mathematical and Computational Applications

MDPI

Article

Classification of Common Bean Landraces of Three Species Using a Neuroevolutionary Approach with Probabilistic Color Characterization

José-Luis Morales-Reyes [1,*], Elia-Nora Aquino-Bolaños [1], Héctor-Gabriel Acosta-Mesa [2], Nancy Pérez-Castro [3] and José-Luis Chavez-Servia [4]

[1] Centre for Food Research and Development, University of Veracruz, Xalapa 91190, Mexico; eliaquino@uv.mx
[2] Artificial Intelligence Research Institute, University of Veracruz, Xalapa 91097, Mexico; heacosta@uv.mx
[3] Agroengineering Institute, University of Papaloapan, Loma Bonita 68400, Mexico; nperez@unpa.edu.mx
[4] National Polytechnic Institute, Hornos 1003, Santa Cruz Xoxocotlán, Oaxaca 71230, Mexico; jchavezs@ipn.mx
* Correspondence: jluismorey@hotmail.com

Abstract

The common bean is a widely cultivated food source. Many domesticated species of common bean varieties, known as landraces, are cultivated in Mexico by local farmers, exhibiting various colorations and seed mixtures as part of agricultural practices. In this work, we propose a methodology for classifying bean landrace samples using three two-dimensional histograms with data in the CIE L*a*b* color space while additionally integrating chroma (C*) and hue (h°) to develop a new proposal from histograms, employing deep learning for the classification task. The results indicate that utilizing three histograms based on L*, C*, and h° brings an average accuracy of 85.74 ± 2.37 compared to three histograms using L*, a*, and b*, which reported an average accuracy of 82.22 ± 2.84. In conclusion, the new color characterization approach presents a viable solution for classifying common bean landraces of both homogeneous and heterogeneous colors.

Keywords: common bean landraces; classification; CNN; histograms; heterogenous color; neuroevolution

1. Introduction

The common bean (*Phaseolus vulgaris* L.) is an essential crop for food security and the rural economy in Mexico and worldwide. According to information from the Agri-Food and Fisheries Information Service (SIAP) [1], after a sharp drop in production in 2023 due to drought conditions, a significant recovery was observed in 2024, reaching nearly 856,000 tons. This rebound highlights the need to value and conserve the genetic diversity of this legume, especially through local varieties such as the common bean landrace, the lima bean (*Phaseolus lunatus* L.), and the ayocote bean (*Phaseolus coccineus* L.), which represent a biocultural heritage of great importance. They are significant global crops, and due to their high protein and carbohydrate content, they constitute essential food sources in human nutrition [2].

One of the most remarkable characteristics of these species is the diversity of seed colors, which has aesthetic implications and correlates with nutritional and functional properties. The seeds of *Phaseolus vulgaris* L. exhibit different hues, from white and yellow to black and red, which influence their commercial acceptance and culinary applications.

Similarly, *Phaseolus lunatus* L. seeds typically exhibit white, cream, or green coloration with mottled patterns [3].

Common bean landrace species are prized for their drought tolerance and adaptability to warm environments, rendering them well suited for water-scarce regions [4]. Thus, the task of classifying *Phaseolus* species is crucial for biodiversity preservation and agricultural advancement, as it enables the selection of resilient and nutritious varieties [5].

Traditionally, human experts have classified *Phaseolus* species using morphological methods, which rely on visible characteristics that can vary due to environmental factors. Additionally, molecular analyses have been employed, but these are often costly, require specialized equipment, and can be invasive. Faced with these disadvantages, using digital images to assess seed color is emerging as a non-destructive, rapid, and accessible alternative. Although this technique also faces challenges related to color variability and lighting conditions, recent research has demonstrated its effectiveness and accuracy in *Phaseolus* seed classification, highlighting the potential of artificial intelligence to automate the process.

A review of the existing literature, with a special emphasis on the incorporation of artificial intelligence techniques, provides insight into the advances and limitations of image-based classification methods for Phaseolus species and other seed species.

The literature review was organized according to the number of feature classes extracted. Table 1 presents these and the respective descriptors employed in the proposals derived from the reviewed articles. Studies focus on classifying beans and other seeds. They analyze features like color, shape, texture, and size. The approaches are described from three classes to one class.

Table 1. Features and descriptors found in reviewed works.

Feature Class	Descriptors (Identifier)
Size (S)	Area (S1), Perimeter (S2), Diameter (S3), Major and Minor Axis Lengths (S4), Convexity (S5), Extent (S6), Solidity (S7), Roundness (S8), Biomass (S9), Height (S10), Width (S11), Weight (S12), Thickness (S13), Entropy (S14).
Shape (H)	Shape Factors (SF1, SF2, SF3, SF4) (H1), Compactness (H2), Roundness (H3), Solidity (H4), Shape Index (H5), Projected Volume (H6), Elliptic Fourier Descriptors (EFDs) (H7), Seed Form (H8).
Color (C)	Mean (C1), Variance (C2), Skewness (C3), Kurtosis (C4) (in RGB, HSV, L*a*b*, or HIS Color Space), 2D Histograms using PMF (C5), Predominant and Secondary Colors (C6), Brightness (C7), 3D Histograms and Color Information Reduction via Gaussian Mixture Model (GMM) (C8).
Texture (T)	Scale-Invariant Feature Transform (SIFT) (T1), Speeded-Up Robust Features (SURF) (T2), Root Scale-Invariant Feature Transform (RootSIFT) (T3), Haralick-Contrast (T4), Correlation (T5), Energy (T6), Homogeneity (T7), Histogram of Curvature (HoC) (T8), Bag-of-Visual Words (BoW) (T9), LBP-Contrast (T10), Correlation (T11), Energy (T12), Homogeneity (T13), Entropy (T14), Gabor Filter-Mean (T15), Standard Deviation (T16), Gray Level Co-occurrence Matrix (GLCM)-Dissimilarity (T17), Correlation (T18), Contrast (T19), Homogeneity (T20), Angular Second Moment (ASM) (T21).

Several works have explored three-class feature extraction using different types of descriptors. Lo Bianco et al. [6] analyzed seed images to classify 67 types of Italian beans based on size, shape, and texture features. They extracted 138 features from digital images and applied stepwise Linear Discriminant Analysis (LDA) on morphological characteristics.

The results showed identification accuracies between 94.3% and 99.7% for different color categories. Furthermore, the system successfully identified the cropping region with over 88% accuracy and differentiated batches of seeds from the same variety grown under different practices with 100% accuracy. However, the authors noted the need for further validation in varying growing conditions and the expansion of the feature set to improve classification performance.

A more advanced approach was presented by Yi et al. [7], who used a multi-kernel SVM to classify seeds based on shape, texture, and color. Their approach achieved 97% accuracy, surpassing the 90% expectation. This study highlighted the importance of texture features in classification.

Garcia et al. [8] developed a computer vision and machine learning system to classify beans. They created a protocol using a Nikon D3300 camera (Nikon Corporation, Tokyo, Japan) and a photo studio box, which improved image quality and reduced shadows. The method employed Otsu thresholding, distance transform, and watershed techniques. A Random Forest algorithm trained on seven attributes achieved an accuracy of 98.5% and an F1-score of 0.98. While the model performed well overall, it struggled slightly with Cargamanto Rojo and MBC 46 due to their visual similarity. The system outperformed contemporary methods, although it was limited to six bean varieties.

The most common approach in digital image seed classification studies is combining two kinds of features. Specifically, five of the seven reviewed papers employ color together with size, shape, or texture, highlighting its importance in this type of analysis, while the other two focus on extracting size and shape.

The work of Kılıc et al. [9] was among the earliest proposals, where they developed a computer vision system that could measure and classify bean samples with an accuracy of 90.6%. The computer vision system was able to identify high-quality white beans 99.3% of the time, outperforming human inspection due to its superior performance, reproducibility, and objectivity. However, factors such as sample size, placement, misclassification, and optimization need to be considered to achieve more accurate size measurements.

Ozktan et al. [10] presented a methodology that employs image processing and machine learning to predict and differentiate 20 common bean genotypes based on their physical attributes, capturing images of the bean seeds and measuring their color parameters. Four machine learning algorithms were applied to predict seed mass. The Random Forest (RF) algorithm predicted bean mass accurately, and the first two principal components explained 73% of the variation in the physical attributes. Hierarchical clustering grouped similar genotypes effectively.

Studies have also explored seed classification by focusing solely on extracting color and texture features, as seen in the works of Mendoza et al. [11], Eric et al. [12], and Djoulde et al. [13].

Mendoza et al. [11] developed a machine vision system for inspecting and predicting the color and quality of canned beans. They extracted color and texture features from images of beans and brine, calibrating RGB values to CIE color spaces. The system showed a strong predictability, with a 0.937 correlation for color and 0.871 for appearance. It correctly grouped 89.7% of the samples.

Similarly, Eric et al. [12] focused on improving cocoa bean classification by extracting color and texture features. An Artificial Neural Network model was trained, and its parameters were fine-tuned using Bayesian optimization. L1L2 regularization, early stopping, and reduced model complexity were applied, resulting in an accuracy of 85.36%.

In contrast, Djoulde et al. [13] used color filter array (CFA) images and an SVM model to classify Penja pepper seeds, achieving 87% accuracy. Images were captured using a custom lightbox and converted to 16-bit grayscale. A broader set of texture features was extracted. It was also found that raw CFA images outperformed demosaiced images in classification accuracy.

Some studies have focused solely on extracting size and shape features for seed classification. For example, Koklu and Özcan [14] used a computer vision system with machine learning to classify seven types of dry beans, extracting 12 shape features from 13,611 images. The SVM model achieved 93.13% accuracy because the color was not distinctive. The major axis length, shape, and suture axis were key contributors, but excluding the suture axis is a limitation. Similarly, Mendigoria et al. [15] employed machine learning to predict and classify dry bean shapes, extracting 16 shape-related features. Their findings indicate that the KNN7 model attained the highest accuracy (93.69%), while GPR performed best in predicting solidity, and RT performed best for roundness and compactness. Both studies demonstrate the effectiveness of size and shape descriptors for bean classification, although differences are observed in the feature sets and modeling approaches.

Several studies have focused exclusively on extracting color features for classification tasks. Early, the work of Nasirahmadi and Behroozi-Khazaei [16] utilized a machine vision system and an Artificial Neural Network (ANN) to classify ten types of beans based on their color attributes, achieving an overall classification accuracy of over 96%. However, due to shared color characteristics, lower accuracy was observed for certain bean types, such as Sarab1 and KS21108. In comparison, Morales-Reyes et al. [17] introduced a computer vision system based on color histograms to classify common bean landraces, achieving an average classification accuracy of 80%. Their method outperformed other color-based techniques, such as spectrophotometer measurements (68.24%) and color averages (CIE L*a*b* at 53.80% and RGB at 44.44%). The study demonstrated that color histograms, particularly 2D and 3D versions, provided a more accurate representation of the color distributions in beans.

Morales-Reyes et al. [18] continued their research with further advancements. They developed a methodology to estimate anthocyanin concentrations in common beans using digital image processing combined with a neuroevolutionary approach. This method incorporated a region-growing algorithm for image segmentation and optimized a Convolutional Neural Network (CNN) using Deep Genetic Algorithm (DeepGA). The results showed over 93% precision in estimating anthocyanin concentrations, particularly when three two-dimensional histograms were used and the luminosity channel was incorporated. Subsequently, the authors [19] refined the technique for estimating anthocyanins, highlighting the challenges of estimating anthocyanin concentrations in beans with heterogeneous coloration. They found that combining 2D histograms and the luminosity channel enhanced precision, offering a promising approach for more accurate estimation in diverse bean landraces.

Sonmez et al. [20] also employed machine learning for classification, but in this case, wheat varieties and hybrids. The study achieved over 99% accuracy using reduced color features extracted from images in different color spaces, although the Naive Bayes algorithm performed somewhat lower (~96%). The results demonstrated the potential of color-based classification for grain identification, though the focus was on wheat rather than beans.

Recently, López-Lobato et al. [21] used a data set of 40 bean landraces from rural Oaxaca, Mexico. Each landrace was represented by a 60 g sample, and its color distribution was captured as a 3D histogram in the CIE L*a*b* color space, resulting in 400 histograms, 10 histograms by sample. The researchers proposed a classification approach using Gaussian mixture models fitted to the histogram data, with the Gini Index algorithm determining the number of Gaussian components. The means of these components were then used to identify primary colors, and classification was performed using the K-Nearest Neighbors algorithm. While the method achieved 100% accuracy in broad color classification, its performance declined to 53.33–80% when distinguishing specific local varieties, particularly black-colored landraces.

Table 2 categorizes and details key aspects of the studies conducted, highlighting the features, descriptors, type of seed, machine learning algorithms, color space, and image acquisition of each work.

Table 2. Detailed description of articles revised.

Authors	Features	Descriptors	Type of Seed	ML Algorithms	Color Space	Image Acquisition
Lo Bianco et al. [6]	S, H, T	C1, S12, S14, T1, T4, T5, T6, T7	Beans (*Phaseolus vulgaris* L.)	LDA and SVM	Gray scale	Flatbed scanner
Yi et al. [7]	C, H, T	C5, C2, C3, C1, H8, H9, T1, T2, T3	Different seed species	NB and SVM	CIE L*a*b*	Motorized multi-purpose zoom microscope
Garcia et al. [8]	C, H, S	H8, C6, C7, S1, S2, S3, S4	Beans (*Phaseolus vulgaris* L.)	RF	RGB	Photo-eBox Plus (PeP)
Kılıc et al. [9]	S, C	C1, C2, C3, C4	Beans	ANN	RGB	Custom-built light black box image capturing
Ozaktan et al. [10]	H, C	S1, S2, S3, S4, S5, S6, S7, H1, H2, S8, H3, H4	Common bean genotypes from Türkiye	MLP, RF, SVR, and KNN	CIE L*a*b*	Controlled illumination and a digital camera
Mendoza et al. [11]	C, T	C1, C2, C3, C4, T4, T5, T6, T7	Bean (*Phaseolus vulgaris* L.)	Non-linear SVM	RGB, CIE L*a*b*, HSV, and gray scale	Controlled lighting system
Eric et al. [12]		C1, C2, C3, C4, C5, C6, T8, T4, T5, T6	Cocoa beans	SVM, RF, DT, NB, and ANN	RGB	Not mentioned
Djoulde et al. [13]		S6, S1, S10, S12, S11, S7, T10, T4, T5, T6, T7, T15, T16, T17, T18, T19, T20, T21	Pepper seeds	KNN, SGD, SVM, and RF	RGB	Custom-built light box
Koklu and Ozkan [14]	S, H	S1, S2, S3, S4, S5, S6, S7, S8, S9, S10, S11, S12, H1, H2, H3, H4	Turkish beans	SVM, DT, MLP, and KNN	RGB, gray scale	Custom-built illumination box
Mendigoria et al. [15]		S1, S2, S3, S4, S5, S6, S7, S8, S9, H1, H2, H3, H4, H5, H6, H7	Bean (*Phaseolus vulgaris* L.)	LDA, KNN, DT, and NB	CIE L*a*b*	The Prosilica GT2000C camera
Nasirahmadi and Behroozi-Khazaei [16]	C	C1	Iranian bean	MLP-ANN	RGB	Controlled lighting
Morales-Reyes et al. [17–19]		C5	Bean (*Phaseolus vulgaris* L.)	KNN	RGB, HIS, and CIE L*a*b*	Custom-built light and diffuser box
Sönmez et al. [20]		C1, C2, C3, C4	Durum wheat seed	ANN, SVM, KNN, DT, RF, and NB	RGB, HSV, CIE L*a* b*, and YCrCb	Custom-built light black box
López-Lobato et al. [21]		C8	Bean (*Phaseolus vulgaris* L.)	KNN	CIE L*a* b*	NA

Acronyms: Linear Discriminant Analysis (LDA), Support Vector Machine (SVM), Naive Bayes (NB), Random Forest (RF), Artificial Neural Network (ANN), Multilayer Perceptron (MLP), Support Vector Regression (SVR), K-Nearest Neighbors (KNN), Non-linear Support Vector Machine (Non-linear SVM), Decision Tree (DT), and Stochastic Gradient Descent (SGD). The different color spaces considered are red, green, and blue (RGB); CIE 1976 (L*, a*, b*) color space (CIE L*a*b*); hue, saturation, and value (HSV); hue, intensity, and saturation (HIS); luminance and chrominance components (YCrCb).

- Color characterization of each bean landrace using three two-dimensional histograms with the data of each bean landrace in CIE L*a*b* color space.
- The second color characterization proposal uses the same color characterization with the same data in CIE L*a*b* color space; our contribution is using chroma and hue instead of a* and b* to characterize the color.

Mexico is the origin and diversification hub for numerous common bean landraces, which are maintained by various ethnic groups and cultivated and harvested for private consumption by farmers. The researchers primarily focus on creating a classification system for common bean landraces across different species [22].

Most research focuses on grading individual seeds of different bean varieties by characterizing their color, including averages and other values of color, and complementing this with other values of texture and shape characteristics of the seed. However, there is evidence that considers the color distribution of a set of seeds, which are characterized by three two-dimensional histograms, to estimate anthocyanin concentration using a regression task [19]. In this sense, this research work aims to classify common bean landraces into homogeneous and heterogeneous colorations across three different bean species. Due to the complexity and challenges presented by working with landraces of heterogeneous coloration, the use of color characterization using three two-dimensional histograms is proposed. The paper presents the following:

This work also incorporates a neuroevolutionary approach, as a CNN architecture is desired for the custom classification task.

The structure of this document is as follows: Section 2 describes the methodology for assigning labels to each landrace and classifying common bean landraces with heterogeneous and homogeneous coloration, utilizing two-color characterizations through deep learning and neuroevolutionary approaches. Next, Section 3 presents the results obtained from its implementation. Section 4 discusses the findings based on the results reported in this work. Finally, Section 5 presents the conclusions.

2. Materials and Methods

2.1. Workflow of the Study

In this work, the classification of common bean landraces with homogeneous and heterogeneous coloration is performed through digital image processing, as shown in the overall workflow in Figure 1. A series of steps were performed as follows:

1. Gather the set of bean landraces, and obtain a representative sample of each represented by 60 g.
2. Acquire digital photographic images of each bean landrace sample, then apply color calibration using an image reproduction workflow.
3. In this work, it is required to characterize the color of a set of seeds; therefore, the application of an algorithm for the separation of the regions of interest is required.
4. A physical characteristic of the study of this work is color, and a process was defined to identify the color of each bean landrace to facilitate the complex task and reduce its subjectivity when reviewing 60 g of seeds.
5. To characterize the color, we propose considering the color distribution of a set of seeds, using the joint probability distribution for two color characterizations.
6. Grouping of local bean varieties by labels, which were assigned based on the two principal predominant colorations in each sample; moreover, the total samples were randomly separated into 50% of the samples by each color group to create training and test data.
7. To develop a Convolutional Neural Network (CNN) architecture tailored to the classification of common beans, a key step in creating deep learning architectures for a specific task is to use a neuroevolutionary approach to evolve CNNs.
8. Finally, the results were compared using CNNs and two-color characterizations for the classification task of common bean landraces.

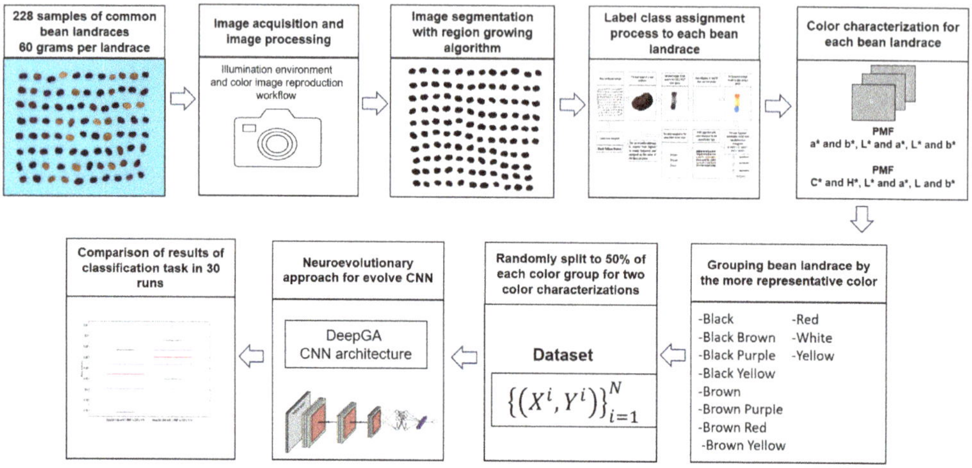

Figure 1. The workflow illustrates the procedure for classifying common bean landraces with heterogeneous and homogeneous coloration.

2.2. Common Bean Landraces

The common bean landraces used in this work were collected from several municipalities in Oaxaca, Mexico. These landraces correspond to three domesticated species (*Phaseolus vulgaris* L., *Phaseolus lunatus* L., and *Phaseolus coccineus* L.). The samples consisted of various colorations, ranging from homogeneous to heterogeneous, and included a mixture of differently colored or variegated seeds. The colors observed in the bean landraces employed in this work included seed coats of red, black, yellow, brown, pink, purple, and white. This color variability in heterogeneous landraces ensures a representative sample of each landrace, represented with a weight of 60 g. Figure 2 shows examples of the common bean landraces.

2.3. Acquisition System and Image Segmentation

The controlled illumination environment for this image acquisition process and protocol involved positioning a sample of bean landraces with individually spaced seeds to reduce occlusions and shadows, along with the optimal image reproduction workflow detailed in [17,18]. In the aluminum box, the camera lens was placed into the hole at the top of the light diffusion box, with regulated lighting and standardized settings, which were crucial for consistent photographic results. Figure 3 displays the workflow, which is summarized below:

1. The image acquisition under standardized conditions using a color reference chart and SONY digital camera model ILCE 3500 with a focal length of 50 mm and exposure configuration: shutter speed 1/60, ISO 100, and Aperture f/8.0.
2. Process the RAW image with the software Darktable 4.4.2 to preserve color data and convert it to a TIFF format with a standard ICC profile. Next, assign the custom ICC profile created with the software calibration tool to the processed TIFF images.
3. Shown in Figure 2, colored paper was used as a contrasting background to differentiate the seed hues. A blue background was employed to accentuate the seed landraces.
4. The RAW images were processed using the same software to create a TIFF image with the standard ICC profile. MATLAB 2023b software was utilized to change the standard ICC to a custom ICC profile and convert sRGB to the CIE L*a*b* color space.

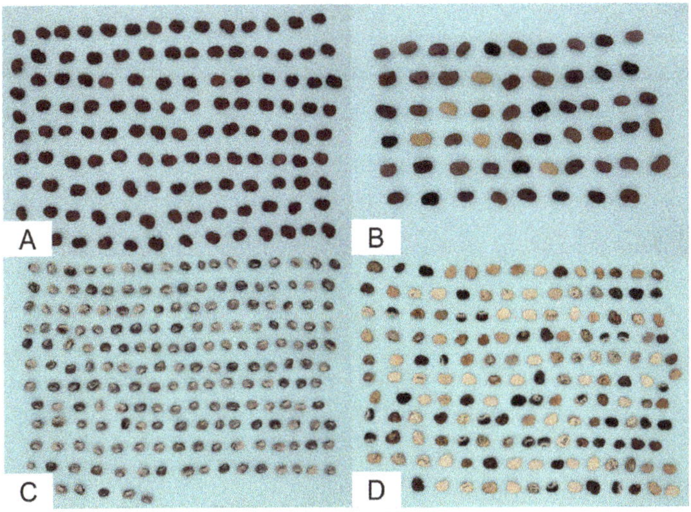

Figure 2. Four cases of coloration were observed in common bean landraces: (**A**) a sample of seeds with homogeneous coloration; (**B**) a sample of a mixture of seeds with different colorations, where each seed has a homogeneous coloration; (**C**) a sample of variegated seed coloration; (**D**) a sample of a mixture of seeds with homogeneous colorations and seeds with variegated coloration.

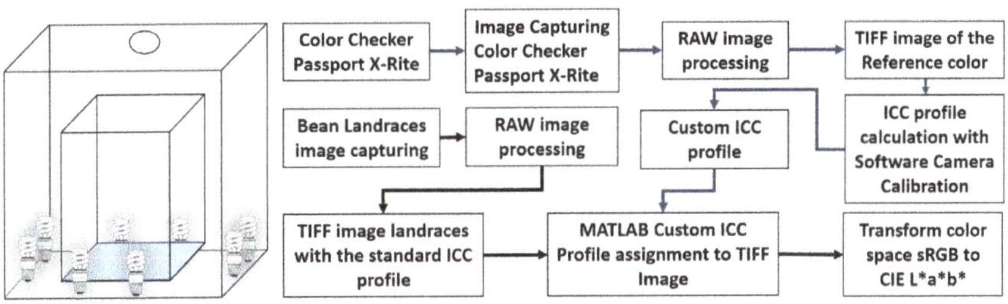

Figure 3. A light-controlled environment is crucial for standardizing image acquisition. The workflow shows the process for image reproduction.

A region-growing algorithm was applied to color images to obtain the regions of interest. Due to the background contrast used during image acquisition, it was defined as an area to select the seed pixel of the algorithm. The algorithm operates by grouping pixels based on a similarity criterion. It starts with the definition of a seed pixel from the image background. The Euclidean distance was used as a similarity measure between neighboring pixels. The appropriate metric to measure color differences using CIE L*a*b* coordinates was Delta E (CIE 1976) defined in Equation (1).

$$\Delta E = \sqrt{\left(L_{np} - L_{sp}\right)^2 + \left(a_{np} - a_{sp}\right)^2 + \left(b_{np} - b_{sp}\right)^2} \tag{1}$$

where ΔE is a color distance computed value of L*a*b*, (L, a, b) of seed pixel (sp), and (L, a, b) of neighboring pixel (np). A standardized metric for quantifying the difference between two colors. The lower the ΔE value, the greater the similarity to the seed pixel.

The result is a binary matrix with equal dimensions to the processed image. In the binary image, the regions of interest are marked with a value of 0, while the region of no interest are marked with a value of 1.

2.4. Objective Color Measurement

Color analysis is often a critical consideration when determining efficacy classification by color. The CIE L*a*b* color space is used by color measurement instruments that report a set of Cartesian coordinates based on the color measurement of a sample. These values represent the color within a three-dimensional space, but it is crucial to understand that they do not convey details of hue and chroma. Chroma quantifies the degree of deviation from gray toward pure chromatic color, whereas hue denotes specific color types, including red, blue, purple, yellow, and others. As shown in Figure 4, the L* channel refers to luminance, with a range of values between 0 and 100, corresponding to black and white, respectively. For any measured color, a* and b* position the color on a rectangular coordinate grid that is perpendicular to the L* axis. The color at the grid's origin (a* = 0, b* = 0) is achromatic (gray). a* positive indicates a purplish-red hue on the horizontal axis, while a* negative indicates a bluish-green hue. On the vertical axis, b* positive denotes yellow, and b* negative is blue.

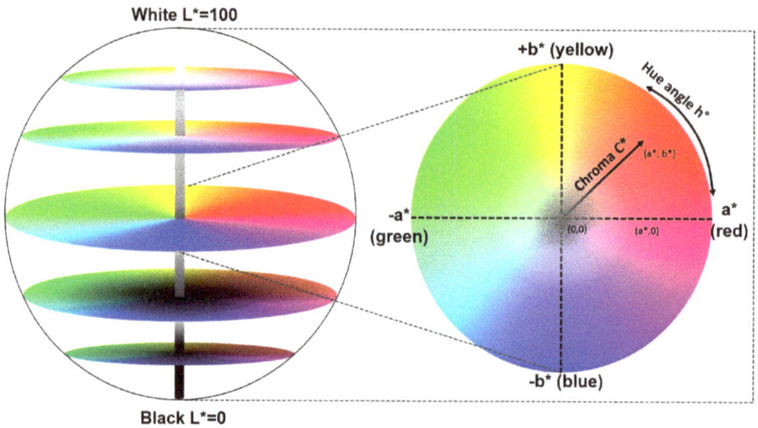

Figure 4. CIE L*a*b* color space is represented by axes L*, a*, and b*, displaying chroma in a color wheel and hue angle.

The chroma C* is calculated as $\sqrt{(a^{*2} + b^{*2})}$ and represents the hypotenuse of a right triangle created by joining the points (0, 0), (a*, 0), and (a*, b*). The hue angle is defined as the angle between the hypotenuse and 0° on the a* (blue-green/red-purple) axis; h is calculated as the arc tangent of b*/a*.

The arc tangent, however, assumes positive values in the first and third quadrants and negative values in the second and fourth quadrants. For correct interpretation, h° must remain positive between 0° and 360° of the color screen; the following pseudocode (Table 3) shows the algorithm for calculating hue [23].

Table 3. Pseudocode for calculating chroma and hue.

Input L a b Value
C = sqrt ((a × a) + (b × b)) Theta = (atan (b/a)/6.2832) × 360 If a > 0 and b >= 0 then h = theta; If a < 0 and b >= 0 then h = 180 + theta; If a < 0 and b < 0 then h = 180 + theta; If a > 0 and b < 0 then h = 360 + theta; return C, h

2.5. Color Characterization Using a Probability Mass Function

In the present study, the color characterization of bean landraces was performed using the CIE L*a*b* color space, which have been used in previous similar studies because they approximate human visual perception. This space allows for the separation of chromaticity from luminosity, facilitating a more detailed examination. In this sense, a probability mass function (PMF) is employed to describe the color distribution within a set of seeds. Specifically, a joint PMF is used to model the relationship between two discrete random variables, X and Y, whose joint probability distribution is expressed as $f(X, Y) = P(X = x, Y = y)$, where $f(X, Y)$ represents the probability of the occurrence of x and y values, subject to standard probability conditions as follows:

1. $f(x, y) \geq 0\, for\, all(x, y)$,
2. $\Sigma x \Sigma y f(x, y) = 1$,
3. $P(X = x, Y = y) = f(x, y)$

Each pixel value in two channels is counted position by position, and the frequency of occurrence of the pixel value is given by Equation (2) to calculate the joint probability of a pair of channels.

$$pmf_{i,j} = \frac{p_{ij}}{n} \quad (2)$$

The overall procedure applied to characterize the color in the CIE L*a*b* color spaces is detailed as follows:

(a) *Color space transformation:* Convert images to CIE L*a*b*.
(b) *First color characterization:* The values of L*, a*, and b* were modified.
    a. Adjust the a* and b* values within the range of [−128 to 127] by adding the absolute value of the lower limit to ensure non-negative representations.
    b. For L*, normalize the values and scale them to the range of [0–255]. Three two-dimensional histograms were generated based on joint probability mass functions (PMFs) for color characterization. Specifically, PMFs were created for (a*, b*), (L*, a*), and (L*, b*) with dimensions of 256 × 256 × 3.
    c. Three two-dimensional histograms were used to characterize the color of each seed that forms the color palette and to characterize the color of each bean landrace integrated into this work.
(c) *Second color characterization:* The values of L* conserved, a*, and b* used to calculate chroma and hue.
    a. Chroma (C*) is calculated by the square root of the sum of a* and b* squares.
    b. Hue (h°) is performed by the arc tangent of b divided by a, and the result is converted to degrees. The procedure is reported in Table 3.
    c. CIE L*C*h°: Three two-dimensional histograms created by PMFs (C*, h°), (L*, C*), (L*, h°), and the color characterization as a 360 × 360 × 3 matrix, preserving joint distributions.

2.6. Gaussian Mixture Model or Gaussian Mixture

In this work, the color distributions of single seeds or all seeds belonging to a sample bean landrace are analyzed by obtaining cloud points in the CIE L*a*b* color space. The Gaussian mixture model possesses several important analytical properties, and it is a fundamental unsupervised learning algorithm in clustering and probability density estimation when the data are unlabeled [24]. To separate the color of variegated seeds, a Gaussian mixture was integrated. A Gaussian mixture is defined by Equation (3).

$$p(\boldsymbol{x}) = \sum_{k=1}^{K} \pi_k \mathcal{N}(\boldsymbol{x}|\boldsymbol{\mu}_k, \boldsymbol{\Sigma}_k) \tag{3}$$

where

$\boldsymbol{x}$: represents a d-dimensional data vector.
K: number of Gaussian distributions (components) in the mixture.
$\boldsymbol{\mu}_k$: centroid (mean vector) of the k-th component.
$\boldsymbol{\Sigma}_k$: matrix describing the shape and orientation of the k-th component.
$N(\boldsymbol{x}|\boldsymbol{\mu}_k, \boldsymbol{\Sigma}_k)$: Gaussian density called a component of the mixture with mean $\boldsymbol{\mu}_k$ and covariance $\boldsymbol{\Sigma}_k$.
$\boldsymbol{\pi}_k$: mixing coefficient, (priori probability that a data belongs to the component).
The parameter $\boldsymbol{\pi}_k$ is subject to the restrictions of Equations (4) and (5).

$$\sum_{k=1}^{K} \pi_k = 1 \tag{4}$$

$$0 \leq \pi_k \leq 1 \tag{5}$$

The main characteristic of any mixture model is its structure, which comprises marginal, conditional, and joint distributions. As a mixture model is directed to solve density estimation problems, the final goal is to identify a distribution over the data vectors $\boldsymbol{x}$, denoted as $p(\boldsymbol{x})$. For this purpose, the joint distribution $p(x,\ z)$ can be considered as in Equation (6).

$$p(x) = \sum_{k=1}^{K} p(x,\ z = k) \tag{6}$$

So, the proposed distribution is the marginal distribution of the joint distribution $p(\boldsymbol{x}, \boldsymbol{z})$.

The joint distribution $p(x,\ z)$ can be defined in terms of a marginal distribution $p(\boldsymbol{z})$ and a conditional distribution $p(\boldsymbol{x}|\boldsymbol{z})$, as in Equation (7).

$$p(\boldsymbol{x}, \boldsymbol{z}) = p(\boldsymbol{z})p(\boldsymbol{x}|\boldsymbol{z}) \tag{7}$$

Regarding the Gaussian mixture model, $\boldsymbol{z}$ is the latent variable indicating the cluster $(z = k)$, and $\boldsymbol{x}$ represents the observed data.

The joint distribution $p(x,\ z = k)$ is factored as Equation (8).

$$p(\boldsymbol{x}, z = k) = p(z = k)p(\boldsymbol{x} \mid z = k) \tag{8}$$

where

$p(z = k) = \pi_k$ (cluster weight, k).
$p(\boldsymbol{x}|z = k) = N(\boldsymbol{x}|\boldsymbol{\mu}_k,\ \boldsymbol{\Sigma}_k)$ (normal distribution of the cluster k).

The conditional distribution of D-dimensional vector $\boldsymbol{x}$ given a particular value of $z = k$ is a multivariate Gaussian distribution and can be written in the form (Equation (9)).

$$N(\boldsymbol{x}|\boldsymbol{\mu}_k,\ \boldsymbol{\Sigma}_k) = \frac{1}{(2\pi)^{D/2}} \frac{1}{|\boldsymbol{\Sigma}_k|^{1/2}} exp\left\{ -\frac{1}{2}(x - \boldsymbol{\mu}_k)^T \boldsymbol{\Sigma}_k^{-1}(x - \boldsymbol{\mu}_k) \right\} \tag{9}$$

where μ_k is a D-dimensional mean vector, Σ_k is a $D \times D$ covariance matrix, and $|\Sigma_k|$ denotes the determinant of Σ_k.

So, with the Gaussian characterization displayed in (8), the structure of the distribution $p(x)$ can be written as in Equation (10).

$$p(x) = \sum_{k=1}^{K} p(x,\ z = k) = \sum_{k=1}^{K} p(z = k) p(x \mid z = k) = \sum_{k=1}^{K} \pi_k \mathcal{N}(x|\mu_k, \Sigma_k) \tag{10}$$

Suppose that the data points $\{x_i\}_{i=1}^{M}$ are drawn independently of the distribution. In that case, we can express the Gaussian mixture model with the likelihood function shown in (11).

$$\mathcal{L}(\mu_k, \Sigma_k|x) = \prod_{i=1}^{M} \sum_{k=1}^{K} \pi_k \mathcal{N}(x_i|\mathbf{\mu}_k,\ \Sigma_k) \tag{11}$$

And the logarithm of the likelihood function is given in Equation (12).

$$lnp(\mathbf{X}|\pi,\ \mu, \Sigma) = \sum_{n=1}^{N} ln\left\{ \sum_{k=1}^{K} \pi_k \mathcal{N}(x_n|\mu_k, \Sigma_k) \right\} \tag{12}$$

A notable issue with applying the maximum likelihood framework to Gaussian mixture models is the occurrence of singularities. As a result, maximizing the log likelihood function poses challenges, since these singularities are persistent and arise when one of the Gaussian components "collapses" at a particular data point. To avoid the singularities, we can employ appropriate heuristics, such as detecting when a Gaussian component is collapsing and resetting its mean to a randomly chosen value, while also adjusting its covariance to some meaningful value, and then continuing with the optimization.

The Expectation-Maximization algorithm (EM algorithm) is a sophisticated method for finding maximum likelihood solutions for models with latent variables. The model parameters were estimated using the Expectation-Maximization (EM) algorithm, which iteratively maximizes the likelihood of the observed data. The EM algorithm alternates between two steps: the Expectation step (E-step) and the Maximization step (M-step), as described in Algorithm 1.

The EM algorithm is repeated until convergence, defined as a negligible change in the log likelihood between successive iterations. The EM algorithm requires significantly more iterations to reach convergence compared to the K-means algorithm, and each cycle requires substantially more computation. It is therefore common to run the K-means algorithm to find a suitable initialization for a Gaussian mixture model, which is subsequently adapted using the EM algorithm. The model is implemented using MATLAB's *fitgmdist* function.

Algorithm 1: Expectation-Maximization for Gaussian Mixture Models

1. Initialize parameters $\boldsymbol{\mu}_k, \boldsymbol{\Sigma}_k, \pi_k$ for each $k = 1, \ldots, K$
2. Compute initial log-likelihood:

$$lnp(\mathbf{X} \mid \boldsymbol{\mu}, \boldsymbol{\Sigma}, \pi) = \sum_{n=1}^{N} ln\left(\sum_{k=1}^{K} \pi_k \mathcal{N}(\boldsymbol{x}_n \mid \boldsymbol{\mu}_k, \boldsymbol{\Sigma}_k)\right)$$

3. **Repeat**

   a. **E-step:** Compute responsibilities

$$\gamma(z_{nk}) = \frac{\pi_k \mathcal{N}(x_n|\boldsymbol{\mu}_k,\boldsymbol{\Sigma}_k)}{\sum_{j=1}^{K} \pi_j \mathcal{N}(x_n|\boldsymbol{\mu}_j,\boldsymbol{\Sigma}_j)}$$

   b. **M-step:** Update parameters

$$N_k = \sum_{n=1}^{N} \gamma(z_{nk})$$

$$\boldsymbol{\mu}_k = \frac{1}{N_k} \sum_{n=1}^{N} \gamma(z_{nk})\boldsymbol{x}_\mathbf{n}$$

$$\boldsymbol{\Sigma}_k = \frac{1}{N_k} \sum_{n=1}^{N} \gamma(z_{nk})(\boldsymbol{x}_\mathrm{n} - \boldsymbol{\mu}_k)(\boldsymbol{x}_\mathrm{n} - \boldsymbol{\mu}_k)^T$$

$$\pi_k = \frac{N_k}{N}$$

   c. **Recompute log-likelihood:**

$$lnp(\mathbf{X} \mid \boldsymbol{\mu}, \boldsymbol{\Sigma}, \pi) = \sum_{n=1}^{N} ln\left(\sum_{k=1}^{K} \pi_k N(\boldsymbol{x}_n \mid \boldsymbol{\mu}_k, \boldsymbol{\Sigma}_k)\right)$$

4. **Until:** the convergence of parameters or log-likelihood

2.7. Label Class Assignment to Common Bean Landraces

Since color is a physical characteristic related to chemical composition, the common bean landraces used in this work were processed to assign labels to each bean landrace and then described by color. The label class assignment procedure used in this methodology was part of the color quantification described in the work by [25]. Figure 5 illustrates the workflow used for assigning labels to each one.

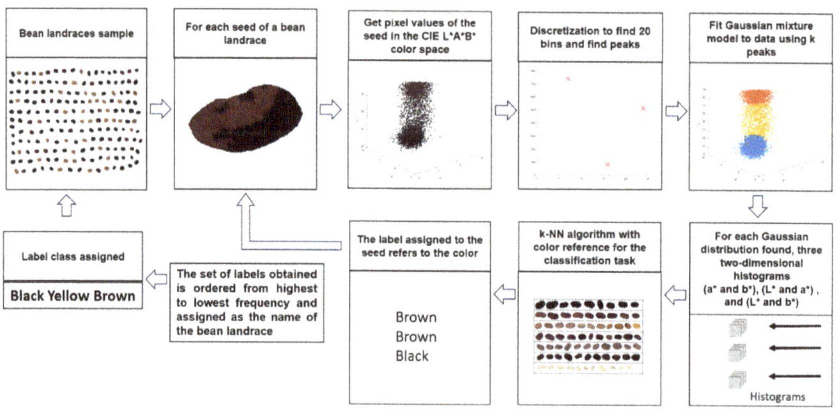

Figure 5. A workflow that visually illustrates the methodology for assigning class labels to each bean landrace.

Due to the complexity of manually assigning a label to each bean landrace weighing 60 g, the task is intricate for samples composed of a mixture of seeds with homogeneous colorations and seeds with variegated colorations and can be quite subjective. We established a procedure to assign a label generated through a solution that includes color characterization and a machine learning algorithm, as shown below:

1. For each bean landrace, the binary image obtained from segmentation was used to apply digital image processing and to analyze each region of interest for its color distribution. For this purpose, connected components were used.
2. Discretize the data into 20 bins and search for histogram peaks. In the MATLAB program 2023b, the function used was *findpeaks*.
3. Given the point cloud, a Gaussian mixture distribution model (GMModel) with k components was fitted to the data using the *fitgmdist* function. The parameter value for k corresponds to the number of identified peaks.
4. A triple two-dimensional histogram was created for each component to characterize the colors of the seeds and obtain labels that describe their color.
5. To identify colors and assign labels, it was essential to define a color palette based on the hues found in native bean varieties. It was noted that uniform seed colorations also appear in variegated seeds. Consequently, a palette featuring seeds of uniform colors was created, and a classification algorithm was implemented to leverage the knowledge base established and conduct similarity searches based on color. A machine learning algorithm was used to generate and assign labels to each seed, achieving this goal.
6. The labels derived from analyzing each seed of every local variety of common bean were organized into color categories based on their presence in the sample, arranged from highest to lowest frequency. For bean varieties exhibiting heterogeneous coloration or a mixture of seeds in different colors, the assigned label combined the two most representative labels in the sample, reflecting the most frequently occurring colorations.

Color Palette Reference and K-Nearest Neighbors Algorithm

Manually labeling a 60 g sample representing a heterogeneous coloration of beans is quite challenging and to minimize subjectivity in this task, it is necessary to develop an automated process to assign a label to each seed per bean landrace, so that the set of labels obtained will allow each bean landrace to be described by its color. For this purpose, color references were developed using information derived from seeds of homogeneous coloration due to their similar shades. A data set was compiled with the color information of selected seeds from various bean landraces. In this way, with the support of an expert, a set of seed samples was selected from the different images to create six color groups. The chosen seed color was characterized using PMFs composed of channels (a*, b*), (L*, a*), and (L*, b*). For each seed, three two-dimensional histograms were then generated to create the color palette.

Figure 6 shows a set of seeds for each type of coloration detected in the samples of this work.

The K-Nearest Neighbors (k-NN) is a supervised learning algorithm that predicts the category of new observations based on the majority class of K-Nearest Neighbors. Its operation relies on the locations of points in multidimensional space using a distance metric; it calculates the distance from the new observation to all the points in the training set. The K-Nearest Neighbors are selected, and the highest frequency class is assigned to the unknown observation through a voting process. The cityblock distance is suitable for comparing histograms [26] (see Equation (13)).

$$d_T(\boldsymbol{a},\boldsymbol{b}) = \sum_{j=1}^{n} |a_j - b_j| \tag{13}$$

where $a = (a_1, a_2, \ldots, a_n)$, $b = (b_1, b_2, \ldots, b_n)$, a and b are histograms, and n-points represent the value frequencies.

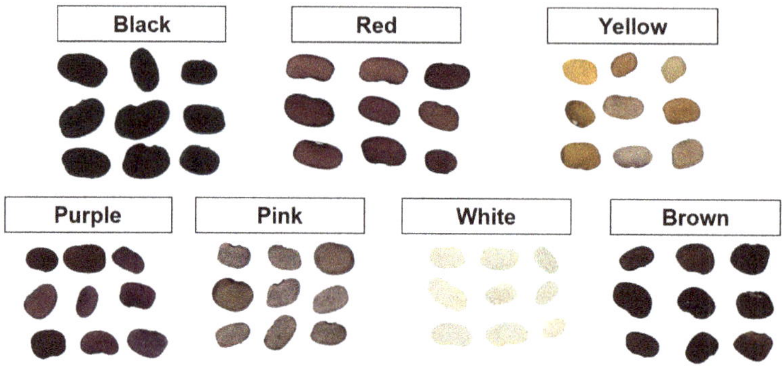

Figure 6. Seven color groups for the knowledge base; the seed for color reference represents training data for the machine learning algorithm k-NN.

The k-NN method stores a training data set instead of undergoing a training phase. When an unknown observation is received, classification or prediction calculations take place. To identify its neighbors and assign them a label, the distance between the query point and the base points is calculated using a metric.

A k-NN classification model is represented in this work using the *fitcknn* function from the MATLAB program 2023b, and the training data set used was the color reference represented by a set of three two-dimensional histograms.

In the process of assigning a class to each bean landrace, to ensure the correct assignment of labels to the seed, steps were performed as shown in Figure 5. In summary, the first step was to obtain the color distribution of the seed, and discretization of the data to find peaks of frequency. The number of peaks was used for the value of k components of a Fit Gaussian mixture model to data using a k-component Gaussian mixture model; for each component corresponding to a new observation in the k-NN model, the parameter k was set to 9, 21, 31, 41, and 51 neighbors; from the acquired labels, the label with the highest frequency was assigned. This same process was performed for each seed.

Once the process of assigning labels to all seeds was completed and given the colorimetric variability of the heterogeneously colored bean landraces, the next step was to order the set of labels and group from highest to lowest frequency to assign the two labels with the highest frequency as class labels. To correspond to coloration for maximal presence in the sample, it is important to note, some colors that make up the palette may not appear on the labels due to their minimal presence, as is the case with pink seeds. For the case of the homogeneously colored bean landrace, a single label was assigned due to its uniform coloration.

2.8. Data Splitting

A total of 228 samples of common bean landraces with different shades were considered. This included homogeneously colored bean landraces with uniformly colored seeds and heterogeneously colored bean landraces with mixed seeds of various shades. As a result, the data set consists of 12 color groups, as shown in Table 4. In this preliminary assessment, the designated label refers to the two colors most prominently featured in the bean landrace of mixed coloration. However, these colors may not be reflected in the class labels of common bean landraces due to their limited occurrence.

Table 4. The number of samples for each color group used in this paper.

Group Color	Number of Samples	Group Color	Number of Samples
Black	78	Black Purple	11
Brown	5	Black Yellow	6
Red	31	Brown Purple	10
White	8	Brown Red	6
Yellow	16	Brown Yellow	11
Black Brown	39	Purple Yellow	7

The process involved random sampling from each color group of bean landraces with a 50% sample separation to generate training and test data.

Subsequently, two color characterizations were created from each separation: the first conformed to three two-dimensional histograms using CIE L*a*b* color space data, and the second was represented by three two-dimensional histograms employing CIE L*C*h° data.

2.9. Convolutional Neural Networks

The color characterization is represented by histograms that are $256 \times 256 \times 3$ matrices, and CNNs are suitable for receiving this type of matrix. The basic structure of the CNN consists of convolutional layers that implement filters (kernels) used for the convolution process on images, generating feature maps. An image can be defined as a two-dimensional function $f(x, y)$, where x and y are spatial coordinates; the amplitude f of a coordinate pair is referred to as the level of the image. The image contains M rows and N columns, and the value of the origin coordinate is $(x, y) = (0, 0)$; the following coordinate is represented by $(x, y) = (0, 1)$, and the filter is a grid of discrete numbers called convolutional kernel and defined as $w(x, y)$; to define the size of an mxn kernel, the following expressions result from applying $m = 2a + 1$ and $n = 2b + 1$, let a and b be non-negative integers [27].

The operation between the image and the kernel simply involves moving them from one point to another on the image. At each point (x, y), the response of the kernel at that location is calculated as the sum of the products of the kernel coefficients and the corresponding image pixels in the area covered by the convolution kernel, as expressed in Equation (14).

$$R = w_1 z_1 + w_2 z_2 + \ldots + w_{mn} z_{mn} = \sum_{i=1}^{mn} w_i z_i \tag{14}$$

where R of an $m \times n$ kernel at any point (x, y), w represents the kernel coefficients, z are the values of the gray levels of the image, and mn is the total number of kernel coefficients.

The process of convolution of an image f of size $M \times N$ with a kernel of size $m \times n$ is given by the following Equation (15) and graphically represented in Figure 7.

$$(w * f)(x,y) = \sum_{s=-a}^{a} \sum_{t=-b}^{b} w(s,t) f(x-s, y-t) \tag{15}$$

where $x = 0, 1, 2, \ldots, M-1$, $y = 0, 1, 2, \ldots, N-1$, and $(w * f)(x,y)$ is the output of a complete process of convolution of an image.

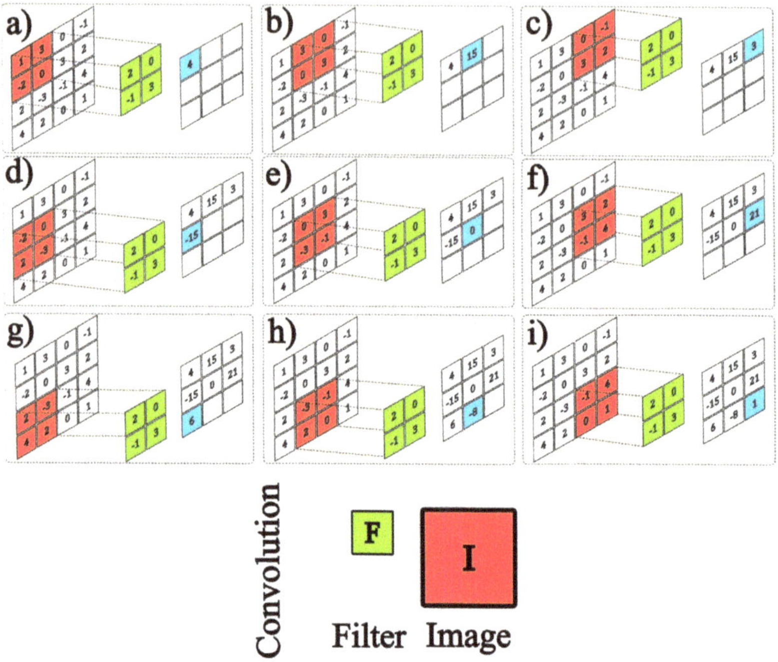

Figure 7. An example of the convolution process involves moving the kernel through the image, from position (**a**–**i**), to extract feature maps taken of [28].

The convolution has several properties. The convolution is as follows:

- Commutative: $w * f = f * w$
- Associative: $f * (w1 * w2) = (f * w1) * w2)$
- Distributive: $f * (w1 + w2) = (f * w1) + (f * w2)$

The convolutional layer implements kernels that are used for the convolution process on the images, generating the aforementioned feature maps, and the pooling layers reduce the dimensions of feature maps generated in the convolutional layers. Like convolutional layers, reduction layers utilize filters to derive a new value from the neighboring pixels. Two strategies, mean reduction and maximum reduction, are commonly used to calculate the value from the filters. The average reduction obtains the average value of all pixels within the filter, and the max-reduction layer obtains the maximum value [29].

The batch normalization algorithm is a technique for transforming input values of each layer into values with zero mean and constant standard deviation [30].

In a fully connected layer, every unit is linked to all units in the preceding layer. Typically, in a CNN, these layers are positioned near the end of the architecture. Fully connected layers convert the resulting feature maps from the reduction layer into a vector representing an ANN [29].

The ANN comprises a collection of basic units known as artificial neurons, linked by weights. These neurons take inputs from their peers and pass along their outputs to others in the form of a simple scalar value. A layer in a neural network consists of a cluster of neurons operating at the same depth or level. These networks utilize basis functions structured similarly to Equation (16), meaning each basis function is a non-linear function derived from a linear combination of the inputs, with the coefficients in this combination being adaptable parameters [24].

$$y(\boldsymbol{x}, \boldsymbol{w}) = f\left(\sum_{j=1}^{M} w_j \phi_j(\boldsymbol{x})\right) \tag{16}$$

where w_j represent the coefficients, ϕ_j are the parameters, $\boldsymbol{x}$ is a input vector, $\boldsymbol{w}$ correspond all weight and bias parameters grouped into a vector, and $f(\cdot)$ is a non-linear activation function. This leads to the basic neural network model, which can be described as a series of functional transformations for the first layer of the network, with input variables $x_i, \ldots, x_D$, expressed in Equation (17).

$$a_j = \sum_{i=1}^{D} w_{ji} x_j + w_{j0} \tag{17}$$

where w_{ji} are the weights, w_{j0} as biases, and a_j are known as activations.

Each activation is then transformed using a differentiable, non-linear activation function $h(\cdot)$ (see Equation (18)).

$$z_j = h(a_j) \tag{18}$$

where z_j represents the hidden units; the non-linear functions $h(\cdot)$ are generally chosen to be functions such as the ReLU function for to give output unit activations. For a second layer of the network expressed in Equation (19).

$$a_k = \sum_{j=1}^{M} w_{kj} z_j + w_{k0} \tag{19}$$

where $j = 1, \ldots, M$ correspond to M linear combination, $k = 1, \ldots, K$, K is the total number of outputs, w_{kj} are the weights second layer. The output unit activations (a_k) are transformed with a suitable activation function to produce a set of network outputs y_k. Therefore, each output unit's activation is transformed using the ReLU function (see Equation (20)).

$$y_k = \sigma(a_k) \tag{20}$$

where $\sigma(a_k)$ is a ReLU function and mathematically defined in Equation (21).

$$\sigma(a_k) = max(0,\, a_k) \tag{21}$$

where a_k is the input to the neuron, the function returns a_k if a_k is greater than 0.

If a_k is less than or equal to 0, the function returns 0.

Finally, the overall network function for the ReLU function output unit activation takes the form of Equation (22).

$$y_k(\boldsymbol{x}, \mathbf{w}) = \sigma\left(\sum_{j=1}^{M} w_{kj} z_j\, h\left(\sum_{i=1}^{D} w_{ji} x_i + w_{j0}\right) + w_{k0}\right) \tag{22}$$

The ANN model is a set of input variables $\{x_i\}$ to a set of output variables $\{y_k\}$ controlled by a vector $\boldsymbol{w}$ of adjustable parameters.

2.10. Neuroevolutionary and DeepGA Algorithm

Neuroevolution, also known as Evolutionary Neural Networks, is a machine learning technique that uses evolutionary algorithms to optimize Artificial Neural Networks, including their weights, architectures, and hyperparameters [31].

One of the most well-known types of evolutionary algorithms, extensively applied to neural network optimization, is the Genetic Algorithm (GA) [18]. GA is a class of search algorithms inspired by natural selection, where the fittest individuals have a higher probability of survival and reproduction. These algorithms evolve a population of candidate solutions, each represented as a set of genes, utilizing selection, mutation, and crossover operators to create improved solutions over time [19]. In the context of neuroevolution, the genes typically represent the connection weights and biases of the neural network architecture. The Genetic Algorithm then explores this parameter space to find an optimal set of weights that maximizes the neural network's performance on a given task.

DeepGA is a neuroevolution algorithm that utilizes a hybrid coding approach to represent Convolutional Neural Networks (CNNs) at two levels [20]. The first level consists of convolutional blocks, each serving as a layer with various filters and sizes. These layers feature a stride of 1, zero padding, batch normalization, and a rectified linear unit (ReLU) activation function. Additionally, this level includes a fully connected block to encode the number of neurons. The second level employs binary coding to describe the connections between layers: 1 indicates a connection, while 0 signifies no connection. This approach leads to a CNN architecture with fewer layers. DeepGA has been optimized [32] and utilized to optimize the design of neural networks for various image classification and regression tasks, including breast cancer diagnosis [21], vehicle make and model recognition [22], steering angle estimation [23], and anthocyanin level estimation in common bean landraces [14].

2.11. Metric Performance

We assessed the Convolutional Neural Network using the optimal architecture obtained from DeepGA. The results showcased the network's accuracy in classifying common bean landraces.

The accuracy is calculated as the ratio of the total number of correct predictions made by the algorithm to the total number of data points (see Equation (23)).

$$Accuracy = \frac{correctly\ classified\ images}{total\ images} \tag{23}$$

2.12. Experiment Design

The experiment was designed to achieve the above-mentioned objectives by comparing classification results obtained using two color characterizations and deep learning. A total of 30 runs were conducted using the common bean landrace data set, each involving a random separation of the data to create training and testing sets for the two different color characterizations. Two data sets corresponding to these color characterizations were employed to develop the neuroevolved architectures using DeepGA. Table 5 presents the values assigned to the hyperparameters of the DeepGA setup for the classification task, particularly to ensure consistent conditions across the experiments.

Table 5. Hyperparameter values for DeepGA in the classification task for evolving CNNs. All other parameters retained their original settings values.

Hyperparameters of Evolutionary Algorithm	Value	Hyperparameters of CNN	Value
Population size	15	Epochs	50
Generations number	50	Learning rate	0.001
Crossover rate	0.7	Optimization method	ADAM
Mutation rate	0.5	Loss function	Cross-entropy

CNN Architecture Optimized Through DeepGA

Two architectures were obtained with DeepGA. The first architecture, depicted in Figure 8, consists of three convolutional layers with batch normalization and ReLU activation. All convolutional layers incorporate 3×3 average pooling with a stride of 2×2. The first convolutional layer contains eight filters of 2×2, the second convolutional layer has 16 filters of 3×3, and the third convolutional layer has eight filters of 2×2. Finally, the architecture was complemented with two fully connected layers, each with 128 and 12 neurons, and the first fully connected layer included a ReLU activation.

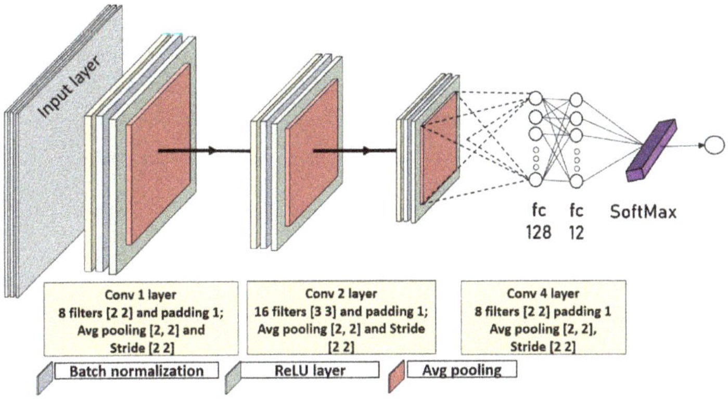

Figure 8. The CNN architecture evolved by DeepGA, utilizing color characterization represented by three two-dimensional histograms: (a* and b*), (L* and a*), and (L* and b*).

The second evolved architecture is illustrated in Figure 9. The solution reported by DeepGA consisted of five convolutional layers and four fully connected layers, all of which contained batch normalization and ReLU layers. The first convolutional layer has 16 filters of 4×4; the second one has eight filters of 2×2; the third one has eight filters of 3×3; the fourth one has 128 filters of 3×3; and the fifth one has eight filters of 3×3. The architecture includes four skip connections. The max pooling from the first convolutional layer has three connections leading to input convolutional layers 3, 4, and 5. The average pooling of the second convolutional layer connects to the input of the fourth convolutional layer, followed by four fully connected layers with 16, 128, 256, and 12 neurons.

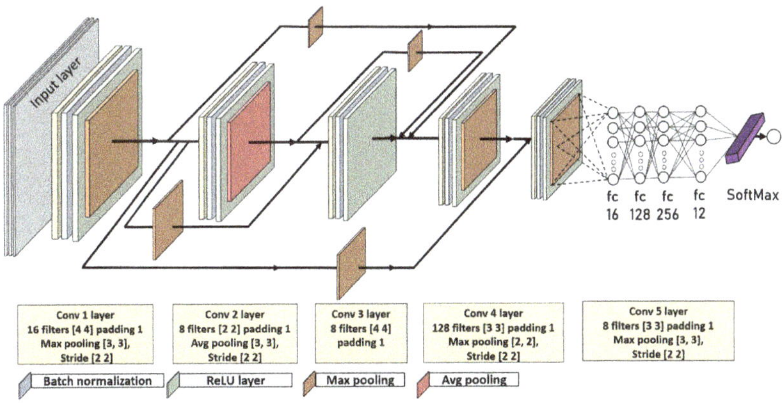

Figure 9. CNN architecture evolved by DeepGA using the color characterization conformed with three two-dimensional histograms (C* and h°), (L* and C*), (L* and h°).

Two architectures of DeepGA were evaluated to compare classification results based on the color characterizations of three two-dimensional CIE L*a*b* histograms and the contributions of three two-dimensional CIE L*C*h° histograms. Each architecture was trained for 500 epochs on each data set over 30 runs.

A normality test, specifically the Shapiro–Wilk test, was conducted to analyze the differences in classification results using two color characterizations and deep learning. In this normality test, a 95% confidence level was established to accept the null hypothesis of normality, indicating that the results follow a normal distribution.

3. Results

The classification results using the architectures obtained with DeepGA and two-color characterizations are displayed in Table 6.

Table 6. Results from 30 runs of classifying bean landraces of various colors are presented. The maximum, minimum, and mean values obtained in two color characterizations using the architectures reported by the DeepGA algorithm.

Models		DeepGA Architecture	DeepGA Architecture
Color characterization technique		PMF of a* and b* PMF of L* and a* PMF of L* and b*	PMF of C* and h° PMF of L* and C* PMF of L* and h°
Accuracy in 30 runs	Max	87.39	91.89
	Min	75.68	80.18
	Mean	82.22 ± 2.84	85.74 ± 2.37

The outcomes from the trials, which exhibited accuracies close to the mean for each color characterization, were used to depict the confusion matrix. Figure 10 shows two confusion matrices.

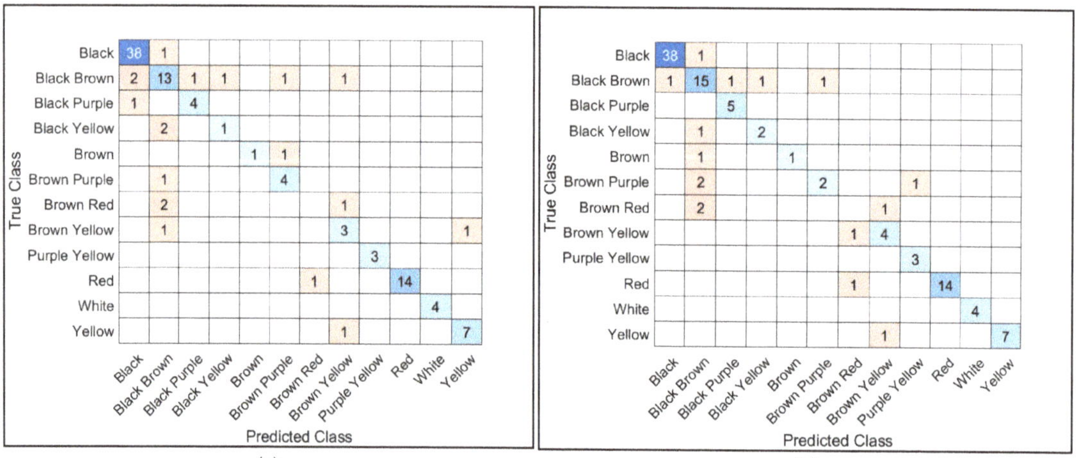

(a) (b)

Figure 10. Confusion matrix of runs exhibiting accuracy comparable to the average of the 30 tests across 12 classes: (**a**) Confusion matrix showing classification results from the DeepGA evolved architecture, with color characterization represented in three two-dimensional histograms of (a* and b*), (L* and a*), (L* and b*). (**b**) Confusion matrix displaying results achieved using color characterization from three histograms of (C* and h°), (L* and C*), (L* and h°), alongside their corresponding architecture provided by DeepGA.

Figure 11 shows the convergence plots of the training process of the CNN in the runs with accuracy close to the mean accuracy reported in Table 3.

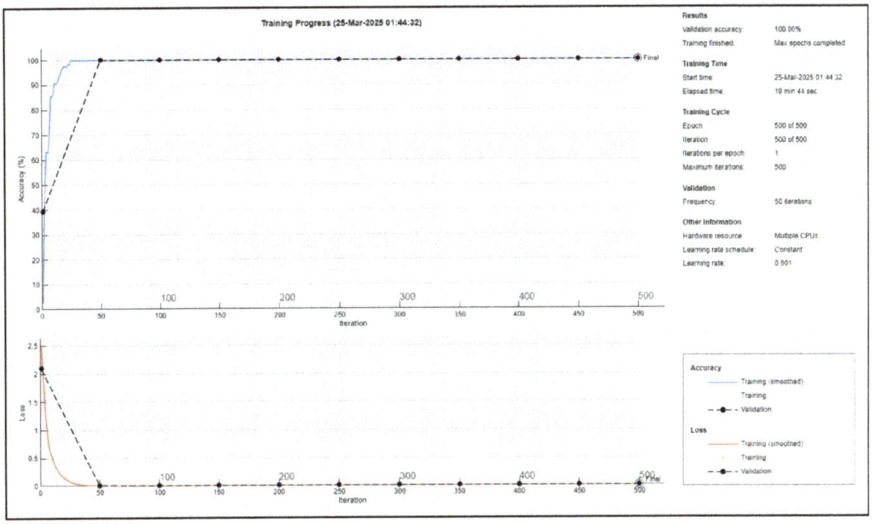

(a)

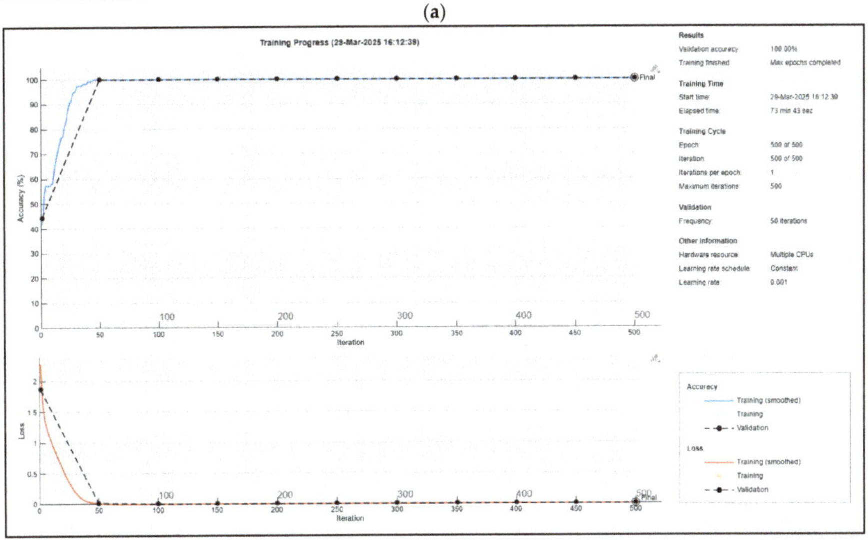

(b)

Figure 11. Convergence plots of the training process for the architectures generated by DeepGA feature two color characterizations: (**a**) The process of architecture, with color characterization illustrated in three two-dimensional histograms of (a* and b*), (L* and a*), (L* and b*). (**b**) The process utilizing color characterization from three histograms of (C* and h°), (L* and C*), (L* and h°), alongside their corresponding architectures provided by DeepGA.

Statistical Results

When comparing the performance of models trained using the CIE L*a*b* and CIE L*C*h° color representations, we found that the accuracy distributions for both followed a normal distribution. The independent samples t-test revealed a statistically significant difference between the two groups (p-value = 2.6409×10^{-6}).

Boxplot analysis revealed differences in the dispersion of the results (see Figure 12). The model based on CIE L*C*h° had a more compact box, suggesting lower variability in accuracy across runs. Two outlying observations were noted, situated on either side of the main distribution, and may be related to variability during the training phase. In contrast, the model using the CIE L*a*b* representation exhibited greater central dispersion, as evidenced by a longer box and extended whiskers. No outliers were detected, but the overall variability was higher than the L*C*h–based model. These findings suggest that the model trained with CIE L*C*h° achieved higher average accuracies and demonstrated more stable behavior.

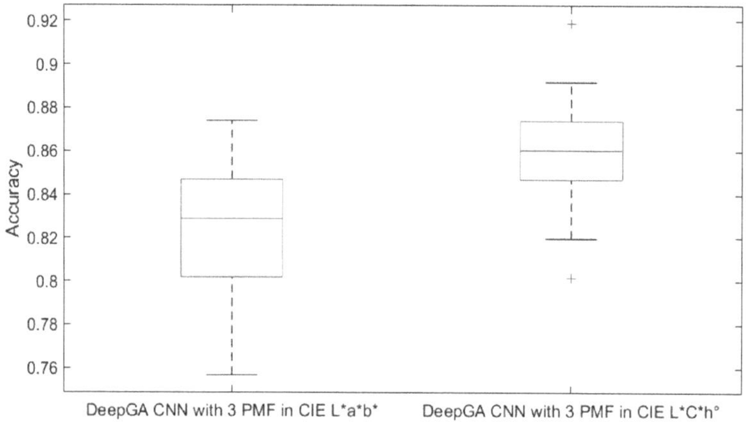

Figure 12. A box plot illustrating the comparative results of homogeneous and heterogeneous coloration bean landraces classification tasks.

4. Discussion

Mexico has hundreds of domesticated and wild bean landraces in various colors. Implementing an automatic classification solution reduces subjectivity in color organization. Furthermore, the colors of bean landraces are linked to bioactive compounds, enabling us to analyze this relationship.

Several studies classify bean varieties using averages of color, texture, or morphological properties to characterize seeds [8,11,18]. In this work, due to the complexity of labeling portions of 60 g by each bean landrace, which contain approximately 100 to 200 seeds depending on the size of the seeds, the complexity increase per the variability of their heterogeneous colors, it was necessary to define a methodology for this task; additionally, we explore the color characterization of a set of seeds, and in that sense, we have examined the use of PMF in two color characterizations.

The methodology used to assign class labels that describe each landrace by coloration allowed us to automatically organize the color groups. This was necessary to create the database, rather than relying on manual assignment again, as reported in previous work for a small number of seeds (20 seeds) [17]. The challenge involved heterogeneous color landraces, which consisted of a mixture of seeds with various color patterns. Additionally, a second challenge arose with variegated color seeds due to their lack of a single-color pattern.

The DeepGA algorithm is essential because it provides an evolved network architecture. In this work, two CNN architectures were required to perform the classification process of bean landraces. For this reason, the same values of the hyperparameters were retained. Unlike other cases where the architectures reported by DeepGA are identical [19], this work has different reported architectures. As shown in Figure 9, a more complex architecture was developed for new color characterization, demonstrating the complexity of the work.

The results obtained from the architecture created by DeepGA, using the color characterization of three two-dimensional histograms (constructed with the L*, a*, and b* channels), reported a mean accuracy of 82.22 $\pm$ 2.84, a maximum accuracy of 87.39, and a minimum accuracy of 75.68, which are lower than those reported by the second architecture evolved by DeepGA and our proposed color characterization of three two-dimensional histograms with the L*, C*, and h° information, which achieved a mean accuracy of 85.74 $\pm$ 2.37, a maximum accuracy of 91.89, and a minimum accuracy of 80.18.

Based on the results, the information provided by chroma and hue (C* and h°) enhances our understanding, as chroma indicates the color purity that varies from the center to the periphery of the CIE L*a*b* color circle. In contrast, hue indicates the angle of the color on the circumference. Therefore, this information is crucial for the deep learning model to accurately identify the colors of the test set samples.

In Figure 10, we observe the confusion matrices from the runs close to the mean of each color characterization. In Figure 10a, it is evident that the classification errors occur in landraces with heterogeneous colors. For example, the bean landraces labeled as Black Brown exhibit a higher classification error, which is an important factor contributing to their color variability. Although the dominant colors are black and brown, these landraces also contain seeds of other colorations, making classification complicated due to the differing colorimetric patterns. The values of the channels in CIE L*a*b* share the same scale, which can be a disadvantage for the similarity of values in landraces that exhibit different colorimetric patterns. In contrast, these values are on a different scale when using chroma and hue. This distinction aids in differentiating between classes, as illustrated in Figure 10b, where a reduction in classification error is observed.

The difference in accuracy reported by both classification models is significant, as illustrated in Figure 12, where notable differences in the results of the two-color characterizations are observed. Therefore, this new proposal accommodates significant differences, making it a suitable solution for classifying bean landraces of both homogeneous and heterogeneous colorations.

5. Conclusions

Initially, images of each bean landrace were obtained, followed by a color calibration procedure to ensure consistent results and prevent chromatic deviations. The definition of a color palette and the application of the k-NN algorithm enabled the accurate assignment of labels to the set of bean landraces used in this study, thereby reducing the subjectivity inherent in the manual classification of bean landraces. The development of a method to correctly separate the colors of variegated seeds allowed the assignment of labels based on the number of colors present.

The color characterization determines the results; for that purpose, two color characterizations were compared to know the classification results of common bean landraces. In that sense, the DeepGA algorithm was used to have custom architectures. The results showed a significant difference. Therefore, the color characterization represented by three two-dimensional histograms (C* and h°), (L* and C*), (L* and h°), and the neuroevolved CNN architecture with DeepGA offered higher accuracy.

In this work, we analyzed the classification of homogeneous and heterogeneous colored bean landraces, considering a reduced number of heterogeneous samples. As future work, we propose the following: i. A greater number of samples of bean landraces with heterogeneous coloration is needed to better represent the diversity of colors present in different bean species. ii. To improve the label assignment method, the total color distribution present in a sample of bean landraces should be considered to identify the different colors rather than each seed individually.

Author Contributions: Conceptualization, J.-L.M.-R. and E.-N.A.-B.; methodology, J.-L.M.-R. and E.-N.A.-B.; software, J.-L.M.-R.; validation, E.-N.A.-B. and H.-G.A.-M.; formal analysis, J.-L.M.-R.; investigation, J.-L.M.-R.; resources, E.-N.A.-B. and J.-L.C.-S.; data curation, J.-L.M.-R. and E.-N.A.-B.; writing—original draft preparation, J.-L.M.-R. and N.P.-C.; writing—review and editing, E.-N.A.-B. and H.-G.A.-M.; visualization, J.-L.M.-R. and N.P.-C.; supervision, E.-N.A.-B. and H.-G.A.-M. All authors have read and agreed to the published version of the manuscript.

Funding: This research received no external funding.

Data Availability Statement: The data sets employed in this article are not readily available since they are part of an ongoing study. Requests for access to the data sets should be directed to eliaquino@uv.mx and heacosta@uv.mx.

Acknowledgments: The first author acknowledges the Secretaría de Ciencia, Humanidades, Tecnología e Innovación (SECIHTI) of Mexico for granting support for the realization of this investigation through scholarship 712056 awarded for postdoctoral studies at the Centre for Food Research and Development in the University of Veracruz.

Conflicts of Interest: The authors declare no conflicts of interest.

References

1. Servicio de Información Agroalimentaria y Pesquera (SIAP). Expectativas Agroalimentarias Agosto 2024. Available online: https://www.gob.mx/cms/uploads/attachment/file/940838/Agosto_2024.pdf (accessed on 10 April 2025).
2. Smith, M.R.; Dinglasan, E.; Veneklaas, E.; Polania, J.; Rao, I.M.; Beebe, S.E.; Merchant, A. Effect of Drought and Low P on Yield and Nutritional Content in Common Bean. *Front. Plant Sci.* **2022**, *13*, 814325. [CrossRef] [PubMed]
3. Aquino-Bolaños, E.N.; Garzón-García, A.K.; Alba-Jiménez, J.E.; Chávez-Servia, J.L.; Vera-Guzmán, A.M.; Carrillo-Rodríguez, J.C.; Santos-Basurto, M.A. Physicochemical Characterization and Functional Potential of *Phaseolus vulgaris* L. and *Phaseolus Coccineus* L. Landrace Green Beans. *Agronomy* **2021**, *11*, 803. [CrossRef]
4. López, C.M.; Pineda, M.; Alamillo, J.M. Differential Regulation of Drought Responses in Two *Phaseolus vulgaris* Genotypes. *Plants* **2020**, *9*, 1815. [CrossRef] [PubMed]
5. Polania, J.A.; Chater, C.C.C.; Covarrubias, A.A.; Rao, I.M. Phaseolus Species Responses and Tolerance to Drought. In *The Plant Family Fabaceae*; Hasanuzzaman, M., Araújo, S., Gill, S.S., Eds.; Springer: Singapore, 2020; pp. 319–336, ISBN 978-981-15-4751-5.
6. Bianco, M.L.; Grillo, O.; Cremonini, R.; Sarigu, M.; Venora, V. Characterisation of Italian Bean Landraces ("*Phaseolus vulgaris*" L.) Using Seed Image Analysis and Texture Descriptors. *Aust. J. Crop Sci.* **2015**, *9*, 1022–1034.
7. Yi, X.; Eramian, M.; Wang, R.; Neufeld, E. Identification of Morphologically Similar Seeds Using Multi-Kernel Learning. In Proceedings of the 2014 Canadian Conference on Computer and Robot Vision, Montreal, QC, Canada, 6–9 May 2014; IEEE: New York, NY, USA, 2014; pp. 143–150.
8. Garcia, M.; Chaves, D.; Trujillo, M. An Automatic Bean Classification System Based on Visual Features to Assist the Seed Breeding Process. In *Trends and Advancements of Image Processing and Its Applications*; Johri, P., Diván, M.J., Khanam, R., Marciszack, M., Will, A., Eds.; EAI/Springer Innovations in Communication and Computing; Springer International Publishing: Cham, Switzerland, 2022; pp. 165–176, ISBN 978-3-030-75944-5.
9. Kılıç, K.; Boyacı, İ.H.; Köksel, H.; Küsmenoğlu, İ. A Classification System for Beans Using Computer Vision System and Artificial Neural Networks. *J. Food Eng.* **2007**, *78*, 897–904. [CrossRef]
10. Ozaktan, H.; Çetin, N.; Uzun, S.; Uzun, O.; Ciftci, C.Y. Prediction of Mass and Discrimination of Common Bean by Machine Learning Approaches. *Environ. Dev. Sustain.* **2023**, *26*, 18139–18160. [CrossRef]
11. Mendoza, F.A.; Kelly, J.D.; Cichy, K.A. Automated Prediction of Sensory Scores for Color and Appearance in Canned Black Beans (*Phaseolus vulgaris* L.) Using Machine Vision. *Int. J. Food Prop.* **2017**, *20*, 83–99. [CrossRef]
12. Eric, O.; Gyening, R.-M.O.M.; Appiah, O.; Takyi, K.; Appiahene, P. Cocoa Beans Classification Using Enhanced Image Feature Extraction Techniques and a Regularized Artificial Neural Network Model. *Eng. Appl. Artif. Intell.* **2023**, *125*, 106736. [CrossRef]
13. Djoulde, K.; Ousman, B.; Hamadjam, A.; Bitjoka, L.; Tchiegang, C. Classification of Pepper Seeds by Machine Learning Using Color Filter Array Images. *J. Imaging* **2024**, *10*, 41. [CrossRef] [PubMed]

14. Koklu, M.; Ozkan, I.A. Multiclass Classification of Dry Beans Using Computer Vision and Machine Learning Techniques. *Comput. Electron. Agric.* **2020**, *174*, 105507. [CrossRef]
15. Mendigoria, C.H.; Concepcion, R.; Dadios, E.; Aquino, H.; Alaias, O.J.; Sybingco, E.; Bandala, A.; Vicerra, R.R.; Cuello, J. Seed Architectural Phenes Prediction and Variety Classification of Dry Beans (*Phaseolus vulgaris*) Using Machine Learning Algorithms. In Proceedings of the 2021 IEEE 9th Region 10 Humanitarian Technology Conference (R10-HTC), Bangalore, India, 30 September–2 October 2021; IEEE: New York, NY, USA, 2021; pp. 1–6.
16. Nasirahmadi, A.; Behroozi-Khazaei, N. Identification of Bean Varieties According to Color Features Using Artificial Neural Network. *Span. J. Agric. Res.* **2013**, *11*, 670–677. [CrossRef]
17. Morales-Reyes, J.L.; Acosta-Mesa, H.G.; Aquino-Bolanos, E.N.; Herrera-Meza, S.; Cruz-Ramirez, N.; Chávez-Servia, J.L. Classification of Bean (*Phaseolus vulgaris* L.) Landraces with Heterogeneous Seed Color Using a Probabilistic Representation. In Proceedings of the 2021 IEEE International Autumn Meeting on Power, Electronics and Computing (ROPEC), Ixtapa, Mexico, 10–12 November 2021; IEEE: New York, NY, USA, 2021; pp. 1–7.
18. Morales-Reyes, J.L.; Acosta-Mesa, H.-G.; Aquino-Bolaños, E.-N.; Herrera Meza, S.; Márquez Grajales, A. Anthocyanins Estimation in Homogeneous Bean Landrace (*Phaseolus vulgaris* L.) Using Probabilistic Representation and Convolutional Neural Networks. *J. Agric. Eng.* **2023**, *54*. [CrossRef]
19. Morales-Reyes, J.-L.; Aquino-Bolaños, E.-N.; Acosta-Mesa, H.-G.; Márquez-Grajales, A. Estimation of Anthocyanins in Heterogeneous and Homogeneous Bean Landraces Using Probabilistic Colorimetric Representation with a Neuroevolutionary Approach. *MCA* **2024**, *29*, 68. [CrossRef]
20. Sönmez, M.E.; Sabancı, K.; Aydın, N. Classification of Wheat Rootstock and Their Hybrids According to Color Features by Machine Learning Algorithms. *Int. J. Appl. Math. Electron. Comput.* **2022**, *10*, 39–48. [CrossRef]
21. López-Lobato, A.-L.; Avendaño-Garrido, M.-L.; Acosta-Mesa, H.-G.; Morales-Reyes, J.-L.; Aquino-Bolaños, E.-N. Bean Landraces Color Identification Through Image Analysis and Gaussian Mixture Model. In *Advances in Computational Intelligence. MICAI 2024 International Workshops*; Martínez-Villaseñor, L., Ochoa-Ruiz, G., Montes Rivera, M., Barrón-Estrada, M.L., Acosta-Mesa, H.G., Eds.; Lecture Notes in Computer Science; Springer Nature Switzerland: Cham, Switzerland, 2025; Volume 15465, pp. 112–124, ISBN 978-3-031-83881-1.
22. Aquino-Bolaños, E.; García-Díaz, Y.; Chávez-Servia, J.; Carrillo-Rodríguez, J.; Vera-Guzman, A.; Heredia-Garcia, E. Anthocyanins, Polyphenols, Flavonoids and Antioxidant Activity in Common Bean (*Phaseolus vulgaris* L.) Landraces. *Emir. J. Food Agric.* **2016**, *28*, 581. [CrossRef]
23. McGuire, R.G. Reporting of Objective Color Measurements. *HortSci* **1992**, *27*, 1254–1255. [CrossRef]
24. Bishop, C.M. *Pattern Recognition and Machine Learning*; Information Science and Statistics; Springer: New York, USA, 2006; ISBN 978-0-387-31073-2.
25. Morales-Reyes, J.-L.; Aquino-Bolaños, E.-N.; Acosta-Mesa, H.-G. Color Quantification in Common Bean Landraces Using a Supervised Learning Technique. In *Advances in Computational Intelligence. MICAI 2024 International Workshops*; Martínez-Villaseñor, L., Ochoa-Ruiz, G., Montes Rivera, M., Barrón-Estrada, M.L., Acosta-Mesa, H.G., Eds.; Lecture Notes in Computer Science; Springer Nature Switzerland: Cham, Switzerland, 2025; Volume 15465, pp. 167–178, ISBN 978-3-031-83881-1.
26. Gustavo, E.A.P.A.B.; Diego, F.S. How K-Nearest Neighbor Parameters Affect Its Performance. Available online: https://citeseerx.ist.psu.edu/document?repid=rep1&type=pdf&doi=b83da505b60e32469152b986cbd6199842403b11 (accessed on 15 April 2025).
27. Gonzalez, R.C.; Woods, R.E. *Digital Image Processing*, 4th ed.; Pearson India: Uttar Pradesh, India, 2018; ISBN 978-93-5306-298-9.
28. Khan, S.; Rahmani, H.; Shah, S.A.A.; Bennamoun, M. *A Guide to Convolutional Neural Networks for Computer Vision*; Synthesis Lectures on Computer Vision; Morgan & Claypool Publishers: San Rafael, CA, USA, 2018; ISBN 978-1-68173-021-9.
29. Guo, Y.; Liu, Y.; Oerlemans, A.; Lao, S.; Wu, S.; Lew, M.S. Deep Learning for Visual Understanding: A Review. *Neurocomputing* **2016**, *187*, 27–48. [CrossRef]
30. Bjorck, J.; Gomes, C.; Selman, B.; Weinberger, K.Q. Understanding Batch Normalization. In Proceedings of the Advances in Neural Information Processing Systems, Montreal, QC, Canada, 3–8 December 2018; Bengio, S., Wallach, H., Larochelle, H., Grauman, K., Cesa-Bianchi, N., Garnett, R., Eds.; Curran Associates, Inc.: Red Hook, NY, USA, 2018; Volume 31, pp. 7705–7716.
31. Galvan, E.; Mooney, P. Neuroevolution in Deep Neural Networks: Current Trends and Future Challenges. *IEEE Trans. Artif. Intell.* **2021**, *2*, 476–493. [CrossRef]
32. Barradas-Palmeros, J.-A.; López-Herrera, C.-A.; Acosta-Mesa, H.-G.; Mezura-Montes, E. Efficient Neural Architecture Search: Computational Cost Reduction Mechanisms in DeepGA. In *Advances in Computational Intelligence. MICAI 2024 International Workshops*; Martínez-Villaseñor, L., Ochoa-Ruiz, G., Montes Rivera, M., Barrón-Estrada, M.L., Acosta-Mesa, H.G., Eds.; Lecture Notes in Computer Science; Springer Nature Switzerland: Cham, Switzerland, 2025; Volume 15465, pp. 125–134, ISBN 978-3-031-83881-1.

Mathematical and Computational Applications

MDPI

Article

Permeability Prediction Using Vision Transformers

Cenk Temizel [1,*], Uchenna Odi [2], Kehao Li [3], Lei Liu [4], Salih Tutun [3] and Javier Santos [5]

[1] TerraPacific, 5900 Balcones Dr., Austin, TX 78731, USA
[2] Aramco Americas, Houston, TX 77002, USA
[3] John M. Olin Business School, Washington University in St. Louis, St. Louis, MO 63130, USA
[4] Hildebrand Department of Petroleum and Geosystems Engineering, University of Texas at Austin, Austin, TX 78712, USA
[5] Los Alamos National Laboratory, Los Alamos, NM 87545, USA
* Correspondence: cenktemizel@gmail.com

Abstract

Accurate permeability predictions remain pivotal for understanding fluid flow in porous media, influencing crucial operations across petroleum engineering, hydrogeology, and related fields. Traditional approaches, while robust, often grapple with the inherent heterogeneity of reservoir rocks. With the advent of deep learning, convolutional neural networks (CNNs) have emerged as potent tools in image-based permeability estimation, capitalizing on micro-CT scans and digital rock imagery. This paper introduces a novel paradigm, employing vision transformers (ViTs)—a recent advancement in computer vision—for this crucial task. ViTs, which segment images into fixed-sized patches and process them through transformer architectures, present a promising alternative to CNNs. We present a methodology for implementing ViTs for permeability prediction, its results on diverse rock samples, and a comparison against conventional CNNs. The prediction results suggest that, with adequate training data, ViTs can match or surpass the predictive accuracy of CNNs, especially in rocks exhibiting significant heterogeneity. This study underscores the potential of ViTs as an innovative tool in permeability prediction, paving the way for further research and integration into mainstream reservoir characterization workflows.

Keywords: permeability prediction; CNN; ViTs

1. Introduction

Predictions of permeability play a role in characterizing reservoirs as they help us understand how fluids flow through porous materials, like rocks in the earth's surface or subsurface areas known as reservoirs. Special Core Analysis (SCAL) has been used for years to predict and evaluate rock permeability in reservoirs by analyzing the cores from drilling sites and well logs along with methods like measuring the physical properties of rocks. Although these traditional methods are effective to some extent at predicting the permeability of reservoir rocks, they come with limitations due to the amount of data needed and the complexity of the rock formations being studied. The field has experienced a change towards digital transformation by leveraging advanced computational methods, like machine learning and deep learning, to improve the prediction capabilities of permeability.

Advanced deep learning technologies like neural networks (CNN) have brought significant advancements to industries like petroleum engineering by effectively enhancing seismic interpretation and reservoir simulation processes. CNNs' capabilities for analyzing sections and digital rock images have shown potential for accurate permeability predictions [1]. Nonetheless, vision transformers (ViTs), an innovation in AI technology, are now being seen as groundbreaking developments with the potential to revolutionize the field further. ViTs differ from CNNs in that they break down images into patches and scrutinize them similarly to how transformers manage sequences in natural language processing, as described by [2]. This novel method has sparked inquiries about the use of ViTs for predicting permeability from rock images due to their capacity to analyze intricate image data.

This research project focuses on exploring the capabilities of vision transformers (ViTs) for predicting permeability by building upon previous studies and delving into the obstacles and possibilities they offer. By comparing ViTs with conventional CNN models, this investigation aims to assess how effective ViTs are at predicting permeability in the realm of digital rock physics.

The unique aspect of this research is its utilizing ViTs to predict permeability in the field of petroleum engineering. This domain has received little exploration thus far compared to the extensively researched CNNs. ViTs' distinct ability to manage image data at a granular level brings a fresh viewpoint. This research delves into the theoretical potential of ViTs and tackles real-world obstacles, like the requirement for extensive datasets, that have historically restricted their utilization in this field. Drawing from datasets, such as the one compiled by Santos and colleagues in 2022 [3] that feature three shapes and outcomes from simulations, this study looks to tackle these obstacles head-on and push forward the application of vision transformers for forecasting permeability within porous materials.

Rahmanifard's [4] research examined how AI methods are utilized in the petroleum sector, focusing on the impressive effectiveness of these techniques for enhancing different operations, like predicting the permeability levels of reservoirs. His study underlined the advantages of integrating AI methods to address intricate challenges in characterizing reservoir formations. This goal resonates with this research's aim of advancing permeability prediction through sophisticated AI models like ViTs.

Furthermore, the research by Kuang and others in 2021 [5] highlighted the impact that AI could have on petroleum exploration and development. That paper explored how AI tools, like learning and optimization, were currently used for estimating reservoir parameters and real-time production optimization tasks. Kuang and colleagues stressed that AI's future role in the petroleum industry would include advanced production machinery, automated data analysis and interpretation, and the creation of tailored software solutions. These findings back up the investigation of ViTs for predicting permeability, since they mark the frontier in utilizing AI for intricate geological and engineering challenges.

Moreover, the research carried out by Ng and colleagues in 2021 [6] shed light on the growing influence of machine learning and metaheuristic algorithms on proxy modeling for reservoir simulation tasks. The study underscored the integration of machine learning with algorithms as an effective strategy to create proxy models that can notably cut down the computational time without compromising the accuracy of reservoir simulations. This integrated method has demonstrated encouraging outcomes across different reservoir engineering tasks, such as the enhancement and quantification of uncertainty, which further solidifies the capacity of cutting-edge AI methods like vision transformers (ViTs) to transform the forecasting of permeability and other intricate modeling duties in reservoir characterization.

Muther's recent research [7] highlighted how crucial optimization is in fracturing for effective reservoir management. It showcased the success of combining reservoir simulations with neural networks and innovative socio-inspired algorithms to enhance fracture design. The outcomes underscored the effectiveness of sophisticated optimization strategies, like multi-cohort intelligence (multi-CI) and teaching–learning-based optimization (TLBO), in contrast to conventional approaches, such as particle swarm optimization

(PSO) and genetic algorithms (GAs). The findings also reinforced the need for investigations into cutting-edge AI models, such as ViTs, for predicting permeability, since these models could present benefits when dealing with intricate optimization tasks in reservoir characterization.

The study conducted by Zhang and colleagues in 2018 [8] underscored the growing significance of intelligence models for enhancing and mimicking reservoir operations, especially deep learning algorithms such as long short-term memory (LSTM). They highlighted how LSTM models excel at managing scheduling challenges in reservoir management compared to conventional AI models by offering superior prediction accuracy and computational efficiency. The study results support the idea that advanced AI methods like vision transformers (ViTs) could transform modeling assignments in reservoir characterization by completing tasks, such as predicting permeability.

In his work published in 2023, Kubeyev [9] introduced a strategy for tackling the computational hurdles linked to multi-physics numerical modeling tasks focused on simulating fractures with intricate shapes and forms. The research showcased the effectiveness of using a deep learning algorithm to forecast physical permeability characteristics based on images of fractures alone without needing data on fluid velocity—a usual prerequisite for such simulations. The research demonstrated that deep learning can substitute for a portion of the physics-oriented modeling procedure by employing a convolutional neural network (CNN) trained with data derived from digitized rough fracture surfaces and computed permeability values. This strategy notably cuts down the computation time without compromising the precision levels and has proven to be an advantageous asset in multi-physics modeling scenarios where conventional techniques have proven to be excessively demanding computationally. The effective utilization of deep learning in this scenario underscores the capabilities of AI models such as vision transformers (ViTs) to improve the accuracy of predicting permeability during reservoir characterization.

Therefore, this study connects the conventional and cutting-edge AI methods for forecasting permeability levels, smoothly bridging the gap between the two realms of AI techniques for permeability prediction. The research seeks to enhance the efficiency and precision of predicting permeability by employing vision transformers, a move that could reshape digital rock physics significantly. The results of this investigation will offer valuable perspectives on using advanced AI for characterizing reservoirs, paving the path for future advancements in this field.

2. Related Literature

Estimating reservoir characteristics like permeability is important for understanding the structures and fluid movement patterns in oil fields and gas reservoirs. The typically used techniques to determine porosity and permeability involve core testing and complex mathematical models or petrophysical simulations. However, advancements in machine learning (ML) and deep learning (DL) have introduced ways to tackle these issues by providing cost-effective, precise, and scalable solutions for evaluating reservoir properties.

Yang and colleagues [10] introduced a deep learning model to forecast reservoir permeability and porosity using authentic logging data from diverse areas. Their method effectively cuts down on the expenses and intricacies linked with traditional approaches while upholding their strong dependability across various geological conditions. This model harnesses advanced learning capabilities to manage the intricate and nonlinear connections between the logging data and reservoir characteristics, presenting a reliable substitute for traditional methods.

Expanding on the progress made in learning techniques, Meng and colleagues [11] developed a new neural network that combines CNN and transformer architectures to overcome the shortcomings of standard 3D CNN models when predicting the permeability of porous materials. This hybrid model has enhanced efficiency, accuracy, and adaptability by utilizing 2D image sequences and integrating characteristics. It shows improvements, especially when working with limited data or in novel scenarios, due to its application of transfer learning. Their research emphasizes that transfer learning-based models show promise for addressing the obstacles linked to sparse data in reservoir engineering, a prevalent issue within the field.

In a study by Zhang and colleagues [12], they expanded the use of transformers in reservoir simulations by creating an enhanced vision transformer neural network (IViT-NN). This advanced model serves as a learning surrogate for addressing history-matching challenges and boosts the speed at which production data is generated, proving to be a crucial asset for tasks like history matching and predicting production outcomes. The performance of this model, producing results comparable to those achieved with complete reservoir simulations, highlights the promise of ViTs for improving the effectiveness and precision of intricate reservoir modeling assignments.

Advancements in using machine learning methods to enhance reservoir engineering have also been made. In a study by Liu and colleagues [13], they tackled the ongoing issue of spatial variability in geostatistical models that has long troubled traditional approaches. Their research showcases the effectiveness of self-attention mechanisms like vision transformer models for enhancing the accuracy of deep learning forecasts in scenarios with substantial spatial diversity. This method not only performs better than traditional CNN models, but also fits in well with the changing trends in machine learning applications within different scientific domains demonstrated by [14]. Using ViTs to address variations marks a crucial advancement in reservoir characterization.

A research project by Liu and colleagues [15] explored how materials are structured by examining factors like the specific surface area tortuousness and pore size. Their approach involved a two-phase machine learning system that utilized 11 metrics to evaluate the structure and reaction rates derived from simulations at the pore level. The research showcases how machine learning methods can be effectively applied to study how nanoconfinement impacts continuum models. Liu and colleagues [15] introduced a method to link fine-scale and coarse-scale models using machine learning emulators to improve the accuracy when predicting permeability in reservoir characterization tasks.

The advancements in imaging technologies have brought about discoveries in understanding the differences in carbonate rocks using X-ray imaging techniques at different levels of scale, such as CT scans and micro/nano CT imaging methods, while facing difficulties in combining these insights into a unified model for precise upscaling measurements, as shown by several recent research papers by Eberhard et al. [16] and Kamrava et al. [17]. Graczyk [18] utilized convolutional neural networks (CNNs) to analyze CT scans to forecast carbonate rocks' permeability. However, CNN models' resource-intensive natures and lack of transparency restrict their usefulness for scaling up. Andrew [19] presented a machine learning approach in 2020 that merged the vectorization of datasets with a regression based on decision trees, providing an understandable and scalable resolution. This approach tackled some of the constraints linked to vision transformers (ViTs), proposing that integrating ViTs with machine or deep learning could offer an efficient and adaptable solution for intricate real-world situations while maintaining accuracy.

A study by Kubeyev [9] introduced a new deep learning method to forecast the physical permeability traits of fractures with intricate shapes and sizes. The approach involved utilizing images of fractures to teach a convolutional neural network (CNN), which can anticipate permeability without relying on data about fluid speeds, a departure from conventional practices. The outcomes indicated that deep learning has the potential to streamline physics-based modeling procedures by cutting down on the computation time without compromising accuracy. This research focused heavily on the advantages of incorporating learning into multi-physics modeling, especially for tasks that are too computationally intensive for conventional numerical methods.

In 2021 Ng and colleagues [6] conducted a study that emphasized the growing importance of machine learning and metaheuristic algorithms for creating intelligent proxy models for reservoir simulation tasks. They found that by integrating machine learning with algorithms, they could create proxy models that reduce the computing time while maintaining high levels of accuracy. This innovative approach has potential in reservoir engineering tasks, such as optimization and uncertainty assessment. The research highlights the possibilities that AI techniques like ViTs can offer for transforming permeability predictions and other intricate modeling tasks in reservoir characterization.

In a study by Zhang and colleagues in 2018 [8] on long short-term memory (LSTM), they delved into the use of LSTM networks for optimizing and simulating reservoir operations to showcase how these models excel at solving scheduling issues in reservoir management compared to traditional AI models, due to their accuracy in making predictions and their computational efficiency improvements. The research findings by Zhang et al. also highlight the future of cutting-edge AI techniques like vision transformers (ViTs), which could potentially transform complex modeling tasks related to reservoir characterization, such as predicting permeability levels.

In their study published in 2023, Meng and colleagues [11] introduced a new deep learning approach called Transformer to effectively predict reservoir permeability and porosity using actual logging data. The Transformer model combines one convolutional layer with LSTM and transformer layers to accurately capture the variations in the depth over time in logging data—a crucial factor for precise subsurface analysis. Firstly, extracting the features from the logging data using 1-dimensional convolutional layers and then establishing the complex mapping connections between the logging data and reservoir parameters through the LSTM layers are the primary steps taken by the model. Using an encoder with self-attention helps improve the feature extraction, enabling the model to make accurate and reliable predictions across various geographical areas more effectively. Their research shows that an RPTransformer performs better than machine learning models, such as random forest and other deep learning models like multilayer LSTM and LSTNet, especially when it comes to generalization and managing uncertainties in practical scenarios. This study underscores the possibilities of incorporating learning structures into reservoir parameter prediction, which could pave the way for exciting advancements in this field.

The literature shows a trend toward incorporating cutting-edge AI technologies like vision transformers into analyses of reservoir properties and permeability forecasts. The research highlights how these methods can address the shortcomings of traditional techniques by providing improved efficiency and accuracy on a larger scale. As a result, the current exploration of ViTs and other advanced AI models marks a progression in reservoir engineering, setting the stage for advancements that will boost our capacity to forecast and regulate subsurface assets more effectively.

While vision transformers are relatively new in earth science applications, a growing number of studies have begun exploring their potential. For example, Meng et al. [11] and Liu et al. [13] applied transformer-based models to predict permeability and reaction rates in porous media using digital rock images and structural features. Additionally, Zhang and Li [12] introduced an improved ViT framework for history-matching and reservoir simulation tasks, demonstrating its ability to replicate full-physics models with significantly reduced computational costs. These pioneering efforts highlight the versatility of

ViTs in geoscientific domains involving complex spatial patterns. However, most existing works have focused either on history-matching or 2D applications, whereas our study uniquely applies 3D ViT modeling for direct permeability prediction at the pore scale. This underscores the novelty and technical contribution of our approach within the broader evolution of ViT usage in the earth sciences.

3. Operational Aspects of Special Core Analysis (SCAL) and Digital Rock Physics

Special Core Analysis (SCAL) and digital rock physics (DRP) enhance our understanding of reservoir characteristics and optimize hydrocarbon recovery. SCAL involves conducting laboratory experiments on core samples to assess their permeability, wettability, and electrical properties. These experiments are essential for comprehending the flow of fluids through the media of reservoir rocks [20–22].

The transition from SCAL to DRP represents an operational change. DRP utilizes imaging technologies like micro-CT scanning to generate detailed 3D models of rock samples. This digital transformation enables us to analyze structures and fluid distribution with precision without being constrained by the limitations of conventional core analysis methods. One important aspect of integrating SCAL with DRP is the requirement for resources. The analysis of 3D images requires powerful computing platforms and specialized software capable of handling extensive datasets and performing complex simulations [23,24].

Furthermore, the integration of SCAL and DRP calls for collaboration. Various engineering, geoscience, and digital transformation disciplines must collaborate closely to interpret rock models accurately. This collaboration extends to developing models that simulate reservoir conditions and fluid interactions. The accuracy of DRP models heavily relies on the quality of the input data. Hence, one of the challenges is ensuring that digital images accurately reflect the properties of rock samples. This often requires aligning the models with the measurements obtained from SCAL experiments. Another aspect to consider is the constantly improving imaging technology. Higher resolutions and faster simulation techniques have made analyzing rock samples in detail possible. However, this also means that the analysis software and computational methods must be continuously updated [25,26]. Additionally, training and expertise in DRP is necessary. Personnel must be well-trained in operating resolution imaging equipment and interpreting rock physics data. This involves understanding the limitations and uncertainties associated with the models. Data management and security have also become increasingly important. Since DRP generates large volumes of data, it is essential to store and manage the data, provide access to the relevant stakeholders, and to ensure data integrity and confidentiality [27,28]. Lastly, integrating SCAL data with reservoir simulation models is important. This integration will help make decisions regarding reservoir management and optimization strategies more streamlined and effective. However, it requires data transfer and compatibility among the software tools used in SCAL, DRP, and reservoir simulations [29,30].

4. Methodology

This study employs a comprehensive approach to model development, dataset utilization, and data preprocessing to predict the permeability of porous media. The methodology is divided into several key subsections, each addressing a critical component of the research process.

5. Model Development

The primary focus of this research is developing an advanced deep learning framework for permeability prediction. The model, a hybrid of CNN–Transformer architecture, is designed to efficiently process and analyze 3D porous media data. The CNN layers are utilized for the initial feature extraction, leveraging their capacity to capture spatial dependencies in imaging data. In contrast, the Transformer layers are employed to handle complex relationships and enhance predictive accuracy. Integrating these architectures aims to address the limitations of traditional methods and previous deep learning models, particularly in terms of the computational efficiency and generalization to diverse datasets.

In the proposed architecture, the CNN layers are positioned at the front of the network to extract the local spatial features from the 3D porous media input. These layers are well-suited for capturing fine-scale geometric patterns, such as pore shapes and connectivity. The extracted spatial feature maps are then passed to the Transformer layers, which apply window-based self-attention to capture the long-range dependencies and contextual relationships across the 3D volume. This combination allows the model to leverage both the local details (from the CNN) and the global structural context (from the Transformer), creating a synergistic framework that improves prediction accuracy while maintaining computational efficiency.

5.1. Dataset Description

Transport phenomena in media are widespread. They have applications in various fields, ranging from hydrocarbon extraction and CO_2 storage to cutting-edge technologies like battery design and desalination [31,32]. Understanding and quantifying the influence of porous structures on transport processes requires focusing on the key properties, such as permeability and electrical conductivity. These properties determine how easily fluids flow through a medium and how well it conducts electrical currents, making them crucial for modeling, design, and a nuanced understanding of the underlying physics [16,33–35]. Despite efforts to establish relationships based on descriptors like porosity, creating a universal model remains a formidable challenge [3].

The complex impact of the length scale and pore space geometry on the flow and other properties adds complexity to this pursuit. Different methodologies, including laboratory measurements, X-ray micro relationships, and 3D fluid mechanics simulations, have been used to estimate the transport properties, each with its advantages and limitations [36–39]. One promising avenue for future exploration involves utilizing machine learning (ML) models as substitutes for estimating the properties from images. This approach has shown potential for expediting the predictions of properties at the microscopic level [31,40,41].

Despite the advancements achieved so far, there remains an expanse of uncharted territory within the realm of pore-scale machine learning. Further research is needed before we can delve into this domain, due to the difficulties in acquiring and processing data. Nevertheless, there is still potential within the realm of pore-scale machine learning (ML). Many current efforts are focused on models trained using either 3D samples ($<128^3$) [41] or larger samples ($>256^3$), often concentrating on one type of geometry, like sphere packs [42]. One notable exception to this trend is an initiative that utilized 90,000 microstructures from 9 distribution families, which were down-sampled to 96^3 for applications in 3D machine learning. In contrast to fields where large and diverse datasets have driven ML breakthroughs, porous media research faces challenges from the datasets used, which limit effective comparisons between modeling techniques and obscure the influence of confounding variables, such as fluid solvers and numerical implementations, on ML models' characteristics [3].

To address this gap, this work (Table 1) aimed to create a dataset encompassing complex scenarios across 3D simulations, empirical functional forms, and machine learning applications in porous media. This diversity covered dimensions including the lithology of the media, boundary conditions, geometric resolution, and simulated physical processes. This work generated three types of microstructures: Gaussian random fields, spinodal decomposition simulations, and non-overlapping ellipsoid systems. Each type of microstructure consisted of 10,000 instances, with varying porosities and characteristic lengths. These instances were then converted into voxel arrays. Volume sizes were selected accordingly to ensure efficiency. Correlation functions ranging from integer radii value bins of 1 to 96 voxels [43] were selected.

Table 1. Overview of this work's progression for permeability prediction study. This table outlines the key steps involved in the methodology of the study, from data collection to model testing. Each step is described with the associated actions, providing a structured view of the research workflow.

Step	Description
Start	Data Collection: DRP 372 Dataset
	- 217 samples from 125 projects
	- Lithologies include subsurface rocks, soils, biofilms, and more
Data Processing	Filtering Data
	- Select key petrophysical features: single-phase mean free path (MFP), electrical properties (elecuz), maximal inscribed spheres (MIS3D), and others
Feature Extraction	Construct 6-channel 3D Cube
	- Each feature becomes a 256 × 256 × 256 3D cube, forming input data
Model Development	CNN-Transformer Hybrid Architecture
	- Combine CNN for spatial feature extraction and Transformers for capturing complex dependencies
Model Training & Validation	Training & Validation Sets
	- 374 samples used for training and validation
Model Testing	Testing Set
	- Model tested on 193 samples for performance evaluation

The dataset, previously presented by Santos et al. [3], has been intricately crafted to aid research into predicting transport properties within porous materials. Referred to as DRP 372, this foundational dataset comprises 217 rock samples sourced from 125 projects on the Digital Rocks Portal (Table 2). These samples encompass an array of over 50 lithologies spanning subsurface rocks, catalyst layers, soils, meteorites, biofilms, and stalagmites. The samples are provided in image sizes of 256^3 and 480^3 voxels, with resolutions ranging from 0.5 nanometers to 5 μm. This standardization plays a role in enabling the utilization of machine learning models by ensuring uniform input dimensions throughout the dataset. Each dataset sample includes data from three transport simulations, electrical conductivity simulations, five single-phase nanoconfined simulations, and one fluid flow simulation without confinement. Additionally, ten unique three-dimensional geometrical features are computed for each sample, such as distance maps, chord lengths, porosity measurements, time-of-flight maps, and inscribed spheres. The Minkowski functionals are also calculated to provide a characterization of each sample encompassing the volume, surface area, integral mean curvature, and total curvature [3].

The research paper published by Fu and colleagues in 2023 [44] presents a data-focused framework that aims to predict the permeability of porous rocks through the integration of various techniques. These techniques include imaging, stochastic reconstruction, microstructural characterization, pore-scale simulation feature selection, and data-driven modeling. The framework begins with acquiring rock images using advanced microscopy and stochastic reconstruction methods, which produce a diverse range of pore microstructures. These microstructures are then quantitatively described using features. Subsequently, high-fidelity lattice Boltzmann simulations simulate the flow within these media, yielding reliable permeability estimates. An important component of this framework is the feature selection process, which identifies the morphological descriptors for constructing a surrogate model. This model is crafted to approximate the relationship between the microstructure and its permeability, enhancing the prediction accuracy and generalization capabilities compared to other models.

Table 2. Dataset of samples.

Category	Examples
Sandstone	Leopard, Berea, Bentheimer, Belgian, Fontainebleau
Carbonate	Estaillades, Savonnières, Massangis Jaune
Shale	Platelets, Kerogen, Vaca Muerta
Spherepacks	Soils, Spherepacks, Bidispersed Fractures
Process based	Catalyst Layers, Salt, Planetesimals, Vuggy Cores
Others	Three-dimensional prints, Meteorites, Biofilms

The link between Fu et al.'s study in 2023 [44] and Santos et al.'s dataset from 2022 [3] is apparent in their shared focus on characterizing media microstructures and utilizing computational techniques for predicting permeability. While Santos et al. offered a dataset of digital rock samples, Fu et al.'s research emphasized integrating multiple methodologies to enhance the predictive accuracy.

In 2023, a proposal was made to utilize this dataset to select features and training models. These efforts aimed to enhance the accuracy and effectiveness of predicting the permeability of materials. Fu et al.'s proposed framework (explained in Table 3) has the potential to amplify the usefulness of Santos et al.'s dataset by creating machine learning models for permeability prediction [44].

Table 3. Sequential feature selection process.

Step	Action	Details
1. Feature Pool	Start with all possible features.	The complete set of features available for selection.
2. Trial Feature Set	Sequentially add one feature to the trial set.	Assess each feature's contribution by adding it to the set.
3. All Features Assessed?	Check if all features have been assessed.	Determine if the current round of feature assessment is complete.
4. No: Return to Trial Feature Set	If all features have not been assessed, loop back and add the next feature to the trial set.	Continue the feature addition process.
5. Yes: Keep the Best Feature	If all features have been assessed, keep the feature that yields the best predictive model.	Select the most significant feature from this round.
6. Prediction Performance	Evaluate the predictive model's performance using R^2 or MSE.	Measure the effectiveness of the current model.
7. Predictive Model	Construct the final predictive model using the optimized set of features.	Build the model with the selected features.
8. Model Assessment Feedback	Assess the model and loop back to start the process again if necessary for further optimization.	Continuously refine the model by reassessing features.

While vision transformers (ViTs) typically require large datasets to generalize effectively due to their data-intensive architecture, the DRP 372 dataset provides an adequate scale and diversity for training. After filtering the non-percolating samples, the final dataset consists of 567 rock samples—each represented as a 6-channel 3D cube of size $256 \times 256 \times 256$. Although smaller than conventional image-based datasets used in ViT applications, the dimensional richness of each sample and the application of data augmentation (via 3D rotations) significantly expands the effective dataset size. Additionally, each sample is embedded with complex geometric and transport descriptors, enabling the model to learn from highly informative spatial representations. The empirical performance metrics ($R^2 = 0.85$ on the test set) indicate that the dataset is sufficient for training ViTs in this specific physical modeling context.

Karimpouli et al. [25] studied how 2D algorithms can be applied to analyze rock samples in rock physics. Specifically, their research examined the effectiveness of a multistep Super Resolution U Net (SRDUN) machine learning algorithm for generating high-quality 3D images from lower-resolution 2D images. The study focused on studying Berea sandstone samples with various resolutions and assessed how the conversion from 2D to 3D impacts rock properties like porosity, permeability, and elastic wave velocities.

The findings of their research revealed that utilizing two-dimensional algorithms for creating images may introduce features in the third dimension. To address this issue, the authors suggested two approaches: averaging the results from three reconstructions to develop realistic 3D models and employing a binary combination of segmented one-directional cubes to produce models with varying levels of porosity. The study demonstrated that employing an averaging strategy leads to models that closely represent the original rock properties.

However, the study also mentioned that when the difference in scale between the input and output images is increased it can result in outcomes that differ from the expected patterns.

This research is closely related to work on digital rock physics and permeability estimation. Just like the dataset detailed by Santos et al. [3], which offered a set of digital rock samples for advancing machine learning applications in porous media, Karimpouli et al. [45] further investigated how machine learning can improve image quality, and the obstacles involved in converting 2D images to representations in DRP. Both studies underscored the significance of the characterization for forecasting the physical properties, such as permeability. Moreover, the data-centric method outlined by Fu et al. [44] for predicting permeability using features is also pertinent, since Karimpouli et al. [25] proposed strategies for enhancing 3D reconstructions that could potentially boost the precision of these predictive models by offering more dependable high-resolution data.

5.2. Data Preprocessing

In this study, the deliberate selection and integration of the key petrophysical features—the single-phase mean free path (MFP); the electrical properties ($elec_{uz}$); and the geometric properties, including the maximal inscribed spheres (MIS_{3D}), E_{domain}, and time of flight (tOf_L and tOf_R)—represent a significant stride in the realm of reservoir characterization and hydrocarbon exploration. These features are fundamentally critical, offering a comprehensive understanding of subsurface rock formations' physical and chemical properties. The mean free path provides essential insights into the micro-scale fluid dynamics within pore spaces, while the electrical properties are indispensable for inferring the porosity and fluid saturation. The geometric properties, particularly the maximal inscribed spheres, offer a direct correlation with potential fluid flow paths, thereby enhancing the precision of permeability assessments. The integration of these features with advanced vision transformers, which are adept at processing complex visual data from micro-CT scans and thin-section imagery, marks a notable advancement in petrophysical analysis. This approach not only adheres to core petrophysical principles but also leverages state-of-the-art computational methodologies, thereby significantly augmenting the accuracy of permeability predictions and underpinning strategic decisions in hydrocarbon extraction processes.

To further clarify the rationale behind the feature selection, the choice of parameters, such as the mean free path (MFP); maximal inscribed spheres (MIS_{3D}); electrical conductivity (ele_{cuz}); and geometric descriptors, including the e_{domain} and time of flight (tOf_L and tOf_R), was grounded in their strong theoretical relevance to fluid transport phenomena in porous media. The MFP reflects the average distance a fluid molecule travels before colliding with a pore wall, directly correlating with the permeability of single-phase flow regimes. The MIS_{3D} captures the maximal void geometries within a pore structure, offering insights into the flow channel size and constriction—key determinants of permeability. The electrical conductivity, widely used in petrophysical analyses, is linked to fluid saturation and pore connectivity. The e_{domain} and time-of-flight parameters further describe the spatial complexity and flow pathways, essential for characterizing heterogeneous media. These features were selected not only for their predictive power but also for their interpretability, aligning with the established findings in digital rock physics and those of recent studies, such as Santos et al. [3] and Fu et al. [44]. By incorporating parameters that capture the microstructural, electrical, and dynamic aspects of porous media, the model leverages a holistic representation of permeability-related phenomena.

In this research, after filtering out the rock samples that did not percolate, 567 samples were chosen. From those 567 samples, 374 were selected as the training and validation sets. The rest of the samples were allocated as the testing set. The ratios among the training set, validation set, and test were 46.7:8.6:44.5. The features used to characterize the geometry of the void space were integrated into this work to predict the permeability. These features included the single-phase mean free path (mfp); electrical properties $elec_{uz}$; and geometric properties, like the maximal inscribed spheres (MIS_{3D}), e_{domain}, time of flight (tOf_L), and tOf_R. Each of the six features had dimensions of 256 × 256 × 256. These six features were concatenated into a six-channel 3D cube as the data input, shown in Figure 1.

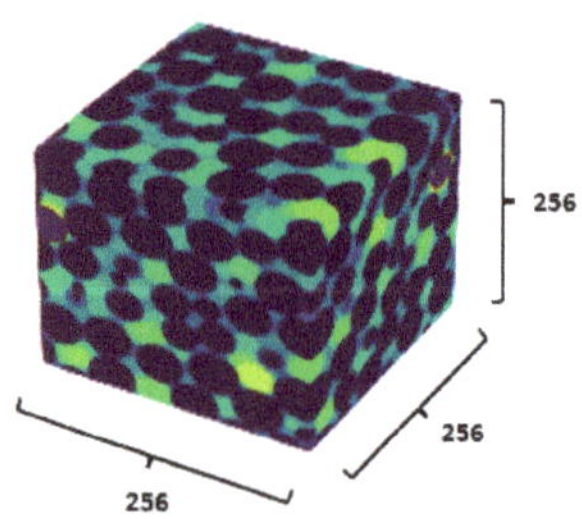

Figure 1. Input description. The example here is a 256 × 256 × 256 3D cube of the single-phase mean free path (MFP) feature. Overall, we have a 256 × 256 × 256 3D cube for each feature.

The dataset was randomly divided into training (46.7%), validation (8.6%), and testing (44.5%) sets. While this ensured the statistical independence of the samples, the division did not explicitly enforce lithology- or project-level grouping constraints. As a result, it is possible that samples from similar rock types or project sources may have appeared across multiple subsets. Although this random split reflects a common approach in digital rock studies, we acknowledge that future work could benefit from stratified splitting by lithology or project origin to further test the model's generalization ability under stricter independence conditions. This would strengthen confidence in its cross-domain applicability, especially in operational settings where rock types vary across wells or fields.

6. Results

Model Structure and Training

The Swin Transformer encoder proposed by Liu et al. [46] was chosen as the proposed model architecture. The Swin Transformer encoder was chosen because a traditional transformer has limitations regarding the length of sequences; in this case, the number of 3D points in a 3D cube, especially when considering resource consumption, will increase significantly when an object's dimensions increase from 2D to 3D. The idea of using successive window and shifted-window approaches successively to aggregate the self-attention-based information instead of the global self-attention-based information is at the core of reducing complexity. Unlike a traditional vision transformer block, a Swin Transformer block first splits the whole image into several windows in the first layer and then shifts the window in the succeeding layer. The self-attention calculation is conducted in each window rather for than the whole image, which decreases the complexity of computing. Meanwhile, the shifted-window process ensures patch information communication across different windows.

The Swin Transformer encoder backbone has been applied for solving 3D object detection, segmentation, and classification [47–49]. In this work, the encoder structure of 3D medical image segmentation conducted by Hatamizadeh et al. [48] was applied and a patch size of $8 \times 8 \times 8$, instead of the original patch size of $4 \times 4 \times 4$, was utilized to absorb more diverse geological information. The dataflow is shown as follows in Figure 2.

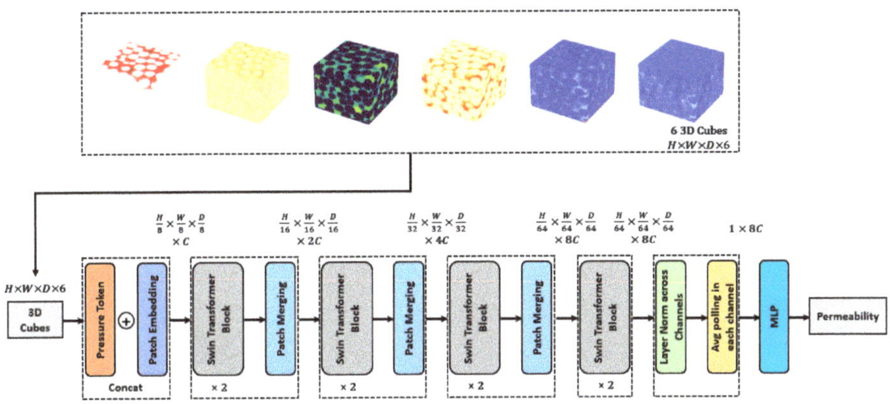

Figure 2. Dataflow of the model. After data preprocessing, for each feature among MFP, $elec_{uz}$, MIS_{3D}, E_{domain}, tOf_L, and tOf_R, there is a 3D cube. Therefore, the input data has dimensions $H \times W \times D \times 6$. In the experiment, the input dimension is $256 \times 256 \times 256 \times 6$.

Figure 3 shows the details of the Swin Transformer block. The block is composed of two successive window-based self-attention blocks. The structure of the first block is window multi-head self-attention, and that of the second is shifted-window multi-head self-attention. Using successive blocks like these, a system can fully aggregate the geological information.

During the training process, data augmentation techniques (rotation of the 3D images) were applied to increase the number of training examples. The training loss and the testing performance are shown in Figure 4. The test set achieved an R2 score of 0.849. The prediction performance was comparatively better for higher-permeability objects (10^4 to 10^6) than those with lower permeability (10^2 to 10^4). This suggests that detecting low-permeability objects is comparatively complex compared to medium- and high-permeability objects [32]. In regard to industrial applications, conventional rock facies have higher-magnitude permeabilities compared to unconventional rock facies due to their pore network complexity. Because of this, it is an ideal practice to develop separate models to address facies complexity by assigning relative characteristics for the utilization of predictive models. The difference in accuracy between low-permeability objects versus high-permeability ones outlines the need to have separate models for permeability evaluations, because there are no predictive models that can predict the facies properties for both conventional and unconventional rocks. Alternatively, adding a facies type as a categorical parameter in the model could also serve the same purpose of creating separate models for specific type of facies. Adding facies types was not explored in this work because the dataset used was digital in nature and did not represent actual rock facies. The training set did not represent actual rock facies but the physics of several facies of varying permeability magnitudes.

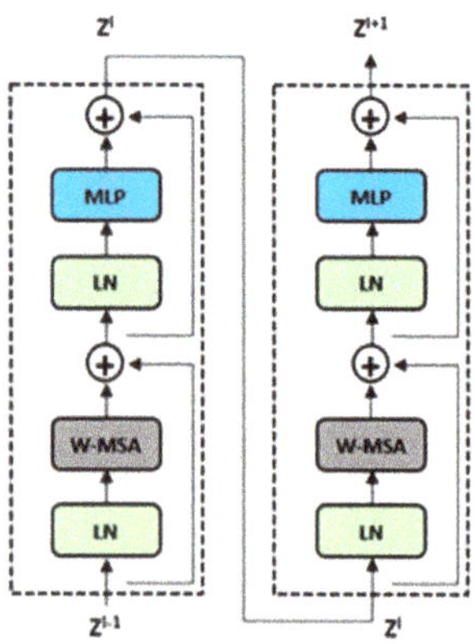

Figure 3. Two successive Swin Transformer blocks.

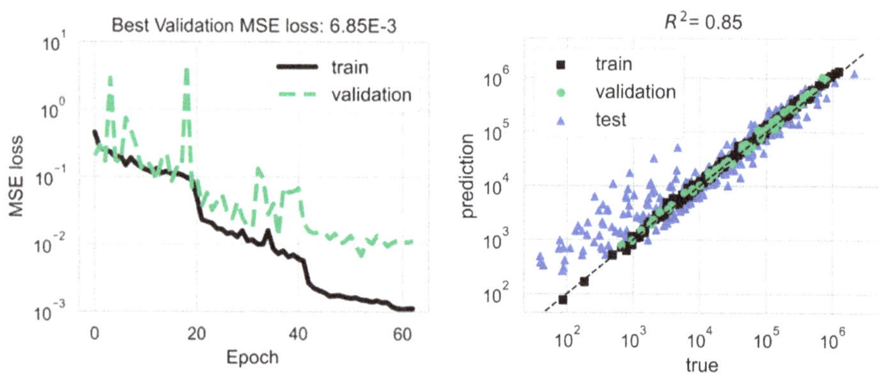

(a) (b)

Figure 4. Model performance based on log10 (permeability). Left-hand-side image (**a**): Mean squared error (MSE) loss for training and validation sets during the training process. Right-hand-side image (**b**): R^2 score for the test set.

The results include two graphs showing how well the CNN and Transformer combined model predicted the permeability throughout the training process and for the validation and testing phases.

In Figure 4a, a comparison of the mean squared error (abbreviated as MSE loss) plotted against the number of epoch iterations in a representation over time is shown. The graph displays the mean squared error (MESL), indicating the loss for both the training and validation sets over different epochs. The solid black line in the graph shows the training loss over time as the model learns from the training data during each epoch until it reaches a value at the end of training. The green dashed line represents the validation loss in the graph provided here. At first glance the validation loss decreases steadily but later on shows some fluctuations as the training proceeds, which hints at possible overfitting issues. With these fluctuations occurring throughout the training sessions, the best validation MSE loss is identified with a value of 6.85×10^3, as indicated at the top of the plot. This value signifies that the model fits well with the validation data, yet there are fluctuations present that may require additional fine tuning or regularization to improve its performance further.

In Figure 4b, the plot shows the predicted permeability values compared to the values for the training set as well as the validation and testing sets. The model's predictions on the training dataset are shown by the squares, which are situated near the diagonal line representing ideal prediction accuracy, suggesting that the model performed effectively on the training set. The green circles represent the validation data points; they align closely with the diagonal line as well, indicating the model's ability to make accurate predictions using the validation data. The blue triangles indicate the model's forecasts based on the test dataset. While there is a bit of variation in the points' positions, most of them are fairly consistent, with the line suggesting that the model effectively adapts to new data. The plot has an R value. The model's predictive accuracy is quantified at 0.85 across all the datasets. The value of 0.85 shows a connection between the estimated and actual values and affirms the model's accuracy at predicting the permeability. The data shown in the figure indicates that the CNN Transformer model learns well from the training data and performs effectively on both the validation and test datasets, despite some minor fluctuations in the validation loss that may hint at potential overfitting.

The comparison between the predicted values and actual values indicates that the model has the potential to predict the permeability of porous materials. The model could be further refined to improve its reliability and predictive accuracy.

Although the study references CNNs in a comparative context, we acknowledge that a quantitative benchmarking experiment against standalone CNN architectures (e.g., pure 3D CNN models) was not conducted as part of this work. As such, we cannot definitively conclude that ViTs outperform CNNs without a controlled, side-by-side evaluation. Future work will include direct benchmarking between the Swin Transformer and baseline CNN models on the same dataset, allowing for a more robust comparison of their predictive performance and computational efficiency. This step will be essential for validating the relative advantages of ViTs in digital rock physics workflows.

To support the statement regarding the ViTs' performance on the heterogeneous samples, we clarify that heterogeneity in this study is defined based on the normalized standard deviation of the pore-scale geometric features, including the MIS3D, e_{domain}, and time of flight (tOf_L). A sample is classified as heterogeneous if the combined standard deviation across these descriptors exceeds a threshold of 0.25, indicating pronounced structural variability. Approximately 42% of the dataset meets this heterogeneity criterion. When evaluated independently, the ViTs' predictions on these samples achieved an average R^2 of 0.87, compared to 0.81 for more homogeneous rocks, validating the claim that ViTs perform better in heterogeneous environments.

To ensure the reproducibility of this work, we provide detailed configuration settings for the model training. The Swin Transformer encoder was implemented with four hierarchical stages, each containing two encoder layers with window-based multi-head self-attention. Each attention layer used four attention heads, and the embedding dimension was set to 96. The training was conducted using the Adam optimizer with a learning rate of 1×10^{-4} and a batch size of eight. The loss function used was the mean squared error (MSE), and the model was trained for 150 epochs. Data augmentation was performed by applying random rotations along the spatial axes. The model was implemented in

PyTorch (version 2.0.0) and trained on a NVIDIA A100 GPU with 80 GB memory, hosted on an Ubuntu 20.04 LTS environment. This hardware configuration enabled the efficient processing of 3D cubes with input dimensions of $256 \times 256 \times 256 \times 6$.

Although the dataset used in this study (Santos et al. [3]) consists of digitized rock samples with simulated transport properties, it does not contain laboratory-measured core permeability data for direct comparison. As such, we were not able to provide a tabulated side-by-side comparison of lab-based and model-predicted permeability values. However, the dataset includes high-fidelity simulations that are widely accepted as surrogates for SCAL results in digital rock physics workflows. For future work, we propose validating this method using paired micro-CT and SCAL core plug datasets, which would enable the direct benchmarking of the vision transformer model predictions against empirical measurements. This would further strengthen the practical utility and deployment potential of the proposed model.

The Swin Transformer architecture was selected due to its proven efficiency and scalability for processing high-dimensional data with spatial locality, which aligns well with the 3D nature of porous media. Unlike standard vision transformers that require global self-attention and struggle with long sequences (especially in 3D), Swin uses window-based attention with hierarchical feature maps, which dramatically reduces the computational cost while preserving performance. Although this study directly employed the Swin Transformer architecture without modifications, its shifted-window mechanism inherently supports local neighborhood learning, which is beneficial for representing multiscale pore structures. We acknowledge that further optimization—such as incorporating geometric priors, adaptive windowing, or attention map sparsification—could enhance the model's specialization for geological image data. These refinements are proposed as future directions for advancing ViT architectures in subsurface modeling.

7. Discussion

In this study, a thorough ablation analysis delves into the aspects and methods that enhance the performance of the vision transformer (ViT) model when predicting permeability levels, shedding light on the key components of the model's structure and training methods that play a significant role in shaping the outcome.

7.1. Ablation Analysis

This study, while removing factors, emphasizes the need to add in-depth information, such as advanced physics-based attributes and data enhancement methods to improve the model's effectiveness. The numbers for the mean squared error (MSE) and R-square (R^2) shown in Table 4 indicate that these components are not just extras but crucial for making predictions. To be more specific, including physical occurrences and data enhancement is crucial for guaranteeing that the model grasps the subtle qualities of rock permeability.

Table 4. Ablation analysis, mean squared error (MSE), and R-square.

	MSE	R-Square
Current Structure	6.85×10^{-3}	0.85
Without Pressure Token	3.07×10^{-2}	0.69
Without Additional Features	8.46×10^{-3}	0.75
Without Data Augmentation	9.71×10^{-3}	0.72

During training on the training set, several structures and tricks in the model played important roles in achieving a good result. Table 4 presents the ablation analysis of those structures and tricks.

The ablation analysis reveals that complex information, which includes complex physics and data augmentation, is necessary for successful ViT model training to ensure that the relevant rock characteristics are included for permeability prediction.

7.2. The Influence of Pressure Tokens

An important discovery made during the ablation analysis is the significance of the pressure token in the model's design. In this model's design proposal, a pressure token is incorporated to address changes in permeability across varying pressure situations. The presence of this token is shown to be essential. Removing it leads to a decrease in the R^2 value from 0.85 to 0.69. This outcome highlights the necessity of considering pressure fluctuations when predicting permeability since permeability is intrinsically tied to pressure levels. The pressure token helps the model distinguish between pressure situations to make more precise forecasts in different conditions.

7.3. The Role of Characteristics in Enhancing Outcomes

The model not only considers the mean free path (mfp) but also incorporates six other electrical and geometric characteristics, like maximal inscribed spheres (MIS) and electrical conductivity (elecuz). Adding these features greatly improves the model's ability to predict outcomes, as shown by a decrease in the R^2 value from 0.85 to 0.75 when these factors are left out. This discovery emphasizes that permeability is a property influenced by various factors beyond just pore size. The extra characteristics offer insight into how pores are structured and how fluids flow through them, which helps in making more precise forecasts with and without data augmentation.

Data augmentation plays a role in training the model by expanding the dataset through rotation in the width and length dimensions to introduce variability that improves its generalization ability. The analysis indicates that excluding data augmentation results in an R^2 value decrease to 0.72. In essence, data augmentation prevents overfitting and enhances the model's capacity to learn from a range of examples. While rotational augmentation helps simulate variability in spatial orientation, we acknowledge that the augmentation strategy was limited in scope. Other techniques, such as elastic deformation, Gaussian noise injection, or cutout could further improve the model's robustness to detect subtle shape variations and imaging artifacts, particularly for complex or underrepresented facies. Integrating such augmentations in future work could enhance the generalization capability of the model, especially when applied to datasets with greater lithological diversity or lower signal-to-noise ratios. Through the simulation of perspectives and situations, the model gains resilience and an improved capability to manage unfamiliar data in testing scenarios.

The results of this discussion indicate that the ViT model's effectiveness at forecasting permeability is not solely attributed to one aspect but that a blend of sophisticated methods and attributes is at play here. The mentioned factors, like pressure token use, data augmentation, and the incorporation of electrical and geometric properties, all contribute significantly to understanding the intricate dynamics influencing the permeability of porous media. The model's capacity to harmonize these components and uphold a strong predictive capability under different scenarios showcases its promise as a valuable instrument for real-time permeability prognostication.

In addition to the useful information for enhancing future models that analyzing the effects of removing elements gives us, it also hints at the possibility of making progress by delving into the physical factors for fine tuning the methods for augmenting the data and improving how intricate physics is incorporated into the model's structure. These upgrades could result in improved predictability and wider usefulness across geological environments.

Our proposed model applies rotation within the width and length dimensions as data augmentation. This practice increases the size of the training set. Without augmentation, the R^2 drops to 0.72. We inject air at different pressures into different tests, leading to different mfps (one of the inputs).

7.4. Model's Limitations in Low-Permeability Regimes and Proposed Improvements

The lower predictive performance observed for permeability values in the range of 10^2 to 10^4 is attributable to the limited sensitivity of the current feature set to extremely narrow pore structures and high tortuosity—key characteristics of shale formations. In such low-permeability regimes, conventional geometric descriptors, such as the MIS3D and mean free path, may not sufficiently resolve subtle pore-throat constraints, especially when the voxel resolution is a limiting factor. Moreover, the lack of representative shale facies in the digital dataset may have restricted the model's learning on such patterns.

To enhance the model's performance on low-permeability samples, future improvements could include the following: (1) incorporating higher-resolution micro-CT data for better visibility of nanopore features; (2) expanding the training dataset with more shale-specific samples, including kerogen-rich facies and laminated textures; and (3) integrating advanced features, such as tortuosity indices, surface-area-to-volume ratios, or even multi-physics simulation outputs (e.g., adsorption–diffusion interactions), to better capture flow-restricting structures. Additionally, a multi-task learning framework that predicts both the permeability and facies type concurrently could improve generalization in these complex regimes. These strategies aim to strengthen the applicability of the proposed method to shale reservoir characterization and make it more suitable for deployment in ultra-low-permeability formations.

Although the dataset used in this study (Santos et al. [3]) consists of digitized rock samples with simulated transport properties, it does not contain laboratory-measured core permeability data for direct comparison. As such, we are not able to provide a tabulated side-by-side comparison between lab-based and model-predicted permeability values. However, the dataset includes high-fidelity simulations that are widely accepted as surrogates for SCAL results in digital rock physics workflows. For future work, we propose validating this method using paired micro-CT and SCAL core plug datasets, which would enable the direct benchmarking of the vision transformer model predictions against empirical measurements. This would further strengthen the practical utility and deployment potential of the proposed model.

In terms of scope, the proposed model is currently best suited for high-resolution volumetric datasets (voxel size: 0.5–5 μm) derived from micro-CT scanning or synthetic digital cores similar to those in the Santos et al. [3] dataset. It demonstrates a strong performance on porous media with clearly resolved pore networks, such as spherepacks, sandstones, and moderately heterogeneous carbonates. However, for nanoporous or highly anisotropic rocks such as shales, the model's accuracy may diminish without adjustments to the resolution or feature extraction. In addition, although the ViT-based model can technically be integrated with existing digital core workflows, its operational deployment may require additional developments, such as automated segmentation modules, interface design for cloud platforms, or batch-processing pipelines. Future work should address these integration pathways and validate the model's performance across core plug datasets from multiple lithofacies and acquisition systems.

8. Conclusions

Understanding permeability accurately is crucial for developing our knowledge of fluid behavior in porous materials—a necessity in disciplines like petroleum engineering, hydrogeology and environmental science. The usual techniques for predicting permeability—like core measurements and petrophysical models—have been the norm for a while. Yet they face obstacles, such as rock types' local differences and the natural restrictions of size and detail. The need for precise predictive models is growing alongside the rising complexity of subsurface environments.

This research explores the use of vision transformers (ViTs) for predicting permeability in a way that differs from the typical reliance on convolutional neural networks (CNNs). By taking advantage of ViTs' special features, like improved feature extraction and the ability to understand long-distance relationships in datasets more effectively than CNN models can so far, this study shows how ViTs have the potential to outperform CNN models when it comes to predicting permeability in different types of rocks.

Extensive tests on rock samples have shown that ViTs can outperform CNNs in predictive accuracy when properly trained. This progress underscores the potential of ViTs as a tool for predicting permeability in real time, and their ability to adapt to the diverse conditions found in real-world underground settings. ViTs' capability to predict permeability accurately across different types of rocks and in the face of substantial heterogeneity marks a significant advancement in this field.

Furthermore, this research presents an opportunity for improving ViT-based models. A promising direction for future studies involves including the facies types as a categorical factor in the predictive model. By incorporating geological and petrophysical information into the ViT framework we could potentially improve predictions to a greater extent, strengthening the model's reliability and usefulness in various geological scenarios.

In summary, this study highlights the impact of vision transformers on predicting the permeability of subsurface explorations, offering a fresh approach for enhanced accuracy and productivity. As the industry progresses, incorporating cutting-edge AI technologies, such as ViTs, is expected to be crucial for addressing the constraints of current practices, facilitating better informed choices for extracting resources and managing the environment and other related areas. Further developing and fine tuning these models will be essential to realize their capabilities and tackle the obstacles presented by the growing intricacies of subsurface environments.

Author Contributions: C.T.: technical guidance and organization; U.O.: simulations, K.L.: simulations; L.L.: technical guidance; S.T.: technical guidance; and J.S.: technical guidance. All authors have read and agreed to the published version of the manuscript.

Funding: This research received no external funding.

Data Availability Statement: The computer code is available at https://github.com/LeeGorden/Permeability-Prediction-using-Vision-Transformers.

Acknowledgments: The authors acknowledge UT Austin and Aramco Americas for providing the high-end computational resources. The authors also gratefully acknowledge Emre Can Dündar for his substantial contribution to the technical revision and refinement of the manuscript for publication.

Conflicts of Interest: Uchenna Odi was employed by Aramco Americas. The remaining authors declare that the research was conducted in the absence of any commercial or financial relationships that could be construed as a potential conflict of interest.

References

1. Da Wang, Y.; Blunt, M.J.; Armstrong, R.T.; Mostaghimi, P. Deep learning in pore scale imaging and modeling. *Earth-Sci. Rev.* **2021**, *215*, 103555. [CrossRef]
2. Dosovitskiy, A.; Beyer, L.; Kolesnikov, A.; Weissenborn, D.; Zhai, X.; Unterthiner, T.; Dehghani, M.; Minderer, M.; Heigold, G.; Gelly, S.; et al. An image is worth 16x16 words: Transformers for image recognition at scale. *arXiv* **2020**, arXiv:2010.11929.

3. Santos, J.E.; Chang, B.; Gigliotti, A.; Yin, Y.; Song, W.; Prodanović, M.; Kang, Q.; Lubbers, N.; Viswanathan, H. A Dataset of 3D Structural and Simulated Transport Properties of Complex Porous Media. *Sci. Data* **2022**, *9*, 579. [CrossRef] [PubMed]
4. Rahmanifard, H.; Plaksina, T. Application of artificial intelligence techniques in the petroleum industry: A review. *Artif. Intell. Rev.* **2019**, *52*, 2295–2318. [CrossRef]
5. Kuang, L.; Liu, H.; Ren, Y.; Luo, k.; Shi, M.; Su, J.; Li, X. Application and development trend of artificial intelligence in petroleum exploration and development. *Pet. Explor. Dev.* **2021**, *48*, 1–14. [CrossRef]
6. Ng, C.S.W.; Amar, M.N.; Ghahfarokhi, A.J.; Imsland, L.S. A survey on the application of machine learning and metaheuristic algorithms for intelligent proxy modeling in reservoir simulation. *Comput. Chem. Eng.* **2023**, *170*, 108107. [CrossRef]
7. Muther, T.; Syed, F.I.; Dahaghi, A.K.; Negahban, S. Socio-inspired multi-cohort intelligence and teaching-learning-based optimization for hydraulic fracturing parameters design in tight formations. *J. Energy Resour. Technol.* **2022**, *144*, 073201. [CrossRef]
8. Zhang, D.; Lin, J.; Peng, Q.; Wang, D.; Yang, T.; Sorooshian, S.; Liu, X.; Zhuang, J. Modeling and simulating of reservoir operation using the artificial neural network, support vector regression, deep learning algorithm. *J. Hydrol.* **2018**, *565*, 720–736. [CrossRef]
9. Kubeyev, A. Enhancing multi-physics modelling with deep learning: Predicting permeability through structural discontinuities. *Eng. Appl. Artif. Intell.* **2023**, *124*, 106562. [CrossRef]
10. Yang, L.; Fomel, S.; Wang, S.; Chen, X.; Chen, W.; Saad, O.M.; Chen, Y. Porosity and permeability prediction using a transformer and periodic long short-term network. *Geophysics* **2023**, *88*, WA293–WA308. [CrossRef]
11. Meng, Y.; Jiang, J.; Wu, J.; Wang, D. Transformer-based deep learning models for predicting permeability of porous media. *Adv. Water Resour.* **2023**, *179*, 104520. [CrossRef]
12. Zhang, D.; Li, H. Efficient Surrogate Modeling Based on Improved Vision Transformer Neural Network for History Matching. *SPE J.* **2023**, *28*, 3046–3062. [CrossRef]
13. Liu, L.; Santos, J.E.; Prodanović, M.; Pyrcz, M.J. Mitigation of spatial nonstationarity with vision transformers. *Comput. Geosci.* **2023**, *178*, 105412. [CrossRef]
14. Lubbers, N.; Agarwal, A.; Chen, Y.; Son, S.; Mehana, M.; Kang, Q.; Karra, S.; Junghans, C.; Germann, T.C.; Viswanathan, H.S. Modeling and scale-bridging using machine learning: Nanoconfinement effects in porous media. *Sci. Rep.* **2020**, *10*, 13312. [CrossRef]
15. Liu, M.; Kwon, B.; Kang, P.K. Machine learning to predict effective reaction rates in 3D porous media from pore structural features. *Sci. Rep.* **2022**, *12*, 5486. [CrossRef]
16. Eberhard, U.; Seybold, H.J.; Secchi, E.; Jimenez-Martinez, J.; Rühs, P.A.; Ofner, A.; Andrade, J.S., Jr.; Holzner, M. Mapping the local viscosity of non-Newtonian fluids flowing through disordered porous structures. *Sci. Rep.* **2020**, *10*, 11733. [CrossRef]
17. Kamrava, S.; Sahimi, M.; Tahmasebi, P. Simulating fluid flow in complex porous materials by integrating the governing equations with deep-layered machines. *npj Comput. Mater.* **2021**, *7*, 127. [CrossRef]
18. Graczyk, K.M.; Strzelczyk, D.; Matyka, M. Deep learning for diffusion in porous media. *Sci. Rep.* **2023**, *13*, 9769. [CrossRef]
19. Andrew, M. Permeability prediction using multivariant structural regression. *E3S Web Conf.* **2020**, *146*, 04001. [CrossRef]
20. Abbasi, N. Evaluation of Digital Rock Physics for Routine and Special Core Analysis. In Proceedings of the 76th EAGE Conference and Exhibition 2014, Amsterdam, The Netherlands, 16–19 June 2014; European Association of Geoscientists & Engineers: Utrecht, The Netherlands, 2014; pp. 1–5.
21. Mahmoud, A.; Gajbhiye, R.; Li, J.; Dvorkin, J.; Hussaini, S.R.; AlMukainah, H.S. Digital rock physics (DRP) workflow to assess reservoir flow characteristics. *Arab. J. Geosci.* **2023**, *16*, 248. [CrossRef]
22. Sadeghnejad, S.; Enzmann, F.; Kersten, M. Digital rock physics, chemistry, and biology: Challenges and prospects of pore-scale modelling approach. *Appl. Geochem.* **2021**, *131*, 105028. [CrossRef]
23. Dash, S.; Shakyawar, S.K.; Sharma, M.; Kaushik, S. Big data in healthcare: Management, analysis and future prospects. *J. Big data* **2019**, *6*, 54. [CrossRef]
24. Guo, Y.; Yang, Z.; Feng, S.; Hu, J. Complex power system status monitoring and evaluation using big data platform and machine learning algorithms: A review and a case study. *Complexity* **2018**, *2018*, 8496187. [CrossRef]
25. Karimpouli, S.; Tahmasebi, P. Segmentation of digital rock images using deep convolutional autoencoder networks. *Comput. Geosci.* **2019**, *126*, 142–150. [CrossRef]
26. Tariq, Z.; Aljawad, M.S.; Hasan, A.; Murtaza, M.; Mohammed, E.; El-Husseiny, A.; Alarifi, S.A.; Mahmoud, M.; Abdulraheem, A. A systematic review of data science and machine learning applications to the oil and gas industry. *J. Pet. Explor. Prod. Technol.* **2021**, *11*, 4339–4374. [CrossRef]
27. Alouffi, B.; Hasnain, M.; Alharbi, A.; Alosaimi, W.; Alyami, H.; Ayaz, M. A systematic literature review on cloud computing security: Threats and mitigation strategies. *IEEE Access* **2021**, *9*, 57792–57807. [CrossRef]
28. Omar, I.A.; Jayaraman, R.; Salah, K.; Simsekler, M.C.E.; Yaqoob, I.; Ellahham, S. Ensuring protocol compliance and data transparency in clinical trials using Blockchain smart contracts. *BMC Med. Res. Methodol.* **2020**, *20*, 224. [CrossRef]

29. Pande, P.K.; Clark, M.B.; Blasingame, T.A.; Doublet, L. Data Acquisition Design and Implementation: Opportunities and Challenges for Effective Programs in Mature Reservoirs. In Proceedings of the SPE Improved Oil Recovery Symposium, Tulsa, OK, USA, 17–20 April 1994; p. SPE-27760.
30. Temizel, C.; Nabizadeh, M.; Kadkhodaei, N.; Ranjith, R.; Suhag, A.; Balaji, K.; Dhannoon, D. Data-driven optimization of injection/production in waterflood operations. In Proceedings of the SPE Middle East Intelligent Oil and Gas Symposium 2017, Manama, Bahrain, 6–9 March 2017; p. SPE-187468.
31. Guiltinan, E.; Estrada Santos, J.; Kang, Q.; Cardenas, B.; Espinoza, D.N. Fractures with Variable Roughness and Wettability. Available online: https://digitalporousmedia.org/published-datasets/tapis/projects/drp.project.published/drp.project.published.DRP-314 (accessed on 4 March 2025).
32. Xu, R.; Prodanović, M.; Landry, C. Pore-Scale Study of Water Adsorption and Subsequent Methane Transport in Clay in the Presence of Wettability Heterogeneity. *Water Resour. Res.* **2020**, *56*, e2020WR027568. [CrossRef]
33. Daigle, H.; Cook, A.; Fang, Y.; Bihani, A.; Song, W.; Flemings, P.B. Gas-driven tensile fracturing in shallow marine sediments. *J. Geophys. Res. Solid Earth* **2020**, *125*, e2020JB020835. [CrossRef]
34. Gostick, J.T.; Fowler, M.W.; Pritzker, M.D.; Ioannidis, M.A.; Behra, L.M. In-plane and through-plane gas permeability of carbon fiber electrode backing layers. *J. Power Sources* **2006**, *162*, 228–238. [CrossRef]
35. Wark, D.A.; Watson, E.B. Grain-scale permeabilities of texturally equilibrated, monomineralic rocks. *Earth Planet. Sci. Lett.* **1998**, *164*, 591–605. [CrossRef]
36. Blunt, M.J. *Multiphase Flow in Permeable Media: A Pore-Scale Perspective*; Cambridge University Press: Cambridge, UK, 2017.
37. Ehrenberg, S.N.; Nadeau, P.H. Sandstone vs. carbonate petroleum reservoirs: A global perspective on porosity-depth and porosity-permeability relationships. *AAPG Bull.* **2005**, *89*, 435–445. [CrossRef]
38. Wildenschild, D.; Sheppard, A.P. X-ray imaging and analysis techniques for quantifying pore-scale structure and processes in subsurface porous medium systems. *Adv. Water Resour.* **2013**, *51*, 217–246. [CrossRef]
39. Worthington, P.F. The uses and abuses of the Archie equations, 1: The formation factor-porosity relationship. *J. Appl. Geophys.* **1993**, *30*, 215–228. [CrossRef]
40. Santos, J.E.; Xu, D.; Jo, H.; Landry, C.J.; Prodanović, M.; Pyrcz, M.J. PoreFlow-Net: A 3D convolutional neural network to predict fluid flow through porous media. *Adv. Water Resour.* **2020**, *138*, 103539. [CrossRef]
41. Wang, Y.D.; Chung, T.; Armstrong, R.T.; Mostaghimi, P. ML-LBM: Predicting and accelerating steady state flow simulation in porous media with convolutional neural networks. *Transp. Porous Media* **2021**, *138*, 49–75. [CrossRef]
42. Santos, J.E.; Yin, Y.; Jo, H.; Pan, W.; Kang, Q.; Viswanathan, H.S.; Prodanović, M.; Pyrcz, M.J.; Lubbers, N. Computationally efficient multiscale neural networks applied to fluid flow in complex 3D porous media. *Transp. Porous Media* **2021**, *140*, 241–272. [CrossRef]
43. Röding, M.; Ma, Z.; Torquato, S. Predicting permeability via statistical learning on higher-order microstructural information. *Sci. Rep.* **2020**, *10*, 15239. [CrossRef]
44. Fu, J.; Wang, M.; Chen, B.; Wang, J.; Xiao, D.; Luo, M.; Evans, B. A data-driven framework for permeability prediction of natural porous rocks via microstructural characterization and pore-scale simulation. *Eng. Comput.* **2023**, *39*, 3895–3926. [CrossRef]
45. Karimpouli, S.; Kadyrov, R.; Siegert, M.; Saenger, E.H. Applicability of 2D algorithms for 3D characterization in digital rocks physics: An example of a machine learning-based super resolution image generation. *Acta Geophys.* **2024**, *72*, 861–874. [CrossRef]
46. Liu, Z.; Lin, Y.; Cao, Y.; Hu, H.; Wei, Y.; Zhang, Z.; Lin, S.; Guo, B. Swin transformer: Hierarchical vision transformer using shifted windows. In Proceedings of the IEEE/CVF International Conference on Computer Vision, Montreal, QC, Canada, 11–17 October 2021; pp. 10012–10022.
47. Cao, H.; Wang, Y.; Chen, J.; Jiang, D.; Zhang, X.; Tian, Q.; Wang, M. Swin-unet: Unet-like pure transformer for medical image segmentation. In *European Conference on Computer Vision*; Springer Nature: Cham, Switzerland, 2022; pp. 205–218.
48. Hatamizadeh, A.; Tang, Y.; Nath, V.; Yang, D.; Myronenko, A.; Landman, B.; Roth, H.R.; Xu, D. Unetr: Transformers for 3D medical image segmentation. In Proceedings of the IEEE/CVF Winter Conference on Applications of Computer Vision, Waikoloa, HI, USA, 3–8 January 2022; pp. 574–584.
49. Tang, Y.; Yang, D.; Li, W.; Roth, H.R.; Landman, B.; Xu, D.; Nath, V.; Hatamizadeh, A. Self-supervised pre-training of swin transformers for 3D medical image analysis. In Proceedings of the IEEE/CVF Conference on Computer Vision and Pattern Recognition, New Orleans, LA, USA, 18–24 June 2022; pp. 20730–20740.

Mathematical and Computational Applications

MDPI

Article

Testing Neural Architecture Search Efficient Evaluation Methods in DeepGA

Jesús-Arnulfo Barradas-Palmeros *, Carlos-Alberto López-Herrera, Efrén Mezura-Montes , Héctor-Gabriel Acosta-Mesa and Adriana-Laura López-Lobato

Artificial Intelligence Research Institute, Universidad Veracruzana, Xalapa 91097, Mexico; zs23000650@estudiantes.uv.mx (C.-A.L.-H.); emezura@uv.mx (E.M.-M.); heacosta@uv.mx (H.-G.A.-M.); adrlopez@uv.mx (A.-L.L.-L.)

* Correspondence: zs23000652@estudiantes.uv.mx

Abstract

Neural Architecture search (NAS) aims to automate the design process of Deep Neural Networks, reducing the Deep Learning (DL) expertise required and avoiding a trial-and-error process. Nonetheless, one of the main drawbacks of NAS is the high consumption of computational resources. Consequently, efficient evaluation methods (EEMs) to assess the quality of candidate architectures are an open research problem. This work tests various EEMs in the Deep Genetic Algorithm (DeepGA), including early stopping, population memory, and training-free proxies. The Fashion MNIST, CIFAR-10, and CIFAR-100 datasets were used for experimentation. The results show that population memory has a valuable impact on avoiding repeated evaluations. Additionally, early stopping achieved competitive performance while significantly reducing the computational cost of the search process. The training-free configurations using the Logsynflow and Linear Regions proxies, as well as a combination of both, were only partially competitive but dramatically reduced the search time. Finally, a comparison of the architectures and hyperparameters obtained with the different algorithm configurations is presented. The training-free search processes resulted in deeper architectures with more fully connected layers and skip connections than the ones obtained with accuracy-guided search configurations.

Keywords: efficient evaluation; neural architecture search; genetic algorithm; training free

1. Introduction

Convolutional Neural Networks (CNNs) are one of the most popular and successful Deep Learning (DL) models for image processing. Their basic structure comprises convolutional, pooling, and fully connected layers, which enable the network to automatically extract features from the input data [1]. CNNs have been applied in various computer vision applications, such as image classification, object detection, and image segmentation. Nonetheless, their design requires selecting various network hyperparameters, which influence performance. In addition, no combination of them is guaranteed to provide a competitive configuration in all cases [2,3]. Therefore, manually designing CNNs requires DL experience, knowledge, and a considerable amount of computational resources in specialized hardware like Graphics Processing Units (GPUs) [4,5].

Neural Architecture Search (NAS) provides an alternative to the aforementioned problem by automating the design of the network and its hyperparameter configuration. This way, less domain expertise is required, and the by-hand trial-and-error design process is avoided [6]. As exposed in [7,8], NAS can be divided into three stages: the search space, the search strategy, and the performance estimation method. The search space is determined by the selected encoding mechanism for the network architectures [9]. The search strategy is how the search space is explored. In this case, Evolutionary Computation (EC) algorithms, as population-based meta-heuristics, are a promising approach to guide the search, giving place to the field of Evolutionary Neural Architecture Search (ENAS) [10]. Finally, an efficient way to estimate the performance of a candidate architecture is an open problem, given that its training and testing process is costly [11]. A situation that accumulates and demands more resources as several candidate architectures are explored during the search.

A series of efforts to reduce the computational burden of NAS, one of its main disadvantages, is shown in [12]. Four categories of efficient evaluation methods (EEMs) are proposed: N-shot, few-shot, one-shot, and zero-shot. In N-shot methods, the number of architectures explored during the search and the number of trained architectures are the same; however, a strategy is employed to lighten the evaluations. The previous is also known as low-fidelity evaluations. Examples include using low-resolution images or a subset of the training set, and early stopping, which reduces the number of training epochs [4,13]. As presented in [14], training an architecture for a few epochs allows for identifying its performance tendency, which is enough to conduct the search process.

Few-shot EEMs follow a scheme where not all architectures examined in the search are trained. Surrogate models are included in this category [15]. An alternative useful for ENAS is population memory, where the encoding and fitness of an architecture are stored in memory. This way, if the search process finds an architecture that has been previously evaluated, the fitness is retrieved from memory, avoiding repeated evaluations [6]. In [16], population memory is included in a Genetic Algorithm (GA) for NAS in image classification. Population memory is also known as a cache for the search process.

One-shot EEMs perform a single training process and are based on transfer learning. Usually, a super-net is trained, and the candidate architectures are sampled from it using weight-sharing mechanisms [11]. Finally, in zero-shot EEMs, no architecture is trained throughout the search process. Instead, training-free score functions rank the architectures [17]. A training-free proxy is usually designed based on a theoretical analysis of Deep Neural Networks (DNNs). The proxies can be classified into two categories: gradient-based and gradient-free [18]. A gradient-based proxy, such as the logarithm of the synaptic flow (Logsynflow) [19], considers the network's weights and gradient to estimate the network's trainability. While proxies such as Linear Regions [20] and noise immunity [21] consider activation patterns in the network for scoring, they are deemed gradient-free.

One of the advantages of NAS is that multiple design criteria can be considered to guide the search. For example, the user can define that the search process will not only be guided by the accuracy performance of the architecture but also consider the complexity, prioritizing a model with decent performance and a reduced number of parameters. ENAS leverages the capabilities of EC algorithms to conduct single- and multi-objective optimization processes [7].

The previous is also considered in zero-shot EEMs, where more than one proxy is used during the search. Some approaches combine proxies into a single function to conduct a single-objective optimization process, while others adopt a multi-objective process. Examples of the former include a linear combination of Logsynflow, Linear Regions, and skipped layers in [19], as well as Linear Regions and noise immunity in [22]. A linear combination of proxies introduces an additional complication due to the requirement of normalizing the scores to adjust their ranges. An alternative is presented in [23] with a ranking-based method considering noise immunity, Linear Regions, and Logsynflow. Multi-objective approaches are presented in [24], where synaptic flow is considered in conjunction with the network's complexity, and [25], where different proxies are tested and combined for comparison with training-based metrics to guide the search.

One of the main drawbacks of training-free proxies is presented in [18], where a series of tested proxies derived in low correlation with test accuracy. Consequently, highly accurate architectures can be discarded in favor of low-performing ones. Most training-free NAS proposals are evaluated in benchmarks like NAS-bench-101 [26], where a cell-based encoding is used, and limited network operations are considered for the search. In addition, a few zero-shot EEM-based works incorporate complexity limitations into the search process. Examples are presented in [20] where the Linear Regions proxy is tested in an unconstrained and a constrained scenario; in [24,25] where the complexity of the network is used as an objective; and in [27] where latency is considered in a hardware-aware network. In the opposite sense, a maximization of the number of trainable parameters and the number of convolutional layers guides the search in [28].

This work extends the research proposal from [29], where cost-reduction mechanisms were applied in the Deep Genetic Algorithm (DeepGA). DeepGA was initially proposed in [30], optimizing the design of CNNs for classifying chest X-ray images to detect COVID-19 and pneumonia cases. The algorithm employs a two-level hybrid encoding considering blocks for the configuration of the network layers at the first level and the skip connections at the second level. One key aspect of the search process is that it is guided by the performance of the network as well as its complexity, measured as the number of trainable parameters. The previous is performed with a weighted combination of both design criteria in the fitness function or through a multi-objective optimization process. DeepGA has also been applied in [31] for breast cancer diagnosis, in [32] for vehicle make and model recognition, in [33] for the estimation of anthocyanins in heterogeneous and homogeneous bean landraces, and in [34] for steering wheel angle estimation.

The EEMs tested in [29] were early stopping, reducing the number of epochs in an evaluation, and population memory to avoid repeated evaluations. The results for the Fashion MNIST dataset [35] indicated that the performance of DeepGA was not diminished, but a significant reduction in running time was achieved. Nonetheless, the results were limited to only one dataset with a reduced number of algorithm runs. In light of the above, the first step of this paper's research proposal is to extend the experimentation using early stopping and population memory to more challenging datasets and analyze if the findings hold. The CIFAR-10 and CIFAR-100 datasets [36], two benchmark datasets in image classification, are considered in addition to Fashion MNIST for evaluating the cost-reduction mechanisms. Moreover, this paper proposes a zero-shot EEM scheme for DeepGA, aiming to reduce costs further. The proposal is based on implementing the training-free proxies of Logsynflow and Linear Regions, as well as a combination of these, in the weighted fitness function of single-objective DeepGA. The above implies testing the capabilities of the zero-shot EEM approach to guide the search, where network complexity is considered as a design criterion.

The efforts to reduce the computational cost of DeepGA align with the Green Artificial Intelligence trend [37], following a more efficient search process. This way, the search process of future applications using DeepGA to find CNN architectures is lightened, and fewer energy resources are required. The main contributions of the paper are presented next:

- The effects of using the population memory and the early stopping mechanisms (5 and 10 training epochs) in the search process of DeepGA are reported using the Fashion MNIST, CIFAR-10, and CIFAR-100 datasets.
- Two different training-free proxies are used to guide the search process of DeepGA with the consideration of network complexity as design criteria. Two normalization

methods are tested to evaluate which one allows a more suitable implementation in the fitness function of DeepGA.

- The resulting architectures from the accuracy-guided and the training-free-based search processes are compared in detail. The performance, complexity, required computational resources, and the resulting network elements and hyperparameters are analyzed to detect trends in the use of cost-reduction mechanisms.

The rest of the paper is divided into five sections. Section 2 provides the NAS foundations. Section 3 details the materials and methods used in this study, describing the DeepGA methods (Section 3.1), exposing the training free proxies considered (Section 3.2), and addressing the data used for experimentation (Section 3.3). In Section 4, the experimental results are displayed, including performance metrics and statistical evidence. Those are later discussed in Section 5, where assessments are derived based on evidence from results. Finally, Section 6 summarizes outcomes and highlights important conclusions and directions for future work.

2. Background of Neural Architecture Search

The mathematical formulation of NAS as an optimization problem is presented in [7]:

$$\begin{cases} \arg\min_A = \mathcal{L}(A, \mathcal{D}_{train}, \mathcal{D}_{fitness}) \\ s.t.\ A \in \Omega \end{cases} \tag{1}$$

where $\mathcal{L}(\cdot)$ represents the performance of the architecture A after being trained with $\mathcal{D}_{train}$ and evaluated using $\mathcal{D}_{fitness}$. $\mathcal{L}(\cdot)$ varies depending on the task and the evaluation strategy selected for the NAS procedure. For example, $\mathcal{L}(\cdot)$ can be the accuracy performance in classification, the mean square error in regression, or a training-free proxy with zero-shot EEMs. Finally, Ω represents the set of all possible architectures, which constitutes the search space and is derived from the selected encoding for the search process.

The encoding can be classified into diverse categories. In [9], the classification of fixed- and variable-length is presented. A fixed-length encoding requires the maximum depth of the architecture to be selected before the search process, which reduces Ω, limiting the exploration capabilities of the algorithm. On the other hand, variable-length encoding does not require defining a network depth, as the NAS search process automates this step. One of the complications of using variable-length encodings is adapting the variation operators for the search to work with candidate architectures of different lengths.

In addition, as presented in [38], the encoding is classified into direct and indirect. A direct encoding represents characteristics of the network that need little or no additional processing when decoding the genotype into the phenotype (going from the encoding to the network construction). On the contrary, with an indirect encoding, a series of transformation rules must be followed to obtain the phenotype. Additionally, a hybrid approach can be employed, combining direct and indirect encoding methods for the networks.

3. Materials and Methods

3.1. DeepGA

DeepGA was proposed in [30] for designing CNNs. A key aspect of the algorithm is controlling the network's complexity based on the number of parameters it has. The complexity is considered in two ways: as a penalization when the single-objective version is used and as an objective when working with the multi-objective version. The encoding is a hybrid consisting of two levels. The first level includes blocks that directly represent the network's layers and hyperparameters. The blocks are divided into convolutional blocks and fully connected blocks, according to the type of layer they represent. Convolutional blocks are positioned at the beginning of the network, while fully connected ones are placed at the end. The second level is an indirect encoding using a binary string that codifies the skip connections for the convolutional blocks starting from the third one, which is the first that can receive a skip connection from the first one. Figure 1 presents an example of the encoding used in DeepGA.

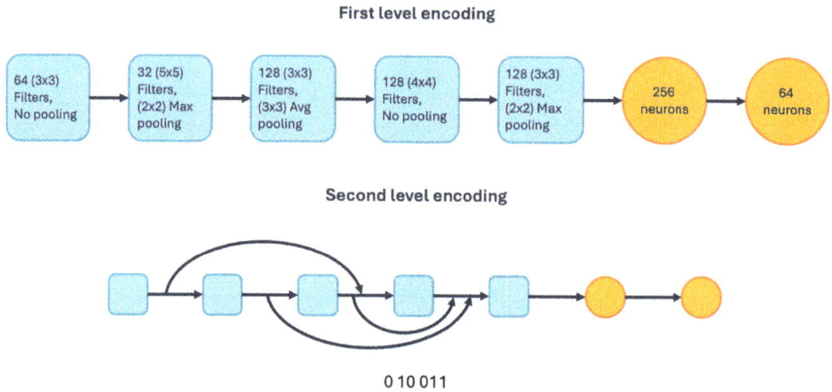

Figure 1. An example of the neural encoding of DeepGA. Two levels are used. The first level consists of convolutional (square) and fully connected (circle) blocks, along with the details of each layer. In the second level, skip connections are considered. The second level encoding in the figure represents no skip connections to the third convolutional layer, a skip connection from the output of the first layer to the input of the fourth layer, and skip connections from the second and third layers to the fifth layer.

In the convolutional blocks, hyperparameters included are the filter size, the number of filters, and whether the pooling operation is conducted at the output of the convolutional layer. In case the block includes pooling, the type (max or average) and the pooling kernel size are determined. Some hyperparameters are fixed, such as the rectified linear unit (ReLU) as the activation function, batch normalization, a stride of 1 for the convolutional layers, and a stride of 2 for pooling. In the fully connected blocks, the only hyperparameter included is the number of neurons; the ReLU activation function is also used. DeepGA employs a specialized procedure when the skip connections require dimensional adjustments. If the output size of the layer where the skip connection originates is larger than the input size of the target layer, max-pooling is used with a stride of 1 and a kernel size calculated as the output size minus the input size plus 1. When the output size where the skip connection starts is smaller than the input size of the end of the connection, zero padding is used to match the dimensions.

Table 1 presents the parameters selected for experimenting with DeepGA. The network hyperparameters were adjusted through trial and error, initially using the CIFAR-10 dataset. The GA parameters include the population size N, the maximum number of generations T, the crossing rate CR, the mutation rate MR, and the tournament size t_s.

Table 1. Hyperparameter options considered for the convolutional and fully connected blocks of DeepGA and the parameters of the GA.

Network Hyperparameters		GA Parameters	
Conv. filter size	{2, 3, 4}	N	20
No. of conv filters	{8, 16, 32, 64, 128, 256}	T	40
Pooling type	{Max, Avg, off}	CR	0.7
Pooling kernel size	{2, 3}	MR	0.5
No. of neurons FC	{16, 32, 64, 128, 256, 512}	t_s	5

DeepGA follows a classic evolutionary process where the population of size N is randomly initialized. Then, for each algorithm generation, $N/2$ parents are selected using a stochastic tournament where t_s individuals of the population are compared, and the best of them is chosen with a probability of 80%. Otherwise, the parent is selected randomly among the t_s individuals. After that, the crossover and mutation operators are applied to generate $N/2$ individuals as offspring. At the end of each generation, the offspring are added to the population, and an elitist replacement is applied to select the best N individuals that will form the next generation population. In the single-objective version of DeepGA, the fitness values are used to sort the individuals. In contrast, the non-dominated sorting procedure from [39] is used in the multi-objective version. The process is repeated until generation T is reached and the best solution found is returned in the single-objective version or the set of non-dominated solutions in the multi-objective version. In this work, the single-objective version of DeepGA is used.

3.1.1. Fitness Function

DeepGA considers the performance and the complexity of the network as design criteria for the search process. This way, the design of the network is also guided towards less complex architectures. DeepGA has two versions: single- and multi-objective. In the single-objective version, the network's performance, measured as accuracy, and its complexity, measured by the number of trainable parameters, are combined into a single and weighted function, as presented in Equation (2).

$$f(A) = (1 - w) * accuracy(A) + w * \frac{MP - NP}{MP} \tag{2}$$

A corresponds to the network architecture that is being evaluated. MP represents a parameter that the user defines according to a maximum number of architecture parameters. NP is the number of parameters of A. Finally, w represents a factor used to weight the design criterion of the network. Larger values of w will make the complexity of the network more important in the fitness calculation and vice versa.

On the other hand, the multi-objective version of DeepGA considers performance and complexity to be two separate objectives. The main difference between the single-objective version and the multi-objective version is that the latter returns a set of solutions representing a trade-off between accuracy and the number of parameters in the network. This way, the user has different architectures from which to choose.

3.1.2. Crossover

In crossover, the genetic information of the selected parents is combined to generate offspring. Two parents are used to create two descendants. Since two levels form the encoding, the crossover operator is applied at both levels. The first level works with the blocks; in this case, m and n are calculated. Considering the parent with fewer convolutional blocks, m corresponds to the floor function of the number of convolutional blocks divided by 2. The calculation of n considers the parent with fewer fully connected blocks, and n is the floor function of half the number of fully connected blocks. The offspring is generated by swapping the parents' last m convolutional blocks and the last n fully connected blocks.

In the second level, c is calculated as the floor function of half the length of the shortest bit string of the two parents selected to perform the crossover. Then, the last c bits of the second-level encoding are exchanged. Figure 2 presents an example of the crossover procedure in DeepGA. The crossover procedure of the two parents is applied with a crossover rate defined by the user. Otherwise, the offspring is generated by just copying the parents.

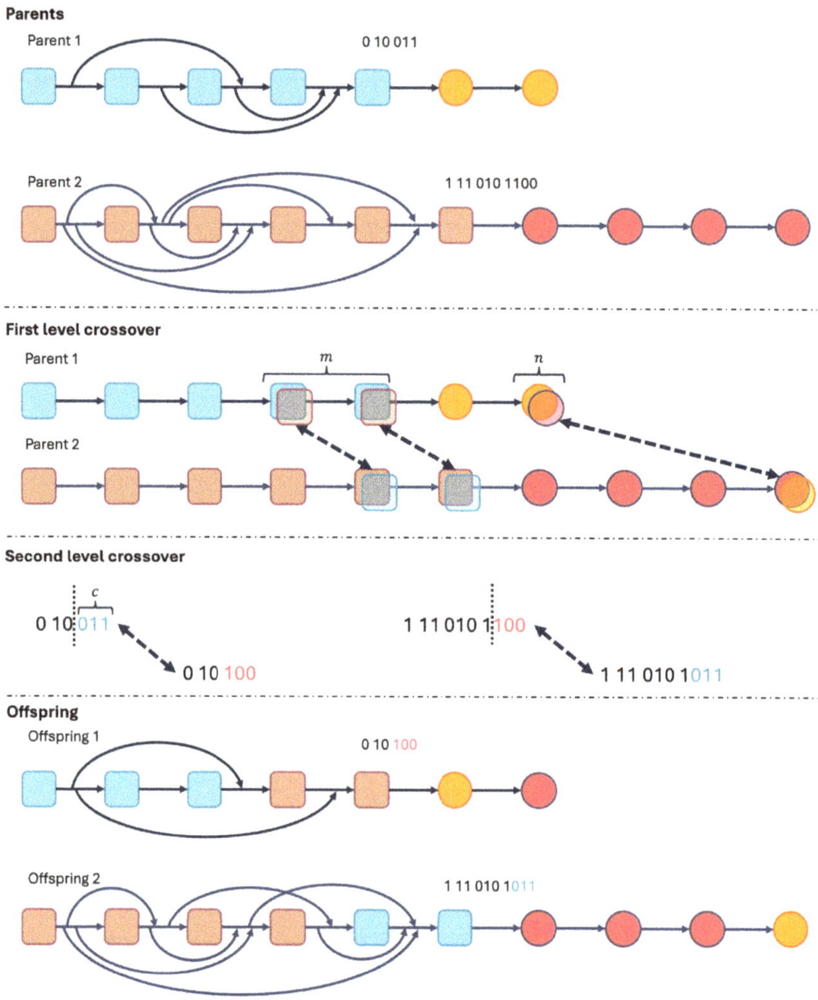

Figure 2. An example of the crossover procedure in DeepGA. The operator works on two levels, taking two parents as input and returning two individuals as offspring. First, a fraction of the blocks is exchanged, and then, a portion of the bits in the bit string is swapped.

3.1.3. Mutation

The mutation operator applies changes to an individual. DeepGA mutation modifies both levels of the encoding. The modifications are applied according to two random numbers, r_1 and r_2, from a uniform distribution in the range (0, 1). If $r_1 \geq 0.5$, one of the blocks is restarted, changing the hyperparameters encoded there. The type of block to be reinitialized is subject to r_2. If $r_2 \leq 0.5$, one of the convolutional blocks is randomly chosen and restarted. Otherwise ($r_2 > 0.5$), the randomly chosen block to be restarted is one of the fully connected ones. This mutation process is complemented by a bit flip in the second-level encoding, which changes one skip connection. Figure 3 presents an example of the mutation where a block is restarted.

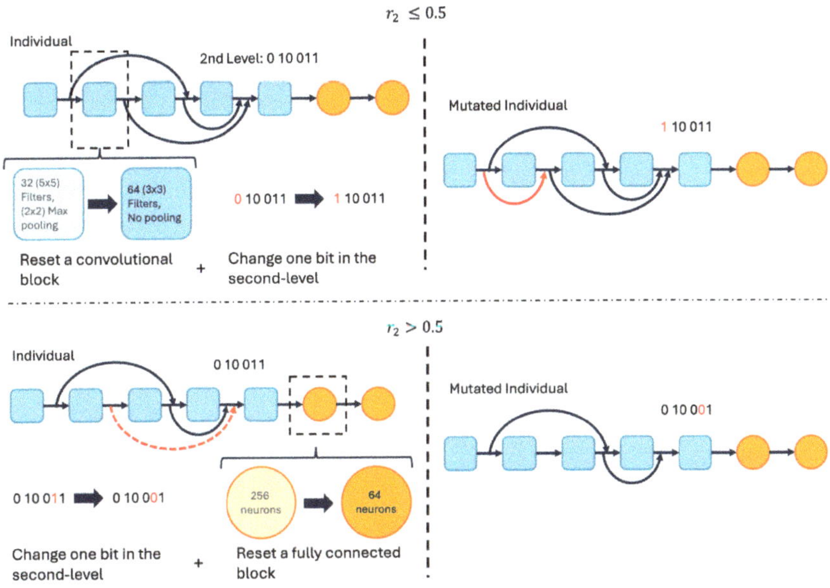

Figure 3. Mutation of restarting a block applied when $r_1 \geq 0.5$.

If $r_1 < 0.5$, a block is added to the encoding. When $r_2 \leq 0.5$, a convolutional block with a random initialization of its hyperparameters is inserted in a position selected by chance. The addition of a convolutional block requires changes to the second level encoding, where the required bits (randomly selected) are attached to the positions where needed to complete the representation of skip connections. Alternatively, if $r_2 > 0.5$, the block to be added is a fully connected one. Similarly to the addition of the convolutional block, the fully connected block to be added is randomly initialized, and the position is determined at random. Figure 4 presents an example of applying the mutation, adding a block to the encoding.

3.2. *Training-Free Proxies*

Given that no architecture is trained during the search process, zero-shot EEMs using training-free score functions can achieve an extreme computational cost reduction in NAS [18]. This work tests two score functions: Logsynflow, as a gradient-based proxy, and Linear Regions, as a gradient-free proxy. The works of [19,23] inspired the selection of these proxies. The rationale behind the choice is to have one of the proxies, the Logsynflow, considering the network's trainability, and the other, the Linear Regions, evaluating the network's expressive capacity. In addition, the combination of them will complement each other.

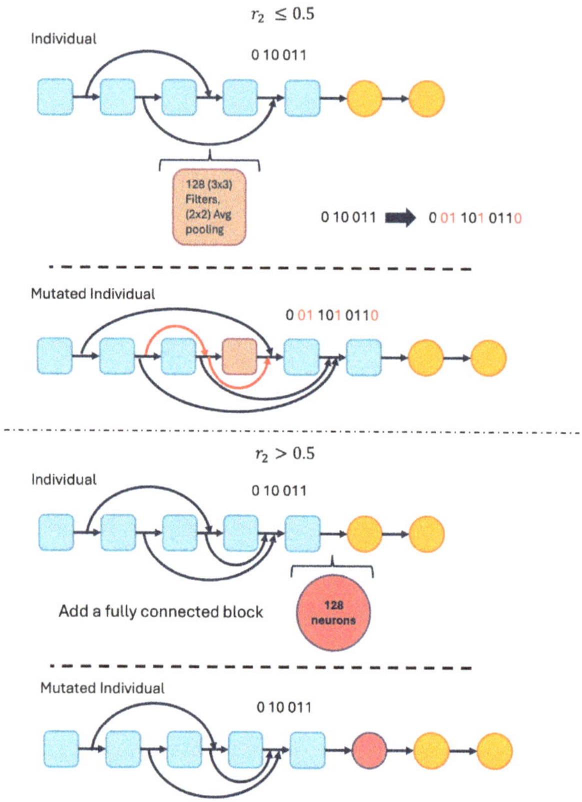

Figure 4. Mutation of adding one block applied when $r_1 < 0.5$.

Nonetheless, as presented in [18], the training-free proxies tend to prefer more complex networks. The Linear Regions proxy that considers the expressive capacity finds potential in models with immense width and depth, given their ability to represent almost any complex function with small error. On the other hand, the trainability of the networks, considered by Logsynflow, is also better in wider networks of similar depth. The above considerations highlight the need to constrain the complexity of the networks in the DeepGA search process, incorporating the number of parameters as a design criterion. The integration of the training-free proxies in the fitness function of DeepGA requires the scores to be scaled similarly to the complexity term of the equation. More details of each proxy are provided next, along with two options for normalizing the metric values and incorporating them into DeepGA.

3.2.1. Logsynflow

The calculation of the synaptic flow was proposed in [40] as a technique for network pruning. The calculation of the score (s) is performed using the weight vector θ and the gradient vector $\frac{\partial \mathcal{R}}{\partial \theta}$ as presented in Equation (3). $\mathcal{R}$ represents a scalar loss function calculated with a feedforward pass in the network with parameters θ.

$$s = \theta \cdot \frac{\partial \mathcal{R}}{\partial \theta} \tag{3}$$

In [19], the method is utilized as a training-free proxy, although some adaptations are made. The calculation of $\frac{\partial \mathcal{R}}{\partial \theta}$ is performed with a pass of a matrix of ones with the same shape as a mini-batch of the input to the network, and the gradients are computed with the output going backward. Then, it was proposed to scale the value with a logarithm to avoid gradient explosion as presented in Equation (4). This calculation gives way to the Logsynflow metric. The batch normalization layers are temporarily omitted during Logsynflow calculation to avoid interfering with the gradient flow.

$$s = \theta \cdot log\left(\frac{\partial \mathcal{R}}{\partial \theta} + 1\right) \tag{4}$$

3.2.2. Linear Regions

The Linear Regions proxy, also called NAS without training (NASWOT) score or logdet proxy, was proposed in [20] using a binary code to examine the activation patterns in an untrained network with the forward pass of a minibatch ($\mathbf{X} = \{x_i\}_{i=1}^{M}$) of the data. It is based on the ReLU activation function, so it is classified in [17] as a model-dependent score function. Given its nature, ReLU allows the binarization of the activation pattern, distinguishing between active (multiplied by 1) and inactive units (multiplied by 0) and serving as indicator variables. When an input image x_i passes through the network, the indicator variables in the ReLU function form a binary code c_i.

The intuition from using c_i is that two inputs with similar binary codes are more challenging for the network to separate, and therefore, they reside in the same linear region. The Hamming distance $d_H(c_i, c_j)$ is used to measure the dissimilarity of the inputs i and j. With this, the kernel matrix $\mathbf{K}_H$ is calculated as presented in Equation (5). N_A is the number of ReLU functions considered in the network for the calculation.

$$\mathbf{K}_H = \begin{bmatrix} N_A - d_H(c_1, c_1) & \cdots & N_A - d_H(c_1, c_M) \\ \vdots & \ddots & \vdots \\ N_A - d_H(c_M, c_1) & \cdots & N_A - d_H(c_M, c_M) \end{bmatrix} \tag{5}$$

Finally, the score is calculated using the logarithm of the determinant of $\mathbf{K}_H$ as presented in Equation (6).

$$s = log\, \mathbf{K}_H \tag{6}$$

3.2.3. Normalization

The ranges of the training-free proxies do not present an upper bound. This way, they must be normalized to combine them in a fitness function or to correctly apply the complexity term as in the fitness function of DeepGA (Equation (2)). In [19], a max normalization of the scores is performed by dividing the score s_i by the maximum score in the population s_{max} as presented in Equation (7). This normalization form sets a lower bound of 0 and an upper bound of 1 for the solution with the s_{max}.

$$s_{norm} = \frac{s_i}{s_{max}} \tag{7}$$

An alternative is presented in [22,28] as the z-score normalization. In z-score normalization, the mean (μ) is subtracted from the value and then divided by the standard deviation (σ) as presented in Equation (8). Nonetheless, the z-score is not guaranteed to be in the range of $[0, 1]$; therefore, using a sigmoid function is proposed as shown in Equation (9). The max and z-score normalization are tested during experimentation with the training-free proxies.

$$s_{norm} = \frac{s_i - \mu}{\sigma} \tag{8}$$

$$s_{norm} = \frac{1}{1 + e^{-\frac{s_i - \mu}{\sigma}}} \quad (9)$$

For combining the two training-free proxies into the fitness function of DeepGA, some changes are proposed in Equation (10). $s1_{norm}$ represents the calculation and normalization of the Logsynflow score, and $s2_{norm}$ refers to the calculation and normalization of the linear region's score. Using $\frac{(1-w)}{2}$ expects an equal contribution of the scores.

$$f(A) = \frac{(1-w)}{2} * s1_{norm}(A) + \frac{(1-w)}{2} * s2_{norm}(A) + w * \frac{MP - NP}{MP} \quad (10)$$

3.3. Data for Experimentation

Three datasets are used for experimentation: Fashion-MNIST [35], CIFAR-10, and CIFAR-100 [36]. In the three cases, the suggested train/test split of each dataset is considered. Fashion-MNIST consists of 70,000 grayscale images of clothing items, each with a size of 28 × 28 pixels. The data split considers 60,000 images for training and 10,000 test images. The dataset contains ten classes.

CIFAR-10 and CIFAR-100 contain 60,000 color images of 32 × 32 pixels of diverse objects. The datasets were proposed with a suggested partition of 50,000 training images and 10,000 test images. The images in CIFAR-10 are divided into ten balanced classes. This way, the training and test subsets contain 5000 and 1000 images of each class, respectively. CIFAR-100 is similar, but the images are divided into 100 classes. The training and testing subsets contain 500 and 100 images of each class, respectively. As presented in [9], CIFAR-10 and CIFAR-100 are datasets considered benchmarks for evaluating the performance of NAS algorithms.

No data augmentation was considered in this work, as the primary motivation was to test the cost reduction mechanisms. Using additional data during search, especially with accuracy-guided configurations, would require more resources and extend the time necessary to evaluate the architectures. The batch size of 24 used in [30] is kept in the experimentation.

4. Results

The experimentation was divided into two: the accuracy-guided search and the training-free search. The population memory mechanism is used in all the configurations for experimentation. For a fair comparison, the best architecture found in each run is trained for 50 epochs, a configuration proposed in [29]. In the accuracy-guided search, the early stopping mechanism is used in DeepGA to assess the effects on the performance of the resulting architecture and the computational resources required (see Section 4.1). Section 4.2 presents the results of the training-free search. The normalization strategies are first evaluated using the training-free proxies. Then, the Logsynflow and linear region proxies are used independently to guide the search in DeepGA. Finally, a combination of Logsynflow and Linear Regions is used for searching. A comparison among the configurations tested is provided. At the end of this section (Section 4.3), details of the resulting architectures from the different algorithm configurations are compared.

The experimentation consisted of ten runs for each configuration in DeepGA. The value of w was set to 0.1 for the accuracy-guided configurations. The networks were trained using the Adam optimizer with a learning rate of 1×10^{-4} and the cross-entropy loss function. The code was executed using Google Colab Pro+ virtual environments with an NVIDIA T4 GPU. The CPU corresponds to a 2.2 GHz Intel Xeon. The code is based on the PyTorch library [41], and the 2.6.0 version was used.

4.1. Accuracy-Guided Search

Two configurations of DeepGA are tested, considering five and ten training epochs, as in [29], to evaluate individuals during the search and analyze the effect of early stopping mechanisms. The performance of both algorithm configurations is presented in Table 2. The tested configurations are identified as Accuracy-10 and Accuracy-5, respectively. The Wilcoxon signed-rank test is performed for pairwise comparison, yielding p-values of 0.7519 for Fashion MNIST, 0.0273 for CIFAR-10, and 0.1930 for CIFAR-100. According to the CIFAR-10 dataset statistics, the configuration with five epochs performed better. Conversely, no significant differences were detected in the methods for the Fashion MNIST and CIFAR-100 datasets. The considerations above show that the early stopping mechanism is capable of maintaining a competitive performance while using fewer training epochs in an evaluation.

Table 2. Accuracy performance of DeepGA using the accuracy-guided configurations. The best values for each dataset are marked in bold.

Dataset	Configuration	Best	Mean	Std Dev	Worst
Fashion MNIST	Accuracy-10	**0.9333**	0.9248	0.0045	0.9180
	Accuracy-5	0.9302	**0.9256**	**0.0038**	**0.9189**
CIFAR-10	Accuracy-10	0.8339	0.8145	**0.0133**	0.7840
	Accuracy-5	**0.8542**	**0.8290**	0.0156	**0.8094**
CIFAR-100	Accuracy-10	0.5566	**0.5341**	**0.0236**	**0.4938**
	Accuracy-5	**0.5650**	0.5173	0.0288	0.4749

Table 3 presents the average complexity of the models considering the number of training parameters and a measure of the mega FLOPS in the model. It is observed that the Accuracy-5 configuration yielded networks with a larger number of parameters. A similar tendency is seen with the MFLOPS, with the only difference occurring with the CIFAR-100 dataset, where Accuracy-10 required more MFLOPS.

Table 3. Average network complexity in terms of trainable parameters and MFLOPS for the accuracy guided configurations of DeepGA. Standard deviation is shown in parentheses.

Dataset	Configuration	No. Parameters	MFLOPS
Fashion MNIST	Accuracy-10	243,438.0 (64,931.6)	140.3 (81.7)
	Accuracy-5	247,103.6 (77,268.6)	156.0 (88.1)
CIFAR-10	Accuracy-10	660,554.8 (233,352.3)	232.0 (210.1)
	Accuracy-5	842,744.4 (247,342.7)	350.6 (126.0)
CIFAR-100	Accuracy-10	1,159,852.0 (337,531.2)	457.9 (394.1)
	Accuracy-5	1,420,398.4 (687,143.5)	258.1 (147.4)

Table 4 presents the number of evaluations and the computational time required by the DeepGA configurations. The time measure is divided into the Search time of the procedure and the time needed for the final evaluation. Additionally, the reduction in search time achieved by the Accuracy-5 configuration compared to Accuracy-10 is presented. It is observed that the number of evaluations is similar between the configurations. The population memory has the effect of reducing the total number of evaluations. The search process without memory would have required 420 evaluations. This way, population memory avoids between 43% and 46% of the evaluations. The achieved time reduction ranges, on average, from 45.99% to 64.47%. As presented above, Accuracy-5 exhibits competitive performance, and it is now evident that it results in a considerable time reduction.

Table 4. Time comparison for the accuracy-guided DeepGA. Standard deviation is shown in parentheses.

Dataset	Configuration	Evaluations	Search Time (h)	Diff. (%)	Final Eval (h)
Fashion MNIST	Accuracy-10	226.8 (24.4)	17.07 (3.86)	-	0.39 (0.11)
	Accuracy-5	231.9 (24.8)	9.22 (1.63)	45.99	0.38 (0.07)
CIFAR-10	Accuracy-10	237.6 (18.8)	22.51 (4.68)	-	0.48 (0.19)
	Accuracy-5	238.1 (28.5)	10.55 (3.24)	53.15	0.50 (0.20)
CIFAR-100	Accuracy-10	226.6 (27.4)	26.32 (13.66)	-	0.70 (0.49)
	Accuracy-5	224.5 (31.7)	9.35 (2.91)	64.47	0.41 (0.11)

As mentioned earlier, 50 epochs were used to evaluate the best architecture found in each run. Table 5 presents the mean results of the accuracy-guided search considering a longer training for the final evaluation. 100 and 200 were considered, respectively. The Wilcoxon rank sum test is also conducted based on the results of the longer training. With CIFAR-100 and Fashion MNIST, no significant difference is found in any of the cases. For CIFAR-10, the superiority of the method that uses five epochs during the search is not detected when the final evaluation is performed with 100 and 200 epochs. An interesting trend is observed in the CIFAR-100 and Fashion MNIST results, where the performance is even worse in some cases when training is longer. The previous observations can indicate overfitting in the network. More analysis and mechanisms to counter it are expected in future changes to the algorithm. Conversely, the results with CIFAR-10 improve if more training epochs are set for the final evaluation.

Table 5. Results of training the architectures found by the accuracy-guided search process considering a larger number of epochs. Statistical tests are included, and significant differences are marked in bold.

Dataset	Configuration	50 Epochs	100 Epochs	200 Epochs
Fashion MNIST	Accuracy-10	0.9248	0.9263	0.9250
	Accuracy-5	0.9256	0.9244	0.9244
Wilcoxon p-value		0.752	0.240	1.000
CIFAR-10	Accuracy-10	0.8145	0.8195	0.8287
	Accuracy-5	0.8290	0.8311	0.8384
Wilcoxon p-value		**0.027**	0.275	0.275
CIFAR-100	Accuracy-10	0.5341	0.5332	0.5379
	Accuracy-5	0.5173	0.5154	0.5143
Wilcoxon p-value		0.193	0.193	0.160

4.2. Training-Free Search

Logsynflow, Linear Regions, and a combination of both proxies are incorporated to guide the search in DeepGA. Nonetheless, as mentioned in Section 3.2, the training-free proxies must be normalized to be used in the fitness function of DeepGA (Equation (2)) as a substitute for the accuracy metric. Max and z-score normalization were tested with different values of w to perform the search process with DeepGA. Ten runs of each configuration were conducted, and the final evaluation was omitted. Tables 6–8 presents the results.

Table 6. Testing the max and z-score normalization schemes with the training-free proxies in DeepGA using the Fashion MNIST dataset.

Proxy	w	Max-Norm		z-Score	
		Score	No. Parameters	Score	No. Parameters
Logsynflow	0.1	161,083.75	5,970,253.2	179,482.57	6,593,799.6
	0.2	154,234.79	4,365,031.6	138,346.88	3780,935.6
	0.3	106,755.63	2,133,017.2	103,994.28	2384,149.2
	0.4	92,342.59	1,227,825.2	104,566.19	1804,906.8
	0.5	81,351.06	1,282,738.0	83,542.26	1265,634.8
NASWOT	0.1	300.50	908,006.0	317.63	5,992,382.0
	0.2	293.06	409,642.8	309.08	3,658,186.0
	0.3	286.07	217,086.8	306.55	2,546,362.8
	0.4	276.33	139,384.4	301.60	1,442,433.2
	0.5	279.46	93,854.0	296.90	898,262.0

Table 7. Testing the max and z-score normalization schemes with the training-free proxies in DeepGA using the CIFAR-10 dataset.

Proxy	w	Max-Norm		z-Score	
		Score	No. Parameters	Score	No. Parameters
Logsynflow	0.1	195,166.95	8,364,607.6	187,851.74	8,839,062.8
	0.2	136,235.81	3,950,958.8	180,108.78	5,814,657.2
	0.3	99,455.17	2,127,498.0	112,331.76	2,480,414.8
	0.4	92,613.55	1,191,590.0	90,275.61	1,865,106.8
	0.5	86,799.67	967,518.8	95,720.37	1,425,199.6
NASWOT	0.1	310.59	656,959.6	328.21	6,082,338.8
	0.2	303.97	391,150.8	328.11	4,015,110.8
	0.3	300.73	220,789.2	317.39	1,793,818.0
	0.4	292.67	126,898.8	317.61	1,748,256.4
	0.5	286.37	58,062.8	315.35	1,054,491.6

Table 8. Testing the max and z-score normalization schemes with the training-free proxies in DeepGA using the CIFAR-100 dataset.

Proxy	w	Max-Norm		z-Score	
		Score	No. Parameters	Score	No. Parameters
Logsynflow	0.1	252,375.81	7,918,436.0	242,474.17	8,063,005.6
	0.2	193,637.93	3,513,457.6	208,765.72	4,834,309.6
	0.3	155,851.48	1,624,516.0	177,344.79	3,352,762.4
	0.4	140,611.86	1,207,996.8	169,114.30	2,570,465.6
	0.5	126,446.96	918,656.8	142,069.35	1,370,908.0
NASWOT	0.1	312.55	720,357.6	328.39	6,557,964.8
	0.2	304.11	330,736.8	324.20	3,213,864.0
	0.3	299.88	227,526.4	322.15	2,154,715.2
	0.4	293.43	134,703.2	319.70	1,863,878.4
	0.5	288.21	98,028.0	315.27	1,204,232.8

It is observed that the max-normalization guides the search towards less complex architectures when the Linear Regions proxy is used. The z-score normalization presents a more consistent behavior with both proxies, which is the desired behavior given that Logsynflow and Linear Regions will be combined to guide the search. The proxies tend to favor more complex architectures, so the value of w is crucial for finding a network configuration with limited complexity. $w = 0.4$ and the z-score normalization are selected for the experimentation with the training-free proxies and their combination.

4.2.1. Fashion MNIST

Table 9 presents the accuracy performance of the resulting architectures with the training-free proxies guiding the search using the Fashion MNIST dataset. The accuracy-guided search results are also included for comparison. It is seen that the highest values are obtained with the training-free configuration. Nonetheless, the Friedman non-parametric test is conducted to analyze if there are significant differences among the means of the populations of results. With a p-value of 0.083, the test did not indicate a significant difference in the accuracy performance. Figure 5 presents a boxplot of the accuracy results. It is observed that the medians of the results are positioned closely. The Logsynflow configuration has the highest standard deviation, as shown in the respective box, which spans more than the other configurations.

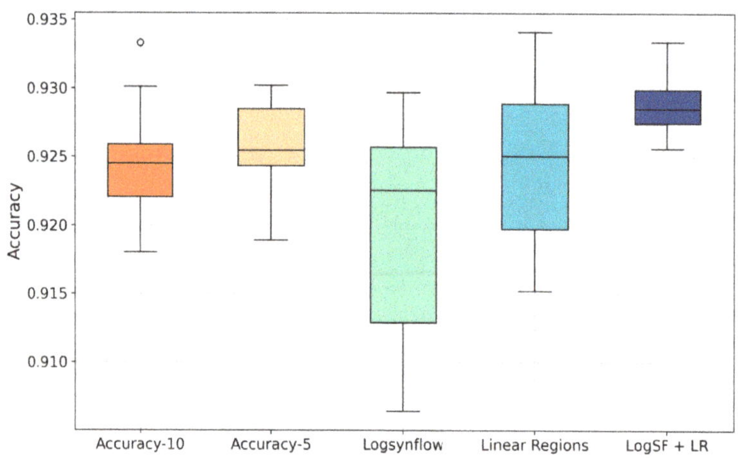

Figure 5. Boxplot of the accuracy performance of the accuracy-guided and training-free search in DeepGA using the Fashion MNIST dataset.

Table 9. DeepGA performance incorporating the training-free proxies to guide the search using the Fashion MNIST dataset. The best result is marked in bold.

Configuration	Best	Mean	Std Dev	Worst
Accuracy-10	0.9333	0.9248	0.0045	0.9180
Accuracy-5	0.9302	0.9256	0.0038	0.9189
Logsynflow	0.9297	0.9198	0.0081	0.9064
Linear Regions	**0.9341**	0.9243	0.0062	0.9152
LogSF + LR	0.9334	**0.9288**	**0.0024**	**0.9256**

The comparison presented in Table 10 corresponds to the average network complexity of the resulting models with the different configurations tested. The number of trainable parameters and the MFLOPS are included. It is observed that the training-free configurations resulted in networks with a considerably higher complexity. In the analysis of the MFLOPS, the Logsynflow configuration achieves a similar number of MFLOPS compared to the accuracy-based search. Conversely, the Linear Regions configuration and the combination of proxies have a considerably higher number of MFLOPS.

Table 10. Average complexity of the resulting networks of the configurations of DeepGA with EEMs using the Fashion MNIST dataset. The standard deviation is shown in parentheses.

Configuration	No. Parameters	MFLOPS
Accuracy-10	243,438.0 (64,931.6)	140.3 (81.7)
Accuracy-5	247,103.6 (77,268.6)	156.0 (88.1)
Logsynflow	1,804,906.8 (636,449.4)	153.3 (179.5)
Linear Regions	1,442,433.2 (474,220.6)	1806.4 (755.9)
LogSF + LR	1,750,311.6 (471,406.5)	1306.6 (607.2)

The effects of using the training-free proxies regarding the computational time are presented in Table 11. The training-free used more evaluations. Nonetheless, the search time reduction achieved by the zero-shot approach is above 99.81%. The training-free DeepGA completes the search in a matter of seconds. Regarding the final evaluation, it is observed that the Linear Regions proxy and the combined version with Logsynflow required more time to be completed. This observation aligns with being the architectures with considerably higher MFLOPS.

Table 11. Time comparison of the search process of DeepGA with EEMs using the Fashion MNIST dataset. The standard deviation is shown in parentheses.

Configuration	Evaluations	Search Time (h)	Diff (%)	Final Eval. (h)
Accuracy-10	226.8 (24.4)	17.071 (3.857)	-	0.389 (0.113)
Accuracy-5	231.9 (24.8)	9.220 (1.632)	45.99	0.384 (0.074)
Logsynflow	315.3 (27.2)	0.018 (0.002)	99.89	0.520 (0.178)
Linear Regions	295.9 (24.4)	0.028 (0.003)	99.84	2.009 (0.930)
LogSF + LR	311.8 (17.6)	0.032 (0.002)	99.81	1.589 (0.485)

4.2.2. CIFAR-10

Table 12 presents the accuracy performance of the different EEMs incorporated in DeepGA for the CIFAR-10 dataset. The highest values are obtained with the Accuracy-5 configuration. Figure 6 presents a box plot visualization of the results. It is seen that the accuracy-guided configurations are positioned above the training-free ones. In addition, Accuracy-10 and Accuracy-5 obtained the smallest standard deviation. An interesting point to observe is that the best result of the LogSf + LR configuration is higher than the best result from Accuracy-10. Statistical tests are conducted for a deeper analysis. The Friedman test detected significant differences among the means of the populations with a p-value of 2.18×10^{-5}.

Table 12. DeepGA performance incorporating the training-free proxies to guide the search using the CIFAR-10 dataset. The best result is marked in bold.

Configuration	Best	Mean	Std Dev	Worst
Accuracy-10	0.8339	0.8145	**0.0133**	0.7840
Accuracy-5	**0.8542**	**0.8290**	0.0156	**0.8094**
Logsynflow	0.8083	0.7646	0.0257	0.7315
Linear Regions	0.8180	0.7853	0.0189	0.7643
LogSF + LR	0.8382	0.7800	0.0345	0.7416

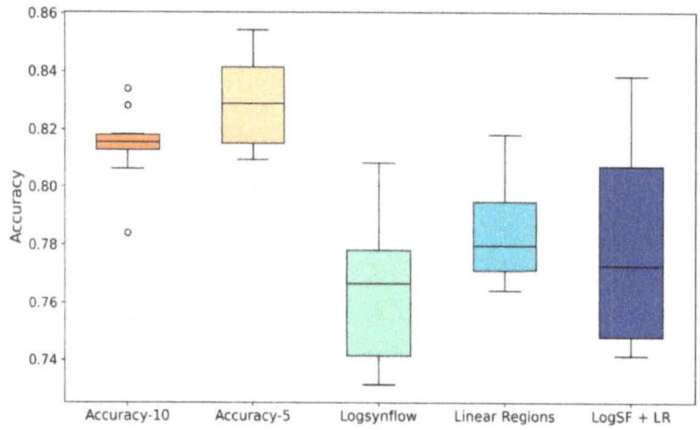

Figure 6. Boxplot of the accuracy performance of the accuracy-guided and training-free search in DeepGA using the CIFAR-10 dataset.

The Nemenyi post-hoc test was used for a deeper analysis. The results are presented in Table 13. In this case, Accuracy-5 outperformed all the training-free configurations. On the other hand, the Accuracy-10 configuration only outmatched the Logsynflow configuration; no significant differences were detected when compared with the Linear Regions and the combined configurations. Unlike the reported pairwise comparison of the accuracy-guided search configurations, the Nemenyi post hoc procedure did not detect significant differences between using 5 or 10 training epochs during the search. Finally, there were no significant differences among the training-free configurations, i.e., no training-free configuration was better than the others.

Table 13. Nemenyi post hoc analysis for the results with the CIFAR-10 dataset. The values where statistical differences are detected are marked in bold.

	Acc-10	Acc-5	Logsynflow	Linear Regions	LogSF + LR
Acc-10	1	0.8600	**0.0062**	0.1571	0.1141
Acc-5	0.8600	1	**0.0001**	**0.0101**	**0.0062**
Logsynflow	**0.0062**	**0.0001**	1	0.7899	0.8600
Linear Regions	0.1571	**0.0101**	0.7899	1	0.9999
LogSF + LR	0.1141	**0.0062**	0.8600	0.9999	1

Table 14 presents the average complexity of the networks generated by DeepGA with the EEMs using the CIFAR-10 dataset. The trends are similar to those observed with the Fashion MNIST dataset. The training-free configurations present a considerably higher number of training parameters. Regarding the FLOPS, Linear Regions is again the configuration with the highest value, followed by the configuration with the combination of the training free proxies. Logsymflow required, on average, the least number of MFLOPS.

The time comparison is presented in Table 15. The search time reduction achieved by the zero-shot search processes exceeds 99.8%. The final evaluation took considerably more time with the Linear Regions configuration and LogSF+LR, the configurations with the highest MFLOPS values.

Table 14. Average complexity of the resulting networks of the configurations of DeepGA with EEMs using the CIFAR-10 dataset. The standard deviation is shown in parentheses.

Configuration	No. Parameters	MFLOPS
Accuracy-10	660,554.8 (233,352.3)	232.0 (210.1)
Accuracy-5	842,744.4 (247,342.7)	350.6 (126.0)
Logsynflow	1,865,106.8 (504,233.2)	152.9 (260.7)
Linear Regions	1,748,256.4 (1,071,596.6)	2989.5 (1784.1)
LogSF + LR	1,884,343.6 (672,313.7)	1801.9 (1461.3)

Table 15. Time comparison of the search process of DeepGA with EEMs using the CIFAR-10 dataset. The standard deviation is shown in parentheses.

Configuration	Evaluations	Search Time (h)	Diff (%)	Final Eval. (h)
Accuracy-10	237.6 (18.8)	22.509 (4.682)	-	0.478 (0.187)
Accuracy-5	238.1 (28.5)	10.545 (3.237)	53.15	0.499 (0.197)
Logsynflow	291.2 (29.0)	0.017 (0.002)	99.92	0.468 (0.235)
Linear Regions	294.4 (28.5)	0.027 (0.003)	99.88	4.192 (2.152)
LogSF + LR	317.7 (15.9)	0.034 (0.003)	99.85	3.086 (3.575)

4.2.3. CIFAR-100

The accuracy performance of the DeepGA configurations using EEMs is presented in Table 16, considering the CIFAR-100 dataset. It is seen that the best values are obtained with the accuracy-guided search. In this case, the Accuracy-10 is the configuration that has the highest mean value, but Accuracy-5 achieved the highest of the best values. An interesting behavior is observed in the worst cases of the training-free configurations with the CIFAR-100 dataset, where the search process resulted in architectures with particularly low performance. Figure 7 presents a box plot with the accuracy results. It is observed that the most compact boxes correspond to the accuracy-guided configurations, which are characterized by small standard deviation values. As shown in the figure, the worst result of the Linear Regions configuration, which exhibits poor performance, is an outlier.

Table 16. DeepGA performance incorporating the training-free proxies to guide the search using the CIFAR-100 dataset. The best result is marked in bold.

Configuration	Best	Mean	Std Dev	Worst
Accuracy-10	0.5566	**0.5341**	**0.0236**	**0.4938**
Accuracy-5	**0.5650**	0.5173	0.0288	0.4749
Logsynflow	0.5093	0.3324	0.1111	0.1587
Linear Regions	0.3777	0.2889	0.1075	0.0100
LogSF + LR	0.4981	0.3644	0.0929	0.2232

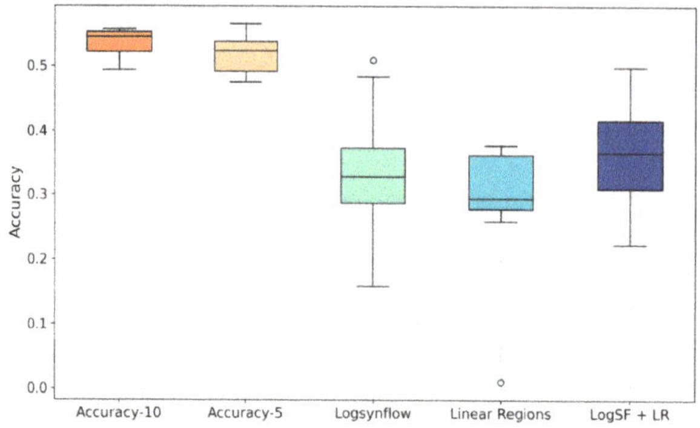

Figure 7. Boxplot of the accuracy performance of the accuracy-guided and training-free search in DeepGA using the CIFAR-100 dataset.

Statistical tests were conducted. The Friedman test detected, with a p-value of 1.45×10^{-5}, that there are significant differences among the means of the results for the CIFAR-100 dataset. The Nemenyi post hoc procedure is then used. The details are presented in Table 17. It is seen that Accuracy-10 outperformed all of the training-free configurations. Nonetheless, no significant differences were detected when considering Accuracy-5 and the Logsynflow and LogSF + LR configurations. Additionally, no significant differences were observed among the training-free configurations.

Table 17. Nemenyi post hoc analysis for the results with the CIFAR-100 dataset. The values where statistical differences are detected are marked in bold.

	Acc-10	Acc-5	Logsynflow	Linear Regions	LogSF + LR
Acc-10	1	0.9153	**0.0062**	**0.0002**	**0.0037**
Acc-5	0.9153	1	0.0808	**0.0062**	0.0559
Logsynflow	**0.0062**	0.0808	1	0.9153	0.9999
Linear Regions	**0.0002**	**0.0062**	0.9153	1	0.9550
LogSF + LR	**0.0037**	0.0559	0.9999	0.9550	1

The network complexity comparison for the CIFAR-100 datasets is presented in Table 18. Similarly to the other datasets, the trends in the number of parameters are that the training-free configurations resulted in higher network complexity. Nonetheless, the average number of parameters from Accuracy-5 is closer to the values of LogSf + LR than the same comparison with Fashion MNIST and CIFAR-10. The Linear Regions proxy exhibits consistent behavior in MFLOPS; it is again the configuration that requires a considerably higher number of MFLOPS.

Table 18. Average complexity of the resulting networks of the configurations of DeepGA with EEMs using the CIFAR-100 dataset. The standard deviation is shown in parentheses.

Configuration	No. Parameters	MFLOPS
Accuracy-10	1,159,852.0 (337,531.2)	457.9 (394.1)
Accuracy-5	1,420,398.4 (687,143.5)	258.1 (147.4)
Logsynflow	2,570,465.6 (428,558.4)	342.5 (225.2)
Linear Regions	1,863,878.4 (741,634.9)	3536.7 (1288.5)
LogSF + LR	1,766,450.4 (331,559.1)	1486.8 (852.3)

Table 19 presents the time comparison for the CIFAR-100 dataset. The number of evaluations is higher in the training-free search process. However, the reduced cost of each evaluation in the zero-shot approaches is minimal compared to the accuracy-guided search. Therefore, the search time is immensely reduced by at least 97.42%. The final evaluations in the Linear Regions and LogSF + LR configurations are the most expensive.

Table 19. Time comparison of the search process of DeepGA with EEMs using the CIFAR-100 dataset. The standard deviation is shown in parentheses.

Configuration	Evaluations	Search Time (h)	Diff (%)	Final Eval. (h)
Accuracy-10	226.6 (27.4)	26.319 (13.664)	-	0.700 (0.492)
Accuracy-5	224.5 (31.7)	9.351 (2.910)	64.47	0.406 (0.115)
Logsynflow	327.2 (21.6)	0.020 (0.001)	99.92	0.811 (0.371)
Linear Regions	307.8 (17.4)	0.030 (0.003)	99.89	5.174 (2.067)
LogSF + LR	316.8 (23.3)	0.039 (0.005)	99.85	2.346 (1.303)

4.3. Comparison of the Architectures

The first step in comparing the resulting architectures across different configurations of DeepGA with EEMs is to visualize the differences in the elements considered for the networks. Figure 8 presents the architectures from the best result of each configuration with the CIFAR-10 dataset (Table 12 presents their accuracy performance). The differences are evident. The accuracy-guided configurations considered resulted in architectures with no skip connections. The training-free search obtained deeper networks, which aligns with their larger number of parameters. The network with more convolutional layers (9) was the one obtained with the Linear Regions configuration. In addition, 15 skip connections were considered.

From Figure 8, the top-performing architecture is the one from Accuracy-5, which is the one presented in the figure with the smallest depth. The main difference between Accuracy-5 and Accuracy-10 in this case is the number of fully connected layers. The architecture with the second-best performance is the one from LogSF + LR, which features the most significant number of fully connected layers. The above observations demonstrate the difficulty in designing CNNs; there is a large number of possible designs and many paths that can be explored. Thus, the importance of NAS lies in automating the design process.

For a deeper understanding of the differences in the resulting architectures from the different DeepGA configurations, a comparison among their characteristics is presented in this subsection. For each architecture, the mean values of the following design and hyperparameter configurations are considered:

- Number of convolutional layers.
- Number of fully connected layers.
- Average number of filters per convolutional layer.
- Average filter size selected for the convolutional layers.
- Average number of neurons per fully connected layer.
- The frequency of using max pooling.
- The frequency of using average pooling.
- Average kernel size for pooling.
- Number of skip connections.

The results are presented in Table 20 for the Fashion MNIST dataset, in Table 21 for CIFAR-10, and in Table 22 for the CIFAR-100 dataset.

The training-free configurations yielded deeper networks, featuring more convolutional and fully connected layers. Notably, it is observed that the accuracy-guided resulting architectures have a reduced number of fully connected layers, whereas the training-free configurations select more of them. With the accuracy-guided configurations, the primary difference observed between the configurations for the CIFAR-100 and CIFAR-10 datasets is the number of neurons in the fully connected layers. The previous explains the additional complexity of the CIFAR-100 architectures. Finally, the number of skip connections is considerably higher in the architectures from the training-free configurations.

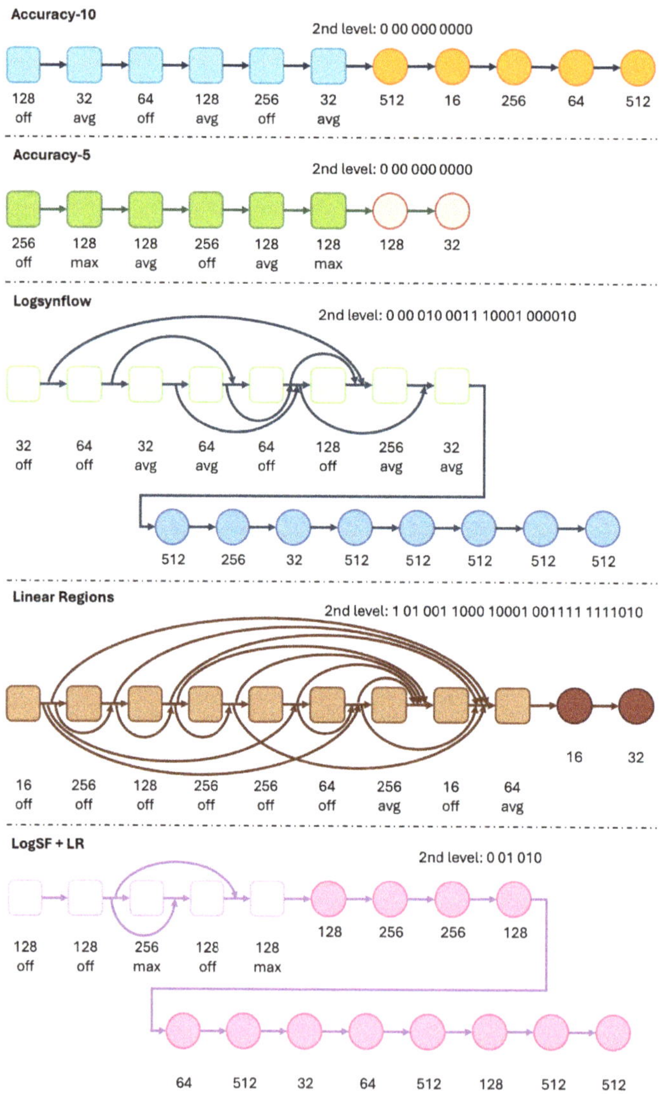

Figure 8. Representation of the best performing architectures obtained with the different DeepGA configurations. The square blocks represent convolutional layers; their number of filters and pooling type are displayed under the block. Circles represent fully-connected blocks, and the number of neurons is displayed below the block.

Table 20. Mean values of network characteristics and hyperparameter configuration from the resulting architectures of applying DeepGA with EEMs using the Fashion MNIST dataset. The highest value is marked in bold as reference.

Configuration	Accuracy-10	Accuracy-5	Logsynflow	Linear Regions	LogSF + LR
No. Conv	4.3	4.6	**7.1**	6.7	6.7
No. FC	2.3	2.3	**9.8**	4.2	7.3
No. Filters/Conv	72.2	76.1	85.0	**150.1**	133.2
Mean Filter size	2.9	**3.0**	**3.0**	2.8	2.7
No. Neurons/FC	84.5	78.5	**383.5**	86.4	333.6
Freq Max pool	0.6	0.8	**1.6**	1.2	1.0
Freq Avg pool	0.7	0.6	**1.2**	0.8	0.8
Freq pool Off	3.0	3.2	4.3	4.7	**4.9**
Pooling kernel size	2.5	2.5	**2.6**	**2.6**	**2.6**
No. Skip Conns	1.8	2.0	**5.2**	3.4	5.1

Table 21. Mean values of network characteristics and hyperparameter configuration from the resulting architectures of applying DeepGA with EEMs using the CIFAR10 dataset. The highest value is marked in bold as reference.

Configuration	Accuracy-10	Accuracy-5	Logsynflow	Linear Regions	LogSF + LR
No. Conv	5.6	5.1	6.0	**7.6**	7.0
No. FC	3.0	2.8	**9.1**	3.5	**9.1**
No. Filters/Conv	119.3	127.7	71.2	**149.9**	125.5
Mean Filter size	3.2	3.0	**3.3**	2.7	2.9
No. Neurons/FC	154.1	97.4	**429.6**	112.9	302.1
Freq Max pool	1.4	**1.5**	1.3	0.9	0.8
Freq Avg pool	1.6	1.5	**1.9**	1.4	1.2
Freq pool Off	2.6	2.1	2.8	**5.3**	5.0
Pooling kernel size	2.5	**2.6**	2.5	2.5	2.3
No. Skip Conns	2.4	1.2	4.1	**8.1**	5.6

Table 22. Mean values of network characteristics and hyperparameter configuration from the resulting architectures of applying DeepGA with EEMs using the CIFAR-100 dataset. The highest value is marked in bold as reference.

Configuration	Accuracy-10	Accuracy-5	Logsynflow	Linear Regions	LogSF + LR
No. Conv	5.3	4.8	**8.5**	7.1	6.8
No. FC	1.5	1.4	**11.7**	4	7.2
No. Filters/Conv	119.2	129.0	79.8	**168.8**	138.7
Mean Filter size	2.8	3.0	**3.1**	2.5	2.6
No. Neurons/FC	317.9	337.1	**403.5**	57.9	336.2
Freq Max pool	1.4	**2.4**	1.5	0.6	1.3
Freq Avg pool	**1.4**	0.4	1.0	0.9	0.9
Freq pool Off	2.5	2.0	**6.0**	5.6	4.6
Pooling kernel size	2.5	**2.6**	**2.6**	2.3	2.5
No. Skip Conns	2.9	2.2	**10.1**	5.7	4.4

Focusing on the number of filters per convolutional layer and the number of neurons in the fully connected ones, interesting patterns emerge. Linear Regions is the configuration that positions more filters on average in the convolutional layers. The behavior is consistent for the three datasets. In addition, Linear Regions positions a small number of neurons in the fully connected layers, as evident in the descriptions of the architectures for the CIFAR-100 dataset. On the other hand, Logsynflow consistently places more neurons in the fully connected layers and fewer filters in the convolutional layers. The combination of the proxies results in a middle point for both values.

5. Discussion

Early stopping, population memory, and training-free proxies are used in this paper as EEMs for NAS. Each of the mechanisms accelerated the search process of DeepGA in designing CNNs for image classification. First, as proposed in [29], 5 and 10 training epochs are used for the accuracy-based search process. The results showed that performing the search with only 5 epochs provides competitive results compared to the 10-epoch configuration. Consequently, time reductions of 45.99%, 64.47%, and 53.15% are achieved for Fashion MNIST, CIFAR-100, and CIFAR-10, respectively. Nonetheless, the resulting architecture is more complex with Accuracy-5.

Using the z-score normalization with a sigmoid function for scaling the training-free proxies resulted in a more consistent behavior than max normalization. The approach mentioned above enables the incorporation of training-free proxies into fitness functions that combine more than one proxy, as well as considering other design criteria, such as complexity limitations in DeepGA. The results showed that the training-free methods were partially competitive compared to the accuracy-guided search. The training-free methods were competitive with the Fashion MNIST data. In addition, no significant differences were detected in particular comparison cases, like Accuracy-5 and Logsynflow in CIFAR-100, or Linear Regions and Accuracy-10 in CIFAR-10. Nonetheless, in both datasets, an accuracy-based configuration outperformed all training-free configurations. It was observed that as the difficulty of the dataset increases, the proxies struggle to remain competitive.

No training-free configuration outperformed the others: using a combination of proxies does not yield better performance than using one of them independently. Nevertheless, it was observed that the resulting architectures from the combination of proxies presented trade-offs for particular network characteristics, such as the number of filters and number of neurons per convolutional and fully connected layers, respectively. The key point for using training-free proxies as EEMs is the expected high time reduction, which is confirmed in the results with a computational time reduction of above 99%. The comparison of the characteristics from the resulting architectures showed that the training-free configurations found deeper networks with considerably more fully connected layers and used more skip connections. Those network characteristics imply that training-free configurations tend to find more complex architectures than accuracy-based ones. Notably, the configurations that considered the Linear Regions proxy resulted in considerably more FLOPS than the other configurations, thereby increasing the time required for the final evaluation.

Lastly, the population memory mechanism enabled DeepGA to avoid more than 40% of the evaluations in the accuracy-based configurations and at least 20% of them in the training-free configurations. The percentage of avoided evaluations indicates the number of repeated architectures that the algorithm explores. It provides insights into the work of the selected variation operators of an EC algorithm and its parameter configuration.

6. Conclusions

This paper evaluates various EEMs in DeepGA, following an ENAS process that considers both accuracy-guided and training-free configurations. Early stopping resulted in competitive performance and considerable time reduction, highlighting the importance of selecting the number of training epochs in efficient NAS. The training-free option presented an extreme cost reduction but was only partially competitive in performance. Finally, population memory avoided repeated evaluations, resulting in further cost savings. Nonetheless, the findings are limited to three datasets, ten runs, and the consideration of only two different training-free proxies.

Future work is stated to extend the experimentation to other datasets and consider additional training-free search configurations and proxies. The focus is on improving the performance of the training-free NAS algorithm, particularly in cases where network complexity is limited. The use of a multi-objective configuration is also a proposed research direction. ENAS procedures can take advantage of the low cost of training-free proxies in the algorithm, utilizing a hybrid search process similar to surrogate models, where the expensive evaluation has limited use, while the low-cost evaluation is employed for exploration. Another possibility is considering the rich initialization of the algorithm's population using training-free proxies to identify promising areas of the search space. Additionally, the lightweight proxies can be tested as a mechanism for parameter tuning in ENAS algorithms, where experimentation involves testing a series of parameter combinations.

Author Contributions: Conceptualization, J.-A.B.-P., C.-A.L.-H., E.M.-M., H.-G.A.-M. and A.-L.L.-L.; methodology, J.-A.B.-P., C.-A.L.-H. and E.M.-M.; software, J.-A.B.-P. and C.-A.L.-H.; validation, E.M.-M., H.-G.A.-M. and A.-L.L.-L.; formal analysis, J.-A.B.-P., E.M.-M. and H.-G.A.-M.; investigation, J.-A.B.-P.; resources, E.M.-M. and H.-G.A.-M.; writing—original draft preparation, J.-A.B.-P. and C.-A.L.-H.; writing—review and editing, E.M.-M., H.-G.A.-M. and A.-L.L.-L.; visualization, J.-A.B.-P., C.-A.L.-H. and A.-L.L.-L.; supervision, J.-A.B.-P., C.-A.L.-H., E.M.-M., H.-G.A.-M. and A.-L.L.-L.; project administration, J.-A.B.-P. and E.M.-M. All authors have read and agreed to the published version of the manuscript.

Funding: This research received no external funding

Data Availability Statement: The CIFAR-10 and CIFAR-100 datasets [36] used for experimenation are publicly available at https://www.cs.toronto.edu/~kriz/cifar.html (accessed on 15 April 2025). The fashion MNIST [35] is available at https://github.com/zalandoresearch/fashion-mnist (accessed on 15 April 2025).

Acknowledgments: The first (CVU 1142850) and second (CVU 1075919) authors acknowledge support from the Mexican Ministry of Science, Humanities, Technology and Innovation (SECIHTI for Secretaría de Ciencia, Humanidades, Tecnología e Innovación) in the form of a scholarship to pursue graduate studies at the Universidad Veracruzana.

Conflicts of Interest: The authors declare no conflicts of interest.

Abbreviations

The following abbreviations are used in this manuscript:

CNNs	Convolutional Neural Networks
DL	Deep Learning
DNNs	Deep Neural Networks
GPUs	Graphics Processing Units
NAS	Neural Architecture Search
EC	Evolutionary Computation
ENAS	Evolutionary Neural Architecture Search
EEM	Eficient Evaluation Method

GA	Genetic Algorithm
DeepGA	Deep Genetic Algorithm
ReLU	Rectified linear unit

References

1. Taye, M.M. Theoretical Understanding of Convolutional Neural Network: Concepts, Architectures, Applications, Future Directions. *Computation* **2023**, *11*, 52. [CrossRef]
2. Li, Z.; Liu, F.; Yang, W.; Peng, S.; Zhou, J. A Survey of Convolutional Neural Networks: Analysis, Applications, and Prospects. *IEEE Trans. Neural Netw. Learn. Syst.* **2022**, *33*, 6999–7019. [CrossRef] [PubMed]
3. Zhao, X.; Wang, L.; Zhang, Y.; Han, X.; Deveci, M.; Parmar, M. A review of convolutional neural networks in computer vision. *Artif. Intell. Rev.* **2024**, *57*, 99. [CrossRef]
4. Li, N.; Ma, L.; Xing, T.; Yu, G.; Wang, C.; Wen, Y.; Cheng, S.; Gao, S. Automatic design of machine learning via evolutionary computation: A survey. *Appl. Soft Comput.* **2023**, *143*, 110412. [CrossRef]
5. Telikani, A.; Tahmassebi, A.; Banzhaf, W.; Gandomi, A.H. Evolutionary Machine Learning: A Survey. *ACM Comput. Surv.* **2021**, *54*, 161. [CrossRef]
6. Li, N.; Ma, L.; Yu, G.; Xue, B.; Zhang, M.; Jin, Y. Survey on Evolutionary Deep Learning: Principles, Algorithms, Applications, and Open Issues. *ACM Comput. Surv.* **2023**, *56*, 41. [CrossRef]
7. Liu, Y.; Sun, Y.; Xue, B.; Zhang, M.; Yen, G.G.; Tan, K.C. A Survey on Evolutionary Neural Architecture Search. *IEEE Trans. Neural Netw. Learn. Syst.* **2023**, *34*, 550–570. [CrossRef] [PubMed]
8. Ren, P.; Xiao, Y.; Chang, X.; Huang, P.y.; Li, Z.; Chen, X.; Wang, X. A Comprehensive Survey of Neural Architecture Search: Challenges and Solutions. *ACM Comput. Surv.* **2021**, *54*, 76. [CrossRef]
9. Mishra, V.; Kane, L. A survey of designing convolutional neural network using evolutionary algorithms. *Artif. Intell. Rev.* **2023**, *56*, 5095–5132. [CrossRef]
10. Ünal, H.T.; Başçiftçi, F. Evolutionary design of neural network architectures: A review of three decades of research. *Artif. Intell. Rev.* **2022**, *55*, 1723–1802. [CrossRef]
11. Poyser, M.; Breckon, T.P. Neural architecture search: A contemporary literature review for computer vision applications. *Pattern Recognit.* **2024**, *147*, 110052. [CrossRef]
12. Song, X.; Xie, X.; Lv, Z.; Yen, G.G.; Ding, W.; Lv, J.; Sun, Y. Efficient Evaluation Methods for Neural Architecture Search: A Survey. *IEEE Trans. Artif. Intell.* **2024**, *5*, 5990–6011. [CrossRef]
13. Yang, S.; Tian, Y.; Xiang, X.; Peng, S.; Zhang, X. Accelerating Evolutionary Neural Architecture Search via Multifidelity Evaluation. *IEEE Trans. Cogn. Dev. Syst.* **2022**, *14*, 1778–1792. [CrossRef]
14. Sun, Y.; Xue, B.; Zhang, M.; Yen, G.G. Evolving Deep Convolutional Neural Networks for Image Classification. *IEEE Trans. Evol. Comput.* **2020**, *24*, 394–407. [CrossRef]
15. Liang, J.; Lou, Y.; Yu, M.; Bi, Y.; Yu, K. A survey of surrogate-assisted evolutionary algorithms for expensive optimization. *J. Membr. Comput.* **2024**, *7*, 108–127. [CrossRef]
16. Sun, Y.; Xue, B.; Zhang, M.; Yen, G.G.; Lv, J. Automatically Designing CNN Architectures Using the Genetic Algorithm for Image Classification. *IEEE Trans. Cybern.* **2020**, *50*, 3840–3854. [CrossRef] [PubMed]
17. Wu, M.T.; Tsai, C.W. Training-free neural architecture search: A review. *ICT Express* **2024**, *10*, 213–231. [CrossRef]
18. Li, G.; Hoang, D.; Bhardwaj, K.; Lin, M.; Wang, Z.; Marculescu, R. Zero-Shot Neural Architecture Search: Challenges, Solutions, and Opportunities. *IEEE Trans. Pattern Anal. Mach. Intell.* **2024**, *46*, 7618–7635. [CrossRef] [PubMed]
19. Cavagnero, N.; Robbiano, L.; Caputo, B.; Averta, G. FreeREA: Training-Free Evolution-based Architecture Search. In Proceedings of the 2023 IEEE/CVF Winter Conference on Applications of Computer Vision (WACV), Waikoloa, HI, USA, 2–7 January 2023; pp. 1493–1502. [CrossRef]
20. Mellor, J.; Turner, J.; Storkey, A.; Crowley, E.J. Neural Architecture Search without Training. In Proceedings of the 38th International Conference on Machine Learning, Virtual, 18–24 July 2021; Volume 139, pp. 7588–7598.
21. Wu, M.T.; Lin, H.I.; Tsai, C.W. A Training-Free Neural Architecture Search Algorithm Based on Search Economics. *IEEE Trans. Evol. Comput.* **2024**, *28*, 445–459. [CrossRef]
22. Wu, M.T.; Lin, H.I.; Tsai, C.W. A Training-free Genetic Neural Architecture Search. In Proceedings of the 2021 ACM International Conference on Intelligent Computing and Its Emerging Applications, Jinan, China, 28–29 December 2021; pp. 65–70. [CrossRef]
23. Hsieh, C.H.; Tsai, C.W. Rank-based Training-Free NAS Algorithm. In Proceedings of the 2023 International Conference on Intelligent Computing and Its Emerging Applications, Kaohsiung, Taiwan, 14–16 December 2023; pp. 30–35. [CrossRef]
24. Vo, A.; Pham, T.N.; Nguyen, V.B.; Luong, N.H. Training-Free Multi-Objective and Many-Objective Evolutionary Neural Architecture Search with Synaptic Flow. In Proceedings of the 11th International Symposium on Information and Communication Technology, Hanoi, Vietnam, 1–3 December 2022; pp. 1–8. [CrossRef]

25. Luong, N.H.; Phan, Q.M.; Vo, A.; Pham, T.N.; Bui, D.T. Lightweight multi-objective evolutionary neural architecture search with low-cost proxy metrics. *Inf. Sci.* **2024**, *655*, 119856. [CrossRef]
26. Ying, C.; Klein, A.; Christiansen, E.; Real, E.; Murphy, K.; Hutter, F. NAS-Bench-101: Towards Reproducible Neural Architecture Search. In Proceedings of the 36th International Conference on Machine Learning, Long Beach, CA, USA, 9–15 June 2019; Volume 97, pp. 7105–7114.
27. Thanh, T.H.; Doan, L.; Luong, N.H.; Huynh Thi Thanh, B. THNAS-GA: A Genetic Algorithm for Training-free Hardware-aware Neural Architecture Search. In Proceedings of the Genetic and Evolutionary Computation Conference, Melbourne, Australia, 14–18 July 2024; pp. 1128–1136. [CrossRef]
28. Lin, J.C.; Tsai, C.W. A Lightweight Training-Free Method for Neural Architecture Search. In Proceedings of the 2024 IEEE Congress on Evolutionary Computation (CEC), Yokohama, Japan, 30 June–5 July 2024; pp. 1–8. [CrossRef]
29. Barradas-Palmeros, J.A.; López-Herrera, C.A.; Acosta-Mesa, H.G.; Mezura-Montes, E. Efficient Neural Architecture Search: Computational Cost Reduction Mechanisms in DeepGA. In Advances in Computational Intelligence. Proceedings of the MICAI 2024 International Workshops, Tonantzintla, Mexico, 21–25 October 2024; Martínez-Villaseñor, L., Ochoa-Ruiz, G., Montes Rivera, M., Barrón-Estrada, M.L., Acosta-Mesa, H.G., Eds.; Springer: Cham, Switzerland, 2025; pp. 125–134. [CrossRef]
30. Vargas-Hákim, G.A.; Mezura-Montes, E.; Acosta-Mesa, H.G. Hybrid encodings for neuroevolution of convolutional neural networks: A case study. In Proceedings of the Genetic and Evolutionary Computation Conference Companion, Lille, France, 10–14 July 2021; pp. 1762–1770. [CrossRef]
31. Llaguno-Roque, J.L.; Barrientos-Martínez, R.E.; Acosta-Mesa, H.G.; Romo-González, T.; Mezura-Montes, E. Neuroevolution of Convolutional Neural Networks for Breast Cancer Diagnosis Using Western Blot Strips. *Math. Comput. Appl.* **2023**, *28*, 72. [CrossRef]
32. Vázquez-Santiago, D.I.; Acosta-Mesa, H.G.; Mezura-Montes, E. Vehicle Make and Model Recognition as an Open-Set Recognition Problem and New Class Discovery. *Math. Comput. Appl.* **2023**, *28*, 80. [CrossRef]
33. Morales-Reyes, J.L.; Aquino-Bolaños, E.N.; Acosta-Mesa, H.G.; Márquez-Grajales, A. Estimation of Anthocyanins in Heterogeneous and Homogeneous Bean Landraces Using Probabilistic Colorimetric Representation with a Neuroevolutionary Approach. *Math. Comput. Appl.* **2024**, *29*, 68. [CrossRef]
34. Velazco-Muñoz, J.D.; Acosta-Mesa, H.G.; Mezura-Montes, E. Reducing Parameters by Neuroevolution in CNN for Steering Angle Estimation. In *Pattern Recognition, Proceedings of the MCPR 2024, Xalapa, Mexico, 19–22 June 2024*; Mezura-Montes, E., Acosta-Mesa, H.G., Carrasco-Ochoa, J.A., Martínez-Trinidad, J.F., Olvera-López, J.A., Eds.; Springer: Cham, Switzerland, 2024; pp. 377–386.
35. Xiao, H.; Rasul, K.; Vollgraf, R. Fashion-MNIST: A Novel Image Dataset for Benchmarking Machine Learning Algorithms. *arXiv* **2017**, arXiv:1708.07747v2. [CrossRef]
36. Krizhevsky, A. *Learning Multiple Layers of Features from Tiny Images*; Technical Report; Computer Science Department, University of Toronto: Toronto, ON, Canada, 2009.
37. Bolón-Canedo, V.; Morán-Fernández, L.; Cancela, B.; Alonso-Betanzos, A. A review of green artificial intelligence: Towards a more sustainable future. *Neurocomputing* **2024**, *599*, 128096. [CrossRef]
38. Vargas-Hákim, G.A.; Mezura-Montes, E.; Acosta-Mesa, H.G. A Review on Convolutional Neural Network Encodings for Neuroevolution. *IEEE Trans. Evol. Comput.* **2022**, *26*, 12–27. [CrossRef]
39. Deb, K.; Pratap, A.; Agarwal, S.; Meyarivan, T. A fast and elitist multiobjective genetic algorithm: NSGA-II. *IEEE Trans. Evol. Comput.* **2002**, *6*, 182–197. [CrossRef]
40. Tanaka, H.; Kunin, D.; Yamins, D.L.; Ganguli, S. Pruning neural networks without any data by iteratively conserving synaptic flow. In Proceedings of the Advances in Neural Information Processing Systems, Virtual, 6–12 December 2020; Volume 33, pp. 6377–6389.
41. Paszke, A.; Gross, S.; Massa, F.; Lerer, A.; Bradbury, J.; Chanan, G.; Killeen, T.; Lin, Z.; Gimelshein, N.; Antiga, L.; et al. PyTorch: An imperative style, high-performance deep learning library. In Proceedings of the 33rd International Conference on Neural Information Processing Systems, Vancouver, BC, Canada, 8–14 December 2019.

Mathematical and Computational Applications

MDPI

Article

Application of the Kurganov–Tadmor Scheme in Curvilinear Coordinates for Supersonic Flow

Sebastián Bertolo [1], Sergio Elaskar [1,2,*] and Luis Gutiérrez Marcantoni [1]

[1] Department of Aerospace Engineering, Faculty of Exact, Physical and Natural Sciences, National University of Cordoba, Córdoba 5000, Argentina; sebastian.bertolo@mi.unc.edu.ar (S.B.); lfgmarcantoni@unc.edu.ar (L.G.M.)

[2] Institute of Advanced Studies in Engineering and Technology (IDIT), CONICET and National University of Cordoba, Córdoba 5000, Argentina

* Correspondence: selaskar@unc.edu.ar

Abstract

In this current study, we developed a second-order Kurganov–Tadmor scheme in curvilinear coordinates to analyze the external supersonic flow over bodies of various shapes. This scheme is capable of handling interfaces across different regions of the domain. We utilized a fourth-order Runge–Kutta temporal integrator and conducted several test cases to validate the performance of the new scheme. The results from the analyzed tests indicate that the new method produces highly accurate outcomes.

Keywords: Kurganov–Tadmor scheme; curvilinear coordinates; CFD; supersonic flow

1. Introduction

Supersonic flow plays a critical role in aerospace engineering, with applications in both internal and external aerodynamics. The determination of high-velocity flow properties around bodies has been the focus of extensive theoretical, numerical, and experimental studies [1–6].

Computational Fluid Dynamics (CFD) simulations are increasingly employed to analyze supersonic flows [6–11]. The selection of the numerical method is pivotal in these simulations. One widely used scheme is the one developed by Kurganov and Tadmor, which is extensively cited in the scientific literature [12–18]. This central scheme is independent of the problem's eigenstructure and utilizes precise information on local propagation velocities. It also represents the non-smooth part of the solution in terms of its cell averages integrated over Riemann fans of different sizes. Also, in Ref. [12], the authors have demonstrated that the scalar version of the Kurganov–Tadmor high-resolution central scheme is non-oscillatory. It satisfies the total-variation diminishing property in the one-dimensional case and the maximum principle in two-dimensional domains.

The Kurganov and Tadmor method has demonstrated robustness and effectiveness in simulating systems of hyperbolic equations [12]. By applying this method in curvilinear coordinates, it is possible to adapt more effectively to complex geometries that are often encountered in external flow problems [14]. Furthermore, the use of meshes with varying topologies provides flexibility in discretizing the study domain, which is crucial for accurately capturing the flow details in specific regions of interest.

The original development of the Kurganov–Tadmor scheme was for a Cartesian coordinate system [12]. Consequently, studies involving bodies of arbitrary geometry often utilized meshes with non-orthogonal element distributions. This study investigates the implementation of the Kurganov and Tadmor method in curvilinear coordinates for simulating external supersonic flows. A new methodology is introduced to enable the use of meshes with different topologies, thereby facilitating the optimal treatment of the interfaces between them. The validity of this methodology is confirmed through solutions of the well-established Euler equations [2], employing a fourth-order Runge–Kutta temporal integrator [19]. We introduce a second-order central scheme designed for systems of hyperbolic conservation laws on curvilinear grids, which builds upon previous work by [14]. At the core of our methodology is the ability to partition the domain into multiple subdomains and a novel approach for handling the interfaces between these subdomains. Additionally, the new method shows second-order accuracy, delivering more precise results compared to the traditional Kurganov–Tadmor–Petrova (KNP) scheme. This advancement not only improves precision but also enhances the reliability of outcomes.

The Euler equations are a set of nonlinear hyperbolic differential equations that delineate the flow of compressible gas without accounting for mass forces, viscosity, and heat transfer by radiation and conduction [2,20,21]. Although this work particularly focuses on solving these equation systems, the scheme presented here can be extended to other types of governing equations formulated in curvilinear coordinates, such as the Burger equation [9].

This work is divided into four sections, starting with the introduction. Section 2 elaborates on the numerical method used, its application, treatment of region interfaces, and the time step condition. Section 3 details the cases to be analyzed, including a cylinder, a wedge, and a blunt body, along with the obtained results. Finally, Section 4 presents the conclusions drawn from this work.

2. Numerical Method

In this section, we present the numerical scheme developed in this study. First, we outline the fundamental equations: the two-dimensional Euler equations in curvilinear coordinates. Next, we introduce the Kurganov–Tadmor scheme. The following subsection presents the temporal scheme used to solve the equation system over time, and finally, we describe the interface treatment.

2.1. Fundamental Equations

In our analysis of non-viscous supersonic flow, we will be focusing on the two-dimensional Euler equations due to their widespread use.

The Euler equations are derived from the Navier–Stokes equations [22] by neglecting diffusive effects. They are used to describe the flow of fluid in which thermal conductivity and viscosity are not significant. These fluids are referred to as ideal fluids [20]. While we refer the reader to fluid mechanics books for their development and properties in Cartesian coordinates, we also recommend consulting references [9,20].

For our current work, we are exploring the presentation of these equations concerning an arbitrary curvilinear coordinate system. This involves utilizing a general coordinate transformation

$$x = x(\xi, \eta) \qquad y = y(\xi, \eta). \tag{1}$$

The two-dimensional unsteady Euler equations in curvilinear coordinates can be written as [23]

$$\frac{\partial \rho}{\partial t}+\frac{1}{h_\xi h_\eta}\frac{\partial}{\partial \xi}[h_\eta(\rho u_\xi)]+\frac{1}{h_\xi h_\eta}\frac{\partial}{\partial \eta}[h_\xi(\rho u_\eta)]=0 \tag{2a}$$

$$\frac{\partial(\rho u_\xi)}{\partial t}+\frac{1}{h_\xi h_\eta}\frac{\partial}{\partial \xi}\left[h_\eta\left(\rho u_\xi^2+p\right)\right]+\frac{1}{h_\xi h_\eta}\frac{\partial}{\partial \eta}[h_\xi(\rho u_\eta u_\xi)]=\frac{1}{h_\xi h_\eta}\frac{\partial h_\eta}{\partial \xi}\left(\rho u_\eta^2+p\right)-\frac{\rho u_\xi u_\eta}{h_\xi h_\eta}\frac{\partial h_\xi}{\partial \eta} \tag{2b}$$

$$\frac{\partial(\rho u_\eta)}{\partial t}+\frac{1}{h_\xi h_\eta}\frac{\partial}{\partial \xi}[h_\eta(\rho u_\xi u_\eta)]+\frac{1}{h_\xi h_\eta}\frac{\partial}{\partial \eta}\left[h_\xi\left(\rho u_\eta^2+p\right)\right]=\frac{1}{h_\xi h_\eta}\frac{\partial h_\xi}{\partial \xi}\left(\rho u_\xi^2+p\right)-\frac{\rho u_\xi u_\eta}{h_\xi h_\eta}\frac{\partial h_\eta}{\partial \xi} \tag{2c}$$

$$\frac{\partial(E)}{\partial t}+\frac{1}{h_\xi h_\eta}\frac{\partial}{\partial \xi}[h_\eta u_\xi(E+p)]+\frac{1}{h_\xi h_\eta}\frac{\partial}{\partial \eta}[h_\xi u_\eta(E+p)]=0. \tag{2d}$$

where h_ξ and h_η are the transformation scale factors, which are defined according to the coordinate systems. Also, ρ is the density, p the pressure, E the energy, and (u_ξ, u_η) the velocity vector.

The used state equation is that of a perfect gas

$$\rho = p R T, \tag{3}$$

where R is the gas constant, and T the temperature. Therefore, the energy can be defined as

$$E=\frac{1}{2}\rho\left(u_\xi^2+u_\eta^2\right)+\frac{p}{\gamma-1}. \tag{4}$$

The previous set of equations in matrix form results in

$$\frac{\partial U}{\partial t}+\frac{1}{h_\xi h_\eta}\frac{\partial}{\partial \xi}h_\eta F(U)+\frac{1}{h_\xi h_\eta}\frac{\partial}{\partial \xi}h_\xi G(U)=S(U), \tag{5}$$

where $U=(\rho, \rho u_\xi, \rho u_\eta, E)^T$ is the vector of conservative variables. $F(U)$ and $G(U)$ are the flow vectors, and $S(U)$ is the source term.

The system given by Equation (5) is conservative, allowing the application of the numerical method introduced here.

2.2. Kurganov–Tadmor Scheme

The numerical scheme here employed to solve the system of equations described in the previous subsection is the one developed by Kurganov and Tadmor. This scheme was described in Ref. [12].

Every numerical method involves discretizing the continuous governing equations to calculate variables at specific discrete points within the domain, known as nodes. To accomplish this, the domain is divided into small control volumes or cells. In the case of this two-dimensional scheme, surfaces are utilized, and nodes are positioned at their centers. The node within each cell represents the average value of the variable over the entire cell

$$\overline{U}(\xi,\eta,t)=\frac{1}{V_{\xi,\eta}}\int\int_{V_{\xi,\eta}}U(\xi,\eta,t)h_\xi h_\eta d\xi d\eta, \tag{6}$$

where the $V_{\xi.\eta}$ corresponds to the surface of each cell. The evaluation of this surface will be explained in the next paragraphs. Therefore, Equation (5) is integrated in a domain $V_{\xi,\eta}$ x$[t, t+\Delta t]$

$$\overline{U}(\xi,\eta,t+\Delta t)=\overline{U}(\xi,\eta,t)+\int_t^{t+\Delta t}\left[\overline{\frac{1}{h_\xi h_\eta}\frac{\partial}{\partial \xi}h_\eta F(U)}+\overline{\frac{1}{h_\xi h_\eta}\frac{\partial}{\partial \eta}h_\xi G(U)}-\overline{S(U)}\right]dt. \tag{7}$$

To evaluate the integral equation, each cell is subdivided into smaller regions based on the impact of the Riemann problem on each interface. To determine the value of the variable at the interface, a Riemann problem is solved, which indicates that within a time interval Δt, the waves will influence specific portions of the cell. This scheme is illustrated in Figure 1 for a two-dimensional domain. It is important to note that regions near the edges receive influence from neighboring cells [13].

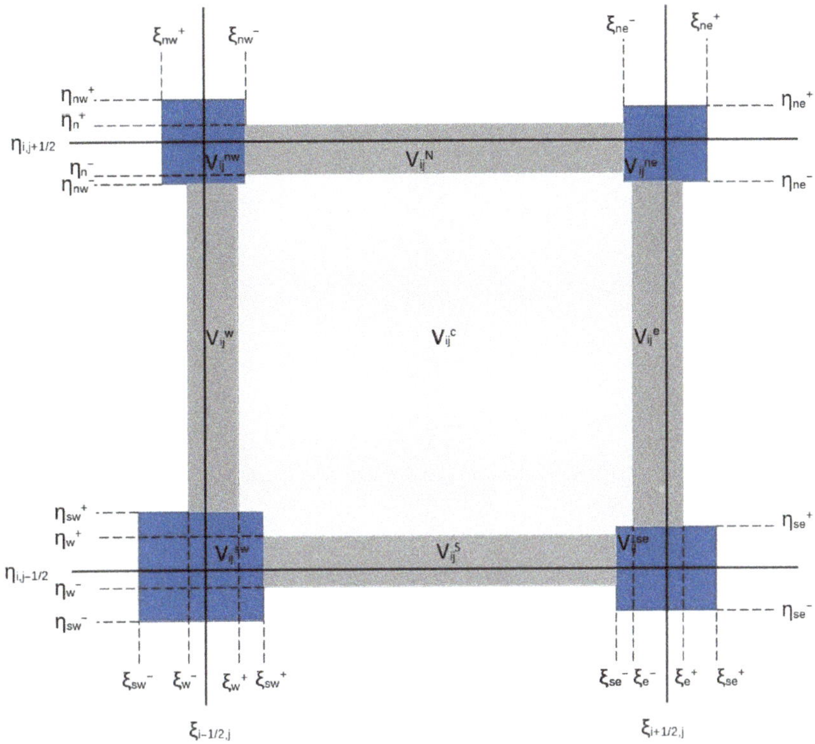

Figure 1. Cell's sub-division.

We assume that the variables have a linear distribution within each cell. Therefore, their value can be calculated as

$$\widetilde{U}_{i,j}^{n}(\xi,\eta) = \overline{U}_{i,j}^{n} + \left(u'_{\xi}\right)_{i,j}^{n}(\xi - \xi_{i,j}) + \left(u'_{\eta}\right)_{i,j}^{n}(\eta - \eta_{i,j}). \tag{8}$$

In this equation, u'_{ξ} and u'_{η} are the velocity derivatives in each direction; the calculation of these derivatives will be detailed later.

The coordinates that define each subdomain are obtained according to

$$\begin{aligned} \xi_e^{\pm} &= \xi_{i+\frac{1}{2},j} + \frac{a^{\pm}_{i+\frac{1}{2},j}\Delta t}{h_{\xi}(\xi_{i+\frac{1}{2}},\eta_j)} & \qquad \xi_w^{\pm} &= \xi_{i-\frac{1}{2},j} + \frac{a^{\pm}_{i-\frac{1}{2},j}\Delta t}{h_{\xi}(\xi_{i-\frac{1}{2}},\eta_j)} \\ \eta_n^{\pm} &= \eta_{i,j+\frac{1}{2}} + \frac{b^{\pm}_{i,j+\frac{1}{2}}\Delta t}{h_{\eta}(\xi_i,\eta_{j+\frac{1}{2}})} & \qquad \eta_s^{\pm} &= \eta_{i,j-\frac{1}{2}} + \frac{b^{\pm}_{i,j-\frac{1}{2}}\Delta t}{h_{\eta}(\xi_i,\eta_{j-\frac{1}{2}})}. \end{aligned} \tag{9}$$

where a and b are the local velocities at the interfaces; in practice, they can be determined as

$$
\begin{aligned}
a^{+}_{i+\frac{1}{2},j} &= max\left\{\lambda_{max}\left(\frac{\partial F}{\partial U}\left(U^{+}_{i+\frac{1}{2},j}\right)\right),\lambda_{max}\left(\frac{\partial F}{\partial U}\left(U^{-}_{i+\frac{1}{2},j}\right)\right)\right\}\\
a^{-}_{i+\frac{1}{2},j} &= min\left\{\lambda_{min}\left(\frac{\partial F}{\partial U}\left(U^{+}_{i+\frac{1}{2},j}\right)\right),\lambda_{min}\left(\frac{\partial F}{\partial U}\left(U^{-}_{i+\frac{1}{2},j}\right)\right)\right\}\\
b^{+}_{i,j+\frac{1}{2}} &= max\left\{\lambda_{max}\left(\frac{\partial G}{\partial U}\left(U^{+}_{i,j+\frac{1}{2}}\right)\right),\lambda_{max}\left(\frac{\partial G}{\partial U}\left(U^{-}_{i,j+\frac{1}{2}}\right)\right)\right\}\\
b^{-}_{i,j+\frac{1}{2}} &= min\left\{\lambda_{min}\left(\frac{\partial G}{\partial U}\left(U^{+}_{i,j+\frac{1}{2}}\right)\right),\lambda_{min}\left(\frac{\partial G}{\partial U}\left(U^{-}_{i,j+\frac{1}{2}}\right)\right)\right\}.
\end{aligned}
\tag{10}
$$

For the edges, there is the influence of waves coming from neighboring interfaces. Therefore, the velocities can be calculated as

$$
\begin{aligned}
A^{+}_{i\pm\frac{1}{2},j+\frac{1}{2}} &= max\left\{a^{+}_{i\pm\frac{1}{2},j},a^{+}_{i\pm\frac{1}{2},j+1}\right\} & A^{-}_{i\pm\frac{1}{2},j+\frac{1}{2}} &= min\left\{a^{-}_{i\pm\frac{1}{2},j},a^{-}_{i\pm\frac{1}{2},j+1}\right\}\\
A^{+}_{i\pm\frac{1}{2},j-\frac{1}{2}} &= max\left\{a^{+}_{i\pm\frac{1}{2},j},a^{+}_{i\pm\frac{1}{2},j-1}\right\} & A^{-}_{i\pm\frac{1}{2},j-\frac{1}{2}} &= min\left\{a^{-}_{i\pm\frac{1}{2},j},a^{-}_{i\pm\frac{1}{2},j-1}\right\}\\
B^{+}_{i+\frac{1}{2},j\pm\frac{1}{2}} &= max\left\{b^{+}_{i,j\pm\frac{1}{2}},b^{+}_{i+1,j\pm\frac{1}{2}}\right\} & B^{-}_{i+\frac{1}{2},j\pm\frac{1}{2}} &= min\left\{b^{-}_{i,j\pm\frac{1}{2}},b^{-}_{i+1,j\pm\frac{1}{2}}\right\}\\
B^{+}_{i-\frac{1}{2},j\pm\frac{1}{2}} &= max\left\{b^{+}_{i,j\pm\frac{1}{2}},b^{+}_{i-1,j\pm\frac{1}{2}}\right\} & B^{-}_{i-\frac{1}{2},j\pm\frac{1}{2}} &= min\left\{b^{-}_{i,j\pm\frac{1}{2}},b^{-}_{i-1,j\pm\frac{1}{2}}.\right\}
\end{aligned}
\tag{11}
$$

Once these velocities are known, the coordinates are (see Figure 1)

$$
\begin{aligned}
\xi^{\pm}_{se} &= \xi_{i+\frac{1}{2}} + \frac{A^{\pm}_{i+\frac{1}{2},j-\frac{1}{2}}\Delta t}{h_\xi(\xi_{i+\frac{1}{2}},\eta_{j-\frac{1}{2}})} & \xi^{\pm}_{sw} &= \xi_{i-\frac{1}{2}} + \frac{A^{\pm}_{i-\frac{1}{2},j-\frac{1}{2}}\Delta t}{h_\xi(\xi_{i-\frac{1}{2}},\eta_{j-\frac{1}{2}})}\\
\xi^{\pm}_{ne} &= \xi_{i+\frac{1}{2}} + \frac{A^{\pm}_{i+\frac{1}{2},j+\frac{1}{2}}\Delta t}{h_\xi(\xi_{i+\frac{1}{2}},\eta_{j+\frac{1}{2}})} & \xi^{\pm}_{nw} &= \xi_{i-\frac{1}{2}} + \frac{A^{\pm}_{i+\frac{1}{2},j-\frac{1}{2}}\Delta t}{h_\xi(\xi_{i-\frac{1}{2}},\eta_{j+\frac{1}{2}})}\\
\eta^{\pm}_{sw} &= \eta_{j-\frac{1}{2}} + \frac{B^{\pm}_{i-\frac{1}{2},j-\frac{1}{2}}\Delta t}{h_\eta(\xi_{i-\frac{1}{2}},\eta_{j-\frac{1}{2}})} & \eta^{\pm}_{se} &= \eta_{j-\frac{1}{2}} + \frac{B^{\pm}_{i+\frac{1}{2},j-\frac{1}{2}}\Delta t}{h_\eta(\xi_{i+\frac{1}{2}},\eta_{j-\frac{1}{2}})}\\
\eta^{\pm}_{nw} &= \eta_{j+\frac{1}{2}} + \frac{B^{\pm}_{i-\frac{1}{2},j+\frac{1}{2}}\Delta t}{h_\eta(\xi_{i-\frac{1}{2}},\eta_{j+\frac{1}{2}})} & \eta^{\pm}_{ne} &= \eta_{j+\frac{1}{2}} + \frac{B^{\pm}_{i+\frac{1}{2},j+\frac{1}{2}}\Delta t}{h_\eta(\xi_{i+\frac{1}{2}},\eta_{j+\frac{1}{2}})}.
\end{aligned}
\tag{12}
$$

The solution method consists of obtaining in the first stage the average value of the variable in each sub-cell of Figure 1 for the time $t+\Delta t$; subsequently, the average of them is evaluated in the cell to find $\overline{U}_{\xi,\eta,t+\Delta t}$. That is, in the first stage, the average value of the variable in each sub-region is calculated as

$$
\overline{w}^{t+\Delta t}_{D} = \frac{\int\int_{V_D} U(\xi,\eta,t)h_\xi h_\eta d\xi d\eta}{V_D} + \int_t^{t+\Delta t}\left[\overline{\frac{1}{h_\xi h_\eta}\frac{\partial}{\partial\xi}h_\eta F(U)} + \overline{\frac{1}{h_\xi h_\eta}\frac{\partial}{\partial\eta}h_\xi G(U)} - \overline{S(U)}\right]dt \tag{13}
$$

$$D \in sw,\ se,\ s,\ ne,\ nw,\ n,\ e,\ w,\ c$$

where the zones $sw, se, s, ne, nw, n, e, w, c$ are shown in Figure 1, and V_D are the surfaces of each sub-cell.

Note that $\overline{U}$ represents the average U for the entire cell, while $\overline{w}$ indicates the average U for each sub-cell.

A linear variation of the vector w is proposed in each sub-cell

$$\begin{aligned}\widetilde{w}_{\xi,\eta,t^{n+1}} = \sum_i \sum_j \Bigg\{ & \left[\overline{w}^{n+1}_{i+\frac{1}{2},j} + (u'_\xi)^{n+1}_{i+\frac{1}{2},j}(\xi - \xi_{i+\frac{1}{2}}) + (u'_\eta)^{n+1}_{i+\frac{1}{2},j}(\eta - \eta_j) \right]_{[\xi_e^-,\xi_e^+]x[\eta_{se}^+,\eta_{ne}^-]} \\ & + \left[\overline{w}^{n+1}_{i,j+\frac{1}{2}} + (u'_\xi)^{n+1}_{i,j+\frac{1}{2}}(\xi - \xi_i) + (u'_\eta)^{n+1}_{i,j+\frac{1}{2}}(\eta - \eta_{j+\frac{1}{2}}) \right]_{[\xi_{nw}^+,\xi_{ne}^-]x[\eta_n^-,\eta_n^+]} \\ & + \left[\overline{w}^{n+1}_{i,j} \right]_{[\xi_w^+,\xi_e^-]x[\eta_s^+,\eta_n^-]} \Bigg\},\end{aligned} \tag{14}$$

where $\widetilde{w}_{\xi,\eta,t^{n+1}} = \widetilde{w}(\xi,\eta,t+\Delta t)$, and $\overline{w}$ is given by Equation (13). Subsequently

$$\overline{U}^{t+\Delta t}_{i,j} = \frac{1}{\Delta V_{i,j}} \int_{\xi_{i-\frac{1}{2}}}^{\xi_{i+\frac{1}{2}}} \int_{\eta_{i-\frac{1}{2}}}^{\eta_{i+\frac{1}{2}}} \widetilde{w}(\xi,\eta,t+\Delta t) h_\xi h_\eta d\xi d\eta, \tag{15}$$

where $\Delta V_{i,j}$ is the surface of the cell i,j.

To solve the integrals, we use the midpoint quadrature technique, which is defined by the following expression for an arbitrary function f [24]

$$\int_a^b \int_c^d f(\xi,\eta) d\xi d\eta = f\left(\frac{c+d}{2}, \frac{a+b}{2}\right)(b-a)(d-c). \tag{16}$$

In Cartesian coordinates, the surface of an element is represented as $dV = dxdy$. In the case of curvilinear coordinates, considering the relevant relations, this surface can be expressed as $dV = h_\xi h_\eta d\xi d\eta$. Therefore, the surface of a general domain P is given by

$$V_P = \int_P dV = \int_a^b \int_c^d h_\xi(\xi,\eta) h_\eta(\xi,\eta) d\xi d\eta = h_\xi\left(\frac{c+d}{2}, \frac{a+b}{2}\right) h_\eta\left(\frac{c+d}{2}, \frac{a+b}{2}\right)(b-a)(d-c). \tag{17}$$

Then, Equation (15) can be evaluated as

$$\overline{U}^{t+\Delta t}_{i,j} = \frac{1}{V_{i,j}} \left[\sum_D V_D \overline{w}^{t+\Delta t}_D \right] \qquad D \in sw, se, s, ne, nw, n, e, w, c \tag{18}$$

It is crucial to conduct an order analysis because the terms resulting from the order of Δt^2 in the preceding expression make zero contribution as will be explained later. Let us take into account that in the case of the variable w, we have

$$\overline{w}^{t+\Delta t}_D = Of(1) + O(\Delta t) + \ldots, \quad \Delta t \ll 1. \tag{19}$$

That is, the order of $\overline{w}$ is approximately $Of(1)$; therefore, those surfaces resulting from order Δt^2 or higher will not contribute to Equation (15).

The size of the surfaces (volume) is analyzed as

$$\begin{aligned} V_{ne} &= \int_{\xi_{ne}^-}^{\xi_{i+\frac{1}{2},j}} \int_{\eta_{ne}^-}^{\eta_{i,j+\frac{1}{2}}} h_\xi(\xi,\eta) h_\eta(\xi,\eta) d\xi d\eta = A^-_{i+\frac{1}{2},j+\frac{1}{2}} B^-_{i+\frac{1}{2},j+\frac{1}{2}} h_\xi(\xi_{i+\frac{1}{2},j+\frac{1}{2}}) h_\eta(\xi_{i+\frac{1}{2},j+\frac{1}{2}}) \Delta t^2 \\ V_e &= \int_{\xi_e^-}^{\xi_{i+\frac{1}{2},j}} \int_{\eta_{se}^+}^{\eta_{ne}^-} h_\xi(\xi,\eta) h_\eta(\xi,\eta) d\xi d\eta \\ &= \left(\Delta\eta + \frac{\Delta t B^-_{i+\frac{1}{2},j+\frac{1}{2}}}{h_\eta(\xi_i + \frac{1}{2}, \eta_{j+\frac{1}{2}})} - \frac{\Delta t B^+_{i+\frac{1}{2},j-\frac{1}{2}}}{h_\eta(\xi_i + \frac{1}{2}, \eta_{j-\frac{1}{2}})} \right) \left(\frac{-\Delta t a^-_{i+\frac{1}{2},j}}{h_\xi(\xi_i + \frac{1}{2}, \eta_j)} \right) h_\xi(\xi_{i+\frac{1}{2},j}) h_\eta(\xi_{i+\frac{1}{2},j}) \\ &= -\Delta\eta\, \Delta t\, a^-_{i+\frac{1}{2},j} h_\eta(\xi_{i+\frac{1}{2},j}) + O\Delta t^2. \end{aligned} \tag{20}$$

Note from the previous analysis that the surface on the edge ne is of order Δt^2, while in e the lowest order is Δt. If a similar analysis were carried out for all the sub-surfaces of the cell, nw, se, and sw, it would be found that all the edges are of order Δt^2. Therefore, they would not need to be computed.

According to the order analysis, Equation (15) can be developed

$$\overline{U}_{i,j}^{t+\Delta t} = \frac{1}{V_{i,j}}\left[V_e\overline{w}_e^{t+\Delta t} + V_w\overline{w}_w^{t+\Delta t} + V_s\overline{w}_s^{t+\Delta t} + V_n\overline{w}_n^{t+\Delta t} + V_c\overline{w}_c^{t+\Delta t}\right], \tag{21}$$

where each variable $\overline{w}$ must be evaluated in the corresponding subdomain (sub-cell) to obtain the proposed scheme.

2.2.1. $V_{i+\frac{1}{2},j}$ Domain

Here, we calculate the variables inside the surface $[\xi_e^-, \xi_e^+]x[\eta_{se}^+, \eta_{ne}^-]$. This domain is indicated as sub-cell V_{ij}^e in Figure 1:

$$\begin{aligned}\overline{w}_{i+\frac{1}{2},j}^{t+\Delta t} =& \frac{1}{V_{i+\frac{1}{2},|j}}\int_{\xi_e^-}^{\xi_e^+}\int_{\eta_{se}^+}^{\eta_{ne}^-} U(\xi,\eta,t)h_\xi h_\eta d\xi d\eta = \frac{1}{V_{i+\frac{1}{2},j}}\int_{\xi_e^-}^{\xi_{i+\frac{1}{2}}}\int_{\eta_{se}^+}^{\eta_{ne}^-} U(\xi,\eta,t)h_\xi h_\eta d\xi d\eta \\ &+ \frac{1}{V_{i+\frac{1}{2},j}}\int_{\xi_{i+\frac{1}{2}}}^{\xi_e^+}\int_{\eta_{se}^+}^{\eta_{ne}^-} U(\xi,\eta,t)h_\xi h_\eta d\xi d\eta = \frac{-a_{i+\frac{1}{2},j}^-}{a_{i+\frac{1}{2},j}^+ - a_{i+\frac{1}{2},j}^-}\frac{U_{(i+\frac{1}{2},j)}^t + U_{e-}^t}{2} \\ &+ \frac{a_{i+\frac{1}{2},j}^+}{a_{i+\frac{1}{2},j}^+ - a_{i+\frac{1}{2},j}^+}\frac{U_{(i+\frac{1}{2},j)}^t + U_{e+}^t}{2}.\end{aligned} \tag{22}$$

For the numerical flows and the source term, we obtain

$$\frac{1}{V_{i+\frac{1}{2},j}}\int_{\xi_e^-}^{\xi_e^+}\int_{\eta_{se}^+}^{\eta_{ne}^-}\frac{1}{h_\xi h_\eta}\frac{\partial}{\partial\xi}h_\eta F(U)h_\xi h_\eta d\xi d\eta = \frac{[F(U_e^+) - F(U_e^-)]}{\Delta t\left(a_{i+\frac{1}{2},j}^+ - a_{i+\frac{1}{2},j}^-\right)}. \tag{23}$$

where $F(U_e^\pm) = F(U(\xi_e^\pm, \eta_j, t)$.

$$\int_t^{t+\Delta t}\overline{\frac{1}{h_\xi h_\eta}\frac{\partial}{\partial\xi}h_\eta F(U)}dt = \frac{[F(U(\xi_e^+,\eta_j,t+\Delta t/2)) - F(U(\xi_e^-,\eta_j,t+\Delta t/2))]}{\left(a_{i+\frac{1}{2},j}^+ - a_{i+\frac{1}{2},j}^-\right)}. \tag{24}$$

The flow G and the source S are

$$\int_t^{t+\Delta t}\left[\frac{1}{V_{i+\frac{1}{2},j}}\int_{\xi_e^-}^{\xi_e^+}\int_{\eta_{se}^+}^{\eta_{ne}^-}\frac{1}{h_\xi h_\eta}\frac{\partial}{\partial\eta}h_\xi G(U)h_\xi h_\eta d\xi d\eta\right]dt = O\Delta t + \ldots. \tag{25}$$

$$\int_t^{t+\Delta t}\left[\frac{1}{V_{i+\frac{1}{2},j}}\int_{\xi_e^-}^{\xi_e^+}\int_{\eta_{se}^+}^{\eta_{ne}^-} S(U)h_\xi h_\eta d\xi d\eta\right]dt = O\Delta t + \ldots. \tag{26}$$

When both the flow G and the source S are inserted into Equation (21), they are of a higher order and do not contribute to the analysis. Therefore, the variable is obtained as

$$\begin{aligned}w_{i+\frac{1}{2},j}^{t+\Delta t} =& \frac{-a_{i+\frac{1}{2},j}^-}{a_{i+\frac{1}{2},j}^+ - a_{i+\frac{1}{2},j}^-}\frac{U_{i+\frac{1}{2},j}^t + U_{e-}^t}{2} + \frac{a_{i+\frac{1}{2},j}^+}{a_{i+\frac{1}{2},j}^+ - a_{i+\frac{1}{2},j}^+}\frac{U_{i+\frac{1}{2},j}^t + U_{e+}^t}{2} \\ &+ \frac{1}{\left(a_{i+\frac{1}{2},j}^+ - a_{i+\frac{1}{2},j}^-\right)}[F(U(\xi_e^+,\eta_j,t+\Delta t/2)) - F(U(\xi_e^-,\eta_j,t+\Delta t/2))].\end{aligned} \tag{27}$$

Then, to incorporate it into Equation (21), its mean value in the domain V_{ij}^{e} is evaluated

$$\overline{w}_{e}^{t+\Delta t} = \frac{1}{V_{i,j}^{e}} \int_{\xi_{e}^{-}}^{\xi_{i+\frac{1}{2}}} \int_{\eta_{se}^{+}}^{\eta_{ne}^{-}} \widetilde{w}_{i+\frac{1}{2},j}^{t+\Delta t} h_{\xi} h_{\eta} d\xi d\eta = w_{i+\frac{1}{2},j}^{t+\Delta t} - U_{\xi}^{t+\Delta t}\left(h_{\xi}(\xi_{i+\frac{1}{2}},\eta_{j}) a_{i+\frac{1}{2},j}^{-} \Delta t\right), \quad (28)$$

where $w_{i+\frac{1}{2},j}^{t+\Delta t}$ is given by Equation (27). Finally, we get

$$\begin{aligned} V_{e}\overline{w}_{e}^{t+\Delta t} =& V_{e}\overline{w}_{i+\frac{1}{2},j}^{t+\Delta t} = h_{\eta}(\xi_{i+\frac{1}{2}},\eta_{j}) \Delta\eta \Delta t \frac{a_{i+\frac{1}{2},j}^{-}}{a_{i+\frac{1}{2},j}^{+} - a_{i+\frac{1}{2},j}^{-}} \left[a_{i+\frac{1}{2},j}^{-} \frac{U_{i+\frac{1}{2},j}^{t} + U_{e^{-}}^{t}}{2} - \right. \\ & \left. a_{i+\frac{1}{2},j}^{+} \frac{U_{i+\frac{1}{2},j}^{t} + U_{e^{+}}^{t}}{2} + F(U(\xi_{e}^{-},\eta_{j},t+\Delta t/2)) - F(U(\xi_{e}^{+},\eta_{j},t+\Delta t/2)) \right]. \end{aligned} \quad (29)$$

2.2.2. $V_{i,j+\frac{1}{2}}$ Domain

This domain corresponds to the sub-cell V_{ij}^{n} in Figure 1. For the current domain, we are utilizing the same approach as previously explained:

$$\begin{aligned} w_{i,j+\frac{1}{2}}^{t+\Delta t} =& \frac{-b_{i,j+\frac{1}{2}}^{-}}{b_{i,j+\frac{1}{2}}^{+} - b_{i,j+\frac{1}{2}}^{-}} \frac{U_{(i,j+\frac{1}{2})}^{t} + U_{n^{-}}^{t}}{2} + \frac{b_{i,j+\frac{1}{2}}^{+}}{b_{i,j+\frac{1}{2}}^{+} - b_{i,j+\frac{1}{2}}^{-}} \frac{U_{(i,j+\frac{1}{2})}^{t} + U_{n^{+}}^{t}}{2} \\ & + \frac{1}{\left(b_{i,j+\frac{1}{2}}^{+} - b_{i,j+\frac{1}{2}}^{-}\right)} \left[G(U(\xi_{i},\eta_{n}^{+},t+\Delta t/2)) - G(U(\xi_{i},\eta_{n}^{-},t+\Delta t/2))\right]. \end{aligned} \quad (30)$$

Next, to include it into Equation (21), we evaluate its average value within the domain V_{ij}^{n}

$$\overline{w}_{n}^{t+\Delta t} = \frac{1}{V_{i,j}^{n}} \int_{\xi_{e}^{-}}^{\xi_{i+\frac{1}{2}}} \int_{\eta_{se}^{+}}^{\eta_{ne}^{-}} \widetilde{w}_{i+\frac{1}{2},j}^{t+\Delta t} h_{\xi} h_{\eta} d\xi d\eta = w_{i,j+\frac{1}{2}}^{t+\Delta t} - U_{\xi}^{t+\Delta t}\left(h_{\xi}(\xi_{i,j+\frac{1}{2}}) b_{i,j+\frac{1}{2}}^{-} \Delta t\right), \quad (31)$$

where $w_{i,j+\frac{1}{2}}^{t+\Delta t}$ is obtained from Equation (30). Finally, we obtain

$$\begin{aligned} V_{n}\overline{w}_{n}^{t+\Delta t} =& V_{n}\overline{w}_{i,j+\frac{1}{2}}^{t+\Delta t} = \Delta\xi \Delta t h_{\xi}(\xi_{i},\eta_{j+\frac{1}{2}}) \frac{b_{i,j+\frac{1}{2}}^{-}}{b_{i,j+\frac{1}{2}}^{+} - b_{i,j+\frac{1}{2}}^{-}} \left[b_{i,j+\frac{1}{2}}^{-} \frac{U_{(i,j+\frac{1}{2})}^{t} + U_{n^{-}}^{t}}{2} \right. \\ & \left. - b_{i,j+\frac{1}{2}}^{+} \frac{U_{(i,j+\frac{1}{2})}^{t} + U_{n^{+}}^{t}}{2} + G(U(\xi_{i},\eta_{n}^{-},t+\Delta t/2)) - G(U(\xi_{i},\eta_{n}^{+},t+\Delta t/2)). \right] \end{aligned} \quad (32)$$

2.2.3. $V_{i,j}$ Domain

We calculate the sub-cell V_{ij}^{c} of Figure 1. The study of the central subdomain is developed as the difference between the entire cell and its extremes. Therefore, we have

$$\begin{aligned} V_{i,j}^{c}\overline{w}_{c}^{t+\Delta t} =& V_{c}\overline{w}_{c}^{t+\Delta t} = V_{i,j}\overline{U}_{i,j}^{t} - \\ & \Delta\eta\Delta t\left[h_{\eta}(\xi_{i+\frac{1}{2}},\eta_{j})F(U(\xi_{i+\frac{1}{2}},\eta_{j},t+\Delta t/2) - h_{\eta}(\xi_{i-\frac{1}{2}},\eta_{j})F(U(\xi_{i-\frac{1}{2}},\eta_{j},t+\Delta t/2))\right] \\ & - \Delta\xi\Delta t\left[h_{\xi}(\xi_{i},\eta_{j+\frac{1}{2}})G(U(\xi_{i},\eta_{j+\frac{1}{2}},t+\Delta t/2) - h_{\eta}(\xi_{i},\eta_{j+\frac{1}{2}})G(U(\xi_{i},\eta_{j+\frac{1}{2}},t+\Delta t/2))\right] \\ & - \Delta\xi\Delta\eta h_{\xi}(\xi_{i},\eta_{j})h_{\eta}(\xi_{i},\eta_{j})S(U(\xi_{i},\eta_{j},t+\Delta t)) \\ & - \left[V_{e}w_{e}^{t+\Delta t} + V_{w}w_{w}^{t+\Delta t} + V_{s}w_{s}^{t+\Delta t} + V_{n}w_{n}^{t+\Delta t}\right] + O\Delta t^{2}. \end{aligned} \quad (33)$$

2.2.4. Final Formulation

For the subdomains s and e, we employ the same methodology used for e and n, yielding very similar expressions.

If we replace the obtained values $V_D\overline{w}_D^{t+\Delta t}$ in Equation (21), and we evaluate the limit $\Delta t \to 0$ of the expression, we reach the following semi-discrete equation:

$$\frac{d\overline{U}}{dt} = \lim_{\Delta t \to 0} \frac{\overline{U}_{i,j}^{t+\Delta t} - \overline{U}_{i,j}^{t}}{\Delta t} = -\frac{F_{i+\frac{1}{2},j} - F_{i+\frac{1}{2},j}}{V_{i,j}} - \frac{G_{i,j+\frac{1}{2}} - G_{i,j+\frac{1}{2}}}{V_{i,j}} + S_{i,j}, \tag{34}$$

where

$$\begin{aligned} F_{i+\frac{1}{2},j} &= \frac{\Delta\eta h_\eta\left(\xi_{i+\frac{1}{2}},\eta_j\right)}{a^+_{i+\frac{1}{2},j} - a^-_{i+\frac{1}{2},j}} \\ &\left\{a^+_{i+\frac{1}{2},j}F\left(U^-_{i+\frac{1}{2},j}\right) - a^-_{i+\frac{1}{2},j}F\left(U^+_{i+\frac{1}{2},j}\right) - a^+_{i+\frac{1}{2},j}a^-_{i+\frac{1}{2},j}\left[U^-_{i+\frac{1}{2},j} - U^+_{i+\frac{1}{2},j}\right]\right\} \\ G_{i,j+\frac{1}{2}} &= \frac{\Delta\xi h_\xi\left(\xi_i,\eta_{j+\frac{1}{2}}\right)}{b^+_{i,j+\frac{1}{2}} - b^-_{i,j+\frac{1}{2}}} \\ &\left\{b^+_{i,j+\frac{1}{2}}G\left(U^-_{i,j+\frac{1}{2}}\right) - b^-_{i,j+\frac{1}{2}}G\left(U^+_{i,j+\frac{1}{2}}\right) - b^-_{i,j+\frac{1}{2}}b^+_{i,j+\frac{1}{2}}\left[U^-_{i,j+\frac{1}{2}} - U^+_{i,j+\frac{1}{2}}\right]\right\} \\ V_{i,j} &= h_\xi(\xi_i\eta_j)h_\eta(\xi_i,\eta_j)\Delta\xi\Delta\eta. \end{aligned} \tag{35}$$

To develop the numerical integration scheme in time through Equation (34), the following considerations must be taken into account:

- In this research, we considered that terms greater than $O\Delta t$ in Equation (21) did not contribute, as the limit applied in the final step of $\Delta t \to 0$ results in a null value.
- From the outset of the analysis, we worked with scale factors affected by the limit of $\Delta t \to 0$ while executing integrals, as it yields simpler expressions without affecting the development.
- The conservative variables at the interface after the limit is applied result as

$$\begin{aligned} U^+_{i+\frac{1}{2},j} &= U^t_{i+1,j} - \frac{\Delta\xi}{2}(U'_\xi)^t_{i+1,j} & U^-_{i+\frac{1}{2},j} &= U^t_{i,j} + \frac{\Delta\xi}{2}(U'_\xi)^t_{i,j} \\ U^+_{i,j+\frac{1}{2}} &= U^t_{i,j+1} - \frac{\Delta\eta}{2}(U'_\eta)^t_{i,j+1} & U^-_{i,j+\frac{1}{2}} &= U^t_{i,j} + \frac{\Delta\eta}{2}(U'_\eta)^t_{i,j}. \end{aligned} \tag{36}$$

The numerical derivatives will be obtained through the limiter *minmod* with $\theta = 1$

$$\begin{aligned} (U'_\xi)^t_{i,j} &= minmod\left(\theta\frac{U^n_{i,j} - U^n_{i-1,j}}{\Delta\xi}, \theta\frac{U^n_{i+1,j} - U^n_{i-1,j}}{2\Delta\xi}, \theta\frac{U^n_{i+1,j} - U^n_{i,j}}{\Delta\xi}\right) \\ (U'_\eta)^t_{i,j} &= minmod\left(\theta\frac{U^n_{i,j} - U^n_{i,j-1}}{\Delta\eta}, \theta\frac{U^n_{i,j+1} - U^n_{i,j+1}}{2\Delta\eta}, \theta\frac{U^n_{i,j+1} - U^n_{i,j}}{\Delta\eta}\right). \end{aligned} \tag{37}$$

- The analysis in this section applies to domains where all cells are of uniform size.
- If a rectangular coordinate system is used with unitary metrics, the two-dimensional Kurganov–Tadmor scheme is obtained.

2.3. Time Integration

To advance the semi-discrete equation in time, we employ the fourth-order Runge–Kutta scheme proposed by [19].

When the domain is partitioned into small cells, it results in an array of elements with specific sizes. Subsequently, the time step for the final scheme to verify the TVD (total variation diminishing) property must be determined.

In this study, we utilize the same time step condition as established in the article by [12]. The interface velocities are selected as follows:

$$a^{+}_{i+\frac{1}{2},j} = -a^{-}_{i+\frac{1}{2},j} = a_{i+\frac{1}{2},j}, \quad b^{+}_{i,j+\frac{1}{2}} = -b^{-}_{i,j+\frac{1}{2}} = b_{i,j+\frac{1}{2}}. \tag{38}$$

Consistent with the approach outlined in [12], the time step is constrained by

$$max\left(\frac{\Delta t\Delta\eta}{V_{i,j}} max_U|h_\eta F'(U)|, \frac{\Delta t\Delta\xi}{V_{i,j}} max_U|h_\xi G'(U)|\right) \le \frac{1}{8}. \tag{39}$$

2.4. Interface Treatment

In practical applications, it is often not feasible to use a single mesh distribution to discretize the entire analysis domain. Instead, the domain is segmented into different regions with different orientations of the elements. When this occurs, an interface is created between two regions that have distinct geometric properties but share a common curve.

The approach employed in this study is a generalization for curvilinear coordinates, based on previous work detailed in the article [25]. To illustrate this concept, consider a scenario where the interface is normal to the ξ coordinate direction for both domains. The left region is denoted by the prefix L, while the right region is denoted by R as shown in Figure 2.

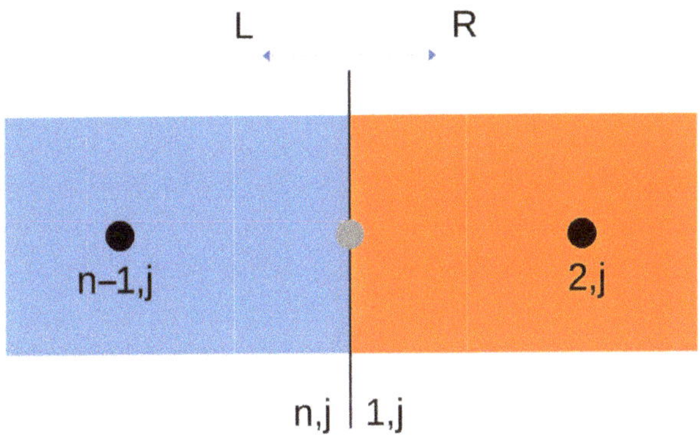

Figure 2. Regions interface.

In the provided figure, the control point shaded in grey is common to both regions. For the left side, it serves as the final node in the ξ direction of the array, marking the beginning of the orange region. It is essential for the variable at this node to hold the same value for both domains.

In this study, we opt to employ the same approach used in previous works to determine the average value on either side of the interface

$$\overline{U}^{L}_{n,j} = \int_{\eta_{j-\frac{1}{2}}}^{\eta_{j+\frac{1}{2}}} \int_{\xi_{i-\frac{1}{2}}}^{\xi_i} U(\xi,\eta,t)d\xi d\eta \qquad \overline{U}^{R}_{1,j} = \int_{\eta_{j-\frac{1}{2}}}^{\eta_{j+\frac{1}{2}}} \int_{\xi_i}^{\xi_{i+\frac{1}{2}}} U(\xi,\eta,t)d\xi d\eta. \tag{40}$$

Then, the same steps implemented in Section 2.2 must be carried out. When developing, it is important to consider that when the interface corresponds to the first or last node of the element in a specific direction, the variable's slope is zero. As a result, the scheme's order is locally reduced at the edges.

We arrive at a semi-discrete expression for the variables on both sides of the interface. In the case of the right side, it results in

$$\frac{d\overline{U}^R}{dt} = \frac{F^R_{i+\frac{1}{2},j}}{V^R_{i,j}} - \frac{G^R_{i,j+\frac{1}{2}} - G^R_{i,j+\frac{1}{2}}}{V^R_{i,j}} + S_{i,j}, \quad V^R_{i,j} = \frac{\Delta\xi}{2}\Delta\eta h_\xi(\eta_{i+\frac{1}{4}},j)h_\eta(\eta_{i+\frac{1}{4}},j), \quad i = 1 \tag{41}$$

$$\begin{aligned} F^R_{i+\frac{1}{2},j} &= \frac{\Delta\eta h_\eta\left(\xi_{i+\frac{1}{2}},\eta_j\right)}{a^+_{i+\frac{1}{2},j} - a^-_{i+\frac{1}{2},j}} \\ &\left\{a^+_{i+\frac{1}{2},j}F\left(U^-_{i+\frac{1}{2},j}\right) + a^-_{i+\frac{1}{2},j}F\left(U^+_{i+\frac{1}{2},j}\right) + a^+_{i+\frac{1}{2},j}a^-_{i+\frac{1}{2},j}\left[U^-_{i+\frac{1}{2},j} - U^+_{i+\frac{1}{2},j}\right]\right\} \\ G^R_{i,j+\frac{1}{2}} &= \frac{\Delta\xi h_\xi\left(\xi_{i+\frac{1}{4}},\eta_{j+\frac{1}{2}}\right)}{2\left(b^+_{i,j+\frac{1}{2}} - b^-_{i,j+\frac{1}{2}}\right)} \\ &\left\{b^+_{i,j+\frac{1}{2}}G\left(U^-_{i,j+\frac{1}{2}}\right) - b^-_{i,j+\frac{1}{2}}G\left(U^+_{i,j+\frac{1}{2}}\right) - b^-_{i,j+\frac{1}{2}}b^+_{i,j+\frac{1}{2}}\left[U^-_{i,j+\frac{1}{2}} - U^+_{i,j+\frac{1}{2}}\right]\right\}. \end{aligned} \tag{42}$$

while the left-side results in

$$\frac{d\overline{U}^L}{dt} = \frac{F^L_{i-\frac{1}{2},j}}{V^L_{i,j}} - \frac{G^L_{i,j+\frac{1}{2}} - G^L_{i,j+\frac{1}{2}}}{V^L_{i,j}} + S_{i,j}, \quad V^L_{i,j} = \frac{\Delta\xi}{2}\Delta\eta h_\xi(\eta_{i-\frac{1}{4}},j)h_\eta(\eta_{i-\frac{1}{4}},j), \quad i = n \tag{43}$$

$$\begin{aligned} F^L_{i-\frac{1}{2},j} &= \frac{\Delta\eta h_\eta\left(\xi_{i-\frac{1}{2}},\eta_j\right)}{a^+_{i-\frac{1}{2},j} - a^-_{i-\frac{1}{2},j}} \\ &\left\{-a^+_{i-\frac{1}{2},j}F\left(U^-_{i-\frac{1}{2},j}\right) - a^-_{i-\frac{1}{2},j}F\left(U^+_{i-\frac{1}{2},j}\right) - a^+_{i-\frac{1}{2},j}a^-_{i-\frac{1}{2},j}\left[U^-_{i-\frac{1}{2},j} - U^+_{i-\frac{1}{2},j}\right]\right\} \\ G^R_{i,j+\frac{1}{2}} &= \frac{\Delta\xi h_\xi\left(\xi_{i-\frac{1}{4}},\eta_{j+\frac{1}{2}}\right)}{2\left(b^+_{i,j+\frac{1}{2}} - b^-_{i,j+\frac{1}{2}}\right)} \\ &\left\{b^+_{i,j+\frac{1}{2}}G\left(U^-_{i,j+\frac{1}{2}}\right) - b^-_{i,j+\frac{1}{2}}G\left(U^+_{i,j+\frac{1}{2}}\right) - b^-_{i,j+\frac{1}{2}}b^+_{i,j+\frac{1}{2}}\left[U^-_{i,j+\frac{1}{2}} - U^+_{i,j+\frac{1}{2}}\right]\right\}. \end{aligned} \tag{44}$$

Using the numerical integrator, we determine the variables for the next time. The value in the interface will be the average of these variables:

$$U_{i,j} = \frac{V^L_{i,j}u^L_{i,j} + V^R_{i,j}u^R_{i,j}}{V^R_{i,j} + V^L_{i,j}}. \tag{45}$$

This process also applies if the interface is oriented in the η direction. Other situations may arise where in one domain it is in the η direction and in the other it is in the ξ direction. The developed software encompasses all possible interactions.

3. Numerical Tests

In this section, we conduct a study of the external flow over bodies by employing the method outlined in the previous section. The codes for the implementation were developed by the authors using the Julia programming language.

To handle the boundary conditions, we utilize two types: Dirichlet, where the variable value is defined, and Neumann, where the zero gradient is defined.

The initial two tests, involving flow over a cylinder and flow over a blunt body, were conducted to validate our software and the numerical techniques we have implemented. The third test, which involves flow over a wedge, includes interfaces between different zones within the physical domain and utilizes the new methodology introduced in this study.

3.1. Flow over a Cylinder

The analysis is confined to two-dimensional cases. Therefore, the flow around a circle is studied. Due to the dual symmetry of the issue at hand, we consider only a quarter of the domain as illustrated in Figure 3a. Figure 3b shows the used mesh of 40,000 elements or cells.

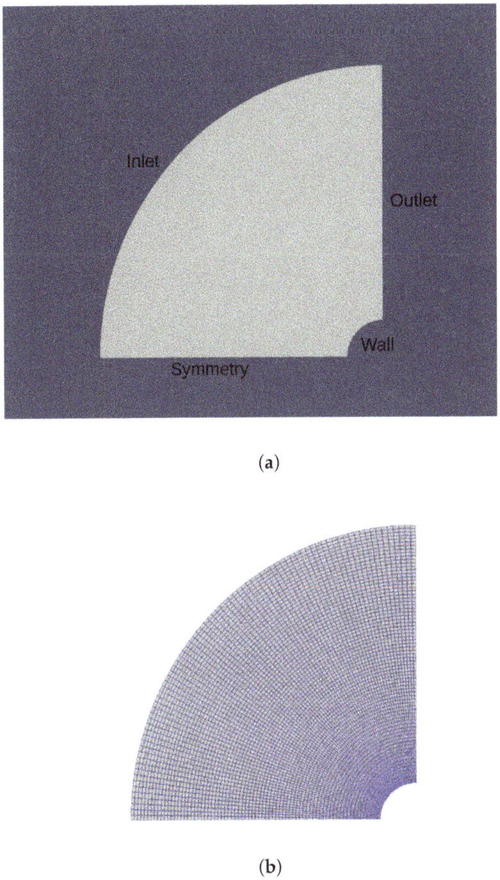

Figure 3. Flow over a cylinder. (**a**) Domain and boundary conditions. (**b**) Mesh.

In this test, as it is a single region, there is no interface to consider. The coordinates used for the domain are polar, with $\xi = r$ and $\eta = \theta$.

In this assessment, the test is performed under ambient conditions characterized by p_∞ = 101,325 Pa and $T_\infty = 298$ K. The inlet velocity is oriented horizontally and has a Mach number of 2 ($M = 2$). It is crucial to emphasize that the velocity is expressed in Cartesian coordinates, necessitating its conversion and evaluation in the corresponding polar coordinates.

The implemented boundary conditions for this test are described in Table 1.

Table 1. Boundary conditions for the cylinder test.

	u	v	p	T
Inlet	Dirichlet $u_\xi = u_{\xi amb}$	Dirichlet $u_\eta = v_{\xi amb}$	Dirichlet $p = p_{amb}$	Dirichlet $T = T_{amb}$
Outlet	Dirichlet $u_\xi = 0$	Neumann	Neumann	Neumann
Symmetry	Neumann	Dirichlet $u_\eta = 0$	Neumann	Neumann
Wall	Dirichlet $u_\xi = 0$	Neumann	Neumann	Neumann

We perform multiple simulations using meshes with varying numbers of cells. Figure 4 illustrates the pressure field acquired in each simulation.

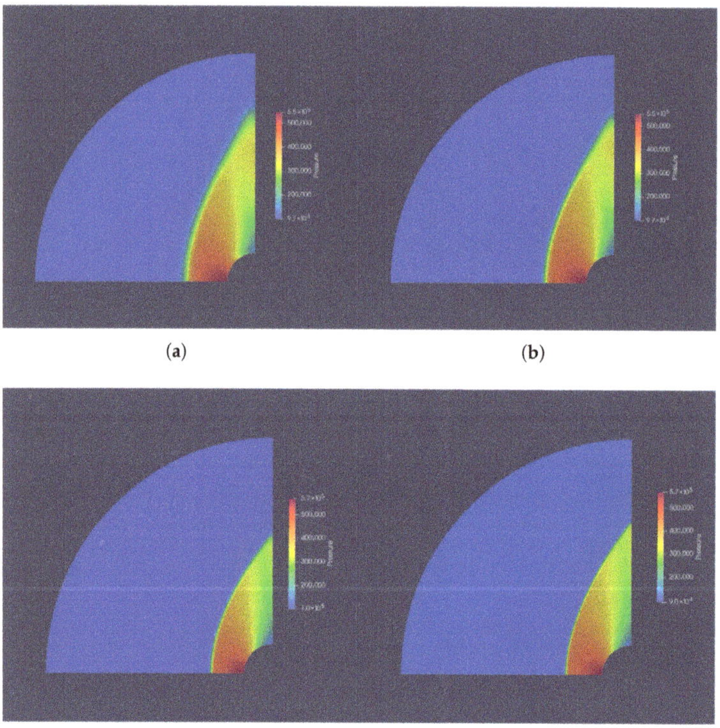

(a) (b)

(c) (d)

Figure 4. Cylinder: pressure distribution for different numbers of cells, $t = 0.3$ s: (**a**) 2700 cells, (**b**) 6000 cells, and (**c**) 14,000 cells. (**d**) 40,000 cells.

At the symmetry axis $y = 0$, the shock wave can be studied as a normal shock. Consequently, we can apply the normal shock wave relations in this specific zone [2]. For the current test, with a Mach number of 2, the ratio of stagnation pressure after shock to static inlet pressure is $\frac{p_0}{p_\infty} = 5.6403$. Table 2 displays the percentage error of the method's result compared to $\frac{p_0}{p_\infty}$.

Table 2. Errors in cylinder simulation.

Number of Cells	p_0/p_∞	% Error
2700	5.3924	4.39
6000	5.4345	3.65
14,400	5.5805–5.4903	1.06–2.659
40,000	5.5953	0.79

3.2. Flow over a Blunt Body

This case involves the analysis of the supersonic external flow over a blunt body, represented by a parabolic cylinder. The equation defining the parabola is as follows:

$$x = 0.769\,y^2 - 1 \tag{46}$$

Given the geometry, a single domain is used while working in parabolic coordinates. The relationship between parabolic and Cartesian coordinates is

$$x = \frac{1}{2}\left(\xi^2 - \eta^2\right) - 0.6749, \qquad y = \xi\eta, \qquad h_\xi = h_\eta = \sqrt{\xi^2 + \eta^2} \tag{47}$$

Note that if we use $\eta = 0.80635$ in Equation (47), we recover Equation (46).

Figure 5a illustrates the physical domain and boundary conditions, while Figure 5b shows the mesh consisting of 102,400 elements. In addition, Table 3 describes the implemented boundary conditions.

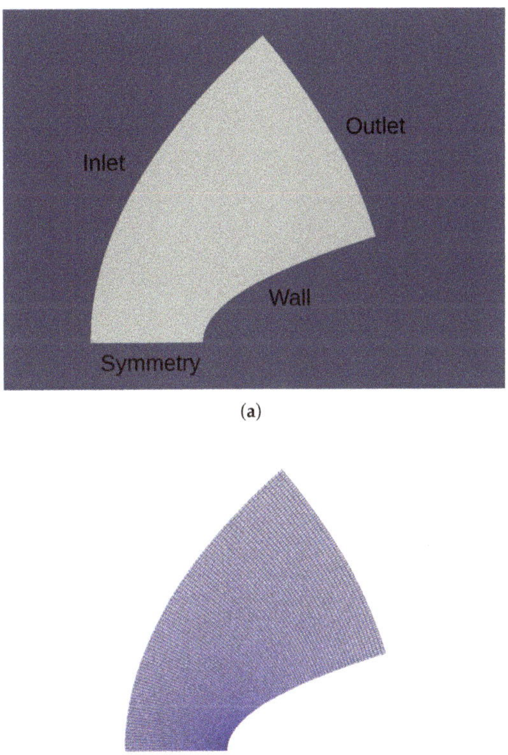

(a)

(b)

Figure 5. Flow over a blunt body. (**a**) Domain and boundary conditions. (**b**) Mesh.

Table 3. Boundary conditions for the blunt body test.

	u	v	p	T
Inlet	Dirichlet $u_\xi = u_{\xi amb}$	Dirichlet $v_\xi = v_{\xi amb}$	Dirichlet $p = p_{amb}$	Dirichlet $T = T_{amb}$
Outlet	Neumann	Neumann	Neumann	Neumann
Symmetry	Dirichlet $u_\xi = 0$	Neumann	Neumann	Neumann
Wall	Neumann	Dirichlet $u_\eta = 0$	Neumann	Neumann

Again, we consider the following ambient conditions: $p_\infty = 101,325$ Pa, $T_\infty = 298$ K, and an external velocity with a Mach number equal to two ($M = 2$) specified in terms of the Cartesian coordinates x.

The present test is similar to the cylinder, as normal shock wave relations apply when analyzing the axis where $y = 0$. Thus, according to [2], the relationship is expressed as $p_0/p_\infty = 21.0698$, where p_0 is the stagnation pressure after the shock wave.

Note that for a coarse mesh, the error is less than 5%. Furthermore, for a dense mesh, the error reduces to less than 1%.

Figure 6 displays the resulting pressure distribution for meshes with different numbers of cells. Table 4 presents the percentage error of p_0/p_∞ for various meshes.

Table 4. Errors in blunt body simulation.

Numbers of Elements	p_0/p_∞	**% Error**
8100	20.2456	3.912
44,100	20.5666	2.38
102,000	20.9445	0.595

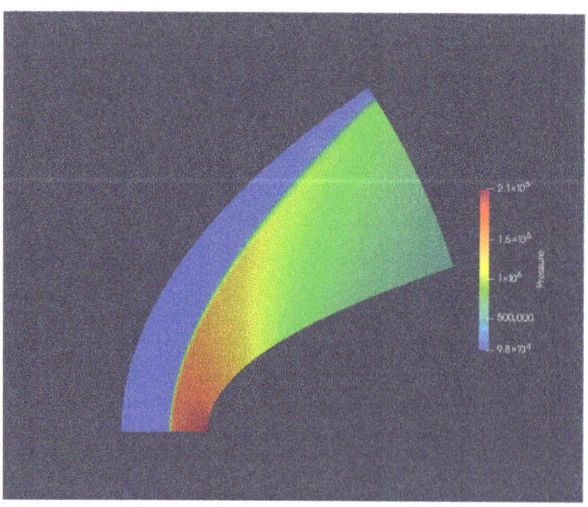

(a)

Figure 6. *Cont.*

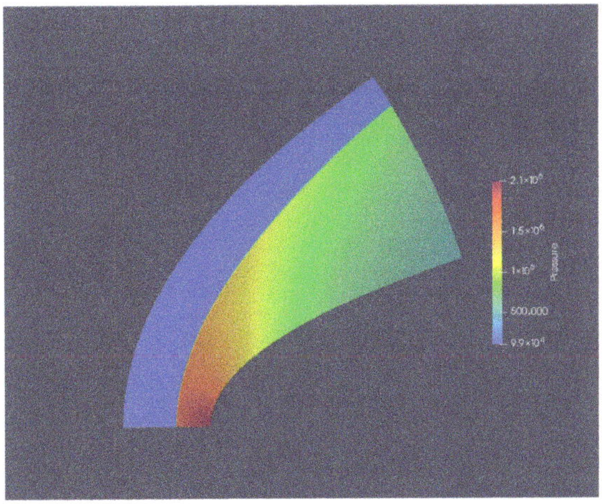

(**b**)

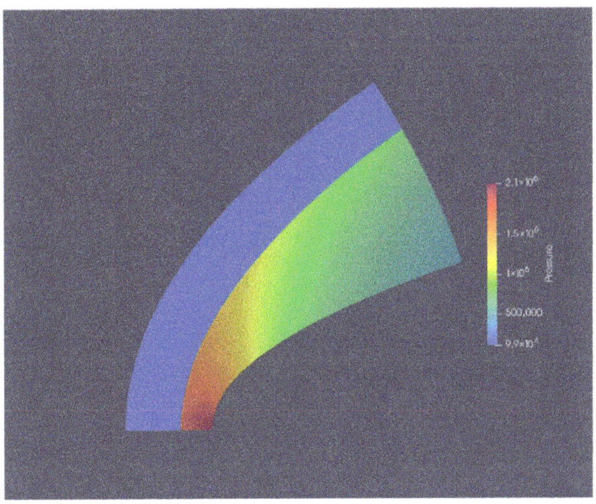

(**c**)

Figure 6. Blunt body: pressure distribution for different numbers of elements, $t = 0.1$ s: (**a**) 8100 cells, (**b**) 44,200 cells, and (**c**) 102,400 cells.

3.3. *Flow over a Wedge*

We analyze the flow around a wedge. Due to the domain's symmetry, we simulate only half of it. The exact steady-state solution of this problem is presented in [2].

This test comprises three subdomains and two interfaces as shown in Figure 7a. Additionally, Table 5 presents the boundary conditions for each subdomain, and Figure 7b depicts the implemented mesh (26,400 cells).

The external ambient conditions are as follows: the static pressure is p_∞ = 101,325 Pa, the static temperature is $T_\infty = 298$ K, and the Mach number is $M = 2$ in the horizontal direction.

Based on [2], for the current case with supersonic flow over a wedge, the static pressure ratio before and after the shock wave is $p_2/p_\infty = 2.82$. This pressure relation was confirmed for all developed simulations. The angle formed by the shock wave with the horizontal axis is also crucial, and it should be $\beta = 32.24°$. Using the numerical scheme with 30,000 cells, an angle of $\beta = 32.07°$ was obtained, resulting in a 0.5% error. Figure 8 shows the numerical results.

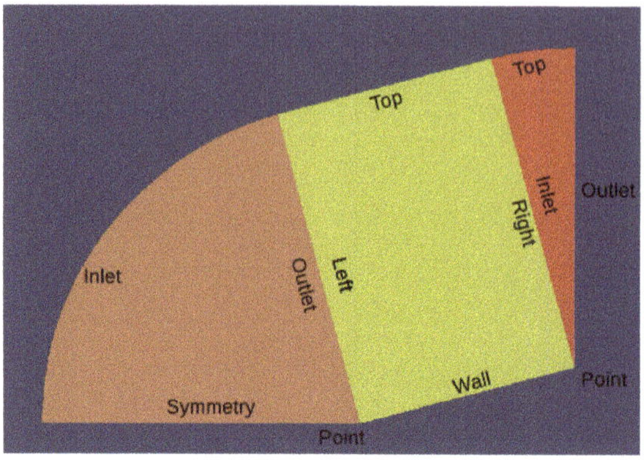

(**a**)

(**b**)

Figure 7. Flow over a wedge. (**a**) Domain and boundary conditions, (**b**) Mesh.

Table 5. Boundary conditions for the edge's test.

		Subdomain 1		
	u	v	p	T
Inlet	Dirichlet $u_\xi = u_{\xi amb}$	Dirichlet $v_\xi = v_{\xi amb}$	Dirichlet $p = p_{amb}$	Dirichlet $T = T_{amb}$
Outlet	interface	interface	interface	interface
Symmetry	Neumann	Dirichlet $u_\eta = 0$	Neumann	Neumann
Point	Neumann	Neumann	Neumann	Neumann
		Subdomain 2		
	u	v	p	T
Left	interface	interface	interface	interface
Right	interface	interface	interface	interface
Top	Neumann	Neumann	Neumann	Neumann
Wall	Neumann	Dirichlet $u_\eta = 0$	Neumann	Neumann

Table 5. *Cont.*

	Subdomain 3			
	u	v	p	T
Inlet	interface	interface	interface	interface
Outlet	Neumann	Neumann	Neumann	Neumann
Top	Neumann	Neumann	Neumann	Neumann
Point	Neumann	Neumann	Neumann	Neumann

Table 2 displays the error in the shock wave angle for five meshes. We can note how the numerical solutions approach the analytical one as the mesh becomes increasingly dense.

From Figures 4, 6, and 8, we can observe that the numerical diffusion introduced by the new scheme to capture the shock waves decreases as the mesh becomes denser. This is evidenced by the reduction in the area experiencing pressure changes around the shock waves. In addition, the numerical diffusion introduced by the new method is less than that generated by OpenFOAM using the KNP scheme.

To calculate the order of the scheme, we use the following equation [26,27]:

$$s_{ij} = \frac{\log\left(\frac{|u_j - u_i|}{|u_{j+1} - u_j|}\right)}{\log(N_j/N_i)} \tag{48}$$

where s_{ij} is the method's order, u_i and N_i are the numerical solution and the number of elements of the mesh i, respectively. The numerical value under consideration is the angle of the shock wave.

We apply Equation (48) to the values in Table 6 and find $s_{12} = 0.045$, $s_{23} = 1.81$, and $s_{34} = 2.1$. Therefore, the new scheme converges to second-order accuracy.

Table 6. Errors in wedge simulation. The columns represent the mesh number, the number of elements in the mesh, the numerical solution for the shock wave angle, and the percentage error relative to the analytical solution.

Mesh	Number of Cells	Shock Wave Angle	% Error
1	3750	31.47°	2.39
2	10,400	31.69°	1.7
3	13,000	31.90°	1.05
4	26,400	32.04°	0.62
5	30,000	32.07°	0.52

We would like to emphasize that the angle of the shock wave calculated by OpenFOAM using a mesh of 30,000 elements is 32.84°. In contrast, the angle determined by our newly introduced method is 32.07°, while the analytical value for the shock wave angle is 32.24°. These results indicate that the new scheme effectively and accurately evaluates the phenomenon under investigation.

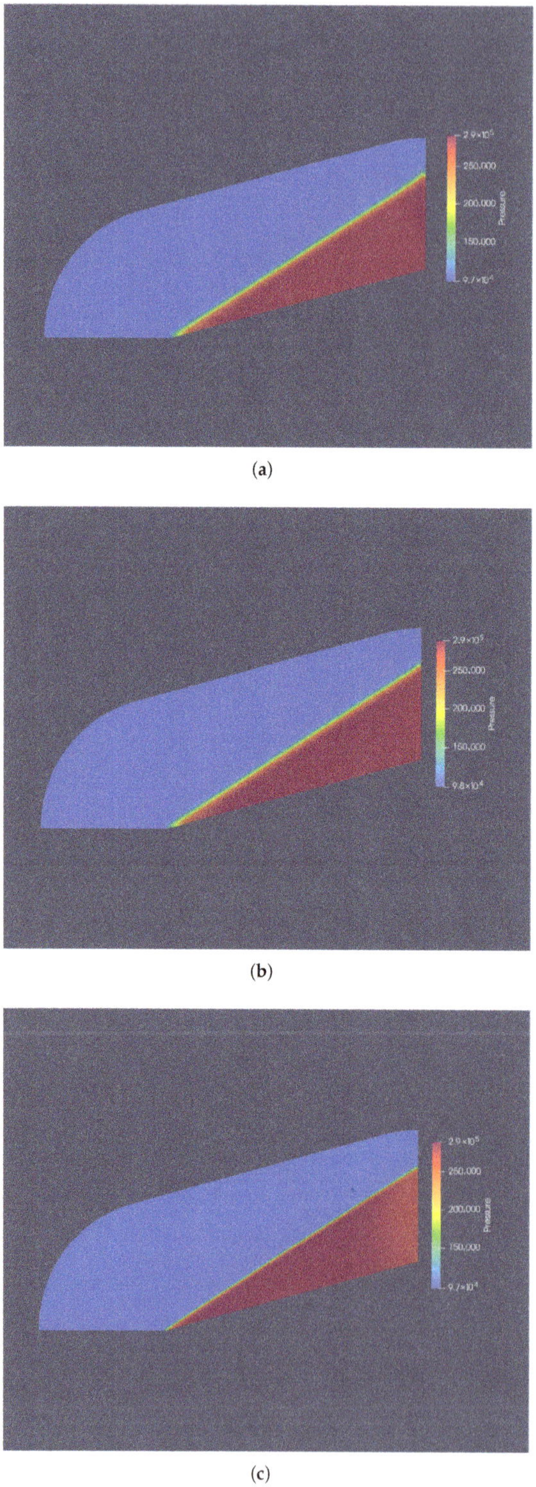

Figure 8. Edge: pressure distribution for different numbers of elements, $t = 0.8$ s: (**a**) 10,400 cells, (**b**) 13,000 cells, and (**c**) 26,400 cells.

4. Conclusions

In this research, we extend the Kurganov–Tadmor scheme for solving Euler equations in two-dimensional curvilinear coordinates.

To determine the average vector of conservative variables, denoted as $\overline{U}$, we first divide the cell into eight sub-cells. Each sub-cell's average is influenced by the neighboring cells, and we assess these influences. Subsequently, we apply Equation (21) to compute $\overline{U}$ for the entire cell, ensuring an accurate representation of the average across the complete structure. This method accounts for spatial interactions and enhances the reliability of our calculated averages. We employ a fourth-order Runge–Kutta temporal integrator and incorporate an interface treatment to handle several mesh types. This scheme can manage interfaces across different regions of the physical domain.

To validate its performance, we test the scheme on three different cases: supersonic flow over a cylinder, a blunt body, and a wedge. For the three tests, the numerical results are promising, indicating that this method is a feasible approach for simulating flow around various objects. Its ability to handle different coordinate systems within the same domain, connected through the interface treatment, demonstrates excellent convergence as the mesh resolution increases.

We note that implementing meshes with different topologies can restrict the time step, thus increasing the total CPU time of the simulation.

The proposed method is especially beneficial for analyzing a variety of external flows over objects. It allows the division of the domain into independent zones, each with its coordinate system. These zones are interconnected through the interface treatment previously described.

The new method achieves second-order accuracy and provides more precise results than the classical Kurganov–Tadmor–Petrova scheme when both methods use similar meshes. This improvement underscores its potential as a valuable tool for enhancing computational precision.

The study presented herein represents a preliminary step in the development of a novel numerical scheme. Subsequent research will be essential in assessing its potential.

Author Contributions: Conceptualization, S.B. and S.E.; methodology, S.B.; software, S.B.; validation, S.B. and L.G.M.; formal analysis, S.B. and S.E.; investigation, S.B., S.E. and L.G.M.; resources, S.B. and S.E.; data curation, S.B. and L.G.M.; writing—original draft preparation, S.B., S.E. and L.G.M.; writing—review and editing, S.B., S.E. and L.G.M.; visualization, S.B. and L.G.M.; supervision, S.E.; project administration, S.E.; funding acquisition, S.E. All authors have read and agreed to the published version of the manuscript.

Funding: This research was funded by the Project 33620180100218CB, Secretary of Science and Technology of the National University of Córdoba, and PIP-2021-2023-GI-11220200101463CO of CONICET.

Data Availability Statement: The authors will be able to provide data and tools upon reasonable request.

Acknowledgments: The authors would like to thank José Tamagno for their teachings.

Conflicts of Interest: The authors declare no conflicts of interest.

References

1. Anderson, J. *Hypersonic and High Temperature Gas Dynamics*; McGraw-Hill: Boston, MA, USA, 1989.
2. Anderson, J. *Modern Compressible Flow: With Historical Perspective*, 3rd ed.; McGraw-Hill: Boston, MA, USA, 2003.
3. LeVeque, R. *Finite Volume Methods for Hyperbolic Problems*, 1st ed.; Cambridge University Press: Cambridge, UK, 2004.
4. Bakhtiyarov, S.; Adanur, S. Airflow over Wavy Yarn in Air-Jet Filling Insertion. *Math. Comput. Appl.* **1999**, *4*, 1–7. [CrossRef]
5. Wang, B.; Garg, N. Third-order numerical scheme for Euler equations of gas dynamics using Jordan canonical based splitting flux. *Comput. Fluids* **2024**, *281*, 106370. [CrossRef]

6. Trojak, W.; Dzanic, T. Positivity-preserving discontinuous spectral element methods for compressible multispecies flows. *Comput. Fluids* **2024**, *280*, 106343. [CrossRef]
7. Tamagno, J.; Elaskar, S.; Ríos, G. Numerical simulation of time-dependent reacting flows in pulse facilities. *Appl. Numer. Math.* **2003**, *47*, 515–530. [CrossRef]
8. Falcinelli, O.; Elaskar, S.; Tamagno, J. Reducing the numerical viscosity in non-structured three-dimensional finite volumes computations. *J. Spacecr. Rocket AIAA* **2008**, *45*, 406–408. [CrossRef]
9. Toro, E. *Riemann Solvers and Numerical Methods for Fluid Dynamics*, 3rd ed.; Springer: Berlin, Germany, 2009.
10. EsfandAbadi, M.; Mohammadi, A.; Djavareshkian, M. Design and analysis of supersonic inlet for ramjet engines: Aerodynamic considerations and performance optimization. *J. Aerosp. Sci. Technol.* **2024**, *17*, 47–59.
11. Araya, G. Unsteady subsonic/supersonic flow simulations in 3D unstructured grids over an acoustic cavity. *Fluids* **2024**, *9*, 92. [CrossRef]
12. Kurganov, A.; Noelle, S.; Petrova, G. Semidiscrete central-upwind schemes for hyperbolic conservation laws and hamilton-jacobi equations. *J. Sci. Comput.* **2001**, *23*, 707–740. [CrossRef]
13. Kurganov, A.; Tadmor, E. New high-resolution central schemes for nonlinear conservation laws and convection–diffusion equations. *J. Comput. Phys.* **2000**, *160*, 241–282. [CrossRef]
14. Illenseer, T.; Duschl, W. Two-dimensional central-upwind schemes for curvilinear grids and application to gas dynamics with angular momentum. *Comput. Phys. Commun.* **2009**, *180*, 2283–2302. [CrossRef]
15. Greenshields, C.; Weller, H.; Gasparini, L.; Reese, J. Implementation of semi-discrete, non-staggered central schemes in a colocated, polyhedral, finite volume framework, for high-speed viscous flows. *Int. J. Numer. Math. Fluids* **2010**, *63*, 1–21. [CrossRef]
16. Gutiérrez Marcantoni, L.; Tamagno, J.; Elaskar, S. rhocentralrffoam: An openfoam solver for high speed chemically active flows—Simulation of planar detonations. *Comput. Phys. Commun.* **2017**, *219*, 209–222. [CrossRef]
17. Gutiérrez Marcantoni, L.; Tamagno, J.; Elaskar, S. Numerical study on the impact of chemical modeling on simulating methane-air detonations. *Fuel* **2019**, *240*, 289–298. [CrossRef]
18. Weng, Z.; Mével, R. Implementation of an openfoam solver for shock and detonation simulation at high pressure. *Comput. Fluids* **2023**, *265*, 10601. [CrossRef]
19. Kreiss, H.; Ortiz, O. *Introduction to Numerical Methods for Time Dependent Differential Equations*; Wiley: Hoboken, NJ, USA, 2014.
20. Landau, L.; Lifshitz, E. *Mecánica de Fluidos, Vol, 6, Colección de Física Teórica*; Reverté: Barcelona, Spain, 1986.
21. Whitham, G. *Linear and Nonlinear Waves*; John Wiley & Sons: New York, NY, USA, 1974.
22. Aris, R. *Vectors, Tensors, and the Basic Equations of Fluid Mechanics*; Dover Publications: Mineola, NY, USA, 1989.
23. Tannehill, J.; Anderson, D.; Pletcher, R. *Computational Fluid Mechanics and Heat Transfer*, 2nd ed.; Taylor & Francis: Washington, DC, USA, 1997.
24. Chapra, S.; Canale, R. *Numerical Methods for Engineers*, 7th ed.; McGraw-Hill Education: New York, NY, USA, 2015.
25. Montes, P.; Reula, O. New numerical interface scheme for the Kurganov-Tadmor second-order method. *arXiv* **2021**, arXiv:2105.03452.
26. Roache, P. *Verification and Validation in Computational Science and Engineering*; Hermosa: Albuquerque, NM, USA, 1998
27. Oberkampf, W.; Trucano, T. Verification and validation in computational fluid dynamics. *Prog. Aerosp. Sci.* **2002**, *38*, 209–272. [CrossRef]

Mathematical and Computational Applications

MDPI

Systematic Review

Measuring Circular Economy with Data Envelopment Analysis: A Systematic Literature Review

Svetlana V. Ratner [1,2,3,*], Andrey V. Lychev [3], Elisaveta D. Muravleva [3] and Daniil M. Muravlev [3]

1 Department of Economic and Mathematical Modelling, Peoples' Friendship University of Russia, 6 Miklukho-Maklaya St., 117198 Moscow, Russia

2 Laboratory for Scientometric Analysis and International Rankings, Armenian State University of Economics, Nalbandyan 128, Yerevan 0025, Armenia

3 College of Computer Sciences, National University of Science and Technology "MISIS", 4 Leninsky Ave., Bldg. 1, 119049 Moscow, Russia; lychev@misis.ru (A.V.L.); m2002852@edu.misis.ru (E.D.M.); m2008409@edu.misis.ru (D.M.M.)

* Correspondence: ratner_sv@pfur.ru

Abstract

This article presents a systematic literature review of data envelopment analysis (DEA) models used to evaluate circular economy (CE) practices. The review is based on 151 peer-reviewed articles published between 2015 and 2024. By analyzing this collection, this review categorizes different DEA models and their levels of application, discusses the data sources utilized, and identifies the prevailing methodologies and evaluation criteria used to measure the CE performance. Despite the extensive literature on measuring the circular economy using DEA, a critical evaluation of existing DEA approaches that highlights their strengths and weaknesses is still missing. Our analysis shows that DEA models provide valuable insights when assessing circular strategies, namely, R2—Reduce, R8—Recycling, and R9—Recovering. Over 40% of the surveyed literature focuses on China, with nearly 20% on the European Union. Other regions are sparsely represented within our sample, highlighting a potential gap in the current research landscape.

Keywords: circular economy; data envelopment analysis; literature review; recycling; sustainable development

MSC: 91B74; 90B30; 90C05

JEL Classification: Q53; Q58; C61; C67

1. Introduction

Measuring the circular economy (CE) presents a number of significant challenges, as highlighted in the existing literature [1–4]. This is largely due to the differing interpretations of the CE concept, often simplifying it to merely material recirculation. Most existing metrics, such as waste generation, material footprint, recycling rates, and others, fail to adequately represent the complexities of multifunctionality and the consequences of material downcycling. While the fundamental principles and overarching vision of CE are well-articulated and widely understood, translating these into measurable progress presents a significant hurdle. Consequently, there is currently no universally adopted monitoring framework or standardized metrics to robustly evaluate its implementation and impact [5,6]. This difficulty in quantification stems from various inherent complexities.

The various 'R' principles (3Rs, 6Rs, etc.) used in the literature also differ [2]. Starting as a set of hierarchical strategies aimed at optimizing resource efficiency, minimizing waste generation, and reducing environmental impact throughout a product's life cycle (Reduce, Reuse, Recycle), they later evolved into more comprehensive frameworks (such as 6R, 9R, 10R, and 12R), integrating strategies that intervene at earlier stages of the product life cycle.

Therefore, a wide range of measurement approaches exists that cover different aspects and are seemingly unrelated to each other. The research landscape related to the CE transition is characterized as fragmented and granular [5]. Defining efficiency indicators in a circular economy is highly complex [7]. Researchers find it challenging to develop indicators that accurately measure CE performance levels, particularly with regard to waste reduction, reuse, and recycling. These difficulties include uncertainty of system boundaries, the necessity to measure counterfactual parameters (i.e., estimating the amount of waste that would have been generated without CE strategies), and the tendency to ignore hidden trade-offs (e.g., the high energy consumption involved in recycling processes). The definition and establishment of these indicators are challenging.

Currently, there is no widely accepted monitoring framework or standardized metrics for evaluating progress toward a CE [5,6]. The CE concept is not clearly defined, and there is no commonly accepted definition. This makes it difficult to determine which elements should be measured. Furthermore, the various 'R' principles (3Rs, 6Rs, etc.) used in the literature also vary [2]. A wide range of measurement approaches exists that cover different aspects and are seemingly unrelated to each other. The research landscape related to the CE transition is characterized as fragmented and granular [5]. Defining efficiency indicators in a circular economy is highly complex [7]. Researchers find it difficult to develop indicators that accurately measure CE performance levels, particularly with regard to waste reduction, reuse, and recycling. The definition and establishment of these indicators are challenging.

Current measurements of resource productivity and efficiency are considered unsatisfactory in the context of the circular economy [8]. These metrics often fail to fulfill the circular economy's primary objective of preserving the value of products, components, and materials for as long as possible [9]. Moreover, only a few CE metrics assess features related to maintaining value [5]. The lack of necessary data is also a significant limitation. Without adequate data, it is difficult to define indicators, which requires companies to invest considerable time and economic resources. Data collection can be challenging, partly due to a lack of information exchange between researchers and company managers, potentially due to confidentiality issues [10]. Efforts are often hindered by discrepancies, gaps, and contrasts in data [6]. Moreover, the measurement and assessment of circular performance is not yet a common practice in companies. Indicators struggle to directly influence business practice. There may also be low stakeholder participation in the design of indicators [11].

Another challenge is the apparent lack of interest in analyzing the middle-of-life (MoL) phase of a product's life cycle [1]. Existing methodologies tend to focus more on the stages from production to disposal than on the initial development phase (BoL). Furthermore, while environmental and economic factors are frequently considered, social equity is less often incorporated into CE indicators that combine the 3Rs principles [12].

These challenges highlight the ongoing need for further research, as well as the development of common methods and strategies, to enable the systematic and practical measurement and assessment of the degree of circularity across different systems and levels.

In recent years, data envelopment analysis (DEA) has become a popular methodological approach for measuring the performance, efficiency, and dynamic evolution of various aspects of CE [13–15]. One reason for its popularity is that the CE inherently involves undesirable outputs such as pollution and waste. DEA models can incorporate these factors by treating them as inputs to be minimized or as specific outputs, often using methods such as the slacks-based measure (SBM) or directional distance function (DDF) [13,16–18]. Furthermore, the DEA can decompose systems to evaluate the efficiency of internal subsystems (e.g., industrial production, environmental treatment, recycling, and wastewater treatment) and individual factors (inputs and outputs) within them [14,15].

In many recent studies, network DEA models have been widely used to recognize that CE systems have internal structures and interconnected stages. These models break down the system into stages (e.g., production, treatment, and recycling) and analyze the efficiency of each stage and of the system as a whole. This approach moves beyond the 'black box' view of traditional DEA [19–21]. In summary, the DEA provides a flexible and objective framework for evaluating the complex, multi-input, multi-output systems inherent in the circular economy. Over the last five years, various extensions such as network, dynamic, game-theoretic, and fuzzy DEA models have been developed to address the specific structural, temporal, and data characteristics of CE performance evaluation.

However, prior to applying the DEA, there is a challenge in properly defining and selecting the key criteria, as well as the appropriate inputs and outputs, for evaluating urban or industrial circular economies. Existing indicator systems are sometimes criticized for being too general, lacking management or potential indicators, or for not fully capturing the circular loop and its link to sustainable development [15]. Furthermore, as there are many different types of DEA models, selecting the most suitable model structure, orientation (input vs. output), and assumptions (e.g., constant or variable returns to scale, CCR/CRS vs. BCC/VRS) for a particular CE context necessitates careful consideration and expertise [22,23].

This study aims to conduct a systematic literature review of work published between 2015 and 2024 on measuring the circular economy (or certain aspects of it) using DEA. The specific research questions for this review are as follows:

RQ1: To reveal the state of the art by identifying the strengths and weaknesses of existing DEA approaches for measuring the multifaceted circular economy.

RQ2: To identify specific knowledge gaps and methodological challenges and inform future research aimed at providing more accurate, dynamic, and actionable insights to promote CE development.

2. Methodology

To answer these research questions, we perform a systematic literature review using the PRISMA protocol. This review was registered at Open Science Framework (OSF) and publicly available at https://osf.io/y4dxe (accessed on 1 July 2025).

The systematic review was conducted using journal articles retrieved from both Google Scholar and Scopus. In the Scopus database, the search query

```
TITLE-ABS-KEY: {(“DEA” OR “data envelopment analysis”) AND “circular economy”}
```

was applied, yielding a total of 117 articles. Given the limited number of results obtained from Scopus, the review was supplemented with publications from Google Scholar, which offers a broader scope of sources. Due to the constraints of Google Scholar's search functionality, relevant publications were collected for each year from 2015 to 2024 using the Publish or Perish software, version 8.17.4863.9118.

As a result of data extraction, a total of 6684 records were obtained. The flowchart of the selection procedure according to the PRISMA protocol is presented in Figure 1. After the eligibility evaluation, 1431 papers were excluded based on the exclusion criteria described in Table 1. Next, a full-text search was conducted on the articles to identify the occurrence of the keywords "data envelopment analysis" and "circular economy". As a result, 3574 articles were excluded because they did not contain these keywords. The remaining 1323 publications were analyzed by two researchers, who are the authors of this paper, based on an agreement on several inclusion and exclusion criteria (see Table 1). If the article does not present calculations based on the DEA model, incorporating variables that include indicators related to the circular economy, it is excluded.

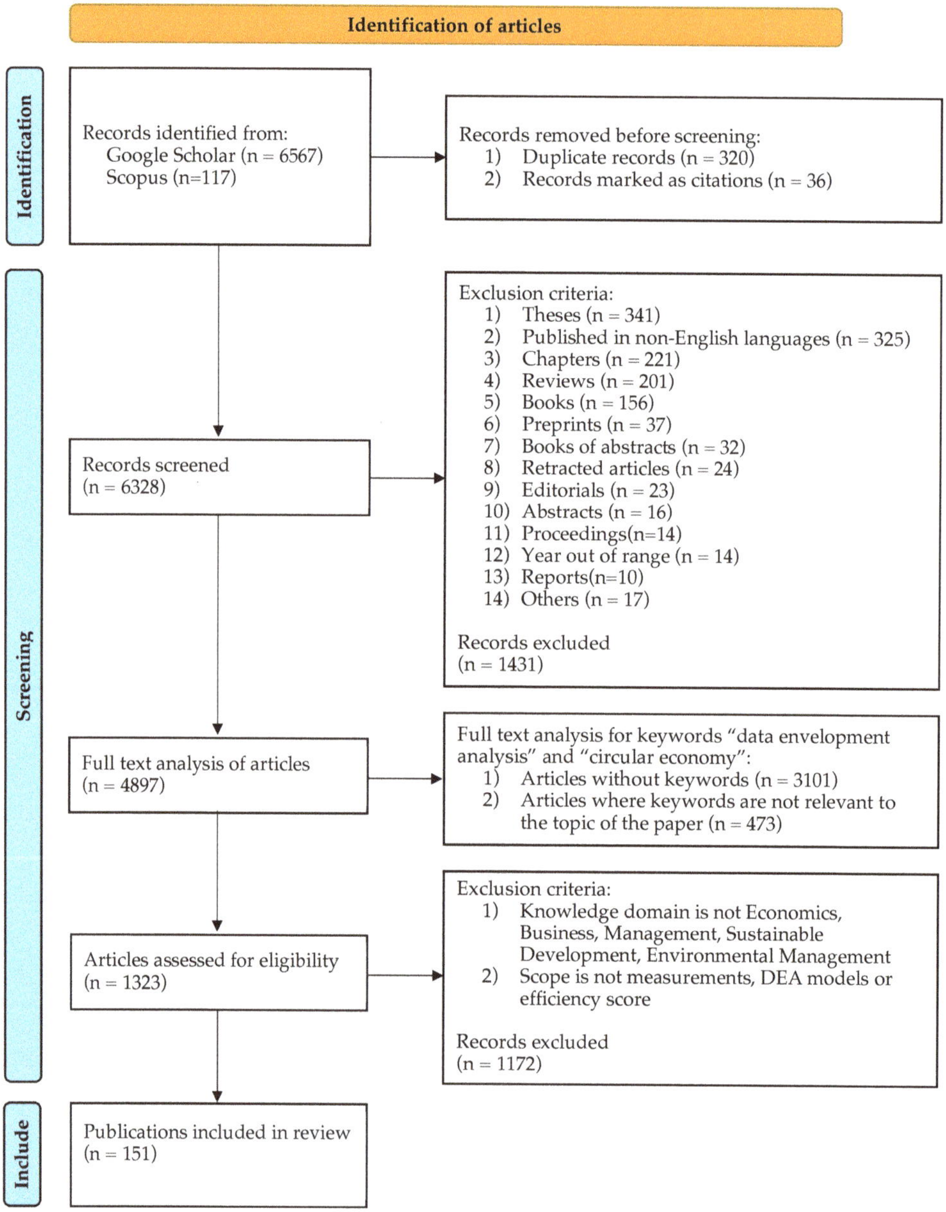

Figure 1. PRISMA flowchart of the selection procedure.

Table 1. Selection criteria.

Criteria	Inclusion Criteria	Exclusion Criteria
Type of article	Peer-reviewed scholarly journal articles (full papers)	Theses or dissertations, books, chapters in edited books, reviews, retracted articles, conference papers (if they are not published in journals), abstracts, books of abstracts, editorials, preprints, working papers, reports (science and policy, technical, study, annual), bibliographies, literature listings, newsletters, resumes, seminars, indexes in journals, datasets, presentations, handbooks
Keywords	The article contains keywords "data envelopment analysis" and "circular economy"	The article does not contain keywords; keywords are mentioned only in tables or references
Time	Published in 2015–2024	Published before 2015; published in 2025; available online, but not published
Language	Written in the English language	Published in non-English languages
Knowledge domain	Economics, Business, Management, Sustainable Development, Environmental Management	Others
Scope	Measurements, DEA models, efficiency score	Others
Methodology	Original theoretical and experimental studies	Bibliometric analysis, Systematic literature reviews, Meta-analysis of experimental studies

The two researchers applied these criteria independently in order to decrease bias. According to [24,25], this method is considered to be a best practice for literature review. Finally, 151 articles were included in the literature review. Based on this corpus, we conducted bibliometric and content analyses to identify underlying models and reveal emerging trends in the application of DEA to the circular economy.

3. Bibliometric and Content analysis

In this section, we present a bibliometric analysis of 151 selected papers on measuring the circular economy with DEA from 2015 to 2024. A comprehensive summary of the selected papers can be found in Supplementary Materials (Tables S1 and S2).

Figure 2 shows the annual number of publications from 2015 to 2024. The data reveal a substantial increase in research activity concerning the application of DEA models to evaluate the efficiency of the circular economy over the past decade. Between 2015 and 2018, an average of approximately three articles were published each year. However, starting in 2019, there has been a significant increase in the volume of publications, with a tenfold increase in recent years. The average annual growth rate of 50% indicates a high level of interest and demonstrates increasing academic engagement in this field. It is expected that the number of studies related to the circular economy will continue to rise annually. The exponential trend line fitted to the number of publications aligns closely with observed data, reinforcing the expectation that the utilization of DEA models in assessing circular economy initiatives will experience sustained growth.

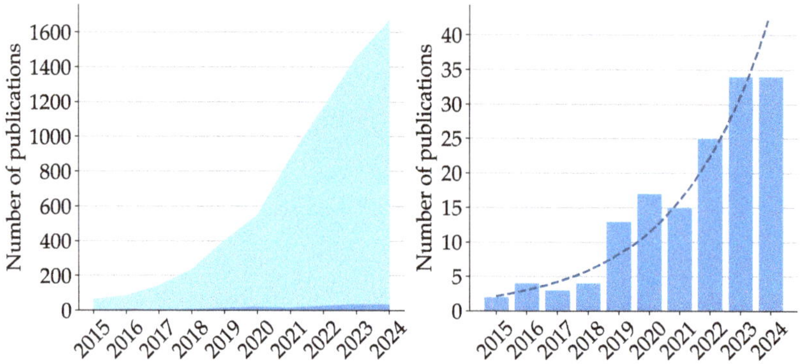

Figure 2. Annual number of publications on measuring the circular economy with DEA from 2015 to 2024 (**left**) retrieved from Google Scholar and Scopus, and (**right**) selected for analysis.

Figure 3 presents a pie chart illustrating how publications are distributed across different publishers. Elsevier is the dominant publisher, contributing around half of all articles examining the application of DEA models to measure the efficiency of the circular economy. MDPI and Springer are the second largest, collectively representing around 25% of the total publications. Wiley and IOP publishers follow with shares of 6% and 2.6% respectively. Due to Elsevier's leading position, this analysis provides a further breakdown of its publications by journal. This analysis reveals that most of the relevant articles have been published in the *Journal of Cleaner Production* and *Waste Management*, emphasizing the practical focus of the analyzed studies.

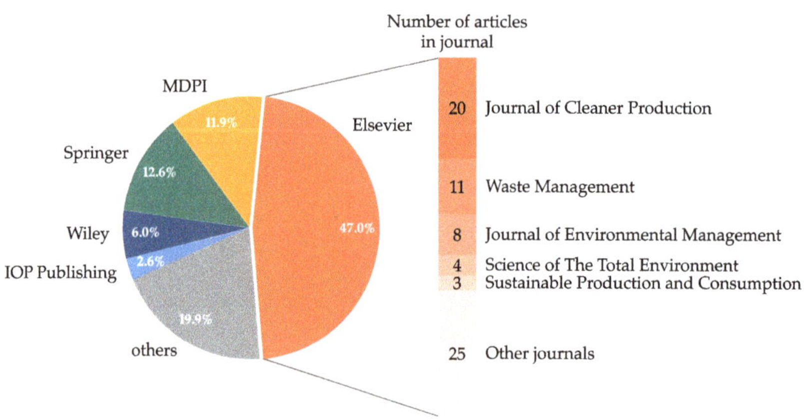

Figure 3. Distribution of articles by publishers.

Figure 4 shows how keywords were used in the 151 papers selected for the systematic review. The figure illustrates the annual evolution and emergence of top research keywords. Most of the keywords depicted in the chart have emerged since 2019 due to an increase in the volume of publications during this period. The presence of the keywords 'DEA' and 'circular economy' among the top-ranked terms can be attributed to the specific search criteria used to select the relevant publications. Overall, the frequency of keywords remains relatively stable over the analyzed period. Certain terms such as 'waste management', 'municipal waste management', and 'Malmquist index' exhibit an upward trend, indicating increasing scholarly interest in the assessment of waste management systems and evaluating productivity change over time. Conversely, the usage of terms like 'recycling efficiency' demonstrates a declining pattern, suggesting a potential shift in the research focus of DEA models.

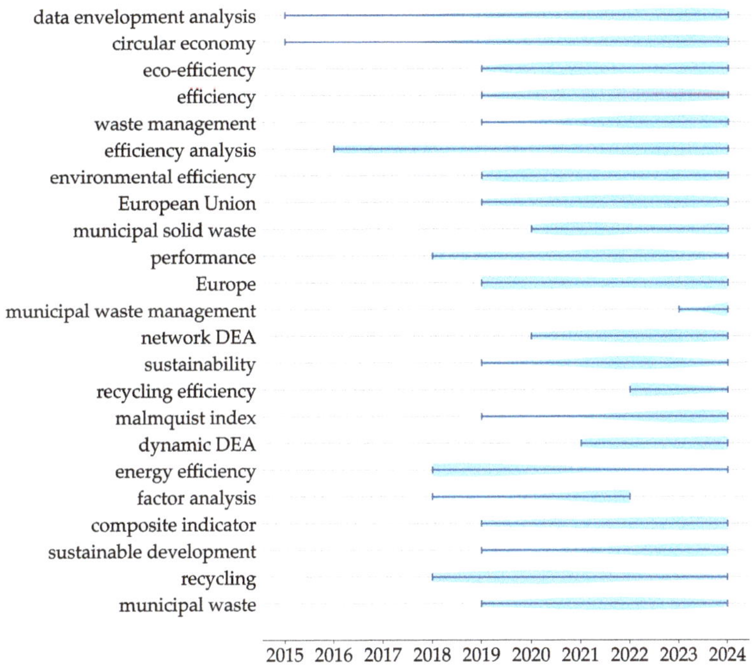

Figure 4. Timeline of the most frequently used keywords.

Table 2 presents the most significant studies identified within the analyzed corpus. It comprises ten highly cited publications focused on measuring the circular economy with DEA, published between 2015 and 2024. It is noteworthy that the majority of these influential works—seven out of ten—were published during 2019–2020, suggesting that recent research has been based particularly on methodologies developed during that period and built upon findings established then. This concentration underscores the pivotal role of studies from these years in shaping current approaches within the field. It is interesting to note that nine out of ten articles were published in journals from Elsevier, and one article in a journal from Wiley.

The most cited article [26] explores the impact of economic openness and R&D investment on green economic growth in the context of the circular economy. For this purpose, the authors use econometric models, explicitly incorporating pure technical efficiency as one of the factors. Wu et al. [27] applied a two-stage DEA model with additive and non-cooperative efficiency measures to assess the efficiency of industrial production processes across provincial regions in China. In this model, input resources are shared between the first and second stages. Undesirable intermediate outputs generated during the production stage are considered as waste products that are processed in the disposal stage, resulting in recovered resources, which are subsequently reused as inputs within the first stage. Halkos and Petrou [28] analyzed waste generation efficiency in EU countries. A comparative analysis was conducted, examining the DEA results in conjunction with the recycling rates for each country during the study period. This analysis demonstrated a relationship between countries' DEA efficiency scores and their recycling rates. Giannakitsidou et al. [29] used DEA models to measure the performance of EU countries in managing and exploiting their MSW. Expósito and Velasco [30] conducted an analysis of MSW recycling across regions in Spain. Mavi and Mavi [31] conducted an assessment of the energy efficiency across OECD countries. To ensure comparability, a common set of weights in the DEA model is employed to evaluate all OECD nations uniformly. Additionally, the Malmquist productivity index is utilized to analyze temporal changes in efficiency over the specified period. Pagotto and Halog [32] integrated material flow analysis (MFA) and DEA to evaluate resource efficiency and assess the potential for enhancing competitiveness within the Australian agri-food sector. Fan and Fang [33] evaluated the levels of CE development across regions in China and proposed strategic recommendations to promote CE initiatives, thus facilitating the country's transition toward a more sustainable development paradigm. Liu et al. [34] evaluated the eco-efficiency of a circular economy system in China's coal mining regions, utilizing emergy theory combined with DEA to provide a comprehensive assessment. Jiang et al. [35] proposed a data-driven methodology that integrates R clustering, DEA, and gray relational analysis (GRA) to evaluate the ecological performance of remanufacturing processes, thereby facilitating the development of more effective strategic solutions.

Table 2. Top 10 highly cited papers published from 2015 to 2024.

Authors	Title	Year	Citations	Cites per Year
Song, X.; Zhou, Y.; Jia, W. [26]	How do economic openness and R&D investment affect green economic growth?—evidence from China	2019	184	28.68
Wu, J.; Zhu, Q.; Ji, X.; Chu, J.; Liang, L. [27]	Two-stage network processes with shared resources and resources recovered from undesirable outputs	2016	143	15.19
Halkos, G.; Petrou, K.N. [28]	Assessing 28 EU member states' environmental efficiency in national waste generation with DEA	2019	138	21.51
Mavi, N.K.; Mavi, R.K. [31]	Energy and environmental efficiency of OECD countries in the context of the circular economy: Common weight analysis for Malmquist productivity index	2019	133	20.73
Pagotto, M.; Halog, A. [32]	Towards a Circular Economy in Australian Agri-food Industry: An Application of Input-Output Oriented Approaches for Analyzing Resource Efficiency and Competitiveness Potential	2016	131	13.91
Fan, Y.; Fang, C. [33]	Circular economy development in China-current situation, evaluation and policy implications	2020	130	24.00
Liu, X.; Guo, P.; Guo, S. [34]	Assessing the eco-efficiency of a circular economy system in China's coal mining areas: Emergy and data envelopment analysis	2019	109	16.99
Giannakitsidou, O.; Giannikos, I.; Chondrou, A. [29]	Ranking European countries on the basis of their environmental and circular economy performance: A DEA application in MSW	2020	107	19.75
Expósito, A.; Velasco, F. [30]	Municipal solid-waste recycling market and the European 2020 Horizon Strategy: A regional efficiency analysis in Spain	2018	104	14.02
Jiang, Z.; Ding, Z.; Zhang, H.; Cai, W.; Liu, Y. [35]	Data-driven ecological performance evaluation for remanufacturing process	2019	101	15.74

Note: The total number of citations was obtained from Scopus in May 2025.

An important aspect of content analysis is examining the geographical distribution of research objects. This offers insights into the level of global interest and engagement with the DEA applications in the circular economy domain. In the analyzed papers, international research was conducted across four regions—the EU, EEA, OECD, and V4 countries. The remaining studies encompassed a total of 20 countries, of which approximately 50% are situated in Europe.

Table 3 presents the distribution of articles by country (or territory) of study. The table indicates that out of 151 articles, approximately 43% are devoted to assessing the efficiency of the circular economy in China. Researchers predominantly apply DEA at the national level, with Chinese provinces serving as the decision-making units (DMUs). The principal data source for such studies is the China Statistical Yearbook, which offers a comprehensive array of statistical information. While it offers a broad quantitative data set, it also includes key statistics related to resource utilization, waste management, recycling, and environmental protection that are essential for evaluating circularity.

Table 3. Geographical scope.

Country/Territory	Number of Studies	Primary Level of Analysis	Primary Data Source
China	65	National	China Statistical Yearbook
EU	28	International	Eurostat database
Italy	8	National	The Italian Institute for Environmental Protection and Research (ISPRA)
Chile	8	National	National System for the Declaration of Waste (SINADER)
Spain	7	Regional	Regional databases of autonomous communities
OECD	3	International	OECD database
Taiwan	3	National	Database of Taiwan Environmental Protection Administration
Brazil	2	National	National Sanitation Information System (SNIS) database

The EU countries are next in terms of geographical coverage. The application of the DEA method to the analysis of CE in EU countries was documented in a total of 28 articles, which accounted for 19% of the selected studies. The main data source for these studies was the Eurostat database, which provides a comprehensive collection of data relevant to measuring the efficiency of the circular economy within EU member states. The available data focused on resource use, waste management, recycling, and material flows, enabling the assessment of how effectively economies were transitioning toward circularity.

A total of eight articles focused on research conducted in Italy and Chile, respectively. In both cases, the primary level of analysis was at the national scale, primarily due to the accessibility of data collected by governmental authorities at the provincial level. The datasets were obtained from the database of the Italian Institute for Environmental Protection and Research (ISPRA) and the National System for the Declaration of Waste (SINADER). These databases contained important indicators of the circular economy, particularly in the context of waste management and resource efficiency, and were aggregated at the national level. In contrast, research on the CE in Spain was conducted exclusively at the regional level. A total of seven such studies were identified.

Three studies on the CE within OECD countries were grounded in data obtained from the OECD database. In the cases of Taiwan and Brazil, the analysis was primarily conducted at the national level. Regional data were obtained from the respective databases provided by environmental ministries. The Brazilian SNIS database provided municipal-level information and was administered by the Ministry of Regional Development. Regional environmental data for Taiwan were provided by the Ministry of Environment through an open data platform.

Figure 5 categorizes the selected studies into distinct levels to clarify the scale at which each study operates. It shows that 22 articles were conducted at the local level. These papers primarily examined operational practices or case studies related to resource management and circular economy implementation at the organizational or technological level. A total of 21 papers focused on the regional level, utilizing provincial databases to facilitate comparisons within one or more administrative regions. Additionally, 71 studies were conducted at the national level, representing the largest category within the dataset. This prevalence is primarily attributable to the existence of comprehensive and systematically maintained databases curated by government organizations, which support large-scale national analyses. At the international level, 37 country-specific studies were identified, mainly focusing on research within EU and OECD member countries.

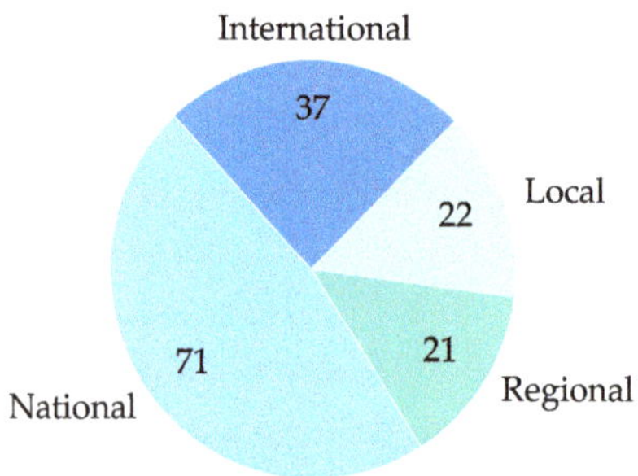

Figure 5. Number of papers by the level of analysis.

The distribution of studies across these levels reflects both the availability of relevant data sources and the scope of research interests within the field. The observed distribution of papers across different levels of analysis was largely influenced by the availability of data sources. Specifically, the predominance of studies at the national level could be linked to the existence of comprehensive databases that enabled analysis across various regions or provinces. Conversely, the relative scarcity of regional- and local-level studies may have been attributed to challenges related to obtaining datasets at the municipal or organizational level, which often required extensive primary data collection or access to proprietary information. Therefore, the current distribution reflects not only research priorities but also the practical constraints imposed by data availability, highlighting the critical role that existing data sources played in shaping analysis within the CE field.

As illustrated in Figure 6, the majority of researchers demonstrate a preference for well-established, single-stage DEA models for evaluating the efficiency of the circular economy. This preference is primarily driven by the availability of existing software tools that facilitate their calculations. Conversely, network models, as highlighted in [36], have recently begun to gain traction and are gradually becoming more common within the literature. These studies typically employ two-stage models, a choice largely influenced by their simple structure and the relative ease of implementation. The adoption of a more complex network DEA models often require the development of specialized mathematical models adapted to specific problems, which can pose significant methodological challenges. Consequently, such studies constitute a minority within this review, reflecting both the developmental stage of these models and their higher implementation complexity.

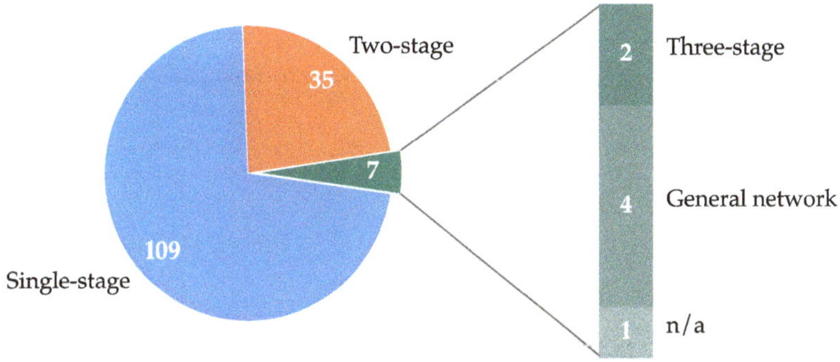

Figure 6. Network structure of DEA models.

Figure 7 represents the distribution of papers by technology type used for constructing the production possibility set of DEA models. Note that the total number of technologies exceeds the total number of articles. This is because papers that proposed multiple DEA models with different RTS assumptions were counted multiple times. The diagram shows that both CRS and VRS types were used with comparable frequency; however, the CRS assumption was utilized slightly more often. The application of other types of technology was exceedingly limited.

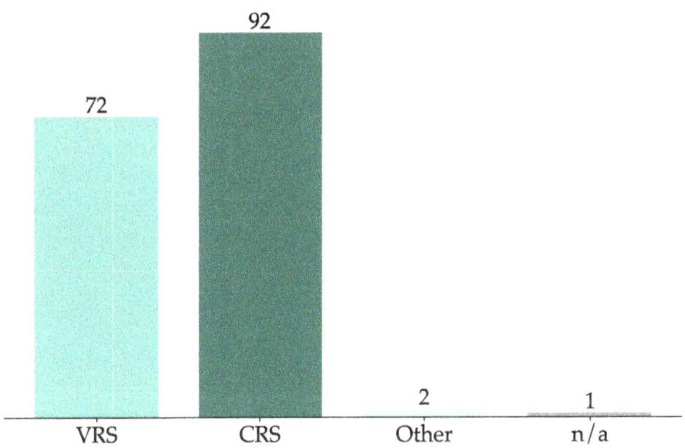

Figure 7. Number of articles by DEA technology type.

Table 4 summarizes the measures of efficiency used in single-stage DEA models. The majority of the studies employed conventional CCR and BCC models with radial measures of efficiency. The slack-based measure was used in 17% of single-stage models, making it the second most frequently used method. However, it is worth noting that SBM was the predominant efficiency assessment method within network DEA models. Compared to SBM, the DDF measure was used less frequently. Benefit of the Doubt, the Russell measure, and other methods for assessing efficiency are generally scarce, and their application by researchers remained irregular. This pattern persisted within circular economy studies, reflecting a narrow application of different efficiency assessment techniques in the field.

Table 4. Measure of efficiency in single-stage DEA models.

Measure of Efficiency	Publications	Percentage (%)
Radial	69	63.30
Slack-based	18	16.51
DDF	11	10.09
Benefit of the Doubt	3	2.75
Russell	2	1.84
Other	6	5.51
Total	109	100.00

Combining DEA with other methods is an important aspect of CE research. This integration allows for the development of new knowledge and improved modeling capabilities. Our analysis reveals that the majority of the examined studies employed DEA as the main metric for evaluating efficiency in the circular economy. Furthermore, approximately half of the analyzed papers relied solely on DEA to calculate performance estimates and draw conclusions based on these results to answer research questions and provide policy recommendations.

Table 5 provides a comprehensive summary of the methods employed in conjunction with DEA. This table illustrates the diversity of approaches used for measuring CE in combination with DEA. A noteworthy trend among the examined papers is the prevalence of second-stage analyses that aim to identify the causes of inefficiency. This approach usually involves statistical methods with respect to exogenous factors and often uses truncated regression (tobit) models. In many papers, DMUs are geographically linked, representing countries, regions, municipalities, or cities. Consequently, specialized geographic regression methods, such as geographically weighted regression, Moran's I, and spatial migration analysis, are employed to reveal geographical patterns. The Malmquist index and its generalizations, including the Malmquist–Luenberger productivity index, are frequently utilized to assess the dynamic performance of units. Factor analysis is commonly combined with DEA to reduce the number of input and output variables, thereby enhancing the overall efficiency of the analysis. Cluster analysis is typically applied following DEA to identify groups of similar DMUs based on their efficiency scores.

Table 5. Combination of DEA with other methods.

Category	Methods, Publications
Statistical analysis	Convergence analysis [14,37–40], OLS [30,41–45], Tobit model [16,30,39,46–53], other regression analysis [26,54–57], Panel regression [45,58,59], Non-parametric regression [60], Kernel density estimation [17,61], Kruskal–Wallis test [42,59,61–67], Mann–Whitney test [61,63,68], Kolmogorov–Smirnov test [42,46,61], Wilcoxon test [69,70]
Factor analysis	Principal component analysis [71–76]
Cluster analysis	[35,47,74,77,78]
Network analysis	Gravitational model [79], Social network analysis [76,79], Augmented gravity model [80]
Spatial analysis	Moran's I [16,79,81–83], Geographically weighted regression [79,84], Spatial Durbin model [79,81,83], Exploratory spatial data analysis [79], Geographic detector [84], Spatial migration analysis [17], Spatial lag model [81], Spatial error model [81]

Table 5. *Cont.*

Category	Methods, Publications
Temporal analysis	Malmquist productivity index [31,38,45,48,54,85–92], Malmquist–Luenberger productivity index [66,86,93]
Other	Multiple-criteria decision analysis [37,82,94], Analytic hierarchy process [72,95], Grey relational analysis [35,96], Coupling coordination degree analysis [82,97], Material flow analysis [32,98], Decoupling index [99], Exploratory data analysis [23], Improved fruit fly optimization algorithm [96], Artificial neural networks [100], Net present value calculation [101]

4. Discussion and Policy Implications

To evaluate how DEA models capture the principles of the CE, the existing literature was analyzed through the lens of the R-ladder framework. Several different R-ladders are currently known in the literature, which more or less capture the concept of the circular economy.

The classic 3R principle of the circular economy—Reduce, Reuse, Recycle—originally formed the basis of circular thinking and waste management strategies. It was initially conceived as a waste prevention strategy to promote more efficient resource utilization, mitigate waste generation, and lessen overall environmental impact. The progressive evolution of R-concepts in recent years reflects a more sophisticated understanding of how to optimize resource efficiency and minimize environmental impact throughout a product's entire life cycle. A guiding principle across these frameworks is the inherent hierarchy—strategies positioned higher in the hierarchy (corresponding to lower R numbers) are generally more desirable as they preserve greater value and have a smaller environmental footprint. The various R frameworks (3R, 6R, 9R, 10R, and 12R) are not merely additive; they build on each other by integrating more nuanced strategies that intervene earlier in the product life cycle, thereby preserving higher material and functional value. Strategies such as 'Refuse' and 'Rethink' are considered to have the greatest impact, whereas 'Recycle' and 'Recover' are generally seen as last-resort options within the hierarchy. The growing number of R-terms in the literature reflects the increasing complexity and holistic nature of CE implementation across diverse economic sectors. By implementing these strategies, the circular economy aims to create a more sustainable and resource-efficient system that moves away from the linear 'take-make-dispose' model.

In this study, we rely on the popular 9R concept—a set of strategies focused on minimizing waste and maximizing resource utilization. These strategies include Refuse, Rethink, Reduce, Reuse, Repair, Refurbish, Remanufacture, Repurpose, Recycle, and Recover. They are often presented in hierarchical order, with the earlier 'Rs' being preferable as they prevent waste at the source (see Table 6).

In each DEA model, the set of inputs and outputs determined which aspect of the circular economy was being measured. Next, frequency analysis was used to determine which R-strategies are most frequently evaluated in the literature using DEA (see Table 7).

Our analysis reveals a significant gap between the hierarchical ideal of the circular economy and the practical application of DEA in measuring it. The literature can be categorized based on the R-strategies that current DEA models are equipped to measure, highlighting a clear bias toward lower-value, end-of-life processes.

The most commonly measured aspect of the CE is the performance of the recycling (or waste management with recycling) system (R8). Both environmental aspects of this efficiency and purely economic aspects, i.e., the efficiency of recycling business models, are measured. In addition, several studies in our sample have focused on comparing the characteristics of several different recycling technologies and several different organizational designs.

Table 6. R-strategies of the circular economy.

R-Strategy	Explanation
R0 Refuse	Actively choosing not to consume or use products that are unsustainable or unnecessary.
R1 Rethink	A fundamental rethinking of products and systems to find more sustainable alternatives.
R2 Reduce	Minimizing resource consumption and waste generation through efficient production processes and mindful consumption.
R3 Reuse	Using items for other uses.
R4 Repair	Fixing broken products to extend their lifespan and prevent them from being discarded.
R5 Refurbish	Renovating or upgrading products to make them functional again, often with updated features.
R6 Remanufacture	Creating new products from used components, often with the same functionality as the original product.
R7 Repurpose	Finding new and creative uses for discarded items, giving them a new life.
R8 Recycle	Processing used materials into new products, closing the loop on material life cycles.
R9 Recover	Recovering energy or materials from waste that cannot be recycled or reused.

Table 7. The frequency of measuring CE according to the characteristics of the R-strategy.

R-Strategy	Publications	Percentage (%)
R0 Refuse	[28,102,103]	1.40
R1 Rethink	[102,103]	0.93
R2 Reduce	[14–16,23,26,28,31,32,34,39,42,43,45,53,57,59,69–71,78,79,82–84,88,98,99,102–125]	23.72
R3 Reuse	[28,29,33,102]	1.86
R4 Repair	[28,29,96,102]	1.86
R5 Refurbish	[29,56,74,76,87,89,102,126]	3.72
R6 Remanufacture	[29,35,56,74,76,87,89,102,126]	4.19
R7 Repurpose	[21,29,102,127]	1.86
R8 Recycle	[13,14,16–18,20–23,27,29,30,37–41,44,45,47–52,54–58,60–68,72–77,79–81,83,85–97,99–103,115,117–119,122,126–167]	53.02
R9 Recover	[20–22,37,40,46,47,52,73,89,90,102,129,145,148,149]	7.44

Temerbulatova et al. [136] present a typical example of a model measuring recycling efficiency, using 27 EU countries as DMUs. The inputs of the model are X_1—generation of municipal waste per capita (kg per capita); X_2—water exploitation index; X_3—final energy consumption (million tons of oil equivalent); and X_4—social progress index (SPI). The outputs of the model are Y_1—circular material use rate (% of total material use) and Y_2—municipal waste recycling rate (%). According to the model's logic, efficient countries are those that achieve the highest indicators for waste recycling and the reuse of recovered materials, while minimizing municipal waste generation, water, energy consumption, and social capital input. In essence, efficient countries possess the most effective material recycling systems, which aligns with stage R8 of the circular economy principles.

The second most popular dimension of CE, measured with DEA, is the efficient use of resources, primarily natural resources such as energy and water, but in some cases, financial resources also. Most often, resource efficiency is measured at the sectoral, regional, or even national level. Improving resource efficiency can be attributed to the R2 strategy (Reduce). The same type of strategy was applied to models in which the volume or share of renewable energy produced was taken into account as one of the outputs. In this case, we assumed that the use of RES reduces the use of other nonrenewable natural resources.

A typical example of a DEA model measuring resource efficiency (R2) is presented by Xian et al. [43]. This study evaluates the efficiency of the 10 administrative districts of Shenzhen City, treating them as DMUs, using the following inputs and outputs. The inputs included in the model are: X_1—energy input (gasoline for production and supply of water + diesel for production and supply of water) (ton of SCE); X_2—water input (industrial water consumption + residential water consumption) (m^3); X_3—completed investment in water resource management (Yuan). The following indicators are used as outputs in the model: Y_1—GDP (Yuan); Y_2—undesirable output (treated wastewater − reuse of wastewater + discarded wastewater) (m^3). The model has a simple one-stage structure. According to the optimization algorithm's logic, the most efficient administrative districts are those that achieve maximum economic output (GDP) and minimum wastewater production, with the least possible consumption of energy, water, and investment resources. This implies the most efficient use of water and energy in production processes and effective water resource management. This approach aligns with the R-ladder concept's R2 stage, which focuses on reducing the use of natural resources.

Next in popularity is the R9 strategy. Typically, it reflects the performance of recycling and waste management systems. It can be distinguished as a separate strategy only by the inputs and outputs of the DEA model, which take into account energy consumption and recovery.

The remaining strategies are difficult to define unambiguously, as different aspects of the circular economy are intertwined in most DEA models. In particular, when using an indicator like the "circular material use rate" (https://ec.europa.eu/eurostat/web/products-manuals-and-guidelines/-/ks-gq-18-013, accessed on 27 June 2025) as an output of the model, a high efficiency score may indicate both the development of a recycling system and the development of higher rungs of the R-ladder, such as R4—Repair, R5—Refurbish, and R6—Remanufacture. When the DEA model is built to evaluate the efficiency of a production system, in our opinion, the use of strategies R7 and R3 is unlikely, as production processes are highly standardized and often do not allow the reuse of equipment, materials, and raw materials. However, when it comes to households and municipalities, the use of the R3 or even R0 strategy is quite likely and can be indirectly detected in the reduction of household waste generation. Therefore, all strategies that relate to product life cycle prolongation are labeled as probable in most of the papers.

For a more complex conceptual model, consider the one constructed by Castellano et al. [103], where the DMUs included 54 OECD countries and several other nations. The inputs of this model were X_1—material footprint and X_2—hazardous waste per capita. It is important to note that these indicators were not traditional resources; rather, they represented undesirable outputs of the economic system. However, in the DEA, a common practice is to ensure the minimization of such undesirable outputs (like hazardous waste or material footprint) is to treat them as inputs within the model. This approach aligns with DEA's principle of minimizing inputs to achieve efficiency and was frequently employed in environmental efficiency studies. A wide range of indicators served as outputs of the model, as follows: Y_1—domestic material consumption, Y_2—municipal waste recovered, Y_3—number of companies publishing sustainability reports, Y_4—sustainable public procurement policies and action plans, Y_5—global citizenship education and education for sustainable development in curricula, Y_6—global citizenship education and education for sustainable development in teacher education, Y_7—global citizenship education and education for sustainable development in national education policies.

In this scenario, the most effective countries are those that generate the smallest environmental footprint and the least hazardous waste per capita. Simultaneously, they achieve the highest rates of waste recycling (R8, R9), prioritize domestic resource consumption (thereby reducing reliance on other resource types, R2), and actively promote R0—Rethink and R1—Refuse through enhanced corporate and civic environmental responsibility. It is important to note that the prevalence of R0—Rethink and R1—Refuse practices is measured indirectly in this model. This exemplifies a key advantage of DEA as a methodology—its capacity to measure latent variables, which are not directly quantifiable, by forming complex combinations of input and output indicators. However, our sample included very few studies that used such an approach

Only one paper considered all rungs of the R-ladder due to the fact that the data were collected by a survey method [102]. This made it possible to determine exactly what strategy is used by the surveyed enterprises.

It is also worth mentioning that, in contemporary literature, DEA is often combined with other methods. Our sample also includes articles where DEA is combined, most often with regression, less often with spatial models [16,39,52,62,111]. However, in these studies, the efficiency indicator of a circular process or system is first calculated using DEA, and then regression is applied to identify the determinants of the already calculated efficiency. That is, nothing changes in the very approach to measuring the efficiency (in this case, circularity) of the studied process or system. Thus, the use of additional methods does not contribute to improving the measurability of circular processes and/or systems.

Therefore, the analysis demonstrates the following critical disconnect: DEA models are most frequently applied to the least desirable circular economy strategies (Recycling and Recovery). It is worth noting that this is not an inherent flaw in the DEA methodology itself, but rather a direct consequence of a systemic lack of clear and specific statistical indicators for higher-order R-strategies. The "measurable" aspects of the CE are those that generate easily quantifiable data (e.g., tons of waste recycled, energy recovered), while the more impactful, preventative strategies (e.g., product redesign, conscious non-consumption) remain statistically invisible.

This creates a significant risk of misinterpretation. Relying on current DEA applications alone could lead to the conclusion that the circular economy is primarily about waste management, rather than a fundamental redesign of our production and consumption systems. The ambiguity of indicators like the "circular material use rate" further compounds this issue, as it conflates low-value recycling with high-value product life extension, preventing a nuanced evaluation of circular progress. Unfortunately, the potential of constructing informative indices reflecting the effectiveness of all circular economy strategies using DEA has not yet been fully realized in practice due to the lack of clear statistical indicators measuring the effectiveness of actions aimed at prolonging the product life cycle. The first steps of the hierarchy of R-strategies could only be determined indirectly from data on the development of innovation, circular economy education, and waste reduction.

Another area in which DEA applications for measuring CE could be improved is that, although methods exist [168], not all CE-related DEA studies include undesirable outputs (e.g., pollution and residual waste), which lead to incomplete assessments. Furthermore, few DEA-based studies translate their results into policy recommendations for accelerating the transition to a circular economy. The link between efficiency scores and actionable strategies is weak.

Drawing upon the analysis presented in this review, several critical and urgent policy implications for the effective transition toward a circular economy emerge. Firstly, statistical agencies must significantly enhance their data infrastructure. This requires the proactive development and implementation of new statistical indicators designed to capture activities at the top of the 'R-ladder' hierarchy. Quantifiable metrics relating to product repair rates, refurbishment volumes, the penetration of reuse platforms, and the adoption of genuinely circular business models are essential for accurately assessing CE progress and the effectiveness of related interventions.

Secondly, policymakers must be wary of policy distortion resulting from an undue reliance on existing metrics. Current assessment frameworks often inadvertently prioritize end-of-pipe solutions, such as recycling (R8) and energy recovery (R9), which can create perverse incentives. This can lead to resources being misallocated toward less impactful recovery operations at the expense of critical investments in upstream innovation, such as waste prevention (R0), extended product longevity (R1), and fundamental system-level redesign (R2).

Thirdly, this review highlights the importance of promoting methodological diversity in assessment. Although quantitative tools such as data envelopment analysis (DEA) can provide valuable insights, they should be used alongside a wider range of assessment tools. As existing research has highlighted, survey-based methodologies can be an effective way of capturing the adoption and diffusion of higher-order circular strategies. Integrating qualitative data and detailed case studies is essential to provide a more comprehensive and contextualized understanding of the challenges and successes of CE implementation.

Finally, direct policy support for innovation in measurement and practice is crucial, particularly with regard to 'Rethink' and 'Refuse' strategies. As these strategies are inherently linked to shifts in design paradigms, consumption patterns, and educational initiatives, they require dedicated funding for research and development. This includes supporting pilot projects that rigorously test new circular business models, as well as investing in comprehensive educational programs that foster sustainable consumption. While the direct impact of these programs may not be quantifiable by traditional efficiency models. Such targeted investments are essential for catalyzing systemic change and ensuring a truly effective circular transition.

5. Conclusions

This systematic literature review of DEA applications within the CE context reveals a significant growth in scholarly interest in recent years. This increasing attention is accompanied by an evolution in the complexity of DEA models employed, with network and dynamic DEA approaches becoming increasingly prevalent. This methodological sophistication reflects a desire to capture the multifaceted and temporally evolving nature of CE performance.

The observed popularity of DEA stems from its capacity to generate comprehensive performance indices by leveraging readily available statistical data. These indices offer a valuable lens through which to evaluate the development level of various CE dimensions, providing a more holistic understanding than is attainable through the isolated analysis of individual statistical indicators. Specifically, DEA-derived efficiency scores serve as latent variables, effectively synthesizing the complex interplay of factors contributing to CE performance. These scores represent an indirect, but insightful, measure of aspects that are either impossible or excessively time-consuming to quantify directly.

Our analysis indicates that DEA models yield particularly informative insights when evaluating the implementation of circular strategies, i.e., R2—Reduce, R8—Recycling, and R9—Recovering. However, the current capabilities of the DEA appear limited in comprehensively assessing the extent and effectiveness of other circular economic strategies. While opportunities exist to manipulate indicators for indirect reflection of specific aspects, a pressing need remains for further development of the statistical framework employed in measuring the circular economy.

Regarding the geographical distribution of the surveyed literature, a significant proportion, exceeding 40%, focuses on China. The European Union is also prominently represented, accounting for nearly 20% of the studies. Conversely, other geographical regions are sparsely represented within our sample, highlighting a potential gap in the current research landscape.

Supplementary Materials: The following supporting information can be downloaded at https://www.mdpi.com/article/10.3390/mca30050102/s1, Table S1: Summary of selected articles for the systematic literature review, and Table S2: Overview of DEA models used for measuring circular economy performance.

Author Contributions: Conceptualization, S.V.R.; methodology, S.V.R. and A.V.L.; software, E.D.M. and D.M.M.; validation, S.V.R. and A.V.L.; formal analysis, A.V.L., E.D.M. and D.M.M.; investigation, E.D.M. and D.M.M.; resources, S.V.R., E.D.M. and D.M.M.; data curation, E.D.M. and D.M.M.; writing—original draft preparation, S.V.R. and A.V.L.; writing—review and editing, S.V.R. and A.V.L.; visualization, A.V.L., E.D.M. and D.M.M.; supervision, S.V.R.; project administration, S.V.R.; funding acquisition, S.V.R. All authors have read and agreed to the published version of the manuscript.

Funding: This research was funded by the Russian Science Foundation (project No. 23-11-00197). https://rscf.ru/en/project/23-11-00197/ (accessed on 10 July 2025).

Data Availability Statement: The original contributions presented in this study are included in the article. Further inquiries can be directed to the corresponding authors.

Acknowledgments: The authors thank the journal editor and anonymous reviewers for their guidance and constructive suggestions.

Conflicts of Interest: The authors declare no conflicts of interest. The funders had no role in the design of the study; in the collection, analyses, or interpretation of data; in the writing of the manuscript; or in the decision to publish the results.

Abbreviations

The following abbreviations are used in this manuscript:

BCC	Banker, Charnes, Cooper
CCR	Charnes, Cooper, Rhodes
CE	Circular Economy
CRS	Constant Returns-to-Scale
DDF	Directional Distance Function
DEA	Data Envelopment Analysis
DMU	Decision Making Unit
EEA	European Economic Area
EU	European Union
GRA	Grey Relational Analysis
MFA	Material Flow Analysis
OECD	Organization for Economic Co-operation and Development
SBM	Slacks-Based Measure
VRS	Variable Returns-to-Scale

References

1. Rosa, P.; Sassanelli, C.; Rocca, R.; Terzi, S. A Review of Circularity Performance Assessment Methods. In Proceedings of the XXIV Summer School "Francesco Turco"—Industrial Systems Engineering, Brescia, Italy, 11–13 September 2019; pp. 293–299.
2. Sánchez-Ortiz, J.; Rodríguez-Cornejo, V.; Del Río-Sánchez, R.; García-Valderrama, T. Indicators to Measure Efficiency in Circular Economies. *Sustainability* **2020**, *12*, 4483. [CrossRef]
3. Corona, B.; Shen, L.; Reike, D.; Rosales Carreón, J.; Worrell, E. Towards sustainable development through the circular economy—A review and critical assessment on current circularity metrics. *Resour. Conserv. Recycl.* **2019**, *151*, 104498. [CrossRef]
4. Pan, Y.; Hashemizadeh, A. Circular economy-based assessment framework for enhancing sustainability in renewable energy development with life cycle considerations. *Environ. Impact Assess. Rev.* **2023**, *103*, 107289. [CrossRef]
5. Parchomenko, A.; Nelen, D.; Gillabel, J.; Rechberger, H. Measuring the circular economy—A Multiple Correspondence Analysis of 63 metrics. *J. Clean. Prod.* **2019**, *210*, 200–216. [CrossRef]
6. De Pascale, A.; Arbolino, R.; Szopik-Depczyńska, K.; Limosani, M.; Ioppolo, G. A systematic review for measuring circular economy: The 61 indicators. *J. Clean. Prod.* **2021**, *281*, 124942. [CrossRef]
7. Potting, J.; Hekkert, M.; Worrell, E.; Hanemaaijer, A. Circular economy: Measuring innovation in the product chain. In *Technical Report 2544*; Policy Report; PBL Netherlands Environmental Assessment Agency: The Hague, The Netherlands, 2016.
8. Bocken, N.M.P.; de Pauw, I.; Bakker, C.; van der Grinten, B. Product design and business model strategies for a circular economy. *J. Ind. Prod. Eng.* **2016**, *33*, 308–320. [CrossRef]
9. Pauliuk, S. Critical appraisal of the circular economy standard BS 8001:2017 and a dashboard of quantitative system indicators for its implementation in organizations. *Resour. Conserv. Recycl.* **2018**, *129*, 81–92. [CrossRef]
10. Park, K.; Kremer, G.E.O. Text mining-based categorization and user perspective analysis of environmental sustainability indicators for manufacturing and service systems. *Ecol. Indic.* **2017**, *72*, 803–820. [CrossRef]
11. Sassanelli, C.; Rosa, P.; Rocca, R.; Terzi, S. Circular economy performance assessment methods: A systematic literature review. *J. Clean. Prod.* **2019**, *229*, 440–453. [CrossRef]
12. Moraga, G.; Huysveld, S.; Mathieux, F.; Blengini, G.A.; Alaerts, L.; Van Acker, K.; de Meester, S.; Dewulf, J. Circular economy indicators: What do they measure? *Resour. Conserv. Recycl.* **2019**, *146*, 452–461. [CrossRef] [PubMed]
13. Li, D.; Wang, M.Q.; Lee, C. The waste treatment and recycling efficiency of industrial waste processing based on two-stage data envelopment analysis with undesirable inputs. *J. Clean. Prod.* **2020**, *242*, 118279. [CrossRef]
14. Ding, L.L.; Lei, L.; Wang, L.; Zhang, L.F.; Calin, A.C. A novel cooperative game network DEA model for marine circular economy performance evaluation of China. *J. Clean. Prod.* **2020**, *253*, 120071. [CrossRef]
15. Wang, S.; Lei, L.; Xing, L. Urban circular economy performance evaluation: A novel fully fuzzy data envelopment analysis with large datasets. *J. Clean. Prod.* **2021**, *324*, 129214. [CrossRef]
16. Lu, C.; Zhang, Y.; Li, H.; Zhang, Z.; Cheng, W.; Jin, S.; Liu, W. An integrated measurement of the efficiency of China's industrial circular economy and associated influencing factors. *Mathematics* **2020**, *8*, 1610. [CrossRef]
17. Zhang, L.; Zhuang, Y.; Chiu, Y.H.; Pang, Q.; Chen, Z.; Shi, Z. Measuring urban integrated water use efficiency and spatial migration path in China: A dynamic two-stage recycling model within the directional distance function. *J. Environ. Manag.* **2021**, *298*, 113379. [CrossRef] [PubMed]
18. Lombardi, G.V.; Gastaldi, M.; Rapposelli, A.; Romano, G. Assessing efficiency of urban waste services and the role of tariff in a circular economy perspective: An empirical application for Italian municipalities. *J. Clean. Prod.* **2021**, *323*, 129097. [CrossRef]
19. Shabanpour, H.; Yousefi, S.; Farzipoor Saen, R. Forecasting sustainability of supply chains in the circular economy context: A dynamic network data envelopment analysis and artificial neural network approach. *J. Enterp. Inf. Manag.* **2025**, *38*, 68–93. [CrossRef]
20. Huang, H.C.; Hu, C.F. Performance measurement for the recycling production system using cooperative game network data envelopment analysis. *Sustainability* **2021**, *13*, 11060. [CrossRef]
21. Sun, J.; Li, G.; Wang, Z. Technology heterogeneity and efficiency of China's circular economic systems: A game meta-frontier DEA approach. *Resour. Conserv. Recycl.* **2019**, *146*, 337–347. [CrossRef]
22. Callao, C.; Martinez-Nu nez, M.; Latorre, M.P. European Countries: Does common legislation guarantee better hazardous waste performance for European Union member states? *Waste Manag.* **2019**, *84*, 147–157. [CrossRef]
23. Taboada, G.L.; Seruca, I.; Sousa, C.; Pereira, Á. Exploratory data analysis and Data Envelopment Analysis of construction and Demolition Waste management in the European Economic Area. *Sustainability* **2020**, *12*, 4995. [CrossRef]
24. Petticrew, M.; Roberts, H. *Systematic Reviews in the Social Sciences: A Practical Guide*; John Wiley & Sons, Ltd.: Hoboken, NJ, USA, 2006. [CrossRef]
25. Staples, M.; Niazi, M. Experiences using systematic review guidelines. *J. Syst. Softw.* **2007**, *80*, 1425–1437. [CrossRef]
26. Song, X.; Zhou, Y.; Jia, W. How do economic openness and R&D investment affect green economic growth?—Evidence from China. *Resour. Conserv. Recycl.* **2019**, *146*, 405–415. [CrossRef]

27. Wu, J.; Zhu, Q.; Ji, X.; Chu, J.; Liang, L. Two-stage network processes with shared resources and resources recovered from undesirable outputs. *Eur. J. Oper. Res.* **2016**, *251*, 182–197. [CrossRef]
28. Halkos, G.; Petrou, K.N. Assessing 28 EU member states' environmental efficiency in national waste generation with DEA. *J. Clean. Prod.* **2019**, *208*, 509–521. [CrossRef]
29. Giannakitsidou, O.; Giannikos, I.; Chondrou, A. Ranking European countries on the basis of their environmental and circular economy performance: A DEA application in MSW. *Waste Manag.* **2020**, *109*, 181–191. [CrossRef]
30. Expósito, A.; Velasco, F. Municipal solid-waste recycling market and the European 2020 Horizon Strategy: A regional efficiency analysis in Spain. *J. Clean. Prod.* **2018**, *172*, 938–948. [CrossRef]
31. Mavi, N.K.; Mavi, R.K. Energy and environmental efficiency of OECD countries in the context of the circular economy: Common weight analysis for malmquist productivity index. *J. Environ. Manag.* **2019**, *247*, 651–661. [CrossRef]
32. Pagotto, M.; Halog, A. Towards a circular economy in Australian agri-food industry: An application of input-output oriented approaches for analyzing resource efficiency and competitiveness potential. *J. Ind. Ecol.* **2016**, *20*, 1176–1186. [CrossRef]
33. Fan, Y.; Fang, C. Circular economy development in China-current situation, evaluation and policy implications. *Environ. Impact Assess. Rev.* **2020**, *84*, 106441. [CrossRef]
34. Liu, X.; Guo, P.; Guo, S. Assessing the eco-efficiency of a circular economy system in China's coal mining areas: Emergy and data envelopment analysis. *J. Clean. Prod.* **2019**, *206*, 1101–1109. [CrossRef]
35. Jiang, Z.; Ding, Z.; Zhang, H.; Cai, W.; Liu, Y. Data-driven ecological performance evaluation for remanufacturing process. *Energy Convers. Manag.* **2019**, *198*, 111844. [CrossRef]
36. Ratner, S.V.; Shaposhnikov, A.M.; Lychev, A.V. Network DEA and Its Applications (2017–2022): A Systematic Literature Review. *Mathematics* **2023**, *11*, 2141. [CrossRef]
37. Castillo-Giménez, J.; Monta nés, A.; Picazo-Tadeo, A.J. Performance and convergence in municipal waste treatment in the European Union. *Waste Manag.* **2019**, *85*, 222–231. [CrossRef]
38. Zhang, L.; Yang, S.; Dong, Z. Evaluating disparities and convergence of financial support efficiency for resource recycling industry in China. *J. Clean. Prod.* **2023**, *398*, 136655. [CrossRef]
39. Zou, W.; Yang, Y.; Yang, M.; Zhang, X.; Lai, S.; Chen, H. Analyzing efficiency measurement and influencing factors of China's marine green economy: Based on a two-stage network DEA model. *Front. Mar. Sci.* **2023**, *10*, 1020373. [CrossRef]
40. Chioatto, E.; Fedele, A.; Ciro Liscio, M.; Sospiro, P. Testing data envelopment analysis models on the performance of European Union regions in sustainable waste management. *Waste Manag.* **2024**, *175*, 170–182. [CrossRef]
41. Lacko, R.; Hajduová, Z.; Zawada, M. The efficiency of circular economies: A comparison of Visegrád Group countries. *Energies* **2021**, *14*, 1680. [CrossRef]
42. Lee, D.H. Production efficiency and economic benefit evaluation of biohydrogen produced using macroalgae as a biomass feedstock in Asian circular economies. *Int. J. Hydrogen Energy* **2022**, *47*, 40532–40551. [CrossRef]
43. Xian, C.; Yang, S.; Fan, Y.; Wu, H.; Gong, C. Coupling efficiency assessment of food–energy–water (FEW) nexus based on urban resource consumption towards economic development: The case of Shenzhen megacity, China. *Land* **2022**, *11*, 1783. [CrossRef]
44. Gu, Z.; Tian, C.; Zheng, Z.; Zhang, S. Favorable fiscal self-sufficiency enables local governments to better improve the environmental governance—Evidence from China's lower-pollution areas. *Sustainability* **2022**, *14*, 16202. [CrossRef]
45. Huang, S. The impact of globalization on comprehensive environmental efficiency and its sub-stage efficiencies: An adjusted range adjusted measure network data envelopment analysis model approach. *Environ. Prog. Sustain. Energy* **2023**, *42*, e14121. [CrossRef]
46. Lee, D.H. Efficiency and economic benefit of dark-fermentative biohydrogen production in Asian circular economies: Evaluation using soft-link methodology with data envelopment analysis (DEA) and computable general equilibrium model (CGE). *Int. J. Hydrogen Energy* **2020**, *45*, 3688–3698. [CrossRef]
47. Ríos, A.M.; Picazo-Tadeo, A.J. Measuring environmental performance in the treatment of municipal solid waste: The case of the European Union-28. *Ecol. Indic.* **2021**, *123*, 107328. [CrossRef]
48. Xu, X.; Zhou, Q.; Chen, X.; Li, Y.; Jiang, Y. The efficiency of green technology innovation and its influencing factors in wastewater treatment companies. *Separations* **2022**, *9*, 263. [CrossRef]
49. Molinos-Senante, M.; Maziotis, A.; Sala-Garrido, R.; Mocholí-Arce, M. Factors influencing eco-efficiency of municipal solid waste management in Chile: A double-bootstrap approach. *Waste Manag. Res.* **2023**, *41*, 457–466. [CrossRef]
50. Wang, N.; Chai, X.; Guo, Z.; Guo, C.; Liu, J.; Zhang, J. Hierarchy performance assessment of industrial solid waste utilization—tracking resource recycling and utilization centers in China. *Environ. Sci. Pollut. Res. Int.* **2023**, *30*, 83330–83340. [CrossRef]
51. Fu, D.; Huang, Y.; Li, M.; Wang, C. Research on the Measurement of Ecological Performance Levels and Influencing Factors in the Yangtze River Delta Region. *Int. Core J. Eng.* **2023**, *9*, 230–238. [CrossRef]
52. Osińska, M. The determinants of municipal solid waste management efficiency in EU countries. *Econ. Environ.* **2024**, *88*, 637. [CrossRef]

53. Yang, L.; Chen, S.; Chiu, Y.H.; Chang, T.H.; Wang, Y. Reassessment of industrial eco-efficiency in China under the sustainable development goals: A meta two-stage parallel entropy dynamic DDF-DEA model. *J. Clean. Prod.* **2024**, *447*, 141275. [CrossRef]
54. Shang, Y.; Song, M.; Zhao, X. The development of China's Circular Economy: From the perspective of environmental regulation. *Waste Manag.* **2022**, *149*, 186–198. [CrossRef] [PubMed]
55. Sala-Garrido, R.; Mocholi-Arce, M.; Molinos-Senante, M.; Maziotis, A. Measuring technical, environmental and eco-efficiency in municipal solid waste management in Chile. *Int. J. Sustain. Eng.* **2022**, *15*, 71–85. [CrossRef]
56. Marques, A.C.; Teixeira, N.M. Assessment of municipal waste in a circular economy: Do European Union countries share identical performance? *Clean. Waste Syst.* **2022**, *3*, 100034. [CrossRef]
57. Martínez, J.M.G.; Puertas, R.; Martín, J.M.M.; Ribeiro-Soriano, D. Digitalization, innovation and environmental policies aimed at achieving sustainable production. *Sustain. Prod. Consum.* **2022**, *32*, 92–100. [CrossRef]
58. Yang, R.; Wu, S.; Wong, C.W.Y.; Liu, K.; Miao, X.; Chen, Y.; Wang, S.; Tang, Y. The recent ecological efficiency development in China: Interactive systems of economy, society and environment. *Technol. Econ. Dev. Econ.* **2023**, *29*, 217–252. [CrossRef]
59. Liu, D.; Liu, T.; Zheng, Y.; Zhang, Q. The construction efficiency study of China National Ecological Civilization Pilot Zone with network SBM model: A city-based analysis. *Environ. Sci. Pollut. Res. Int.* **2023**, *30*, 47685–47698. [CrossRef]
60. Struk, M.; Bod'a, M. Factors influencing performance in municipal solid waste management —A case study of Czech municipalities. *Waste Manag.* **2022**, *139*, 227–249. [CrossRef]
61. lo Storto, C. Measuring ecoefficiency of municipal solid waste management in Apulia to account for governance heterogeneities. *Clean. Waste Syst.* **2024**, *7*, 100131. [CrossRef]
62. Romano, G.; Molinos-Senante, M. Factors affecting eco-efficiency of municipal waste services in Tuscan municipalities: An empirical investigation of different management models. *Waste Manag.* **2020**, *105*, 384–394. [CrossRef]
63. Delgado-Antequera, L.; Gémar, G.; Molinos-Senante, M.; Gómez, T.; Caballero, R.; Sala-Garrido, R. Eco-efficiency assessment of municipal solid waste services: Influence of exogenous variables. *Waste Manag.* **2021**, *130*, 136–146. [CrossRef]
64. Llanquileo-Melgarejo, P.; Molinos-Senante, M.; Romano, G.; Carosi, L. Evaluation of the impact of separative collection and recycling of municipal solid waste on performance: An empirical application for Chile. *Sustainability* **2021**, *13*, 2022. [CrossRef]
65. Llanquileo-Melgarejo, P.; Molinos-Senante, M. Evaluation of economies of scale in eco-efficiency of municipal waste management: An empirical approach for Chile. *Environ. Sci. Pollut. Res. Int.* **2021**, *28*, 28337–28348. [CrossRef] [PubMed]
66. Llanquileo-Melgarejo, P.; Molinos-Senante, M. Assessing eco-productivity change in Chilean municipal solid waste services. *Util. Policy* **2022**, *78*, 101410. [CrossRef]
67. Hernández-Chover, V.; Castellet-Viciano, L.; Fuentes, R.; Hernández-Sancho, F. Circular economy and efficiency to ensure the sustainability in the wastewater treatment plants. *J. Clean. Prod.* **2023**, *384*, 135563. [CrossRef]
68. Hu, J.L.; Honma, S.; Chang, T.M. Recycling efficiencies in Japan's administrative regions: Findings from network data envelopment analysis. *Circ. Econ. Sustain.* **2024**, *4*, 1–21. [CrossRef]
69. Huang, K.Y.; Chang, T.H.; Chiu, Y.H.; Yang, C.Y.; Lin, T.Y. Considering climate change and regional differences: An efficiency assessment of coal mine use and land restoration. *Nat. Resour. Forum* **2023**, *47*, 578–601. [CrossRef]
70. Li, Y.; Du, L.; Chiu, Y.H. Energy poverty impact on sustainable development of water resources in China: The study of an entropy recycling dynamic two-stage SBM model. *Water* **2024**, *16*, 876. [CrossRef]
71. Li, L.; Lei, Y.; Pan, D.; Si, C. Research on sustainable development of resource-based cities based on the DEA approach: A case study of Jiaozuo, China. *Math. Probl. Eng.* **2016**, *2016*, 5024837. [CrossRef]
72. He, X.; Zhang, J. Supplier selection study under the respective of low-carbon supply chain: A hybrid evaluation model based on FA-DEA-AHP. *Sustainability* **2018**, *10*, 564. [CrossRef]
73. Robaina, M.; Murillo, K.; Rocha, E.; Villar, J. Circular economy in plastic waste—Efficiency analysis of European countries. *Sci. Total Environ.* **2020**, *730*, 139038. [CrossRef]
74. Nazarko, J.; Chodakowska, E.; Nazarko, Ł. Evaluating the transition of the European Union member states towards a circular economy. *Energies* **2022**, *15*, 3924. [CrossRef]
75. Daraio, C.; Di Leo, S.; Simar, L. Viable eco-efficiency targets for waste collection communities. *Sci. Rep.* **2024**, *14*, 15038. [CrossRef] [PubMed]
76. de Oliveira Frascareli, F.C.; Furlan, M.; Mariano, E.B.; Jugend, D. A macro-level circular economy index: Theoretical proposal and application in European Union countries. *Environ. Dev. Sustain.* **2024**, *26*, 18297–18331. [CrossRef]
77. Yamada, T.; Hasegawa, S.; Kinoshita, Y.; Yamada, S.; Inoue, M.; Rosebrock, C.; Bracke, S. Process integration concept for waste reduction among manufacturing planning, modularization and validation. *Procedia Manuf.* **2018**, *21*, 337–344. [CrossRef]
78. Yan, D.; Kong, Y.; Ye, B.; Shi, Y.; Zeng, X. Spatial variation of energy efficiency based on a Super-Slack-Based Measure: Evidence from 104 resource-based cities. *J. Clean. Prod.* **2019**, *240*, 117669. [CrossRef]
79. Han, X.; Zhang, X.; Lei, H. Analysis of the spatial association network structure of water-intensive utilization efficiency and its driving factors in the Yellow River Basin. *Ecol. Indic.* **2024**, *158*, 111400. [CrossRef]

80. Yao, C.; Liu, G.; Hao, X.; Liu, Y. Symbiotic integration of waste disposal capability within a city cluster: The case of the Yangtze River Delta. *J. Environ. Manag.* **2023**, *330*, 117166. [CrossRef]
81. Zhang, L.; Du, X.; Chiu, Y.H.; Pang, Q.; Wang, X.; Yu, Q. Measuring industrial operational efficiency and factor analysis: A dynamic series-parallel recycling DEA model. *Sci. Total Environ.* **2022**, *851*, 158084. [CrossRef]
82. Wang, M.; Yang, C.; Deng, M.; Tao, J.; Jing, X.; Zhao, C. Spatial-temporal differentiation of coupling coordination degree for green finance and green innovation efficiency: A case study in China. *Environ. Sci. Pollut. Res. Int.* **2023**, *30*, 70621–70635. [CrossRef]
83. Chen, P. The spatial impacts of the circular economy on carbon intensity—New evidence from the super-efficient SBM-DEA model. *Energy Environ.* **2024**, *35*, 47–63. [CrossRef]
84. Zhuang, Y.; Zhang, L.; Chiu, Y.H.; Guo, Z.; Chu, Y.; Du, X. Evaluating the recycling efficiency of industrial water use systems in China: Basin differences and factor analysis. *J. Environ. Manag.* **2022**, *316*, 115313. [CrossRef] [PubMed]
85. Ding, L.L.; Lei, L.; Wang, L.; Zhang, L.F. Assessing industrial circular economy performance and its dynamic evolution: An extended Malmquist index based on cooperative game network DEA. *Sci. Total Environ.* **2020**, *731*, 139001. [CrossRef] [PubMed]
86. Llanquileo-Melgarejo, P.; Molinos-Senante, M. The impact of recycling on the productivity of Municipal Solid Waste: A comparison of the Malmquist and Malmquist-Luenberger Productivity Indexes. *Int. J. Sustain. Eng.* **2023**, *16*, 236–247. [CrossRef]
87. Banjerdpaiboon, A.; Limleamthong, P. Assessment of national circular economy performance using super-efficiency dual data envelopment analysis and Malmquist productivity index: Case study of 27 European countries. *Heliyon* **2023**, *9*, e16584. [CrossRef]
88. Xiao, L.; Ye, H.; Xu, S.; Lin, T. Assessment of waste management efficiency using subjective and objective indicators in 26 major Chinese cities. *Ecosyst. Health Sustain.* **2023**, *9*, 0024. [CrossRef]
89. García-Valderrama, T.; Sánchez-Ortiz, J.; Pérez-González, M.D.C.; Puentes-Gra na, M.D.C. Relationship between recycling, circular economy and eco-innovation in Europe. Application of a dynamic network data envelopment analysis model. *Bus. Strategy Environ.* **2024**, *33*, 5955–5974. [CrossRef]
90. Marišová, E.; Fandel, P. Municipal waste management performance: A focus on Slovakia and its LAU-1 districts. *Acta Polytech. CTU Proc.* **2024**, *46*, 65–84. [CrossRef]
91. Meleddu, M.; Vecco, M.; Mazzanti, M. The role of voluntary environmental policies towards achieving circularity. *Ecol. Econ.* **2024**, *219*, 108134. [CrossRef]
92. Li, H.; Lu, C.C.; Yang, C.Y.; Chung, Y.C. Evaluating the resource recovery efficiency of garbage removal and disposal in Taiwan. *Waste Manag. Res.* **2024**, *42*, 569–582. [CrossRef]
93. Romano, G.; Molinos-Senante, M.; Carosi, L.; Llanquileo-Melgarejo, P.; Sala-Garrido, R.; Mocholi-Arce, M. Assessing the dynamic eco-efficiency of Italian municipalities by accounting for the ownership of the entrusted waste utilities. *Util. Policy* **2021**, *73*, 101311. [CrossRef]
94. Bellver-Domingo, Á.; Fuentes, R.; Hernández-Sancho, F.; Carmona, E.; Picó, Y.; Hernández-Chover, V. MCDA-DEA approach to construct a composite indicator for effluents from WWTPs considering the influence of PPCPs. *Environ. Sci. Pollut. Res. Int.* **2023**, *30*, 47234–47247. [CrossRef] [PubMed]
95. Hmamed, H.; Benghabrit, A.; Cherrafi, A.; Hamani, N. Achieving a sustainable transportation system via economic, environmental, and social optimization: A comprehensive AHP-DEA approach from the waste transportation sector. *Sustainability* **2023**, *15*, 15372. [CrossRef]
96. Yuan, G.; Yang, Y.; Tian, G.; Zhuang, Q. Comprehensive evaluation of disassembly performance based on the ultimate cross-efficiency and extension-gray correlation degree. *J. Clean. Prod.* **2020**, *245*, 118800. [CrossRef]
97. Wang, X.; Zhou, H.; Liu, J. Measurement and coupling analysis of the efficiency of resource-based treatment of municipal solid waste in Chengdu–Chongqing area. *Energy Sci. Eng.* **2024**, *12*, 4641–4661. [CrossRef]
98. Rebolledo-Leiva, R.; Vásquez-Ibarra, L.; Entrena-Barbero, E.; Fernández, M.; Feijoo, G.; Moreira, M.T.; González-García, S. Coupling Material Flow Analysis and Network DEA for the evaluation of eco-efficiency and circularity on dairy farms. *Sustain. Prod. Consum.* **2022**, *31*, 805–817. [CrossRef]
99. Pais-Magalh aes, V.; Moutinho, V.; Marques, A.C. Scoring method of eco-efficiency using the DEA approach: Evidence from European waste sectors. *Environ. Dev. Sustain.* **2021**, *23*, 9726–9748. [CrossRef]
100. Afinogentov, A.A.; Bagdasarova, Y.A.; Derevyanov, M.Y.; Pleshivtseva, Y.E. Application of neural networks to assess the resource value of oil-contaminated waste storage facilities. *IOP Conf. Ser. Earth Environ. Sci.* **2022**, *988*, 022073. [CrossRef]
101. Uhlemann, J.P.R.; Oude Lansink, A.; Leahy, J.J.; Dalhaus, T. Do investments in phosphorus recovery from dairy processing wastewater pay off? *J. Environ. Manag.* **2024**, *357*, 120606. [CrossRef]
102. Garrido, S.; Rodríguez-Antón, J.; Amado, C.A.F.; Santos, S.; Dias, L.C. Development and application of a composite circularity index. *J. Environ. Manag.* **2023**, *337*, 117752. [CrossRef]
103. Castellano, R.; De Bernardo, G.; Punzo, G. Sustainable well-being and sustainable consumption and production: An efficiency analysis of Sustainable Development Goal 12. *Sustainability* **2024**, *16*, 7535. [CrossRef]
104. Guo, L.S. Agricultural foods economic efficiency evaluation based on DEA. *Adv. J. Food Sci. Technol.* **2015**, *8*, 472–475. [CrossRef]

105. Xia, Q.; Li, M.; Wu, H.; Lu, Z. Does the Central Government's environmental policy work? Evidence from the provincial-level environment efficiency in China. *Sustainability* **2016**, *8*, 1241. [CrossRef]
106. Guo, X.; Zhu, Q.; Lv, L.; Chu, J.; Wu, J. Efficiency evaluation of regional energy saving and emission reduction in China: A modified slacks-based measure approach. *J. Clean. Prod.* **2017**, *140*, 1313–1321. [CrossRef]
107. Li, W.; Li, Z.; Liang, L.; Cook, W.D. Evaluation of ecological systems and the recycling of undesirable outputs: An efficiency study of regions in China. *Socio-Econ. Plan. Sci.* **2017**, *60*, 77–86. [CrossRef]
108. Wang, Q.; Sun, Y.; Yuan, X.; Cao, D.; Zuo, J.; Gao, Z. Addressing the efficiency of the core ecological industrial chain: A DEA approach. *J. Clean. Prod.* **2017**, *156*, 235–243. [CrossRef]
109. Halkos, G.; Petrou, K.N. Analysing the energy efficiency of EU Member States: The potential of energy recovery from waste in the circular economy. *Energies* **2019**, *12*, 3718. [CrossRef]
110. Wu, J.; Huang, D.; Zhou, Z.; Zhu, Q. The regional green growth and sustainable development of China in the presence of sustainable resources recovered from pollutions. *Ann. Oper. Res.* **2020**, *290*, 27–45. [CrossRef]
111. Ren, W.; Zhang, Z.; Wang, Y.; Xue, B.; Chen, X. Measuring regional Eco-efficiency in China (2003–2016): A "full world" perspective and network data envelopment analysis. *Int. J. Environ. Res. Public Health* **2020**, *17*, 3456. [CrossRef]
112. Chen, D.; Ma, Y.; Yang, R.; Sun, J. Performance analysis of China's regional circular economy from the perspective of circular structure. *J. Clean. Prod.* **2021**, *297*, 126644. [CrossRef]
113. Wang, M.; Huang, Y.; Li, D. Assessing the performance of industrial water resource utilization systems in China based on a two-stage DEA approach with game cross efficiency. *J. Clean. Prod.* **2021**, *312*, 127722. [CrossRef]
114. Chen, Y.; Liu, L. Improving eco-efficiency in coal mining area for sustainability development: An emergy and super-efficiency SBM-DEA with undesirable output. *J. Clean. Prod.* **2022**, *339*, 130701. [CrossRef]
115. Cierpiał-Wolan, M.; Stec-Rusiecka, J.; Twaróg, D.; Bilińska, K.; Dewalska-Opitek, A.; Wierzbiński, B. Relationship between renewable biogas energy sources and financial health of food business operators. *Energies* **2022**, *15*, 5797. [CrossRef]
116. Jakubelskas, U.; Skvarciany, V. Circular economy practices as a tool for sustainable development in the context of renewable energy: What are the opportunities for the EU? *Oeconomia Copernic.* **2023**, *14*, 833–859. [CrossRef]
117. Ji, L.; Sun, Y.; Liu, J.; Chiu, Y.H. Analysis of the circular economy efficiency of China's industrial wastewater and solid waste—based on a comparison before and after the 13th Five-Year Plan. *Sci. Total Environ.* **2023**, *881*, 163435. [CrossRef]
118. Zhang, D.; Dong, X. From the perspectives of pollution governance and public health: A research of China's fiscal expenditure on energy conservation and environmental protection. *Int. J. Environ. Res. Public Health* **2023**, *20*, 6018. [CrossRef]
119. Murillo, K.P. The importance of discriminant metrics in efficiency analysis. *WSEAS Trans. Bus. Econ.* **2023**, *20*, 2425–2435. [CrossRef]
120. Zhuang, Y.; Zhang, L.; Chiu, Y.H.; Pang, Q.; Wang, X.; Yu, Q. Layer-by-layer investigation of the black box: A case of assessing the industrial water-related system in China. *J. Environ. Manag.* **2023**, *344*, 118353. [CrossRef]
121. Qin, J.; Wang, M. Assessing the performance of industrial water resource systems in China with total constraints on water consumption and pollution emissions. *Environ. Sci. Pollut. Res. Int.* **2023**, *30*, 110251–110279. [CrossRef]
122. Shabanpour, H.; Dargusch, P.; Wadley, D.; Saen, R.F.; Lieske, S.N. A breakthrough in macro-scale circularity and eco-efficiency assessment: A case study of OECD countries. *J. Environ. Manag.* **2024**, *360*, 121070. [CrossRef]
123. Huang, H.C.; Liu, F.B.; Hu, C.K.; Hu, C.F. Efficiency measurement of the water recycling system in a fuzzy environment. *Sustain. Water Resour. Manag.* **2024**, *10*, 124. [CrossRef]
124. Yanhong, F.; Zhongfu, W. Improved data envelopment analysis model based on geometric mean model. *Int. J. Comput. Appl. Technol.* **2019**, *61*, 8. [CrossRef]
125. Rebolledo-Leiva, R.; Barros, M.V.; Entrena-Barbero, E.; Vásquez-Ibarra, L.; Fernández, M.; Feijoo, G.; Teresa Moreira, M.; González-García, S. Embedding Water-Energy-Food nexus and circularity assessment for organization benchmarking: A case study for dairy farms. *Waste Manag.* **2024**, *189*, 410–420. [CrossRef]
126. D'Adamo, I.; Daraio, C.; Di Leo, S.; Gastaldi, M.; Rossi, E.N. Driving EU sustainability: Promoting the circular economy through municipal waste efficiency. *Sustain. Prod. Consum.* **2024**, *50*, 462–474. [CrossRef]
127. Zhou, J.; Zhang, R. Efficiency evaluation of industrial solid waste recycling utilization based on improved DEA model. *IOP Conf. Ser. Earth Environ. Sci.* **2019**, *295*, 032024. [CrossRef]
128. Wu, J.; Zhu, Q.; Chu, J.; Liang, L. Two-stage network structures with undesirable intermediate outputs reused: A DEA based approach. *Comput. Econ.* **2015**, *46*, 455–477. [CrossRef]
129. Marques, R.C.; Sim oes, P.; Pinto, F.S. Tariff regulation in the waste sector: An unavoidable future. *Waste Manag.* **2018**, *78*, 292–300. [CrossRef]
130. Gobbi, C.N.; Sanches, V.M.L.; Guimar aes, M.J.d.O.C.; Freitas, M.A.V.d.; Pacheco, E.B.A.V. Efficiency in the environmental management of plastic wastes at Brazilian ports based on data envelopment analysis. *Mar. Pollut. Bull.* **2019**, *142*, 377–383. [CrossRef]

131. Chen, F.; Yao, W. Evaluation of circular economy efficiency in Eastern China. *IOP Conf. Ser. Earth Environ. Sci.* **2020**, *453*, 012030. [CrossRef]
132. Yang, H.; Zhang, S.; Ye, W.; Qin, Y.; Xu, M.; Han, L. Emission reduction benefits and efficiency of e-waste recycling in China. *Waste Manag.* **2020**, *102*, 541–549. [CrossRef]
133. Gastaldi, M.; Lombardi, G.V.; Rapposelli, A.; Romano, G. The efficiency of waste sector in Italy: An application by Data Envelopment Analysis. *Environ. Clim. Technol.* **2020**, *24*, 225–238. [CrossRef]
134. Derevyanov, M.Y.; Pleshivtseva, Y.E.; Afinogentov, A.A. Simulation and evaluation of the efficiency of oil-contaminated wastes recycling system. *IOP Conf. Ser. Earth Environ. Sci.* **2020**, *459*, 042058. [CrossRef]
135. Li, X.N.; Feng, Y.; Chiu, Y.H.; Lin, T.Y.; Chiu, S.Y. Recycling water and sludge disposal efficiency in China's sewage treatment industry. *Manag. Decis. Econ.* **2021**, *42*, 1703–1717. [CrossRef]
136. Temerbulatova, Z.S.; Zhidebekkyzy, A.; Grabowska, M. Assessment of the effectiveness of the European Union countries transition to a circular economy: Data Envelopment Analysis. *Econ. Strategy Pract.* **2021**, *16*, 142–151. [CrossRef]
137. Lu, L.C.; Chiu, S.Y.; Chiu, Y.H.; Chang, T.H. Three-stage circular efficiency evaluation of agricultural food production, food consumption, and food waste recycling in EU countries. *J. Clean. Prod.* **2022**, *343*, 130870. [CrossRef]
138. Wang, H.F.; Hu, C.F. Carbon emission abatement allocation of a recycling production system in a fuzzy environment. *J. Uncertain Syst.* **2022**, *15*, 2243005. [CrossRef]
139. Milanović, T.; Savić, G.; Martić, M.; Milanović, M.; Petrović, N. Development of the waste management composite index using DEA method as circular economy indicator: The case of European Union countries. *Pol. J. Environ. Stud.* **2022**, *31*, 771–784. [CrossRef]
140. Yadollahi, A.H.; Ebrahimnejad, A.; Kazemi Matin, R. Centralized resource reallocation in two-stage network structures with undesirable products. *Comput. Appl. Math.* **2022**, *41*, 228. [CrossRef]
141. Huang, H.C.; Liu, F.B.; Hu, C.F. A slacks-based measure approach for efficiency measurement of recycling production systems with imprecise data. *J. Math.* **2022**, *2022*, 4909856. [CrossRef]
142. Bronner, M.; See, K.F.; Yu, M.M. Circular water economy performance evaluation based on dynamic network data envelopment analysis. *J. Clean. Prod.* **2022**, *367*, 132474. [CrossRef]
143. Ren, F.R.; Chen, K.J.; Tian, Z.; Zhang, Y. The investment and treatment efficiencies of industrial solid waste in China's Yangtze and non-Yangtze River Economic Belts. *J. Mater. Cycles Waste Manag.* **2022**, *24*, 900–916. [CrossRef]
144. Gennitsaris, S.; Sagani, A.; Sofianopoulou, S.; Dedoussis, V. Integrated LCA and DEA approach for circular economy-driven performance evaluation of wind turbine end-of-life treatment options. *Appl. Energy* **2023**, *339*, 120951. [CrossRef]
145. Liu, F.B.; Hu, C.F. Fuzzy game approach network data envelopment analysis models for the waste management performance evaluation. *Int. J. Fuzzy Syst.* **2023**, *25*, 3193–3203. [CrossRef]
146. Volsuuri, E.; Owusu-Sekyere, E.; Zarouk Imoro, A.; Napoleon Bellua, S. Assessing the efficiency of solid waste collection services in urban Ghana. *Waste Manag. Bull.* **2023**, *1*, 71–81. [CrossRef]
147. Yang, H. Research on development efficiency of circular economy of silk road economic belt: Based on super efficiency DEA model. *Inf. Syst. Econ.* **2023**, *4*, 16–23. [CrossRef]
148. Chioatto, E.; Khan, M.A.; Sospiro, P. Sustainable solid waste management in the European Union: Four countries regional analysis. *Sustain. Chem. Pharm.* **2023**, *33*, 101037. [CrossRef]
149. Radovanov, B.; Marcikić-Horvat, A.; Stojić, D.; Sedlak, O.; Bobera, D. Assessing circular economy performance of European countries and Serbia using data envelopment analysis. *Eur. J. Appl. Econ.* **2023**, *20*, 1–11. [CrossRef]
150. Ferraro, A.; Garofalo, A.; Marchesano, K. Measuring differences in efficiency in waste collection and disposal services from the EU targets in Campania municipalities. *Environ. Ecol. Stat.* **2023**, *30*, 81–101. [CrossRef]
151. Gupta, N.; Vishwakarma, A. Multi-level data envelopment approach for performance evaluation of MSW generated in urban area of madhya pradesh, India. *Pol. J. Environ. Stud.* **2023**, *32*, 3577–3589. [CrossRef]
152. Maziotis, A.; Molinos-Senante, M. A comprenhesive Eco-efficiency analysis of wastewater treatment plants: Estimation of optimal operational costs and greenhouse gas emissions. *Water Res.* **2023**, *243*, 120354. [CrossRef]
153. Lin, T.Y.; Chiu, Y.H.; Lin, Y.N.; Chang, T.H. Profit-seeking enterprise production and business waste treatment efficiency in Taiwan. *Environ. Dev. Sustain.* **2023**, *25*, 10661–10683. [CrossRef]
154. Huang, J.; Wen, J.; He, F. Research on evaluation of power battery recycling efficiency of new energy vehicle based on DEA. *Ind. Eng. Innov. Manag.* **2023**, *6*, 71–77. [CrossRef]
155. Lin, H.Y.; Rijal, S. Comparative study of eco-performance evaluation for municipal solid waste management practices. *Int. J. Appl. Sci. Eng.* **2024**, *21*, 2022363. [CrossRef]
156. Hosseinpoor, A.; Ghorbanpour, A.; Shabandarzadeh, H. Evaluating the Efficiency of Circular Economies in Persian Gulf Countries in Terms of Municipal Solid Waste Management. *Q. J. Quant. Econ.* **2024**, *21*, 87–106. [CrossRef]
157. Shabanpour, H.; Dargusch, P.; Wadley, D.; Farzipoor Saen, R. A breakthrough in circular economy: Using a closed-loop framework to assess the circularity of supply chains. *J. Clean. Prod.* **2024**, *444*, 141265. [CrossRef]

158. Ndoka, E.; Alimehmeti, G. A challenging path or full of opportunities. A comparison of the performance of circular economy in the Western Balkan countries. *Rom. J. Econ.* **2024**, *59*, 316–332.
159. Lei, A.; Yang, L.; Chiu, Y.H.; Niu, Y.Y.; Chang, T.H. Reassessment of the efficiency of China's industrial circular economy considering quality of life: A meta recycle SBM dynamic under exogenous model. *Environ. Dev. Sustain.* **2024**, *27*, 19435–19466. [CrossRef]
160. Guan, X.G.; Ren, F.R.; Fan, G.; Zhang, Q.Q.; Wu, T.F. Dynamic evaluation and sensitivity analysis of China's industrial solid waste management efficiency based on ecological environment cycle perspective. *Front. Environ. Sci.* **2024**, *12*, 1462975. [CrossRef]
161. Sala-Garrido, R.; Mocholi-Arce, M.; Maziotis, A.; Molinos-Senante, M. Eco-efficiency approach in sustainable waste management: An uncertainty analysis for Chile. *Environ. Sci. Policy* **2024**, *160*, 103859. [CrossRef]
162. Lingjuan, T.; Hongjuan, Y. Evolution characteristics and influencing factors of the human-earth system in minority areas of Yunnan, China. *J. Resour. Ecol.* **2024**, *15*, 372–384. [CrossRef]
163. Molinos-Senante, M.; Maziotis, A.; Sala-Garrido, R. Estimating the eco-efficiency of urban waste services towards sustainable waste management. *Sustain. Dev.* **2024**, *32*, 5677–5691. [CrossRef]
164. Shi, Z.; Wu, Y.; Chiu, Y.H.; Pang, Q.; Zhang, L. Optimizing the allowance allocations of water consumption, industrial solid waste and carbon emissions in China. *Process Saf. Environ. Prot.* **2024**, *183*, 835–847. [CrossRef]
165. Gholian-Jouybari, F.; Khazaei, M.; Farzipoor Saen, R.; Kia, R.; Bonakdari, H.; Hajiaghaei-Keshteli, M.; Ramezani, M. Developing environmental, social and governance (ESG) strategies on evaluation of municipal waste disposal centers: A case of Mexico. *Chemosphere* **2024**, *364*, 142961. [CrossRef] [PubMed]
166. Dyckhoff, H.; Souren, R.; Clermont, M. Performance assessment of waste sorting: Component-based approach to incorporate quality into data envelopment analysis. *EURO J. Decis. Process.* **2024**, *12*, 100048. [CrossRef]
167. das Mercês Costa, I.; Dias, M.F.; Robaina, M. Evaluation of the efficiency of urban solid waste management in Brazil by data envelopment analysis and possible variables of influence. *Waste Dispos. Sustain. Energy* **2024**, *6*, 283–295. [CrossRef]
168. Seiford, L.M.; Zhu, J. Modeling undesirable factors in efficiency evaluation. *Eur. J. Oper. Res.* **2002**, *142*, 16–20. [CrossRef]

Mathematical and Computational Applications

MDPI

Article

Thrinax radiata Seed Germplasm Dynamics Analysis Assisted by Chaos Theory

Hilario Martines-Arano [1,*], Marina Vera-Ku [2], Ricardo Álvarez-Espino [2], Luis Enrique Vivanco-Benavides [3,4], Claudia Lizbeth Martínez-González [4] and Carlos Torres-Torres [4,*]

1 Escuela Superior Tepeji del Río, Universidad Autónoma del Estado de Hidalgo, Pachuca de Soto 42860, Mexico

2 SECIHTI-Laboratorio Regional Para el Estudio y Conservación de Germoplasma (GermoLab), Centro de Investigación Científica de Yucatán (CICY), Parque Científico Tecnológico de Yucatán, Km. 5.5 Carretera Sierra Papacal-Chuburná Puerto, Mérida 97302, Mexico; marina.vera@cicy.mx (M.V.-K.); ricardo.alvarez@cicy.mx (R.Á.-E.)

3 División de Ingeniería en Sistemas Computacionales, Tecnológico Nacional de México, Tecnológico de Estudios Superiores de Coacalco, Coacalco de Berriozábal, San Francisco Coacalco 55700, Mexico; lvivancob1900@alumno.ipn.mx

4 Sección de Estudios de Posgrado e Investigación, Escuela Superior de Ingeniería Mecánica y Eléctrica Unidad Zacatenco, Instituto Politécnico Nacional, Ciudad de México 07738, Mexico; clmartinezg@ipn.mx

* Correspondence: hilario_martines@uaeh.edu.mx (H.M.-A.); ctorrest@ipn.mx (C.T.-T.)

Abstract

This study examines the contrast in the nonlinear dynamics of *Thrinax radiata* Lodd. ex Schult. & Schult. f. Seed germplasm explored by optical and electrical signals. By integrating chaotic attractors for the modulation of the optical and electrical measurements, the research ensures high sensitivity monitoring of seed germplasm dynamics. Reflectance measurements and electrical responses were analyzed across different laser pulse energies using Newton–Leipnik and Rössler chaotic attractors for signal characterization. The optical attractor captured laser-induced changes in reflectance, highlighting nonlinear thermal effects, while the electrical attractor, through a custom-designed circuit, revealed electromagnetic interactions within the seed. Results showed that increasing laser energy amplified voltage magnitudes in both systems, demonstrating their sensitivity to energy inputs and distinct energy-dependent chaotic patterns. Fractional calculus, specifically the Caputo fractional derivative, was applied for modeling temperature distribution within the seeds during irradiation. Simulations revealed heat transfer about 1 °C in central regions, closely correlating with observed changes in chaotic attractor morphology. This interdisciplinary approach emphasizes the unique strengths of each method: optical attractors effectively analyze photoinduced thermal effects, while electrical attractors offer complementary insights into bioelectrical properties. Together, these techniques provide a realistic framework for studying seed germplasm dynamics, advancing knowledge of their responses to external perturbations. The findings pave the way for future applications and highlight the potential of chaos theory for early detection of structural and bioelectrical changes induced by external energy inputs, thereby contributing to sample protection. Our results provide quantitative dynamical descriptors of laser-evoked seed responses that establish a tractable framework for future studies linking these metrics to physiological outcomes.

Keywords: chaotic attractors; fractional calculus; instrumentation; sensing; *Thrinax radiata*

1. Introduction

Germplasm is any tissue or plant material that can be used for the reproduction of a new plant. DNA is the hereditary molecule within cells, whereas germplasm refers to living genetic resources (e.g., seeds, tissues, or propagules) that preserve and transmit genetic variation. It is the basis of plant reproduction and genetic diversity, present in seeds, tissues, and other vegetative organs [1]. Plant reproduction generates and maintains genetic variation; germplasm denotes the living genetic resources that conserve and make that variation available for breeding, research, and conservation. It plays a crucial role in agriculture and horticulture, as it is the basis of critical plant genetic information passed down from one generation to the next. Seeds house the embryo and its genome as living genetic resources (germplasm); however, developmental outcomes also depend on epigenetic states, maternal effects, and environmental conditions [2]. Biological studies are essential, as they enable the development of strategies to improve seed viability, optimize germination rates, and contribute to sustainable agricultural practices. Therefore, understanding the complex dynamics of seed germplasm under divergent environmental and experimental regimes is crucial [3]. Seed germination has a long tradition of population-based threshold models (thermal/hydro/hydrothermal time) in which germination rate increases approximately linearly with temperature or water potential within sub-optimal ranges [4]. In parallel, differential-equation and nonlinear statistical frameworks are widely used [5].

Consistent with processual perspectives that treat time as constitutive of plant function, we adopt a time-aware dynamical framing of seed germplasm behavior rather than static endpoints [6].

Thrinax radiata Lodd. ex Schult. & Schult. f., known as the chit palm in the Yucatán Peninsula, is an ecologically and culturally significant species whose conservation is a priority. This palm is endemic to the Caribbean region, southern Florida, and certain parts of Mexico, where it has been traditionally used for construction, handicrafts, and thatching [7]. Additionally, medicinal uses have been reported in Maya communities, where its leaves are applied as poultices to stop bleeding, and its roots are infused to treat kidney stones and nervous disorders. Despite its ethnobotanical value, *Thrinax radiata* has been classified as a threatened species in Mexico [8], primarily due to habitat destruction caused by human activities such as tourism, agriculture, and cattle ranching, as well as unregulated exploitation [9].

Seed studies, including morphological characterization, provide an insight towards viability assessment and a study of factors affecting germination and survival and the conservation of *Thrinax radiata* germplasm is crucial to ensure the persistence of this species in its natural ecosystem and its sustainable use. In this context, the establishment of germplasm banks and the development of advanced methodologies for its analysis and preservation become critically important. Specifically, the application of analytical models based on chaos theory and laser technology offers an innovative strategy for exploring the germplasm dynamics of this palm.

Chaos theory enables the characterization of the complex response of seeds to external stimuli, providing mathematical tools such as the Newton–Leipnik and Rössler attractors to model these dynamic processes. Additionally, irradiation with a 532 nm Nd:YVO_4 pulsed laser, combined with optical and electrical measurements, facilitates the early detection of structural and bioelectrical changes in seeds, allowing for the evaluation of their viability and resistance to adverse environmental factors, ensuring minimal disruption and maximizing sample preservation [10]. Seed germination can be predicted with useful accuracy within sub-optimal ranges using population-based threshold fitted to appropriate measurements; predictive performance typically declines near supra-optimal conditions or under heterogeneous stress. Chaos theory defines the ground rules of nonlinear, deterministic systems that show and possess the attribute of being unpredictable. Some chaotic attractors like that of Rössler and Newton–Leipnik are now being used as efficient tools for modeling such dynamic biological processes [11]. As indicators of internal sensitivity towards external stimuli, these attractors describe the response patterns along with the variability of seed responses [12]. At the same time, laser ablation enables the localized assessment of thermal effects on seed germplasm [13]. The effects of different energy levels on the actions of seeds, both at the macroscopic and microscopic levels, can be understood by changing the energy of the laser pulse [14]. Moreover, the use of fractional calculus, particularly the Caputo fractional derivative, allows for the simulation of temperature distribution induced by laser irradiation, providing insights into thermal effects and dynamics on seed internal structures [15]. By considering the fractional derivatives within the analysis of temperature distributions during laser irradiation, it renders possible the influence of memory effects and anomalous diffusion processes which classical integer-order models would not account for [16].

By memory effects we mean history-dependent signal behavior, whereby identical instantaneous conditions can elicit different responses depending on prior inputs. Operationally, this manifests as long-range temporal correlations and non-exponential relaxations; in our modeling, we represent it with a fractional-order term $0 < \alpha < 1$.

Optical reflectance variations supplement such a study as they furnish in-the-moment optical science data for changes in seed surface properties. These reflectance measurements can also capture structural and compositional changes induced by laser ablation and thus provide a profile on how seeds would interact with different thermal conditions in light [17]. The combination of optical reflectance and thermal simulations shall provide a comprehensive view into the responses of seed germplasm while linking microscale physical phenomena to macroscale biological behaviors [18]. Further, electrical potentials in seeds that were subjected to laser irradiation act as an indication of the alterations in their underlying biophysical states. Change in electrical conductivity and impedance indicates the effect of localized heating, the redistribution of moisture content, and possible structural changes [19]. When combining these electrical measurements with the dynamic models which arise from chaotic attractors, it becomes quite feasible to analyze and quantify the relationship between both thermal effects and germplasm dynamics as fully as possible [20].

This research explores the potential of chaos theory for the assistance of laser technology and fractional calculus in analyzing *Thrinax radiata* seeds dynamics. The integration of these techniques does not only contribute to a better understanding of the biological processes underlying seed conservation but also offers innovative tools for monitoring and protecting endangered species. Accordingly, we present a dynamical analysis framework for non-destructive, time-resolved characterization of seed responses under controlled irradiation, without inferring biological outcomes such as viability or conservation efficacy. The findings may open new avenues in seed science, species conservation, and crop improvement, highlighting the potential of interdisciplinary approaches in plant germplasm research.

2. Materials and Methods

2.1. Description of the Biological Material Studied, Image Acquisition and Processing

Thrinax radiata Lodd. ex Schult. & Schult. f. (Arecaceae), commonly called Chit. is a monocot palm that can grow up to 8 m tall, it grows in coastal areas from Florida to Nicaragua. However, the Mexican Official Standard classifies it as an endangered species and its conservation in Botanical Gardens has been promoted for years. The fruits are fleshy drupes of white color that contain one brown spherical seed (5 mm of diameter) with linear under-development embryo of 1–2 mm length. The *Thrinax radiata* seeds are tolerant to desiccation but lose viability if preserved at low temperatures. Due to its morpho-physiological traits and storage behavior, are considered as intermediate or recalcitrant seeds for its conservation in traditional seed banks [21]. Mature fruits and seeds were collected in field collections at the Regional Laboratory for the Study and Conservation of Germplasm (GermoLab-CICY, 21°07′48.12″ N, 89°46′45.93″ W; 5 m a.s.l.). Initial moisture content of seeds was 15.13%, with 100% of viability (in tetrazolium test) and 93.3% of germination under controlled laboratory conditions (25–32 °C, and photoperiod of 12/12 h light/darkness). Seeds provenance are individuals planted outside their habitat in the GermoLab-CICY field collections. The seeds for this study were collected in November 2022, air-dried in a laminar flow chamber and stored at room temperature (25 °C) in an airtight glass jar until its use. Details of the methods used to evaluate viability, germination, and storage behavior of the *Thrinax radiata* seed samples studied has been previously reported in detail [21].

High-resolution digital images of *Thrinax radiata* were acquired under controlled lighting conditions and against a neutral, non-reflective background, ensuring consistency across all samples. Seeds were arranged in well-defined subsets to facilitate individualized morphological analysis. The implemented pipeline yielded accurate segmentation in over 95% of the processed images. A total of N = 3 seeds were evaluated and the experiments repeated by triplicate; each processed independently under the same irradiation protocol. Photographic images of *Thrinax radiata* seeds were captured using a triple digital camera (50 MP/12 MP/5 MP, Samsung Galaxy A54, Nueva Delhi, India) equipped with optical image stabilization, under controlled lighting conditions to ensure consistency across shots. The seeds were arranged in subsets on a neutral background to facilitate image segmentation. The acquired images were processed using the Python (version 3.12.7) programming language, employing the OpenCV library for preprocessing tasks such as grayscale conversion, filtering, and segmentation through thresholding techniques. Subsequently, the scikit-image library was used to extract relevant morphological and textural features, including area, shape, convexity, and contrast. The effectiveness of this image preparation approach for seed analysis is supported by Nucci et al. [22], who employed computer vision to segment images of Guavira seeds for classification into viable and non-viable categories.

2.2. Chaotic Attractors Generation

For modulating monitoring signals, we generated two chaotic systems exhibiting just one attractor: the Rössler and the Newton–Leipnik attractors. These dynamic systems were selected for their simplicity in their coefficients in the differential equations.

The Rössler attractor is a three-dimensional system of ordinary differential equations introduced by Otto Rössler in 1976 [23]. It was designed to show chaotic behavior in a simpler form compared to the Lorenz system.

The Rössler system was defined mathematically as:

$$\frac{dx}{dt} = -y - z, \tag{1}$$

$$\frac{dy}{dt} = x + ay, \tag{2}$$

$$\frac{dz}{dt} = b + z(x - c), \tag{3}$$

where a, b, and c are parameters that influence the system dynamics. The used chaotic parameters were $a = 0.2$, $b = 0.2$, $c = 5.7$. The system exhibits a single scroll attractor when it is in the chaotic regime and x, y and z represent the state variables of the system theoretically assumed.

The Newton–Leipnik system was defined as [24]:

$$\frac{dx}{dt} = -0.4x + y + 10yz, \tag{4}$$

$$\frac{dy}{dt} = -x - 0.4y + 5xz, \tag{5}$$

$$\frac{dz}{dt} = -\alpha z - 5xy, \tag{6}$$

where α acts as a damping and control parameter that influences the attractor dynamic behavior. $\alpha = 0.4$ for this case as a typical chaotic parameter. The Newton–Leipnik system features both scroll-like and spiral shapes.

2.3. Optical Monitoring of Seed Reflectance via Chaotic Attractors

In order to monitor the optical behavior of *Thrinax radiata* seeds under pulsed laser excitation, a system was designed to capture real-time reflectance changes associated with photoinduced thermal and structural modifications. A Nd:YVO_4 pulsed laser (Spectra-Physics Explorer® One™ XP, Santa Clara, CA, USA) at 532 nm was used to irradiate the seed, while a chaotic signal, modeled using the Rössler attractor, was employed to interpret the reflectance variations as a function of energy input.

The optical monitoring setup included a focus-tunable lens (Optotune EL-10–30-TC Series, Dietikon, Switzerland) with a focal range from +40 mm to +900 mm, which was controlled by a chaotic signal generated by an Arduino Uno. Two plano-convex lenses (focal lengths 10 cm and 12 cm) directed the laser beam onto the sample, ensuring consistent beam profile and spot size.

Optical reflectance was recorded using a fiber optic spectrometer (Ocean Optics USB2000, Orlando, FL, USA) and a calibrated PIN photodetector (Model: 818-BB-21, Newport, Irvine, CA, USA). These measurements allowed us to detect subtle surface alterations in reflectivity in real time. The morphology of the chaotic attractor varied with laser pulse energy, revealing thermal sensitivity and seed surface reactivity to external perturbation.

In order to determine the photoinduced temperature in the biological probe, generated by the Nd:YVO_4 pulsed laser system, we combined the experimental data and the fractional Newton cooling equation.

Figure 1 shows the representation of experimental setup used for optical monitoring of reflectance in *Thrinax radiata* seeds irradiated with a Nd:YVO_4 pulsed laser operating at 532 nm. This method enables real-time detection of laser-induced structural changes using chaos theory to interpret variations in the seed's optical properties.

The laser beam is first directed through a focus-tunable lens, whose focal range is modulated by a chaotic signal generated electronically. The beam then passes through a planoconvex lens, which focuses it precisely onto the surface of the seed. This optical path allows for controlled energy delivery and facilitates the evaluation of photoinduced thermal effects.

The reflected light from the seed is captured by a fiber-optic spectrometer, which analyzes spectral variations in reflectance at different laser energy levels. Spectral data are transmitted in real time to a laptop, where the optical response is recorded and visualized as chaotic attractor trajectories, derived from the reflectance signal modulated by the light–seed interaction.

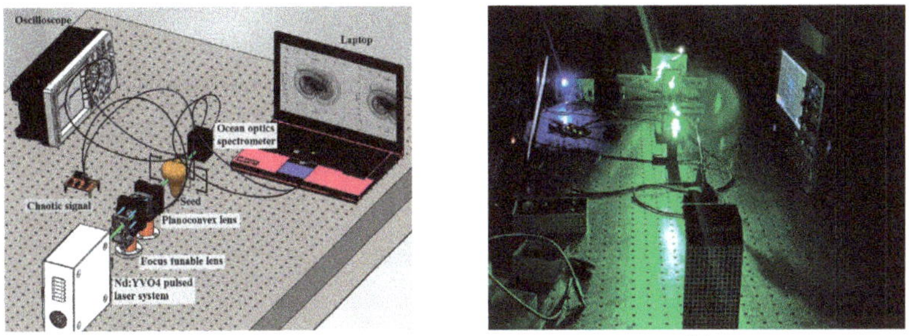

(**a**) (**b**)

Figure 1. Optical monitoring of seed. (**a**) Scheme of the experimental setup for optical monitoring of *Thrinax radiata* seeds assisted by chaotic attractors; (**b**) Experimental setup for optical monitoring.

2.4. Electrical Monitoring of Seed Bioelectrical Response

Thrinax radiata seeds were irradiated using a Nd:YVO_4 pulsed laser at 532 nm. Some energy levels were tested (1 µJ to 6 µJ, 10 ns pulse duration, 10 Hz repetition rate) with irradiation times between 30–120 s and a fixed spot size of 1 mm. These parameters were selected to evaluate both low and high energy regimes and their influence on seed ablation and thermal response.

In parallel with the optical approach, an electrical monitoring system was established to evaluate the bioelectrical response of *Thrinax radiata* seeds during laser irradiation. This method involved generating a chaotic electrical signal based on the Newton–Leipnik attractor, propagated through an experimental circuit into which the seed was directly integrated.

The Arduino Uno microcontroller (Arduino, Scarmagno, Italy) was used to simulate the chaotic system, while a Tektronix TDS014B oscilloscope (Tektronix, Beaverton, OR, USA) displayed evolving attractor patterns, enabling real-time tracking of the seed electrical behavior.

A DC power supply ensured stability throughout the procedure, and all data acquisition was managed by a high-performance computing system (Omen by HP, Intel i7-9750H, 2.60 GHz).

Figure 2 provides a visual representation of the experimental setups used to study the effects of laser irradiation on *Thrinax radiata* seeds. Figure 2a is a schematic illustration of the experimental setup: It outlines the overall configuration, showcasing the key components used to irradiate the seed with a laser beam and monitor its response. Whereas Figure 2b expresses the experimental setup for a nonfocused laser beam: Here, the laser beam is directed at the seed without the use of focusing optics, allowing for a broader distribution of energy across the seed surface. A Nd:YVO_4 pulsed laser system is carefully calibrated to ensure precise energy delivery, minimizing excessive thermal load while maximizing sensitivity to seed germplasm changes.

The beam passes through a planoconvex lens to focus it and is reflected by a mirror before hitting the sample. The chaotic attractor was generated using an Arduino board, which was connected directly to the irradiated seed and later it was connected to an oscilloscope displaying the attractor waveform. A laptop (Omen by HP, 15″ Intel© Core™ i7-9750H CPU, 2.60 GHz, Windows 10) was also part of the setup, used to control and monitor the experiment.

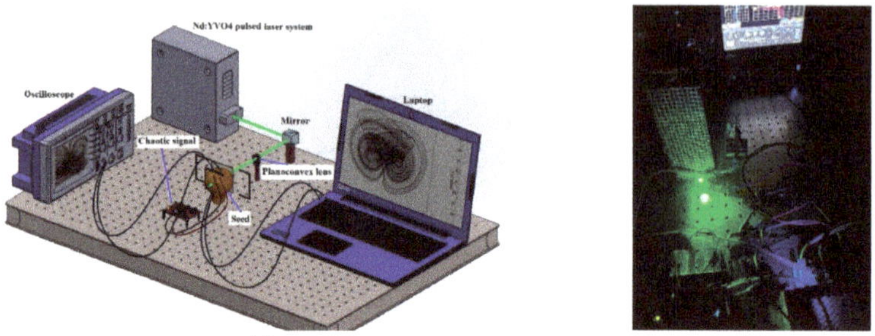

(a) (b)

Figure 2. Visual representation of the experiments; (**a**) Schematic illustration of the experimental setup for laser irradiation on the seed; (**b**) Experimental setup for non-focused laser beam.

3. Results

3.1. Morphological Characterization of Thrinax radiata Seeds

Analyses were conducted on three seeds, unless stated otherwise, figures show one representative seed with consistent trends across specimens. The extracted parameters enabled clear differentiation between seeds with regular morphology and those exhibiting surface or structural irregularities. Figure 3 presents a representative subset of *Thrinax radiata* seeds used in this study. The visual consistency achieved across samples can support the suitability for phenotypic characterization, seed quality assessment (see Materials and Methods Section 2.1), and long-term germplasm optical monitoring.

Figure 3. Representative subset of *Thrinax radiata* seeds subjected to digital image analysis for morphological and textural characterization.

3.2. Chaotic Attractor-Based Simulation for Monitoring Seed Morphodynamics

In order to simulate and monitor potential nonlinear biological changes in *Thrinax radiata* seeds, two chaotic attractors were numerically implemented and analyzed: the Rössler and Newton–Leipnik systems. Both attractors were selected for their ability to exhibit bounded yet complex trajectories in three-dimensional phase space; biological instability can be identified as a modification in the signals that provide feedback in the chaotic system.

Using Equations (1)–(3) for simulating the stable attractors and using $a = 0.2$, $b = 0.2$ and $c = 5.7$ for Rössler system, it exhibits a single-scroll chaotic attractor. In the simulated Rössler dynamics used in the manuscript the largest Lyapunov exponent is ≈ 0.071 per model time unit, indicating sustained but weak chaos. The correlation fractal dimension is ≈ 2.0, consistent with a low-dimensional attractor. Under a single positive exponent, the Kolmogorov–Sinai entropy is bounded below by λ_1 and thus ≈ 0.071 per unit time, reflecting a moderate rate of information production. The attractor remains bounded and structurally stable, ensuring reproducibility and sensitivity to initial conditions without diverging trajectories. It can be observed in Figure 4a. Whereas, for simulating the Newton–Leipnik attractor we utilized $\alpha = 0.17$ parameters in Equations (4)–(6) generated a complex spiral–scroll hybrid attractor, sensitive to external perturbations yet remaining within a topologically invariant domain. By nonlinear environmental perturbations we mean stimuli whose effects are non-proportional and history-dependent, for example: pulsed irradiance showing thresholds, leading to non-proportional changes in the measured signals. Figure 4 illustrates the numerical simulation results of two classical chaotic systems. Figure 4a shows the Rössler attractor, exhibiting a smooth, spiral-like trajectory indicative of low-dimensional chaos. Figure 4b presents the Newton–Leipnik attractor, which features a more intricate and folded geometry typical of higher-dimensional chaotic dynamics. Both attractors demonstrate the sensitive dependence on initial conditions and nonlinear coupling that define chaotic behavior, providing valuable insights for applications in nonlinear system monitoring and control.

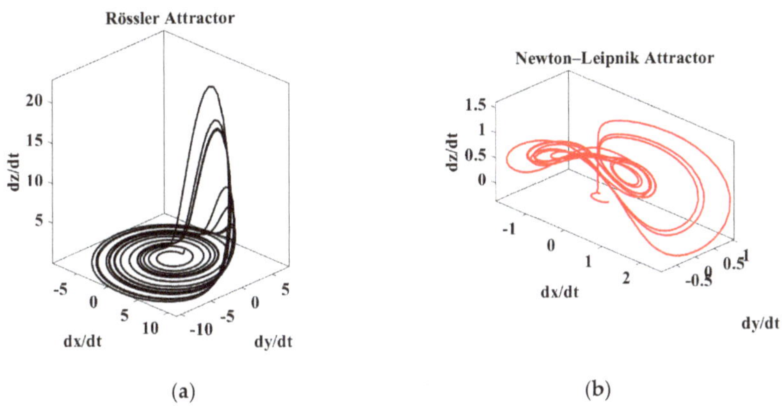

Figure 4. Chaotic attractors simulations. (**a**) Simulated Rössler chaotic attractor displaying the characteristic spiral and folding behavior in three-dimensional phase space. (**b**) Chaotic Newton–Leipnik attractor, scaled for visual clarity, showing complex and sensitive dependence on initial conditions with a distinct double-scroll structure.

3.3. Optical Response of Seed Germplasm

Figure 5 illustrates the experimental results associated with the Newton–Leipnik attractor. The figure captures the attractor evolution under different laser power settings, which ranged from 1 μJ to 6 μJ. The variations in the shape and trajectory of the attractor are directly influenced by the incremental adjustments in laser power. As the laser power increases, the attractor exhibits more pronounced and complex trajectories, reflecting the system nonlinear response to higher energy inputs. These morphological changes in the attractor are closely tied to reflectance measurements taken from the irradiated seeds. Reflectance serves as an indicator of the surface properties and thermal effects induced by the laser. As the seed's optical properties are altered by varying laser energy, corresponding shifts in the attractor structure can be observed.

Figure 6 illustrates the reflectance measurements of the seed under laser irradiation, with the laser power varying between 2 μJ and 6 μJ. The data clearly show that the reflectance behavior depends significantly on the laser power, and the wavelength corresponding to the highest irradiance is centered at 532 nm, matching the wavelength of the laser used in the experiment. At a laser energy of 6 μJ, the reflectance reached its maximum value of 19%, as indicated by the red points. This peak demonstrates the strong optical interaction between the laser and the seed surface at this energy level. For a laser energy of 4 µJ, the reflectance decreased slightly to 17%, represented by the black points. This reduction suggests less optical coupling or surface modification at this lower energy. At the lowest laser power of 2 µJ, the reflectance was observed to be 14%, as indicated by the blue points. This reflects the minimal photothermal effect and optical response of the seed at this energy level. The laser beam was focused on the seed using a plano-convex lens with a focal length of 10 cm. This lens configuration ensured precise and concentrated energy delivery to the target area, which is crucial for achieving the observed reflectance variations.

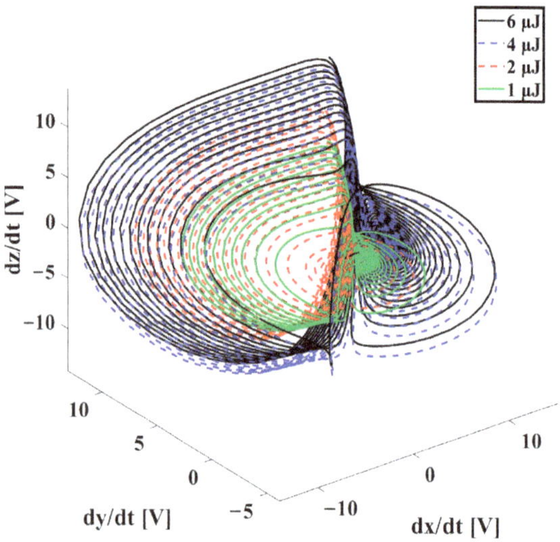

Figure 5. Experimental chaotic shapes of Newton–Leipnik attractor for different pulse energy on the studied seed.

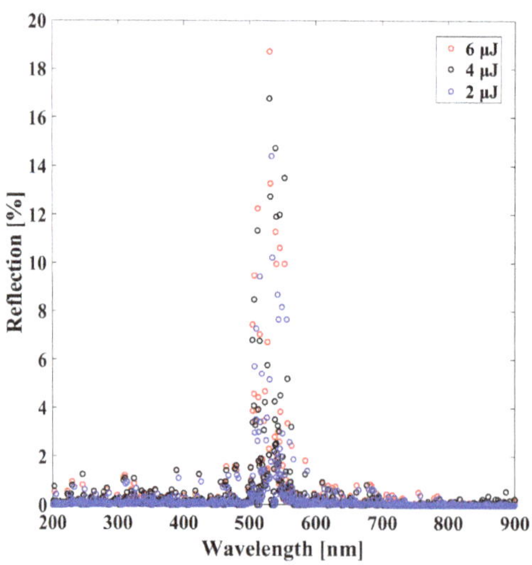

Figure 6. Experimental reflectance spectra of the studied seed focused, in function of different laser energy.

Figure 7 presents the reflectance measurements of the seed under laser irradiation with laser energy ranging from 1 μJ to 6 μJ. At the highest laser energy of 6 μJ, the reflectance reached 15%, indicating the minimal surface reflectivity at this energy level due to potential thermal or optical modifications. For a laser power of 4 μJ, the reflectance was measured at 30%, significantly higher than at 6 μJ, suggesting intermediate laser-material interaction. At a laser energy of 2 μJ, the reflectance peaked at 45%, representing the maximum reflectance among all measurements. This high value indicates minimal surface alteration at lower laser energies. At the lowest energy level of 1 μJ, the reflectance was measured at 16%, suggesting moderate surface reflectance with minimal laser-induced effects.

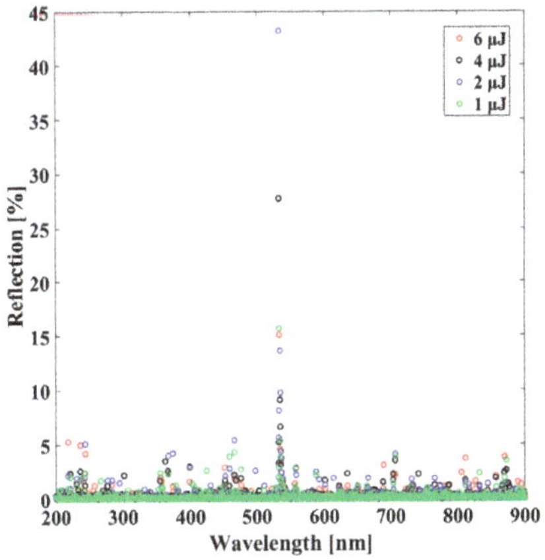

Figure 7. Experimental reflectance spectra of the studied non-focused seed, as a function of laser energy.

The measurements shown in Figures 6 and 7 correspond to different laser beam configurations. Specifically, Figure 6 presents data obtained using a focused laser beam, allowing localized energy delivery and enhanced interaction with the seed surface. In contrast, Figure 7 displays results acquired under a non-focused beam configuration, which distributes energy more broadly across the seed, resulting in distinct reflectance behaviors.

We measured the sensor's output voltage at ten fixed light levels and averaged repeated readings. A straight-line fit $V = a + bl$ was applied; $r \approx 0.9998$, $R^2 \approx 0.9996$, it was used in Figure 8.

Figure 8 illustrates the calibration curve for the optical attractor, where reflectance values are plotted against the stability of the chaotic optical pattern. The optical system exhibits an estimated error margin of ±2.5%, highlighting its sensitivity to laser-induced perturbations. These calibration curves are essential for validating the accuracy and repeatability of the chaotic monitoring techniques, ensuring that the observed structural or bioelectrical changes in the seed germplasm are not due to instrumental fluctuations.

As shown in Table 1, stable optical attractors are characterized by moderate reflectance values (10–20%), preservation of attractor morphology under low induced temperature, symmetrical shapes, and low spectral dispersion. When stability is lost, reflectance exceeds 20%, the attractor structure becomes asymmetrical and erratic, and optical spectrum dispersion increases significantly. Integrating both electrical and optical attractor analyses enables a more accurate and rapid assessment of seed germplasm dynamics compared to conventional germination methods. The calculated error margins for the optical and electrical measurements were ±2.5% and ±2.0%, respectively.

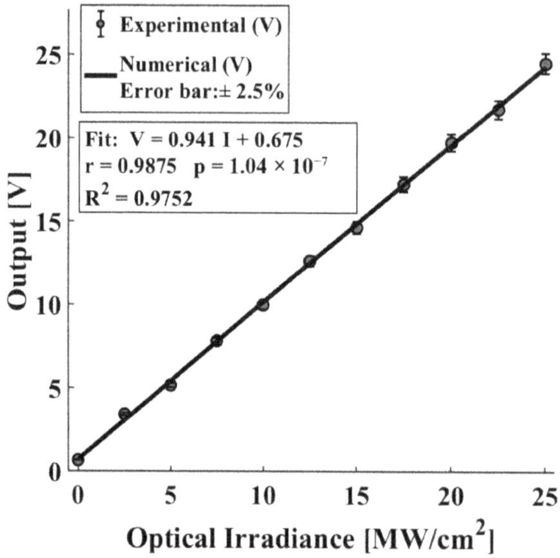

Figure 8. Calibration curve for estimating the error margin of the optical chaotic attractor.

Table 1. Stability of optical chaotic attractors.

Variable	Stable Attractor	Loss of Stability
Reflectance (%)	10–20%	>20% chaotic
Induced Temperature (°C)	Low (attractor shape preserved)	High (attractor deformation)
Attractor Morphology	Symmetrical	Asymmetrical and erratic
Optical Spectrum Dispersion	Low	High

3.4. Electrical Chaotic Attractor Response

In order to evaluate the bioelectromagnetic behavior of the seed under pulsed laser excitation, the chaotic electrical attractor based on the Newton–Leipnik system was recorded using an oscilloscope. The seed was subjected to different laser pulse energies: 2 μJ, 3 μJ, 4 μJ, 5 μJ, and 6 μJ. As the laser energy increased, the electrical response exhibited increasingly complex attractor trajectories, reflecting the seed's enhanced nonlinear electrical activity.

At lower energy (2 μJ), the attractor showed compact and symmetric shapes, indicating a stable and low-response regime. At 3 μJ and 4 μJ, the attractor began to stretch and oscillate with greater amplitude, suggesting early activation of bioelectrical dynamics. At 5 μJ and especially 6 μJ, the attractor became asymmetric and highly irregular, with dense loops and extended lobes, indicating strong chaotic activity induced by thermal and structural changes in the seed tissue. These changes in attractor morphology reflect variations in induced voltage and impedance. Specifically, at 6 μJ, the peak voltage reached up to 3.2 V and impedance showed nonlinear shifts, supporting the sensitivity of this method to detect early-stage bioelectrical transformations.

Upon irradiating the seed with varying pulse energies, we observed significant changes in the shape of the chaotic attractor. Figure 9 illustrates these variations, showing distinct Rössler attractor shapes corresponding to different energy levels. These variations indicate that the energy of the laser pulses directly influences the dynamical state of the seed germplasm. The correlation between pulse energy and attractor morphology suggests a sensitive dependence on initial conditions, a hallmark of chaotic systems.

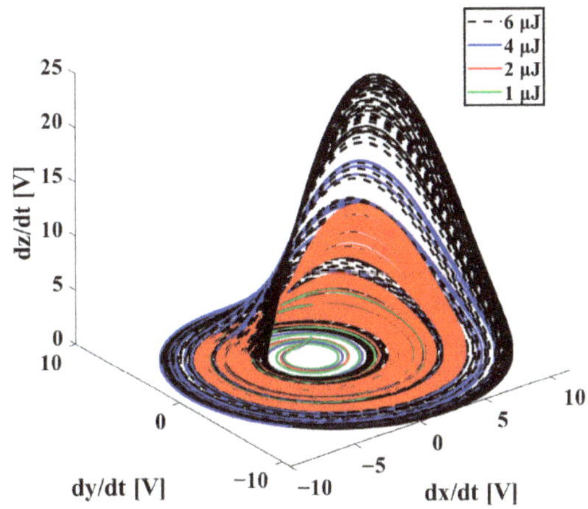

Figure 9. Experimental chaotic shapes of Rölsser attractor for different pulse energy on the studied seed.

Figure 10 shows the Fast Fourier Transform (FFT) spectrum corresponding to the electrical chaotic attractor response of *Thrinax radiata* seeds under laser excitation. The figure provides a frequency-domain representation of the system's nonlinear dynamics, where the stability of the attractor is assessed based on the distribution and sharpness of frequency components.

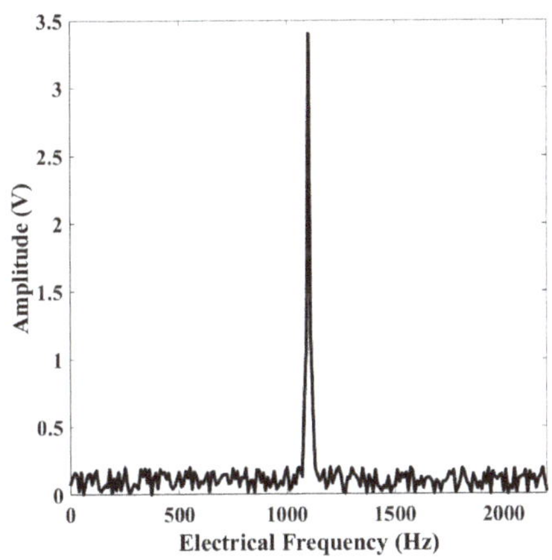

Figure 10. FFT spectrum of the electrical chaotic attractor recorded from *Thrinax radiata* seed under laser irradiation. The spectrum reveals a dominant peak centered around 1100 Hz, indicating stable nonlinear dynamics with low spectral dispersion.

A dominant peak is clearly observed at approximately 1100 Hz, indicating a strong periodic or quasi-periodic component within the electrical signal. The surrounding frequency range displays a relatively low amplitude baseline, suggesting that the attractor maintains a coherent oscillatory structure with minimal spectral dispersion.

This concentration of energy in a narrow frequency band is characteristic of a stable chaotic attractor, as it implies that the system dynamic behavior is constrained within well-defined limits, without exhibiting broadband, irregular frequency components typical of fully developed chaos. Such spectral profiles validate the reliability of the chaotic electrical attractor as a sensitive yet stable tool for bioelectromagnetic monitoring.

The presence of a high-amplitude peak combined with a sharp spectral boundary confirms that the system is in a low-entropy, structured dynamical regime, enabling precise detection of seed responses to laser perturbation. The FFT analysis thereby reinforces the calibration findings and supports the ±2.0% error margin previously established for the electrical monitoring system.

Figure 11 displays the calibration curve used to determine the error margin associated with the electrical chaotic attractor. This curve was constructed by systematically varying the laser pulse energy and recording the corresponding voltage responses from the seed sample using a digital oscilloscope. As the energy increased, the attractor exhibited broader and more irregular loops, which translated into voltage fluctuations with higher standard deviations. The result yielded an average uncertainty of ±2.0% for the electrical measurements across the tested energy range (1–6 μJ).

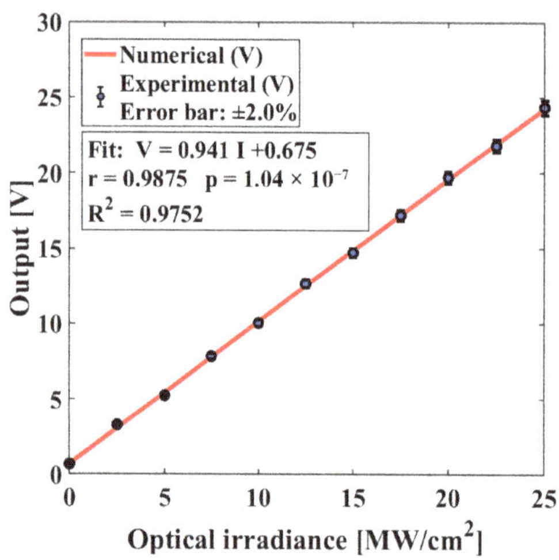

Figure 11. Calibration curve for the error bar in electrical attractor.

Table 2 summarizes the stability criteria for electrical chaotic attractors. Stable attractors are associated with induced voltages below 2.5 V, low impedance, uniform electromagnetic responses, and a narrow frequency range (0–100 Hz) with a sharp peak in the Fourier transform (FT) spectrum. In contrast, loss of stability is indicated by chaotic behavior even below 2.5 V, increased impedance, abrupt electromagnetic fluctuations, and a broad, asymmetric FT spectrum spanning up to 600 Hz.

Table 2. Stability of electrical chaotic attractors.

Variable	Stable Attractor	Loss of Stability
Induced Voltage (V)	<2.5 V (stable)	<2.5 V (chaotic)
Impedance (Ω)	Low (attractor shape preserved)	High (attractor deformation)
Electromagnetic Response	Uniform	Abrupt fluctuations
Oscillation Frequency (Hz)	0–100 Hz (narrow peak in FT)	0–600 Hz (broad and asymmetric FT spectrum)

4. Discussion

Short-term, non-destructive signal dynamics of seeds under controlled laser irradiation; this study does not evaluate long-term germplasm stability or shelf life. Viability was guaranteed in the samples explored before their analysis (see Materials and Methods Section 2.1). This study seeks to put together chaos theory with laser technology to study plant seed germplasm quality and to contrast the light-based or electrical chaotic attractors. Nd:YVO_4 pulsed laser operating at 532 nm was used for seed irradiation and then analyzed the resulting seed germination responses by optically and electrically dual modalities. The optical approach utilized a Rössler chaotic attractor to study the changes in laser-induced reflectance, which included thermal effects supposedly resulted from irradiation, whilst on the other hand, a custom-designed electrical chaotic attractor system connected directly with the seeds captured the electromagnetic response of the seeds even to external stimulation [25]. Reflectance measurements, which are meant to study the dynamic results of thermal energy induced by laser, were performed at different laser pulse energies of 2, 3, 4, 5, 6, and 7 μJ [26]. Meanwhile, electric signals from seeds, subjected to the same conditions, were monitored using the chaotic electrical circuit. The results showed that the voltage magnitudes in optical and electrical attractor systems were increased by laser energy input [27,28]. Therefore, they are highly sensitive to energy input. The optical attractor proved to have nonlinear thermal dynamics that captured how laser energy interferes with reflectance, as in the electrical attractor capturing electromagnetic interactions among some seeds, quite different for looking into their bioelectrical properties [29,30]. For the better comprehension of laser irradiation thermal effects, fractional calculus based on the Caputo fractional derivative was employed [31,32]. This sophisticated mathematical modeling was further able to depict the heat transfer process inside the seeds since it had memory-dependent and non-local characteristics. Through such simulations, the inner regions of the seeds offered simulated temperatures above 1 °C which closely corresponded to changes being observed in the morphology of shapes attractors. Such observations were indicative of the significant contribution that fractional modeling made towards more refined insights into transient thermal phenomena in biological systems.

The relationship between laser ablation and chaotic dynamics was further clarified. Controlled variations in laser energy and irradiation time act as perturbations in the fractional-order model, leading to measurable modifications in attractor morphology. Numerical simulations confirm that these parameter changes induce shifts in the trajectories, consistent with experimental observations. This suggests that laser ablation can serve as a precise tool to adjust chaotic behavior in seed systems, reinforcing the advantages of the fractional modeling approach [33–35]. Additional details are provided in the Supplementary Material.

The main advantages of adopting a fractional-order approach over the classical integer-order models are evident. First, fractional derivatives incorporate memory effects, allowing the present thermal response to depend on past states, which matches the delayed relaxation observed experimentally. Second, the fractional formulation provides a closer agreement with experimental data, capturing non-exponential cooling and anomalous diffusion that the classical model cannot reproduce. Finally, the approach generalizes the traditional Newton's law of cooling, reducing to the integer case, while extending the analysis to nonlinear, history-dependent regimes relevant to irradiated biological systems.

The comparative analysis between light-based and electrical chaotic attractors showed the specific applications and merits. The optical attractor had proved quite effective in analyzing photoinduced thermal dynamics; it can give a direct relationship between laser energy and seed reflectance behavior. On the other hand, the electrical attractor gave some electromagnetic responses of the seeds, capturing bioelectrical signals not visible through optical techniques. By this, the complementary approaches would provide a comprehensive resolution for seed germplasm studies combining thermal and electromagnetic perspectives [36,37].

Optical and electrical detection methods each provide unique advantages and limitations in the study of seed germplasm dynamics. Optical detection, based on reflectance measurements and chaotic attractors, offers high sensitivity to surface modifications and thermal effects induced by laser irradiation [38,39]. This method allows non-contact, high-resolution monitoring of structural and compositional changes, making it particularly useful for detecting subtle alterations in surface properties [40]. However, optical techniques can be affected by scattering, absorption variations, and surface irregularities, which may limit their accuracy in heterogeneous biological samples [41,42].

In contrast, electrical detection methods, such as the chaotic circuit employed in this study, provide direct insight into the bioelectromagnetic properties of seeds [43]. These techniques can reveal information about the internal physiological state, electrical conductivity, and impedance changes induced by laser energy [44,45]. Electrical monitoring is less influenced by surface roughness and can detect responses from deeper regions of the seed, offering complementary data to optical measurements [46,47]. However, electrical methods require direct contact with the sample, which may introduce artifacts due to electrode placement or seed heterogeneity [48]. Additionally, the interpretation of bioelectrical signals can be complex, as it involves multiple interacting variables that influence conductivity and impedance [49,50].

By integrating both techniques, it is possible to obtain a more comprehensive understanding of seed germplasm dynamics. Optical methods excel in detecting surface modifications and laser-induced heating effects, while electrical techniques provide deeper insights into bioelectromagnetic responses [51]. This multimodal approach enhances the robustness of the analysis, reducing the limitations associated with each individual technique.

This interdisciplinary study explores seed germplasm dynamics by integrating chaos theory, laser technology, and fractional calculus. Laser ablation significantly alters the optical and thermal properties of seeds, affecting their reflectance and the morphology of chaotic attractors. Variations in laser energy enable precise tuning of seed responses, suggesting applications in conservation and crop enhancement. Additionally, reflectance changes indicate key thermal and structural effects, with potential applications in optical diagnostics and laser-based treatments. This study did not measure germination rate, viability, or long-term storage performance; therefore, biological implications cannot be established from the present data. Future work will integrate our dynamical descriptors with standardized germination/viability assays across storage conditions to assess relevance for seed conservation.

In this work, we present two highly sensitive measurements as a concept test to explore potential physical differences exhibited by plant/seed stability. This can be a base for a study with an experimental design where the optical technique explores the surface of the sample and the electrical measurement analyzes its interior, considering the complexity of the dynamics.

5. Conclusions

We conclude that chaotic–dynamical descriptors can be robustly extracted from non-destructive measurements of laser-evoked seed responses, providing a methodological basis for subsequent studies that explicitly test links to physiological outcomes. This study analyzes the contrast in the advantages and limitations of optical and electrical monitoring of the nonlinear thermal dynamics exhibited by *Thrinax radiata* seed germplasm. The sensing performance was assisted by modulation related to chaotic attractors. Using both optical and electrical chaotic attractors, the research highlights the complementary insights provided by each method. The optical attractor captured nonlinear thermal effects with high sensitivity, while the electrical attractor provided early-stage detection of bioelectromagnetic changes, ensuring proactive monitoring to prevent potential structural damage in the seeds.

Fractional calculus simulations, employing the Caputo derivative, effectively modeled temperature distributions, emphasizing memory-dependent thermal transfer processes. Central regions of the seeds reached temperatures 1 °C, correlating with changes in attractor morphology. These findings establish a robust framework for linking theoretical chaos dynamics with experimental photothermal responses.

These results highlight the advantages of fractional calculus, particularly its ability to model memory-dependent thermal transport and anomalous diffusion, offering a more accurate description than classical integer-order models.

This study demonstrates that integrating chaos theory, laser technology, and fractional modeling enables high-sensitivity detection of seed germplasm changes, ensuring effective monitoring and protection of biological samples against excessive thermal and structural modifications, with implications for agricultural diagnostics, seed treatment, and conservation. This approach paves the way for innovative applications in biology, materials science, and precision agriculture.

Supplementary Materials: The following supporting information can be downloaded at: https://www.mdpi.com/article/10.3390/mca30050113/s1.

Author Contributions: H.M.-A.: writing—original draft, investigation, writing—review and editing. M.V.-K.: investigation, writing—review and editing. R.Á.-E.: investigation, writing—review and editing. L.E.V.-B.: investigation, writing—review and editing. C.L.M.-G.: investigation, writing—review and editing. C.T.-T.: investigation, writing—review and editing, Conceptualization. The manuscript was written through contribution of all authors. All authors have read and agreed to the published version of the manuscript.

Funding: This research was funded by Instituto Politécnico Nacional (SIP-2025) and Secretaría de Ciencia, Humanidades, Tecnología e Innovación (CF-2023-I-2042).

Data Availability Statement: The original contributions presented in this study are included in the article/Supplementary Material. Further inquiries can be directed to the corresponding authors: Carlos Torres-Torres (ctorrest@ipn.mx), and Hilario Martines-Arano (hilario_martines@uaeh.edu.mx).

Acknowledgments: The authors kindly acknowledge to Instituto Politécnico Nacional, Universidad Autónoma del Estado de Hidalgo, Escuela Superior Tepeji del Río, Centro de Investigación Científica de Yucatán, A.C, and Secretaría de Ciencia, Humanidades, Tecnología e Innovación.

Conflicts of Interest: The authors declare that they have no known competing financial interests or personal relationships that could have appeared to influence the work reported in this paper.

References

1. Luo, Z.; Yao, Z.; Yang, Y.; Wang, Z.; Zou, H.; Huang, L. Genetic fingerprint construction and genetic diversity analysis of sweet potato (*Ipomoea batatas*) germplasm resources. *BMC Plant Biol.* **2023**, *23*, 355. [CrossRef]
2. Priyanka, V.; Kumar, R.; Dhaliwal, I.; Kaushik, P. Germplasm conservation: Instrumental in agricultural biodiversity—A review. *Sustainability* **2021**, *13*, 6743. [CrossRef]
3. Šerá, B.; Hnilička, F. Genetic and environmental factors affecting seed germination. *Plants* **2023**, *12*, 4106. [CrossRef]
4. Ribeiro-Oliveira, J.P.; Ranal, M.A.; Boselli, M.A. Water dynamics on germinating diaspores: Physiological perspectives from biophysical measurements. *Plant Phenomics* **2020**, *2020*, 5196176. [CrossRef]
5. Moltchanova, E.; Sharifiamina, S.; Moot, D.J.; Shayanfar, A.; Bloomberg, M. Comparison of three different statistical approaches (non-linear least-squares regression, survival analysis and Bayesian inference) in their usefulness for estimating hydrothermal time models of seed germination. *Seed Sci. Res.* **2020**, *30*, 64–72.

6. Souza, G.M.; Posso, D.A.; de Carvalho Oliveira, T.F. The quest for time in plant physiology: A processual perspective. *Theor. Exp. Plant Physiol.* **2024**, *36*, 387–398. [CrossRef]
7. Gayosso-Soto, E.; Cohuo, S.; Sánchez-Sánchez, J.A.; Villegas-Sánchez, C.A.; Macario-González, L. Coastal dune vegetation dynamism and anthropogenic-induced transitions in the Mexican Caribbean during the last decade. *Plants* **2024**, *13*, 1734. [CrossRef]
8. Secretaría de Medio Ambiente y Recursos Naturales (SEMARNAT). Norma Oficial Mexicana NOM-059-SEMARNAT-2001. In *Protección Ambiental-Especies Nativas de México de Flora y Fauna Silvestres-Categorías de Riesgo y Especificaciones Para su Inclusión, Exclusión o Cambio-Lista de Especies en Riesgo*; Diario Oficial de la Federación: Ciudad de México, Mexico, 2001.
9. Calvo-Irabién, L.M.; Soberanis, A. Indigenous Management Practices of Chit (*Thrinax radiata*) in Quintana Roo, Mexico. *PALMS* **2008**, *52*, 46–50.
10. Zhang, M.; Wang, Y. Review on chaotic lasers and measurement applications. *J. Light. Technol.* **2021**, *39*, 3711–3723. [CrossRef]
11. Letellier, C.; Olsen, L.F.; Mangiarotti, S. Chaos: From theory to applications for the 80th birthday of Otto E. Rössler. *Chaos* **2021**, *31*, 060402. [CrossRef]
12. Sharif, M.A.; Shahnazary, M.; Pourezzat, M. Modelling heat transfer in laser-soft matter interaction via chaotic Ikeda map. *arXiv* **2022**, arXiv:2201.05682. [CrossRef]
13. Martines-Arano, H.; Palacios-Barreto, S.; Castillo-Cruz, J.; Meda-Campaña, J.A.; García-Pérez, B.E.; Torres-Torres, C. Fractional photodamage triggered by chaotic attractors in human lung epithelial cancer cells. *Int. J. Therm. Sci.* **2022**, *181*, 107734. [CrossRef]
14. Martínez-Ayala, L.; Bornacelli, J.; Misses, M.A.O.; Arano-Martinez, J.A.; Torres-Torres, C.; Martines-Arano, H. Chaos-driven detection of methylene blue in wastewater using fractional calculus and laser systems. *Meas. Sci. Technol.* **2024**, *36*, 015801. [CrossRef]
15. Padder, A.; Almutairi, L.; Qureshi, S.; Soomro, A.; Afroz, A.; Tassaddiq, A. Dynamical analysis of generalized tumor model with Caputo fractional-order derivative. *Fractal Fract.* **2023**, *7*, 258. [CrossRef]
16. Li, L.; Liu, J.-G. A discretization of Caputo derivatives with application to time fractional SDEs and gradient flows. *SIAM J. Numer. Anal.* **2019**, *57*, 2095–2120. [CrossRef]
17. Feng, T.; Chen, G.; Han, H.; Qiao, J. Femtosecond-laser-ablation dynamics in silicon revealed by transient reflectivity change. *Micromachines* **2021**, *13*, 14. [CrossRef]
18. Ma, G.; Fu, C.; Wang, G.; Del Hougne, P.; Christensen, J.; Sheng, P. Polarization bandgaps and fluid-like elasticity in fully solid elastic metamaterials. *Nat. Commun.* **2016**, *7*, 13536. [CrossRef] [PubMed]
19. Karna, P.; Giri, A. Effect of intense laser irradiation on the thermal transport properties of metals. *Phys. Rev. B* **2003**, *107*, 094301. [CrossRef]
20. Nazarimehr, F.; Sprott, J.C. Investigating chaotic attractor of the simplest chaotic system with a line of equilibria. *Eur. Phys. J. Spec. Top.* **2020**, *229*, 1289–1297. [CrossRef]
21. Bacab-Caamal, D.V.; Souza-Perera, R.; Alvarez-Espino, R. Evaluation and short-term conservation of *Thrinax radiata* (Arecaceae) seeds. In *Conservation of Plant Genetic Resources*; Ramírez-Mosqueda, M.A., Zamudio, C., Noyola, A., Eds.; Springer: Berlin/Heidelberg, Germany, 2004.
22. Nucci, H.H.P.; de Azevedo, R.G.; Nogueira, M.C.; Costa, C.S.; de Oliveira Guilherme, D.; Higa, G.T.H.; Pistori, H. Use of computer vision to verify the viability of guavira seeds treated with tetrazolium salt. *Smart Agric. Technol.* **2023**, *5*, 100239. [CrossRef]
23. Rössler, O.E. An equation for continuous chaos. *Phys. Lett. A* **1976**, *57*, 397–398. [CrossRef]
24. Lofaro, T. A model of the dynamics of the Newton–Leipnik attractor. *Int. J. Bifurcat. Chaos* **1997**, *7*, 2723–2733.
25. Lai, Q.; Yang, L. Hyperchaos of neuron under local active discrete memristor simulating electromagnetic radiation. *Chaos* **2024**, *34*, 013145.
26. Abasi, S.; Aggas, J.R.; Garayar-Leyva, G.G.; Walther, B.K.; Guiseppi-Elie, A. Bioelectrical impedance spectroscopy for monitoring mammalian cells and tissues under different frequency domains: A review. *ACS Meas. Sci. Au* **2022**, *2*, 495–516. [CrossRef]
27. Ni, D.; Klämpfl, F.; Schmidt, M.; Hohmann, M. Towards a sensing model using a random laser combined with diffuse reflectance spectroscopy. *Biomed. Opt. Express* **2024**, *15*, 4425–4437. [CrossRef] [PubMed]
28. Prasetyanto, E.A.; Wasisto, H.S.; Septiadi, D. Cellular lasers for cell imaging and biosensing. *Acta Biomater.* **2022**, *143*, 39–51. [CrossRef]
29. Kesgin, B.U.; Teğin, U. Implementing the analogous neural network using chaotic strange attractors. *Commun. Eng.* **2024**, *3*, 99. [CrossRef]
30. Yang, J.; Li, C.; Zhang, Q.; Wu, Z.; Zhang, X.; Liu, P.; Liu, Z.; Tao, C.; Zheng, G.; Yang, Y.; et al. Chaos-enhanced manganese electrolysis: Nodule suppression and improved efficiency using controllable chaotic electrical signals. *Sci. Rep.* **2025**, *15*, 59. [PubMed]
31. Abouelregal, A.E.; Alhassan, Y.; Alsaeed, S.S.; Marin, M.; Elzayady, M.E. MGT photothermal model incorporating a generalized Caputo fractional derivative with a tempering parameter: Application to an unbounded semiconductor medium. *Contemp. Math.* **2024**, *5*, 6556–6581. [CrossRef]

32. Lizama, C.; Trujillo, M. The time fractional approach for the modeling of thermal therapies: Temperature analysis in laser irradiation. *Int. J. Heat Mass Transf.* **2020**, *154*, 119677. [CrossRef]
33. Hernández-Acosta, M.A.; Martines-Arano, H.; Soto-Ruvalcaba, L.; Martínez-González, C.L.; Martínez-Gutiérrez, H.; Torres-Torres, C. Fractional thermal transport and twisted light induced by an optical two-wave mixing in single-wall carbon nanotubes. *Int. J. Therm. Sci.* **2020**, *147*, 106136. [CrossRef]
34. Mondol, A.; Gupta, R.; Das, S.; Dutta, T. An insight into Newton's cooling law using fractional calculus. *Jpn. J. Appl. Phys.* **2018**, *123*, 064901. [CrossRef]
35. Yang, Q.; Chen, D.; Zhao, T.; Chen, Y. Fractional Calculus In Image Processing: A Review. *Fract. Calc. Appl. Anal.* **2016**, *19*, 1222–1249. [CrossRef]
36. Singh, R.N.; Krishnan, P.; Singh, V.K.; Sah, S.; Das, B. Combining biophysical parameters with thermal and RGB indices using machine learning models for predicting yield in yellow rust affected wheat crop. *Sci. Rep.* **2023**, *13*, 18814. [CrossRef] [PubMed]
37. Dziwulska-Hunek, A.; Kornarzyńska-Gregorowicz, A.; Niemczynowicz, A.; Matwijczuk, A. Influence of electromagnetic stimulation of seeds on the photosynthetic indicators in Medicago sativa L. leaves at various stages of development. *Agronomy* **2020**, *10*, 594. [CrossRef]
38. Jaber, M.M.; Hemed, A.A. The chaotic behavior of an optical artificial neuron. *Fiber Integr. Opt.* **2024**, *43*, 235–260. [CrossRef]
39. Wang, Y.; Wu, Z.; Li, B.; Chen, J.; Shen, L.; Yang, H.; Feng, Y.; Chen, X.; Li, M. Hybrid integrated optical chaos circuits with optoelectronic feedback. *Opt. Express* **2024**, *32*, 15923–15935. [CrossRef] [PubMed]
40. Wang, S.; Liu, S.; Liu, Y.; Xiao, S.; Wang, Z.; Fan, Y.; Han, J.; Ge, L.; Song, Q. Direct observation of chaotic resonances in optical microcavities. *Light Sci. Appl.* **2021**, *10*, 135. [CrossRef] [PubMed]
41. Kotha, A.; Harvey, J.E. Scattering effects of machined optical surfaces. In *Optical Scattering in the Optics, Semiconductor, and Computer Disk Industries*; SPIE: Bellingham, WA, USA, 1995.
42. Song, G.; Wang, Y.; Tan, D.Q. A review of surface roughness impact on dielectric film properties. *IET Nanodielectrics* **2022**, *5*, 1–23. [CrossRef]
43. Bonato, M.; Chiaramello, E.; Parazzini, M.; Gajšek, P.; Ravazzani, P. Extremely low frequency electric and magnetic fields exposure: Survey of recent findings. *IEEE J. Electromagn. RF Microw. Med. Biol.* **2023**, *7*, 216–228. [CrossRef]
44. Syugaev, A.V.; Zonov, R.G.; Mikheev, K.G.; Maratkanova, A.N.; Mikheev, G.M. Electrochemical impedance of laser-induced graphene: Frequency response of porous structure. *J. Phys. Chem. Solids* **2023**, *181*, 111533. [CrossRef]
45. Pham, K.H.; Lin, A.K.; Spear, N.A.; Cushing, S.K. Laser-driven ultrafast impedance spectroscopy for measuring complex ion hopping processes. *Rev. Sci. Instrum.* **2024**, *95*, 073004. [CrossRef]
46. Gorji, R.; Skvaril, J.; Odlare, M. Applications of optical sensing and imaging spectroscopy in indoor farming: A systematic review. *Spectrochim. Acta A Mol. Biomol. Spectrosc.* **2024**, *322*, 124820. [CrossRef]
47. Tottrup, C.; Druce, D.; Meyer, R.P.; Christensen, M.; Riffler, M.; Dulleck, B.; Rastner, P.; Jupova, K.; Sokoup, T.; Haag, A.; et al. Surface water dynamics from space: A round robin intercomparison of using optical and SAR high-resolution satellite observations for regional surface water detection. *Remote Sens.* **2022**, *14*, 2410. [CrossRef]
48. Polat, E.O.; Cetin, M.M.; Tabak, A.F.; Bilget Güven, E.; Uysal, B.Ö.; Arsan, T.; Kabbani, A.; Hamed, H.; Gül, S.B. Transducer technologies for biosensors and their wearable applications. *Biosensors* **2022**, *12*, 385. [CrossRef]
49. Kralikova, I.; Babusiak, B.; Smondrk, M. Measurement of the conductive fabric contact impedance for bioelectrical signal acquisition purposes. *Measurement* **2023**, *217*, 113005. [CrossRef]
50. Ge, X.; Guo, Y.; Gong, C.; Han, R.; Feng, J.; Ji, J.; Sun, Z.; Gao, J.; Bian, F.; Xu, Z. High-conductivity, low-impedance, and high-biological-adaptability ionic conductive hydrogels for ear-EEG acquisition. *ACS Appl. Polym. Mater.* **2023**, *5*, 8151–8158. [CrossRef]
51. Ziriax, J.M.; Smith, K.I.; Nelson, D.A.; Ryan, K.L.; Gajsek, P.; D'Andrea, J.A.; Walters, T.J.; Hurt, W.D.; Mason, P.A. Effects of frequency, permittivity, and voxel size on predicted specific absorption rate values in biological tissue during electromagnetic-field exposure. *IEEE Trans. Microw. Theory Tech.* **2000**, *48*, 2050–2058. [CrossRef]

Mathematical and Computational Applications

Article

An Exposition on the Kaniadakis κ-Deformed Decay Differential Equation

Rohan Bolle, Ibrahim Jarra and Jeffery A. Secrest *

Department of Biochemistry, Chemistry, and Physics, Georgia Southern University, Savannah, GA 31419, USA; rb23491@georgiasouthern.edu (R.B.); ij01273@georgiasouthern.edu (I.J.)
* Correspondence: jsecrest@georgiasouthern.edu

Abstract: Kaniadakis deformed κ-mathematics is an area of mathematics that has found relevance in the analysis of complex systems. Specifically, the mathematical framework in the context of a first-order decay κ-differential equation is investigated, facilitating an in-depth examination of the κ-mathematical structure. This framework serves as a foundational platform, representing the simplest non-trivial setting for such inquiries which are demonstrated for the first time in the literature. Finally, additional avenues of study are discussed.

Keywords: κ-statistics; κ-exponential; κ-logarithm; κ-mathematics; κ-deformation; κ-differential equations; Kaniadakis entropy

1. Introduction

In recent decades, the deformed statistics of Kaniadakis [1–6] have gained popularity as they have been applied to a wide array of disciplines such as cosmology [7–10], economics [11,12], and epidemiology [13,14], to cite but a few references. These so-called κ-statistics are predicated upon one parameter of a relativistically inspired generalization of the standard exponential as the κ-exponential (Figure 1(left)),

$$\exp_\kappa(x) \quad = \quad (\sqrt{1+\kappa^2x^2}+\kappa x)^{1/\kappa} \tag{1}$$

and the one-parameter relativistically inspired generalization of the usual logarithm as the κ-logarithm (Figure 1(right)),

$$\ln_\kappa x = \frac{x^\kappa - x^{-\kappa}}{2\kappa} \tag{2}$$

where κ is a deformation parameter (sometimes also known as the entropic index), ranging in values between -1 and 1.

Kaniadakis κ-statistics are important because they provide a generalized statistical framework that extends the classical Boltzmann–Gibbs statistical mechanics to systems where standard assumptions—like extensivity, short-range interactions, or Markovian dynamics—may not hold. This is particularly relevant for complex systems with the following:

1. Long-range interactions;
2. Fractal or multifractal structure;
3. Relativistic effects;
4. Non-equilibrium steady states.

In these types of complex systems, power-law tails instead of exponential ones are generated. The κ-exponential is able to naturally generate distributions such as these.

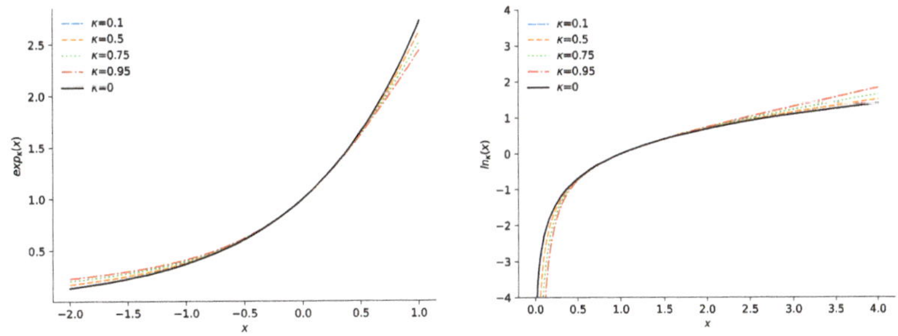

Figure 1. Examples of κ-exponential (**left**) and κ-logarithm (**right**) for various values of the deformation parameter κ. Note that when $\kappa \to 0$, then κ-exponential and κ-logarithm approach the standard exponential and logarithm.

There are some issues with κ-statistics. Outside the specific context of relativistic statistical mechanics (which is the inspiration for κ-statistics), by which the κ-statistics framework was originally motivated, the physical meaning of the deformation parameter κ is often ambiguous. Unlike physical constants (like Planck's constant or the speed of light), κ is typically introduced as a phenomenological parameter without a direct derivation from first principles in many applications.

As a result, many times, it is unclear how to interpret the κ-parameter. In these cases, the κ-parameter effectively becomes a free parameter that can be adjusted in order to fit data and explore different regimes of the distribution functions.

In such cases, κ functions more like a modeling knob than a physically grounded variable, which may limit the predictive power and falsifiability of models that use it.

As the deformation parameter approaches zero,

$$\lim_{\kappa \to 0} \exp_\kappa(x) \quad \to \exp(x) \tag{3}$$

$$\lim_{\kappa \to 0} \ln_\kappa(x) \quad \to \ln(x) \tag{4}$$

the κ-exponential and κ-logarithm approach the standard exponential and natural logarithm, respectively. The κ-exponential and κ-logarithm are inverses of one another,

$$\exp_\kappa(\ln_\kappa(x)) = \ln_\kappa(\exp_\kappa(x)) = x. \tag{5}$$

Probability distributions with power-law tails are ubiquitous in the natural sciences, and this makes these functions interesting. As mentioned above, some examples of phenomena described by the κ-statistics are the cosmic ray spectrum [15], which extends over 13 decades in energy and 33 decades in particle flux, with low-energy particles obeying an exponential distribution, whilst at high energies, the spectrum exhibits a power-law tail. The impact of loads on buildings and structures is effectively modeled [16] using κ-statistics. In this framework, the κ-exponential distribution accurately represents normal design loading conditions, while the tails of the distribution follow a power law pattern, reflecting the effects of loads that exceed the design values.

The natural question to ask within the framework of these deformed statistics is what is the physical meaning of the κ-deformation parameter? This deformation parameter has been introduced to describe deviations from the standard exponential behavior, especially in various probability distributions such as the exponential, Gaussian, weibull, and pareto distributions. In complicated physical systems, these deformations tend to be related to processes composed of short-range interactions, various correlations, or long-term memory effects. These deformations furthermore describe systems that are not in equilibrium or have a complex hierarchical nature, such as fractal systems.

At this point, it is appropriate to draw attention to another well-known generalized deformed statistical framework, Tsallis statistics [17–19], and to briefly compare it with the Kaniadakis formulation. Since the Tsallis framework is more widely recognized in the literature, such a comparison serves to place the present discussion within the broader context of deformed statistical mechanics.

Kaniadakis and Tsallis statistics represent two prominent generalizations of the Boltzmann–Gibbs framework developed to describe complex systems that deviate from classical extensivity. Both theories introduce a single deformation parameter that modifies the standard exponential and logarithmic functions, giving rise to power-law distributions capable of modeling long-range correlations, fractal structures, and non-equilibrium steady states. In Tsallis statistics, the deformation parameter q emerges from nonadditive entropy S_q, leading to q-exponentials that break the additivity of entropy and capture nonextensive thermodynamics. In contrast, Kaniadakis statistics introduce a deformation parameter κ derived from relativistic symmetries, producing κ-exponentials that preserve additivity but deform the underlying algebra in a way that is consistent with special relativity. Consequently, while both frameworks yield heavy-tailed distributions and are reduced to the Boltzmann–Gibbs limit of $q \to 1$ or $\kappa \to 0$, Tsallis statistics are rooted in nonextensive entropy composition, whereas Kaniadakis statistics maintain entropy extensivity within a deformed relativistic mathematical structure.

The motivation of this work arises from the growing significance of Kaniadakis κ-statistics as a relativistically inspired generalization of Boltzmann–Gibbs statistical mechanics. This framework extends the classical exponential and logarithmic functions through the deformation parameter κ, allowing for the description of complex systems characterized by long-range interactions, fractal structures, relativistic effects, and non-equilibrium steady states. Although now applied in diverse areas, as already mentioned, such as cosmology, plasma physics, and information theory, the κ-formalism is often presented with few detailed explanations of its differential foundations accessible to new researchers. This study presents a systematic and accessible analytical exposition of the simplest nontrivial κ-deformed dynamical system, namely the first-order κ-deformed decay differential equation, with the goal of forming a pedagogical connection between classical and deformed calculus frameworks.

The principal result of this work is the introduction and validation of κ-exponential as a solution to the κ-deformed decay differential equation. This relationship demonstrates how deformation modifies the familiar exponential decay law within the κ-statistical framework. The equivalence of this solution is confirmed through a variety of independent analytical and numerical techniques, including direct substitution, separation of variables, the integrating-factor and WKBJ methods, Laplace and Lagrange–Charpit approaches, Picard's iterative method, power-series expansion, and several numerical algorithms (Euler, Adams, and Runge–Kutta). The agreement among these approaches establishes both the internal consistency of κ-differential calculus and also highlights the unity of the deformed and classical frameworks, where each technique illuminates a different aspect of the same underlying structure.

The organization of this paper is as follows. Section 2 provides the motivation and mathematical preliminaries of κ-calculus, including the κ-exponential, κ-logarithm, and their algebraic properties. Section 3 introduces the κ-deformed decay equation and applies multiple analytic methods to obtain its solution. Section 4 extends the analysis to the Laplace and Lagrange–Charpit techniques, while Section 5 presents iterative and series approaches. Section 6 compares several numerical methods with the analytic solution to assess convergence and accuracy. Finally, Section 7 summarizes the findings and outlines future applications to more complex κ-deformed equations, such as κ-logistic, κ-advection, κ-wave, κ-diffusion, and κ-Fokker–Planck models.

2. Preliminaries

Much of the material presented in this section has been adapted and consolidated from established references on κ-mathematics and related works by Kaniadakis and others [1,2,4–6]. It is reproduced here for completeness and to ensure that the exposition is self-contained and accessible to readers new to the κ-formalism.

Arguably, the most interesting aspect of the κ-exponential is that it exhibits an exponential behavior at small values of x,

$$\lim_{x\to 0} \exp_\kappa(x) \sim \exp(x) \tag{6}$$

whilst exhibiting a power law behavior at asymptotic values of x (that is, the tail exhibits a power law structure),

$$\lim_{x\to\pm\infty} \exp_\kappa(x) \sim |2\kappa x|^{\pm 1/|\kappa|} \tag{7}$$

(see Figure 2).

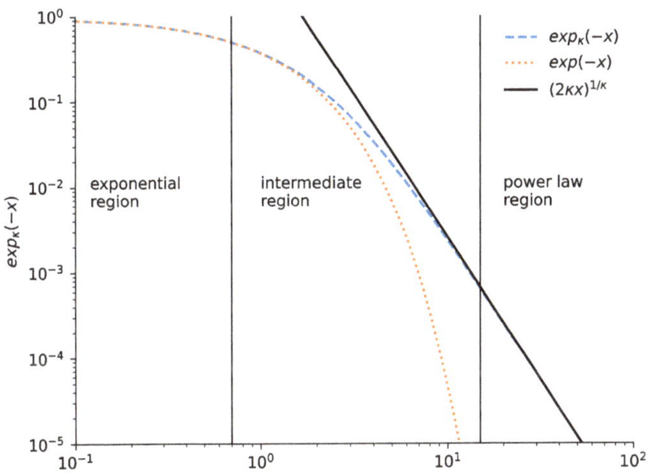

Figure 2. The figure above shows the various regions of the κ-exponential (blue dashed curve), the exponential (red dashed curve), and a power-law (solid black curve). The κ parameter has the value of 0.75 in the above plots.

The Kaniadakis κ-exponential is defined by Equation (1). Expanding the square root using the first-order Taylor series for small x,

$$\exp_\kappa(x) = \left(1 + \frac{1}{2}\kappa^2 x^2 + \kappa x\right)^{\frac{1}{\kappa}}, \tag{8}$$

Applying the logarithm property $a^b = e^{b \ln a}$ reveals that,

$$\exp_\kappa(x) = \exp\left(\frac{1}{\kappa} \ln\left(1 + \frac{1}{2}\kappa^2 x^2 + \kappa x\right)\right). \tag{9}$$

Using the Taylor series expansion of $\ln(1+u)$ for small u,

$$\ln(1+u) = u - \frac{u^2}{2} + O(u^3); \tag{10}$$

thus, the logarithm can be rewritten as

$$\ln\left(1 + \frac{1}{2}\kappa^2 x^2 + \kappa x\right) \approx \kappa x + \frac{1}{2}\kappa^2 x^2 - \frac{1}{2}(\kappa x)^2. \tag{11}$$

Since the last two terms cancel, this results in

$$\ln\left(1 + \frac{1}{2}\kappa^2 x^2 + \kappa x\right) \approx \kappa x. \tag{12}$$

Thus,

$$\exp_\kappa(x) = \exp\left(\frac{1}{\kappa} \cdot \kappa x\right) = \exp(x). \tag{13}$$

The large x approximation of the κ-exponential follows by taking Equation (1), and for large x, the square root term can be approximated using the expansion,

$$\sqrt{1 + \kappa^2 x^2} \approx \kappa|x|, \quad \text{for } x \gg 1. \tag{14}$$

Thus, the term inside the power simplifies to

$$\sqrt{1 + \kappa^2 x^2} + \kappa x \approx 2\kappa x. \tag{15}$$

Raising both sides to the power of $1/\kappa$,

$$\exp_\kappa(x) \approx (2\kappa x)^{\frac{1}{\kappa}}. \tag{16}$$

resulting in,

$$\exp_\kappa(x) \sim |2\kappa x|^{\frac{1}{\kappa}}, \quad \text{for } x \gg 1. \tag{17}$$

Similarly, the κ-logarithm is similar to the usual standard logarithm as small values of x,

$$\lim_{x \to 0} \ln_\kappa(x) \sim \ln(x) \tag{18}$$

as it also exhibits a power law tails for the asymptotic values of x,

$$\lim_{x \to 0^+} \ln_\kappa(x) \sim \frac{1}{|\kappa|} x^{-|\kappa|} \tag{19}$$

$$\lim_{x \to +\infty} \ln_\kappa(x) \sim \frac{1}{2|\kappa|} x^{|\kappa|}. \tag{20}$$

The low x regime result can be seen by taking the Kaniadakis κ-logarithm, Equation (2), and expanding for small κ,

$$x^\kappa = e^{\kappa \ln x} \approx 1 + \kappa \ln x, \tag{21}$$

$$x^{-\kappa} = e^{-\kappa \ln x} \approx 1 - \kappa \ln x. \tag{22}$$

Substituting these results into the definition of the $\ln_\kappa(x)$,

$$\ln_\kappa(x) = \frac{(1 + \kappa \ln x) - (1 - \kappa \ln x)}{2\kappa}. \tag{23}$$

The numerator can be simplified as

$$\ln_\kappa(x) = \frac{1 + \kappa \ln x - 1 + \kappa \ln x}{2\kappa} \tag{24}$$

$$= \frac{2\kappa \ln x}{2\kappa} \tag{25}$$

$$= \ln x. \tag{26}$$

The Kaniadakis κ-logarithm for the small x approximation as $x \to 0^+$ regime can be approximated as

$$x^\kappa = e^{\kappa \ln x} \tag{27}$$

$$x^{-\kappa} = e^{-\kappa \ln x}. \tag{28}$$

Since $\ln x \to -\infty$ for $x \to 0^+$ leads to $x^{-\kappa} \gg x^\kappa$, resulting in

$$\ln_\kappa(x) \approx \frac{-x^{-\kappa}}{2\kappa}. \tag{29}$$

rewriting in terms of absolute value,

$$\ln_\kappa(x) \approx \frac{1}{|\kappa|} x^{-|\kappa|}, \quad \text{for } x \to 0^+. \tag{30}$$

The approximation for Large x as ($x \to +\infty$) can be written as

$$x^\kappa = e^{\kappa \ln x} \tag{31}$$

$$x^{-\kappa} = e^{-\kappa \ln x}. \tag{32}$$

Since $x^\kappa \gg x^{-\kappa}$ for large x, the dominant term in the κ logarithm is

$$\ln_\kappa(x) \approx \frac{x^\kappa}{2\kappa}. \tag{33}$$

Rewriting in absolute-value form,

$$\ln_\kappa(x) \approx \frac{1}{2|\kappa|} x^{|\kappa|}, \quad \text{for } x \to +\infty. \tag{34}$$

There are two identities that are useful when working with κ-mathematics,

$$\text{arsinh}\,(kx) = \ln(\sqrt{1 + \kappa^2 x^2} + \kappa x) \tag{35}$$

and

$$\ln x = \text{arsinh}\left[\frac{1}{2}\left(x - \frac{1}{x}\right)\right]. \tag{36}$$

The algebraic structure $(\mathbb{R}, \oplus)$ of the κ-algebra for $x, y \in \mathbb{R}$ with $\kappa \in [0, 1)$, whose κ-sum composition law is defined via

$$x \oplus y = x\sqrt{1 + \kappa^2 y^2} + y\sqrt{1 + \kappa^2 x^2} = \frac{1}{\kappa} \sinh\left(\text{arsinh}\,(\kappa x) + \text{arsinh}\,(\kappa y)\right),$$

forms an abelian group. The group properties are given below:

1. Associativity: $(x \oplus y) \oplus z = x \oplus (y \oplus z)$,
2. Identity Element: $x \oplus 0 = 0 \oplus x = x$,
3. Inverse Element: $x \oplus (-x) = (-x) \oplus x = 0$, and
4. Commutativity: $x \oplus y = y \oplus x$.

The algebraic structure $(\mathbb{R}, \otimes)$ for the x, y and κ previously described has a κ-product composition law defined via

$$x \otimes y = \frac{1}{\kappa} \sinh\Big(\operatorname{arsinh}(\kappa x) \operatorname{arsinh}(\kappa y)\Big)$$

and this also forms an abelian group. The group properties are given below:

1. Associativity: $(x \otimes y) \otimes z = x \otimes (y \otimes z)$,
2. Identity Element: $x \otimes I = I \otimes x = x, \quad \text{for } I = \kappa^{-1} \sinh(\kappa \otimes x)$,
3. Inverse Element: $x \otimes \bar{x} = \bar{x} \otimes x = I, \quad \text{for } \bar{x} = \kappa^{-1} \sinh\left(\frac{\kappa^2}{\operatorname{arsinh}(\kappa x)}\right)$, and
4. Commutativity: $x \otimes y = y \otimes x$.

Often it is useful to introduce the definition of the κ-number $x_{\{\kappa\}} \in C^{\infty}(\mathbb{R})$ via

$$x_{\{\kappa\}} = \frac{1}{\kappa} \operatorname{arsinh}(\kappa x) \tag{37}$$

and its dual is given as

$$x^{\{\kappa\}} = \frac{1}{\kappa} \sinh(\kappa x). \tag{38}$$

It is easy to show that the κ-differential is given as

$$dx_{\{\kappa\}} = \frac{dx}{\sqrt{1 + \kappa^2 x^2}} \tag{39}$$

and the κ-integral corresponds to,

$$\int f(x) dx_{\{\kappa\}} = \int f(x) \frac{dx}{\sqrt{1 + \kappa^2 x^2}}.$$

The κ-exponential (see Figure 1) is defined by Equation (1) and written in terms of the hyperbolic sine function,

$$\begin{aligned} \exp_{\kappa}(x) &= \exp\left[\frac{1}{\kappa} \operatorname{arsinh}(\kappa x)\right] && (40) \\ &= \exp(x_{\{\kappa\}}), && (41) \end{aligned}$$

where the Taylor series expansion of the κ-exponential is determined to be

$$\begin{aligned} \exp_{\kappa}(x) &= 1 + x + \tfrac{1}{2!}x^2 + (1 - \kappa^2)\tfrac{1}{3!}x^3 + (1 - 4\kappa^2)\tfrac{1}{4!}x^4 \\ &\quad + (1 - \kappa^2)(1 - 9\kappa^2)\tfrac{1}{5!}x^5 + \ldots \end{aligned} \tag{42}$$

with the κ-logarithm (see Figure 1) defined by Equation (2), and writing in terms of the hyperbolic sine function,

$$\ln_{\kappa} x = \frac{1}{\kappa} \sinh(\kappa \ln x), \tag{43}$$

where the Taylor series expansion of the κ-logarithm is determined to be

$$\ln_{\kappa}(1 + x) \approx x - \frac{1}{2}x^2 + \left(1 + \frac{\kappa^2}{2}\right)\frac{1}{3}x^3 - \ldots$$

where the deformation parameter κ exists on the interval $|\kappa| < 1$, and as $\kappa \to 0$, Equations (1) and (2) reduce to the usual logarithm and exponential functions. Equations (1) and (2) are inverses of each other, and thus the following property holds:

$$\ln_\kappa(\exp_\kappa x) = \exp_\kappa(\ln_\kappa x) = x.$$

One of the most ubiquitous equations in physics is the linear first-order homogeneous decay differential equation [20],

$$\frac{df(x)}{dx} + r(x)f(x) = 0 \tag{44}$$

where in this work, the rate function $r(x) = r_0 = 1$ is taken to be constant and the initial condition is $f(0) = 1$. In this particular instance, the rate of decrease is a function, $f(x)$, that is proportional to the value of $f(x)$ itself, which leads to the well-known standard decaying exponential function,

$$f(x) = \exp(-x). \tag{45}$$

This equation describes radioactive half-lives, simple population decay, the discharge of a capacitor, and the rate law for certain first-order molecular reactions. In this work, the homogeneous first-order κ-differential equation (see the slope field in Figure 3),

$$\sqrt{1+\kappa^2x^2}\frac{df(x)}{dx} + r(x)f(x) = 0 \tag{46}$$

will be studied, where again the rate function $r(x) = r_0 = 1$ is taken to be a constant and the initial condition $f(0) = 1$. The solution to this equation is analogous to the solution to Equation (45),

$$f(x) = \exp_\kappa(-x). \tag{47}$$

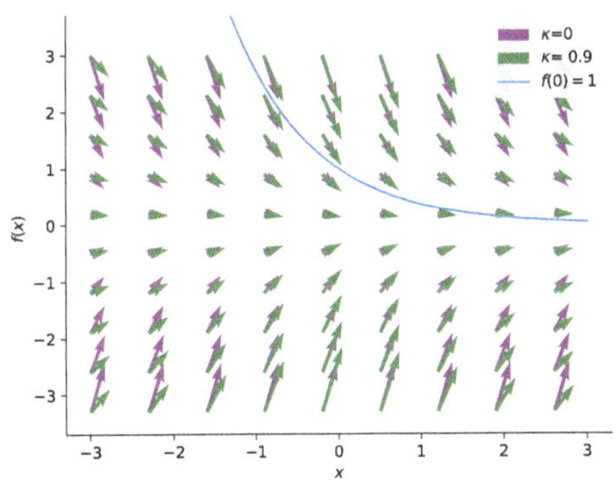

Figure 3. The slope field for the κ-decay differential Equation (46) for $\kappa = 0.9$ and for $\kappa \to 0$, which leads to the standard decay differential Equation (44). The blue curve represents the solution, $f(x) = \exp_\kappa(-x)$, with the initial condition that $f(0) = 1$.

3. Techniques

In order to gain a deeper understanding of the κ-deformed framework, the deformed differential equation described in Equation (46) is solved by a variety of elementary methods to demonstrate the mathematical structure of the differential equation as well as the solution.

1. Validation and verification: Validating and verifying solutions in the context of differential equations are important steps in the process of solving and understanding these

equations and their solutions. These two steps ensure that the obtained solutions are accurate and consistent with the original differential equation and any initial or boundary conditions.

2. Understanding: The κ-deformed statistics are not as well known as standard statistics or other deformed statistics (such as Tsallis statistics). This is an opportunity to investigate these statistics, in particular the deformed exponential and the deformed decay equation, from which a solution can be obtained within a familiar framework. By exploring a variety of methods for solving the same differential equation, valuable experience and insights that contribute to a deeper understanding of both the equation itself and its solutions can be acquired.
3. Rigor: Solving a problem through various methods introduces rigor by subjecting the solution to different analytical approaches, verification steps, and perspectives. This multiplicity of approaches helps ensure the robustness and reliability of the solution. It allows for cross-validation and comparison.
4. Computational efficiency and Applicability: This presents an opportunity to examine this deformed differential equation and corresponding solution and to determine which methods are better for handling the additional complexities introduced by the deformation aspects of both the equation and solutions.

3.1. Direct Substitution

The method of Direct Substitution is a technique used to solve certain types of ordinary differential equations. This method involves substituting a proposed solution into the differential equation to check if it satisfies the differential equation. If the substituted solution works, it is the solution to the differential equation. This method is advantageous when wanting to confirm a guessed and given solution. Assuming the solution has the form of Equation (1) and taking the derivative yields,

$$\begin{aligned}
\frac{df(x)}{dx} &= \frac{d}{dx}\exp_\kappa(-x) \\
&= \frac{d}{dx}\left(\sqrt{1+\kappa^2x^2}-\kappa x\right)^{1/\kappa} \\
&= \frac{-1}{\sqrt{1+\kappa^2x^2}}\exp_\kappa(-x) \\
&= \frac{-1}{\sqrt{1+\kappa^2x^2}}f(x),
\end{aligned}$$

and rearranging leads to Equation (46). This method provides an intuitive way to understand the relationship between the differential equation and the κ-exponential.

3.2. Separation of Variables I

The method of Separation of Variables is one of the most straightforward techniques to determine the solution to a differential equation. This method requires that the differential equation be written in the form

$$m(x)+n(f)\frac{df(x)}{dx}=0,$$

which can then be manipulated into the form

$$\int n(f)df = -\int m(x)dx, \tag{48}$$

where direct integration can be applied in this situation.

The κ-decay equation (46) can be separated into the form of Equation (48) as

$$\int_1^f \frac{df(x)}{f(x)} = -\int_0^x \frac{1}{\sqrt{1+\kappa^2x^2}}dx$$

which leads to

$$\begin{aligned} f(x) &= \exp\left[-\int_0^x \frac{1}{\sqrt{1+\kappa^2x^2}}dx\right] \\ &= \exp\left[-\frac{\operatorname{arsinh}(\kappa x)}{\kappa}\right], \end{aligned}$$

which results in Equation (47).

3.3. *Separation of Variables II*

Another more interesting application of the method of Separation of Variables that was described in Section 3.2 can be applied to the κ-decay equation utilizing the κ-numbers described by Equation (39).

Rewriting Equation (46),

$$\frac{df(x_{\{\kappa\}})}{dx_{\{\kappa\}}} = -f(x_{\{\kappa\}}),$$

separating

$$\int_1^f \frac{df(x_{\{\kappa\}})}{f(x_{\{\kappa\}})} = -\int_0^{x_{\{\kappa\}}} dx_{\{\kappa\}}$$

integrating yields,

$$\ln f(x_{\{\kappa\}}) = -x_{\{\kappa\}}$$

exponentiating both sides,

$$f(x_{\{\kappa\}}) = \exp(-x_{\{\kappa\}})$$

and applying the relationship described by the Equation (37) result in Equation (47).

3.4. *Integrating Factor*

The technique of the Integrating Factor [21,22] is a special implementation of the Separation of Variables technique with the derivative product rule. It should be noted that the integrating factor can be identified as Green's function [23] when dealing with a non-homogenous first-order differential equation. This method requires the first-order differential equation of interest to be of the form

$$\frac{df}{dx} + P(x)f = Q(x), \tag{49}$$

$$I(x)\frac{df}{dx} + I(x)P(x)f = I(x)Q(x),$$

where this looks somewhat like the derivative of $I(x)f(x)$. In order to be a separable equation, the following is required:

$$\frac{dI}{dx} = I(x)P(x),$$

which leads to the separable equation,

$$\frac{df}{dx} = f(x)P(x),$$

where the solution is

$$f(x) = A\exp[I] \tag{50}$$

and the integration factor, $I(x)$, is

$$I = -\int P(x)dx. \tag{51}$$

Examining the κ-decay equation, Equation (46), the quantities $P(x) = \frac{1}{\sqrt{1+\kappa^2x^2}}$ and $Q(x) = 0$, as defined in Equation (49). Using Equations (50) and (51) leads to the result

$$f(x) = A\exp\left[-\int_0^x \frac{1}{\sqrt{1+\kappa^2x^2}}dx\right]$$

which when the initial condition, $f(0) = 1$, is applied, the constant A is determined, and the solution is determined to be Equation (47).

3.5. WKBJ

The Wentzel–Kramers–Brillouin-Jeffreys (WKBJ) method [24,25], though relatively specialized, can be applied to Equation (44) in order to determine the solution. It is assumed that the solution will be of the form

$$f(x) = A\exp\{B(x)\},$$

where A is a constant and $B(x)$ satisfies the differential equation,

$$\sqrt{1+\kappa^2x^2}B(x)' = -1$$

where

$$B(x)' = \frac{dB}{dx} \tag{52}$$

which leads to,

$$\begin{aligned} B(x) &= -\int \frac{dx}{\sqrt{1+\kappa^2x^2}} \\ &= -\frac{\operatorname{arsinh}(\kappa x)}{\kappa}. \end{aligned} \tag{53}$$

Substituting the result for the exponential's exponent, Equation (53), into the test function, Equation (52), leads to

$$f(x) = A \exp\left[-\frac{\operatorname{arsinh}(\kappa x)}{\kappa}\right] \\ = A \exp_\kappa(-x)$$

where $A = 1$ in order to satisfy the initial condition that $f(0) = 1$ results in the solution, Equation (47).

4. Laplace and Lagrange–Charpit Techniques

4.1. Laplace Transform

Laplace transform is a technique to reduce a differential equation into an algebraic equation. The Laplace transform of the function $g(t)$ is denoted by $\mathcal{L}\{g(t)\}$ and $G(s)$ is defined by,

$$\mathcal{L}\{g(t)\} = \int_0^\infty g(t)e^{-st}dt = G(s).$$

It should be noted that, in order to ensure this integral's convergence, $t \in (0, \infty)$ while $x\{\kappa\} \in (-\infty, \infty)$. This is in conflict with the Laplace transform that requires a non-negative domain. In order to ensure the applicability of the Laplace transform, $x\{\kappa\}$ will be restricted to the half-domain, $x\{\kappa\} \in (0, \infty)$.

Rewriting Equation (44) using the κ-numbers defined by Equations (37) and (38),

$$\frac{df(x_{\{\kappa\}})}{dx_{\{\kappa\}}} = -f(x_{\{\kappa\}}),$$

which can be re-written as

$$f'(x_{\{\kappa\}}) + f(x_{\{\kappa\}}) = 0,$$

where the notation of the expression has been simplified using the $'$-notation to describe the derivative with respect to $x_{\{\kappa\}}$. Applying the Laplace transform, $\mathcal{L}$,

$$\mathcal{L}\{f'(x_{\{\kappa\}}) + f(x_{\{\kappa\}})\} = \mathcal{L}\{0\}$$

which leads to

$$\mathcal{L}\{f'(x_{\{\kappa\}})\} + \mathcal{L}\{f(x_{\{\kappa\}})\} = 0, \tag{54}$$

where the Laplace transform of a sum is the sum of Laplace transforms and the Laplace transform of zero is simply zero. Applying the Laplace transform for a derivative,

$$\mathcal{L}\{g(t)'\} = s\mathcal{L}\{g(t)\} - g(0),$$

to Equation (54) leads to

$$\mathcal{L}\{f(x_{\{\kappa\}})\} = \frac{f(0)}{s+1}, \tag{55}$$

using the inverse Laplace transform to Equation (55) leads to

$$f(x_{\{\kappa\}}) = f(0)\mathcal{L}^{-1}\left\{\frac{1}{s+1}\right\},$$

where the inverse Laplace transform is known to be

$$\mathcal{L}^{-1}\left\{\frac{1}{s+\alpha}\right\} = \exp(-\alpha t),$$

which leads to the result

$$f(x_{\{\kappa\}}) = f(0)\exp(-x_{\{\kappa\}})$$

and applying the initial condition that $f(0) = 1$ leads to the result of Equation (47).

4.2. Lagrange–Charpit Method

The Lagrange–Charpit method [26], also known as the Method of Characteristics, is a technique for solving hyperbolic differential equations.

Consider the partial differential equation of the form,

$$a(x,y)\frac{\partial f}{\partial x} + b(x,y)\frac{\partial f}{\partial y} = c(x,y,f). \tag{56}$$

The solution surface $f(x,y)$ is defined by characteristic curves that satisfy the system,

$$\frac{dx}{a} = \frac{dy}{b} = \frac{df}{c}. \tag{57}$$

If $b \neq 0$, the system defines characteristic curves in the (x,y,f) space. However, if $b = 0$, the equation $dy/0$ is not defined, indicating that the solution depends only on x. In such cases, the system reduces to the following,

$$\frac{dx}{a} = \frac{df}{c}, \tag{58}$$

which describes single-variable characteristic curves. This method is now applied to the κ-deformed decay equation, Equation (46), given by

$$\sqrt{1+\kappa^2x^2}\frac{df}{dx} + f = 0. \tag{59}$$

Setting $f(x) = u$ and defining $p = \frac{du}{dx}$, the equation is rewritten as

$$F(x,u,p) = \sqrt{1+\kappa^2x^2}p + u = 0. \tag{60}$$

The Lagrange–Charpit characteristic equations are then given by

$$\frac{dx}{dt} = \frac{\partial F}{\partial p}, \quad \frac{du}{dt} = -\frac{\partial F}{\partial x} - p\frac{\partial F}{\partial u}, \quad \frac{dp}{dt} = -\frac{\partial F}{\partial u}. \tag{61}$$

Computing the necessary derivatives,

$$\frac{\partial F}{\partial p} = \sqrt{1+\kappa^2x^2}, \quad \frac{\partial F}{\partial x} = \frac{\kappa^2xp}{\sqrt{1+\kappa^2x^2}}, \quad \frac{\partial F}{\partial u} = 1. \tag{62}$$

Substituting these into the characteristic equations,

$$\frac{dx}{dt} = \sqrt{1+\kappa^2x^2}, \tag{63}$$

$$\frac{du}{dt} = -1, \tag{64}$$

$$\frac{dp}{dt} = -1. \tag{65}$$

Solving for $x(t)$, the first equation,

$$\frac{dx}{dt} = \sqrt{1+\kappa^2 x^2}, \tag{66}$$

is separable. Integrating both sides,

$$\int \frac{dx}{\sqrt{1+\kappa^2 x^2}} = \int dt. \tag{67}$$

Using the standard integral,

$$\frac{1}{\kappa}\operatorname{arsinh}(\kappa x) = t + C_1. \tag{68}$$

Solving for x,

$$x = \frac{1}{\kappa}\sinh(\kappa(t + C_1)). \tag{69}$$

Solving for $u(t)$ from the second equation,

$$\frac{du}{dt} = -1, \tag{70}$$

and integrating it,

$$u = -t + C_2. \tag{71}$$

Using $t = \frac{1}{\kappa}\operatorname{arsinh}(\kappa x) - C_1$, the substitution yields the following,

$$u = -\frac{1}{\kappa}\operatorname{arsinh}(\kappa x) + (C_1 + C_2). \tag{72}$$

Defining the integration constants as a single constant, $C = C_1 + C_2$, results in

$$u(x) = C - \frac{1}{\kappa}\operatorname{arsinh}(\kappa x). \tag{73}$$

Exponentiating both sides,

$$u(x) = e^C e^{-\operatorname{arsinh}(\kappa x)/\kappa}. \tag{74}$$

Since

$$\operatorname{arsinh}(\kappa x) = \ln\left(\sqrt{1+\kappa^2 x^2} + \kappa x\right), \tag{75}$$

this simplifies to

$$u(x) = e^C \left(\frac{1}{\sqrt{1+\kappa^2 x^2} + \kappa x}\right)^{1/\kappa}. \tag{76}$$

Applying the initial condition $u(0) = 1$,

$$1 = e^C e^{-\operatorname{arsinh}(0)/\kappa}. \tag{77}$$

Since $\operatorname{arsinh}(0) = 0$, it follows that $C = 0$; thus,

$$u(x) = e^{-\operatorname{arsinh}(\kappa x)/\kappa}. \tag{78}$$

Recognizing that,

$$e^{-\mathrm{arsinh}(\kappa x)/\kappa} = \exp_\kappa(-x), \tag{79}$$

leading to the solution, Equation (47).

5. Iterative and Series Approaches

5.1. Picard's Iterative Method

Picard's method [27,28], sometimes known as the Method of Successive Approximations, is a technique where one transforms a differential equation of the form

$$\frac{df}{dx} = G(x, f), \quad f(0) = f_0. \tag{80}$$

The method constructs an iterative sequence according to the integral equation,

$$f_{n+1}(x) = f_0 + \int_0^x G(t, f_n(t))dt. \tag{81}$$

The process begins with an initial approximation $f_0(x)$, typically chosen as the given initial condition, and refines the solution through successive iterations. If the iterations converge, the sequence approaches the exact solution of the differential equation.

Taking the κ-deformed decay equation, Equation (46), and rearranging it into standard form

$$\frac{df}{dx} = -\frac{f}{\sqrt{1+\kappa^2 x^2}}, \quad f(0) = 1 \tag{82}$$

establishes the recursive formulation,

$$f_{n+1}(x) = 1 - \int_0^x \frac{f_n(t)}{\sqrt{1+\kappa^2 t^2}}dt. \tag{83}$$

The first iteration, ($n = 0$), is obtained by setting $f_0(x) = 1$, leading to

$$f_1(x) = 1 - \int_0^x \frac{1}{\sqrt{1+\kappa^2 t^2}}dt. \tag{84}$$

Since the integral is evaluated to be

$$\int_0^x \frac{dt}{\sqrt{1+\kappa^2 t^2}} = \frac{\mathrm{arsinh}(\kappa x)}{\kappa}, \tag{85}$$

it follows that,

$$f_1(x) = 1 - \frac{\mathrm{arsinh}(\kappa x)}{\kappa}. \tag{86}$$

The second iteration, ($n = 1$), substituting $f_1(x)$ into the iteration formula, is

$$f_2(x) = 1 - \int_0^x \frac{1 - \frac{\text{arsinh}(\kappa t)}{\kappa}}{\sqrt{1+\kappa^2 t^2}} dt. \tag{87}$$

Expanding $\text{arsinh}(\kappa t)$ as a Taylor series,

$$\text{arsinh}(\kappa t) = \kappa t - \frac{\kappa^3 t^3}{6} + O(t^5), \tag{88}$$

allows for the approximation

$$\frac{\text{arsinh}(\kappa t)}{\kappa} \approx t - \frac{\kappa^2 t^3}{6}. \tag{89}$$

Thus, the integral simplifies to,

$$f_2(x) = 1 - \int_0^x \left(1 - t + \frac{\kappa^2 t^3}{6}\right) \frac{dt}{\sqrt{1+\kappa^2 t^2}}. \tag{90}$$

Approximating $\frac{1}{\sqrt{1+\kappa^2 t^2}} \approx 1 - \frac{\kappa^2 t^2}{2}$, the integration yields

$$f_2(x) \approx 1 - \left[x - \frac{x^2}{2} + \frac{\kappa^2 x^3}{6} - \frac{\kappa^2 x^3}{6}\right]. \tag{91}$$

Simplifying this,

$$f_2(x) = 1 - x + \frac{x^2}{2}. \tag{92}$$

The next iteration, ($n = 2$), is

$$f_3(x) = 1 - \int_0^x \frac{1 - t + \frac{x^2}{2}}{\sqrt{1+\kappa^2 t^2}} dt. \tag{93}$$

Following the same approximation procedure, the integration leads to

$$f_3(x) = 1 - x + \frac{x^2}{2} - \frac{(1-\kappa^2)x^3}{6}. \tag{94}$$

The Taylor series expansion of the κ-exponential is given by

$$\exp_\kappa(-x) = 1 - x + \frac{x^2}{2} - \frac{(1-\kappa^2)x^3}{6} + O(x^4). \tag{95}$$

A comparison between the computed approximations and the exact expansion confirms that Picard's method successfully reproduces the first three terms of $\exp_\kappa(-x)$ for $|x| < 1$.

The series solution for various highest orders is shown in Figure 4 along with the associated errors.

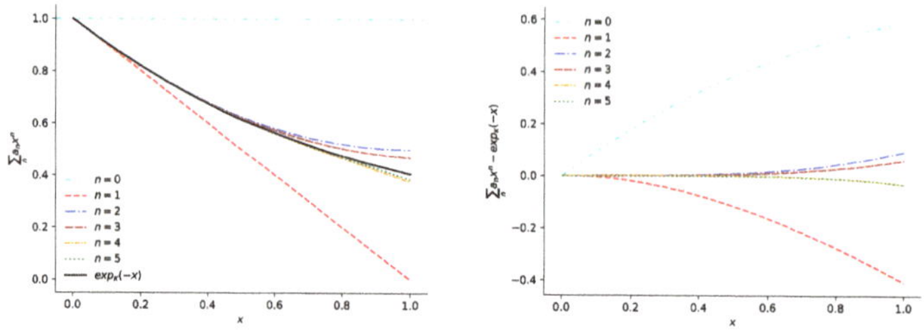

Figure 4. The figure on the left is a comparison between the series solution (of various highest orders) from Picard's method (see Equation (94)), the Power Series Method (see Equation (98)) and the exact solution, $f(x) = \exp_\kappa(-x)$. The figure on the right is the difference between the power series truncated at order n and the κ-exponential.

5.2. Power Series Method

The Power Series Method seeks to determine a series solution by utilizing a trial power series solution [29]. The trial solution, along with its derivative, is taken to be

$$f(x) = \sum_{n=0}^{\infty} a_n x^n = a_0 + a_1 x + a_2 x^2 + a_3 x^3 + a_4 x^4 + a_5 x^5 + \mathcal{O}(x^6) \tag{96}$$

$$\frac{df(x)}{dx} = \sum_{n=1}^{\infty} = a_1 + 2a_2 x + 3a_3 x^2 + 4a_4 x^3 + 5a_5 x^4 + \mathcal{O}(x^5) \tag{97}$$

Substituting the ansatz into Equation (49) results in

$$\begin{aligned}&\sqrt{1+\kappa^2 x^2}\Big(a_0 + a_1 x + a_2 x^2 + a_3 x^3 + a_4 x^4 + a_5 x^5 + \mathcal{O}(x^6)\Big)\\ &= -\Big(a_1 + 2a_2 x + 3a_3 x^2 + 4a_4 x^3 + 5a_5 x^4 + \mathcal{O}(x^5)\Big).\end{aligned}$$

and applying Taylor series to expand the square root,

$$\begin{aligned}\left(1 + \frac{\kappa^{2\,2}}{x} - \frac{\kappa^4 x^4}{8} + \mathcal{O}(x^6)\right) \quad &\Big(a_0 + a_1 x + a_2 x^2 + a_3 x^3 + a_4 x^4 + a_5 x^5 + \mathcal{O}(x^6)\Big)\\ &= -\Big(a_1 + 2a_2 x + 3a_3 x^2 + 4a_4 x^3 + 5a_5 x^4 + \mathcal{O}(x^5)\Big)\end{aligned}$$

Equating coefficients of various powers of x leads to the following relationships:

$$\begin{aligned} a_1 &= -a_0,\\ 2a_2 &= -a_1,\\ 3a_3 + \frac{\kappa^2}{2} a_1 &= -a_2,\\ 4a_4 + \kappa^2 a_2 &= -a_3, \end{aligned}$$

and

$$5a_5 + 3\frac{\kappa^2}{2} a_3 - \frac{\kappa^4}{8} a_1 = -a_4.$$

Using the initial condition that $f(0) = 1$ allows us to solve for a_0, which then allows for the subsequent determination of the other coefficients, yielding

$$\begin{aligned} a_0 &= 1, \\ a_1 &= -1, \\ a_2 &= \frac{1}{2}, \\ a_3 &= \frac{1}{6}(\kappa^2 - 1), \end{aligned}$$

and

$$a_4 = \frac{1}{24}(1 - 4\kappa^2)$$

Substituting these coefficients back into Equation (96) results in

$$f(x) \approx 1 - x + \frac{x^2}{2} + \frac{1}{6}\left(\kappa^2 - 1\right)x^3 + \frac{1}{24}\left(1 - 4\kappa^2\right)x^4 + \mathcal{O}(x^5) \tag{98}$$

which results in the Taylor series described by the κ-decaying exponential, again yielding the solution, Equation (47).

6. Numerical Methods

Analytically solving the majority of ordinary differential equations, especially in physical contexts, is often challenging or even impossible. However, numerous numerical methods are available for effectively addressing and solving these types of equations. The focus of this work will be on the three commonly applied methods of Euler, Adam, and Runge–Kutta.

6.1. Euler's Method

Euler's method serves as an approximation to the solution with initial conditions. While this method may not be the most accurate approximation for practical situations, it stands out as the most straightforward approach for numerical calculation purposes. Rewriting Equation (46),

$$\frac{df(x)}{dx} = G(x, f)$$

where $G(x, f)$ depends on both the independent variable x and the dependent variable $f(x)$ and where the initial condition is $f(x_0) = f_0$, the idea for using Euler's method is to approximate the tangent line of the curve at equally spaced intervals $(x_i, f(x_i))$. The general equation of the tangent line is

$$f = f_0 + G(x_0, f_0)(x - x_0)$$

By choosing points $(x_1, f(x_1))$, a better approximation can be obtained as x_1 gets closer to x_0. As a result, the approximation can further be refined as the distance between x_{n+1} and x_n gets smaller, which in turn allows for an approximation of $f(n)$. This refinement feeds back into even subsequent approximations for $f(n+1)$.

This is written as

$$f_{n+1} = f_n + G(x_n, f_n)h$$

where $h = x_{n+1} - x_n$ is the step size. By iterating through, the approximate numerical solution to the differential equation can be determined.

Euler's method was applied to the κ-deformed decay differential equation, Equation (46), and the results and numerical errors, along with the analytic solution and comparison to other numerical methods, can be seen in Figure 5.

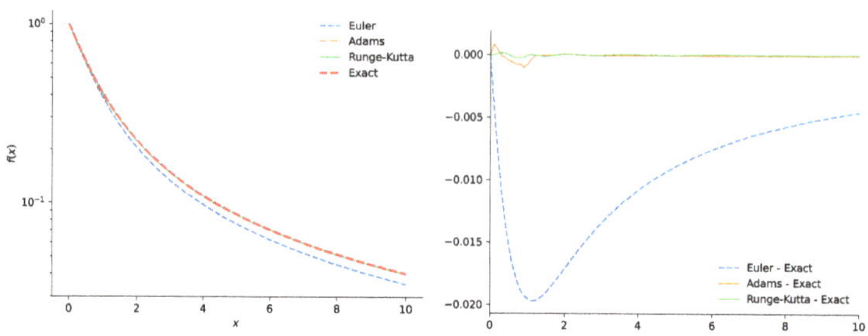

Figure 5. The figure on the left is a comparison between the various numerical methods (Euler, Adam, and Runge–Kutta) and the exact solution to Equation (44). The figure on the right is the difference between various numerical methods and the exact solution.

6.2. Adam's Method

Adam's method is a multi-step algorithm to find approximate solutions to

$$\frac{df(x)}{dx} = G(x, f).$$

This method is attractive due to the fact that it is typically more accurate than Euler's method, and there is a gain in efficiency requiring only the use of the previous two approximations. Using the approximation,

$$f_{n+2} = f_{n+1} + \frac{3}{2}hG(x_{n+1}, f_{n+1}) - \frac{1}{2}f(x_n, y_n)$$

where $h = x_{n+1} - x_n$ is the step size.

Adams's method was applied to the κ-deformed decay differential equation, Equation (46), and the results and numerical errors, along with the analytic solution and comparison to other numerical methods, can be seen in Figure 5.

6.3. Runge–Kutta Method

The Runge–Kutta method is the most widely used technique for the numerical solution of general first-order differential equations and stands out as the most accurate among the numerical methods discussed here. It is employed to generate a highly accurate higher-order numerical method without the need for calculating higher-order derivatives. The general form of the Runge–Kutta method is

$$f_{n+1} = f_n + h\sum_{j=1}^{v} b_j K_j$$

where the fourth-order Runge–Kutta method is given as

$$f_{n+1} = f_n + \frac{h}{6}(K_1 + 2K_2 + 2K_3 + K_4)$$

where $h = x_{n+1} - x_n$ is the step size and the slope estimates of the weighted average are given as

$$\begin{aligned} K_1 &= f(x_n, f_n), \\ K_2 &= f(x_n + \frac{1}{2}h, f_n + \frac{1}{2}K_1), \\ K_3 &= f(x_n + \frac{1}{2}h, f_n + \frac{1}{2}K_2), \end{aligned}$$

and

$$K_4 = f(x_n + h, f_n + K_3).$$

Runge–Kutta's Method was applied to the κ-deformed decay differential Equation (46) and the results and numerical errors along with the analytic solution and comparison to other numerical methods can be seen in Figure 5.

7. Conclusions

The objective of this study was to apply elementary methods to solving the deformed κ-exponential decay differential equation in order to gain experience with deformed statistics, in particular the κ-deformed exponential at the undergraduate level. The application of these techniques to Equation (46) has not been found in the literature, except for the method of Separation of Variables which was applied to

$$\frac{df(x)}{dx} + \frac{\beta}{\sqrt{1+\kappa^2\beta^2x^2}}f(x) = 0$$

with the initial condition that $f(0) = 1$ and where β is a constant. This resulted in a solution,

$$f(x) = \exp_\kappa(-\beta x). \tag{99}$$

Any of the elementary methods that were applied in this work could be applied to Equation (99).

Now that there is experience with the deformed exponential and the deformed decay differential equation, this knowledge can be applied to studying similar differential equations such as the following:

1. the κ-logistic differential equation would be an example of the next level of complexity,

$$\frac{df(x)}{dx} = f(x)\Big(1 - f(x)\Big) \rightarrow \sqrt{1+\kappa^2x^2}\frac{df(x)}{dx} = f(x)\Big(1 - f(x)\Big).$$

   The solution to the standard logistics differential equation as well as the expected deformed solutions,

$$f(x) = \frac{1}{1+\exp(-x)} \rightarrow f(x) = \frac{1}{1+\exp_\kappa(-x)} \tag{100}$$

   where the solutions along with numerical errors have been plotted in Figure 6.
2. analogous differential equations that are important in transport phenomena physics: differential equations such as,

   (a) The κ-advection equation,

$$u\sqrt{1+\kappa^2x^2}\frac{\partial f(x,t)}{\partial x} = -\frac{\partial f(x,t)}{\partial t}$$

   where u is the constant velocity associated with the advection,

(b) κ-wave equation,

$$\kappa^2 x \frac{\partial f(x,t)}{\partial x} + (1+\kappa^2 x^2)\frac{\partial^2 f(x,t)}{\partial x^2} = \frac{1}{v^2}\frac{\partial^2 f(x,t)}{\partial t^2}$$

where v is the speed of the wave,

(c) κ-diffusion equation (and other Schrodinger-like equations),

$$\kappa^2 x \frac{\partial f(x,t)}{\partial x} + (1+\kappa^2 x^2)\frac{\partial^2 f(x,t)}{\partial x^2} = \frac{1}{D}\frac{\partial f(x,t)}{\partial t}$$

where D is the diffusion constant (the κ-diffusion equation has been examined for the first time by [30,31]), and

(d) κ-Fokker–Planck equation,

$$\kappa^2 x D \frac{\partial f(x,t)}{\partial x} + (1+\kappa^2 x^2) D \frac{\partial^2 f(x),t}{\partial x^2} - \mu\sqrt{1+\kappa^2 x^2}\frac{\partial f(x,t)}{\partial x} = \frac{\partial f(x,t)}{\partial t}$$

where D is a diffusion constant and μ is a drift constant. The κ-Fokker–Planck equation has been preliminary studied by [32,33].

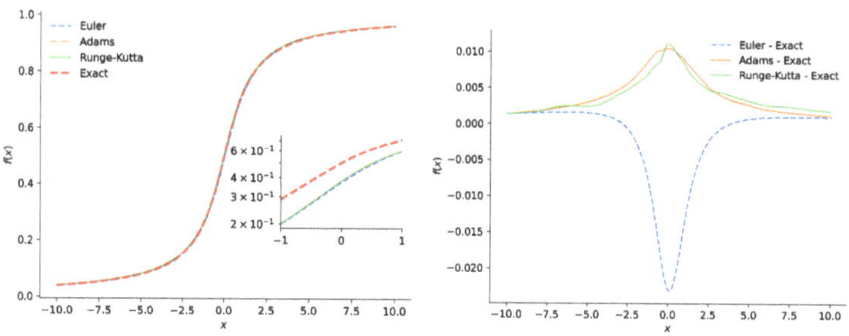

Figure 6. The figure on the left is a comparison between the various numerical methods (Euler, Adam, and Runge–Kutta) and the exact solution to the κ-deformed logistic equation, Equation (100). The figure on the right is the difference between various numerical methods and the exact solution.

3. Fractional differential equations: these differential equations of non-integer order are used to more accurately model complex phenomena. They utilize fractional derivative operators such as the Caputo derivative. Preliminary work in this emerging field can be found in [34].
4. Expansion of techniques: methods such as Laplace and Fourier transforms [35,36] have only begun to be investigated and there is still much work to do. In this work, the Laplace transform was performed using the κ-numbers. In the works cited, the authors investigated the κ-Laplace transform and the κ-Fourier transform.

Author Contributions: Conceptualization, J.A.S.; methodology, R.B., I.J. and J.A.S.; software, R.B. and I.J.; validation, R.B., I.J. and J.A.S.; formal analysis, R.B., I.J. and J.A.S.; investigation, R.B., I.J. and J.A.S.; writing—original draft preparation, R.B. and I.J.; writing—review and editing, R.B., I.J. and J.A.S.; supervision, J.A.S.; project administration, J.A.S. All authors have read and agreed to the published version of the manuscript.

Funding: This research received no external funding.

Data Availability Statement: No new data were created or analyzed in this study. Data sharing is not applicable to this article.

Acknowledgments: J. A. Secrest would like to thank J. M. Conroy at the State University of New York at Fredonia for many enlightening and stimulating conversations about the κ-formalism. R. Bolle and I. Jarra gratefully acknowledge the financial support of the College of Science and Mathematics at Georgia Southern University.

Conflicts of Interest: The authors declare no conflicts of interest.

References

1. Kaniadakis, G. Non-linear kinetics underlying generalized statistics. *Phys. A Stat. Mech. Appl.* **2001**, *296*, 405–425. [CrossRef]
2. Kaniadakis, G. Statistical mechanics in the context of special relativity. *Phys. Rev. E* **2002**, *66*, 056125. [CrossRef]
3. Kaniadakis, G.; Scarfone, A.M. A new one-parameter deformation of the exponential function. *Phys. A Stat. Mech. Appl.* **2002**, *305*, 69–75. [CrossRef]
4. Kaniadakis, G. Statistical mechanics in the context of special relativity. II. *Phys. Rev. E* **2005**, *72*, 036108. [CrossRef] [PubMed]
5. Guha, P. Balanced gain-loss dynamics of particle in cyclotron with friction, κ-defomed logarithmic Lagrangians and fractional damped systems. *Eur. Phys. Plus* **2022**, *137*, 64. [CrossRef]
6. Guha, P. The κ-deformed entropic Lagrangians, Hamiltonian dynamics and their applications. *Eur. Phys. J. Plus* **2022**, *137*, 932. [CrossRef]
7. Luciano, G.G. Gravity and Cosmology in Kaniadakis Statistics: Current Status and Future Challenges. *Entropy* **2022**, *24*, 1712. [CrossRef]
8. Abreu, E.M; Neto, J.A.; Mendes, A.C.; Bonilla, A.; de Paula, R.M. Cosmological considerations in Kaniadakis statistics. *Europhys. Lett.* **2018**, *124*, 30003. [CrossRef]
9. Lourek, I.; Tribeche, M. On the role of the κ-deformed Kaniadakis distribution in nonlinear plasma waves. *Phys. A Stat. Mech. Appl.* **2016**, *441*, 215–220. [CrossRef]
10. Abreu, E.M.C.; Neto, J.A. Statistical approaches and the Bekenstein bound conjecture in Schwarzschild black holes. *Phys. Lett. B* **2022**, *835*, 137565. [CrossRef]
11. Clementi, F. The Kaniadakis Distribution for the Analysis of Income and Wealth Data. *Entropy* **2023**, *25*, 1141 . [CrossRef]
12. Clementi, F.; Gallegati, M.; Kaniadakis, G. A New Model of Income Distribution: The κ-Generalized Distribution. *J. Econ.* **2012**, *105*, 63–91. [CrossRef]
13. Kaniadakis, G.; Baldi, M.M.; Deisboeck, T.S.; Grisolia, G.; Hristopulos, D.T.; Scarfone, A.M.; Sparavigna, A.; Wada, T.; Lucia, U. The κ-statistics approach to epidemiology. *Sci. Rep.* **2020**, *10*, 19949. [CrossRef] [PubMed]
14. Kaniadakis, G. Novel class of susceptible–infectious–recovered models involving power-law interactions. *Phys. A Stat. Mech. Appl.* **2024**, *633*, 129437. [CrossRef]
15. Luciano, G.G. Kaniadakis entropy in extreme gravitational and cosmological environments: A review on the state-of-the-art and future prospects. *Eur. Phys. J. B* **2024**, *97*, 80. [CrossRef]
16. Bushinskaya, A.; Timashev, S. Application of Kaniadakis κ-statistics to Load and Impact Distributions. In Proceedings of the 6th International Conference on Construction, Architecture and Technosphere Safety, Sochi, Russia, 10–16 September 2023; Springer: Cham, Switzerland, 2023.
17. Tsallis, C. Possible generalization of Boltzmann–Gibbs statistics. *J. Stat. Phys.* **1988**, *52*, 479–487. [CrossRef]
18. dos Santos, R.J.V. Generalization of Shannon's theorem for Tsallis entropy. *J. Math. Phys.* **1997**, *38*, 4104–4107. [CrossRef]
19. Lyra, M.L.; Tsallis, C. Nonextensivity and multifractality in low-dimensional dissipative systems. *Phys. Rev. Lett.* **1998**, *80*, 53–56. [CrossRef]
20. Hobbie, R.K.; Roth, B.J. Exponential Growth and Decay. In *Intermediate Physics for Medicine and Biology*; Springer: New York, NY, USA, 2007.
21. Krogstad, S. Generalized integrating factor methods for stiff PDEs. *J. Comput. Phys.* **2005**, *203*, 72–88. [CrossRef]
22. Anco, S.C.; Bluman, G. Integrating factors and first integrals for ordinary differential equations. *Eur. J. Appl. Math.* **1998**, *9*, 245–259. [CrossRef]
23. Melnikov, Y.A.; Borodin, V.N. *Green's Functions: Potential Fields on Surfaces*; Springer: New York, NY, USA, 2017.
24. Peters, J.M.H. Elementary but unusual methods of solving ordinary differential equations. *Int. J. Math. Educ. Sci. Technol.* **1982**, *13*, 295–297. [CrossRef]
25. Keller, H.B.; Keller, J.B. Exponential-Like Solutions of Systems of Linear Ordinary Differential Equations. *Rev. Soc. Ind. Appl. Math.* **1962**, *10*, 246–259. [CrossRef]
26. Delagado, M. The Lagrange–Charpit Method. *Rev. Soc. Ind. Appl. Math.* **1997**, *39*, 298–304.
27. Tisdell, C.C. On Picard's iteration method to solve differential equations and a pedagogical space for otherness. *Int. J. Math. Educ. Sci. Technol.* **2019**, *50*, 788–799. [CrossRef]
28. Schelkunoff, S.A. Solution of linear and slightly nonlinear differential equations. *Quart. Appl. Math.* **1946**, *3*, 348–355. [CrossRef]

29. Haarsa, P.; Pothat, S. The Frobenius Method on a Second-Order Homogeneous Linear ODEs. *Adv. Stud. Theor. Phys.* **2014**, *3*, 1145–1148. [CrossRef]
30. da Silva, M.V.; Martinez, A.S.; Gonçalves, A.C. Effective medium temperature for calculating the Doppler broadening function using Kaniadakis distribution. *Ann. Nucl. Energy* **2021**, *161*, 108500. [CrossRef]
31. Wada, T.; Scarfone, A.M. On the Kaniadakis Distributions Applied in Statistical Physics and Natural Sciences. *Entropy* **2023**, *25*, 292. [CrossRef]
32. Gomez, I.S.; da Costa, B.G.; dos Santos, M.A.F. Inhomogeneous Fokker–Planck equation from framework of Kaniadakis statistics. *Commun. Nonlinear Sci. Numer. Simul.* **2023**, *119*, 107131. [CrossRef]
33. Hirica, I.E.; Pripoae, C.L.; Pripoae, G.T.; Preda, V. Lie Symmetries of the Nonlinear Fokker-Planck Equation Based on Weighted Kaniadakis Entropy. *Mathematics* **2022**, *10*, 2776. [CrossRef]
34. Perovano, A.P.; Silva, F.S. Fractional operators with Kaniadakis logarithm kernels. *Intermaths* **2022**, *3*, 37–49. [CrossRef]
35. Scarfone, A.M. κ-deformed Fourier transform. *Phys. A Stat. Mech. Appl.* **2017**, *480*, 63–78. [CrossRef]
36. Kaniadakis, G. Theoretical Foundations and Mathematical Formalism of the Power-Law Tailed Statistical Distributions. *Entropy* **2013**, *15*, 3983–4010. [CrossRef]

Mathematical and Computational Applications

MDPI

Article

Mathematical Modeling and Analysis of Tumor Growth Models Integrating Treatment Therapy

Mohsin Kamran [1], Johari Yap Abdullah [2,3,*], Afaf Syahira Ahmad Satmi [2], Maya Genisa [4], Abdul Majeed [1] and Tayyaba Nadeem [1]

1 Division of Science and Technology, Department of Mathematics, University of Education Lahore, Lahore 54770, Pakistan; mohsin.kamran@ue.edu.pk (M.K.); abdulmajeed@ue.edu.pk (A.M.); tayyaba90ms@gmail.com (T.N.)

2 Oral & Maxillofacial Radiology, School of Dental Sciences, Health Campus, Universiti Sains Malaysia, Kota Bharu 16150, Malaysia; afafsyahira@usm.my

3 Dental Research Unit, Center for Transdisciplinary Research (CFTR), Saveetha Institute of Medical and Technical Sciences, Saveetha Dental College, Saveetha University, Chennai 602105, India

4 Biomedical Sciences Programme, School of Postgraduate, YARSI University, Jakarta 10510, Indonesia; maya.genisa@yarsi.ac.id

* Correspondence: johariyap@usm.my; Tel.: +60-9-767-5560

Abstract: This study presents a comparative analysis of tumor growth models based on logistic, exponential, and Gompertz formulations. Their response to therapeutic intervention is examined to identify which model shows better behavior with minimal decline of immune cells. The framework incorporates three main cell populations as follows: natural killer cells, cytotoxic T cells, and tumor cells, along with treatment effects. Dynamical properties such as positive invariance, existence, boundedness, and equilibrium stability are investigated. Numerical simulations indicate that the logistic model gives more favorable treatment outcomes compared to the exponential and Gompertz models. The results also show a faster decline of immune cell populations in the exponential and Gompertz models than in the logistic model under varying drug flux.

Keywords: mathematical modeling; logistic; exponential; Gompertz growth model

1. Introduction

Cancer comes from the Greek word karkinos, meaning crab. It was first reported in the 1600s and is defined as the abnormal growth of cells that can invade and spread to other parts of the body [1]. Tumor is a fatal disease and is the second leading cause of mortality worldwide [2,3]. Tumors are classified as benign or malignant, as shown in Table 1. Figure 1 shows MRI images of a tumor.

In recent years, mathematical oncology has developed many models to study cancer dynamics. These models provide a theoretical framework for exploring immune-oncological pathways [4,5]. They allow the study of immune system dynamics, tumor behavior, treatment strategies, and the prediction of outcomes of new therapies [6–10]. Mathur [11] explored how mathematical models can guide treatment beyond standard regimens. Yin et al. [12] reviewed models addressing solid tumor dynamics and drug resistance. Their work supports model-based approaches for analyzing treatment response and resistance. The authors in [13] provided a model to measure the hormesis of anti-tumor drugs and identify the critical antibody dose. Lopez et al. [14] developed a model that includes tumor, healthy host cells, and immune effector cells. Abernathy [15] studied oncolytic virotherapy using a logistic growth model. Bao et al. [16] analyzed the effects of immunotherapy and chemotherapy, showing that combination therapy is necessary for complete tumor removal. Claret et al. [17] developed a tumor growth inhibition model that links drug exposure with tumor size data and survival outcomes. Unni et al. [18] proposed a model that integrates therapy and immune interactions involving dendritic cells, natural killer cells, and cytotoxic T cells. Azizi et al. [19] summarized the key applications of mathematical modeling in oncology, including immunology, heterogeneity, personalized therapy, tumor progression, and trial optimization. Magni and Lavezzi et al. [20,21] reviewed tumor progression models and their role in laboratory and animal studies. Poggesi et al. [22] developed an ODE-based model to describe cancer growth in xenograft studies. Pang et al. [6] analyzed tumor behavior using standard models and found chemotherapy to be effective in reducing tumor cells. Mishra et al. [23] used a fractional model to study chemotherapy effects on both tumor and normal cells. Their results showed that regular drug dosing can suppress tumor growth. Bunonyo et al. [24] studied exponential tumor growth with combined therapy and concluded that multi-treatment strategies are more effective. Tosca et al. [25] applied a PK–TGI model to support dose selection in early trials. Rocchetti and Simeoni et al. [26,27] proposed PK-PD models to study tumor response under cytostatic therapy. Butner et al. [28] developed a model and used it to study the tumor growth and immune response parameters to stratify patients on long-term tumor burden. Pang [29] designed an immune response model with bifurcations. Valle et al. [30] created a six-dimensional model to explain tumor evolution under therapy. Ronchi et al. [31] built a framework to estimate tumor doubling time and survival curves from xenograft data. Raeisi et al. [32] studied colon cancer spread using a mathematical model. Makhlouf et al. [33] modeled interactions between tumor cells, NK cells, CD4+, CD8+ T cells, and circulating lymphocytes under therapy.

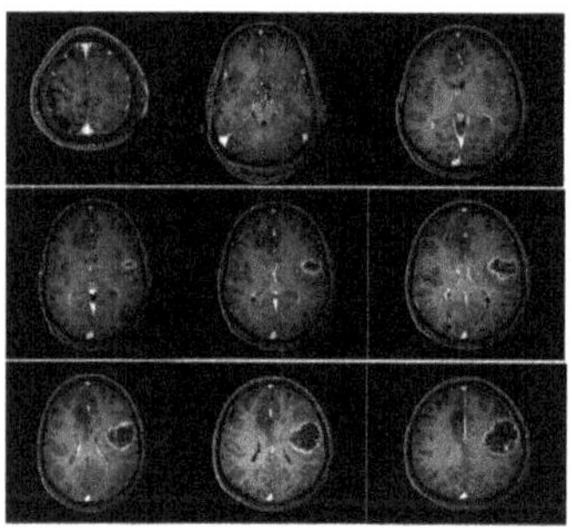

Figure 1. Tumor images.

Table 1. Differences between cancerous and non-cancerous tumors.

Trait	Benign	Malignant
Nuclear size	Small	Large
Ratio of nuclear size to cytoplasmic volume	Low	High
Nuclear shape	Regular	Pleomorphic (irregular shape)
Mitotic index	Low	High
Tissue organization	Normal	Disorganized
Differentiation	Well differentiation	Poorly differentiated
Tumor boundary	Well defined	Poorly defined

The tumor growth law fundamentally determines model stability, tumor progression, and treatment response. Logistic, exponential, and Gompertz formulations represent distinct biological behaviors—bounded and stable growth, unrestricted and unstable proliferation, and decelerating yet parameter-sensitive expansion, respectively [14,18,24,29]. Therefore, choosing an appropriate growth model is vital for accurately predicting tumor dynamics and optimizing therapeutic strategies.

The novelty of this work is a unified framework that integrates the following three tumor growth laws: logistic, Gompertz, and exponential combined with NK and CTL immune responses under chemotherapy. Unlike studies limited to single models, this work compares therapeutic outcomes across models. The results show that the logistic model suppresses tumors while better preserving immune cells. This comparative approach provides new insights and supports the design of improved therapy strategies. The framework considers NK cells, CTLs, and tumor cells and studies their response to treatment. Dynamical properties, including stability, existence, boundedness, and invariance are analyzed. The model is solved numerically using the Runge–Kutta method Python 3.11.

This paper has seven sections. Section 1 is the introduction. Section 2 presents tumor growth models and their formulations. Section 3 describes the combined model. Sections 4 and 5 explain the system dynamics, including boundedness, existence, invariance, and stability. Section 6 presents the results and discussion. Section 7 presents some concluding remarks.

2. Mathematical Models of Tumor Growth

2.1. Tumor Growth Models

Several growth functions have been studied in epidemiology and ecology. First-order ordinary differential equations are widely used to predict tumor growth by describing changes in tumor volume over time. The most common formulations are exponential and logistic models [34,35].

2.1.1. Exponential Models

- Malthusian Model: $\frac{dT}{dt} = cT,\ c > 0$, T is tumor volume in m^3 and c is growth rate in $m^3\ day^{-1}$.
- Power Law Model: $\frac{dT}{dt} = cT^m,\ c > 0,\ m > 0$, and m is a real constant.
- Migration Model: $\frac{dT}{dt} = cT + K,\ c > 0,\ K > 0$, where K is the migration rate.
- Gompertz Model: $\frac{dT}{dt} = \alpha e^{-bt}T,\ \alpha > 0,\ b > 0$, where α is the intrinsic growth parameter and b is the parameter of growth deceleration.

2.1.2. Generalized Logistic Model

The generalized form of the logistic equation is as follows [35]:

$$\frac{dT}{dt} = pT^m\left[1 - \left(\frac{T}{K}\right)^{\delta}\right]^{\lambda}, \tag{1}$$

where m, δ, and λ are nonnegative exponents and p is the tumor growth rate in $m^3\ day^{-1}$. From Equation (1), we can deduce all forms of models as follows: The above equation turns into an exponential equation for $m = 1$ and $\lambda = 0$ as

$$\frac{dT}{dt} = pT.$$

The logistic model can be obtained by putting $m = \delta = \lambda = 1$ in Equation (1) as,

$$\frac{dT}{dt} = pT\left[1 - \left(\frac{T}{K}\right)\right],$$

and for $m = 2/3$, $\delta = 1/3$, and $\lambda = 1$ we have a Von Bertalanffy equation model expressed as,

$$\frac{dT}{dt} = pT^{2/3}\left[1 - \left(\frac{T}{K}\right)^{1/3}\right].$$

where p is the growth rate and q is the growth deceleration parameter. Equation (1) expresses Richard's model for $m = 1$ and $\lambda = 1$ as

$$\frac{dT}{dt} = pT\left[1 - \left(\frac{T}{K}\right)^{\delta}\right].$$

3. Formulation of the Mathematical Model

The key parameters and their biological interpretation are outlined as follows:

- $\aleph$: Natural killer cells: provide an immediate, nonspecific anti-tumor defense.
- Ł: Cytotoxic T lymphocytes: delayed, specific immune response that strengthens and sustains tumor clearance after activation.
- τ: Tumor cells.
- $a_1\tau(1 - a_2\tau)$: Tumor proliferation.
- $a_3\tau\aleph$: Immune-mediated tumor killing by NK cells.
- $\beta_1\tau$Ł: Immune-mediated tumor killing by CTL.
- $b_\tau \tau C$: Drug-induced cytotoxicity.
- $b_\aleph \aleph C$: Drug-related immune cell death.
- $b_{Ł}$ŁC: Drug-related immune cell death.
- wŁ, $\rho\aleph$: Natural death of CTL and NK cells.
- $r\tau\aleph$: Immune cell activation.

This study considers three tumor models that involve three cell populations as follows: tumor cells $\tau(t)$, natural killer (NK) cells $\aleph(t)$, and cytotoxic T cells Ł(t). Their dynamics are described under the influence of chemotherapy drug concentration $C(t)$. Each cell population is modeled using an ordinary differential equation of the following form [18]:

$$\frac{d[.]}{dt} = P(.) - Q(.) - K_{[.]}[.]. \tag{2}$$

where $P[.]$ and $Q[.]$ represent proliferation, competition, and inhibition functions, and $K[.]$ describes the effect of chemotherapy. It is assumed that natural killer cells grow logistically through the term $a_4\aleph(1 - a_5\aleph)$, where a_4 and a_5 express the growth rate and reciprocal of the carrying capacity, respectively. Additionally, natural killer cells are influenced by the interaction of NK cells and tumor cells [35] denoted by $-a_6\tau\aleph$ and the interaction with the drug by $-b_\aleph \aleph C$. Also, the inactivation or natural death of NK cells has been denoted by $-\rho\aleph$. Here, the parameters a_6, ρ, and $b_\aleph$ express death of NK cells by tumor, natural death of NK cells, and death of NK cells by the drug, respectively. Thus, the differential equation describing the dynamics of NK cells is as follows:

$$\frac{d\aleph(t)}{dt} = a_4\aleph(1 - a_5\aleph) - a_6\tau(t)\aleph(t) - \rho\aleph(t) - b_\aleph\aleph(t)C(t). \tag{3}$$

Cytotoxic (CD8+ T) cells play a crucial role in the immune system's ability to eliminate tumor cells. Tumor-specific CD8+ T lymphocytes are active while tumor cells are present but become inactive after some encounters [36,37]. They are recruited by tumor cells in a linear fashion as $r\tau\aleph$. The cytotoxic cell population impacted by the interactions of cytotoxic cells with the tumor and drug are expressed by the terms $\beta_2\tau Ł$ and $b_Ł ŁC(t)$, respectively. Moreover the natural death of cytotoxic cells is represented by the term $-wŁ$. Here, r, β_2, $b_Ł$, and w represents the activation rate of CD8+ cells, death of CD8+ by the tumor, death of CD8+ by drug, and natural death of CD8+ cells, respectively. Thus the dynamical equation of CD8+ cells is as follows:

$$\frac{dŁ(t)}{dt} = r\tau(t)\aleph(t) - wŁ(t) - \beta_2\tau(t)Ł(t) - b_Ł ŁC(t). \quad (4)$$

It is supposed that tumor grows through a logistic function $a_1\tau(1 - a_2\tau)$. Here, parameters a_1 and a_2 represents the per capita growth rate and the inverse of tumor capacity [38]. The tumor growth has been impacted by the interactions of natural killer cells represented by $-a_3\tau\aleph$, cytotoxic cells $-\beta_1\tau Ł$, and therapy $-b_\tau\tau C(t)$ [36,39]. Where a_3, β_1, and b_τ describe tumor death by natural killer cells, tumor death by cytotoxic cells, and tumor cell death by the drug, respectively. Thus, tumor dynamics can be expressed as

$$\frac{d\tau(t)}{dt} = a_1\tau(1 - a_2\tau) - a_3\tau(t)\aleph(t) - \beta_1\tau(t)Ł(t) - b_\tau\tau(t)C(t). \quad (5)$$

The dynamical equation expressing chemotherapy drug intervention is

$$\frac{dC}{dt} = \kappa - C_o C(t). \quad (6)$$

where κ and C_o describe chemotherapy drug influx and drug decay, respectively. Table 2 lists the parameters and their dimensions.

Table 2. Numeric values of parameters.

Parameter	Description	Unit	Value	Reference
a_1	growth rate of tumor cells	day^{-1}	4.31×10^{-1}	[18]
a_2	tumor carrying capacity	$cell^{-1}$	5.14×10^{-1}	[10]
a_3	tumor death by NK cells	day^{-1}	3.5×10^{-6}	[18]
a_4	growth rate of NK cells	day^{-1}	5.14×10^{-1}	[10]
a_5	carrying capacity of NK cells	$cell^{-1}$	1.0×10^{-7}	[18]
a_6	NK cell death by tumor	$cell^{-1}\ day^{-1}$	1.0×10^{-7}	[18]
β_1	tumor death by cytotoxic cells	$cell^{-1}\ day^{-1}$	1×10^{-4}	Assumed
β_2	cytotoxic cell death by tumor	$cell^{-1}\ day^{-1}$	3.42×10^{-10}	[10]
w	natural death of CTLs	day^{-1}	2×10^{-2}	[18]
r	activation rate of CTLs	day^{-1}	1.6×10^{-7}	Assumed
ρ	natural death of NK cells	day^{-1}	4.12×10^{-2}	Assumed
$b_\aleph$	death rate of NK cells by drug	day^{-1}	6×10^{-1}	[10]
$b_Ł$	death rate of CD8+ cells by drug	day^{-1}	0.0009	Assumed
b_τ	death rate of tumor cells by drug	day^{-1}	8×10^{-1}	[10]
κ	drug influx	day^{-1}	0.85, 1.15, 1.90, 5.15	Assumed
C_o	drug decay	day^{-1}	0.95, 1.25, 2.10, 5.25	Assumed

Thus, the complete logistic model is

$$\begin{aligned} \frac{d\aleph(t)}{dt} &= a_4\aleph(t)(1-a_5\aleph(t)) - a_6\tau(t)\aleph(t) - \rho\aleph(t) - b_\aleph\aleph(t)C(t), \\ \frac{dŁ(t)}{dt} &= r\tau(t)\aleph(t) - wŁ(t) - \beta_2\tau(t)Ł(t) - b_ŁŁ(t)C(t), \\ \frac{d\tau(t)}{dt} &= a_1\tau(t)(1-a_2\tau(t)) - a_3\tau(t)\aleph(t) - \beta_1\tau(t)Ł(t) - b_\tau\tau(t)C(t), \\ \frac{dC}{dt} &= \kappa - C_oC(t). \end{aligned} \tag{7}$$

with initial conditions $\tau(0) = \tau_0 \geq 0,\ \aleph(0) = \aleph_0 \geq 0,\ Ł(0) = Ł_0 \geq 0$, and $C(0) = c_0 \geq 0$.

4. Dynamics

4.1. Positive Invariance

We check positive invariance by analyzing the vector field on the system boundaries. Each variable is set to zero to see if the flow points inward or is tangent.

For $\aleph(t) = 0$,

$$\frac{d\aleph(t)}{dt}|_{\aleph=0} = a_4(0)(1-a_5(0)) - a_6\tau(t)(0) - \rho(0) - b_\aleph(0)C(t), \implies \aleph' = 0 \text{ at } \aleph = 0,$$

Thus, no flow leaves through $\aleph = 0$.

For $Ł(t) = 0$,

$$\frac{dŁ(t)}{dt}|_{Ł=0} = r\tau(t)\aleph(t) - w(0) - \beta_2\tau(t)(0) - b_Ł(0)C(t), \implies Ł' = r\tau\aleph \geq 0,$$

Since $r,\ \tau,\ \aleph\ \geq 0$, the flow is nonnegative. No flow leaves through $Ł = 0$. For $\tau = 0$,

$$\frac{d\tau(t)}{dt}|_{\tau=0} = a_1(0)(1-a_2(0)) - a_3(0)\aleph(t) - \beta_1(0)Ł(t) - b_\tau(0)C(t) = 0.$$

So, $\tau' = 0$, and no flow leaves through $\tau = 0$.

Similarly, for $C = 0$,

$$\frac{dC}{dt}|_{C=0} = \kappa - C_0(0) = 0, \implies \kappa \geq 0,$$

The flow is positive at $C = 0$. So no outflow occurs. Since all derivatives on the boundaries are nonnegative, the vector field points inward or is tangent. Therefore, the positive orthant is invariant.

4.2. Boundedness

To show boundedness, define

$$V = \aleph + Ł + \tau + C,$$

and compute its time derivative along the system trajectories. First we will compute $\frac{dV}{dt}$ as follows:

$$\frac{dV}{dt} = \frac{d\aleph}{dt} + \frac{dŁ}{dt} + \frac{d\tau}{dt} + \frac{dC}{dt}. \tag{8}$$

Using the system (11) and Equation (8), we have

$$\begin{aligned}\frac{dV}{dt} &= a_4\aleph(t)(1-a_5\aleph(t)) - a_6\tau(t)\aleph(t) - \rho\aleph(t) - b_\aleph\aleph(t)C(t) \\ &+r\tau(t)\aleph(t) - w\text{Ł}(t) - \beta_2\tau(t)\text{Ł}(t) - b_\text{Ł}\text{Ł}(t)C(t)+ \\ &a_1\tau(t)(1-a_2\tau(t)) - a_3\tau(t)\aleph(t) - \beta_1\tau(t)\text{Ł}(t) - b_\tau\tau(t)C(t)+ \\ &\kappa - C_oC(t).\end{aligned} \tag{9}$$

Arranging the terms by variables and signs, we have

$$\begin{aligned}\frac{dV}{dt} &= a_4\aleph - a_4a_5\aleph^2 - a_6\tau\aleph - \rho\aleph - b_\aleph\aleph C + r\tau\aleph - w\text{Ł} - \beta_2\tau\text{Ł} - b_\text{Ł}\text{Ł}C \\ &+a_1\tau - a_1a_2\tau^2 - a_3\tau\aleph - \beta_1\tau\text{Ł} - b_\tau\tau C + \kappa - C_0C.\end{aligned} \tag{10}$$

By analyzing the signs of terms in the above equation, we have

- Negative quadratic terms: $-a_4a_5\aleph^2$ and $-a_1a_3\tau^2$ help to control growth.
- Negative linear terms: $-\rho\aleph$, $-w\text{Ł}$, and $-C_0C$ provide damping.
- Mixed terms are negative or zero as variables are nonnegative.
- $a_4\aleph$, $r\tau\aleph$, $a_1\tau$, and κ are positive terms.

For greater values of $\aleph$, Ł, τ, and C, negative quadratic and linear terms dominate positive linear terms, implying that if $V > M$, for $M > 0$, then $V' < 0$. Hence, solutions enter and remain in a bounded set.

4.3. Existence

Consider the system

$$\begin{aligned}\frac{d\aleph(t)}{dt} &= a_4\aleph(t)(1-a_5\aleph(t)) - a_6\tau(t)\aleph(t) - \rho\aleph(t) - b_\aleph\aleph(t)C(t), \\ \frac{d\text{Ł}(t)}{dt} &= r\tau(t)\aleph(t) - w\text{Ł}(t) - \beta_2\tau(t)\text{Ł}(t) - b_\text{Ł}\text{Ł}(t)C(t), \\ \frac{d\tau(t)}{dt} &= a_1\tau(t)(1-a_2\tau(t)) - a_3\tau(t)\aleph(t) - \beta_1\tau(t)\text{Ł}(t) - b_\tau\tau(t)C(t), \\ \frac{dC}{dt} &= \kappa - C_oC(t).\end{aligned} \tag{11}$$

with initial conditions $\tau(0) = \tau_0 \geq 0$, $\aleph(0) = \aleph_0 \geq 0$, $\text{Ł}(0) = \text{Ł}_0 \geq 0$, and $C(0) = c_0 \geq 0$.

Now define the system in vector form as follows: $x(t) = [\aleph(t),\ \text{Ł}(t),\ \tau(t),\ C(t)]^T$. Thus, we have,

$$\frac{dx}{dt} = f(t,x).$$

Since each component of the function is a polynomial in x, all expressions are continuous in all variables. Also, these expressions are polynomial or rational functions so they are differentiable functions.

A function is Lipschitz continuous if the following holds:

$$\|f(t,x) - f(t,y)\| \leq L\|x-y\|,$$

Now the Jacobian matrix of model (11) at a general point is

$$J = \begin{bmatrix} a_4 - 2a_4a_5\aleph - a_6\tau - \rho - C & 0 & -a_6\aleph & -\aleph \\ r\tau & -w - \beta_2\tau - C & r\aleph - \beta_2\text{Ł} & -\text{Ł} \\ -a_3\tau & -\beta_1\tau & a_1 - 2a_1a_2\tau - a_3\aleph - \beta_1\text{Ł} - C & -\tau \\ 0 & 0 & 0 & -C_0 \end{bmatrix}, \tag{12}$$

From above, we can see that all partial derivatives are continuous and bounded on any compact subset. Thus, $f(t, x)$ is locally Lipschitz in x. Hence, the initial value problem has a unique local solution in some interval $[0, T]$, for some $T > 0$.

5. Stability Analysis

For nonlinear systems, stability is studied around equilibrium points. The system is first linearized, and the Jacobian matrix is computed. Eigenvalues of the Jacobian determine stability. The Routh–Hurwitz theorem is applied for higher-order cases. The Jacobian of system (11) at a general point is

$$J = \begin{bmatrix} a_4 - 2a_4a_5\aleph - a_6\tau - \rho - C & 0 & -a_6\aleph & -\aleph \\ r\tau & -w - \beta_2\tau - C & r\aleph - \beta_2Ł & -Ł \\ -a_3\tau & -\beta_1\tau & a_1 - 2a_1a_2\tau - a_3\aleph - \beta_1Ł - C & -\tau \\ 0 & 0 & 0 & -C_0 \end{bmatrix}, \tag{13}$$

Equilibrium points are obtained by setting $\tau' = Ł' = \aleph' = C' = 0$.

$$\begin{aligned} a_4\aleph(t)(1 - a_5\aleph(t)) - a_6\tau(t)\aleph(t) - \rho\aleph(t) - b_\aleph\aleph(t)C(t) &= 0, \\ r\tau(t)\aleph(t) - wŁ(t) - \beta_2\tau(t)Ł(t) - b_ŁŁ(t)C(t) &= 0, \\ a_1\tau(t)(1 - a_2\tau(t)) - a_3\tau(t)\aleph(t) - \beta_1\tau(t)Ł(t) - b_\tau\tau(t)C(t) &= 0, \\ \kappa - C_oC(t) &= 0. \end{aligned}$$

This implies the following:

$$\aleph = \frac{a_4 - a_6\tau - \rho - C}{a_4a_5} = \frac{a_4 - a_6\tau - \rho - \frac{\kappa}{C_0}}{a_4a_5}, \text{ where, } C = \frac{\kappa}{C_o}, \; Ł = \frac{r\aleph\tau}{w + C + \beta_2\tau}$$

and

$$\tau = \frac{a_1 - a_3\aleph - \beta_1Ł - C}{a_1a_2}.$$

Three cases are identified as follows:
(I). *(Steady State or dead state)* All populations (tumor and immune cells) go to zero, i.e., $\aleph = Ł = \tau = 0$. This represents a biologically unrealistic outcome but mathematically corresponds to system extinction. So, the equilibrium point is $E_0(0, 0, 0, \frac{\kappa}{C_o})$.

The Jacobian matrix of Equation (11) at point E_0 is

$$J(E_0) = \begin{bmatrix} a_4 - \rho - \frac{\kappa}{C_o} & 0 & 0 & 0 \\ 0 & -w - \frac{\kappa}{C_o} & 0 & 0 \\ 0 & 0 & a_1 - \frac{\kappa}{C_o} & 0 \\ 0 & 0 & 0 & -C_o \end{bmatrix}, \tag{14}$$

The eigenvalues of $J(E_0)$ are $\lambda_1 = a_4 - \rho - \frac{\kappa}{C_o}$, $\lambda_2 = -w - \frac{\kappa}{C_o}$, $\lambda_3 = a_1 - \frac{\kappa}{C_o}$, and $\lambda_4 = -C_o$, From here, we conclude that E_0 is locally asymptotically stable if $\lambda_1 < 0$ and $\lambda_3 < 0$, i.e., $\kappa > C_o(a_4 - \rho)$ or $\kappa > a_1C_o$., and E_0 is unstable if $\kappa = C_oa_1$ or $\kappa = C_o(a_4 - \rho)$ and is stable for $\kappa > max\,\{a_1C_o, C_o(a_4 - \rho)\}$.

Thus, the following stability results can be obtained.

- E_0 will be locally stable if $\kappa > max\,\{a_1C_o, C_o(a_4 - \rho)\}$.
- E_0 is unstable if $\kappa = C_oa_1$ or $\kappa = C_o(a_4 - \rho)$.

(II). *(Tumor-free state)* Tumor cells vanish, i.e., $\tau = 0$, while immune cells and possibly drug concentration settle at positive levels. This indicates successful therapy or immune clearance, where the body eliminates cancer and maintains immune activity. So, the equilibrium point is $E_1\left(\frac{a_4-\rho-\frac{\kappa}{C_o}}{a_4a_5},0,0,\frac{\kappa}{C_o}\right)$ and the Jacobian matrix of Equation (11) at the E_1 point is

$$J(E_1)=\begin{bmatrix} -\left(a_4-\rho-\frac{\kappa}{C_o}\right) & 0 & -a_6\left(\frac{a_4-\rho-\frac{\kappa}{C_o}}{a_4a_5}\right) & 0 \\ 0 & -w-\frac{\kappa}{C_o} & r\left(\frac{a_4-\rho-\frac{\kappa}{C_o}}{a_4a_5}\right) & 0 \\ 0 & 0 & a_1-a_3\left(\frac{a_4-\rho-\frac{\kappa}{C_o}}{a_4a_5}\right)-\frac{\kappa}{C_o} & 0 \\ 0 & 0 & 0 & -C_o \end{bmatrix}, \quad (15)$$

The eigenvalues of $J(E_1)$ are $\lambda_5 = -\left(a_4-\rho-\frac{\kappa}{C_o}\right)$, $\lambda_6 = -w-\frac{\kappa}{C_o}$, $\lambda_7 = a_1 - a_3\left(\frac{a_4-\rho-\frac{\kappa}{C_o}}{a_4a_5}\right)$, and $\lambda_8 = -C_o$. For the tumor-free state, λ_5 and λ_7 must be negative, so from the above expressions $a_4 > \rho-\frac{\kappa}{C_o}$; thus, $\lambda_5 < 0$, and for $\lambda_7 < 0$ we must have $\kappa > \left(\frac{(a_1a_4a_5-a_3a_4+a_3\rho)C_o}{a_4a_5-a_3}\right)$.

Using the Routh–Hurwitz theorem [40] the following conditions of stability are obtained.

- E_1 is stable if $\lambda_5 < 0$, $\lambda_7 < 0$, i.e., for $\kappa > \left(\frac{(a_1a_4a_5-a_3a_4+a_3\rho)C_o}{a_4a_5-a_3}\right)$.
- E_1 is unstable if $\kappa = \left(\frac{(a_1a_4a_5-a_3a_4+a_3\rho)C_o}{a_4a_5-a_3}\right)$.

(III). *(Tumor-present state)* Tumor persists at a positive equilibrium along with immune cells (NK and CTLs) and drug concentration. This reflects a chronic or controlled tumor burden, where the cancer is not eradicated but stabilized under immune and drug pressure. Thus, the equilibrium point becomes as follows: $E_2\left(0,0,\frac{a_1-\frac{\kappa}{C_o}}{a_1a_2},\frac{\kappa}{C_o}\right)$. So the Jacobian matrix of Equation (11) at E_2 is

$$J(E_2)=\begin{bmatrix} \left[a_1-\rho-\frac{\kappa}{C_o}-a_6\Lambda\right] & 0 & 0 & 0 \\ r\Lambda & \left[-w-\frac{\kappa}{C_o}-\beta_2\Lambda\right] & 0 & 0 \\ -a_3\Lambda & -\beta_1\Lambda & -\left[a_1-2a_1a_2\Lambda-\frac{\kappa}{C_o}\right] & \Lambda \\ 0 & 0 & 0 & -C_o \end{bmatrix}, \quad (16)$$

where $\Lambda = \left(\frac{a_1-\frac{\kappa}{C_o}}{a_1a_2}\right)$. The eigenvalues of $J(E_2)$ are $\lambda_9 = \left[a_1-\rho-\frac{\kappa}{C_o}-a_6\Lambda\right]$, $\lambda_{10} = -w-\frac{\kappa}{C_o}-\beta_2\Lambda$, $\lambda_{11} = a_1-2a_1a_2\Lambda-\frac{\kappa}{C_o}$. For the tumor-present state to be locally stable, λ_9 & λ_{11} should be negative. After simplifying the expressions of λ_9 and λ_{11}, one can have $a_1-\rho-\frac{\kappa}{C_o} < 0$. So $\lambda_9 < 0$. When $a_1-\frac{\kappa}{C_o}-\rho > 0$ and $\lambda_9 < 0$, we have $\kappa > \left(\frac{(a_1a_2(a_1-\rho)-a_1a_6)C_o}{a_1a_2-a_6}\right)$.

The stability results indicate that when the drug influx rate κ exceeds the combined thresholds of tumor growth a_1 and immune activation parameters, the system reaches a stable tumor-free equilibrium, representing tumor elimination with preserved immune activity. Conversely, insufficient drug influx or high decay C_o leads to a stable tumor-present state, corresponding to therapeutic failure or residual disease. Clinically, this reflects that optimizing chemotherapy dosage and immune-related parameters such as NK cell growth a_4 and cytotoxic activity β_1 is critical for maintaining long-term tumor control and preventing immune exhaustion.

Now, assume that the tumor and natural killer cells follow exponential growth. Thus, the mathematical model of exponential growth is expressed as follows:

$$
\begin{aligned}
\frac{d\aleph(t)}{dt} &= a_4\aleph(t) - a_6\tau(t)\aleph(t) - \rho\aleph(t) - b_{\aleph}\aleph(t)C(t), \\
\frac{dŁ(t)}{dt} &= r\tau(t)\aleph(t) - wŁ(t) - \beta_2\tau(t)Ł(t) - b_{Ł}Ł(t)C(t), \\
\frac{d\tau(t)}{dt} &= a_1\tau(t) - a_3\tau(t)\aleph(t) - \beta_1\tau(t)Ł(t) - b_{\tau}\tau(t)C(t), \\
\frac{dC}{dt} &= \kappa - C_oC(t).
\end{aligned}
\tag{17}
$$

with initial conditions $\tau(0) = \tau_0 \geq 0,\ \aleph(0) = \aleph_0 \geq 0,\ Ł(0) = Ł_0 \geq 0$, and $C(0) = c_0 \geq 0$.

The tumor model of Gompertz growth is expressed as follows:

$$
\begin{aligned}
\frac{d\aleph(t)}{dt} &= a_4\aleph(t)e^{-a_5t} - a_6\tau(t)\aleph(t) - \rho\aleph(t) - b_{\aleph}\aleph(t)C(t), \\
\frac{dŁ(t)}{dt} &= r\tau(t)\aleph(t) - wŁ(t) - \beta_2\tau(t)Ł(t) - b_{Ł}Ł(t)C(t), \\
\frac{d\tau(t)}{dt} &= a_1\tau(t)e^{-a_2t} - a_3\tau(t)\aleph(t) - \beta_1\tau(t)Ł(t) - b_{\tau}\tau(t)C(t), \\
\frac{dC}{dt} &= \kappa - C_oC(t).
\end{aligned}
\tag{18}
$$

with initial conditions $\tau(0) = \tau_0 \geq 0,\ \aleph(0) = \aleph_0 \geq 0,\ Ł(0) = Ł_0 \geq 0$, and $C(0) = c_0 \geq 0$. The formulation of tumor growth dynamics markedly determines the pattern and stability of equilibrium states in tumor–immune–drug systems. The logistic framework, constrained by a carrying capacity, portrays limited proliferation and typically yields stable tumor-free or controlled equilibria when treatment efficacy is adequate [14,18]. Conversely, the exponential representation implies unrestricted growth potential, often resulting in unstable or unbounded tumor expansion unless counteracted by intensive therapeutic intervention [24,29]. The Gompertz formulation, characterized by the gradual slowing of growth with tumor enlargement, exhibits intermediate stability that can fluctuate with therapeutic strength [15]. Collectively, logistic growth tends to promote more stable and biologically realistic control outcomes, whereas exponential and Gompertz laws describe faster or treatment-sensitive tumor progression.

The stability analysis of the tumor–immune–chemotherapy model reveals that its long-term dynamics are primarily governed by the chemotherapy drug influx and decay rates. Tumor-free equilibrium stability is achieved when the influx rate surpasses a threshold defined by the tumor growth and immune response parameters, leading to tumor elimination and sustained immune activity. When this condition is not satisfied, the system tends toward a tumor-present equilibrium, signifying treatment inefficacy or tumor persistence. Immune-related parameters, including natural killer cell proliferation and death rates, also affect the system's capacity to maintain immune surveillance. Overall, the analysis underscores the necessity of optimizing treatment parameters to balance tumor suppression and immune preservation, providing a foundation for effective chemotherapy design and scheduling.

6. Results and Discussion

This section presents the numerical results of the proposed models using the Runge–Kutta method. The initial populations of tumor cells, natural killer cells, cytotoxic T cells, and the drug are assumed to be 20, 50, 30, and 5, respectively, over a time span of 100 days.

Figure 2 illustrates the effect of chemotherapy on different cell populations, including NK and tumor cells exhibiting logistic growth, keeping all other parameters fixed. In the first case, with drug concentration $\kappa = 0.85$ and decay rate $C_0 = 0.95$, the tumor population decreases rapidly. NK cells initially decline but later recover, suggesting that the immune response is not significantly weakened and the patient has significant immune strength against the tumor. The second case, with κ increased to 1.15 and $C_0 = 1.25$, shows further tumor reduction while healthy cells remain largely unaffected, which indicates a preserved immune system. In the third case, with $\kappa = 1.95$ and $C_0 = 2.10$, the tumor continues to regress while only limited damage is observed in healthy cells, indicating that the immune system has been adjusted with drug concentration. When κ increases to 5.15, the results indicate a sharp decline in the NK and CTL populations, reflecting the adverse effects of drugs on the immune system.

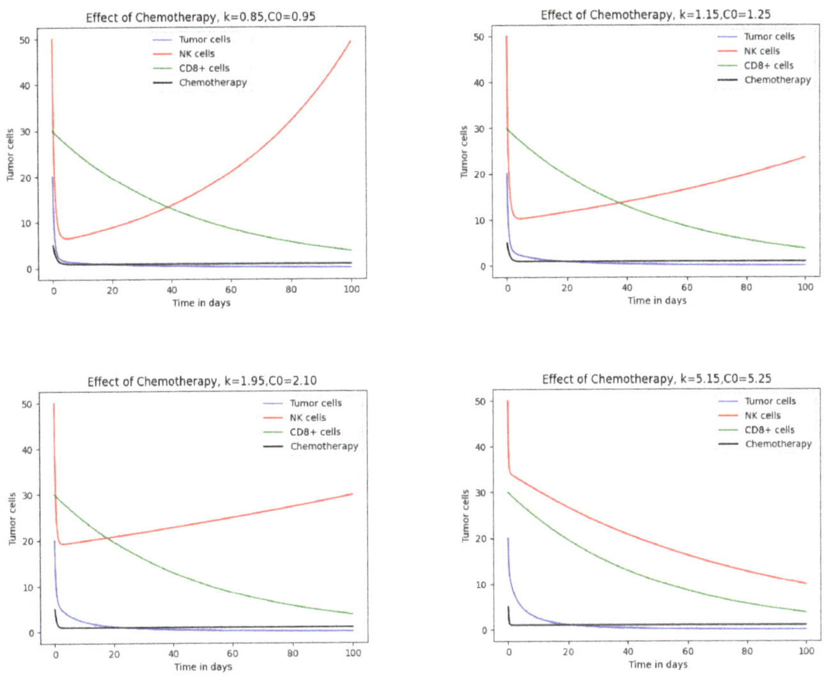

Figure 2. Impact of chemotherapy on tumor and immune cells for the logistic growth model.

Figure 3 presents the effect of chemotherapeutic drugs on cell populations under exponential growth. Tumor and immune cell dynamics were examined for $\kappa = 0.85$, 1.15, 1.90, and 5.15 with decay rates $C_0 = 0.75$, 1.25, 2.10, and 5.35, respectively. In the first case, with $\kappa = 0.85$ and $C_0 = 0.95$, tumor cells are completely eliminated while natural cells remain unaffected. NK cells decline initially but later recover due to drug influx. Such a situation is unlikely because realistically, at the initial stage, the whole tumor has been eradicated. Although tumor cells are eliminated, the treatment also affects healthy cells. At higher values, such as $\kappa = 5.15$, both tumor and immune cell populations decrease sharply. In severe cases, NK cells are entirely eliminated, indicating host mortality. Increasing κ from 0.85 to 1.15, 1.90, and 5.15 produces marked changes in tumor and immune cell behavior, as shown in Figures 2 and 3, where $\kappa = 5.15$ and $C_0 = 5.35$. These results demonstrate that chemotherapy consistently destroys tumor cells but also damages healthy cells. A comparison of Figures 2 and 3 shows that drug effects on healthy cells are less pronounced under logistic growth, while exponential growth leads to greater impairment. Thus, the logistic growth model yields more favorable outcomes than exponential growth for the same parameter values.

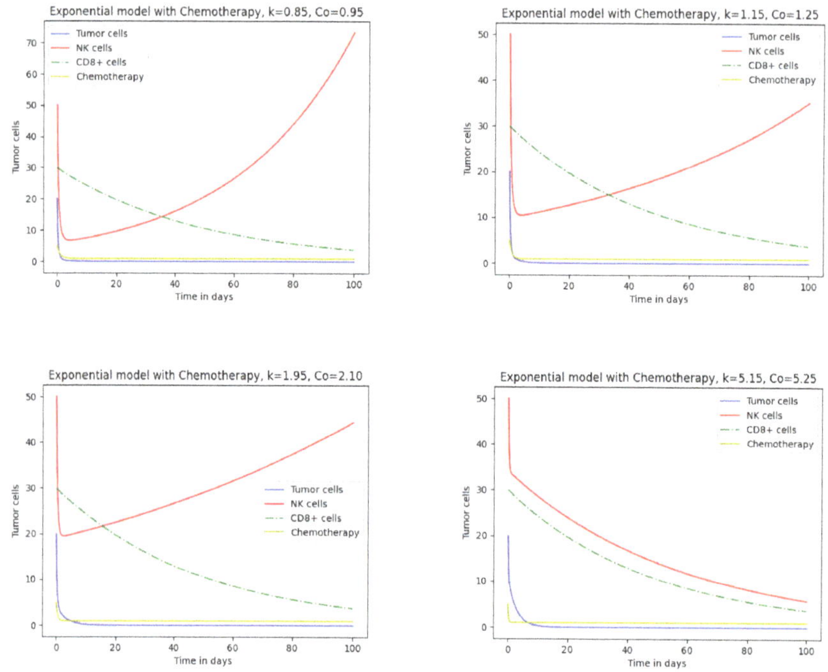

Figure 3. Impact of chemotherapy on tumor and immune cells for the exponential growth model.

Figure 4 presents the response of tumor cells, NK cells following Gompertz growth, and CTLs described in model (18) under chemotherapy. At lower drug influx and decay rates, tumor and CTL cells show a behavior similar to that in the logistic and exponential models. As κ increases from 0.85 to 1.15, 1.90, and 5.15, tumor cell elimination remains consistent with logistic and exponential results, while immune cells display distinct patterns. NK cells decline sharply at first, followed by a gradual decrease. A comparison of exponential and Gompertz models shows similar NK cell behavior, while in the logistic model, the decline of NK cells is less pronounced. Tumor reduction across all three models is comparable, but immune cell dynamics differ, reflecting variations in immune response capacity to therapy. The comparison of results extracted from these models is summarized in Table 3.

Figure 5 demonstrates the variational effect of drug killing parameters like $b_{\aleph}$, $b_{\mathcal{T}}$, and $b_{\mathcal{L}}$ on tumor and immune cells, keeping the rest of the parameters fixed. From Figure 5b, it can be observed that, as we take $b_{\aleph} = 5 \times 10^{-1}$, the graph initially falls and then rises, indicating sustainability in NK cells with drug and NK cell interaction. While the NK cell population becomes zero for $b_{\aleph} = 0.7$, which means the patient's death, realistically, it is unlikely that all immune cells are destroyed in the patient. Figure 5c depicts the effect of $b_{\mathcal{T}}$ on tumor cells, and from here it is observed that for smaller values of $b_{\mathcal{T}}$, such as 0.0001 and 0.002, the tumor cells rise drastically, indicating the intensity of tumor cells, and for the complete eradication of the tumor, drug influx should be reviewed. While for larger values of $b_{\mathcal{T}} = 8 \times 10^{-1}$, 3×10^{-2}, and 3×10^{-1}, the tumor cells first rise and then start declining, as shown in Figures 5a and 5c, respectively. Figure 5d expresses the rapid decline in cytotoxic T lymphocytes for smaller values of $b_L = 0.0009$ and 0.09, indicating a weak immune system; for $b_L = 0.9$, CTL cells gradually decline; and for $b_L = 1, 2, 5$, the graph shows no extraordinary changes. Moreover, when varying the parameters β_1, a_3, ρ, and r from the defined values, they do not cause any major change in tumor and immune cells. Meanwhile, growth rate and decay rate parameters cause drastic changes and sometimes produce implausible outcomes.

Moreover, the graphs illustrate that initially, when drug influx is absent and the immune system is inactive, the tumor is present. And, as with the activation of the immune system and drug concentration, the tumor starts to reduce, and with the passage of time, it will be eliminated along with the decline of healthy immune cells, as shown in Figures 2–4. The elimination of the tumor population and the decline of immune cells vary in each model, depicting variable immune system strengths.

Table 3. Comparison of the logistic, exponential, and Gompertz models.

Logistic	Exponential	Gompertz
Parameters: 16	Parameters: 14	Parameters: 16
State variables: 4	State variables: 4	State variables: 4
Identical behavior of tumor cells for $\kappa = 0.85$	Identical behavior of tumor cells for $\kappa = 0.85$	Identical behavior of tumor cells for $\kappa = 0.85$
Tumor and cytotoxic T cells decline rapidly for $\kappa = 0.85$, 1.15, and 1.90 while NK cells show variation	Tumor and cytotoxic T cells decline rapidly for $\kappa = 0.85$, 1.15, and 1.90 while NK cells show variation	Tumor and cytotoxic T cells decline rapidly for $\kappa = 0.85$, 1.15, and 1.90 while NK cells show variation
The decline of NK and CTL cells is rapid but better than exponential and Gompertz for $\kappa = 5.15$	Immune cells decrease more rapidly as compared to logistic for $\kappa = 5.15$	The decline of NK and CTL cells is more rapid than logistic but identical to exponential for $\kappa = 5.15$

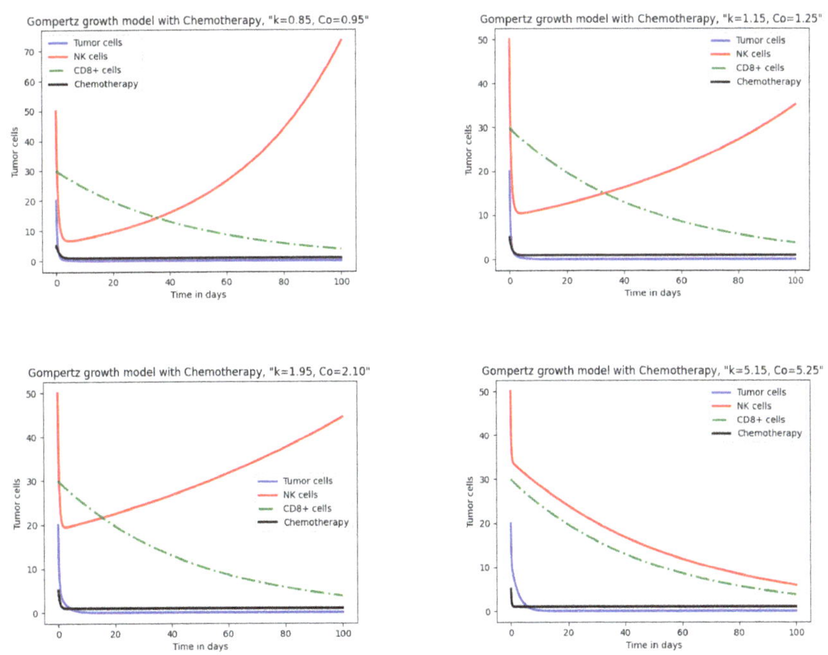

Figure 4. Impact of chemotherapy on tumor and immune cells for the Gompertz growth model.

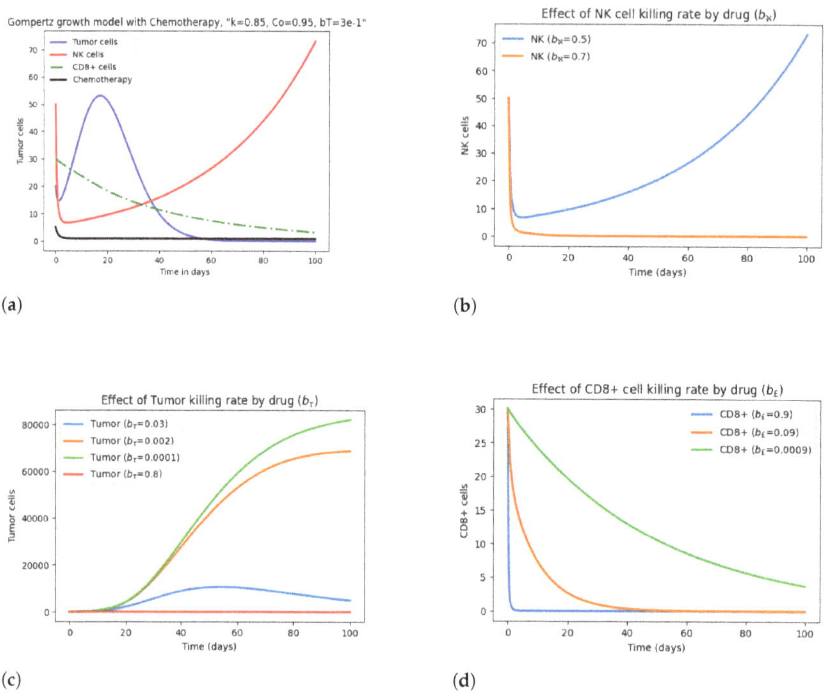

Figure 5. Effect of drug killing parameters $b_{\mathcal{L}}$, $b_{\aleph}$, and b_T on tumor and immune cells.

7. Conclusions

Predicting tumor response to therapy is complex because tumor growth and immune interactions differ across models. Therefore, comparative analysis is important for designing effective treatment strategies. In this context, this study compared logistic, exponential, and Gompertz tumor growth models under chemotherapy. The models incorporated natural killer cells, cytotoxic T lymphocytes, and tumor cells to assess the effects of therapy. The comparison of existing works vs. the current work is presented in Table 4. Dynamical analysis confirmed the existence, boundedness, invariance, and stability of solutions. The results demonstrated that the logistic model provides better outcomes as it preserves immune cells while reducing tumor size. In contrast, the exponential and Gompertz models showed faster immune cell depletion under drug influence. Consequently, these findings suggest that the logistic model may support long-term tumor control and serve as a basis for combination therapies. Table 4 presents a summary of existing works versus the current work. Despite these contributions, the study has limitations. It does not include other immune components such as dendritic cells, cytokines, angiogenesis, and tumor heterogeneity. It also does not optimize parameters or integrate clinical datasets. To address these gaps, future work will extend the framework by adding these components, applying bifurcation analysis, using genetic algorithms for parameter optimization, and validating results with clinical data. Overall, the logistic model appears more effective for preserving immune function during chemotherapy and may provide a foundation for designing improved tumor therapy strategies.

Table 4. Comparison with existing works.

Reference	State Variables/Therapy	Growth Model
[4]	6, Chemotherapy and chemo-immunotherapy	Logistic
[5]	2, Radiotherapy	Logistic
[6]	3, Immunotherapy and chemotherapy	Logistic
[10]	4, Chemotherapy	Logistic
[14]	4, Chemotherapy	Logistic
[15]	4, Virotherapy	Logistic
[16]	4, Chemotherapy and immunotherapy	Logistic
[18]	6, Chemo-immunotherapy	Logistic and Linear
[19]	3, Immunotherapy	Logistic
[23]	4, Chemotherapy, fractional derivative, and diffusion term	Logistic
[24]	4, Chemotherapy, radiotherapy, and immunotherapy	Exponential
[29]	3, Interaction of immune cells and tumor cells	Exponential
[30]	6, Chemo-immunotherapy	Logistic
[32]	4, Fractional informed neural network	Logistic
[33]	6, Chemotherapy	Logistic
Current Paper	4, Chemotherapy	Logistic, Gompertz, and Exponential

Author Contributions: All authors contributed equally. Methodology and software were implemented by M.K. The introduction, literature review, and concluding remarks were written by A.M. and T.N. Results and graphics were elaborated by M.K., A.S.A.S., and M.G. The organization and proofreading were done by A.M. and J.Y.A. All authors have read and agreed to the published version of the manuscript.

Funding: This research received no external funding.

Data Availability Statement: Restrictions apply to the availability of these data. Data were obtained from USM Specialist Hospital and are available from the authors with the permission of USM Specialist Hospital.

Conflicts of Interest: The authors have no conflict of interest.

References

1. Kumar, Y.; Gupta, S.; Singla, R.; Hu, Y.C. A systematic review of artificial intelligence techniques in cancer prediction and diagnosis. *Arch. Comput. Methods Eng.* **2022**, *29*, 2043–2070. [CrossRef]
2. Biemar, F.; Foti, M. Global progress against cancer-challenges and opportunities. *Cancer Biol. Med.* **2013**, *10*, 183–186.
3. IARC Newsletter. Available online: https://www.iarc.who.int/iarcnewsletter/ (accessed on 9 September 2025).
4. Robertson-Tessi, M.; El-Kareh, A.; Goriely, A. A model for effects of adaptive immunity on tumor response to chemotherapy and chemoimmunotherapy. *J. Theor. Biol.* **2015**, *380*, 569–584. [CrossRef] [PubMed]
5. Liu, Z.; Yang, C. A mathematical model of cancer treatment by radiotherapy. *Math. Comput. Simulat.* **2014**, *7*, 172923. [CrossRef]
6. Pang, L.; Lin, S.; Zhong, Z. Mathematical modelling and analysis of the tumor treatment regimens with pulsed immunotherapy and chemotherapy. *Comput. Math. Methods Med.* **2016**, *2016*, 6260474. [CrossRef]
7. Shu, Y.; Huang, J.; Dong, Y.; Takeuchi, Y. Mathematical modeling and bifurcation analysis of pro- and anti-tumor macrophages. *Appl. Math. Mol.* **2020**, *88*, 758–773. [CrossRef]
8. Roesch, K.; Hasenclever, D.; Scholz, M. Modelling Lymphoma Therapy and Outcome. *Bull. Math. Biol.* **2014**, *76*, 401–430. [CrossRef] [PubMed]
9. Dagher, O.; King, T.R.; Wellhausen, N.; Posey, A.D. Combination Therapy for Solid Tumors: Taking a Classic CAR on New Adventures. *Cancer Cell* **2020**, *38*, 621–623. [CrossRef]

10. Song, G.; Liang, G.; Tian, T.; Zhang, X. Mathematical modeling and analysis of tumor chemotherapy. *Symmetry* **2022**, *14*, 704. [CrossRef]
11. Mathur, D.; Barnett, E.; Scher, H.I.; Xavier, J.B. Optimizing the future: How mathematical models inform treatment schedules for cancer. *Trends Cancer* **2022**, *8*, 506–516. [CrossRef]
12. Yin, A.; Moes, D.J.A.; van Hasselt, J.G.; Swen, J.J.; Guchelaar, H.J. A review of mathematical models for tumor dynamics and treatment resistance evolution of solid tumors. *CPT Pharmacometrics Syst. Pharmacol.* **2019**, *8*, 720–737. [CrossRef]
13. Xiao, Y.; Shen, J.; Zou, X. Mathematical modeling and dynamical analysis of anti-tumor drug dose-response. *Math. Biosci. Eng.* **2022**, *19*, 4120–4144. [CrossRef]
14. López, A.G.; Seoane, J.M.; Sanjuán, M.A.F. A validated mathematical model of tumor growth including tumor-host interaction, cell-mediated immune response and chemotherapy. *Bull. Math. Biol.* **2014**, *76*, 2884–2906. [CrossRef] [PubMed]
15. Abernathy, Z.; Abernathy, K.; Stevens, J. A mathematical model for tumor growth and treatment using virotherapy. *AIMS Math.* **2020**, *5*, 4136–4150. [CrossRef]
16. Bao, K.; Liang, G.; Tian, T.; Zhang, X. Mathematical modeling of combined therapies for treating tumor drug resistance. *Math. Biosci.* **2024**, *371*, 109170. [CrossRef]
17. Claret, L.; Girard, P.; Hoff, P.M.; Van Cutsem, E.; Zuideveld, K.P.; Jorga, K.; Fagerberg, J.; Bruno, R. Model-based prediction of phase III overall survival in colorectal cancer on the basis of phase II tumor dynamics. *J. Clin. Oncol.* **2009**, *27*, 4103–4108. [CrossRef]
18. Unni, P.; Seshaiyer, P. Mathematical modeling, analysis, and simulation of tumor dynamics with drug interventions. *Comput. Math. Methods Med.* **2019**, *2019*, 4079298. [CrossRef] [PubMed]
19. Azizi, T. Mathematical Modeling of Cancer Progression. *AppliedMath* **2024**, *4*, 1065–1079. [CrossRef]
20. Carrara, L.; Lavezzi, S.M.; Borella, E.; De Nicolao, G.; Magni, P.; Poggesi, I. Current mathematical models for cancer drug discovery. *Expert Opin. Drug Discov.* **2017**, *12*, 785–799. [CrossRef]
21. Lavezzi, S.M.; Borella, E.; Carrara, L.; De Nicolao, G.; Magni, P.; Poggesi, I. Mathematical modeling of efficacy and safety for anticancer drugs clinical development. *Expert Opin. Drug Discov.* **2018**, *13*, 5–21. [CrossRef]
22. Magni, P.; Simeoni, M.; Poggesi, I.; Rocchetti, M.; De Nicolao, G. A mathematical model to study the effects of drugs administration on tumor growth dynamics. *Math. Biosci.* **2006**, *200*, 127–151. [CrossRef]
23. Mishra, M.N.; Aljohani, A.F. Mathematical modelling of growth of tumour cells with chemotherapeutic cells by using Yang–Abdel–Cattani fractional derivative operator. *J. Taibah Univ. Sci.* **2022**, *16*, 1133–1141. [CrossRef]
24. Bunonyo, K.W.; Ebiwareme, L. Tumor growth mathematical modeling and application of chemo-immunotherapy and radiotherapy treatments. *Int. J. Stat. Appl. Math.* **2022**, *7*, 123–132. [CrossRef]
25. Tosca, E.M.; Terranova, N.; Stuyckens, K.; Dosne, A.G.; Perera, T.; Vialard, J.; Perez-Ruixo, J.J.; Magni, P.; Poggesi, I. A translational model-based approach to inform the choice of the dose in phase 1 oncology trials: The case study of erdafitinib. *Cancer Chemother. Pharmacol.* **2022**, *89*, 117–128. [CrossRef] [PubMed]
26. Rocchetti, M.; Germani, M.; Del Bene, F.; Poggesi, I.; Magni, P.; Pesenti, E.; De Nicolao, G. Predictive pharmacokinetic–pharmacodynamic modeling of tumor growth after administration of an anti-angiogenic agent, bevacizumab, as single-agent and combination therapy in tumor xenografts. *Cancer Chemother. Pharmacol.* **2013**, *71*, 1147–1157. [CrossRef]
27. Simeoni, M.; Magni, P.; Cammia, C.; De Nicolao, G.; Croci, V.; Pesenti, E.; Germani, M.; Poggesi, I.; Rocchetti, M. Predictive pharmacokinetic-pharmacodynamic modeling of tumor growth kinetics in xenograft models after administration of anticancer agents. *Cancer Res.* **2004**, *64*, 1094–1101. [CrossRef]
28. Butner, J.D.; Wang, Z.; Elganainy, D.; Al Feghali, K.A.; Plodinec, M.; Calin, G.A.; Dogra, P.; Nizzero, S.; Ruiz-Ramírez, J.; Martin, G.V.; et al. A mathematical model for the quantification of a patient's sensitivity to checkpoint inhibitors and long-term tumour burden. *Nat. Biomed. Eng.* **2021**, *5*, 297–308. [CrossRef]
29. Pang, L.; Liu, S.; Zhang, X.; Tian, T. Mathematical modeling and dynamic analysis of anti-tumor immune response. *J. Appl. Math. Comput.* **2020**, *62*, 473–488. [CrossRef]
30. Valle, P.A.; Coria, L.N.; Salazar, Y. Tumor clearance analysis on a cancer chemo-immunotherapy mathematical model. *Bull. Math. Biol.* **2019**, *81*, 4144–4173. [CrossRef]
31. Tosca, E.M.; Ronchi, D.; Rocchetti, M.; Magni, P. Predicting tumor volume doubling time and progression-free survival in untreated patients from patient-derived-xenograft (PDX) models: A translational model-based approach. *AAPS J.* **2024**, *26*, 92. [CrossRef]
32. Raeisi, E.; Yavuz, M.; Khosravifarsani, M.; Fadaei, Y. Mathematical modeling of interactions between colon cancer and immune system with a deep learning algorithm. *Eur. Phys. J. Plus* **2024**, *139*, 345. [CrossRef]
33. Makhlouf, A.M.; El-Shennawy, L.; Elkaranshawy, H.A. Mathematical Modelling for the Role of CD4+ T Cells in Tumor-Immune Interactions. *Comput. Math. Methods Med.* **2020**, *2020*, 7187602. [CrossRef]
34. Wang, J. Modeling Cancer Growth with Differential Equations. In Proceedings of the SIMIODE, Denver, CO, USA, 1–4 August 2018; pp. 45–48.

35. Ira, J.I.; Islam, M.S.; Misra, J.C.; Kamrujjaman, M. Mathematical modelling of the dynamics of tumor growth and its optimal control. *Preprints* **2020**. [CrossRef]
36. Adam, A.; Bellomo, N. Basic models of tumor immune system interactions-identification, analysis and predictions. In *A Survey of Models for Tumor-Immune System Dynamics*; Birkhauser: Basel, Switzerland, 1997.
37. Kirschner, D.; Panetta, J.C. Modeling immunotherapy of the tumor—Immune interaction. *J. Math. Biol.* **1998**, *37*, 235–252. [CrossRef] [PubMed]
38. de Pillis, L.G.; Radunskaya, A. A mathematical model of immune response to tumor invasion. In *Computational Fluid and Solid Mechanics*; Elsevier Science: Amsterdam, The Netherlands, 2003; pp. 1661–1668.
39. Diefenbach, A.; Jensen, E.R.; Jamieson, A.M.; Raulet, D.H. Rae1 and H60 ligands of the NKG2D receptor stimulate tumour immunity. *Nature* **2001**, *413*, 165–171. [CrossRef] [PubMed]
40. Chen, L. *Mathematical Models and Methods in Ecology*; Science Press: Beijing, China, 1988; pp. 174–198.

Mathematical and Computational Applications

MDPI

Article

Reinforcement Learning-Driven Evolutionary Stackelberg Game Model for Adaptive Breast Cancer Therapy

Fatemeh Tavakoli [1], Davud Mohammadpur [1], Javad Salimi Sartakhti [2] and Mohammad Hossein Manshaei [3,*]

[1] Department of Electrical and Computer Engineering, University of Zanjan, Zanjan 45371-38791, Iran; dmp@znu.ac.ir (D.M.)
[2] Department of Electrical and Computer Engineering, University of Kashan, Kashan 87317-53153, Iran; salimi@kashanu.ac.ir
[3] Department of Computer Science, Hunter College, City University of New York, New York, NY 10065, USA
* Correspondence: mohammad.manshaei@hunter.cuny.edu

Abstract: In this paper, we present an integrative framework based on Evolutionary Stackelberg Game Theory to model the strategic interaction between a physician, acting as a rational leader, and a heterogeneous population of treatment-sensitive and treatment-resistant breast cancer cells. The model incorporates ecological competition, evolutionary adaptation, and spatial heterogeneity, enabling prediction of tumor progression under clinically relevant treatment protocols. Using tumor volume data obtained from breast cancer-bearing mice treated with Capecitabine and Gemcitabine, we estimated treatment and subject-specific parameters via the GEKKO optimization package in Python. Benchmarking against classical tumor growth models (Exponential, Logistic, and Gompertz) showed that while classical models capture monotonic growth, they fail to reproduce complex, non-monotonic behaviors such as treatment-induced regression, rebound, and phenotypic switching. The game-theoretic approach achieved superior alignment with experimental data across Maximum Tolerated Dose, Dose-Modulation Adaptive Therapy, and Intermittent Adaptive Therapy protocols. To enhance adaptability, we integrated reinforcement learning (RL) for both single-agent and combination chemotherapy. The RL agent learned dosing policies that maximized tumor regression while minimizing cumulative drug exposure and resistance, with combination therapy exploiting dose diversification to improve control without exceeding total dose budgets. Incorporating reaction diffusion equations allowed the model to capture spatial dispersal of sensitive (cooperative) and resistant (defector) phenotypes, revealing that spatially aware adaptive strategies more effectively suppress resistant clones than non-spatial approaches. These results demonstrate that evolutionarily informed, spatially explicit, and computationally optimized strategies can outperform conventional fixed-dose regimens in reducing resistance, lowering toxicity, and improving efficacy. This framework offers a biologically interpretable tool for guiding evolution-aware, patient-tailored cancer therapies toward improved long-term outcomes.

Keywords: breast cancer modeling; Stackelberg game theory; adaptive therapy; phenotypic dynamics; diffusion; treatment-sensitive cells; treatment-resistant cells

1. Introduction

Breast cancer is a biologically complex and heterogeneous disease, often leading to drug resistance and treatment failure. Traditional approaches such as the maximum tolerated dose (MTD) aim for aggressive tumor eradication but frequently accelerate the emergence of resistant clones [1,2]. Adaptive therapy offers a promising alternative by dynamically adjusting drug dosage to maintain a manageable tumor burden and suppress resistance through intratumoral competition [3,4].

To design such evolution-informed strategies, computational modeling plays a crucial role. Frameworks including cellular automata, differential equations, agent-based simulations, and especially game-theoretic models [5–8] enable researchers to simulate tumor dynamics and optimize treatment protocols. Among these, evolutionary game theory provides biologically realistic insights into strategic interactions among cancer cells [9,10]. Recent models based on Stackelberg evolutionary games conceptualize the physician as a rational leader who anticipates the adaptive responses of cancer cells [11,12].

Building on this foundation, our study introduces the Breast Cancer Stackelberg game model to analyze the strategic interactions between a physician and a heterogeneous tumor cell population. The schematic representation of this hierarchical leader–follower interaction framework is presented in Figure 1, highlighting the physician's role as a rational leader who anticipates and influences the evolutionary responses of cancer cells.

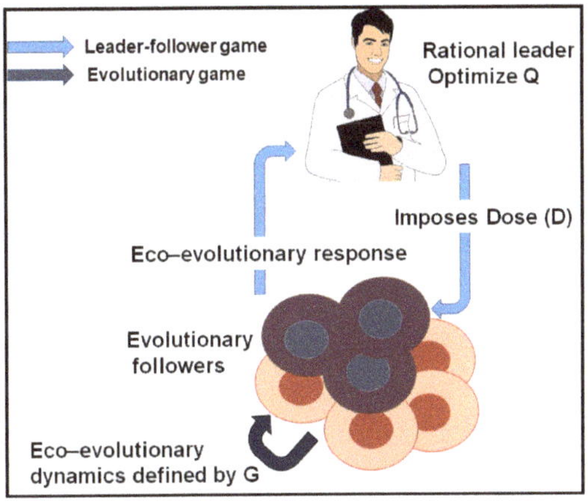

Figure 1. The structure of evolutionary Stackelberg game in cancer.

To complement our theoretical framework, we utilized experimental data from xenograft mice treated with Capecitabine and Gemcitabine, as reported in [13]. Moving beyond purely theoretical approaches, we incorporate patient-specific tumor measurements to estimate key biological parameters through the Python-based GEKKO optimization package (version 1.3.0), enhancing model realism and predictive accuracy. The resulting model closely reproduces observed tumor behavior under three therapeutic protocols: dose-modulated adaptive therapy, intermittent adaptive therapy, and MTD regimens.

To capture the strategic interplay between treatment-sensitive and -resistant cancer cell populations, we formulate their interactions as a Stackelberg evolutionary game. In this hierarchical framework, the physician acting as a rational leader selects treatment doses to optimize a predefined objective function linked to patient quality of life. We evaluate three therapeutic strategies: MTD, ecologically enlightened therapy (EET), and evolutionarily enlightened therapy (EVT), following the conceptual framework introduced by Stein et al. [14]. Our analysis, applied to our own dataset, demonstrates that EVT consistently achieves the best outcomes: minimizing drug usage, reducing resistance emergence, and maximizing the objective function. In contrast, the MTD strategy accelerates resistance and compromises treatment durability.

In EET, the physician dynamically adjusts dosing based on observed resistance levels, leading to a static Nash equilibrium, where both the cancer cells' resistance and the physician's dosage mutually stabilize in response to one another. However, in EVT, the physician anticipates the future adaptive responses of cancer cells, achieving a Stackelberg equilibrium in which resistant populations settle into a stable eco-evolutionary state. This foresight allows the physician to proactively steer tumor evolution toward more manageable trajectories.

Further, to address spatial heterogeneity in the tumor microenvironment, we integrate reaction-diffusion equations into the model. This extension captures phenotypic diffusion and spatial expansion of resistant clones, underscoring the critical role of spatial dynamics in shaping treatment outcomes and resistance patterns.

Building on this calibrated framework, we integrate reinforcement learning (RL) to design adaptive treatment strategies for both single-agent and dual-drug settings. In the single-agent case, the RL agent learns dosing policies that balance tumor regression against cumulative drug exposure and resistance suppression. For combination therapy, the agent dynamically allocates doses between Capecitabine and Gemcitabine within pharmaco dynamic and toxicity constraints, exploiting dose diversification to improve tumor control without exceeding total dose budgets. In both scenarios, the RL-driven policies adapt to evolving tumor states, offering a flexible and data-informed approach to therapy optimization.

By leveraging limited early-stage tumor data, our approach enables reliable forecasts of tumor evolution and facilitates comparative evaluation of alternative treatment strategies, including their long-term efficacy and resistance outcomes. This predictive capability suggests that the framework may serve as a useful decision-support tool for designing personalized, evolution-aware cancer therapies that combine biologically grounded modeling with adaptive, AI-driven treatment planning.

The remainder of this paper is organized as follows. Section 2 presents a Stackelberg-based evolutionary modeling framework that strategically captures tumor progression by explicitly representing the interactions among heterogeneous breast cancer cell populations. Section 3 presents the main findings, including parameter estimation from experimental data, analysis of sensitive and resistant cell dynamics, spatial modeling of phenotype dispersal within the tumor microenvironment, and reinforcement learning-based optimization of adaptive therapy (single-drug and dual-drug). Finally, Section 4 discusses the broader implications of our findings, highlighting how the integration of game theory, reinforcement learning, and spatial ecology can inform the design of evolutionarily informed, resistance-aware treatment protocols in precision oncology.

2. Stackelberg Game Framework for Breast Cancer Therapy

The Stackelberg-Based Evolutionary Model provides a strategic framework for analyzing tumor progression by incorporating hierarchical interactions between breast cancer cells. By leveraging game theory principles, this model optimizes treatment strategies, balancing the competition between sensitive and resistant cell populations to enhance therapeutic efficacy.

This model enables physicians to make informed treatment decisions by dynamically adjusting drug dosages based on tumor response. Through its predictive capabilities, it offers personalized approaches that mitigate resistance development, ultimately improving patient outcomes in breast cancer therapy.

In this study, we propose an evolutionary Stackelberg game theory model to describe interactions among breast cancer cells. To evaluate the model's applicability to physician–tumor dynamics, we analyzed experimental data from mice treated with two distinct therapeutic agents: Capecitabine and Gemcitabine. Model parameters were estimated based on observed data for each protocol, enabling a comparative evaluation of drug dosage effects and tumor burden variations.

The model was subsequently extended to incorporate two cancer cell populations, treatment-sensitive and treatment-resistant cells, allowing for a more comprehensive analysis of their spatial diffusion dynamics within a two-dimensional framework. This extension provides deeper insights into tumor evolution and treatment optimization, enhancing the predictive capabilities of the proposed model in guiding therapeutic decision-making.

Evolutionary Stackelberg game theory offers a promising framework for optimizing cancer treatment strategies. Within this approach, breast cancer therapy is modeled as an interaction between the physician and a heterogeneous population of cancer cells To capture the evolutionary dynamics of tumor growth and phenotypic adaptations leading to resistance over time, a fitness generating function (G-function) is employed. This function accounts for logistic tumor growth, which is effectively suppressed by multiple anticancer drugs. The generating function is defined as

$$G(u,x,D) = r\left[1 - \frac{x}{K(u)}\right] - \frac{D}{k+bu}. \tag{1}$$

r indicates intrinsic growth rate and x is normalized tumor burden. The expression $\frac{D}{k+bu}$ represents the drug-induced death rate, where D denotes the administered drug dose, k represents the intrinsic resistance of cancer cells, and b quantifies the impact of resistance traits on diminishing drug efficacy. In this framework, D takes values between 0 and 1, with $D = 1$ corresponding to MTD. The carrying capacity, denoted as $K(u)$, is modeled as a function of the resistance level u, reflecting the trade-off between resistance and ecological fitness. This formulation follows previous work by Pressley et al. [15], where similar relationships were used to capture treatment-induced evolutionary dynamics:

$$K(u) = K_{\max} \cdot \exp(-g \cdot u). \tag{2}$$

Here, $K_{\max}$ represents the maximum possible carrying capacity, and g determines the magnitude of the resistance-associated cost. This formulation accounts for the impact of resistance on population growth, ensuring that as resistance levels increase, the effective carrying capacity is reduced. The ecological dynamics governing the system are defined as follows:

$$\frac{dx}{dt} = xG(u,x,D). \tag{3}$$

The evolution of cancer cell resistance in response to the physician's treatment choices is governed by specific biological and ecological dynamics. These dynamics define how resistance levels change over time. The formal mathematical representation of these resistance dynamics is defined as follows:

$$\frac{du}{dt} = \sigma\frac{\partial G}{\partial u}, \tag{4}$$

The parameter σ determines the evolutionary speed of resistance adaptation. The following functions describe the calculation of the D value, adjusted for different treatment protocols.

Standard Treatment Protocol: The standard treatment protocol involves the continuous administration of the drug at MTD, ensuring a consistent therapeutic effect. This approach maintains a high level of drug exposure to maximize tumor suppression, although it may lead to increased side effects and potential resistance over time.

Dose Modulation Adaptive Therapy: In this adaptive therapy protocol, drug dosage is dynamically adjusted based on tumor burden fluctuations. If the tumor burden decreases by more than 10% compared to the previous measurement, the dose is reduced by 50%, preventing unnecessary drug exposure. Conversely, if the tumor burden increases by more than 10%, the dose is increased by 50%, ensuring sufficient drug pressure to counteract tumor progression.

Additionally, treatment is suspended when the tumor burden falls below a predefined threshold, allowing for drug holidays to minimize toxicity and prevent unnecessary intervention. Therapy is resumed once tumor growth surpasses the threshold again, ensuring effective control of disease progression. The parameters governing this adaptive strategy include $\alpha = 0.5$ and $\beta = 0.1$, which regulate the degree of dose modulation. The dose adjustment function for this protocol is defined as

$$D(x_i) = \begin{cases} (1+\alpha)D_{i-1} & \text{if } x_i > (1+\beta)x_{i-1}, \\ (1-\alpha)D_{i-1} & \text{if } x_i \leq (1-\beta)x_{i-1}, \\ D_0 & \text{otherwise.} \end{cases} \quad (5)$$

Here, D_0 represents the initial dose at the start of treatment, D_{i-1} is the drug dose in phase $(i-1)$, and i indicates the current stage. The variable x_i denotes the tumor burden at time step i, while x_{i-1} corresponds to the burden measured in the previous interval. The time steps i and $i-1$ represent consecutive measurement intervals, each corresponding to one unit of time based on the experimental sampling schedule.

Intermittent Adaptive Therapy Protocol: This protocol initiates treatment by administering the drug at MTD. If the tumor burden decreases to less than 50% of its initial value, treatment is temporarily discontinued to minimize unnecessary drug exposure and reduce toxicity. However, if the tumor burden exceeds its original load, therapy is resumed at the MTD for each drug. The function D for this protocol is defined as

$$D(x_i) = \begin{cases} 0 & \text{if } x_i < 0.5x_0, \\ 1 & \text{if } x_i > x_0, \\ D_0 & \text{otherwise.} \end{cases} \quad (6)$$

Here, $D_0 = \text{MTD}$ denotes the maximum tolerated dose. This innovative approach provides a comprehensive depiction of tumor population dynamics and the evolutionary trajectories of cellular resistance mechanisms in response to therapeutic interventions. By employing this modeling technique, evolutionary game theory offers critical insights into the complex interactions between therapeutic strategies and tumor evolution. These findings contribute to the development of personalized treatment protocols, enabling the optimization of therapeutic outcomes and improving long-term cancer management.

3. Results

This section is organized into six interconnected parts, each addressing a key component of the study. First, in Estimation of Model Parameters (Section 3.1), we present the methodology for deriving both treatment-specific and patient-specific parameters from experimental tumor volume data, ensuring accurate calibration of the model to individual and regimen-level characteristics. Second, in Sensitive and Resistant Cell Interactions (Section 3.2), we investigate the ecological and evolutionary dynamics between treatment-sensitive and treatment-resistant phenotypes, highlighting their competitive interplay under different therapeutic protocols. Third, in Integration of Experimental Data into the Simulation Framework (Section 3.4), we explain how real-world data is incorporated into the simulation environment and how it informs model behavior and predictions. Fourth, in Diffusion in Sensitive and Resistant Cells (Section 3.3), we incorporate spatial heterogeneity through reaction-diffusion modeling to capture the dispersal patterns of both phenotypes and assess their impact on tumor progression and treatment response Fifth, in Application of Reinforcement Learning for Adaptive Cancer Therapy (Section 3.5), we evaluate the performance of an RL-based framework in learning dosing strategies that balance tumor regression, cumulative drug exposure, and resistance suppression. Finally, in Extension from Single-Agent to Combination Therapy Modeling (Section 3.6), we expand the RL approach to dual-drug regimens, analyzing dose allocation under pharmacodynamic and toxicity constraints. This structured presentation enables a comprehensive evaluation of the model's predictive capabilities and its potential to inform the design of evolutionarily informed, resistance-aware cancer therapies.

3.1. Estimation of Model Parameters

To evaluate the proposed model for cancer cell interactions with the physician, experimental data from treated mice were analyzed. Initially, the dataset underwent MinMax scaling normalization to standardize values, ensuring uniformity and consistency in the analytical process. This preprocessing step allowed for a more accurate comparison of treatment effects and model predictions. Tumors were classified into two distinct categories increasing (Up) and decreasing (Down) based on their initial response to treatment. This classification criterion is based on the tumor's early trend upon treatment initiation, distinguishing between cases where the tumor shows immediate growth versus regression. Clinically, patients are categorized as non-responders if their tumor burden increases initially, while those showing early tumor shrinkage are labeled as responders. Notably, this initial reaction to treatment may provide valuable predictive insights into future tumor progression, making it a meaningful clustering approach.

Parameter estimation was conducted using the Python package GEKKO, a specialized tool for machine learning and optimization tasks. The model incorporates both treatment-specific and patient-specific parameters to enhance predictive accuracy. The treatment-specific parameters $g, k, b, K_{\max}$ define therapeutic response mechanisms.These parameters are estimated independently for each therapy. while the patient-specific parameters σ, r, u_0 account for individual variations in disease progression and treatment sensitivity.

The distinction between treatment-specific and patient-specific parameters is grounded in both biological reasoning and modeling precedent. In our framework, parameters such as $K_{\max}$ which denotes the effective carrying capacity of the tumor under therapy are modeled as treatment-specific because they reflect the pharmacodynamic impact of the administered drug on tumor growth constraints. Prior studies have shown that therapeutic agents can modulate the tumor microenvironment, vascularization, and immune infiltration, all of which influence the maximum sustainable tumor burden under treatment [3,16]. In contrast, parameters like intrinsic growth rate (r) or resistance kinetics (σ, u_0) are considered patient-specific, as they are more tightly linked to host biology, genetic background, and tumor phenotype [17,18].

The variables and parameters of the model are summarized in Table 1. The optimal parameters for each group were selected based on their ability to achieve the best fit with observed data. A summary of their values is provided in Table 2, highlighting key parameter estimates.

Table 1. Variables and parameters of the model. Parameter ranges were informed by prior literature, particularly the study by Benzekry et al. on resistance modeling in non-small cell lung cancer [19], which provides biologically plausible bounds for resistance-related dynamics.

Parameter	Description	Range
r	Intrinsic growth rate	$[0,1]$
σ	Evolution speed	$(0,0.1]$
u_0	Initial resistance to treatment	Non-negative
k	Intrinsic resistance	$[0,20]$
$K_{\max}$	Maximum carrying capacity	Non-negative
b	Benefit of resistance traits reducing drug efficacy	$[0,20]$
g	Cost of resistance	$[0,1]$
x	Normalized tumor burden (scaled)	$[0,1]$
D	Drug dosage amount	$[0,1]$
u	Resistance intensity to treatment	Non-negative

Table 2. The model parameters have been estimated.

	Increasing				Decreasing				
Therapy	b	k	$K_{\max}$	g	b	k	$K_{\max}$	g	**Mouse**
Capecitabine Therapy									
MTD	1.0	10.33	1.0	0.04	–	–	–	–	19,20,21,22,23,24
Dose modulation	–	–	–	–	19.92	1.02	1.0	0.99	31,34
Intermittent	1.0	9.98	1.0	0.18	1.0	19.99	1.0	0.83	25,26,27,29,28,30
Gemcitabine Therapy									
MTD	1.0	5.53	1.0	0.1	19.99	19.99	1.0	1.0	1,2,4,3,5,6
Dose modulation	1.0	7	1.0	0.05	19.93	18	1.0	0.89	13,15,16,17,18
Intermittent	1.0	6.55	1.0	1.0	1.0	3.38	1.0	0.13	7,8,9,10,11,12

Note: Parameter values were estimated using the GEKKO optimization package. The variation in parameter b reflects differences in tumor response dynamics across treatment protocols, as determined by nonlinear least-squares fitting to experimental data.

The parameters $b, k, K_{\max}$ and g were estimated under the assumption that they are treatment-specific but remain constant across all patients receiving the same therapeutic regimen. In contrast, the parameters σ, r, and the initial value of u were considered patient-specific, as summarized in Table 1. These subject-specific parameters were estimated independently for each tumor, with the primary objective of minimizing the discrepancy between observed experimental data and the predictions generated by the model.

Figure 2 illustrate actual tumor growth data and corresponding model-generated graphs based on the estimated parameters for a subset of mice, providing a visual representation of the model's predictive accuracy and its ability to capture tumor dynamics. As illustrated in the figure, the graph representing the actual data for Mice 2, 5, 12, 22, 25, and 31 closely aligns with the graph generated using the estimated parameters. This similarity indicates the accuracy and reliability of the parameter estimation process. The specific parameters associated with each mouse (u_0, σ, r) are detailed in the figure caption, providing insights into individual variations in tumor progression and response to treatment. Such consistency validates the effectiveness of the modeling approach in capturing key biological dynamics.

Since we have assumed that a specific set of parameters namely $K_{\max}, b, g$ and k are treatment-specific, we can utilize them to simulate potential outcomes for patients who received different therapeutic protocols. This simulation enables comparative analysis of treatment efficacy, providing insights into how variations in drug administration strategies may have influenced tumor progression and patient responses.

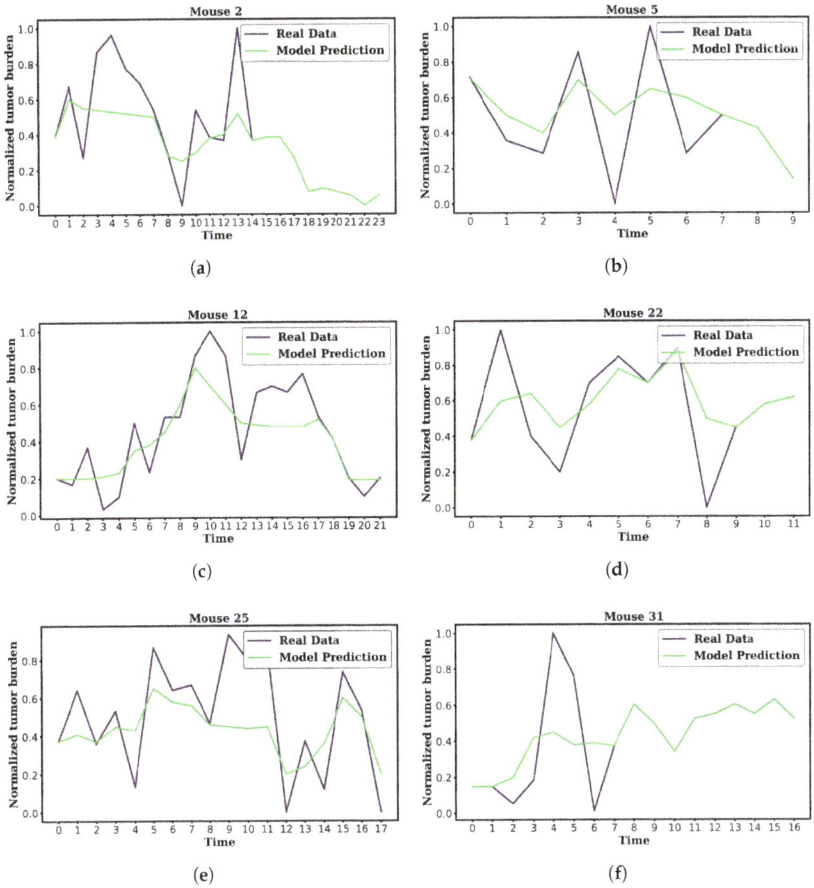

Figure 2. Comparison between experimental data and simulated population dynamics for Mice 2, 5, 12, 22, 25, and 31 using subject-specific estimated parameters. (**a**) Mouse 2: $r = 0.20$, $u_0 = 1.5478$, $\sigma = 0.0499$; (**b**) Mouse 5: $r = 0.2$, $u_0 = 10.0$, $\sigma = 0.05$; (**c**) Mouse 12: $r = 0.1999$, $u_0 = 1.1651$, $\sigma = 0.05$; (**d**) Mouse 22: $r = 0.2001$, $u_0 = 9.5948$, $\sigma = 0.0499$; (**e**) Mouse 25: $r = 0.1907$, $u_0 = 0.5102$, $\sigma = 0.0499$; (**f**) Mouse 31: $r = 0.2039$, $u_0 = 3.1046$, $\sigma = 0.05$.

While the model generally captures the overall trends in tumor growth and treatment response, its predictions do not fully align with experimental data in certain cases—particularly for subjects exhibiting oscillatory or non-monotonic behavior. These discrepancies likely stem from the simplified structure of the model, which does not explicitly incorporate key biological mechanisms such as immune system interactions, microenvironmental influences, and stochastic variability. Moreover, the parameter estimation process was intentionally constrained to biologically plausible ranges to prevent overfitting and ensure interpretability, which may have further limited the model's flexibility in reproducing complex dynamics. Despite these limitations, the framework remains effective in capturing key features of tumor ecology and provides a foundation for evaluating adaptive treatment strategies.

In order to demonstrate the advantages of our game-theoretic modeling framework, we first compared its performance against well-established classical tumor growth models that have long served as the foundation of mathematical oncology. Classical models such as the Exponential, Logistic, and Gompertz formulations provide simplified yet analytically tractable descriptions of tumor expansion, each grounded in distinct biological assumptions. The Exponential model presumes unrestricted proliferation, making it suitable for early-stage growth but unrealistic for long-term dynamics due to the absence of resource limitations. The Logistic model introduces a fixed carrying capacity, thereby capturing saturation effects as tumor burden approaches physiological constraints. The Gompertz model, in turn, characterizes a gradual deceleration in growth rate, consistent with empirical observations of reduced proliferation in larger tumors. These paradigms have been extensively studied and benchmarked in both preclinical and clinical contexts, with recent systematic analyses confirming their utility and limitations [20,21].

Following the methodology outlined by Ghaffari Laleh et al. [20], we performed a comparative analysis using a dataset derived from murine tumor volume measurements across various tumor growth models. Tumor burden trajectories were fitted to each of the three classical models, and predictive accuracy was quantified using the Mean Squared Error (MSE) between model-predicted and experimentally measured tumor data. This benchmarking step provided a rigorous reference point for evaluating our game-theoretic framework, which explicitly incorporates ecological and evolutionary interactions between phenotypically distinct subpopulations within the tumor microenvironment. Unlike classical models that treat tumor growth as a homogeneous process, the game-theoretic approach accounts for competition, cooperation, and treatment feedback, thereby enabling the modeling of adaptive responses and evolutionary dynamics. Model parameters were estimated using the GEKKO optimization suite [22], which supports dynamic systems and differential-algebraic equations.

The comparative results revealed that while classical models can adequately reproduce monotonic growth patterns, they consistently fail to capture non-monotonic behaviors such as treatment-induced regressions, rebounds, and phenotypic switching phenomena increasingly recognized in both experimental and clinical datasets. In contrast, the game-theoretic model achieved superior alignment with these complex dynamics, underscoring its potential for more biologically grounded and clinically informative predictions. A summary of MSE values across different therapy strategies is presented in Table 3, highlighting the enhanced predictive accuracy of the game-theoretic framework, particularly in scenarios involving adaptive treatment.

An important advantage of the proposed modeling framework is its ability to incorporate patient- or therapy-specific parameter estimates, enabling the simulation and comparison of multiple therapeutic protocols for the same individual. By calibrating the model to experimental data, it becomes possible to explore how alternative treatment strategies would influence both tumor dynamics and cumulative drug exposure, thereby providing a quantitative basis for personalized therapy design.

Table 3. Mean Squared Error (MSE) comparison across classical tumor growth models and game theory.

Therapy Strategy	Exponential	Logistic	Gompertz	Game Theory
Capecitabine with MTD-Up	0.0788	0.0574	0.0694	0.0300
Capecitabine dose modulation-Down	0.0675	0.0434	0.058	0.0400
Capecitabine intermittent-Up	0.0809	0.0789	0.0803	0.0600
Capecitabine intermittent-Down	0.0533	0.0476	0.0141	0.0100
Gemcitabine with MTD-Up	0.0969	0.0805	0.0873	0.0300
Gemcitabine with MTD-Down	0.0848	0.0786	0.0785	0.0700
Gemcitabine dose modulation-Up	0.0966	0.0642	0.0641	0.0356
Gemcitabine intermittent-Up	0.0640	0.0525	0.1220	0.0400
Gemcitabine intermittent-Down	0.0809	0.0687	0.0700	0.0300

3.2. Sensitive and Resistant Cell Interactions

The analytical framework presented in this section builds upon the Stackelberg evolutionary game theory approach, which has been developed and extended over time in prior work [11,23–25]. In particular, Stein et al. [14] applied and further extended this framework in the context of cancer treatment, and we build on their formulation to explore treatment-induced evolutionary responses under varying therapeutic strategies, including EET and EVT. While the structure follows their established model, our simulations use modified parameters tailored to the current study, resulting in distinct graphical outcomes.

Tumors consist of heterogeneous populations of cancer cells with varying degrees of therapeutic resistance, all competing for limited resources. Adaptive therapy is a dose modulation strategy guided by treatment response, which leverages the intrinsic competition between sensitive and resistant cancer cells to optimize therapeutic efficacy. Treatment response depends on the adaptive capacity of cancer cells; therefore, adaptive therapy can incorporate evolutionary principles to better account for these adaptive dynamics.

By maintaining a substantial population of treatment-sensitive cells through controlled drug dosing or periodic treatment interruptions, adaptive therapy creates an environment in which sensitive cells suppress the proliferation of treatment-resistant subpopulations via competitive interactions. This strategic approach not only delays the emergence of drug resistance but also enhances long-term tumor control, offering a promising alternative to traditional high-dose regimens.

Evolutionary Stackelberg game theory provides a framework for refining cancer treatment strategies. In this context, breast cancer therapy is conceptualized as a dynamic interaction between a physician and a polymorphic population of cancer cells, encompassing both treatment-sensitive and treatment-resistant phenotypes. To model tumor growth dynamics and the evolutionary adaptations of resistance-related traits over time, a fitness-generating function (G-function) is employed. This function simulates the competitive interplay between subpopulations, offering insights into optimal therapeutic interventions that leverage evolutionary principles to suppress resistance and enhance treatment effectiveness.

The dynamics of two tumor subpopulations are described by the following system of equations. The variable x_S represents cells sensitive to treatment, while x_R denotes cells resistant to treatment. Both equations incorporate ecological competition and pharmacodynamic effects. The growth of the sensitive subpopulation x_S is governed by its intrinsic proliferation rate r_S. The term $\alpha_{SS}x_S + \alpha_{SR}x_R$ represents the total competitive pressure experienced by sensitive cells, where α_{SS} denotes intra-type competition among sensitive cells, and α_{SR} captures inter-type competition exerted by resistant cells. The cytotoxic effect of therapy is modeled by the term $\frac{D}{k+b\,u_s}$. Here, D denotes the administered drug dose, and u_s represents the treatment resistance in the sensitive cell population. In this scenario $u_s = 0$:

$$\frac{dx_S}{dt} = x_S\left(r_S\left(1 - \frac{\alpha_{SS}x_S + \alpha_{SR}x_R}{K(u)}\right) - \frac{D}{k + b\,u_s}\right), \qquad u_s = 0. \tag{7}$$

The dynamics of the resistant subpopulation x_R are similarly governed by its intrinsic growth rate r_R. α_{RR} represents intra-type competition among resistant cells, and α_{RS} accounts for inter-type competition from sensitive cells. The treatment effect on resistant cells is captured by the term $\frac{D}{k+b\,u_R}$, where u_R denotes the treatment resistance in the resistant subpopulation:

$$\frac{dx_R}{dt} = x_R\left(r_R\left(1 - \frac{\alpha_{RS}x_S + \alpha_{RR}x_R}{K(u)}\right) - \frac{D}{k + b\,u_R}\right). \tag{8}$$

In our study, the experimental data correspond to tumor burden, which were normalized to the unit interval $[0,1]$ using min–max scaling. Accordingly, $x = x_S + x_R$ denotes the normalized total tumor burden. To optimize treatment decisions, we define the physician's objective function Q as

$$Q(D, u_R, x^*(D, u_R)) = \begin{cases} Q^{\max} - C_1\left(\frac{x^*(D,u_R)}{K}\right)^2 - C_2 u_R^2 - C_3 D^2, \\ (D, u_R) \in \text{stabilization region}, \\ \text{undefined, elsewhere.} \end{cases} \quad (9)$$

In Equation (9), $Q^{\max}$ represents the maximum attainable value of the objective function. The term $x^*(D, u_R))$ corresponds to the ecological equilibrium, while u_R denotes the resistance strategy adopted by treatment-resistant cells and D is treatment dose. The parameters C_1, C_2, and C_3 reflect the relative importance of tumor burden, resistance, and toxicity.

Progression time is defined as the moment when tumor burden exceeds a fraction δ of the carrying capacity. In this study, we set $\delta = 0.7$, and therefore the threshold is given by $\delta K_{max} = 0.7K_{max}$. The goal is to identify treatment doses and resistance levels that keep the tumor below this threshold, enabling sustained control. Tumor behavior is classified into elimination, stabilization, and progression regions.

We adopt the classification of therapeutic strategies proposed by Stein et al. [14], which distinguishes between ecologically and evolutionarily enlightened approaches. These are formalized through Nash and Stackelberg optimization frameworks. The Nash strategy assumes a fixed resistance level and optimizes dose accordingly:

$$D^*(u_R) = \arg\max_D Q(D, u_R, x^*(D, u_R)). \quad (10)$$

This strategy aligns with the intersection of the cancer cells'evolutionary response curve (ESS strategy $u_R^*(D)$) and the physician's best response curve $D^*(u_R)$. The Stackelberg strategy anticipates the cancer cells' evolutionary response:

$$D_S = \arg\max_D Q(D, u_R^*(D), x^*(D, u_R^*(D))). \quad (11)$$

In order to illustrate the comparative outcomes of different therapeutic strategies, we analyzed Mouse 7 under three distinct approaches: MTD, the ecologically enlightened strategy (Nash equilibrium), and the evolutionarily enlightened strategy (Stackelberg equilibrium). The parametrization was based on the framework introduced by Stein et al. [14], adapted to our experimental data (Figure 3). The model was parameterized with $Q^{\max} = 1$, $C_1 = 0.51$, $C_2 = 0.08$, and $C_3 = 0.41$, reflecting the relative weighting of tumor burden, treatment-induced resistance, and therapy toxicity in the physician's objective function. Transition rates between phenotypes were set as $\alpha_{RS} = 0.60$, $\alpha_{RR} = \alpha_{SS} = 1.0$, and $\alpha_{SR} = 0.25$.

Under this parametrization, all three strategies fell within the stabilization region, where tumor burden remains nonzero but manageable. Among them, the Stackelberg equilibrium achieved the highest objective function value, followed by the Nash equilibrium, while MTD resulted in the lowest value. It should be noted that the near-zero dosing outcome observed under the Stackelberg strategy is influenced by the toxicity weight C_3, which strongly penalizes drug administration. This reflects the sensitivity of the framework to parameter selection and highlights the importance of careful calibration and biological validation.

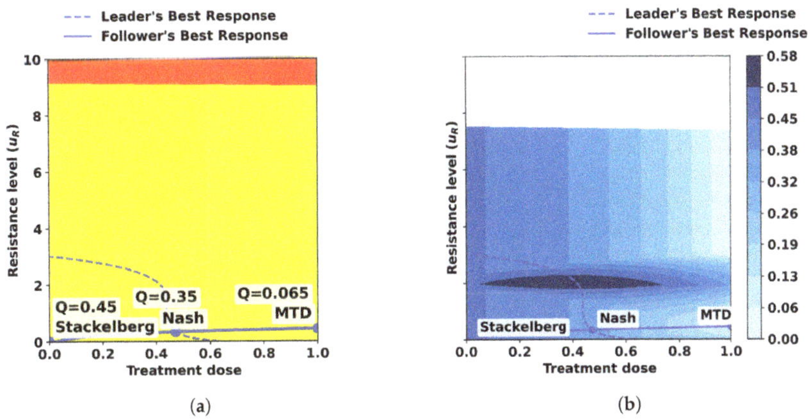

Figure 3. Outcomes of three therapeutic strategies for Mouse 7: MTD, Nash equilibrium, and Stackelberg equilibrium. (**a**) Regions of tumor stabilization (yellow) versus progression (red). (**b**) Physician's objective function under the chosen parametrization.

Furthermore, the Stackelberg strategy not only leads to a lower treatment dose and toxicity compared to both the Nash strategy and MTD but also reduces treatment-induced resistance, demonstrating its potential for optimizing therapeutic outcomes while minimizing adverse effects.

3.3. Diffusion in Sensitive and Resistant Cells

In this study, we adopt a conceptual framework based on evolutionary game theory, in which drug-sensitive cancer cells are represented as cooperative players and drug-resistant cells as opportunistic defectors. This abstraction has been widely used in the literature to model the ecological and evolutionary dynamics of tumor cell populations competing for limited resources within the tumor microenvironment [26–28].

Understanding spatial processes is essential, as tumor growth and treatment response are fundamentally shaped by the interplay between cellular motility, resource availability, and local interactions [27,29]. Although this classification offers a useful lens for analyzing treatment-induced selection pressures and spatial dynamics, we recognize that it simplifies the biological complexity of tumor behavior. For instance, under certain conditions, resistant cells may contribute to tumor-wide benefits—such as VEGF-mediated angiogenesis in hypoxic environments—which improve resource availability for both sensitive and resistant populations. This perspective aligns with recent work that integrates evolutionary game theory and control approaches to cancer therapy optimization [16,30]. These examples challenge the strict cooperator-defector dichotomy and underscore the context-dependent nature of cellular behavior.

To account for this nuance, our model focuses on the ecological consequences of differential diffusion and competition, rather than assigning fixed behavioral roles. By examining the conditions under which cooperative-like traits can suppress or coexist with defector-like strategies.

In spatially structured tumor environments, cells disperse to colonize new territories through migration and diffusion. The rate and pattern of this diffusion strongly influence population distribution and competitive dynamics. Slow diffusion of cooperative cells tends to channel their migration along high-benefit pathways, optimizing resource utilization and reinforcing mutualistic interactions. Conversely, rapid diffusion of defector cells enables them to quickly locate and exploit favorable niches, often undermining cooperative expansion and destabilizing spatial organization [31,32].

These opposing forces cooperative resource optimization versus opportunistic exploitation can drive the coexistence of both phenotypes, producing a spectrum of spatial patterns ranging from stable segregation to dynamic spatial chaos. The local microenvironment is further shaped by the production and consumption of shared resources, which modulate population stability and competitive balance over time. Self-organization arising from these diffusion processes not only strengthens cooperative interactions but also generates habitat diversity, a fundamental driver of ecological complexity in biological systems [27].

Building on the evolutionary dynamics presented in previous sections, we now introduce a two-dimensional migration diffusion model to explicitly capture the role of spatial heterogeneity in shaping interactions between cancer subpopulations. This spatially explicit framework provides deeper insight into the mechanisms governing tumor progression and therapeutic response, offering a quantitative basis for the development of spatially informed, evolution-aware treatment protocols. The model is defined as

$$\frac{dx_S}{dt} = DI_S \nabla^2 x_S + x_S G \tag{12}$$

$$\frac{dx_R}{dt} = DI_R \nabla^2 x_R + x_R G. \tag{13}$$

The functions x_s and x_R represent the densities of cooperative and defector cells at time t, respectively. The diffusion constants DI_S and DI_R determine the migration rates for cooperative and defector cells, while ∇^2 denotes the diffusion operator. This continuous spatial expansion reveals a complex landscape of dynamic pattern formation within tumor microenvironments.

When defector cells exhibit a higher dispersal rate than cooperative cells ($DI_R \geq DI_S$), the resulting spatial dynamics do not support the dominance of cooperators. Instead, defectors engage in persistent exploration of resource-rich pathways. Slow migration fosters cooperator aggregation, stabilizing their presence in favorable regions, whereas rapid migration allows defectors to quickly identify cooperative pathways. However, excessive mobility also undermines their ability to fully exploit any specific pathway efficiently, leading to transient rather than sustained advantage.

Existing models for various cancers frequently evaluate cell fitness based solely on the relative abundance of phenotypes within the population. However, these models often overlook the spatial structure of cells beyond one dimension or fail to incorporate cell diffusion dynamics, which are critical for accurately capturing tumor behavior. In complex biological systems, such as the human body, cells, hormones, and growth factors exhibit mobility, influencing intercellular interactions and overall population dynamics [33–35]. The dispersal of these components plays a fundamental role in tumor progression and response to treatment. The rate at which these elements disperse is governed by the diffusion coefficient in the reaction-diffusion equation, which may vary across different spatial coordinates, further influencing population dynamics.

Since the equations presented in this section are second-order partial differential equations, their solutions require numerical methods for accurate computation. To approximate function values at each point in the spatial domain and across generations, numerical techniques such as the five-point stencil method are employed to solve all replicator equations, ensuring precision and practical applicability in modeling tumor evolution.

As proposed, the breast cancer game model is implemented within a two-dimensional spatial environment, represented as an $n \times n$ computational grid, where n denotes the number of cells along each coordinate direction. Each grid cell contains a type i cancer cell with a probability of p_i, while remaining vacant with a probability of $1 - p_i$, allowing for a probabilistic representation of tumor heterogeneity and spatial distribution.

Figure 4, depicting the diffusion dynamics of Mouse 22 across multiple generations, illustrates tumor progression trends. Specifically, at generation 90, the density of treatment-resistant cells surpasses that of treatment-sensitive cells, highlighting the selective pressures that drive resistance evolution over time.

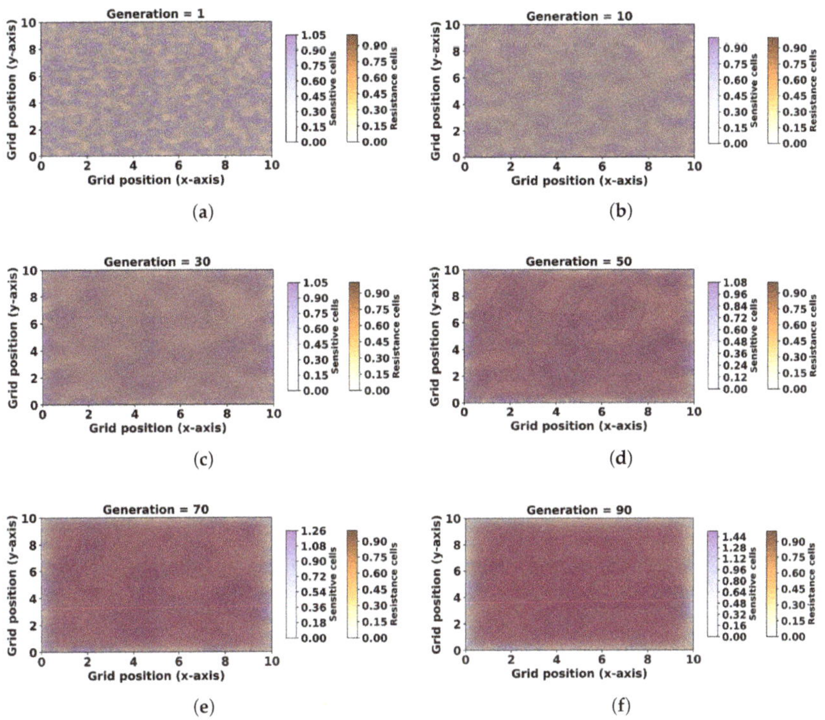

Figure 4. Two-dimensional representation of population dynamics and evolutionary progression under the condition $DI = 0.24$ on a 100×100 grid for Mouse 22, with initial values set to $x_S = 65\%$ and $x_R = 35\%$ of the initial population. (**a**) Population dynamics in generation 1; (**b**) Population dynamics in generation 10; (**c**) Population dynamics in generation 30; (**d**) Population dynamics in generation 50; (**e**) Population dynamics in generation 70; (**f**) Population dynamics in generation 90.

As illustrated in Figure 5, the population dynamics for Mouse 22 exhibit distinct shifts depending on the applied treatment protocol. When the Dose Modulation Adaptive Therapy protocol is implemented, the population predominantly transitions toward treatment-resistant phenotypes. Conversely, under the Intermittent Adaptive Therapy protocol, the population dynamics favor an increase in treatment-sensitive phenotypes, highlighting the differential impact of these therapeutic strategies on cellular evolution.

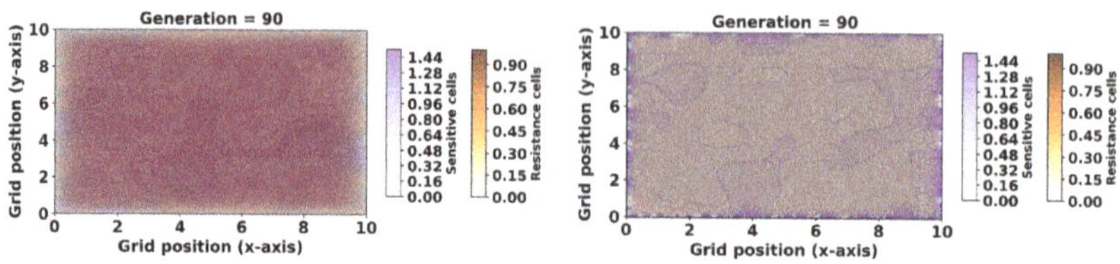

(a) (b)

Figure 5. Two-dimensional representation of population dynamics and evolutionary progression under the condition $DI = 0.24$ on a 100×100 grid for Mouse 22: (**a**) Population state and evolutionary trajectory under the Dose Modulation Adaptive Therapy protocol. (**b**) Population state and evolutionary trajectory under the Intermittent Adaptive Therapy protocol.

3.4. Integration of Experimental Data into the Simulation Framework

To ensure biological relevance and model fidelity, we integrated real-world experimental data into the simulation environment. Specifically, tumor volume measurements obtained from murine xenograft models treated with Gemcitabine and Capecitabine under distinct therapeutic protocols were used as reference datasets. These data served as the foundation for estimating key pharmacodynamic parameters through nonlinear least-squares optimization using the Python-based GEKKO package, a specialized tool for dynamic modeling and parameter fitting.

The estimated parameters informed the construction of a biologically grounded simulation framework capable of capturing tumor dynamics under both single-agent and combination therapies. This calibration process enabled the model to reproduce observed treatment responses and provided a reliable basis for evaluating alternative therapeutic strategies, including reinforcement learning (RL)-based schedules. In our framework, we distinguish between two categories of parameters:

- Therapy-specific parameters (g, k, b, $K_{\max}$): These define the pharmacodynamic characteristics of each drug and are estimated independently for each treatment protocol. They remain constant across patients receiving the same therapy.
- Subject-specific parameters (σ, r, u_0): These capture individual tumor growth behavior, initial tumor burden, and biological variability. They are uniquely estimated for each subject based on their experimental data.

By combining these parameter sets, we simulate multiple treatment protocols for a given patient and assess their relative effectiveness. This enables personalized therapy planning by comparing outcomes such as tumor volume reduction and cumulative drug exposure across different regimens. The simulation framework thus supports the identification of optimal strategies tailored to individual patient profiles, balancing therapeutic efficacy with toxicity constraints.

As illustrated in Figure 6, Mouse 6 was treated experimentally under the Gemcitabine MTD protocol. Model based comparative analysis, however, indicates that if an intermittent adaptive therapy protocol had been applied, a more pronounced reduction in tumor burden could have been achieved, accompanied by a lower cumulative drug dose. These results suggest that intermittent scheduling may improve treatment effectiveness by better controlling the tumor while reducing the overall drug burden for Mouse 6.

Similarly, Figure 7 presents results for Mouse 25, comparing the real-data intermittent adaptive therapy protocol with a model simulated Dose Modulation adaptive therapy. In this case, the Dose Modulation approach produced a greater reduction in tumor burden, but at the expense of increased drug administration. Specifically, while the total dose delivered in the real data protocol was 16 units, the model required 22 units to achieve the observed tumor suppression. Such analyses underscore the capacity of the modeling framework to quantify trade-offs between tumor control and drug exposure, thereby informing the selection of treatment strategies that balance efficacy with toxicity considerations.

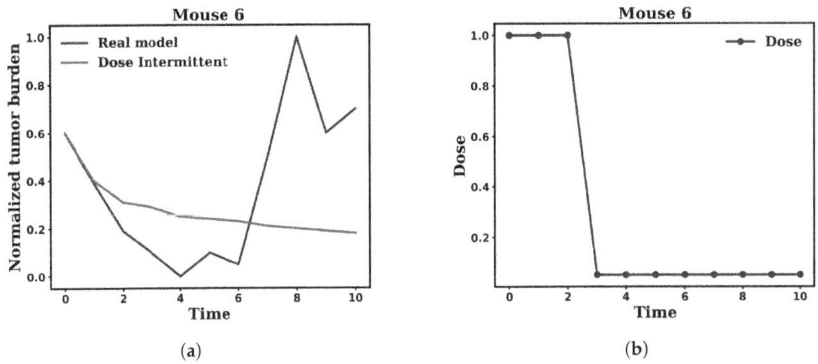

Figure 6. Model-based comparison of (**a**) population dynamics and (**b**) treatment dose rates for mouse 6. While the experimental protocol involved MTD administration of Gemcitabine, simulation results suggest that an intermittent adaptive therapy schedule could have achieved greater tumor suppression with reduced cumulative drug exposure.

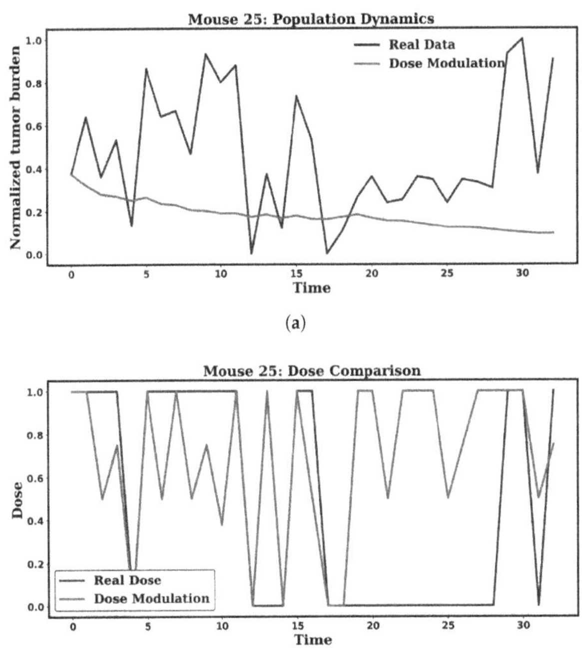

Figure 7. Comparison of (**a**) population dynamics and (**b**) treatment dose rates for mouse 25 under intermittent adaptive therapy (real data) and Dose Modulation adaptive therapy.

3.5. Application of Reinforcement Learning for Adaptive Cancer Therapy

Recent advances in artificial intelligence have facilitated the emergence of reinforcement learning (RL) frameworks capable of optimizing therapeutic strategies in complex and dynamic biological systems. In the context of oncology, RL offers a principled approach to designing adaptive treatment schedules that respond to the evolving state of the tumor and its microenvironment. In this study, we developed a biologically informed RL model to generate personalized chemotherapy protocols for tumor-bearing mice, with the overarching goal of minimizing tumor burden, delaying or preventing the emergence of drug resistance, and avoiding overtreatment, key objectives in precision oncology [17,36].

The RL agent was trained on tumor burden and dosing data, enabling it to learn from the temporal interplay between treatment intensity, tumor regression, and resistance dynamics. The environment was modeled as a discrete-time system, where at each time step the agent observed the current state $s = (X, u)$, with X representing the tumor burden and u denoting the level of resistance. Based on this state, the agent selected an action $a \in \{0, 1, 2, 3\}$ corresponding to no dose, low dose, medium dose, or high dose administration, respectively.

A central component of the RL framework is the reward function, which encodes the therapeutic objectives and guides policy optimization. In our formulation, the reward at each time step was defined as

$$\text{reward} = C_1 \cdot (x_{\text{prev}} - x) - C_2 \cdot D - C_3 \cdot u, \tag{14}$$

where $(x_{\text{prev}} - x)$ quantifies the reduction in tumor burden relative to the previous time step, D is the administered drug dose, and u is the resistance level. The coefficients C_1, C_2, and C_3 are tunable parameters that determine the relative importance of tumor shrinkage, dose minimization, and resistance suppression, respectively. Increasing C_1 prioritizes aggressive tumor reduction, while larger C_2 values penalize excessive drug usage to mitigate toxicity. Similarly, higher C_3 values place greater emphasis on controlling resistance evolution, potentially favoring strategies that maintain a stable, treatment-sensitive tumor subpopulation. By adjusting these weights, the framework can be tailored to different clinical priorities, such as maximizing tumor control in aggressive disease or minimizing toxicity in frail patients.

The agent was trained using tabular Q-learning, a RL algorithm, with learning rate $\alpha = 0.1$, discount factor $\gamma = 0.9$, and exploration rate $\epsilon = 0.1$. The Q-table was updated iteratively according to the Bellman equation:

$$Q(s_t, a_t) \leftarrow Q(s_t, a_t) + \alpha \left[r_t + \gamma \max_{a'} Q(s_{t+1}, a') - Q(s_t, a_t) \right], \tag{15}$$

where r_t is the reward obtained at time t. The discount factor γ controls the trade-off between immediate and long-term gains, with higher values encouraging the agent to adopt strategies that yield sustained tumor control rather than short-lived regressions.

Once trained, the reinforcement learning (RL) agent was applied to an unseen test subject (Mouse 25) within a simulated environment. The simulation was constructed using subject-specific parameters estimated from experimental tumor volume data. To evaluate the agent's performance, its dosing schedule was compared against the actual intermittent adaptive therapy protocol recorded for Mouse 25 in the experimental dataset (Figure 8). The RL-derived schedule achieved a reduction in tumor burden while lowering cumulative drug exposure, demonstrating its ability to balance efficacy with toxicity constraints. Notably, the agent exhibited adaptive dosing behavior—intensifying treatment in response to rising tumor burden and reducing it when resistance levels were low. This behavior, which aligns with clinical intuition, emerges directly from the structure of the reward function used during training. Its performance should be interpreted within the context of the simulation framework and the subject-specific parameter estimates embedded in the model.

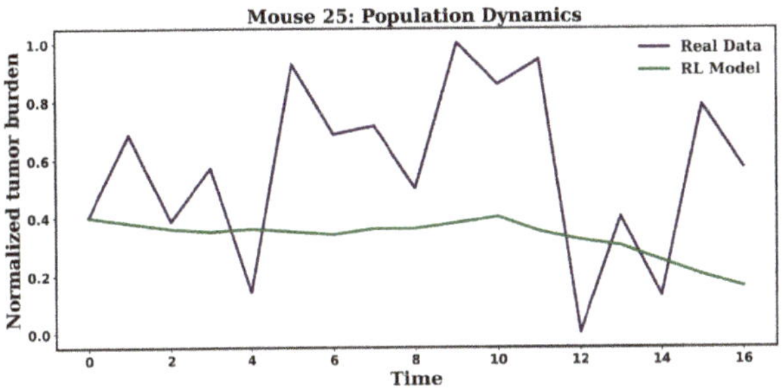

(a)

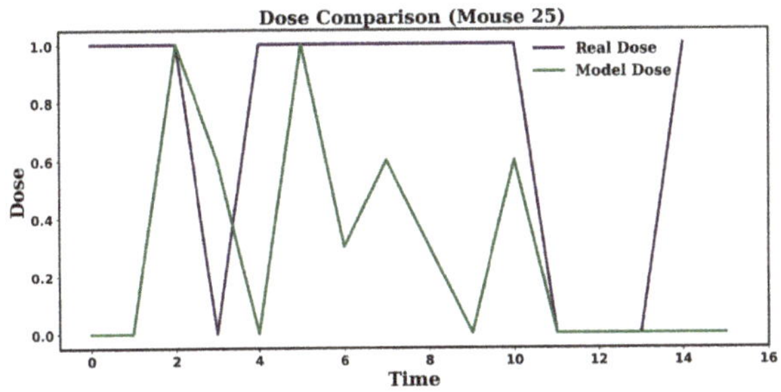

(b)

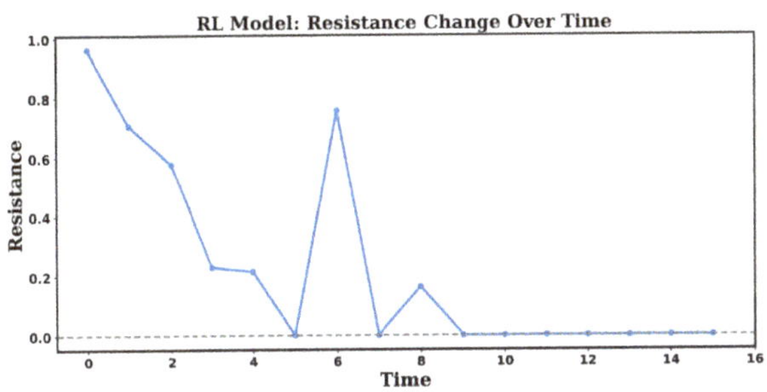

(c)

Figure 8. Illustration of (**a**) population dynamics, (**b**) treatment dose rates for mouse 25 under experimental intermittent adaptive therapy and simulated RL-based schedule ($C_1 = 2$, $C_2 = 0.1$, $C_3 = 0.1$), and (**c**) resistance level trajectories generated by the simulation.

A key strength of our approach lies in the integration of tumor growth and resistance models within the RL framework. By embedding differential equation-based dynamics into the environment, the agent learns policies that are not only data-driven but also biologically interpretable and generalizable across individuals and treatment contexts [37]. This hybrid modeling paradigm enhances clinical relevance, offering a pathway toward evolution-aware, patient-specific cancer therapies that adapt in real time to the shifting landscape of tumor ecology.

After estimating subject-specific parameters for each mouse, it becomes feasible to simulate and assess the effectiveness of various therapeutic strategies in a case-specific manner. Table 4 provides a quantitative comparison of three treatment approaches applied to Mouse 25 over 16 time units. The RL-derived schedule demonstrates more effective performance, achieving the lowest final tumor burden and resistance level while requiring the least cumulative drug exposure. In contrast, the dose modulation strategy effectively reduces tumor burden but entails a higher overall drug consumption.

Table 4. Quantitative comparison of treatment strategies for Mouse 25 over 16 time units. Metrics include Final Tumor Burden (normalized), Total Cumulative Dose, and Final Resistance Level.

Model	Final Tumor Burden (Normalized)	Total Cumulative Dose	Final Resistance Level
Intermittent Dose (Real Data)	0.65	12.0	0.40
Dose Modulation	0.19	7.5	0.05
RL Model	0.16	4.6	0.001

3.6. *Extension from Single-Agent to Combination Therapy Modeling*

Combination chemotherapy, in which two or more cytotoxic or cytostatic agents are administered in a coordinated regimen, is a cornerstone of modern oncology. Such protocols aim to exploit complementary mechanisms of action, reduce the likelihood of cross-resistance, and achieve synergistic tumor suppression while maintaining acceptable toxicity profiles [38]. By targeting distinct molecular pathways or cell cycle phases, combination regimens can enhance therapeutic efficacy compared to single-agent protocols, particularly in heterogeneous tumors where subpopulations may exhibit differential drug sensitivities [38,39]. Clinically, combinations such as Gemcitabine with Capecitabine have been investigated in several malignancies, including pancreatic and breast cancers, with evidence of improved progression-free survival in selected patient cohorts [40,41].

Building on this rationale, we extended our reinforcement learning based tumor dynamics framework originally developed for single agent treatment protocols to capture the dynamics of dual drug interactions. The baseline datasets for the murine experiments comprised tumor volume measurements obtained under regimens of Gemcitabine and Capecitabine. Using these data as a reference, we developed a biologically informed simulation environment that integrates the pharmacodynamic effects of both Gemcitabine (D_G) and Capecitabine (D_C), while enforcing clinically relevant constraints, including an upper bound on the total normalized dose administered at each time step ($D_G + D_C < 1$). This formulation enables the model to explore adaptive dosing strategies that balance efficacy and toxicity within a realistic therapeutic window.

The reinforcement learning agent was trained using the Q-learning algorithm to adaptively allocate doses between the two therapeutic agents, with the overarching objective of maximizing tumor regression while simultaneously minimizing cumulative toxicity and the emergence of drug resistance. The reward function guiding the agent learning process was formulated as:

$$\text{reward} = (x_{\text{prev}} - x) - \lambda_{\text{dose}} \cdot (D_G + D_C) - \beta_{\text{final}} \cdot u, \tag{16}$$

where $(x_{\text{prev}} - x)$ quantifies the reduction in tumor burden between consecutive time steps, $(D_G + D_C)$ denotes the total normalized dose of Gemcitabine and Capecitabine administered at that step, and u represents the current level of treatment resistance within the tumor population. The coefficient λ_{dose} penalizes excessive drug administration to limit cumulative toxicity, while β_{final} penalizes high resistance levels to encourage strategies that maintain treatment sensitivity. In this study, we set $\lambda_{\text{dose}} = 0.08$ and $\beta_{\text{final}} = 0.15$, parameter values selected to balance the competing clinical priorities of maximizing therapeutic efficacy and minimizing adverse effects.

When applied to Mouse 25, the learned combination policy achieved a consistently lower tumor burden compared to the single-agent trajectory, while maintaining a smoother dosing profile and reducing reliance on high-dose pulses (Figure 9). Importantly, the total normalized dose budget was identical to that of the single-agent protocol, indicating that the observed improvement was due to dose diversification rather than escalation. This aligns with prior computational and experimental studies showing that alternating or mixing agents with distinct mechanisms can suppress resistant clones more effectively than monotherapy [42,43].

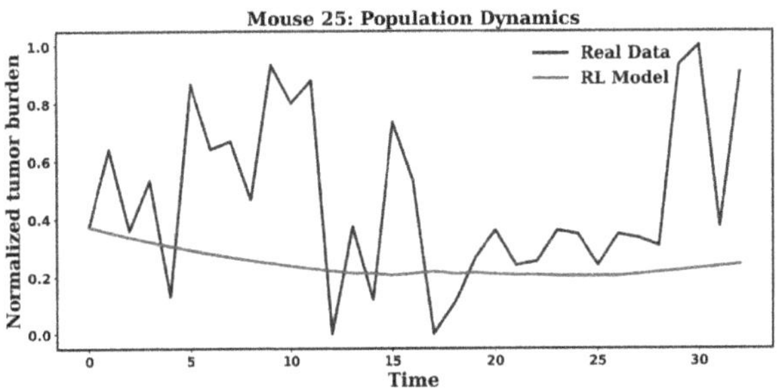

(a)

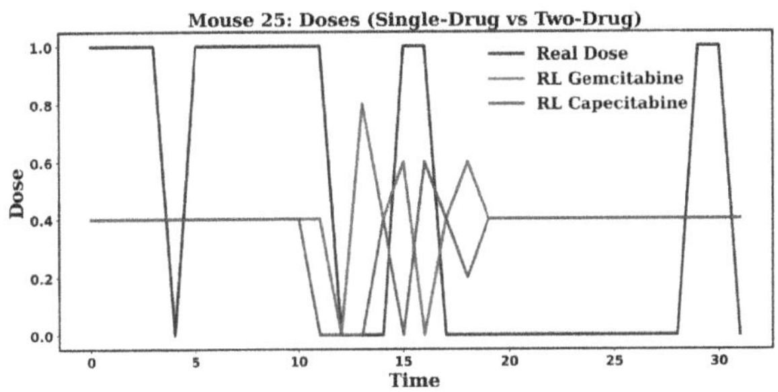

(b)

Figure 9. Comparison of (**a**) population dynamics and (**b**) treatment dose rates for mouse 25 under intermittent adaptive therapy protocol and RL (two drugs).

These results illustrate how reinforcement learning can generalize empirical single-agent data into optimized multi-agent treatment strategies, offering a pathway toward personalized, evolution-aware cancer therapy. By explicitly modeling pharmacodynamic constraints and tumor heterogeneity, the framework can identify dosing schedules that exploit drug complementarity, potentially improving long-term disease control without increasing cumulative toxicity.

4. Discussion and Conclusions

In this study, we developed and systematically evaluated an integrative modeling framework for personalized cancer therapy that combines evolutionary game theory, tumor growth modeling, and reinforcement learning (RL). The central objective was to capture the ecological and evolutionary dynamics of heterogeneous tumor cell populations—comprising both treatment-sensitive and treatment-resistant phenotypes—and to leverage these insights for the design of adaptive, evolution-aware treatment strategies.

At the core of our approach lies an Evolutionary Stackelberg Game formulation, in which the physician is modeled as a rational leader and the tumor cell population as a responsive follower. This leader–follower structure enables the anticipation of tumor evolutionary responses to treatment, allowing the physician's strategy to be optimized in a forward-looking manner. The tumor's ecological dynamics were described using a fitness-generating function (G-function) that incorporates logistic growth, treatment-induced mortality, and resistance-associated fitness costs.

A key strength of this framework is the incorporation of both treatment-specific and subject-specific parameters, estimated directly from experimental data using the Python-based GEKKO optimization package. This calibration step ensures that the model reflects individual variability in tumor growth kinetics and drug response, thereby enhancing predictive accuracy. Using tumor volume data from 70 breast cancer-bearing mice treated with Capecitabine or Gemcitabine, we parameterized the model to simulate three clinically relevant protocols: MTD, Dose Modulation Adaptive Therapy, and Intermittent Adaptive Therapy.

Comparative analysis against classical tumor growth models—Exponential, Logistic, and Gompertz—highlighted the limitations of these traditional approaches. While classical models have been widely used in oncology modeling [44,45], they often fail to capture non-monotonic behaviors such as treatment-induced regressions, rebounds, and phenotypic switching, which are increasingly recognized in both preclinical and clinical settings [3,46]. In contrast, our game-theoretic model aligned more closely with experimental observations, particularly in scenarios involving adaptive or intermittent dosing, underscoring the value of explicitly modeling ecological and evolutionary feedbacks.

Our use of reinforcement learning builds on recent efforts to apply AI-driven optimization to cancer therapy [37,47]. For single-agent therapy, an RL agent trained via Q-learning learned to balance tumor regression against cumulative drug exposure and resistance suppression, as encoded in a multi-term reward function. This approach was then extended to combination therapy by incorporating two drugs—Gemcitabine and Capecitabine—into a pharmacodynamically constrained environment. The RL agent dynamically allocated doses between the two agents, achieving superior tumor control compared to single-agent protocols without exceeding the total dose budget. These results support the hypothesis proposed by Gatenby et al. [3] and further explored by West et al. [48] that dose diversification, rather than escalation, can yield more effective and biologically efficient treatment schedules.

We also examined the spatial dimension of tumor ecology by incorporating reaction-diffusion equations to model the dispersal of sensitive and resistant cells. This builds on prior work demonstrating the role of spatial heterogeneity in resistance evolution [16,29]. In our spatially explicit framework, drug-sensitive cells were conceptualized as cooperators, often exhibiting slower migration and reliance on shared resources, while resistant cells acted as defectors, characterized by higher motility and opportunistic exploitation of spatial niches.

Overall, our findings demonstrate that integrating evolutionary game theory, subject-specific parameter estimation, reinforcement learning, and spatial ecology yields a powerful framework for optimizing cancer therapy. The Evolutionary Stackelberg Game model consistently outperformed classical growth models in reproducing complex tumor dynamics and provided a principled basis for comparing treatment protocols. RL-based adaptive scheduling proved effective for both single- and multi-drug regimens, while spatial modeling illuminated the critical role of phenotypic diffusion in resistance evolution.

This work underscores the importance of explicitly accounting for ecological and evolutionary processes in treatment design. By anticipating tumor adaptation, exploiting competitive interactions between sensitive and resistant cells, and tailoring strategies to individual patient and treatment parameters, such integrative models have the potential to improve long-term tumor control, reduce cumulative toxicity, and ultimately enhance patient outcomes. Future research should focus on validating these approaches in larger, clinically diverse datasets and extending the framework to incorporate immune–tumor interactions, multi-scale modeling, and real-time treatment adaptation.

Author Contributions: F.T. conducted the theoretical modeling and drafted the manuscript. J.S.S. contributed to the mathematical analysis. D.M. and M.H.M. reviewed and edited the final version of the manuscript. All authors have read and agreed to the published version of the manuscript.

Funding: This research received no external funding.

Data Availability Statement: The data used in this study are publicly available and were obtained from the article "Testing Adaptive Therapy Protocols Using Gemcitabine and Capecitabine in a Preclinical Model of Endocrine-Resistant Breast Cancer" (*Cancers* **2024**, *16*, 257) [13]. All relevant information and datasets can be accessed through the original publication.

Conflicts of Interest: The authors declare no conflicts of interest.

References

1. Crawford, S. Is it time for a new paradigm for systemic cancer treatment? Lessons from a century of cancer chemotherapy. *Front. Pharmacol.* **2013**, *4*, 68. [CrossRef]
2. Gatenby, R.A.; Frieden, B.R. Inducing catastrophe in malignant growth. *Math. Med. Biol. J. IMA* **2008**, *25*, 267–283. [CrossRef]
3. Gatenby, R.A.; Silva, A.S.; Gillies, R.J.; Frieden, B.R. Adaptive therapy. *Cancer Res.* **2009**, *69*, 4894–4903. [CrossRef]
4. Belkhir, S.; Thomas, F.; Roche, B. Darwinian approaches for cancer treatment: Benefits of mathematical modeling. *Cancers* **2021**, *13*, 4448. [CrossRef]
5. Deris, A.; Sohrabi-Haghighat, M. Analysis of cancerous tumor growth by the competitive model based on the evolutionary game theory. *Int. J. Nonlinear Anal. Appl.* **2023**, *14*, 1903–1910.
6. Hajdowska, K.; Swierniak, A.; Borys, D. Modelling Changes in Genetic Heterogeneity Using Games with Resources. *Comput. Methods Programs Biomed.* **2025**, *270*, 108916. [CrossRef] [PubMed]
7. Bayer, P.; Gatenby, R.A.; McDonald, P.H.; Duckett, D.R.; Staňková, K.; Brown, J.S. Coordination games in cancer. *PLoS ONE* **2022**, *17*, e0261578. [CrossRef] [PubMed]
8. Tavakoli, F.; Sartakhti, J.S.; Manshaei, M.H.; Basanta, D. Cancer immunoediting: A game theoretical approach. *In Silico Biol.* **2020**, *14*, 1–12. [CrossRef]
9. Maynard Smith, J. The theory of games and the evolution of animal conflicts. *J. Theor. Biol.* **1974**, *47*, 209–221. [CrossRef]
10. Romano, C.; Borri, A.; Di Benedetto, M.D. Stackelberg evolutionary games for cancer modeling and treatment. In Proceedings of the 2024 IEEE 63rd Conference on Decision and Control (CDC), Milan, Italy, 16–19 December 2024; IEEE: Piscataway, NJ, USA, 2024; pp. 7044–7049.
11. Salvioli, M.; Garjani, H.; Satouri, M.; Broom, M.; Viossat, Y.; Brown, J.S.; Dubbeldam, J.; Staňková, K. Stackelberg Evolutionary Games of Cancer Treatment: What Treatment Strategy to Choose if Cancer Can be Stabilized? *Dyn. Games Appl.* **2024**, *15*, 1750–1769. [CrossRef]
12. Reed, D.R.; Metts, J.; Pressley, M.; Fridley, B.L.; Hayashi, M.; Isakoff, M.S.; Loeb, D.M.; Makanji, R.; Roberts, R.D.; Trucco, M.; et al. An evolutionary framework for treating pediatric sarcomas. *Cancer* **2020**, *126*, 2577. [CrossRef]
13. Seyedi, S.; Teo, R.; Foster, L.; Saha, D.; Mina, L.; Northfelt, D.; Anderson, K.S.; Shibata, D.; Gatenby, R.; Cisneros, L.H.; et al. Testing adaptive therapy protocols using gemcitabine and capecitabine in a preclinical model of endocrine-resistant breast cancer. *Cancers* **2024**, *16*, 257. [CrossRef]
14. Stein, J.; Salvioli, M.; Garjani, H.; Dubbeldam, J.; Viossat, Y.; Brown, J.S.; Staňková, K. Stackelberg evolutionary game theory: How to manage evolving systems. *Philos. Trans. R. Soc. B* **2023**, *378*, 20210495. [CrossRef]
15. Pressley, M.; Salvioli, M.; Lewis, D.B.; Richards, C.L.; Brown, J.S.; Staňková, K. Evolutionary dynamics of treatment-induced resistance in cancer informs understanding of rapid evolution in natural systems. *Front. Ecol. Evol.* **2021**, *9*, 681121. [CrossRef]
16. Gluzman, M.; Scott, J.G.; Vladimirsky, A. Optimizing adaptive cancer therapy: Dynamic programming and evolutionary game theory. *Proc. R. Soc. B* **2020**, *287*, 20192454. [CrossRef]
17. Zhang, J.; Cunningham, J.J.; Brown, J.S.; Gatenby, R.A. Integrating evolutionary dynamics into treatment of metastatic castrate-resistant prostate cancer. *Nat. Commun.* **2017**, *8*, 1816. [CrossRef]
18. Fu, F.; Nowak, M.A.; Bonhoeffer, S. Spatial heterogeneity in drug concentrations can facilitate the emergence of resistance to cancer therapy. *PLoS Comput. Biol.* **2015**, *11*, e1004142. [CrossRef]
19. Martinez, V.A.; Laleh, N.; Salvioli, M.; Thuijsman, F.; Brown, J.; Cavill, R.; Kather, J.; Staňková, K. Improving mathematical models of cancer by including resistance to therapy: A study in non-small cell lung cancer. *bioRxiv* **2021**. [CrossRef]

20. Ghaffari Laleh, N.; Lo, W.; Tran, H.; Frieboes, H.B.; Cristini, V.; Lowengrub, J.S.; Enderling, H.; Scott, J.G. Classical mathematical models for prediction of response to chemotherapy and immunotherapy. *PLoS Comput. Biol.* **2022**, *18*, e1009822. [CrossRef]
21. Benzekry, S.; Lamont, C.; Beheshti, A.; Tracz, A.; Ebos, J.M.L.; Hlatky, L.; Hahnfeldt, P. Classical mathematical models for description and prediction of experimental tumor growth. *PLoS Comput. Biol.* **2014**, *10*, e1003800. [CrossRef]
22. Beal, L.D.; Hill, D.J.; Martin, R.; Hedengren, J.D. GEKKO optimization suite. *Processes* **2018**, *6*, 106. [CrossRef]
23. Tian, H.; Guo, Y.; Wang, X. Algorithm of Stackelberg game with multiple leaders followers based on evolutionary game theory. *J. Syst. Eng.* **2005**, *20*, 303.
24. Salvioli, M.; Dubbeldam, J.; Staňková, K.; Brown, J.S. Fisheries management as a Stackelberg Evolutionary Game: Finding an evolutionarily enlightened strategy. *PLoS ONE* **2021**, *16*, e0245255. [CrossRef]
25. Romano, C.; Di Benedetto, M.D.; Borri, A. Stackelberg Evolutionary Games With Modulated Leadership: A Three-Agent Framework for Tumor Immune Dynamics. *IEEE Control. Syst. Lett.* **2025**, *9*, 468–473. [CrossRef]
26. Gatenby, R.A.; Vincent, T.L. An evolutionary model of carcinogenesis. *Cancer Res.* **2003**, *63*, 6212–6220.
27. Basanta, D.; Hatzikirou, H.; Deutsch, A. Studying the emergence of invasiveness in tumours using game theory. *Eur. Phys. J. B* **2008**, *63*, 393–397. [CrossRef]
28. Archetti, M. Evolutionary dynamics of the Warburg effect: Glycolysis as a collective action problem among cancer cells. *J. Theor. Biol.* **2014**, *341*, 1–8. [CrossRef]
29. Kaznatcheev, A.; Peacock, J.; Basanta, D.; Marusyk, A.; Scott, J.G. Fibroblasts and alectinib switch the evolutionary games played by non-small cell lung cancer. *Nat. Ecol. Evol.* **2019**, *3*, 450–456. [CrossRef]
30. Romano, C.; Di Benedetto, M.D.; Borri, A. Evolution-Informed Modeling and Control of Tumor Growth. *IEEE Trans. Autom. Sci. Eng.* 2025, *early access*. [CrossRef]
31. Marusyk, A.; Almendro, V.; Polyak, K. Intratumor heterogeneity: A looking glass for cancer. *Nat. Rev. Cancer* **2012**, *12*, 323–334. [CrossRef]
32. Gatenby, R.A.; Gillies, R.J. A microenvironmental model of carcinogenesis. *Nat. Rev. Cancer* **2008**, *8*, 56–61. [CrossRef]
33. Sartakhti, J.S.; Manshaei, M.H.; Sadeghi, M. MMP–TIMP interactions in cancer invasion: An evolutionary game-theoretical framework. *J. Theor. Biol.* **2017**, *412*, 17–26. [CrossRef]
34. Zeltz, C.; Primac, I.; Erusappan, P.; Alam, J.; Noel, A.; Gullberg, D. Cancer-associated fibroblasts in desmoplastic tumors: Emerging role of integrins. In *Seminars in Cancer Biology*; Elsevier: Amsterdam, The Netherlands, 2020; Volume 62, pp. 166–181.
35. Sartakhti, J.S.; Manshaei, M.H.; Archetti, M. Game theory of tumor–stroma interactions in multiple myeloma: Effect of nonlinear benefits. *Games* **2018**, *9*, 32. [CrossRef]
36. Gatenby, R.A.; Brown, J.S.; Vincent, T.L. The evolution and ecology of resistance in cancer therapy. *Cold Spring Harb. Perspect. Med.* **2020**, *10*, a040972. [CrossRef]
37. Yang, C.-Y.; Shiranthika, C.; Wang, C.-Y.; Chen, K.-W.; Sumathipala, S. Reinforcement learning strategies in cancer chemotherapy treatments: A review. *Comput. Methods Programs Biomed.* **2023**, *229*, 107280. [CrossRef] [PubMed]
38. Al-Lazikani, B.; Banerji, U.; Workman, P. Combination cancer therapy: A road map toward the next generation. *Nat. Rev. Cancer* **2017**, *17*, 293–299.
39. Greco, F.; Vicent, M.J. Combination strategies for cancer therapy: The next generation. *Ther. Deliv.* **2015**, *6*, 165–181.
40. Herrmann, R.; Bodoky, G.; Ruhstaller, T.; Glimelius, B.; Bajetta, E.; Schüller, J.; Saletti, P.; Bauer, J.; Figer, A.; Pestalozzi, B.; et al. Gemcitabine plus capecitabine compared with gemcitabine alone in advanced pancreatic cancer: A randomized, multicenter, phase III trial of the Swiss Group for Clinical Cancer Research (SAKK) and the Central European Cooperative Oncology Group (CECOG). *J. Clin. Oncol.* **2007**, *25*, 2212–2217. [CrossRef]
41. Scheithauer, W.; Schüller, J.; Ulrich-Pur, H.; Schmid, K.; Raderer, M.; Haider, K.; Kwasny, W.; Depisch, D.; Schneeweiss, B.; Lang, F.; et al. Randomised multicentre phase II trial of two different schedules of capecitabine plus gemcitabine in advanced pancreatic cancer. *Br. J. Cancer* **2003**, *89*, 597–602.
42. Geng, Z.; Wang, Y.; Wang, Z.; Wang, Y. Adaptive chemotherapy scheduling via reinforcement learning. *IEEE Trans. Biomed. Eng.* **2020**, *67*, 1430–1441.
43. Komorowski, M.; Celi, L.A.; Badawi, O.; Gordon, A.C.; Faisal, A.A. Reinforcement learning for optimal control of cancer treatment. *PLoS Comput. Biol.* **2018**, *14*, e1005964.
44. Simeoni, M.; Magni, P.; Cammia, C.; De Nicolao, G.; Croci, V.; Pesenti, E.; Germani, M.; Poggesi, I. Predictive pharmacokinetic-pharmacodynamic modeling of tumor growth kinetics in xenograft models after administration of anticancer agents. *Cancer Res.* **2004**, *64*, 1094–1101. [CrossRef]
45. Gerlowski, L.E.; Jain, R.K. Microvascular permeability of normal and neoplastic tissues. *Microvasc. Res.* **1986**, *31*, 288–305. [CrossRef]
46. Enriquez-Navas, P.M.; Kam, Y.; Das, S.; Hassan, S.; Silva, A.S.; Foroutan, P.; Ruiz, E.; Martinez, G.; Minton, S.; Gillies, R.J.; et al. Exploiting evolutionary principles to prolong tumor control in preclinical models of breast cancer. *Sci. Transl. Med.* **2016**, *8*, 327ra24. [CrossRef] [PubMed]

47. Zhao, Y.; Wang, Z.; Li, Y.; Zhang, J. Reinforcement learning for personalized cancer treatment. *PLoS Comput. Biol.* **2020**, *16*, e1008322. [CrossRef]
48. West, J.; You, L.; Zhang, J.; Gatenby, R.A.; Brown, J.S.; Newton, P.K. Towards multidrug adaptive therapy. *Cancer Res.* **2020**, *80*, 1578–1589. [CrossRef]

MDPI AG
Grosspeteranlage 5
4052 Basel
Switzerland
Tel.: +41 61 683 77 34

Mathematical and Computational Applications Editorial Office
E-mail: mca@mdpi.com
www.mdpi.com/journal/mca

www.ingramcontent.com/pod-product-compliance
Lightning Source LLC
Chambersburg PA
CBHW061556220926
51850CB00005B/350
* 9 7 8 3 7 2 5 8 7 4 3 8 5 *